Using 1-2-3® for DOS Release 2.3

Special Edition

Que Development Group

Using 1-2-3® for DOS Release 2.3, Special Edition

Copyright© 1991 by Que® Corporation.

Library of Congress Catalog No.: 91-61986

ISBN 0-88022-727-3

94 93 92 91   4 3 2 1

Interpretation of the printing code: the rightmost double-digit number is the year of the book's printing; the rightmost single-digit number is the number of the book's printing. For example, a printing code of 91-1 shows that the first printing of the book occurred in 1991.

This book is based on Lotus 1-2-3 for DOS Release 2.3, but can be used with Releases 2.01 and 2.2.

Publisher: Lloyd J. Short

Associate Publisher: Karen A. Bluestein

Acquisitions Manager: Terrie Lynn Solomon

Managing Editor: Paul Boger

Product Development Manager: Mary Bednarek

Book Design: Scott Cook

Production Team: Christine Young, Sandy Grieshop, Bob LaRoche, Sarah Leatherman, Jeff Baker, Mary Beth Wakefield, Howard Peirce, Tad Ringo, Johnna VanHoose

Product Director
Joyce J. Nielsen

Production Editor
Kelly D. Dobbs

Editors
Gail S. Burlakoff
H. Leigh Davis
Robin Drake
Donald R. Eamon
Mike La Bonne

Technical Editor
Brian Underdahl

*Composed in Garamond and Macmillan
by Que Corporation*

TRADEMARK ACKNOWLEDGMENTS

Que Corporation has made every effort to supply trademark information about company names, products, and services mentioned in this book. Trademarks indicated below were derived from various sources. Que Corporation cannot attest to the accuracy of this information.

1-2-3, DIF, Symphony, VisiCalc, and Magellan are registered trademarks and Lotus Manuscript is a trademark of Lotus Development Corporation.

Apple and LaserWriter are registered trademarks of Apple Computer, Inc.

dBASE, dBASE II, and dBASE III are registered trademarks and dBASE III Plus and dBASE IV are trademarks of Ashton-Tate Corporation.

Epson FX Series, Epson RX-80, and Epson MX-80 are trademarks of EPSON America, Inc., and EPSON is a registered trademark of Epson Corporation.

Hercules Graphics Card is a trademark of Hercules Computer Technology.

HP and HP ThinkJet are registered trademarks and HP DeskJet and HP LaserJet are trademarks of Hewlett-Packard Co.

IBM, IBM PC, IBM AT, PS/2, Personal System 2, OS/2, and IBM Quietwriter are registered trademarks and ProPrinter and IBM PC XT are trademarks of International Business Machines Corporation.

MS-DOS, Microsoft Windows, and Microsoft Windows Write are registered trademarks of Microsoft Corporation.

NEC P-5 Pinwriter is a registered trademark of NEC Corporation.

PageMaker is a registered trademark of Aldus Corporation.

PostScript is a registered trademark of Adobe Systems Incorporated.

R:BASE is a registered trademark of Microrim, Inc.

Rolodex is a registered trademark of Rolodex Corporation.

SideKick and SideKick Plus are registered trademarks of Borland International, Inc.

Ventura Publisher is a registered trademark of Ventura Software, Inc.

WordPerfect is a registered trademark of WordPerfect Corporation.

Joseph **Desposito** is a microcomputer consultant and free-lance writer specializing in microcomputer topics. Currently, he is a contributing editor for *Computer Craft* magazine. Desposito has held the position of editor-in-chief of *PC Clones* magazine and has worked as senior project leader at *PC Magazine's* PC Labs. He also has served as a technical editor for several magazines, including *Creative Computing, Computers and Electronics*, and *Popular Electronics*. Desposito is a revision author for *1-2-3 Quick Reference for Release 3.1, Using 1-2-3 Release 3.1, 1-2-3 Macro Library*, 3rd Edition, and *Using 1-2-3 Release 2.2*.

David **Paul Ewing** is the president and publisher of New Riders Publishing Company. Prior to his position with New Riders, he was the publishing director of the BestSellers editorial group at Que Corporation. He is the author of Que's *1-2-3 Macro Library* and *Using 1-2-3 Workbook and Instructor's Guide* coauthor of Que's *Using Symphony*, Special Edition, *Using Q&A, Using Javelin* and *1-2-3 Macro Workbook*; and contributing author to *Using 1-2-3*, Special Edition, *1-2-3 QuickStart*, and *Upgrading to 1-2-3 Release 3*.

Bill **Fletcher** is a quality assurance and documentation manager at the Lotus Development Corporation. He is the coauthor of a number of books on using microcomputer software in business applications. He is a revision author for *Using 1-2-3 Release 3.1*.

Joyce **J. Nielsen** is a product development specialist and serves as the 1-2-3 product director for Que Corporation. She received a B.S. degree in quantitative business analysis from Indiana University. Nielson formerly worked as a research analyst for a shopping mall developer, where she developed and documented 1-2-3 applications used nationwide. She worked closely with the authors and editors of this book through manuscript development and editing. In addition to coauthoring this book, she has coauthored *1-2-3 Macro Library*, 3rd Edition; *1-2-3 Release 2.2 QuickStart*, 2nd Edition; and *1-2-3 Release 3.1 QuickStart*, 2nd Edition, all published by Que Corporation.

Anna **Marie Saintonge** has worked with microcomputers and spreadsheets for more than eight years, starting with Software Arts' VisiCalc program. She is a former software engineer and documentation consultant for Lotus Development Corporation where she worked on a number of projects including 1-2-3/G and Agenda. She currently owns her own software design and documentation consulting business in Ellsworth, Maine.

▼ ACKNOWLEDGMENTS

Using 1-2-3 for DOS Release 2.3, Special Edition, is the result of the extraordinary efforts of a team of 1-2-3 and microcomputer book publishing experts. Que Corporation thanks the following individuals for their contributions to this book.

Lloyd Short, Que publisher, for his support throughout the project, and for allowing additional product development time to ensure that this book is the best 1-2-3 Release 2.3 book available.

The authors, **Joe Desposito**, **David Ewing**, **Bill Fletcher**, **Joyce Nielsen**, and **Anna Marie Saintonge**, for providing original and revised text in a timely manner that greatly improves upon previous editions of *Using 1-2-3*. Thanks also to **David Ewing**, former Que publishing director, for assisting with the development of the outline and for providing initial guidance on the content of this book.

Terrie Lynn Solomon, Acquisitions Manager, for coordinating the highly qualified authoring team for this book and for managing the communications and materials sent to and from the authors.

Kelly Dobbs, Senior Editor, for her superlative project management skills, quick and thorough editing, and dedicated commitment to producing a high-quality book that meets Que's standards of excellence.

Editors **Mike La Bonne**, **Robin Drake**, **Gail Burlakoff**, **Don Eamon**, and **Leigh Davis** for their outstanding editing skills and for their adherence to the rigid conventions used in Que's 1-2-3 books.

Brian Underdahl, Technical Editor, for his superb technical review of this book. Brian's technical edit is one of the best we have ever seen.

Tim Stanley, Product Development Specialist, for the valuable developmental and technical contributions he provided throughout the project.

Paul Boger, Managing Editor, for his proficient management skills and for recognizing that extending the project schedule to allow for last minute beta changes would greatly enhance the quality and accuracy of the final product.

Mary Bednarek, Product Development Manager, and **Dorothy Aylward**, Product Development Assistant, for supervising the flow of materials to and from the authors and the technical editor. Thanks also to Mary for her support and encouragement throughout the project.

Jerry Ellis, Technical Support Assistant, for spending countless hours assisting with the development of guidelines for the authors to use when capturing screen shots and for assisting with figure creation when needed.

Stacey Beheler, Acquisitions Coordinator, for her prompt and efficient support throughout the project.

The **Que Production Department**, for their skillful talents in producing a high-quality text and for their dedication to ensuring a quick turn-around time in the final stages of the project. Special thanks to **Hilary Adams, Jeff Baker**, **Joelynn Gifford, Bob LaRoche**, **Sarah Leatherman, Susan VandeWalle, Mary Beth Wakefield**, and **Christine Young**, who took this text from floppies to the final product.

Special thanks also to staff members at Lotus Development Corporation for their support and assistance during the development and production of this book. In particular, public relations personnel **Alexandra Trevelyan** and **Kim Twist**, for coordinating the software distribution among authors and for finding the time to help Que staff when needed. Also, many thanks to beta support contact **Steve Ormsby**, for providing accurate and timely answers to our numerous questions about the content of Release 2.3.

JJN

CONTENTS AT A GLANCE

TABLE OF CONTENTS ▼

Part I   Building the 1-2-3 Worksheet

Part II Creating 1-2-3 Reports and Graphs

Part III   Customizing 1-2-3

Part IV   1-2-3 Release 2.3 Command Reference

Introduction

Since 1983, Que has helped more than two million spreadsheet users learn the commands, features, and functions of Lotus 1-2-3. *Using 1-2-3*—through five editions—has become the standard guide to 1-2-3 for both new and experienced 1-2-3 users worldwide. With the publication of *Using 1-2-3 for DOS Release 2.3*, Special Edition, Que continues its tradition of excellence by providing you the most extensive tutorial and reference coverage available for the new Release 2.3. This book provides complete coverage of 1-2-3 for DOS Release 2.3 to help new spreadsheet users, as well as users who have upgraded to Release 2.3, take advantage of the capabilities of 1-2-3. Users of Releases 2.01 and 2.2 also can benefit from the tutorials and discussions of the main 1-2-3 commands.

Que's unprecedented experience with 1-2-3 and 1-2-3 users helped produce this high-quality, informative book. But a book such as *Using 1-2-3 for DOS Release 2.3*, Special Edition, does not develop overnight. This book represents long hours of work from a team of expert authors and dedicated editors.

The experts who developed *Using 1-2-3 for DOS Release 2.3*, Special Edition, know firsthand the many ways 1-2-3 is used every day. As consultants, trainers, and 1-2-3 users, the authors of *Using 1-2-3 for DOS Release 2.3*, Special Edition, have used 1-2-3 and have taught others how to use 1-2-3 to build many types of applications—from accounting and general business applications to scientific applications. This experience, combined with the editorial expertise of the world's leading 1-2-3 publisher, brings you outstanding tutorial and reference information.

Que began developing the first edition of *Using 1-2-3 for DOS Release 2.3*, Special Edition, immediately after Lotus designers announced that they were planning a new version of 1-2-3. Even before the software was developed, Que's product development editors began searching for the best team of 1-2-3 experts available. This team of authors had to be able to cover the powerful new program comprehensively, accurately, and clearly.

The authors outlined the strategies needed to produce the best book possible on Release 2.3 and analyzed the qualities that made previous editions of *Using 1-2-3* the most popular 1-2-3 books on the market. When Lotus announced 1-2-3 Release 2.3, Que authors began updating the preceding edition of *Using 1-2-3* to cover and illustrate the powerful new Release 2.3 desktop publishing features (Release 2.3's "Wysiwyg" capabilities). The authors tested and developed applications using Wysiwyg features and revised every chapter to incorporate the new features. The revisions were meant to teach 1-2-3 users how to use Release 2.3's Wysiwyg component to create and use 1-2-3 applications to enhance the screen display and printed reports. The result is a comprehensive tutorial and reference, written in the easy-to-follow style expected from Que books. Often, there are differences between Release 2.3 and previous 1-2-3 versions (Releases 2.01 and 2.2) with regard to the wording of prompts in menus. This book shows the Release 2.3 version in the screens and in the text.

For 2.2 users, Appendix D covers the Allways commands. This appendix is arranged like the Wyssiwyg section of the command reference so that you can find needed information quickly.

Because of these efforts, *Using 1-2-3 for DOS Release 2.3*, Special Edition, is the best available guide to 1-2-3 Release 2.3. Whether you are using 1-2-3 for inventory control, statistical analysis, or portfolio management, this book is designed for you. Like all previous editions of this title, *Using 1-2-3 for DOS Release 2.3*, Special Edition, leads you step-by-step from worksheet basics to the advanced features of Release 2.3. Whether you are a new user or an experienced user upgrading to Release 2.3, this book will occupy a prominent place next to your computer, as a tried and valued reference to your most-used spreadsheet program.

Who Should Read This Book?

Using 1-2-3 for DOS Release 2.3, Special Edition, is written and organized to meet the needs of a wide range of readers—from those for whom 1-2-3 Release 2.3 is their first spreadsheet product to those experienced 1-2-3 Release 2.01 and 2.2 users.

If Release 2.3 is your first 1-2-3 package, then this book helps you learn the basics so that you can quickly begin using 1-2-3 for your needs. The first five chapters in particular teach you basic concepts for understanding 1-2-3—commands, the differences and organization of the two command menus in Release 2.3 (the 1-2-3 menu and the Wysiwyg menu), special uses of the keyboard and mouse, features of the 1-2-3 screen, and methods for creating and modifying 1-2-3 worksheets.

If you are an experienced 1-2-3 Release 2.01 or 2.2 user and have upgraded to Release 2.3, you learn all about the new desktop publishing features in Release 2.3 and how to apply them as you develop worksheet applications, create graphs, and print reports and graphs. In particular, you learn how to use the mouse to highlight ranges, move from one part of the worksheet to another, select commands, access the 1-2-3 Help screens, change column widths and row heights, and make selections in dialog boxes. You also learn how to change the way the 1-2-3 worksheet appears on-screen by adding grid lines and drop shadows, changing colors of screen elements, and changing the size and style of characters on the worksheet. *Using 1-2-3 for DOS Release 2.3*, Special Edition, quickly and easily teaches you how to use Wysiwyg features to produce presentation-quality reports and graphics.

Whether you are a new user or a user who has upgraded to Release 2.3, *Using 1-2-3 for DOS Release 2.3*, Special Edition, gives you the tips and techniques necessary to get the most from the program. As you continue to use Release 2.3, you find that the 1-2-3 Release 2.3 command reference, with its easy-to-use format, is a frequently used guide providing you with the steps, reminders, tips, and cautions for using Release 2.3 commands.

The Details of This Book

If you flip quickly through this book, you can get a better sense of its organization and layout. The book is organized to follow the natural flow of learning and using 1-2-3.

Part I—Building the 1-2-3 Worksheet

Chapter 1, "An Overview of 1-2-3 Release 2.3," covers the uses, features, and commands specific to Release 2.3. This chapter explains the "What-you-see-is-what-you-get" desktop publishing capabilities for displaying and printing high-quality worksheets and graphs. Also, this chapter introduces the general concepts for understanding 1-2-3 as a spreadsheet program and introduces the program's major uses—creating worksheets, databases, graphics, and macros.

Chapter 2, "Getting Started," helps you begin using 1-2-3 Release 2.3 for the first time and includes starting and exiting from the program, learning special uses of the keyboard and mouse with 1-2-3, understanding features of the 1-2-3 and Wysiwyg screen display, getting on-screen help, and using the 1-2-3 tutorials.

Chapter 3, "Learning Worksheet Basics," introduces the concepts of worksheets and files and teaches you how to move the cell pointer around the worksheet, enter and edit data, and use Undo. You also learn how to create formulas that link cells among different files and how to use the Viewer add-in to quickly link files.

Chapter 4, "Using Fundamental 1-2-3 Commands," teaches you how to use the 1-2-3 Release 2.3 command menus and the most fundamental commands for building worksheets. For example, in this chapter, you learn how to change the width of a column, clear data from the worksheet, and control the way data displays on-screen. You also learn how to save the worksheet files and leave 1-2-3 temporarily to return to the operating system.

Chapter 5, "Formatting Cell Contents," shows you how to change the way data appears on-screen, including the way values, formulas, and text are displayed. You also learn how to suppress the display of zeros.

Chapter 6, "Using Functions in the Worksheet," covers all types of functions available in 1-2-3: mathematical, date and time, financial and accounting, statistical, database, logical, string, logarithmic, trigonometric, and special.

Chapter 7, "Managing Files," covers commands for saving, erasing, and listing files, as well as commands for combining and extracting data from one file to another. Chapter 7 also includes coverage of the new Enhanced option for Expanded Memory support and the Viewer add-in.

Part II—Creating 1-2-3 Reports and Graphs

Chapter 8, "Printing Reports," shows you how to print a report immediately, create a file for printing at a later time, or create a file to be read by another program. You learn how to print a basic report by using only a few commands. Also, you learn how to enhance a report by using other commands that change page layout, type size, character and line spacing, and enable you to add elements such as headers and footers.

Chapter 9, "Using Wysiwyg To Enhance and Print Reports," focuses on the Wysiwyg formatting and printing features of Release 2.3. This chapter introduces you to the Wysiwyg commands, covering in particular how the main 1-2-3 commands and Wysiwyg commands work together. You learn how to design a worksheet with different sizes and types of characters, and how to highlight worksheet data with special elements such as underlining, shading, boxes, and grids. Automatic print compression and background printing capabilities also are covered. Finally, Chapter 9 teaches you how to use the word processing capabilities available through the **:T**ext command.

Chapter 10, "Creating and Printing Graphs," teaches you how to create graphs from worksheet data. This chapter also covers the additional graph types available with Release 2.3 and the options available to change the titles and scaling. You learn how to add a background grid, data labels, and legends and how to view a graph. You also learn how to print your 1-2-3 graphs through the PrintGraph program provided with Release 2.3.

Chapter 11, "Enhancing and Printing Graphs in Wysiwyg," shows you how to modify, embellish, and print graphs through the extensive **:G**raph commands on the Release 2.3 Wysiwyg menu. You learn how to change the position of a graph on the page; adjust graph settings; add, modify, and rearrange text and geometric shapes; and change the size and rotation of objects displayed on graphs.

Part III—Customizing 1-2-3

Chapter 12, "Managing Data," introduces you to the advantages and limitations of 1-2-3's database and shows you how to create, modify, and maintain data records, including sorting, locating, and extracting data. Chapter 12 also covers the special commands and features of 1-2-3 data management, such as database statistical functions, parsing data to use in the worksheet, and regression analysis.

Chapter 13, "Using Macros," is an introduction to the powerful macro capability of 1-2-3. This chapter teaches you how to create, name, and run macros and how to build a macro library. Also, the chapter covers macro features such as creating a macro automatically by recording keystrokes in Learn mode, naming macros with descriptive names, and invoking macros from a menu.

Chapter 14, "Introducing the Advanced Macro Commands," explains the powerful advanced macro commands in 1-2-3 and includes a complete alphabetized reference of all advanced macro commands with examples of their use.

Part IV—1-2-3 Release 2.3 Command Reference

The command reference is a quick, easy-to-use, and comprehensive guide to the procedures for using almost every command on the command menus. This section also gives many reminders, important cues, and cautions that greatly simplify and expedite the day-to-day use of 1-2-3.

Appendixes

Appendix A, "Installing 1-2-3 Release 2.3," shows you how to install 1-2-3 Release 2.3 for your hardware and operating system and how to modify settings at a later time.

Appendix B, "Using the Auditor Add-In," explains how to use the new Auditor add-in provided with Release 2.3 to identify and check the formulas in your worksheets. All menu options are covered, with specific examples provided.

Appendix C, "Compose Sequences for the Lotus International Character Set," presents a table of the LICS—characters not on the keyboard that can appear on-screen and that can be printed. Your equipment determines which characters in this list you can display and print.

Appendix D, "Allways Commands," is a command reference for 1-2-3 Release 2.2 users. This appendix is an easy-to-use reference for the Allways add-in.

Other Titles To Enhance Your Personal Computing

Although *Using 1-2-3 for DOS Release 2.3*, Special Edition, is a comprehensive guide to Release 2.3, no single book can fill all your 1-2-3 and personal computing needs. Que Corporation publishes a full line of microcomputer books that complement this best-seller.

Several Que books can help you learn and master your operating systems. *Using DOS* is an excellent guide to the IBM-specific PC DOS operating system. Its counterpart—written for all DOS users—is *Que's MS-DOS 5 User's Guide*, Special Edition. Both books provide the same type of strong tutorial and complete command reference found in *Using 1-2-3 for DOS Release 2.3*, Special Edition. If you prefer to "get up and run" with DOS fundamentals in a quick and easy manner, try Que's *MS-DOS 5 QuickStart*, 2nd Edition. This graphics-based tutorial helps you teach yourself the fundamentals of DOS.

If you are using 1-2-3 on a personal computer equipped with a hard disk drive, you already may know that the key to efficient computer use is effective hard disk management. Que's *Using Your Hard Disk* shows you how to get the most from your hard disk by streamlining your use of directories, creating batch files, and more. This well-written text is an invaluable addition to your library of personal computer books.

Learning More about 1-2-3

If *Using 1-2-3 for DOS Release 2.3*, Special Edition, whets your appetite for more information about 1-2-3, you're in good company. More than one million *Using 1-2-3* readers have purchased one or more additional Que books about 1-2-3.

1-2-3 for DOS Release 2.3 Quick Reference is an affordable, compact reference to the most commonly used Release 2.3 commands and functions. It is a great book to keep near your computer when you need to find quickly the function of a command and the steps for using it.

Besides these books, Que publishes several books for new Release 2.3 users. These books include *1-2-3 for DOS Release 2.3 QuickStart* and *1-2-3 for DOS Release 2.3 PC Tutor*. Keep in mind that Que also publishes a complete line of books for 1-2-3 Release 3 users, covering Releases 3 and 3.1.

All of these books can be found in quality bookstores worldwide. In the United States, you can call Que at 1-800-428-5331 to order books or obtain further information.

Part I

Building the 1-2-3 Worksheet

Includes

An Overview of 1-2-3 Release 2.3

Getting Started

Learning Worksheet Basics

Using Fundamental 1-2-3 Commands

Formatting Cell Contents

Using Functions in the Worksheet

Managing Files

An Overview of 1-2-3 Release 2.3

For more than eight years, 1-2-3 has been the dominant spreadsheet software product used in businesses worldwide. Although the market for spreadsheet software grows increasingly competitive, 1-2-3 continues to dominate with more than 10 million users.

Introduced in 1983, 1-2-3 revolutionized microcomputing by quickly replacing the dominant spreadsheet product at the time. 1-2-3 soon became identified with the IBM PC and compatibles as the established tool for financial analysis. With the introduction of Release 2.3, 1-2-3 maintains and improves upon the overall efficiency, command structure, and screen and keyboard features of its earlier versions. In fact, 1-2-3 Release 2.3 not only is fully compatible with all previously released versions but also provides several new features.

In particular, Release 2.3 offers two new dynamic features: the Wysiwyg add-in (from the acronym WYSIWYG—what-you-see-is-what-you-get) and mouse control. Other new features include an on-line tutorial, interactive dialog boxes, enhanced options for expanded memory, and the Auditor add-in and Viewer add-in programs.

Why is 1-2-3 so popular? Because it provides three fundamental applications integrated in one program. Without having to learn three separate kinds of software, you can perform financial analysis with the 1-2-3 worksheet, create database applications, and generate graphics. Commands enabling users to develop all three types of applications are combined on one main menu. The Wysiwyg add-in provides an additional menu system for enhancing on-screen and printed reports and graphics. When you select any of these easily accessed commands, prompts guide you through each step needed to perform a task.

Reminder:
1-2-3 is three applications in one: spreadsheet, database, and graphics.

Besides using the traditional keyboard mode, Release 2.3 enables you to use a mouse in 1-2-3 text mode and Wysiwyg graphics mode. By moving the mouse and pressing its control buttons, you can quickly and easily perform many actions normally executed with a series of keystrokes.

If you are upgrading to Release 2.3, this chapter briefly explains the differences between earlier releases and Release 2.3 and identifies many of the features and commands unique to Release 2.3. In this chapter, you learn about the following topics:

- The features special to Release 2.3 (developed for readers planning to upgrade or who have upgraded from Release 2.01 or 2.2 to Release 2.3)

- The general capabilities of 1-2-3 (presented especially for readers new to 1-2-3)

- Features that identify 1-2-3 as a spreadsheet program, including the capability to create formulas and use functions in 1-2-3

- The commands available for creating, modifying, and using 1-2-3 worksheets

- 1-2-3 file management

- 1-2-3 graphics, including an introduction to enhancements in Release 2.3 graphics

- Database management with 1-2-3

- Printing reports and graphs by using the new Wysiwyg menu and its commands

- Macros and the advanced macro commands

- The hardware and operating system requirements for running 1-2-3 Release 2.3

Comparing Release 2.3 with Earlier Versions

If you have used a previous version of 1-2-3, you will find the program unchanged in its primary functions. For example, you can still use 1-2-3 for simple-to-complex financial applications; for organizing, sorting, extracting, and finding information; and for creating graphs useful for presentations or analyzing data.

The major enhancements to 1-2-3 over earlier versions are the interactive Wysiwyg work environment and mouse support. Mouse control makes 1-2-3 easier than ever to use. With the mouse, you can quickly adjust column widths or row heights, select ranges, make menu selections, and add worksheet windows. *Mouse-driven icons*, which enable you to position the mouse pointer on the icon and click the mouse control button to activate, can be used to scroll the worksheet or access a context-sensitive help feature. When the Wysiwyg add-in is attached, what appears on-screen is nearly identical to the way printed documents appear. This visual representation gives you better control of fonts, colors, lines, borders, and graphs.

Reminder:
1-2-3 Release 2.3 offers Wysiwyg and mouse capabilities.

Additional enhancements to Release 2.3 include the following:

- The Auditor add-in enables you to analyze worksheet formulas and detect errors easily.

- The Viewer add-in enables you to quickly view, browse, or link files on a hard disk.

- Dialog boxes enable you to quickly select options (such as print and graph settings) directly on-screen with either the keyboard or the mouse.

- The interactive Help system has been greatly enhanced and now provides different procedures you can follow and a glossary of 1-2-3 terms.

- The new on-line tutorials, 1-2-3-Go! and Wysiwyg-Go!, provide sample sessions that can be accessed from within 1-2-3 (as an add-in) or directly from DOS.

- The background print feature enables you to print while working in the worksheet.

- The new enhanced memory feature enables you to use expanded memory to increase the maximum size of the worksheet.

Seeing 1-2-3 as an "Electronic" Accountant's Pad

1-2-3 Release 2.3, as well as earlier versions, is like an electronic accountant's pad, or electronic spreadsheet (see fig. 1.1). When you start Release 2.3, the computer screen displays a column and row area into which you can enter text, numbers, or formulas as an accountant does on one sheet of a columnar pad (and with the help of a calculator).

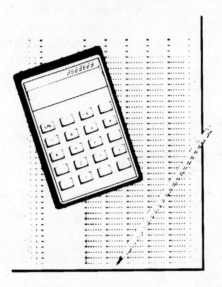

Fig. 1.1. *1-2-3 as an accountant's columnar pad.*

With Release 2.3, as with earlier versions of 1-2-3, the worksheet is the basis for the whole product. Whether you are working with a database application or creating graphs, tasks are done within the structure of the worksheet. You initiate commands from the menu commands that appear at the top of the screen. Figure 1.2 displays the 1-2-3 main menu, and figure 1.3 shows the Wysiwyg main menu. You create graphs from data entered in the worksheet; you perform database operations from data organized into the worksheet's column and row formats; and you store macro programs in worksheet cells.

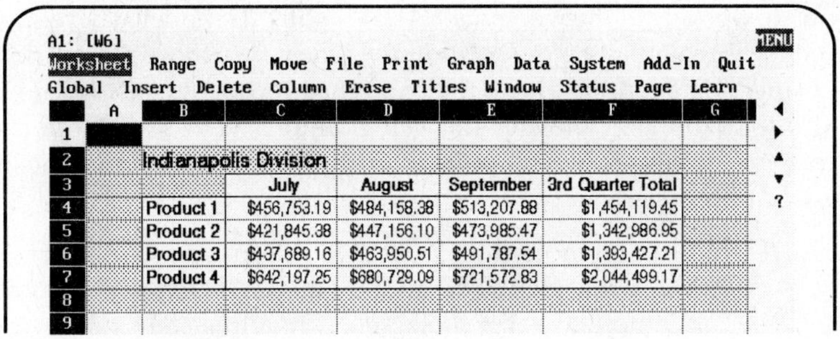

Fig. 1.2. The 1-2-3 main menu.

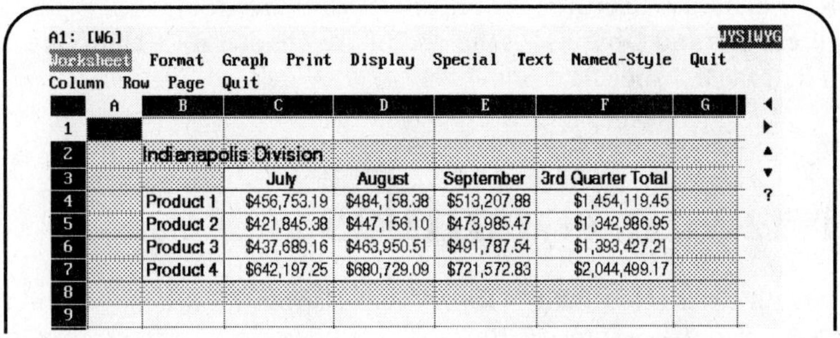

Fig. 1.3. The Wysiwyg main menu.

All data—text, numbers, or formulas—is stored in individual cells in the worksheet. A cell is a rectangular area identified by the intersection of a column and row on the worksheet. For example, if you type a number in the cell two rows down from the top border and three columns to the right of the left border, you have entered the number in cell C2 (see fig. 1.4). Worksheet columns are marked alphabetically from A to Z, then AA to AZ, then BA to BZ, and so on up to IA to IV; rows are marked by numbers 1 to 8192.

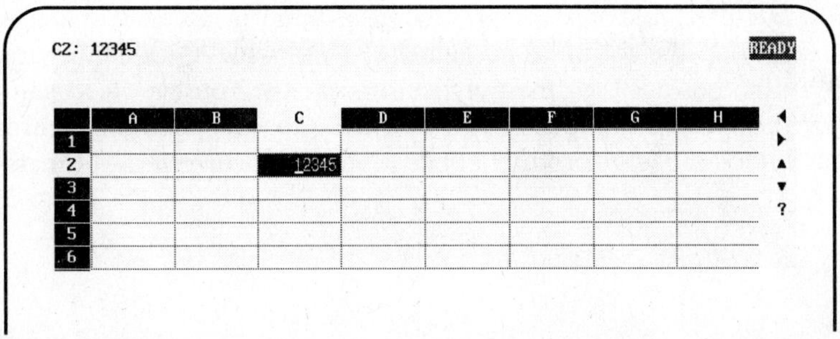

Fig. 1.4. A 1-2-3 worksheet cell entry.

Reminder:
*Use the direction
keys or the mouse
to move the cell
pointer around the
worksheet.*

As you are working in the worksheet, 1-2-3 highlights the cell where you can enter data; this highlight is the *cell pointer*. One way to move the cell pointer is by using the direction keys on the computer keyboard (see Chapter 3 for more information on moving the cell pointer). Release 2.3 offers you another way to move the cell pointer: by moving a mouse and clicking a mouse button.

Potentially, you can fill more than 2,000,000 cells in one worksheet. Most likely, few users have the need or computer equipment to handle this much data. At the minimum, however, Release 2.3 requires 384K (kilobytes) of memory in the computer. To use the Wysiwyg add-in program, you need 512K of memory. If you use Wysiwyg and want to use additional add-ins (such as Viewer and Auditor included with Release 2.3), you need at least 640K of memory. See the section titled "Understanding 1-2-3 Hardware Requirements and Options" at the end of this chapter for a complete list of 1-2-3 Release 2.3 specifications.

Creating Formulas

Because 1-2-3 is used mainly for financial applications, its capability to develop formulas is one of its most sophisticated and yet easy-to-use features. Creating a formula can be as simple as adding the values in two cells on the same worksheet, as shown in the following example:

+A1+B1

Entered in another cell, such as C1, this formula says that the values stored in cells A1 and B1 will be added together and the result will be placed in cell C1. The formula does not depend on the specific values contained in A1 and B1 but adds whatever values are entered. For example, if A1 originally contains the value 4, and B1 the value 3, the formula computes to 7. If you change the value in A1 to 5, the formula in C1 recalculates to 8.

Because 1-2-3 remembers the relationships between cells and does not simply calculate values, you can change a value in a cell and see what happens when the formulas recalculate. This "what-if" capability makes 1-2-3 a powerful tool for many types of analysis. You can, for example, analyze the effect of an expected increase in the cost of goods and determine the price increase your product needs to maintain current profit margins.

You can create formulas that have *operators*—the symbols that indicate the arithmetic operations, such as addition (+), subtraction (–), multiplication (*), and division (/). The value of Release 2.3 formulas, however, is their capability of linking worksheets. By referencing cells in other worksheets, formulas can calculate results from numerous, separate worksheet applications.

Reminder:
With Release 2.3, you can use formulas to link worksheets.

When you create a formula to link data between worksheets, you first identify the worksheet that has the data (identified by the file name of the worksheet); then you follow this file name with a cell reference (or range name). The following example shows a formula that links data between two worksheets:

+<<SALES>>C5

Why do you want to link files? Linking is ideal for consolidating regional sales, department budgets, product forecasts, and so on. You easily can create formulas that consolidate data from other worksheets saved to disk, and these formulas are updated anytime you change the data in the other file.

You can, for example, receive data from separate departments (in separate files) to consolidate. The consolidation file can use formulas to combine the data from each separate file. The process also works in reverse. You can have a central database file as well as separate files to distribute to each department. The individual department files can contain formulas that refer to data in the central database file. See Chapter 3 for more information on creating formulas that link data across files.

Examining Functions

Building applications in 1-2-3 would be difficult if you couldn't calculate complex mathematical, statistical, logical, financial, and other types of formulas. Release 2.3 provides 93 useful functions that enable you to create complex formulas for a wide range of business, scientific, engineering, and other types of applications. Instead of entering complicated formulas containing numerous operators and parentheses, you can use functions as a shortcut. All functions in 1-2-3 begin with the @ sign followed by the name of the function—for example, @SUM, @RAND, and @ROUND. Many functions require that after the function name you enter an *argument*—the specifications the function needs to calculate the formula.

Reminder:
1-2-3 Release 2.3 has 93 predefined functions.

Release 2.3 includes seven categories of functions: mathematical and trigonometric, statistical, financial and accounting, logical, special, date and time, and string. Refer to Chapter 6 for more information on 1-2-3 functions and examples of each of the functions provided with Release 2.3.

Using the Command Menus

The worksheet is the basis for all applications you create, modify, and print in 1-2-3. Into the worksheet cells, you enter data in the form of text, numbers, and formulas. You perform operations on this data with Release 2.3's two command menus: the 1-2-3 main menu and the Wysiwyg main menu. The 1-2-3 menu enables you to format, copy, move, print, create a graph, and perform database operations on this data. The Wysiwyg menu enables you to enhance the look of text and numbers you enter, as well as enhance the look of graphs you create. Figure 1.5, for example, shows a worksheet with numbers formatted as currency. The worksheet has been dressed up with lines, shadows, and fonts selected from the Wysiwyg menu.

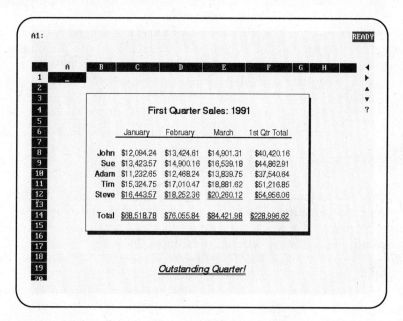

Fig. 1.5. *A worksheet formatted with Wysiwyg commands.*

The 1-2-3 Menu and the Wysiwyg Menu

The 1-2-3 main menu is always available when you start 1-2-3. You access the 1-2-3 menu by pressing the forward slash (/) key. To use the Wysiwyg menu, however, you first must load the Wysiwyg feature into memory. You can install Wysiwyg so that it loads when you start 1-2-3. After the Wysiwyg add-in is loaded, you access the Wysiwyg menu by pressing the colon (:) key. You also can use the mouse to access a menu by moving the mouse pointer to the top of the screen. Then you can use the right mouse button to toggle between the 1-2-3 and Wysiwyg menus.

The commands in the main 1-2-3 and Wysiwyg menus lead to many sublevels of commands. In fact, hundreds of commands are available from these two menus combined. Some commands you use frequently when you create or modify a worksheet application. Other commands, such as specialized database commands, you may rarely or never use. The following sections briefly introduce the commands you probably use most frequently—commands related to creating and modifying worksheet applications.

Reminder:
1-2-3 Release 2.3 offers hundreds of commands, some of which you use every time you create or modify a worksheet.

Using the 1-2-3 Main Menu

1-2-3 provides menu commands that enable you to save and retrieve the worksheet as a file on disk, manage and change the file, and read files in formats different from a 1-2-3 worksheet file format. Another command on the main menu enables you temporarily to leave a worksheet, return to the operating system (for example, to format a disk), and then return to the original worksheet location.

You bring up the 1-2-3 main menu by pressing / or <. If you have a mouse, you can move the mouse pointer to the control panel. Pressing the right mouse button toggles between the 1-2-3 main menu and the Wysiwyg menu.

Understanding the 1-2-3 worksheet structure and the effect of certain commands on the worksheet are your first steps in learning to use 1-2-3 successfully. When you begin working with the 1-2-3 command menu, you find that some commands affect the entire worksheet. For example, if you want to widen all columns of a worksheet, you use the /Worksheet Global Column-Width command.

Other commands in the 1-2-3 main menu affect only a portion or block of cells in the worksheet, called a *range*. A range may be one or up to thousands of cells, all on the same worksheet. Ranges are always a contiguous square or rectangular block of cells. One of the commands in the 1-2-3 main menu, the /Range command, affects only a designated cell or block of cells in the worksheet. If you are a beginning 1-2-3 user, keep in mind that commands can affect the worksheet or just a specific range.

Using the /Worksheet Commands

Worksheet, the first command on the 1-2-3 menu, leads to options that affect either the whole worksheet or columns and rows on the worksheet. With /Worksheet commands, you can change the way numbers and formulas appear in the worksheet—in percentage, currency, or comma formats, and so on. Other commands that affect the overall worksheet include those for inserting and deleting columns or rows. The /Worksheet menu provides a command that enables you to clear the current file from the screen and computer memory and to replace the screen with a new, clean worksheet. You also can hide worksheet columns to keep data confidential or to prevent data from printing on a report.

Reminder:
The /Worksheet commands on the 1-2-3 main menu enable you to change the way data and graphs appear on-screen.

Some /Worksheet commands on the 1-2-3 main menu enable you to change the way data and graphs appear on-screen. You may, for example, freeze certain columns or rows so that they remain on-screen even though you move the cell pointer to other areas of the worksheet. You also can split the screen and display two areas of the worksheet at one time. Another /Worksheet command provides a status report displaying such information as how much memory is available for you to use and what settings are in effect for the worksheet. You also can use one of the /Worksheet commands to record keystrokes in the worksheet, to be used later in a macro.

Using the /Range Commands

Apart from the 1-2-3 main menu commands for copying and moving data from one area of the worksheet to another, one other command, /Range, affects single cells or a rectangular block of cells. Some /Range commands control the way data in one cell or block of cells appears on-screen and when printed. You may, for example, change the way numbers and formulas are displayed; indicate whether you want text to be aligned to the left, right, or center of the cell; and justify the right margin of a block of text that spans many rows of the worksheet. You also can change data from displaying in column format to row format and vice versa. /Range also enables you to protect certain areas of the worksheet so that you or other users do not accidentally change, erase, or overwrite data. Other /Range commands enable you to erase data in one cell or block of cells and search for specified strings of data.

One of the most useful /Range commands—/Range Name—enables you to attach a name to one cell or block of cells. You can create a formula, for example, that totals a column of numbers by entering the function @SUM followed in parentheses by the column's *range name*—@SUM(QTR1). Range names also are useful for printing. For example, rather than defining the exact cell boundaries for an area you want to print, you can name the area and enter the name when you are asked to identify the part of the worksheet you want to print. Other uses for range names include naming parts of a worksheet so that you easily can move the cell pointer from one area to another. These examples are only a few of the many uses for range names.

Reminder:
Range names make the /Range commands easier to use.

Using the /Copy and /Move Commands

/Worksheet and /Range are two of the most frequently used 1-2-3 commands. Two other commands, however, also are used frequently for creating and modifying worksheet applications. As their names indicate, /Copy and /Move enable you to copy and move data from one cell or block of cells to another, respectively.

The /Copy command saves you hours of time by enabling you to duplicate text, numbers, divider and formatting lines, and formulas. Copying formulas is one of the most important functions of this command. You can create a few key formulas and then copy these formulas to other parts of the worksheet, where they can calculate values different from those that the original formula calculates.

When you use /Move, you can move not only the contents of one cell to another but also the contents of a large block of cells to another area of the worksheet or another worksheet. You move a large block with the /Move command by highlighting the cells you want to move and then indicating the top left cell where you want the data to be relocated.

Using the Wysiwyg Menu

Besides the 1-2-3 menu, Release 2.3 offers the Wysiwyg menu. The Wysiwyg menu is like the menu used with the add-in utility program, Impress, and is similar to the Allways menu of Release 2.2. The Wysiwyg menu does not load automatically. You must start 1-2-3 and then load the Wysiwyg menu.

You can press Alt-F10 or select /Add-In to access the Add-In menu, from which you can load Wysiwyg. As mentioned previously in this chapter, you can tell 1-2-3 to load Wysiwyg when you start 1-2-3. Each of these methods is discussed in detail in Chapter 2.

Reminder:
Pressing the right
mouse button
toggles between the
1-2-3 and Wysiwyg
menus.

After you load Wysiwyg, you bring up the Wysiwyg menu by pressing : or, if you have a mouse, by moving the mouse pointer to the control panel. Pressing the right mouse button toggles between the main menu and the Wysiwyg menu. Some of the commands that appear in the Wysiwyg main menu are described in the following sections.

Using the :Worksheet Commands

The Wysiwyg menu :Worksheet commands enable you to adjust column width and row height. The Wysiwyg features enable you to enhance text and numbers by changing the typeface and type size. Although 1-2-3 adjusts the height of a row to accommodate an enlarged typeface, the :Worksheet Row command gives you control over this feature. The Wysiwyg :Worksheet menu also enables you to insert or delete page breaks into rows or columns of a worksheet.

Using the :Format Commands

The Wysiwyg :Format command options improve the appearance of text and numbers when printed. :Format options enable you to specify the font for a range and add or remove bold, italic, and underline attributes. The :Format command also enables you to outline; add or remove horizontal and vertical lines and drop shadows from ranges; and add or remove single, double, or thick underlines from a range. Other options enable you to specify colors for background, text, and negative values in a range. The :Format Shade command enables you to add or remove light, dark, or solid shading from a range.

Using the :Display Commands

The Wysiwyg :Display commands change the way 1-2-3 displays worksheets on-screen. By using :Display, you can specify colors for all parts of the worksheet, namely the worksheet background, data, cell pointer, grid, frame, lines, drop shadows, negative values, and data in unprotected ranges. The :Display Mode command enables you to switch the screen display between graphics display mode and text display mode or between color and black and white. Other :Display commands enable you to add page breaks and grid lines to a worksheet, display up to 60 rows at one time on-screen, and reduce or enlarge cells to display more of the whole worksheet on-screen or zoom in on a portion of the worksheet.

Using the :Text Commands

The Wysiwyg :Text commands give you more control over labels than any previous version of 1-2-3. For example, the :Text Edit command enables you to edit labels directly in the worksheet rather than in the control panel. The :Text Reformat command formats a column of long labels so that they fit within a text range and look like a paragraph. :Text Align, a command similar to 1-2-3's /Range Label command, aligns text at the right, left, or center of a text range.

Using the :Special and :Named-Style Commands

The Wysiwyg :Special commands enable you to copy or move formats from one part of a worksheet to another or copy a format from one file to another. These commands are useful when you want identical formats in several areas of a worksheet or when you want to format worksheets with identical structures, such as monthly expense statements.

The Wysiwyg :Named-Style commands enable you to assign a name to a collection of Wysiwyg formats taken from one cell or range of cells. Then you can apply the style to one or more ranges in the current file. Up to eight named styles can exist in each file.

Understanding 1-2-3 File Management

The type of file you create most often when using Release 2.3 is a *worksheet file*. A worksheet file saves the data, formulas, and text you enter into a worksheet and saves things such as cell formats, text alignments, range names, and settings for protected ranges. These files are stored with a WK1 extension. Worksheet files also may have a BAK extension, indicating that a backup file is saved on disk.

Reminder:
A worksheet file stores the data, formulas, and text entered into a worksheet.

Four other types of Release 2.3 files may be created: text files, marked by a PRN extension; encoded print-image files, marked by an ENC extension; graph-image files, marked by a PIC extension; and Wysiwyg files, marked by an FMT extension.

One of the commands on the 1-2-3 main menu enables you to perform most of the file operations you need when creating and using worksheet applications. The /File command provides a wide range of file management, modification, and protection capabilities. Some of these commands are similar to the operating system commands, such as those that enable you to erase or list files. Other commands relate to specific 1-2-3 tasks and applications. You can, for example, combine data from several files and extract data from one file to another file. "Reserving" a file also is possible, through the use of passwords, so that only one user can write information to and update the file. The /File commands are particularly useful for people who are using 1-2-3 Release 2.3 on a network.

In addition to the 1-2-3 menu options for managing, modifying, and protecting files, the Translate utility enables you to "translate" several file formats that differ from the 1-2-3 worksheet file format. You can, for example, convert files from the following programs and read them into 1-2-3 Release 2.3: dBASE II and III; Multiplan in the SYLK format; Enable 2.0; SuperCalc4; VisiCalc; and other files in DIF format. You also can convert 1-2-3 Release 2.3 files to formats that can be read by 1-2-3 Release 1A; dBASE II and III; Multiplan in the SYLK format; Symphony 1.0; Enable 2.0; SuperCalc4; and other programs that use the DIF format. You need not use the Translate utility to read worksheet files created by 1-2-3 Releases 1A, 2, 2.01, and 2.2; and Symphony 1.0 and 1.2 through 2.2. You also do not need the utility to convert 1-2-3 Release 2.3 files to 1-2-3 Releases 3 and 3.1 or Symphony 1.1 through 2.2.

Enhancing Worksheets with 1-2-3 Graphics

When 1-2-3 was first introduced, business users quickly recognized the advantages of being able to analyze worksheet data with instant graphs produced by the same worksheet program. Release 2.3 enables you to create seven types of graphs: line, bar (vertical and horizontal), XY, stacked-bar, pie, high-low-close-open, and mixed (a bar graph overlaid with a line graph). You also can create three-dimensional bar graphs. Depending on how data is organized in the worksheet, you can create a graph by using the /Graph Group command and by highlighting a range of data.

Beyond creating a simple graph, 1-2-3 /Graph commands enable you to enhance and customize graphs for your needs. You can, for example, add titles and notes, label data points, change the format of values displayed on a graph, create a grid, and change the scaling along the x-axis or y-axis. By naming the settings you have entered to create a graph and by saving the name, you can display and modify the graph whenever you access the file.

Some earlier 1-2-3 releases can analyze data in graph form but are primitive in their capability to produce high-quality graphs on-screen and in printed form. Exceptions are Release 2.2 combined with the Allways add-in and Releases 3 and 3.1. Release 2.3, like its three most recent predecessors (Releases 2.2, 3, and 3.1), supports the most advanced monitor adapters as well as high-quality printers. Depending on the monitor, graphs can be viewed in full-screen view or as part of a Wysiwyg worksheet. The quality of Release 2.3 graphs can be enhanced by options on the 1-2-3 and Wysiwyg menus.

The Wysiwyg :Graph menu enables you to enhance a graph with text, lines, arrows, polygons, rectangles, ellipses, and symbols and enables you to choose colors from a pallet of 224 choices. Release 2.3 gives you two choices for printing graphs: through the separate PrintGraph program or from the Wysiwyg :Print menu. Chapter 10 covers how to use the PrintGraph program, and Chapter 11 describes how to use Wysiwyg to enhance and print graphs from within the worksheet.

Reminder:
Save a graph name so that you can use it again.

Getting Acquainted with 1-2-3 Database Management

The column-row structure used to store data in the 1-2-3 worksheet is similar to the structure of a relational database. 1-2-3 provides true database management commands and functions, enabling you to sort, query, extract, and perform statistical analysis on data. One important advantage of 1-2-3's database manager over independent database programs is that its commands are similar to the other commands used in the 1-2-3 program. Therefore, you can learn how to use the 1-2-3 database manager along with the rest of the 1-2-3 program.

After a database has been built in 1-2-3 (an activity no different from building any other worksheet application), you can perform a variety of functions on the database. Some of these tasks are accomplished with standard 1-2-3 commands. For example, /Worksheet Insert Row adds records to a database. /Worksheet Insert Column adds fields to a database. Editing the

Reminder:
You build data-bases in 1-2-3 like you build any other worksheet application.

contents of a database cell is as easy as editing any other cell; you move the cell pointer to that location, press Edit (F2), and start typing (or use the Wysiwyg **:Text Edit** command).

Data also can be sorted. You can perform sorts by using alphabetic or numeric keys in ascending or descending order. In addition, various kinds of mathematical analyses can be performed on a field of data over a specified range of records. For example, you can count the items in a database that match a set of criteria; compute a mean, variance, or standard deviation; and find the maximum or minimum value in the range. The capability to perform statistical analysis on a database is an advanced feature for database management systems.

1-2-3 also has a special set of statistical functions that operate only on information stored in the database. As with the query commands, the database statistical functions use criteria to determine the records on which they operate.

The combination of these functions and 1-2-3's database commands make this program a capable data manager. 1-2-3's data-management capabilities, however, are not equivalent to such dedicated database languages as dBASE III Plus, dBASE IV, or R:BASE. (1-2-3's data-management capabilities are covered in detail in Chapter 12.)

Printing Reports and Graphs

By using 1-2-3's **Print** command from the 1-2-3 menu or the Wysiwyg menu, you can access several levels of print options that enable you to print worksheet data and graphs for draft review or more formal presentations. The **/Print** command enables you to send data directly from 1-2-3 to the printer or save worksheet data in a text file so that the data can be incorporated into another program, such as a word processing program. You save data and graphs to a file format that retains the selected report enhancements (such as boldface type, underlining, and italic) so that you can print later with an operating system command.

Cue:
Use :Print to combine text and graphics on a report.

With the Wysiwyg **:Print** command, you can combine text and graphics anywhere on a page for sophisticated, publishing-quality output; you can preview all pages, including text and graphics, before printing; you can print in portrait or landscape mode on laser printers; and you can compress a worksheet print range to fit on one page.

1-2-3's printing capabilities give you considerable control over the design of printed output—from simple one-page reports to longer reports that incorporate graphs. Commands available from the 1-2-3 /Print and Wysiwyg :Print menus provide options for developing page-layout features—setting margins, indicating text for headers and footers, telling 1-2-3 to print certain column or row data on every page, and setting the length of the page. Other :Print commands enable you to rotate the position of the graph on the page, change the graph size, and print in draft or final quality.

Besides the commands that affect how the report and graph look when printed, other commands give you greater control over the printing process and operation of the printer. A new background printing feature enables you to send output to a printer while you continue to work within the worksheet. You also can easily clear settings—all or only certain settings— and reenter new ones in their place. Release 2.3 enables you to temporarily stop the process of entering print settings, return to the worksheet to make a change, and then enter settings again, all without losing the initial settings.

Reminder:
With 1-2-3
Release 2.3, you
can print to a printer
while you work in
the worksheet.

Using Macros and the Advanced Macro Commands

One of 1-2-3's most useful features is its macro capability, which enables you to automate and customize 1-2-3 for your special applications. 1-2-3's macro and advanced macro command capability enables you to create, inside the 1-2-3 worksheet, user-defined programs to be used for a variety of purposes. At the simplest level, these programs save time. Just like the memory function keys of some telephones, which "remember" a set of buttons for a frequently used phone number, the macro command reduces, from many to two, the number of keystrokes for a 1-2-3 operation. At a more complex level, 1-2-3's advanced macro commands give the user full-featured programming capability.

Cue:
Use macros to
simplify and speed
up your work in
1-2-3.

By using Release 2.3's Learn feature, you easily can create a macro that records a series of keystrokes automatically. These keystrokes then may be copied to the worksheet as macros. In addition to naming a macro with the backslash (\) and a single letter, Release 2.3 enables you to assign to a macro a descriptive name of up to 15 characters.

Whether you use 1-2-3's macro capability as a typing alternative or as a programming language, you will find that it simplifies and automates many of your 1-2-3 applications. When you create simple keystroke macros, you group together and name a series of normal 1-2-3 commands, text, or numbers. After you name a macro or advanced macro command program, you can activate its series of commands and input data by pressing two keys—the Alt key and a letter key—or by accessing a menu to select the macro name.

Cue:
You can use the advanced macro commands to create interactive macros that pause for user input.

The implications for such typing-alternative macros are limited only by 1-2-3's capabilities. For example, typing the names of months as column headings is a task frequently performed in budget building. A 1-2-3 macro easily can reduce these multiple keystrokes to a couple of keys. Macro programs also can make decisions. These decisions can be based on values found in the worksheet or on input from the user at the time the sequence is executed. By combining the typing-alternative features of 1-2-3's macro capability with the advanced macro commands, you can create interactive programs that pause and wait for user input.

When you begin to use 1-2-3's advanced macro commands, you discover the power available for your special needs. The application developer finds that the advanced macro commands are much like a programming language (such as BASIC). The programming process, however, is simplified significantly by all the powerful features of 1-2-3's worksheet, database, and graphics commands. Whether you want to use 1-2-3 to create simple keystroke macros or to program, Chapters 13 and 14 give you the information you need to get started.

Understanding 1-2-3 Hardware Requirements and Options

Reminder:
You need only an 8086- or 8088-type computer to run 1-2-3 Release 2.3.

1-2-3 Release 2.3 runs on computer systems configured with a hard disk drive and at least one floppy disk drive, a monochrome monitor, and 384K of random access memory (RAM). To run Wysiwyg, you need at least 512K of memory. At minimum, you need only an 8086- or 8088-type of system (a computer with an 8086 or 8088 microprocessor). However, if you use 1-2-3 for serious business purposes, you are likely to have much more sophisticated hardware. The hardware requirements for running Release 2.3 are listed in table 1.1. For a complete listing of supported displays and printers, refer to the Lotus 1-2-3 Release 2.3 documentation.

Table 1.1
1-2-3 Release 2.3 System Requirements

Published by:	Lotus Development Corporation 55 Cambridge Parkway Cambridge, Massachusetts 02142
System Requirements:	IBM PC or IBM PS/2 or compatibles
	Hard disk drive with at least one floppy disk drive
Display:	VGA, EGA, CGA, or Hercules Graphics adapter
Disk capacity:	7M (5M without tutorials)
Memory size:	384K
	512K required for Wysiwyg
	640K required for Wysiwyg and additional add-in(s)
Maximum usable memory:	640K conventional memory
	4M of expanded memory (LIM 3.2)
	12M of expanded memory (LIM 4.0)
Operating System:	DOS Version 2.1 or higher
Optional hardware:	Printer and/or plotter
	Math coprocessor (8087, 80287, 80387SX, 80387)

Summary

Although Release 2.3 offers several powerful new features, the program is still compatible with previous versions of 1-2-3 and can run on 8086- and 8088-type systems.

This chapter has described in general terms the capabilities that make 1-2-3 Release 2.3 an outstanding program. The remaining chapters of this book show you how to use the powerful features of Release 2.3 quickly, easily, and productively.

2

Getting Started

T his chapter helps you get started using 1-2-3 and the Wysiwyg spreadsheet publishing feature. If you are familiar with 1-2-3 but new to Release 2.3, you may find some of the introductory material in this chapter too basic. If you want to begin using the 1-2-3 worksheet immediately, you can skip to Chapter 3. However, if you want to begin using Wysiwyg and other new features, you should read the appropriate sections of this chapter before moving to Chapter 3.

Besides other features, this chapter discusses two new on-line tutorials provided with Release 2.3: 1-2-3-Go! and Wysiwyg-Go!. Many first-time users find these tutorials a helpful introduction to 1-2-3. If you are new to 1-2-3, you can use the tutorials as you read through this book for the first time. If you are new to Release 2.3 but have used previous versions of 1-2-3, the tutorials can be used to learn about Wysiwyg and other new features available with Release 2.3.

This chapter covers the following topics:

- Starting 1-2-3 and Wysiwyg

- Exiting 1-2-3

- Using the Install and Translate Programs

- Using the computer keyboard and mouse with 1-2-3

- Understanding the 1-2-3 and Wysiwyg screen displays

- Using the 1-2-3 Help system and tutorials

- Accessing 1-2-3 from Microsoft Windows

Before you begin, be sure that 1-2-3 Release 2.3 is installed on your computer system. Follow the instructions in Appendix A or the Lotus documentation to complete the installation.

Starting 1-2-3

Cue:

Access 1-2-3 from any directory by adding the 1-2-3 directory name to the PATH statement.

You can start 1-2-3 directly from the operating system or from within the Lotus 1-2-3 Access menu. Most users start directly from the operating system because this method is easier, faster, and uses less memory. Also, from the operating system, you can specify a file name to retrieve when 1-2-3 is loaded. The following sections cover how to start 1-2-3 from the operating system and the Lotus 1-2-3 Access menu, as well as how to start Wysiwyg.

To start 1-2-3 from any operating system prompt each time you use 1-2-3, add the name of your 1-2-3 program directory to the PATH statement of the AUTOEXEC.BAT file. See your operating system manuals for more information on modifying the AUTOEXEC.BAT file.

Starting 1-2-3 from the Operating System

If you have installed 1-2-3 according to the directions in Appendix A (or the Lotus documentation), the 1-2-3 program is now in a subdirectory named \123R23. If you installed 1-2-3 in a different subdirectory, you should substitute that directory name in the following procedures.

To start 1-2-3 directly from the operating system, use the following steps:

1. Change to the drive on which you installed 1-2-3. In most systems, this is drive C, but you may have installed 1-2-3 on drive D, E, or another drive. If 1-2-3 is installed on drive C and drive C is not the current drive, type **C:** and press Enter.

2. Type **CD \123R23** and press Enter to change to the 1-2-3 program directory. (**Note:** You can omit this step if you added the Release 2.3 directory name to the PATH statement of the AUTOEXEC.BAT file, as explained earlier in this chapter.)

3. Type **123** and press Enter to start 1-2-3.

To retrieve a file automatically when you start 1-2-3 from the operating system, you can type **123** followed by a space, a hyphen, the letter **w**, and the file name. If the file is not in the 1-2-3 default directory, you also must include the directory name with the file name. Chapter 7 contains information on how to change the 1-2-3 default directory.

For example, to retrieve the file SALES.WK1 located in the C:\DATA directory (which is not the 1-2-3 default directory), type the following at the operating system prompt and press Enter:

123 -wC:\DATA\SALES

In this example, if the 1-2-3 default directory *is* C:\DATA, you can just type the following and press Enter:

123 -wSALES

Starting 1-2-3 from the Lotus 1-2-3 Access Menu

The Lotus 1-2-3 Access menu is a way to use menus to access not only the 1-2-3 worksheet but also the Release 2.3 PrintGraph, Install, and Translate programs (see fig. 2.1).

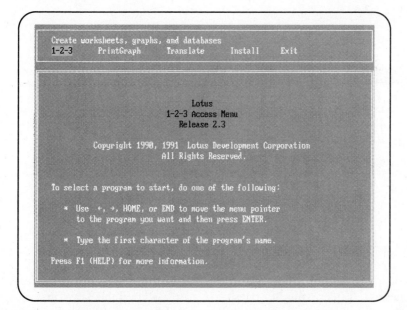

Fig. 2.1. The Lotus 1-2-3 Access Menu screen.

Use the following steps to start the Lotus 1-2-3 Access menu:

1. Change to the drive on which you installed 1-2-3. In most systems, this drive is C, but you may have installed 1-2-3 on drive D, E, or another drive. If 1-2-3 is installed on drive C and drive C is not the current drive, type **C:** and press Enter.

2. Type **CD \123R23** and press Enter to change to the 1-2-3 program directory. (**Note:** You can omit this step if you added the Release 2.3 directory name to the PATH statement of the AUTOEXEC.BAT file, as explained earlier in this chapter.)

3. Type **LOTUS** and press Enter to start the Lotus 1-2-3 Access menu.

The Lotus 1-2-3 Access Menu screen appears (see fig. 2.1). The command menu at the top of the screen displays the following options:

> **1**-2-3   PrintGraph   Translate   Install   Exit

The first option in the Lotus 1-2-3 Access menu, **1**-2-3, starts the main 1-2-3 program. This option is highlighted when the Lotus 1-2-3 Access Menu screen appears. To select the highlighted option, press Enter. If you have moved the highlight to another option, use the right-arrow or left-arrow key (or the Home key) to return to the first option and then press Enter. You also can type the first character of the option (**1** in this example) and then press Enter. After you start 1-2-3, the registration screen appears for a few seconds as the program loads. A blank worksheet appears, and you are ready to start using 1-2-3.

Starting Wysiwyg

To take advantage of the new Wysiwyg features of Release 2.3, you have to load the Wysiwyg add-in into memory. This multistep procedure must be performed each time you start 1-2-3—unless you set 1-2-3 to load and invoke Wysiwyg whenever you start 1-2-3. If you want to learn how to set up your system to invoke Wysiwyg automatically, skip the discussion in the next section.

Starting Wysiwyg Manually

To load Wysiwyg manually, select /Add-In Attach. (You also can press Alt-F10 to access the same menu, unless you have assigned this key combination to another add-in program.) A list of add-in files appears. Highlight

WYSIWYG.ADN, and then press Enter. When you select the file, a menu appears that enables you to attach the Wysiwyg add-in to a function key. Attaching an add-in to a function key means that you can *invoke*, or start, the add-in by pressing the Alt key and a function key.

This procedure is not recommended for Wysiwyg, however, because of easier ways to invoke the add-in. Rather than attaching Wysiwyg to a function key, you should select **No-Key**. If you want to attach Wysiwyg to a function key, select **7**, **8**, **9**, or **10** (for function keys Alt-F7, Alt-F8, Alt-F9, or Alt-F10). After you make your selection, the Wysiwyg copyright screen appears, and then the Wysiwyg worksheet appears. (Unlike other 1-2-3 add-in programs, you need *not* separately invoke Wysiwyg to activate the program.) You must select **Quit** to leave the /Add-In menu.

Starting Wysiwyg Automatically

Loading Wysiwyg manually can take time because you have to follow the same procedure each time you start 1-2-3. You can save time by configuring the system to load Wysiwyg automatically. To set up the system to invoke Wysiwyg automatically, perform the following steps:

1. Select /**W**orksheet **G**lobal **D**efault **O**ther **A**dd-In **S**et.

2. Select a number from 1 to 8. If this is the first add-in you are setting up to load automatically, select **1**.

3. Select WYSIWYG.ADN from the list of files that appears.

4. Decide whether you want to attach Wysiwyg to a function key. You may want to select **No-Key**.

5. Select **Yes** (to automatically activate the application when it is read into memory).

6. Select **Quit Update Quit** to update the 1-2-3 configuration file and return to the worksheet.

The next time you start 1-2-3, and each time thereafter, first the 1-2-3 worksheet loads, and then Wysiwyg loads automatically.

If you want to use a mouse with 1-2-3, you have to load a mouse driver before starting 1-2-3. If you are starting 1-2-3 with a batch file, like the one described in the previous section, you can add commands to it that load the mouse driver. You can also load the mouse driver by adding it to the AUTOEXEC.BAT file, the file that automatically executes commands when you turn the computer on.

Reminder:
You must load the mouse driver separately from 1-2-3.

1-2-3 Release 2.3 does not provide the mouse driver; the company that manufactures the mouse does. Directions for adding a mouse driver are in the documentation you received with the mouse.

If you load a mouse driver before starting 1-2-3, a pointer arrow appears in the center of the screen when Wysiwyg is loaded into memory. If Wysiwyg is not attached, a one-character-wide rectangular cursor appears in the center of the worksheet. The mouse controls the movement of the pointer—if you move the mouse, the pointer moves. You can use the mouse to select commands by pointing to the command and clicking the left mouse button. For example, to leave the /Add-In menu, you move the pointer to **Quit** and click the left mouse button.

Exiting 1-2-3

To exit the 1-2-3 program, press the forward slash (/) key to access the 1-2-3 main menu. Use the right- or left-arrow key (or the End key) to highlight the **Quit** option (see fig. 2.2), and then press Enter.

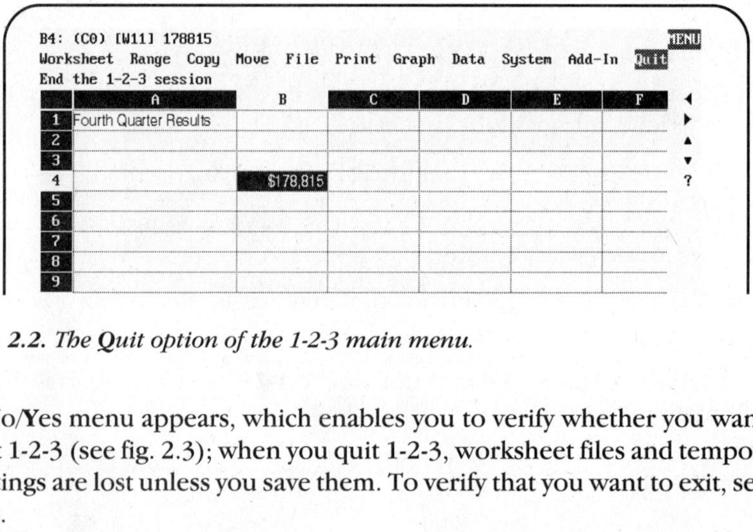

```
B4: (C0) [W11] 178815                                          MENU
Worksheet  Range  Copy  Move  File  Print  Graph  Data  System  Add-In  Quit
End the 1-2-3 session
          A                 B          C         D         E         F
1  Fourth Quarter Results
2
3
4                       $178,815
5
6
7
8
9
```

Fig. 2.2. The Quit option of the 1-2-3 main menu.

A **No/Yes** menu appears, which enables you to verify whether you want to exit 1-2-3 (see fig. 2.3); when you quit 1-2-3, worksheet files and temporary settings are lost unless you save them. To verify that you want to exit, select **Yes**.

Caution:
Remember to save your work before you quit the worksheet.

If you made changes to any worksheets and did not save them, 1-2-3 beeps and prompts you a second time to verify this choice before you exit (see fig. 2.4). If you want to save the changes you have made to a worksheet, select **No**; then save the file and exit from 1-2-3. The commands to save files are introduced in Chapter 4 and covered in detail in Chapter 7. If you do not want to save your file and want to quit, select **Yes**.

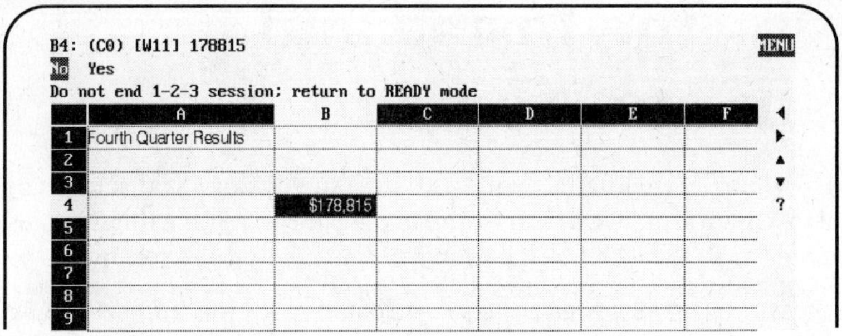

Fig. 2.3. The prompt to verify that you want to quit 1-2-3.

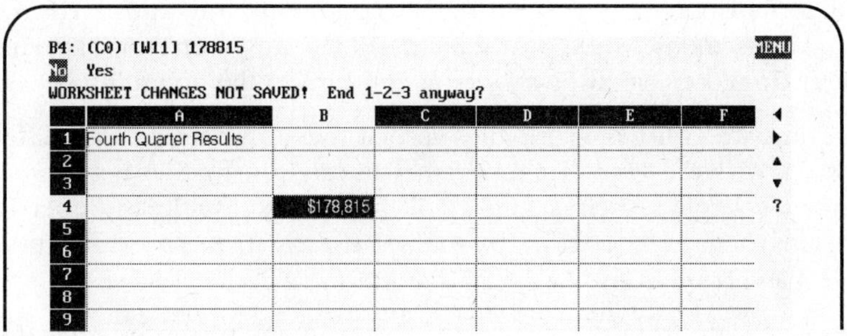

Fig. 2.4. The prompt to remind you to save a worksheet before exiting 1-2-3.

If you started 1-2-3 from the operating system, you return to the operating system when you exit 1-2-3. However, if you started 1-2-3 from the Lotus 1-2-3 Access menu, selecting **Q**uit from the 1-2-3 main menu returns you to the Lotus 1-2-3 Access Menu screen. To exit the Lotus 1-2-3 Access menu and return to the operating system, select **E**xit.

Mouse users can exit 1-2-3 another way. First move the mouse pointer to the control panel. The act of moving the pointer arrow to this section of the display brings up the Wysiwyg or the 1-2-3 menu (whichever menu was last accessed). If Wysiwyg is not attached, the 1-2-3 main menu is generated. Clicking the mouse button on the right toggles between the two menus.

When you see the 1-2-3 menu with MENU displayed in the upper right corner of the screen, point to **Q**uit, click the left button, and then click **Y**es. As before, if you made changes to any worksheets and did not save them, 1-2-3 prompts you a second time to verify this choice before you exit. Click **Y**es again to end your 1-2-3 session. If you used the Lotus 1-2-3 Access menu to start 1-2-3, select **E**xit to return to the operating system.

Using the Install and Translate Programs

Cue:
Use the Install program to change options specified during installation.

The Install program enables you to change the options you set during the initial installation. You can run Install to prepare 1-2-3 for a different display or printer or to select Wysiwyg fonts and change mouse settings.

To access the Install program, choose Install from the Lotus 1-2-3 Access menu. You also can access the Install program from DOS by typing **INSTALL** at the drive and directory containing the 1-2-3 program files. Appendix A carries complete installation instructions.

If you start Install from the Lotus 1-2-3 Access menu, you return to the Lotus 1-2-3 Access menu when you exit Install. If, however, you start Install directly from the operating system, you return to the operating system.

Cue:
Use the Translate program to exchange files between 1-2-3 and other programs.

The Translate utility converts files so that they can be read by a different program. With the Translate program, you can transfer files between 1-2-3 and other programs, such as dBASE II, III, and III Plus; Multiplan; SuperCalc4; programs that can read and write to the DIF format; and previous versions of 1-2-3 and Symphony.

Select **Translate** from the Lotus 1-2-3 Access menu to reach the Translate program. You also can access the Translate program from DOS by typing **TRANS** at the drive and directory containing the 1-2-3 program files. See Chapter 7 for more detailed information on the Translate program.

If you start Translate from the Lotus 1-2-3 Access menu, you return to the Lotus 1-2-3 Access menu when you exit Translate. If, however, you start the Translate program directly from the operating system, you return to the operating system.

Learning the 1-2-3 Keyboard

The most common configurations for keyboards on IBM and IBM-compatible personal computers are shown in figures 2.5, 2.6, and 2.7. The enhanced keyboard, shown in figure 2.7, is now the standard keyboard on all new IBM personal computers and most compatibles. Some compatibles, especially laptops, have different keyboards.

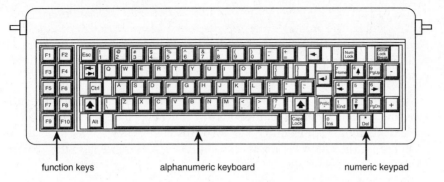

Fig. 2.5. The original IBM PC keyboard.

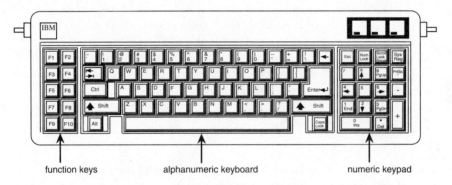

Fig. 2.6. The original IBM AT keyboard.

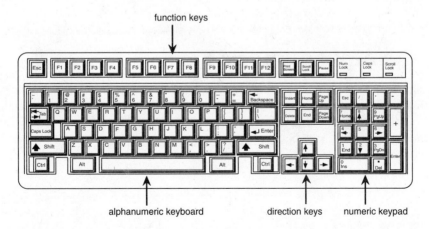

Fig. 2.7. The enhanced keyboard.

The keyboards are divided into four or five sections: the *alphanumeric keys* in the center, the *numeric keypad/direction keys* on the right, and the *function keys* on the left or across the top. The *special keys* are found in various locations. The *direction keys* are found in a separate section on the enhanced keyboard.

Reminder:
Some keys on the keyboard take on special meaning in 1-2-3.

Most keys in the alphanumeric section match the keys on a typewriter, and most maintain their normal functions in 1-2-3. Several keys, however, have special meanings. For example, the forward slash (/) key accesses the 1-2-3 main menu, the colon (:) key accesses the Wysiwyg menu, and the period (.) defines a range of cells.

You use the keys on the numeric keypad (on the right side of the keyboard) to enter numbers or to move the cell pointer or cursor.

The function keys provide special actions. For example, they can be used to access 1-2-3's editing functions, to display graphs, and to call up help messages. These keys are located across the top of the enhanced keyboard and on the left side of the older keyboards. Lotus provides function key templates with each software package to remind the user what each function key does.

The special keys include Del (Delete), Ins (Insert), Esc (Escape), Num Lock, Scroll Lock, Break, and Pause. These keys, which provide certain special actions, are located in different places on different keyboards.

Reminder:
Use the enhanced keyboard's numeric keypad to enter numbers.

Only the enhanced keyboard has a separate section for direction keys—the up-, down-, left-, and right-arrow keys. You can use the enhanced keyboard's numeric keypad to enter numbers and use the keyboard's direction keys to move easily around the worksheet.

The Alphanumeric Keys

Although most of the alphanumeric keys shown in figures 2.5, 2.6, and 2.7 have the same functions as on a typewriter, several keys have special functions in 1-2-3. These keys and their actions are listed in table 2.1. The meaning of these keys becomes clear as they are explained and used in later chapters.

Table 2.1
Alphanumeric Key Operation

Key	Action
→| (Tab)	Moves cell pointer one screen to the right
|← (Shift-Tab)	Moves cell pointer one screen to the left
Caps Lock	Activates capitalization of alphabetic characters when keys for those characters are pressed; displays the CAPS indicator in the status line when active; remains in effect until you press this key again (acts as a toggle)
↑ (Shift)	Changes lowercase letters and characters to uppercase; when not in Num Lock mode, enables you to type numbers on the numeric keypad
Ctrl	When used with the left- or right-arrow key, moves the cell pointer one screen to the left or right in READY mode; when used with Break, returns 1-2-3 to READY mode or halts execution of a macro; when used with F1, activates the last Help screen viewed
Alt	Used with the function keys to provide additional functions, such as activating LEARN mode and performing an Undo operation; also used with letter keys to invoke macros
Backspace	During cell definition or editing, erases the preceding character; cancels a range during some prompts that display the old range
/ (slash)	Calls up the 1-2-3 main menu; also used as a division sign in formulas
< (less-than sign)	Used as an alternative to the slash (/) to call up the 1-2-3 main menu; also used in logical formulas
. (period)	Defines a range of cells or anchors a cell address during pointing; also used as a decimal point when entering values
: (colon)	Calls up the Wysiwyg menu

The Numeric Keypad and the Direction Keys

The keys in the numeric keypad on the right side of IBM PC-style and AT-style keyboards are used mainly for moving the cell pointer or cursor (see figs. 2.5 and 2.6). When Num Lock is off, these keys are used as direction keys. When Num Lock is on (or the Shift key is used), these keys serve as number keys. You can reverse the setting of Num Lock by holding down the Shift key as you press one of the numeric keys. The enhanced keyboard has separate keys for moving the cell pointer or cursor (see fig. 2.7). The actions of the direction keys are explained in Chapter 3; the other special keys on the numeric keypad are discussed later in this chapter.

Cue:
Macros can solve numeric-keypad problems on PC-style and AT-style keyboards.

If you do not have an enhanced keyboard, you can use a macro to move the cell pointer every time you press Enter. You then can keep Num Lock on and use the numeric keypad to enter numbers. You can use different macros to move the cell pointer in different directions.

The Function Keys

The 10 function keys, F1 through F10, are used for special actions in 1-2-3. These keys are located across the top of the enhanced keyboard and on the left side of the other two keyboards. The enhanced keyboard has 12 function keys, but 1-2-3 uses only the first 10. These keys can be used alone or with the Alt or Ctrl key. Table 2.2 lists the function keys and an explanation of each key's action.

Table 2.2
Function Key Operation

Key	Action
F1 (Help)	Accesses the context-sensitive Help system, displays a cross-referenced Help index, and explains error messages that appear in a dialog box on-screen
F2 (Edit)	Puts 1-2-3 into EDIT mode to change the current cell; also enables you to activate a dialog box displayed on-screen
F3 (Name)	Displays a list of names any time a command or formula can accept a range name or a file name. Whenever a list of names is on the third line of the control panel, this key produces a full-screen display of all available names.

Key	Action
F4 (Abs)	In EDIT mode, changes a cell or range address from relative to absolute to mixed; in READY mode, enables you to prespecify ranges in 1-2-3 or Wysiwyg (You also can use a mouse to prespecify range.)
F5 (GoTo)	Moves the cell pointer directly to a specified cell address or range name; when used with F3 (Name), enables you to select a range name that you can jump to
F6 (Window)	Moves the cell pointer to another window when the screen is split; also toggles the display on dialog boxes on-screen.
F7 (Query)	In READY mode, repeats the last /Data Query command; during a /Data Query Find, switches between FIND and READY mode
F8 (Table)	Repeats the last /Data Table command
F9 (Calc)	In READY mode, recalculates all worksheets in memory; if entering or editing a formula, converts the formula to its current value
F10 (Graph)	Displays the current graph if one exists; if no current graph exists, displays a blank screen
Alt-F1 (Compose)	When used with alphanumeric keys, creates international characters that cannot be typed directly by using the keyboard. A list of these characters appears in Appendix C.
Alt-F2 (Step)	Activates STEP mode, enabling you to execute macros one step at a time; acts as a toggle
Alt-F3 (Run)	Generates a list of range names in the current worksheet, enabling you to select the name of a macro to execute
Alt-F4 (Undo)	Reverses all actions made since 1-2-3 was last in READY mode
Alt-F5 (Learn)	Activates the Learn feature and begins recording keystrokes in the prespecified learn range. Press Alt-F5 again to stop recording keystrokes.
Alt-F6	Not defined in Release 2.3

continues

Table 2.2 *(continued)*

Key	Action
Alt-F7 (App1)	Activates an add-in program assigned to this key combination, if one has been assigned
Alt-F8 (App2)	Activates an add-in program assigned to this key combination, if one has been assigned
Alt-F9 (App3)	Activates an add-in program assigned to this key combination, if one has been assigned
Alt-F10 (App4)	Activates an add-in program assigned to this key combination, if one has been assigned; otherwise, displays the /Add-In menu
Ctrl-F1 (Bookmark)	Displays the last Help screen viewed

The Special Keys

Reminder:
Use Esc to cancel a menu or an action; use Break to cancel a menu or a macro.

The special keys provide some important 1-2-3 functions. For example, Break cancels a menu as well as a macro. Esc cancels certain entries and backs up to the previous menu displayed in MENU mode. The Del key deletes a character when you are editing a cell.

Some special keys change the actions of other keys. When you edit data in a cell, you can use the Ins key to change the mode from insert to overtype. Num Lock changes the meaning of the keys on the numeric keypad from direction keys to numeric keys. Scroll Lock changes how the direction keys move the display. Special keys and their functions on the different keyboards are listed in table 2.3.

Using the Mouse with 1-2-3

To use a mouse with 1-2-3, you need mouse driver software that should be loaded from your CONFIG.SYS or AUTOEXEC.BAT file, depending upon which is appropriate for your mouse. Refer to the documentation provided with your mouse for more information. After the mouse software is loaded and the mouse is physically attached to your computer, you can use the mouse with 1-2-3.

A mouse (if one is installed) can replace some of the activities normally completed by using the keyboard in 1-2-3 and Wysiwyg. If you have a mouse installed, the *mouse pointer* (a small arrow) points to the center of the screen when 1-2-3 is loaded. The mouse enables you to quickly select commands, switch between the 1-2-3 and Wysiwyg menus, move the cell and menu pointers, select ranges, specify Help topics, and select items in a dialog box. If Wysiwyg is active, you also can use the mouse to change column widths and row heights. Before using the mouse, you should become familiar with terms such as *point*, *click*, *click-and-drag*, *icon*, and *icon panel*.

Cue:
Instead of pressing several keys, use the mouse to quickly perform an action.

Table 2.3
Special Key Operation

Key	Action
Break	Cancels a macro or a menu and returns 1-2-3 to READY mode. On the PC and AT keyboards, Break is Ctrl-Scroll Lock. On the enhanced keyboard, Break is Ctrl-Pause or Ctrl-Break.
Del	When a cell containing an entry is highlighted, erases the cell entry (similar to /**R**ange Erase); when editing a cell, deletes one character at the cell pointer
Esc	When accessing the command menus, backs up to the preceding menu; at the 1-2-3 or Wysiwyg main menu, returns to READY mode; when entering or editing data in a cell, clears the edit line; cancels a range during some prompts that display the old range; returns from the on-line help facility
Ins	When editing a cell, changes mode to overtype. Any keystrokes typed replace whatever is at the cell pointer. If you press Ins again to return to insert mode, any keystrokes are inserted at the cell pointer (acts as a toggle).
Num Lock	Shifts the actions of the numeric keypad from direction keys to numbers. On the PC and AT keyboards, Ctrl-Num Lock serves as the Pause key.
Pause	Pauses a macro, a recalculation, and some commands until you press any key (other than Pause)
Scroll Lock	Scrolls the entire window when you use the arrow keys. On the PC and AT keyboards, Ctrl-Scroll Lock serves as the Break key.

Understanding Mouse Terminology

To *point* means to move the mouse until the tip of the arrow is covering a specific part of the worksheet. For example, if you are instructed to point to cell B5, then you must move the mouse until the tip of the arrow is *over* cell B5.

When you *click* the mouse, you press and immediately release one of the two buttons on the mouse. (If the mouse has three buttons, only the two outside buttons are active. The center button is not used in 1-2-3.) Normally, you click a mouse button only after you have pointed with the mouse. The left button on the mouse acts as the Enter key. The right button has two functions. Normally, the right button acts as the Esc key; if you are typing text into a cell, for example, pressing the right button erases the text from the edit line and returns 1-2-3 to READY mode. The second function of the right mouse button is to switch between the 1-2-3 menu and the Wysiwyg menu.

Cue:
If you are left-handed, reverse the operations of the two mouse buttons.

When installing 1-2-3, you can reverse the operations of the mouse buttons. For example, you can make the right button the Enter button and the left button the Esc/Switch menu button. This change is helpful if you are left-handed.

Click-and-drag is a combination of pointing, clicking, and moving (dragging) the mouse. When you are using this method, you normally are highlighting a range. To click-and-drag, move the mouse pointer to the desired beginning location—for example, the upper left corner of a range. Press and hold down the left mouse button; do not release the button at this time (this anchors the cell pointer). Move the mouse pointer to the desired ending location, such as the lower right corner of a range, and release the mouse button. The desired range is highlighted. If you are responding to a menu prompt, click the left mouse button again to finish specifying the range. (If you are prespecifying a range, do not click the left mouse button again.)

For example, to select a range from B5 through D10 when prompted for a range, point to cell B5, press and hold down the left mouse button and point to cell D10; then release and press the left mouse button again.

An *icon* is a character that represents an action. These characters, four triangles and a question mark, appear on the right side of the screen—within the *icon panel* (see fig. 2.8). When you point and click on one of the icons, you invoke an action.

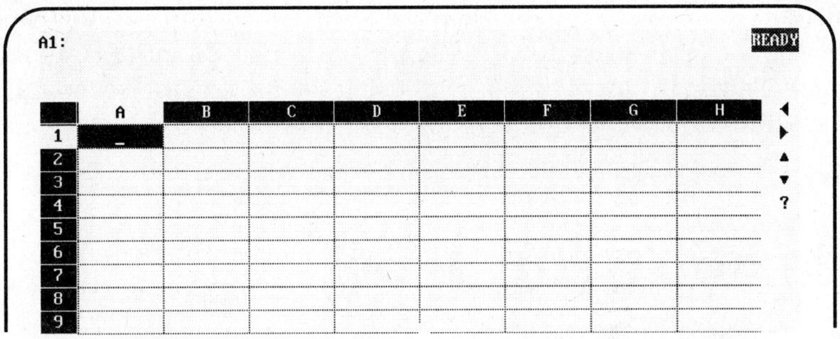

Fig. 2.8. The five mouse icons on the right side of the Release 2.3 screen.

Clicking any of the triangles has the same action as pressing one of the arrow keys; the cell pointer moves one cell in the direction indicated by the triangle. Clicking the question mark selects Help, just as if you pressed the F1 (Help) function key.

Using the Mouse To Select Menu Commands

When you move the mouse pointer into the control panel, a menu automatically appears on-screen as if you pressed the slash or colon key. The menu that appears (1-2-3 or Wysiwyg) depends on the last menu that was active. Pressing the right mouse button switches between the 1-2-3 and Wysiwyg menus.

Reminder:
Press the right mouse button to switch between the 1-2-3 and Wysiwyg menus.

Using the mouse to select an option from a menu is easy. First, activate a menu by moving the mouse pointer to the control panel. After a menu is active, point to a menu option, and click the left mouse button. All options from menus are selected in the same way. If the command requires you to type additional information, you may do so; then press Enter or click the left mouse button in the control panel to accept the entry.

If you press and hold down the left mouse button, you can drag the menu cursor to see each menu item's description. Releasing the button while the mouse pointer is in the control panel selects the highlighted option. To cancel a menu selection without selecting an option, move the mouse pointer out of the control panel.

Using the mouse can greatly increase your speed and productivity. If, however, you have used 1-2-3 in the past, you may be more comfortable using the keyboard. Experiment with using the mouse, the keyboard, or a combination of both to discover which method is best for you.

Learning the 1-2-3 Screen Display

The main 1-2-3 display is divided into three parts: the *control panel* at the top of the screen, the *worksheet area* itself, and the *status line* at the bottom of the screen (see fig. 2.9). The reverse-video *border*, or *frame*, marks the worksheet area. This border contains the letters and numbers that mark columns and rows.

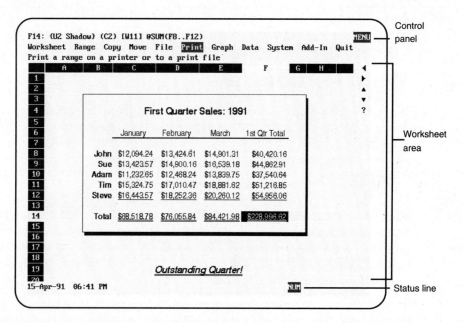

Fig. 2.9. *The three main parts of the 1-2-3 worksheet.*

The Control Panel

The three-line control panel is the area above the reverse-video border. The first line contains information about the current cell. This information can include the address of the cell, the cell's contents, and the protection status (U if unprotected or PR if protected). The cell's address is the column and the row in the form B4 for column B, row 4.

The format and column widths are included if different from the default; these attributes are explained in later chapters. When Wysiwyg is active, information applicable to Wysiwyg, such as row height, graph, and text format, also is displayed in the control panel.

When you use the command menus, the second line of the control panel displays the menu choices, and the third line contains explanations of the current menu item or the next hierarchical menu (see fig. 2.10). As you move the menu pointer from one item to the next in a command menu, the explanation on the third line of the control panel changes.

Cue:
The third line of the control panel displays an explanation of the highlighted command.

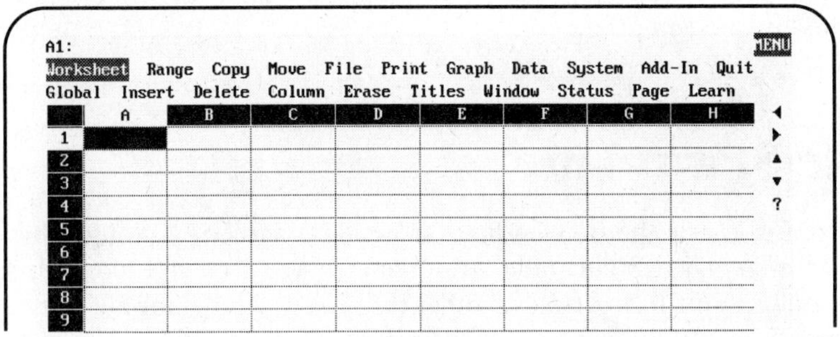

Fig. 2.10. *The 1-2-3 main menu with the Worksheet menu option highlighted.*

When a command prompts you for information, the second line of the control panel displays the prompt (see fig. 2.11). When a command prompts you for a file name, a range name, a graph name, or a print settings name, the third line displays the beginning of this list of names.

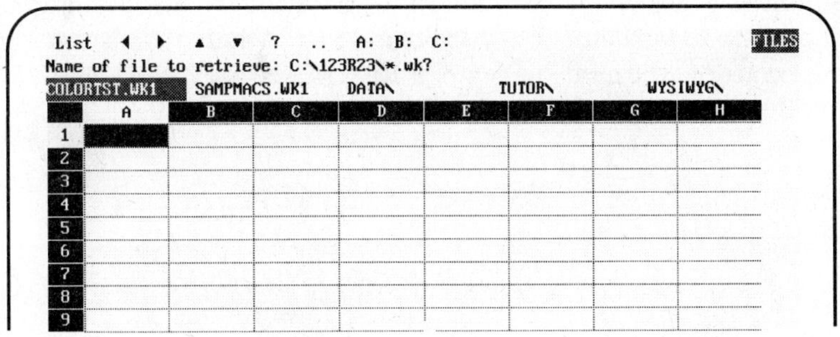

Fig. 2.11. *The display showing command prompts on the second line.*

The first line of the control panel also displays the mode indicator in the upper right corner. The mode indicators are described later in this chapter.

The Worksheet Area

The largest part of the 1-2-3 screen is the worksheet. The 1-2-3 worksheet has 256 lettered columns and 8,192 numbered rows, yct only a portion of the worksheet is displayed on-screen at any time. Information entered into the worksheet is stored in a cell, which is the intersection of a column and a row.

The *cell pointer* marks the location of the current cell in the worksheet area. When you enter data into the worksheet, the data goes into the location marked by the cell pointer.

The Status Line

The status line is the bottom line of the 1-2-3 screen. Although this line normally displays the current date and time, you can change it to reflect the current file name or to display neither the date and time nor file name. The current date and time can be displayed in the status line in two different formats. The status line also contains any status indicators, described later in this chapter.

The Mode Indicators

Reminder:
Mode indicators display the current mode, or state, of 1-2-3.

The *mode indicator* is located in the upper right corner of the control panel. This indicator tells you which mode 1-2-3 is in and what you can do next. Only one mode indicator is displayed at a time. When 1-2-3 is waiting for your next action, the mode indicator is READY (see fig. 2.12). Table 2.4 lists the mode indicators and their meanings.

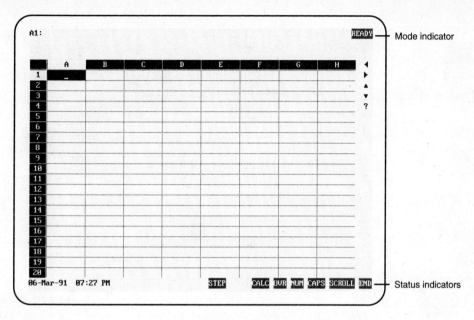

Fig. 2.12. *A mode indicator at the top and status indicators at the bottom of the worksheet.*

Table 2.4
Mode Indicators

Indicator	Description
COLOR	You selected one of the following Wysiwyg commands: **:Graph Edit Color Background** or **:Graph Edit Color Inside**.
CYCLE	You selected the Wysiwyg command **:Graph Edit Select Cycle**.
DRAG	You selected one of the following Wysiwyg commands: **:Graph Edit Add Rectangle**; **:Graph Edit Add Ellipse**; and **:Graph Edit View In**.
EDIT	You are editing a cell entry, editing settings in a dialog box, or you incorrectly entered a formula.
ERROR	1-2-3 encountered an error, and a dialog box is displaying the error on-screen. Press F1 to display an explanation of the error.

continues

Table 2.4 *(continued)*

Indicator	*Description*
FILES	1-2-3 prompted you to select a file name from a list of files.
FIND	1-2-3 is in the middle of a /Data Query Find operation.
FRMT	You selected the 1-2-3 command /Data Parse Format-Line Edit to edit a format line.
HELP	You are in the Help system, and a Help screen is displayed. Press Esc to return to the worksheet.
LABEL	You are entering a label into a cell.
MENU	A menu of 1-2-3 commands is displayed because you pressed slash (/) or the less-than symbol (<) from READY mode.
NAMES	1-2-3 prompted you to select a range name, graph name, or attached add-in name and then displayed a list of names.
PAN	You selected the Wysiwyg command :Graph Edit View Pan.
POINT	Either 1-2-3 prompted you to select a range or you used the direction keys to specify a range while entering a formula.
READY	1-2-3 is waiting for your next entry or command. Ready is the default mode when you start 1-2-3.
SELECT	You selected one of the following Wysiwyg commands: :Format Font (1...8) Replace Other; :Print Config Printer; :Graph Edit Select One; :Graph Edit Select More/Less; or options on the :Graph Edit Edit or :Graph Edit Transform commands.
SETTINGS	A dialog box is active and displayed on-screen.
STAT	1-2-3 is displaying a status screen resulting from the /Worksheet Status or /Worksheet Global Default Status command.
TEXT	You selected the Wysiwyg command :Text Edit.
VALUE	You are entering a number or a formula (a value) into a cell.

Indicator	Description
WAIT	1-2-3 is in the middle of some activity. Do not proceed until the activity finishes and the WAIT indicator disappears.
WYSIWYG	A menu of Wysiwyg commands is displayed because you pressed the colon (:) key from READY mode.

The Status Indicators

1-2-3 displays the *status indicators* in the status line at the bottom of the display. These indicators give you information about conditions that are present. More than one status indicator can be displayed at one time. Each indicator displays in reverse video (see fig. 2.12). The status indicators and their meanings are listed in table 2.5.

Reminder:
Status indicators appear when certain conditions are present in the worksheet.

Table 2.5
Status Indicators

Indicator	Description
CALC	Warns you that parts of the file may not be current. Press Calc (F9) to recalculate the worksheet and clear the indicator.
CAPS	You pressed Caps Lock. All letters are entered as uppercase. Press Caps Lock again to turn off the indicator.
CIRC	A circular reference exists in the worksheet. Use the /Worksheet Status command or the Auditor add-in program to find information on the circular reference.
CMD	You are running a macro.
END	You pressed the End key.
LEARN	The Learn feature has been activated by pressing Alt-F5, and your keystrokes are being recorded in the Learn range. Press Alt-F5 again to clear the indicator and stop recording keystrokes.
MEM	You have fewer than 4,096 characters of memory left and may soon receive a `Memory full` error message.

continues

Table 2.5 *(continued)*

Indicator	Description
NUM	You pressed Num Lock. The keys on the numeric keypad now act as numbers, not direction keys. To use the keys as direction keys, press Num Lock again or press the Shift key.
OVR	You pressed Ins while editing a cell to change to overtype mode. Any keystrokes replace whatever is at that cell pointer position in the cell. Press Ins again to return to insert mode. Keystrokes then are inserted at the cell pointer position.
PRT	Indicates a background print is in progress.
RO	The current file is read-only. The file can be saved only with a different name. Applies to files used on a network or multiuser system.
SCROLL	You pressed Scroll Lock. Whenever you use an arrow key, the entire window moves in the direction of the arrow. To use the arrow keys to move the cell pointer from cell to cell, press Scroll Lock again.
SST	You are executing a macro in single-step mode.
STEP	You turned on single-step mode for macros, but you are not currently running a macro. When you start a macro, this indicator changes to SST.
UNDO	The Undo feature has been activated with the /Worksheet Global Default Other Undo Enable command. You can press Alt-F4 to reverse changes made since 1-2-3 was last in READY mode.

Now that you have learned about several important features of the screen, you may want to see them all together. Figure 2.13 shows a screen with all its parts labeled.

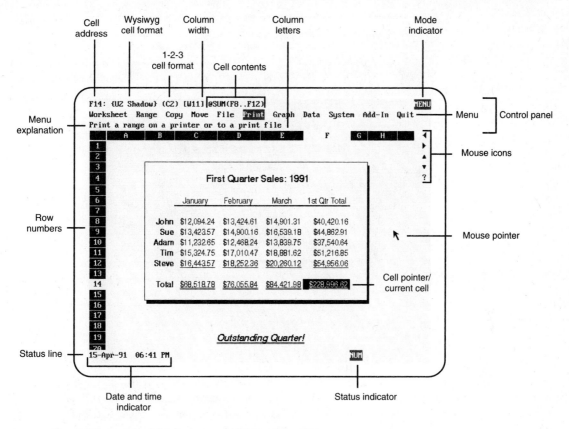

Fig. 2.13. A typical 1-2-3 screen and its various parts.

The Interactive Dialog Boxes

When you choose certain commands in 1-2-3 and Wysiwyg such as /Worksheet Global, /Graph, /Print Printer, /Data Sort, /Data Query, :Format Font, and :Print, 1-2-3 displays a special status screen or *dialog box* (see fig. 2.14). A dialog box shows the current settings associated with a command and helps you keep track of the choices you are making.

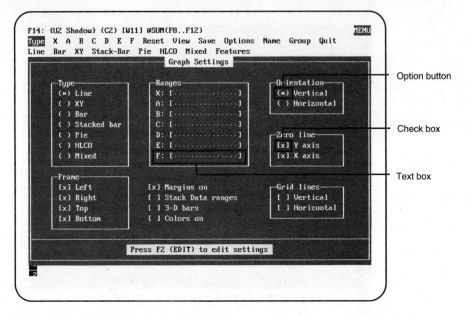

Fig. 2.14. A dialog box.

In addition to showing the settings, dialog boxes enable you to select settings from the screen rather than through menus. You still can use the command menu to select the desired operation, however. The different parts of dialog boxes consist of option buttons, check boxes, text boxes, pop-up dialog boxes, command buttons, and list boxes.

Option buttons appear as parentheses. If an option is selected, an asterisk (*) appears within the parentheses. You can select only one option from a group of option buttons. Check boxes appear as brackets [ ]. If an item is on, or active, the box contains an x. You can select any number of check boxes that appear in a dialog box. Text boxes enable you to type text, a number, or a range name, depending on what the command requires.

When a command requires further options, 1-2-3 may show a pop-up dialog box with more choices or a list box enabling you to choose an item from a list (see fig. 2.15).

To use a dialog box with the keyboard, press F2 (Edit). 1-2-3 highlights a character (usually the first letter) from each of the options in the dialog box (see fig. 2.16). Press the letter of the option you want to change.

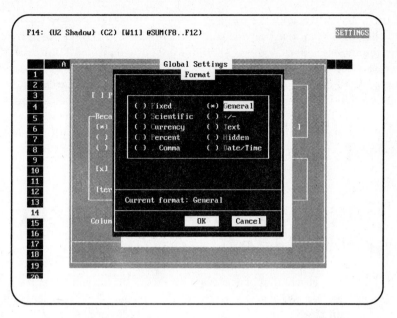

Fig. 2.15. *A pop-up dialog box.*

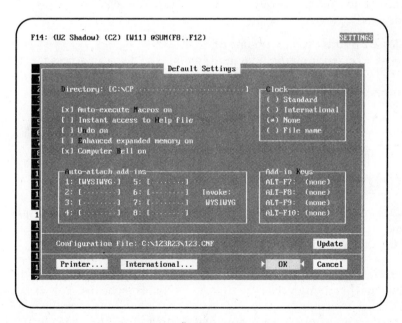

Fig. 2.16. *Options highlighted in a dialog box when you press Edit (F2).*

To use a dialog box with the mouse, move the mouse pointer to an option and click the left mouse button. After you press Edit (F2) or choose an item with the mouse, the dialog box shows at least one command button at the bottom of the dialog box (see fig. 2.16). The OK command button is the most common. Choose OK by pressing Enter when the command button is highlighted or by clicking on the command button. Other command buttons include Cancel and choices that produce another dialog box. Command buttons that produce another dialog box end with an ellipsis (...).

Using the 1-2-3 Help System and On-Line Tutorials

Cue:
Use the Help feature and the on-line tutorials to get assistance with 1-2-3.

1-2-3 includes features that provide help to users: the context-sensitive Help system and the 1-2-3-Go! and Wysiwyg-Go! tutorials. 1-2-3 provides on-line help at the touch of a key. You can be in the middle of any operation and press the Help (F1) key at any time to get one or more screens of explanations and advice on what to do next. You also can access a Help index and a glossary of terms.

Release 2.3 adds two new on-line tutorials, 1-2-3-Go! and Wysiwyg-Go!, that can be accessed from the operating system. You also can access the 1-2-3-Go! tutorial from within 1-2-3. Each of these tutorials provides several lessons on how to use different 1-2-3 and Wysiwyg features.

Using the Context-Sensitive Help System

Press Help (F1) at any time to get to the on-line help facility. If you press Help while in READY mode, the Help Index appears (see fig. 2.17). Choose any of the topics in the Help Index to get to the other help screens.

Reminder:
The Help (F1) key is context-sensitive.

You can press the Help (F1) key at any time, even while executing a command or editing a cell. The Help key is context-sensitive. For example, if you are executing a particular command when you press Help (F1), 1-2-3 displays a help screen about that command (see fig. 2.18).

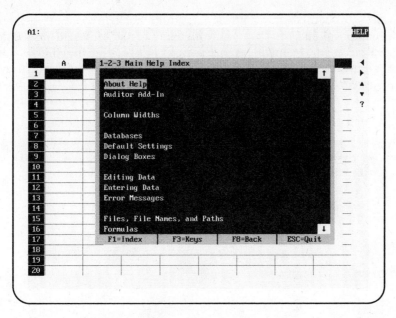

Fig. 2.17. *The 1-2-3 Help Index screen.*

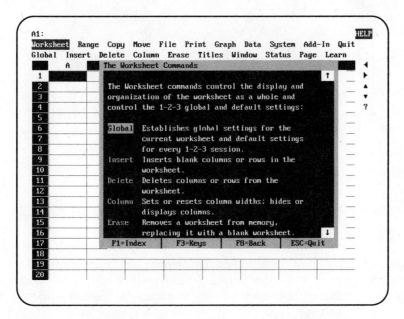

Fig. 2.18. *A context-sensitive help screen that explains the /Worksheet commands.*

Certain parts of the help screen identify additional help topics. To get more information about a topic, move the highlight to that topic and press Enter. You can access the Help Index by pressing F1 again. Other function keys that can assist you with Help are displayed at the bottom of the Help screen. Press the Esc key to return to the 1-2-3 worksheet when you finish consulting the Help system. When you return to the worksheet, you can return to the last Help screen displayed by pressing Ctrl-F1 (Bookmark).

Cue:
Help also is available for Wysiwyg.

You also can access context-sensitive help information if you are working with Wysiwyg. Pressing F1 from the Wysiwyg main menu (with the :Graph option highlighted) brings up the Wysiwyg help screen shown in figure 2.19.

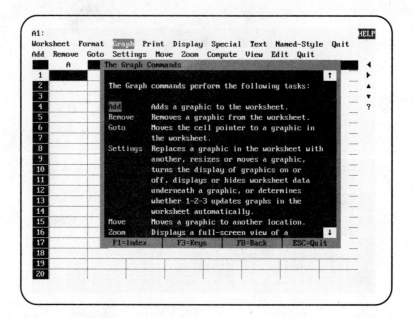

Fig. 2.19. *A Wysiwyg help screen.*

Using the On-Line Tutorials

The on-line tutorials discussed earlier provide help on various 1-2-3 and Wysiwyg procedures and features. 1-2-3-Go! teaches you the basics of how to use 1-2-3. Wysiwyg-Go! shows you how to create professional-looking documents and graphics with the Wysiwyg feature. The 1-2-3-Go! and Wysiwyg-Go! tutorials do not cover all commands and features of 1-2-3 and Wysiwyg but cover enough to give you a basic understanding of 1-2-3 and Wysiwyg. The tutorials do not provide any assistance for users who want to use the mouse. Before you can use the tutorials, you must install them onto your hard disk (see Appendix A).

If you are new to 1-2-3, the best approach is to complete the 1-2-3-Go! tutorial before proceeding with the Wysiwyg-Go! tutorial. After each lesson of 1-2-3-Go!, work with 1-2-3 for a while before you tackle the more advanced topics. Only after you feel comfortable with all the material in the first section of the tutorial should you try the other sections and move on to Wysiwyg-Go!

If you have used previous versions of 1-2-3 before and are new to Release 2.3, you may choose to skip 1-2-3-Go! and proceed directly to Wysiwyg-Go! to try out the new Wysiwyg features.

For further details on 1-2-3 functions and commands, refer to the command reference section or other appropriate sections of this book or to the 1-2-3 documentation.

Using 1-2-3-Go!

The 1-2-3-Go! tutorial is divided into four major sections that cover the following information:

- Building a Worksheet
- Using Graphs
- Using a Database
- Working with Macros

You can access 1-2-3-Go! from within the worksheet or from the operating system. To use 1-2-3-Go! from the worksheet, you first must clear all attached add-ins with /Add-In Clear. Then select /Add-In Attach. Select TUTOR.ADN from the list of add-ins that appears in the control panel. Next, select the function key you want to use to start the tutorial. Finally, select Invoke and select TUTOR from the list of attached add-ins to begin using 1-2-3-Go! The next time you want to use the tutorial in the current 1-2-3 session, you can use the function key you selected when you attached the add-in.

To use 1-2-3-Go! from the operating system, first change to the 1-2-3 program directory. Then type **LEARN123** and press Enter. Follow the instructions on-screen to proceed with the tutorial. Figure 2.20 displays the opening screen of 1-2-3-Go!

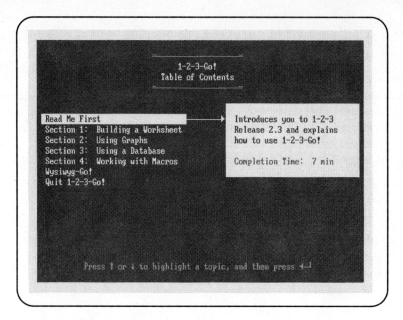

Fig. 2.20. The opening screen of the 1-2-3-Go! tutorial.

Using Wysiwyg-Go!

The Wysiwyg-Go! tutorial also is divided into five major sections. These sections cover the following topics:

- Introduction to Wysiwyg
- Formatting a Worksheet
- Including Graphics in a Worksheet
- Using Text Ranges
- Previewing and Printing

You can access Wysiwyg-Go! only from the operating system. To do this, first change to your 1-2-3 program directory. Then type **LEARNWYS** and press Enter. Follow the instructions on-screen to proceed with the tutorial. Figure 2.21 displays the opening screen of Wysiwyg-Go!

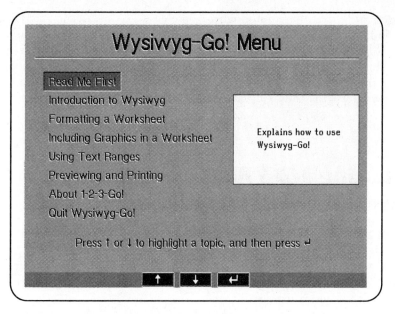

Fig. 2.21. The opening screen of the Wysiwyg-Go! tutorial.

Using 1-2-3 Release 2.3 with Microsoft Windows

Microsoft Windows 3 is a popular operating environment for DOS. Windows 3 enables you to start programs, manage directories and files, and run multiple programs at the same time in multiple windows on-screen. Release 2.3 can be started and operated from this environment. Although 1-2-3 Release 2.3 cannot take full advantage of Windows 3 like a program written specifically for Windows (such as Microsoft Excel), it can return to 1-2-3 applications without exiting Windows, and it can transfer information to other programs while operating in Windows.

Microsoft Windows 3 operates in three modes. *Real Mode* is used to run old Windows applications. *Standard Mode* operates on a computer equipped with an 80286 microprocessor, such as an IBM AT or compatible. Another mode, which works on computers with at least an 80386 microprocessor,

Cue:
You can use 1-2-3 Release 2.3 with the Microsoft Windows 3 operating environment.

is *386-Enhanced Mode*. Although 1-2-3 Release 2.3 operates in Standard or 386-Enhanced mode, you may find that 1-2-3's speed is better in Standard Mode. In 386-Enhanced Mode, however, transferring information to other programs is more versatile. If you are using Wysiwyg, you must operate 1-2-3 in a full screen with 386-Enhanced mode. If you try to run Release 2.3 in a window (instead of a full screen) you may encounter errors that will abort the Microsoft Windows program.

Starting 1-2-3 Release 2.3 from Microsoft Windows

1-2-3 Release 2.3 includes a special file, a *Program Information File* (PIF), which contains information that Windows must have for 1-2-3 to operate from Windows. This information includes the amount of memory that 1-2-3 requires, whether 1-2-3 will run in a window and whether 1-2-3 requires the entire screen.

You can create an icon in Windows' Program Manager to start 1-2-3. You can do it yourself or let Windows create the icon by using the Windows Setup utility found in the Main program group of the Program Manager. Activating this icon starts 1-2-3 from Microsoft Windows 3.

If you are using 1-2-3 in Windows' Standard Mode or if you are using Wysiwyg in 386-Enhanced Mode, then you must run 1-2-3 in *full-screen* mode. 1-2-3 takes the entire screen. You may use the Alt-Esc key to switch from 1-2-3 back to Windows. When you switch back to Windows, 1-2-3 stops whatever it is doing. When you switch back to 1-2-3, however, 1-2-3 picks up where it left off.

1-2-3 operates in Windows just as it does if you do not use Windows. One benefit of using Windows is that you can transfer information from 1-2-3 into a Windows document.

Transferring 1-2-3 Data by Using Microsoft Windows

Cue:
Use 1-2-3 with Microsoft Windows to transfer information.

While using 1-2-3 with Windows, you can copy information from the 1-2-3 screen and place it in other Windows applications such as word processors like WordPerfect or Microsoft Word. If you are using 1-2-3 in full-screen mode, you must transfer the entire screen.

Summary

This chapter presented the information you need to use 1-2-3 for the first time. You learned how to start and exit 1-2-3 from either the operating system or the Lotus 1-2-3 Access menu and how to start Wysiwyg. You learned how to implement the Install and Translate programs. You also learned about the features provided in the 1-2-3 display and how 1-2-3 uses the keyboard and mouse. In addition, you learned how to use the context-sensitive Help system and the on-line tutorials.

This chapter sets the stage so that you can begin to use 1-2-3 for your work. The next chapter presents information on entering and editing data and moving around in worksheets. Chapter 3 also presents additional information about using Wysiwyg.

3

Learning
Worksheet Basics

This chapter presents the skills you need to use 1-2-3, the powerful electronic spreadsheet. If this is your first experience with spreadsheet software, you learn how to use a spreadsheet to analyze and control data, numbers, and formulas. If you are familiar with electronic spreadsheets but are new to 1-2-3 or to Release 2.3, you learn information that helps you better understand the conventions and features of the program.

1-2-3 refers to its spreadsheet as a *worksheet*. In this chapter, you gain access to the power of 1-2-3 by learning how to move around the worksheet with the keyboard and with the mouse. Most of the actions you perform on a worksheet change it in some way. Some of these actions, such as entering and editing data, are covered in this chapter. Also discussed is the Undo feature, which enables you to reverse changes made in error.

You also learn how to correct errors in formulas by using the Auditor add-in provided with Release 2.3 (discussed in Appendix B). Because you use worksheets as final reports, you need a method to organize material. This chapter shows you how to use titles, headings, names, comments, descriptions, and a variety of other entries, called *labels*, to make your worksheets clear and easy to follow.

Finally, this chapter teaches you how to create formulas that link data in a single worksheet as well as formulas that link a cell in one worksheet to a cell in another worksheet. This file-linking capability enables you to create many types of consolidations. The Viewer add-in, new with Release 2.3, enables you to link files quickly. The Viewer program is discussed briefly in this chapter and in more detail in Chapter 7.

This chapter enables you to do the following:

- Work with worksheets and files
- Move the cell pointer around the worksheet with the keyboard or the mouse
- Enter labels, numbers, and formulas
- Edit data
- Use the Undo feature
- Use the linking capabilities

Understanding Files and Worksheets

When you first start 1-2-3, you start with a blank worksheet file and build a worksheet in the computer's memory. To keep the worksheet, you save it in a file on disk with a file name. (Chapter 7 covers files in detail.) In 1-2-3 Releases 2.01, 2.2, and 2.3, a file consists of one worksheet. (In Releases 3 and 3.1, a file can contain up to 256 worksheets.)

Whenever you enter data into the worksheet, the entry goes into the cell at the location of the cell pointer. This highlighted cell is the *current cell*. To move around the worksheet, you move the cell pointer. By moving the cell pointer, you control where you put data in the worksheet. In figure 3.1, for example, data you type goes into cell C7 until you move the cell pointer.

Usually, the current date and time are displayed in the lower left corner of the screen. You can change this default display to the name of the current file. To do so, execute the /Worksheet Global Default Other Clock Filename command. In figure 3.1, the current file is PROFIT.WK1. The worksheet is displayed on-screen.

```
C7: (,2) [W12] +C4-C5                                    READY

        A              B          C          D      E      F    ◀
 1  Fourth Quarter Profit                                       ▶
 2                   Projection   Actual                        ▲
 3                   This Year   Last Year   % Change           ▼
 4  Sales           $315,221.98 $252,422.96  19.92%             ?
 5  Variable costs  $190,965.23  151,173.83  20.84%
 6
 7  Variable Margin  124,256.75  101,249.13  18.52%
 8  Fixed Costs      $41,235.36   36,512.21  11.45%
 9
10  Profit Before Taxes 83,021.39 64,736.92  22.02%
11  Taxes            50,435.52   32,314.98   34.94%
12
13  Profit           32,585.87   31,921.94    2.04%
14
15
16
17
18
19
20
21
22
PROFIT.WK1
```

Fig. 3.1. *A sample worksheet.*

Formulas are operations or calculations that you want 1-2-3 to perform on data. Formulas make 1-2-3 an electronic worksheet, not just a computerized method of displaying data. You enter the numbers and the formulas, and 1-2-3 performs the calculations. If you change a number, 1-2-3 changes the results of the formulas that use that number. For example, if you change the number in C4 or C5 in figure 3.1, the results of the cells containing formulas that depend on these cells change automatically.

Reminder:
Formulas make 1-2-3 an electronic worksheet.

Retrieving Files

To call a file into memory from disk (after it has been saved), use the /File Retrieve command. Then select the desired file name from a list of worksheet files displayed in the control panel (see fig. 3.2). You can press the Name (F3) key to see a full-screen listing of file names.

When you select /File Retrieve, the command brings a new file into memory. However, if you already have a file on-screen and use /File Retrieve, the command replaces the current file with the new file, and the previously loaded file is removed from memory. Therefore, you always should save the current file with /File **Save** *before* retrieving a new file. If you forget this step, however, Release 2.3 reminds you to save before replacing the current file. Chapter 7 contains complete information on saving and retrieving worksheet files.

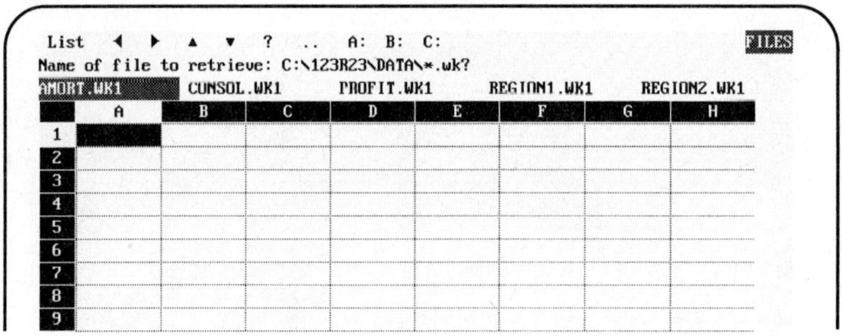

```
List  ◀  ▶  ▲  ▼  ?  ..  A:  B:  C:                      FILES
Name of file to retrieve: C:\123R23\DATA\*.wk?
AMORT.WK1      CUNSOL.WK1      PROFIT.WK1    REGION1.WK1    REGION2.WK1
        A        B        C        D        E        F        G        H
  1
  2
  3
  4
  5
  6
  7
  8
  9
```

Fig. 3.2. *A partial list of worksheet files in the current drive and directory.*

Introducing File Linking

Reminder:
File linking enables you to link a current file to another file.

1-2-3 Release 2.3 enables you to put a formula in the current worksheet that refers to cells in other worksheets stored on disk. This procedure is called *file linking* or *creating file links*.

With this capability, you easily can consolidate data in separate files. Suppose that you have to consolidate data from several departments and each department's data is in a separate file. Your consolidation file can use formulas to link the data from each department file. See "Entering Formulas That Link Files" later in this chapter.

Using linked files instead of one large file gives you the following advantages:

- You can use file linking to build worksheet systems too large to fit into memory at the same time.

- You easily can track information and its specific location.

- You can link files that come from different sources.

Moving around the Worksheet

Moving around the worksheet means moving the *cell pointer*, the high-lighted rectangle that identifies a cell. In figure 3.1, the cell pointer is in cell C7. Characters inside the cell pointer appear in reverse video on the highlighted background. (You can use the Wysiwyg **:D**isplay Options Cell-Pointer Outline command to change the default solid cell pointer to an outline and display the cell contents in normal video.) Data typed into the worksheet goes into the cell at the location of the cell pointer. The *cursor* is the small line that appears within the cell pointer and the control panel when you enter or edit data in a cell. Generally, the cursor shows you the position of the next character typed. Within a menu, the *menu pointer* is the highlight used to select a command.

Reminder:
The cell pointer highlights the current cell.

Because you can enter data only at the location of the cell pointer, you must know how to move the cell pointer to the location you want before you enter data. Also, because you can display only a small part of the worksheet at any one time, you must know how to move the cell pointer to see different parts of the worksheet at different times. The cell pointer is controlled with keyboard keys or—as long as the mouse driver is loaded and a mouse is attached to the computer—with the mouse. The following sections cover moving the cell pointer around the worksheet with the keyboard and the mouse.

Keyboard Control of the Cell Pointer

Many of the same keys move the cell pointer or the cursor, depending on the current mode. These *direction keys* are sometimes referred to as *pointer-movement keys* when they move the cell pointer, and *cursor-movement keys* when they move the cursor. This distinction between pointer-movement and cursor-movement keys can be confusing if you forget that these terms refer to the same keys.

Reminder:
Many of the same keys are used to move the cell pointer and the cursor.

This section discusses the movement of the cell pointer. Cursor movement is covered later in this chapter. Menu-pointer movement is discussed in Chapter 4.

When 1-2-3 is in READY or POINT mode, the direction keys move the cell pointer. In LABEL or VALUE mode, the direction keys end the entry, return to READY mode, and move the cell pointer. In EDIT mode, some direction keys move the cursor in the control panel; other direction keys end the edit, return to READY mode, and move the cell pointer. In MENU mode, the direction keys move the menu pointer to different menu options.

Reminder:
The control panel shows the column letter and row number of the current cell.

The current cell address appears in the upper left corner of the display in the following format: B3. This format represents the column letter followed by the row number. Another way to quickly find the current location of the cell is by observing the reverse-video border. The column border and row border contrast with the rest of the border. Exactly how it contrasts depends on the type of monitor you use.

Using the Basic Direction Keys

Reminder:
Use the arrow keys on the keyboard to move the cell pointer.

The four arrow keys that move the cell pointer are located on the numeric keypad on all keyboards. The enhanced keyboard also has a separate pad for direction keys. The cell pointer moves in the direction of the arrow on the key. If you press and hold the arrow key, the cell pointer continues to move in that direction. When the pointer reaches the edge of the screen, the worksheet continues to scroll in the direction of the arrow. If you try to move past the edge of the worksheet, 1-2-3 beeps a warning.

You can use several other keys to page through the worksheet by moving the cell pointer one screen at a time. Press the PgUp and PgDn keys to move up or down one screen. Press Ctrl-→ or Tab to move one screen to the right; press Ctrl-← or Shift-Tab (hold the Shift key and press Tab) to move one screen to the left. The size of one screen depends on the type of display driver in your system and whether a window is present on-screen. (Windows are discussed in Chapter 4.)

Table 3.1 summarizes the action of the direction keys. Press the Home key to move the cell pointer directly to the home position—usually cell A1. In Chapter 4, you learn how to freeze worksheet titles on-screen—freezing titles changes the home position of a worksheet. The other keys listed in table 3.1 are covered in the following sections.

Table 3.1
Direction Keys

Key	Description
←	In the worksheet, moves the cell pointer one cell to the left; in the control panel, moves the cursor one character to the left in EDIT mode; in the command menu, moves the menu pointer one item to the left in MENU mode

Key	*Description*
→	In the worksheet, moves the cell pointer one cell to the right; in the control panel, moves the cursor one character to the right in EDIT mode; in the command menu, moves the menu pointer one item to the right in MENU mode
↑	Moves the cell pointer up one row
↓	Moves the cell pointer down one row
Tab or Ctrl-→	In the worksheet, moves the cell pointer one screen to the right; in the control panel, moves the cursor five characters to the right in EDIT mode
Shift-Tab or Ctrl-←	In the worksheet, moves the cell pointer one screen to the left; in the control panel, moves the cursor five characters to the left in EDIT mode
PgUp	Moves the cell pointer up one screen
PgDn	Moves the cell pointer down one screen
Home	Moves the cell pointer to the home position (cell A1, unless worksheet titles are set)
End Home	Moves the cell pointer to the lower right corner of the current worksheet
End-→, End-↓, End-←, End-↑	Moves the cell pointer (in the direction of the arrow key) to the next boundary and between a blank cell and a cell that contains data
F5 (GoTo)	Moves the cell pointer directly to the cell address or range name you specify
F6 (Window)	If the window has been split, moves the cell pointer to the next window
Scroll Lock	Toggles the scroll function on and off; when active, moves the entire window when you press one of the four arrow keys

Scrolling the Worksheet

Reminder:
Use Scroll Lock to toggle the scroll function.

The Scroll Lock key toggles the scroll function on and off. When you press the Scroll Lock key, you activate the scroll function, and the SCROLL status indicator appears at the bottom right of the screen.

When you press an arrow key while Scroll Lock is on, the cell pointer stays in the current cell, and the entire window moves in the direction of the arrow key. When the cell pointer reaches the end of the display, and if you continue to press the same arrow key, the cell pointer moves to the next cell as the entire window scrolls. If the SCROLL status indicator is on, press the Scroll Lock key again to turn it off.

Use the scroll function with the arrow keys if you want to see part of the worksheet off-screen without moving the cell pointer from the current cell. For example, in figure 3.3, the cell pointer is in cell B3. Suppose that you want to see the data in column G before you change the contents of B3. If you turn on the scroll function and press the right-arrow key once, the entire window moves to the right. You can see column G, and the cell pointer stays in B3 (see fig. 3.3). To get the same result without using Scroll Lock, you move the mouse until column G appears; then you click cell B3, or you press the right arrow five times to display column G and then press the left arrow five times to return to B3.

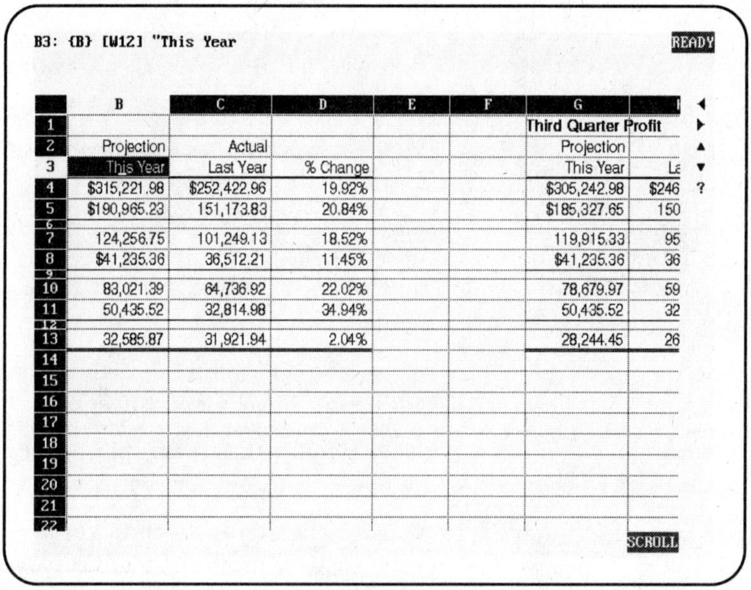

Fig. 3.3. The Scroll Lock key used to move an entire window.

When you use the mouse to move the cell pointer, you see no obvious change in operation until you try to move to a cell not on the current screen. Then Scroll Lock is disabled, and the worksheet scrolls normally.

Scroll Lock has no effect on the other direction keys. If the cell pointer does not move the way you expect it to, check to see whether Scroll Lock has been accidentally turned on. Check for the SCROLL indicator in the lower-right corner of the screen, as shown in figure 3.3. Press Scroll Lock again to turn it off.

Reminder:
Check the scroll indicator if the cell pointer does not move as you expect.

Using the End Key

The End key is used in a special way in 1-2-3. When you press and release the End key, the END status indicator appears in the status line. If you then click one of the triangle icons with the mouse or press one of the arrow keys, the cell pointer moves in the direction of the triangle or arrow key to the next intersection of a blank cell and a cell that contains data. The cell pointer always stops on a cell that contains data if possible. If there are no cells that contain data in the direction of the triangle or arrow key, the cell pointer stops at the edge of the worksheet. After you press the End key, the END indicator stays on only until you click a triangle icon or press an arrow key or the End key again. If you press End in error, just press End again, and the END status indicator disappears.

Reminder:
Use End with an arrow key or triangle icon to move to the next intersection of a blank cell and a cell that contains data.

For example, figure 3.4 shows the cell pointer in cell B3. The END status indicator at the bottom right corner of the screen shows that the End key has been pressed. If you now click the triangle that points to the right or press the right-arrow key, the cell pointer moves right to the first cell that contains data, and the END indicator disappears. In this case, the cell pointer moves to D3, as shown in figure 3.5. If you press the End key and then click the triangle that points right or press the right-arrow key again, the cell pointer moves to the last cell that contains data before a blank cell. In this case, the cell pointer moves to G3, as shown in figure 3.6.

In the preceding example, if no other data is in the worksheet and you press the End key and then click the right-triangle or press the right-arrow key again, the cell pointer moves to the end of the worksheet to cell IV3. If you press End and then click the down-triangle or press the down-arrow key from G3, the cell pointer moves to G14.

Cue:
Use the End key to move directly to the end of a list of data.

If you press the End key and then the Home key, the cell pointer moves to the lower right corner of the *active area.* The active area includes rows and columns that have data or cell formats (covered in Chapter 5).

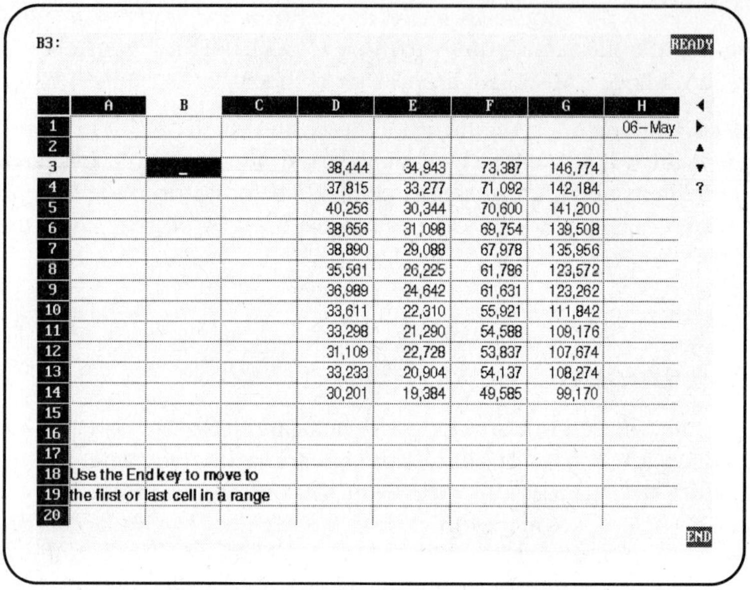

Fig. 3.4. *The END status indicator.*

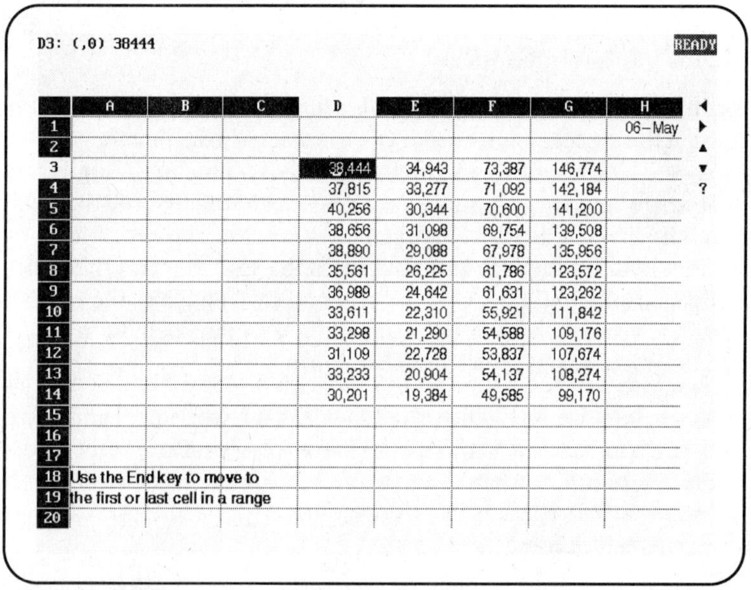

Fig. 3.5. *The cell pointer moved to the first cell that contains data after pressing End-→ from cell B3.*

```
G3: (,0) 146774                                              READY

        A       B       C       D       E       F       G       H    ◄
  1                                                            06-May ►
  2                                                                   ▲
  3                              38,444  34,943  73,387  146,774      ▼
  4                              37,815  33,277  71,092  142,184      ?
  5                              40,256  30,344  70,600  141,200
  6                              38,656  31,098  69,754  139,508
  7                              38,890  29,088  67,978  135,956
  8                              35,561  26,225  61,786  123,572
  9                              36,989  24,642  61,631  123,262
 10                              33,611  22,310  55,921  111,842
 11                              33,298  21,290  54,588  109,176
 12                              31,109  22,728  53,837  107,674
 13                              33,233  20,904  54,137  108,274
 14                              30,201  19,384  49,585   99,170
 15
 16
 17
 18 Use the End key to move to
 19 the first or last cell in a range
 20
```

Fig. 3.6. The cell pointer moved to the last cell that contains data after pressing End-→ again.

If you press End and then Home in figure 3.4, the cell pointer moves to H19. 1-2-3 considers this blank cell the end of the active area because there is an entry in column H (in H1) and an entry in row 19 (in A19). Use End and then Home to find the end of the active area if you want to add a section to the worksheet and not interfere with existing data.

Using the GoTo Key

You can use the GoTo (F5) key to jump directly to any cell in the worksheet. When you press GoTo (F5), 1-2-3 prompts you for an address. When you type the cell address and press Enter, the cell pointer moves directly to that address. The address format is the column letter from A to IV, followed by the row number from 1 to 8192.

Without the GoTo key, especially if you have a large worksheet, you must hold down the mouse button for a long time or press one of the direction keys many times to move from one part of the worksheet to another. With the GoTo key, you can move quickly across large parts of the worksheet.

Reminder:
Use GoTo (F5) to jump to any cell in the worksheet.

Cue:
You can use range names with the GoTo (F5) key.

With a large worksheet, you may find it difficult to remember the addresses for each part of the worksheet. You can, however, use range names with the GoTo (F5) key so that you don't have to remember cell addresses.

You can give a range name to a cell or a rectangular group of cells. *Range name* is a synonym for cell address; for example, you can give cell B56 the range name PROFIT. Range names are easier to remember than cell addresses. If you include range names in the worksheet, you can press GoTo (F5) and then type the range name instead of the cell address. If the range name refers to more than one cell, the cell pointer moves to the upper left corner of the range. After you press GoTo (F5), you also can press Name (F3) to display a list of range names from which you can select the desired range name to jump to. More information about ranges and range names is provided in Chapter 4.

Mouse Control of the Cell Pointer

Cue:
To move the cell pointer with the mouse, use the icon panel at the right side of the screen.

You can use the mouse to move the cell pointer in READY or POINT mode. When in LABEL, VALUE, or EDIT mode, the left mouse button ends the entry and returns to READY mode. You also can use the mouse to move the menu pointer to menu choices when in MENU mode. Several ways exist to move the cell pointer with the mouse. The simplest way is to point to a cell and click the left mouse button. Another way is to use one of the four directional icons on the right side of the worksheet. This set of icons, the *icon panel*, contains four solid triangles, each pointing in a different direction (see fig. 3.1).

Reminder:
Point to one of the triangular mouse icons, hold down the mouse button, and move the pointer off the worksheet to scroll the screen.

Pointing to one of the triangles and clicking the left mouse button moves the cell pointer one cell in the direction of the triangle. If you hold the left mouse button down, the cell pointer keeps moving in the direction of the triangle. If you want to move the cell pointer to a cell not shown on the display, point to the appropriate triangle and hold the left mouse button until the worksheet starts to scroll. When you reach the row or column you want, release the mouse button.

Entering Data into the Worksheet

To enter data into a cell, move the cell pointer to that cell, type the entry, and then press Enter or a direction key. As you type, the entry appears on the second line of the control panel. When you press Enter, the entry appears in the current cell and on the first line of the control panel. If you enter data into a cell that already contains information, the new data replaces the earlier entry.

If you plan to enter data into more than one cell, you do not have to press Enter and then move the cell pointer to the next cell. You can type the entry into the cell and move the cell pointer with one operation; click a triangle icon with the mouse or press one of the direction keys (such as the arrow keys, Tab, PgUp, or PgDn) after typing the entry. However, if the data being input is a value and the final character is +, −, *, /, or ^, a direction key changes you to POINT mode and extends the formula.

Cue:
Use the direction keys to complete an entry and move to another cell.

The two types of cell entries are labels and values. A *label* is a text entry. A *value* is a number or a formula. 1-2-3 determines the type of cell entry from the first character that you enter. 1-2-3 treats the entry as a value (a number or a formula) if you begin with one of the following characters:

> 0 1 2 3 4 5 6 7 8 9 + − . (@ # $

If you begin by entering any other character, 1-2-3 treats the entry as a label. As soon as you type the first character, the mode indicator changes from READY to VALUE or LABEL.

Entering Labels

Labels clarify the meaning of numbers and formulas in the worksheets. The labels in figures 3.1 and 3.3 tell you what the data means. In figures 3.4 through 3.6, the numbers and formulas have no labels, and you have no idea what this data represents.

Cue:
Labels make worksheet numbers and formulas more understandable.

Because a label is a text entry, it can contain any string of characters and can be up to 240 characters long. Labels can include titles, headings, explanations, and notes, all of which can help make your worksheet more readable.

When you enter a label, 1-2-3 adds a *label prefix* to the beginning of the cell entry. The label prefix is not visible on the worksheet but is visible in the control panel (see fig. 3.7). 1-2-3 uses the label prefix to identify the entry as a label and determine how it is displayed and printed.

You can assign one of the following five label prefixes:

Prefix	Meaning
'	Left-aligned (default)
"	Right-aligned
^	Centered
\	Repeating
|	Left-aligned and nonprinting, if located at the beginning of a row of data

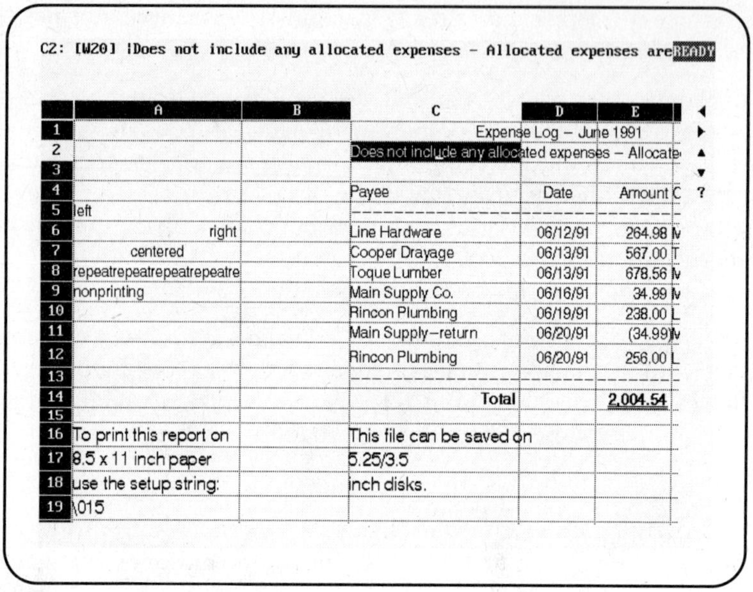

Fig. 3.7. Examples of different label prefixes.

When you enter a label, 1-2-3 by default adds the apostrophe (') for a left-aligned label. To use a different label prefix, type the prefix as the first character of the label.

Cue:
Use right-aligned labels for column headings over columns of numbers or numeric formulas.

In figure 3.7, column A shows examples of the different label prefixes so that you can compare how they appear. Columns C through E show how to use these label prefixes in a typical worksheet. A column of descriptions such as in C6..C12 usually looks best if left-aligned—the normal way to line up text. Column headings should usually align with the data that follows, such as the heading in C4, which is left-aligned to match the *Payee* descriptions. When the entries fill the cell width, as the dates do in column D, the column heading can be aligned either left, right, or center. In this example, the *Date* heading is centered. A centered label is best when the column heading is shorter than the data that follows it. Because numbers and numeric formulas are always right-aligned, the *Amount* column heading in E4 is also right-aligned.

Reminder:
A repeating label changes length to match the column width.

The dashed lines in rows 5 and 13 are repeating labels. The repeating labels fill the entire width of the cell. If you change the column width, the label adjusts to fill the new column width. Keep in mind, however, that Wysiwyg enables you to create solid lines in the worksheet. In most cases, a solid line is preferable to a dashed line.

The note in cell C2 of figure 3.7 has a nonprinting label prefix (|). The prefix displays left-aligned but does not print if the print range starts in the same column as the label. In this example, if the print range starts in C1, the note in C2 does not print. If the print range starts in A1, the note does print. Printing and nonprinting labels are covered in more detail in Chapter 8.

To use a label-prefix character as the first character of a label, first type a label prefix and then type the label-prefix character you want to use as the first character of the label (see cell A19 in fig. 3.7). If you type \015 into A19, the cell displays 015015015015015015 as a repeating label. In this example, you first must type a label prefix (in this case an apostrophe) and then \015.

You must type a label prefix if the first character of the label is a numeric character. If not, as soon as you type the numeric character, 1-2-3 switches to VALUE mode and expects a valid number or formula. If the label is a valid formula, 1-2-3 evaluates it. If it is invalid, 1-2-3 refuses to accept the entry and places you in EDIT mode. (EDIT mode is explained later in this chapter.)

In cell C17 of figure 3.7, you must type a label prefix to precede the label 5.25/3.5. If you do not, 1-2-3 treats the entry as a formula and displays the result of 5.25 divided by 3.5, which is 1.5. In A17 in figure 3.7, you must type a label prefix to precede the label 8.5 x 11 inch paper, or 1-2-3 treats it as an invalid formula. You often encounter this problem when you enter an address, such as **11711 N. College Avenue**.

Reminder:
You must type a label prefix before an entry that looks like a valid formula.

If a label is longer than the cell width, the label appears across the cells to the right as long as these cells are blank (see cells C2..E2 in fig. 3.7). The label in C2 in figure 3.7 is longer than what can be displayed in the window. The cell display can even continue into the next window to the right as long as all these cells are blank (see fig. 3.8).

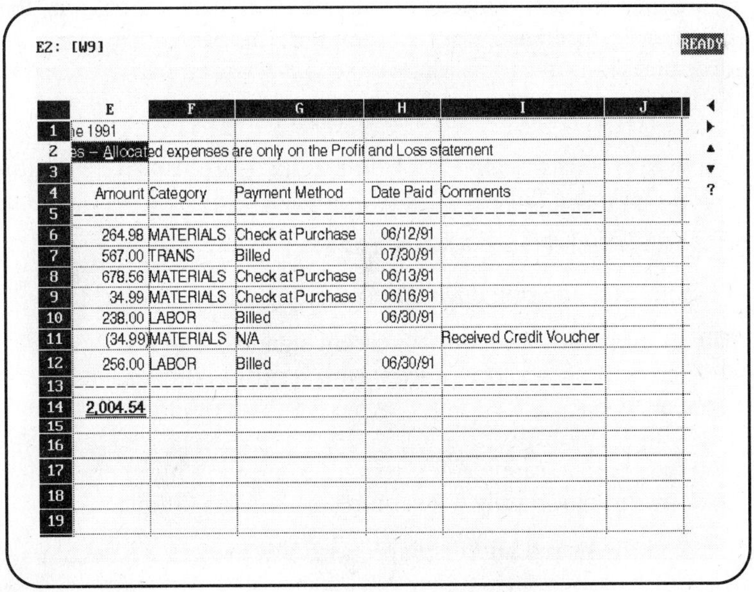

Reminder:
A long label appears across blank cells to its right.

Fig. 3.8. A long label in row 2 continuing into the next window.

Cue:
*In Wysiwyg, use a
double caret (^^) to
center or double
quotation marks
("") to right-justify.*

1-2-3 alone does not correctly center or right-align text that overflows a cell. However, if you have Wysiwyg in memory, you can correct this problem by preceding a label entry with a double caret (^ ^) to center, or a double quotation mark ("") to right-justify the entry. The label entered in cell D1 of figure 3.7 uses the double caret to center the report title over the Date column.

1-2-3 and Wysiwyg include several commands that can change many label prefixes at one time. This subject is covered in Chapter 5.

Entering Numbers

To enter a valid number, you may type any of the 10 digits (0 through 9) and certain other characters according to the following rules. (Reported results are based on the default column width of nine characters with Wysiwyg loaded and the default font of 12-point Swiss displayed):

1. The number may start with a plus sign (+); the sign is not stored when you press Enter.

   +123 is stored and displayed as 123.

2. The number may begin with a minus sign (–); the number is stored as a negative number.

   –123 is stored and displayed as -123.

3. The number may be placed within parentheses ( ); however, the number is stored as a positive number. The parentheses are dropped.

   (123) is stored as (123) and displayed as 123.

4. The number may begin with a dollar sign ($); the sign is not stored when you press Enter.

   $123 is stored and displayed as 123.

5. You may include one decimal point.

6. The number may end with a percent sign (%); the number is divided by 100, and the percent sign is dropped.

   123% is stored and displayed as 1.23.

7. You may type a number in scientific notation. A number is stored in scientific notation only if it requires more than 20 digits.

   123E3 is stored and displayed as 123000.

123E30 is stored as 1.2300000E+32 and displayed as 1.23E+30.

123E–4 is stored and displayed as 0.0123.

1.23E–30 is stored as 1.2300000E-28 and displayed as 1.23E-30.

8. If you enter a number with more than 18 digits, it is rounded off to 18 digits.

12345678998765432198 is stored as 1.23456789E+19 and displayed as 1.2E+19.

9. If you enter a number with more than 14 digits, it is stored in scientific notation.

123456789987654 is stored as 1.23456789E+14 and displayed as 1.2E+14.

If the number is too long to display normally in the cell, 1-2-3 tries to display what it can. If the cell uses the default **G**eneral format and the integer part of the number can fit in the cell width, 1-2-3 rounds off the decimal part of the number that does not fit. In figure 3.9, the numbers in columns C, D, and E are the same; only the column widths are different. In E5, 25.654321 displays truncated to 25. In C6, 1675.1234567 displays rounded off to 1675.123. Cell formats are described in detail in Chapter 5.

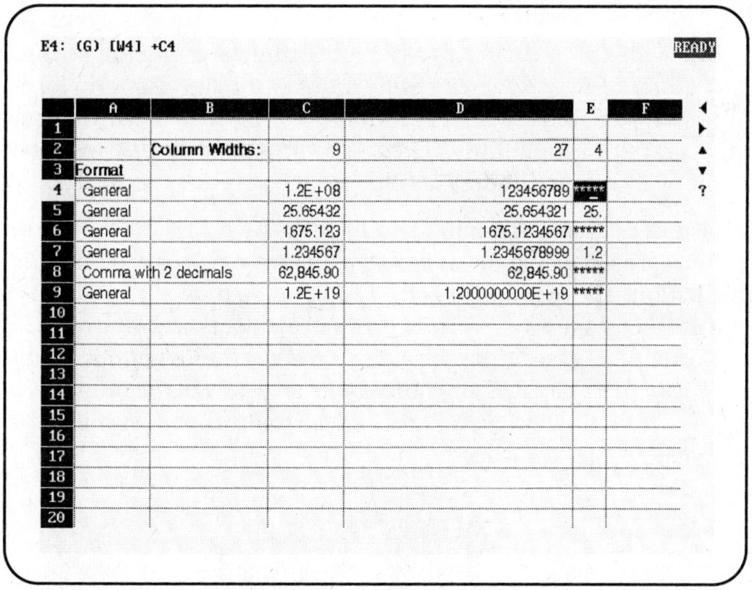

E4: (G) [W4] +C4						READY
	A	B	C	D	E	F
1						
2		Column Widths:	9	27	4	
3	Format					
4	General		1.2E+08	123456789	*****	
5	General		25.65432	25.654321	25.	
6	General		1675.123	1675.1234567	*****	
7	General		1.234567	1.2345678999	1.2	
8	Comma with 2 decimals		62,845.90	62,845.90	*****	
9	General		1.2E+19	1.2000000000E+19	*****	

Fig. 3.9. Asterisks displayed in place of a number too long for the cell width.

Caution:
If the column width is too narrow to display a number, 1-2-3 displays asterisks.

If the cell uses the default General format and the integer part of the number does not fit in the cell, 1-2-3 displays the number by using scientific notation. Example cells in figure 3.9 are C4 and C9. If the cell uses a format other than General or the cell width is too narrow to display in scientific notation and the number cannot fit into the cell width, 1-2-3 displays asterisks (see fig. 3.9).

Entering Formulas

Reminder:
Formulas make 1-2-3 an electronic worksheet by performing calculations automatically.

The real power of 1-2-3 comes from its capability to perform calculations on formulas you enter. In fact, formulas make 1-2-3 an electronic worksheet— not just a computerized way to assemble data for reports. You enter the numbers and formulas into the worksheet, and 1-2-3 calculates the results of all the formulas. As you add or change data, you never have to recalculate the effects of the changes; 1-2-3 does it automatically. In figure 3.1, if you change the Sales or Variable Costs, 1-2-3 recalculates the Variable Margin. In figure 3.7, the total expense in E14 is recalculated each time you add or change an expense amount.

You can enter formulas that operate on numbers, labels, and other cells in the worksheet. Like labels, a formula can be up to 240 characters long. The new Auditor add-in provided with Release 2.3 can be used to quickly locate and identify errors in your formulas. Appendix B explains how to use the Auditor add-in.

You work with three different types of formulas: numeric, string, and logical. *Numeric formulas* work with numbers, other numeric formulas, and numeric functions. *String formulas* work with labels, other string formulas, and string functions. *Logical formulas* are true/false tests that can test numeric or string values. This chapter covers each type of formula.

Reminder:
The formula appears in the control panel; the result of the calculation appears in the worksheet.

Formulas can operate on numbers in the cell, such as 8+26. This formula uses 1-2-3 just as a calculator. A more useful formula uses cell references in the calculation. The formula in cell F1 in figure 3.10 is +B1+C1+D1+E1. The control panel shows the formula. The worksheet shows the result of the calculation; in this case, 183. The power and usefulness of this formula is that the result in F1 changes any time you change any of the numbers in the other cells. This automatic recalculation capability is a powerful feature of the 1-2-3 electronic worksheet.

```
F1:  +B1+C1+D1+E1                                              READY
```

	A	B	C	D	E	F	G	H
1		23	4	56	100	_ 183		
2								
3								
4								
5								
6								
7								
8								
9								

Fig. 3.10. The result of the calculation displayed in the worksheet.

Notice that the formula begins with a plus sign (+B1). If a formula begins with the characters *B1*, 1-2-3 assumes that you are entering a label, and no calculation is performed.

Using Operators in Numeric Formulas

A formula is an instruction to 1-2-3 to perform a calculation. You use *operators* to specify the calculations to perform. The numeric operators are addition, subtraction, multiplication, division, and exponentiation (raising a number to a power). The formula in figure 3.10 uses the plus sign—the addition operator. The simplest numeric formula uses just the plus sign to repeat the value in another cell. In figure 3.9, D4 and E4 contain the formula +C4. The other cells in columns D and E also are formulas that refer to the corresponding cells in column C. In each case, the value of the cell in column C is repeated in columns D and E.

Reminder:
Use operators to specify which calculations a formula is to perform.

When 1-2-3 evaluates a formula, it calculates terms within the formula in a specified sequence. This sequence is called the *order of precedence*. Following are the arithmetic operators listed by their order of precedence in 1-2-3:

Operator	Meaning
^	Exponentiation
+, −	Positive, negative
*, /	Multiplication, division
+, −	Addition, subtraction

If a formula uses all these operators, 1-2-3 calculates the exponents first and then works down the list. If two operators are equal in precedence, it makes no difference which is calculated first. This order of precedence has a definite effect on the result of many formulas. To override the order, use one or more levels of parentheses. Operations inside a set of parentheses are always evaluated first.

The following examples show how 1-2-3 uses parentheses and the order of precedence to evaluate complex formulas. In these examples, numbers are used instead of cell references to make it easier to follow the calculations.

Formula	Evaluation	Result
5+3*2	5+(3*2)	11
(5+3)*2	(5+3)*2	16
-3^2*2	$-(3^2)*2$	−18
$-3^{(2*2)}$	$-(3^{(2*2)})$	−81
5+4*8/4−3	5+(4*(8/4))−3	10
5+4*8/(4−3)	5+((4*8)/(4−3))	37
(5+4)*8/(4−3)	(5+4)*8/(4−3)	72
(5+4)*8/4−3	(5+4)*(8/4)−3	15
$5+3*4^2/6-2*3^4$	$5+(3(*(4^2)/6)-(2*(3^4))$	−149

Using Operators in String Formulas

String formula rules are different from numeric formula rules. A string is a label or string formula. You work with only two string formula operators: you can repeat another string, or you can join (*concatenate*) two or more strings.

The simplest string formula uses only the plus sign to repeat the string in another cell. In figure 3.11, the formula in A6 is +A3. The formula to repeat a numeric cell and to repeat a string cell is the same. In figure 3.9, the formula is considered a numeric formula because it refers to a cell with a number. In figure 3.11, the formula is considered a string formula because it refers to a cell with a string.

```
B10: [W15] +D3&", "&E3                                          READY
```

	A	B	C	D	E	F
1						
2	First Name	Last Name	Address	City	ST	
3	Pat	Thompson	625 East 75th	New York	NY	
4						
5						
6	Pat					
7	PatThompson					
8		Pat Thompson				
9		625 East 75th				
10		New York, NY				
11						
12						
13						
14						
15						
16						
17						
18						
19						
20						

Fig. 3.11. *String formulas used to repeat or concatenate strings.*

The string concatenation operator is the ampersand (&). The formula in A7 in figure 3.11 is +A3&B3. The first operator in a string formula must be a plus sign; any other operators in the formula must be ampersands. If you do not use the ampersand but use any of the numeric operators, 1-2-3 treats the formula as a numeric formula. A cell that contains a label has a numeric value of zero. For example, if you enter the formula +A3+B3 in the worksheet in figure 3.11, the formula is treated as a numeric formula and evaluates to zero.

Reminder:
A string is treated as a value of zero in numeric formulas.

If you use an ampersand in a formula, 1-2-3 treats it as a string formula. If you also use any numeric operators (after the plus sign at the beginning), 1-2-3 considers it an invalid formula. The formulas +A3&B3+C3 and +A3+B3&C3 are invalid. When you enter an invalid formula, 1-2-3 places you in EDIT mode. EDIT mode is covered later in this chapter.

In figure 3.11, the names run together in A7, so you want to put a space between the first and last names. You can insert a string directly into a string formula by enclosing the string in quotation marks (" "). The formula in B8 is +A3&" "&B3. The formula in B10 is +D3&", "&E3. You can write more complex string formulas with string functions, which are covered in Chapter 6.

Cue:
You can insert a string directly into a string formula if you enclose it in quotation marks.

Using Operators in Logical Formulas

Logical formulas are true/false tests. The formulas compare two values and evaluate to 1 if the test is true and 0 if the test is false. Used mainly in database criteria ranges, logical formulas are covered in more detail in Chapters 6 and 12.

The logical operators include the following:

Operator	*Meaning*
<	Less than
>	Greater than
=	Equal to
<=	Less than or equal to
>=	Greater than or equal to
<>	Not equal to
#NOT#	Reverses the results of a test (changes the result from true to false or from false to true)
#OR#	Logical OR to join two tests; the result is true if *either* test is true
#AND#	Logical AND to join two tests; the result is true if *both* tests are true

Figure 3.12 shows examples of logical formulas.

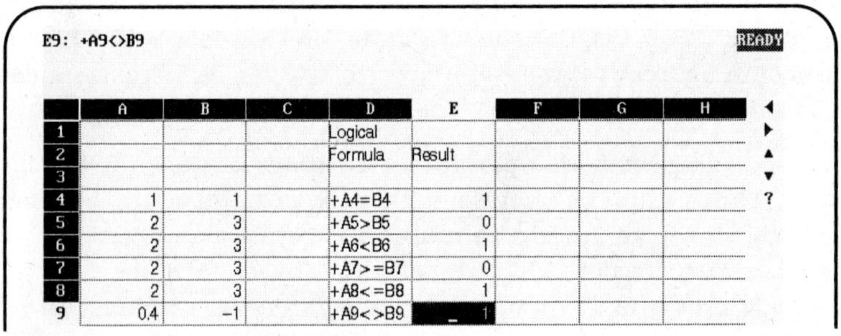

Fig. 3.12. *Logical formulas evaluate to 1 if true or 0 if false.*

Pointing to Cell References

Cue:
Point to the cell you want a formula to use.

Formulas consist mainly of operators and cell references. The formula in figure 3.10 has four cell references. You can type each address, but there is a better way. Whenever 1-2-3 expects a cell address, you can use the mouse or the direction keys to point to the cell. If you use the mouse, you also must use the triangle icons in the icon panel to move the cell pointer. When you move the cell pointer, 1-2-3 changes to POINT mode, and the address of the cell pointer appears in the formula in the control panel.

Move the cell pointer until it is on the correct cell address for the formula you are creating. If this location marks the end of the formula, press Enter. If the formula has more terms, type the next operator and continue the process until you are finished; then press Enter. You can type some addresses and point to others. You have no way to tell whether the cell references in the formula in figure 3.10 were entered by typing or pointing.

Typing an incorrect address in a formula is easy. Pointing to cells is not only faster but also more accurate than typing. The only time typing an address is easier than pointing to the cell or using range names is when the cell reference is far from the current cell and you happen to remember the cell address. For example, if you enter a formula in Z238 and you want to refer to cell I23, it may be faster to just type **I23** than point to it. Experienced 1-2-3 users rarely type addresses.

Reminder:
Pointing to rather than typing cell addresses is faster and more accurate.

Correcting Errors in Formulas

If you mistakenly enter a formula that 1-2-3 cannot evaluate, the program beeps, changes to EDIT mode, and moves the cursor to the approximate location place in the formula where it encountered an error. You cannot enter an invalid formula into a worksheet. For more information about changing a cell in EDIT mode, see "Editing Data in the Worksheet" later in this chapter.

Common errors that make a formula invalid are missing or extra parentheses and mixing numeric and string operators. Other sources of errors are misspelled function names and incorrect arguments in functions (covered in Chapter 6). As mentioned previously in this chapter, you can use the Auditor add-in to help you correct errors in your formulas (see Appendix B). Some common simple errors are as follows:

Formula	Reason Why It's Incorrect
+A1+A2&A3	Mixing numeric and string operators
+A1/(A2−A3	Missing right parentheses
@SIM(A1..A3)	Misspelled @SUM function

You may not know what is wrong or how to fix the formula. You also may want to use the Help system to check the format of a function. Before you can do anything else, you must clear the error. If you press Esc, you erase the entire entry. If you press Esc again, you are back to READY mode, but you have lost the entire formula.

If you know what is wrong with the formula, follow the procedures in "Editing Data in the Worksheet" later in this chapter. If you do not know how to correct the formula, convert it to a label. Because all labels are valid entries, this technique clears the error and enables you to continue working. Follow these steps to convert a formula to a label:

1. Press Edit (F2).

2. Press Home to move to the beginning of the formula.

3. Type an apostrophe as the label prefix (1-2-3 accepts anything preceded by an apostrophe as a label).

4. Press Enter.

Addressing Cells

A cell address in a formula, such as the one in figure 3.10, is known as a *cell reference*. The formula in F1 has four cell references. Normally, when you copy a formula from one cell to another cell, the cell references adjust automatically. If you use the /Copy command to copy the formula in F1 of figure 3.10 to F2, the cell references change to +B2+C2+D2+E2. This automatic change of cell references is *relative addressing*.

You can use absolute instead of relative cell references in formulas. An *absolute address* in a formula does not change when you copy the formula to another cell. You specify an absolute address when you type a formula by preceding the column and row address with a dollar sign ($). For example, +$A$1 is an absolute address. If this address were in cell C10 and you copied it to cell E19, the cell reference would still be +$A$1. To specify an absolute cell address in POINT or EDIT mode, press the Abs (F4) key. You also can make a reference to a cell in a specific worksheet absolute. For example, +$A$1 always refers to cell A1, no matter what cell the address is copied to.

In addition to relative and absolute cell addresses, you also have *mixed addresses*. In a mixed-cell address, part of the address is relative and part is absolute. For example, +A$1 is a mixed address; the column letter can change, but the row number cannot.

Whether a cell reference is relative, absolute, or mixed has no effect on how the formula is calculated. This type of addressing matters only when you copy the formula to another cell. Copying and cell addressing are covered in detail in Chapter 4.

Changing Cell Formats

Several commands change the way numbers and formulas appear in the worksheet. These commands, /Worksheet Global Format and /Range Format, are covered in detail in Chapter 5.

For example, you can force a fixed number of decimal digits so that the numbers in a column line up; add commas and currency symbols; show numbers as percents; and even hide the contents of the cell. Values can be formatted to include commas between thousands and to show 0 to 15 decimal places.

The Wysiwyg menu also enables you to change cell formats. The :Format command changes the appearance of numbers and labels in the worksheet. This command is covered in detail in Chapter 5. With Wysiwyg, you also can change the font, style (bold, italic, underline), and color of a number or label, and change the color of negative numbers. Additionally, you can change the color of cells, reverse data and cell colors, and add lines, boxes, shadows, and shading to cells.

Editing Data in the Worksheet

After you make an entry in a cell, you may want to change the entry. For example, you may have misspelled a word in a label or created an incorrect formula. You can change an existing entry by using the keyboard and mouse with the 1-2-3 menu or the keyboard and mouse with the Wysiwyg menu.

Keyboard Editing

You can replace the contents of a cell by typing a new entry. The new entry completely replaces the old entry. You also can change (edit) the contents of the cell. To edit a cell's contents, move the cell pointer to the cell and press the Edit (F2) key to go into EDIT mode. You also can press Edit (F2) while you are typing an entry. If you make an error entering a formula, 1-2-3 forces you into EDIT mode, and the entry appears on the second line in the control panel.

Reminder:
Edit the contents of a cell by highlighting the cell, pressing Edit (F2), and making the changes.

Table 3.2 describes the actions of keys in EDIT mode. When you are in the EDIT mode, the cursor is in the entry area in the control panel. You use the keys in table 3.2 to move the cursor. As you edit the cell, the contents of the cell as displayed in the first line of the control panel and in the worksheet do not change. The cell's contents change only when you press Enter or click the left mouse button in the control panel to complete the edit. Any key that moves the cell pointer in EDIT mode first completes the entry and then moves the cell pointer.

Cue:
Press Esc twice to
cancel editing and
restore the cell to its
original contents.

If you click the right mouse button or press Esc while in EDIT mode, you clear the edit area. If you then click the right mouse button or press Esc or Enter with a blank edit area, you do not erase the cell; you cancel the edit, and the cell reverts back to the way it was before you pressed Edit (F2).

Table 3.2
Key Actions in EDIT Mode

Key	Action
←	Moves the cursor one character to the left
→	Moves the cursor one character to the right
Tab or Ctrl-→	Moves the cursor five characters to the right
Shift-Tab or Ctrl-←	Moves the cursor five characters to the left
Home	Moves the cursor to the beginning of the entry
End	Moves the cursor to the end of the entry
Backspace	Deletes the character to the left of the cursor
Del	Deletes the character at the cursor
Ins	Toggles between insert and overtype mode
Esc	Clears the edit line; when pressed again, abandons changes and leaves EDIT mode
F2 (Edit)	Switches to VALUE or LABEL mode
Enter	Completes the edit

Wysiwyg Editing

The :Text command on the Wysiwyg menu provides you with additional editing features. With this command, you can edit labels in the worksheet instead of in the control panel. When you choose :Text Edit and specify a cell or range of cells, a vertical-line cursor appears in front of the first character in the label. Move the cursor by using the arrow keys. Delete characters with the Del and Backspace keys; insert characters by typing. End the edit by clicking the right mouse button or by pressing Esc.

The **:Text** command also enables you to reformat columns of long labels to look like a paragraph. When you choose **:Text Reformat** from the Wysiwyg menu and specify a range of labels, Wysiwyg reformats the labels to look like a paragraph.

Using the Undo Feature

When you type an entry or edit a cell, you change the worksheet. If you change the worksheet in error, you can press the Undo (Alt-F4) key to reverse the last change. For example, if you type over an existing entry, you can undo the new entry and restore the old one. When you select commands from either the 1-2-3 menu or the Wysiwyg menu, you often change the worksheet. In most cases, you can press Undo to reverse the changes you have made with the command menus.

Initially, the Undo feature is disabled, so you must invoke a command to enable Undo. To turn on the Undo feature, choose **/Worksheet Global Default Other Undo Enable**. To make this change permanent, choose **/Worksheet Global Default Update**. When Undo is enabled, 1-2-3 must remember the last action that changed the worksheet. This action requires memory. How much memory Undo requires changes with different actions. You should enable Undo on your system and disable it again with **/Worksheet Global Default Other Undo Disable** only if you get low on memory.

If you Undo a change but then decide to restore it, you can undo the undo. If you press Undo at the wrong time and undo an entry, you can recover it. Undo is very useful and powerful. It also is tricky and can surprise you, so use Undo carefully. 1-2-3 remembers the last change to the worksheet and reverses this change when you press Undo. You must understand what 1-2-3 considers a change.

A *change* occurs between the time 1-2-3 is in READY mode and the next time it is in READY mode. Suppose that you press Edit (F2) to go into EDIT mode to change a cell. You can make any number of changes to the cell and then press Enter to save the changes and return to READY mode. If you then press Undo, 1-2-3 returns the worksheet to the way it was at the last READY mode. In this case, 1-2-3 returns the cell to the way it was before you edited the cell.

You can change many cells at one time or even erase everything in memory with one command. These commands are covered in Chapter 4. If you press Undo after a command, you undo all the effects of the command.

With some commands, such as /**Print** (Chapter 8); /**Graph** (Chapter 10); and /**Data** (Chapter 12), you can execute many commands before you return to READY mode. If you press Undo then, you reverse all the commands executed since the last time 1-2-3 was in READY mode.

Caution:
What 1-2-3 considers the last change may not be the last action you performed.

Some commands do not change any cells or settings. Examples of such commands are /**File Save**, /**File Xtract**, /**File Erase**, and /**Print Printer Page**. If you make an entry in a cell, save the file, and then press Undo, you undo the last change, which is the cell entry. Note that Undo is suspended when any add-in except Auditor or Wysiwyg is active.

Using Linked Worksheets

Linked worksheets make it easier to organize large, complex files. If you are new to 1-2-3, you may want to get comfortable with the basics by concentrating on one worksheet. When you are ready to design more complex worksheets, you can expand your expertise by using the file-linking capability of Release 2.3.

The commands related to linking worksheets include the following:

- /**File Admin Link-Refresh** updates the values of cells in the current worksheet linked to cells in other worksheets.

- /**File List Linked** displays a list of source files referred to by linking formulas in the current worksheet.

- /**File Admin Table Linked** creates a table in the worksheet that lists linked files from a specified directory.

A formula can refer to cells in other files. This type of referencing is *file linking*. Figures 3.13, 3.14, and 3.15 show three separate worksheet files. The formula in cell B4 of the Consolidation worksheet in figure 3.15 refers to cell B3 in the Region 1 worksheet shown in figure 3.13.

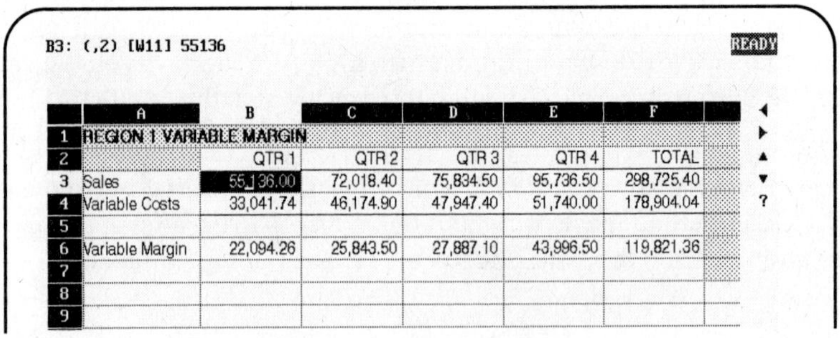

Fig. 3.13. A worksheet that contains regional data to be used in fig. 3.15.

B3: (,2) [W11] 75719   READY

	A	B	C	D	E	F
1	REGION 2 VARIABLE MARGIN					
2		QTR 1	QTR 2	QTR 3	QTR 4	TOTAL
3	Sales	75,719.00	98,363.98	103,749.30	147,947.40	425,779.68
4	Variable Costs	48,720.90	68,308.10	72,849.30	73,844.00	263,722.30
5						
6	Variable Margin	26,998.10	30,055.88	30,900.00	74,103.40	162,057.38
7						
8						
9						

Fig. 3.14. *A second worksheet that contains regional data to be used in fig. 3.15.*

B4: (,2) [W11] +<<REGION1.WK1>>B3   READY

	A	B	C	D	E	F
1	CONSOLIDATED VARIABLE MARGIN					
2		QTR 1	QTR 2	QTR 3	QTR 4	TOTAL
3	Sales					
4	REGION 1	55,136.00	72,018.40	75,834.50	95,736.50	298,725.40
5	REGION 2	75,719.00	98,363.98	103,749.30	147,947.40	425,779.68
6	Variable Costs					
7	REGION 1	33,041.74	46,174.90	47,947.40	51,740.00	178,904.04
8	REGION 2	48,720.90	68,308.10	72,849.30	73,844.00	263,722.30
9						
10	Variable Margin	49,092.36	55,899.38	58,787.10	118,099.90	281,878.74
11						
12						
13						
14						
15						
16						
17						
18						
19						
20						

Fig. 3.15. *A worksheet that contains formulas that link it to the worksheets in figs. 3.13 and 3.14.*

This powerful feature enables you to consolidate data from separate files automatically. Thus, cells B4 through E4 and cells B7 through E7 in the Consolidation worksheet refer to cells B3 through E3 and cells B4 through E4, respectively, in the Region 1 worksheet (see fig. 3.13). And cells B5 through E5 and cells B8 through E8 in the Consolidation worksheet refer to cells B3 through E3 and cells B4 through E4, respectively, in the Region 2 worksheet (see fig. 3.14).

You can use file linking on a network or other multiuser environment. If you think that one or more of these linked files has been updated since you read the file that contained the links, use the /File Admin Link-Refresh command to update these formulas.

Entering Formulas That Link Files

When you write a formula that refers to a cell in another worksheet file, you must type the entire cell reference including the file name (and extension if different from WK1) inside double angle brackets, as in the following example:

+<<REGION1>>B3

This formula appears in the worksheet as follows:

```
+<<REGION1.WK1>>B3
```

If the file is in another directory, you must include the entire path (although the drive letter is optional if on the same drive), as in the following example:

+<<C:\123\DATA\REGION1>>B3

Instead of using the cell reference B3 in the preceding example, you can use a range name. Suppose that you use the /Range Name Create command to assign cell B3 of the Region 1 worksheet the range name REG1QTR1. Then, use the following formula to link cell B4 of the CONSOL worksheet to cell B3 of the Region 1 worksheet (assuming that Region 1 is in the current directory):

+<<REGION1>>REG1QTR1

When you create a linking formula, you can copy the formula to other cells in the worksheet, just like any other formula. If the cell reference is a relative reference, it adjusts the way any relative cell reference does.

Using the Viewer Add-In To Link Files

The Viewer add-in not only enables you to quickly browse and retrieve files, but also enables you to easily link cells between files. Chapter 7 covers the Viewer add-in, including the Browse and Retrieve features. A brief discussion of Viewer's linking capabilities follows.

When you link files, the *source file* is the file that contains the information to be transferred, and the *target file* (the current file) is the file to receive the transferred data.

To use Viewer's link feature, you must have the target file on-screen, with the cell pointer highlighting the target cell or upper left corner of the target range. Then, attach the Viewer by performing the following steps:

1. Select **/Add-In Attach** and select VIEWER.ADN from the list of add-ins that appears. (The 1-2-3 program directory must be the current directory.)

2. Select a function key to be assigned to the Viewer add-in (or select **No-Key**).

3. Select **Invoke** from the /Add-In menu (or select **Quit** and use the Alt-function key combination you assigned in step 2, if any); then select VIEWER from the list of attached add-ins.

4. Select **Link** from the resulting Viewer menu.

A split-screen display appears (see fig. 3.16) with all worksheet files in the current directory displayed in the List window on the left side of the screen. Highlight the source worksheet from the files listed and press → to move to that worksheet, which is displayed in the View window on the right side of the screen. Next, highlight the source cell or range by using the direction keys and then press Enter. The target file returns, and the source cell or range has been copied to the target cell or range.

Note: If the target file contains data that can be overwritten by the source cell or range, a message appears to ask you to confirm the link (see fig. 3.17). Select **Yes** to confirm or **No** to return to the List/ View window. If you select **Yes**, the contents in the target file are deleted.

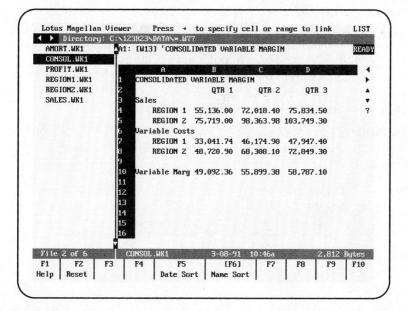

Fig. 3.16. The Viewer add-in screen.

```
B4: (,2) [W11] +<<REGION1.WK1>>B3                                    MENU
No  Yes
LINK WILL WRITE OVER NONBLANK CELLS!  Proceed anyway?
```

	A	B	C	D	E	F
1	CONSOLIDATED VARIABLE MARGIN					
2		QTR 1	QTR 2	QTR 3	QTR 4	TOTAL
3	Sales					
4	REGION 1	55,136.00	72,018.40	75,834.50	95,736.50	298,725.40
5	REGION 2	75,719.00	98,363.98	103,749.30	147,947.40	425,779.68
6	Variable Costs					
7	REGION 1	33,041.74	46,174.90	47,947.40	51,740.00	178,904.04
8	REGION 2	48,720.90	68,308.10	72,849.30	73,844.00	263,722.30
9						
10	Variable Margin	49,092.36	55,899.38	58,787.10	118,099.90	281,878.74
11						
12						
13						
14						
15						
16						
17						
18						
19						
20						

Fig. 3.17. The Viewer prompt to confirm overwriting the contents of a cell.

Summary

In this chapter, you learned how to move around the worksheet with the keyboard and the mouse and how to enter and edit data. You learned how to build different types of formulas, including formulas that refer to other worksheets. You learned how to point to cells in formulas and how to use the various operators. You learned about the important Undo feature, which you can use to undo a change made in error. Finally, you learned how to use the powerful linking capabilities of Release 2.3.

This chapter gives you the basic skills to use 1-2-3. In the next chapter, you learn the basic commands that provide the tools to build and use worksheets effectively.

4

Using Fundamental
1-2-3 Commands

Much of the power of 1-2-3 comes from your use of commands. You use commands to tell 1-2-3 to perform a specific task or sequence of tasks. Commands can change the operation of the 1-2-3 program, or they can operate on a file, a worksheet, or a range. You use commands to print reports, to graph data, to change how data displays in the cell, to save and retrieve files, to copy and move cells, to arrange the display of the worksheet windows on-screen, and to perform many other tasks.

1-2-3 and the PrintGraph program include hundreds of commands. Certain commands are used everytime you use the program; others are used rarely, if ever. Some commands perform general tasks that apply to all worksheets; other specialized commands apply only to special circumstances. In this chapter, you learn how to use command menus and the most fundamental 1-2-3 commands. Subsequent chapters cover more specific commands and features.

You also learn the limitations of these commands. You cannot perform certain actions, such as formatting a floppy disk, within 1-2-3. In this chapter, you learn how to access the operating system without quitting 1-2-3, which enables you to perform operations, such as formatting a floppy disk.

In addition to the detailed explanation of the most important commands in this chapter, this book includes a separate command reference section that lists and describes all the commands in the order presented in the 1-2-3, Wysiwyg, and PrintGraph menus.

This chapter shows you how to do the following:

- Use command menus
- Save files
- Use ranges and range names
- Set column widths
- Insert and delete rows and columns
- Use window and display options
- Protect and hide data
- Control worksheet recalculation
- Move and copy data
- Reference cells with relative and absolute addressing
- Find and replace specified data
- Access the operating system without quitting 1-2-3

Selecting Commands from Command Menus

Reminder:
You can access the 1-2-3 and Wysiwyg command menus from READY mode only.

You execute 1-2-3 commands through a series of menus. To access the 1-2-3 menu, which displays in the second line of the control panel, press the slash (/) key from READY mode. To access the Wysiwyg menu, press the colon (:) key from READY mode. In the 1-2-3 menu, the mode indicator changes to MENU (see fig. 4.1), and in the Wysiwyg menu, the mode indicator changes to WYSIWYG (see fig. 4.2). To access these menus with the mouse, move the mouse pointer into the control panel, and one of the menus appears. To toggle between the 1-2-3 and Wysiwyg menus, click the right mouse button.

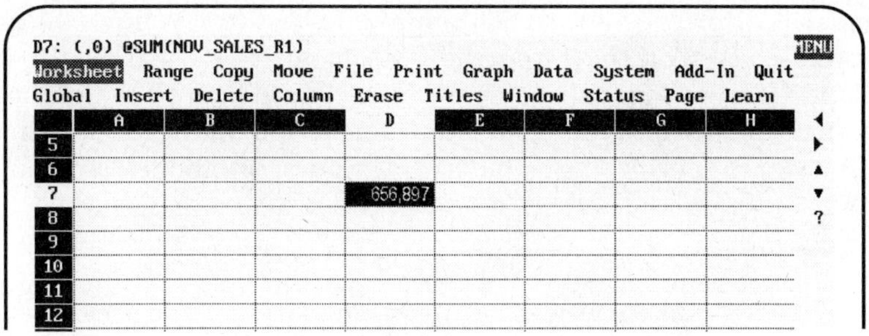

```
D7: (,0) @SUM(NOV_SALES_R1)                                          MENU
Worksheet Range  Copy  Move  File  Print  Graph  Data  System  Add-In  Quit
Global  Insert  Delete  Column  Erase  Titles  Window  Status  Page  Learn
        A         B         C         D         E        F         G        H      ◄
  5                                                                               ►
  6                                                                               ▲
  7                                          656,897                              ▼
  8                                                                               ?
  9
 10
 11
 12
```

Fig. 4.1. The 1-2-3 main menu.

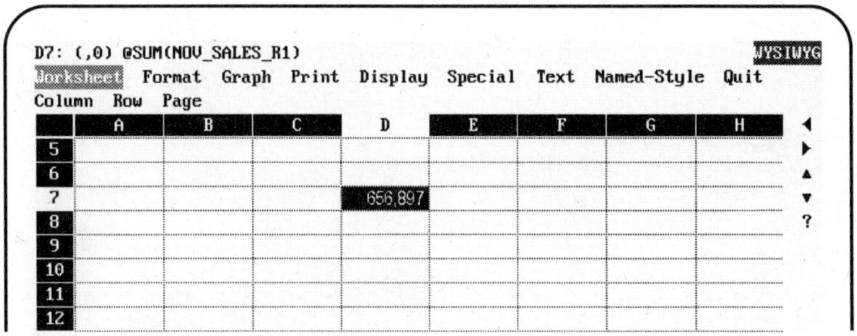

```
D7: (,0) @SUM(NOV_SALES_R1)                                        WYSIWYG
Worksheet Format  Graph  Print  Display  Special  Text  Named-Style  Quit
Column  Row  Page
        A         B         C         D         E        F         G        H      ◄
  5                                                                               ►
  6                                                                               ▲
  7                                          656,897                              ▼
  8                                                                               ?
  9
 10
 11
 12
```

Fig. 4.2. The Wysiwyg main menu.

When you first press the slash or the colon key or when you move the mouse into the control panel area, the **Worksheet** command is highlighted. Remember that both the 1-2-3 and Wysiwyg menus have a **Worksheet** command, and each command leads to additional menus. You can determine the active menu by looking at the rest of the commands in the menu or by observing the mode indicator. The highlight also typically changes color to indicate which of the two menus is active. Below the menu options, on the third line, you find either an explanation of the highlighted menu option or a list of the options in the next menu. In figure 4.1, the third line lists the /Worksheet menu options of the 1-2-3 main menu.

To select a menu option, use the direction keys to move the highlight to a choice and press Enter or point to the selection with the mouse and click the left mouse button. Table 4.1 shows the keys that move the menu pointer, also called the highlight. As you highlight each menu item, the next set of commands displays on the screen's third line. Figure 4.3 shows the menu after you select /Worksheet from the 1-2-3 menu. Notice that the third line in figure 4.1 moved up to become the menu line in figure 4.3. Continue to select menu items until you get to the command you want. Some commands prompt you to specify ranges, file names, values, or other information.

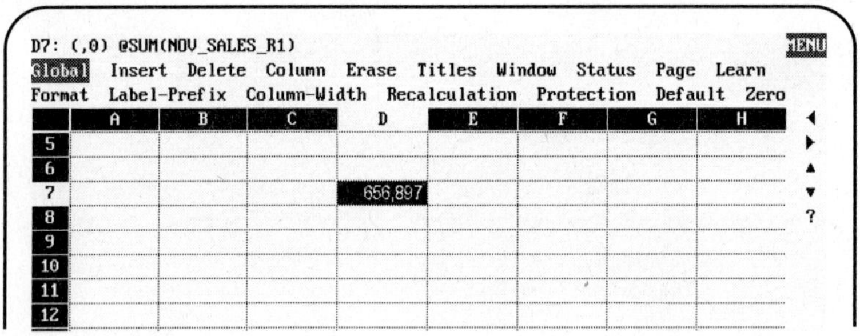

Fig. 4.3. The /Worksheet menu.

Table 4.1
Menu Pointer Movement Keys

Key	Function
→	Moves the pointer one command to the right; if at the last command, wraps to the first command
←	Moves the pointer one command to the left; if at the first command, wraps to the last command
Space bar	Works like the right arrow
Home	Moves the pointer to the first command
End	Moves the pointer to the last command
Enter	Selects the command highlighted by the menu pointer
Esc	Cancels the current menu and returns to the preceding menu; if at the main 1-2-3 or Wysiwyg menu, cancels the menu and returns to READY mode
Ctrl-Break	Cancels the menu and returns to READY mode

After you become familiar with the command menus, you can use a different method to select commands. Type the first letter of each command. You may find this a faster technique than highlighting the command and pressing Enter. Every option on a 1-2-3 or Wysiwyg menu begins with a different character, so 1-2-3 always "knows" the menu option you want. You can type the first letter of the commands you know well and point to commands you rarely use.

Cue:
Type the first character of a command name to select the command

One of the first commands you use is /**R**ange **E**rase. To erase a cell or a range of cells from the keyboard, first press / from READY mode, then select **R**ange, and finally select **E**rase. The prompt `Enter range to erase:` appears (see fig. 4.4). To erase only the current cell, press Enter (see fig. 4.5). (Note that you also can erase a single-cell entry by highlighting the cell and pressing Del). To erase a range, specify the range to erase and press Enter. You learn how to specify ranges in a following section, "Using Ranges," in this chapter.

```
D15: [W11] 'Dept 13                                    POINT
Enter range to erase: D15..D15
```

	A	B	C	D	E	F	G
1	Sales Forecast				This	Next	Following
2					Year	Year	Year
3				Dept 1	23456	34198	37650
4				Dept 2	17693	28762	31495
5				Dept 3	33418	31690	34893
6				Dept 4	16933	19761	23061
7				Dept 5	28610	33388	38964
8				Dept 6	18793	21931	25593
9				Dept 7	23691	27647	32264
10				Dept 8	31520	36784	42927
11				Dept 9	17621	20564	23998
12				Dept 10	16918	19743	23040
13				Dept 11	35971	41978	48988
14				Dept 12	26918	31413	36659
15				Dept 13			
16							
17							
18							
19							
20							

```
18-Feb-91  01:34 AM                           NUM
```

Fig. 4.4. The /Range Erase prompt.

To perform the same operation by using the mouse, move the mouse pointer to the control panel to display the 1-2-3 menu (click the right mouse button, if necessary, to toggle the menu). Point to **R**ange and click the left mouse button. Then click the left mouse button on **E**rase. The same prompt appears as before (see fig. 4.4). To erase the currently highlighted cell, click within the control panel or click twice with the pointer on the cell (see fig. 4.5). To erase a range, specify the range to erase and click the left mouse button. You learn how to specify ranges with the mouse in the section "Using Ranges" later in this chapter.

	A	B	C	D	E	F	G	
D15: [W11]							READY	

	A	B	C	D	E	F	G	
1	Sales Forecast				This	Next	Following	
2					Year	Year	Year	
3				Dept 1	23456	34198	37650	
4				Dept 2	17693	28762	31495	
5				Dept 3	33418	31690	34893	
6				Dept 4	16933	19761	23061	
7				Dept 5	28610	33388	38964	
8				Dept 6	18793	21931	25593	
9				Dept 7	23691	27647	32264	
10				Dept 8	31520	36784	42927	
11				Dept 9	17621	20564	23998	
12				Dept 10	16918	19743	23040	
13				Dept 11	35971	41978	48988	
14				Dept 12	26918	31413	36659	
15								
16								
17								
18								
19								
20								

18-Feb-91 01:35 AM   UNDO   NUM

Fig. 4.5. The current cell erased by using /Range Erase.

You can point to each menu option (using either the mouse or the direction keys) or type the first letter of the option. In this book, the entire command name is shown and the first letter is in boldface. You type only the first letter. For example, to erase a range, select /**R**ange **E**rase.

As you select items from the menus, you can make an occasional error. To correct an error, press Esc or click the right mouse button to return to the preceding menu. Press Esc at the main 1-2-3 or Wysiwyg menu to clear the menu and return to READY mode. If you press Ctrl-Break from any menu, you return directly to READY mode. To clear a main menu with the mouse, move the mouse pointer to the worksheet area; if the menu doesn't clear, click the right mouse button.

Cue:
Use the arrow keys to explore the command menus.

You can explore the command menus without actually executing the commands. Using the direction keys to highlight each menu option in the 1-2-3 menu (see fig. 4.1), read the third line in the control panel to learn more about the option or to see the next menu. Then select each menu option to get to the next menu (see fig. 4.3). Use the 1-2-3 command chart at the back of this book to help guide you through the menus. Figure 4.6 shows the /**W**orksheet **C**olumn **C**olumn-Range menu. You can select one of two column width options from this menu.

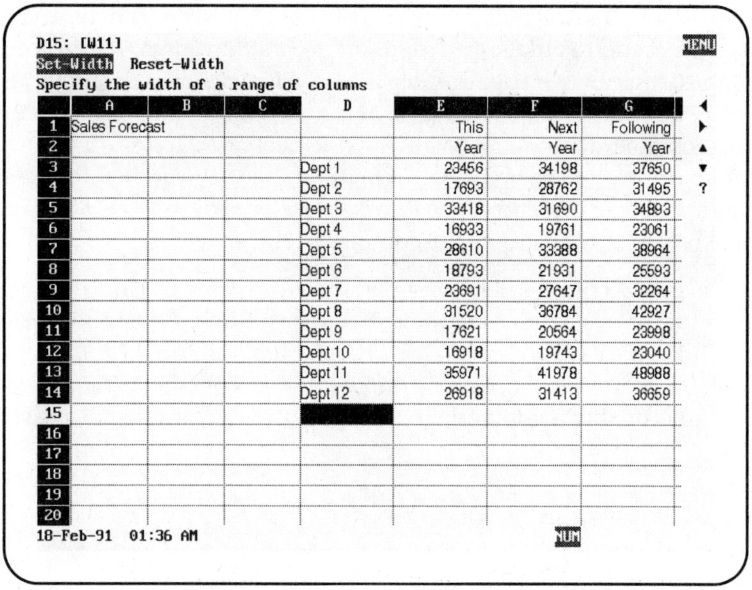

```
D15: [W11]                                                    MENU
Set-Width  Reset-Width
Specify the width of a range of columns
        A         B         C         D         E         F         G       ◄
  1  Sales Forecast                              This      Next    Following  ►
  2                                              Year      Year       Year    ▲
  3                              Dept 1         23456     34198      37650    ▼
  4                              Dept 2         17693     28762      31495    ?
  5                              Dept 3         33418     31690      34893
  6                              Dept 4         16933     19761      23061
  7                              Dept 5         28610     33388      38964
  8                              Dept 6         18793     21931      25593
  9                              Dept 7         23691     27647      32264
 10                              Dept 8         31520     36784      42927
 11                              Dept 9         17621     20564      23998
 12                              Dept 10        16918     19743      23040
 13                              Dept 11        35971     41978      48988
 14                              Dept 12        26918     31413      36659
 15
 16
 17
 18
 19
 20
 18-Feb-91  01:36 AM                                        NUM
```

Fig. 4.6. *The /Worksheet Column Column-Range menu.*

Use the Esc key or click the right mouse button to back out of a menu to the
next higher menu without actually executing the command. Figure 4.7 shows
the result after you press Esc at the /Worksheet Column Column Range menu
in figure 4.6. You now can explore another /Worksheet Column option.

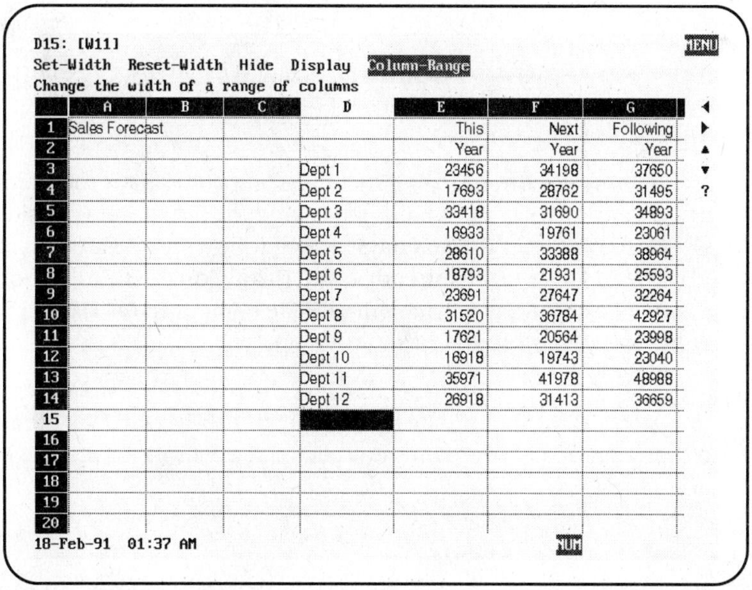

```
D15: [W11]                                                    MENU
Set-Width  Reset-Width  Hide  Display  Column-Range
Change the width of a range of columns
        A         B         C         D         E         F         G       ◄
  1  Sales Forecast                              This      Next    Following  ►
  2                                              Year      Year       Year    ▲
  3                              Dept 1         23456     34198      37650    ▼
  4                              Dept 2         17693     28762      31495    ?
  5                              Dept 3         33418     31690      34893
  6                              Dept 4         16933     19761      23061
  7                              Dept 5         28610     33388      38964
  8                              Dept 6         18793     21931      25593
  9                              Dept 7         23691     27647      32264
 10                              Dept 8         31520     36784      42927
 11                              Dept 9         17621     20564      23998
 12                              Dept 10        16918     19743      23040
 13                              Dept 11        35971     41978      48988
 14                              Dept 12        26918     31413      36659
 15
 16
 17
 18
 19
 20
 18-Feb-91  01:37 AM                                        NUM
```

Fig. 4.7. *The /Worksheet Column menu after you press Esc from the /Worksheet
Column Column-Range menu.*

Reminder:
A /Worksheet command may refer to a single worksheet or to 1-2-3 as a whole.

The 1-2-3 and Wysiwyg menu choices (see figs. 4.1 and 4.2) help guide you to the correct command. For example, all the graph commands are accessed through /Graph or :Graph, and all the data-management commands are accessed through /Data. One important exception is that the /Worksheet commands can refer to an individual worksheet or to 1-2-3 as a whole. For example, use /Worksheet Global Default to change overall 1-2-3 defaults, such as the default directory. The /Worksheet commands affect a larger area of the worksheet than any other command, such as /Range.

If you execute a command by mistake, you normally can Undo the action. For example, if you accidentally erase a range (see figs. 4.4 and 4.5), you can press Undo (Alt-F4) to recover the erased range. Before you can use the Undo feature, you must activate Undo with the /Worksheet Global Default Other Undo Enable command. See Chapter 3 for a complete discussion of Undo.

Saving Your Files

A worksheet file you build exists only in the computer's memory. When you use /Quit to exit 1-2-3 and return to the operating system, you lose your work if you do not first save the current worksheet to disk. When you save a file, you copy the file in memory to a disk and give the file a name. The file then exists not only in memory but as a duplicate file on disk after you quit 1-2-3 or turn off the computer. When you make changes to a file, the changes are made only in the computer's memory until you save the new version of the file to disk.

More information about file operations is included in Chapter 7, where you learn how to read in, use, and save files. For now, you can save your work by giving the /File Save command.

First, select /File Save from the 1-2-3 menu. 1-2-3 prompts for the name of the file to save and displays a default path name for the file. If you did not previously save the file, 1-2-3 displays *.wk1 following the default path name and the names of the files already saved (if any) on the third line of the control panel. You should type a meaningful file name, such as **DEPT1BUD** (a budget file for Department 1).

If you previously saved the file, 1-2-3 displays the name you supplied, such as DEPT1BUD.wk1, as the default file name (see fig. 4.8). To save the file again and keep the same name, press Enter or click the left mouse button within the control panel.

```
A1: 'Department 1 Budget                                    EDIT
Enter name of file to save: C:\123R23\FILES\DEPT1BUD.wk1

        A        B        C      D      E      F      G      H      ◄
    1 Department 1 Budget                                          ►
    2                                                              ▲
    3                                                              ▼
    4                                                              ?
    5
    6
    7
    8
    9
```

Fig. 4.8. The default file name is the same name used the last time the file was saved.

To save the file with a different name, type the file name. The file name you type replaces the existing name. If the file already exists on the disk, 1-2-3 displays the following three-option menu:

    Cancel Replace Backup

Select **R**eplace to write over the previous file. After you select **R**eplace, however, you lose the previous file. If you make an error in a file and then save the file with the same name and select **R**eplace, the previous file is lost. Select **C**ancel to void the /**F**ile **S**ave. If, by mistake, you type a file name that matches another file name, **C**ancel the command so that you do not lose the other file.

If you select **B**ackup, 1-2-3 renames the existing file on disk with a BAK extension and then saves the new file with the WK1 extension. **B**ackup stores the new file and the previous version of the file on the disk.

Caution:
If you choose **Replace** *from the* /**F**ile **S**ave *menu, the previous file with that name is lost.*

Cue:
Choose **Backup** *to keep a backup copy of your file.*

Using Ranges

A range, a rectangular group of cells, is defined by the cell addresses of two opposite corners and is separated by two periods. As shown in figure 4.9, a range can be a single cell (E1..E1), part of a row (A1..C1), part of a column (G1..G5, D13..D20, and F14..F15), or a rectangle that spans multiple rows and columns (B4..E9 and A13..B15). Also, an entire worksheet can be a range.

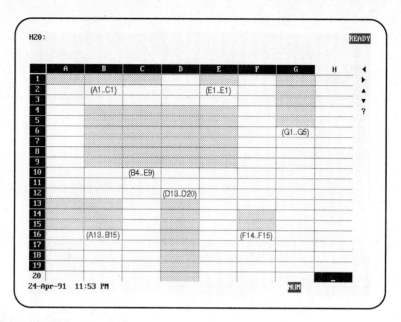

Fig. 4.9. Some 1-2-3 ranges.

Many commands act on one or more ranges. For example, the /Range Erase command prompts you for the range to erase. In the example shown in figure 4.4, the range is a single cell. You can respond to a prompt for a range in several ways. At different times, one method may be more convenient. To specify a range, you can use one of the following methods:

- Type the addresses of the corners of the range.

- Highlight a range in POINT mode (using the arrow keys or the mouse).

- Preselect the range with the F4 key or by using the mouse.

- Type the range name or press Name (F3) and point to the range name if you assigned a name.

Each method is covered in the following sections.

Typing the Addresses of the Range

Caution:
Typing the addresses of the range is the method most prone to error.

Because the first method—typing the addresses of the range—is the most prone to error, you probably will use this method least of the four. This method requires you to type the addresses of any two opposite corners of the range.

You can specify a range by typing the address of the upper left corner, one or two periods, and the address of the lower right corner. 1-2-3 always stores a range with two periods to separate the addresses, but you need to type only one period. 1-2-3 always stores a range by using the upper left and lower right addresses. You can type the upper right and lower left addresses or reverse the order and type the lower address first and then the upper address. 1-2-3 always stores the range using the upper left and lower right coordinates.

For example, to specify the range B4..E9 in figure 4.9, type **B4..E9** or **B4.E9** or **E9..B4** or **E9.B4**. You also can use the other two opposite corners: **B9..E4** or **E4..B9**. In all cases, 1-2-3 stores the range as B4..E9.

You can type cell addresses to specify a range in several situations: when the range does not have a range name; when the range you want to specify is far from the current cell and using the POINT mode is not convenient; or when you happen to know the cell addresses of the range. Experienced 1-2-3 users rarely type cell addresses. Instead, they use one of the following alternative methods: specifying a range in POINT mode, preselecting a range with the F4 key or the mouse, typing range names, or pointing to a range name that already exists.

Highlighting a Range in POINT Mode

The second method, highlighting the cells in the range in POINT mode, is the most common technique. Highlighting can be done with the mouse or the direction keys.

You can point to and highlight a range required for commands and functions in the same manner that you point to a single cell in a formula. Special considerations for highlighting ranges in functions are covered in Chapter 6.

Figure 4.10 shows a sample sales forecast. Suppose that, because of a reorganization, you must erase all the forecasts and enter new data. Figure 4.10 shows the `Enter range to erase:` prompt that appears when you execute **/Range Erase**. The default range in the control panel is the address of the cell pointer, in this example E3..E3. The single cell is shown as a one-cell range. When the prompt shows a single cell as a one-cell range, the cell is said to be anchored. **/Range Erase** and most other **/Range** commands use an anchored, one-cell range as the default range. When the cell is anchored, as you drag the mouse from the anchored cell (move the mouse while holding down the left mouse button) or move the cell pointer with the direction keys, you highlight a range.

```
E3: [W11] 23456                                              POINT
Enter range to erase: E3..E3
```

	A	B	C	D	E	F	G
1	Sales Forecast				This	Next	Following
2					Year	Year	Year
3				Dept 1	23456	34198	37650
4				Dept 2	17693	28762	31495
5				Dept 3	33418	31690	34893
6				Dept 4	16933	19761	23061
7				Dept 5	28610	33388	38964
8				Dept 6	18793	21931	25593
9				Dept 7	23691	27647	32264
10				Dept 8	31520	36784	42927
11				Dept 9	17621	20564	23998
12				Dept 10	16918	19743	23040
13				Dept 11	35971	41978	48988
14				Dept 12	26918	31413	36659
15				Dept 13			
16							
17							
18							
19							
20							

```
18-Feb-91  01:50 AM                                    NUM
```

Fig. 4.10. An anchored range at the location of the cell pointer.

Reminder:
Check the control panel to see whether the cell is anchored.

Figure 4.11 shows the screen after you drag the mouse from E3 to G14 and release the left mouse button or press End-↓ and then End-→. As you move the cell pointer, the highlight expands from the anchored cell. The highlighted range becomes E3..G14, which is the range that appears in the control panel. When you click the left mouse button or press Enter, 1-2-3 executes the command (see fig. 4.12).

Cue:
Use the End key with the arrow keys to highlight ranges.

Typically, pointing and highlighting is faster and easier than typing the range addresses. Also, because you can see the range while you make the selection (see fig. 4.11), you make fewer errors when you point than when you type the range address.

Use the End key when you highlight ranges from the keyboard. The End key moves to the end of a range of occupied cells. To highlight the range from E3..G14 in figure 4.11, press End-↓ and End-→, as in the preceding example. Without the End key, you must press the → twice and the ↓ 11 times.

With some commands, such as /**R**ange **E**rase in this example, the anchored cell starts at the position of the cell pointer. You should move the cell pointer to the upper left corner of the range before you start the command. In figure 4.10, the cell pointer started at E3, the upper left corner of the range that you want to erase.

```
G14: [W11] 36659                                              POINT
Enter range to erase: E3..G14
```

	A	B	C	D	E	F	G	
1	Sales Forecast				This	Next	Following	◄
2					Year	Year	Year	►
3				Dept 1	23456	34198	37650	▲
4				Dept 2	17693	28762	31495	▼
5				Dept 3	33418	31690	34893	?
6				Dept 4	16933	19761	23061	
7				Dept 5	28610	33388	38964	
8				Dept 6	18793	21931	25593	
9				Dept 7	23691	27647	32264	
10				Dept 8	31520	36784	42927	
11				Dept 9	17621	20564	23998	
12				Dept 10	16918	19743	23040	
13				Dept 11	35971	41978	48988	
14				Dept 12	26918	31413	36659	
15				Dept 13				
16								
17								
18								
19								
20								

```
18-Feb-91  03:45 AM                                           NUM
```

Fig. 4.11. *A range highlighted as the cell pointer is moved.*

```
E3: [W11]                                                     READY
```

	A	B	C	D	E	F	G	
1	Sales Forecast				This	Next	Following	◄
2					Year	Year	Year	►
3				Dept 1	–			▲
4				Dept 2				▼
5				Dept 3				?
6				Dept 4				
7				Dept 5				
8				Dept 6				
9				Dept 7				
10				Dept 8				
11				Dept 9				
12				Dept 10				
13				Dept 11				
14				Dept 12				
15				Dept 13				
16								
17								
18								
19								
20								

```
18-Feb-91  03:46 AM        UNDO                    NUM
```

Fig. 4.12. *The highlighted range erased.*

However, when you use other commands (including /Data, /Graph, /Print, and /Range Search from the 1-2-3 menu and :Graph and :Print from the Wysiwyg menu) at the Enter range: prompt, 1-2-3 does not expect the range to start at the current location of the cell pointer. Therefore, the control panel shows the current cell address as a single address and the cell pointer is not anchored.

Cue:

Press the right mouse button, Esc, or Backspace to clear a highlighted range.

You can press the right mouse button, Esc, or Backspace to clear an anchored or incorrectly highlighted range. The highlight collapses to the anchor cell only, and the anchor is removed. For example, if you press, Backspace, Esc, or the right mouse button—as shown in figure 4.10—the highlight becomes E3 and the cell becomes unanchored (see fig. 4.13). Notice that the cell address in the control panel in figure 4.13 is the single address E3, not the one-cell range E3..E3.

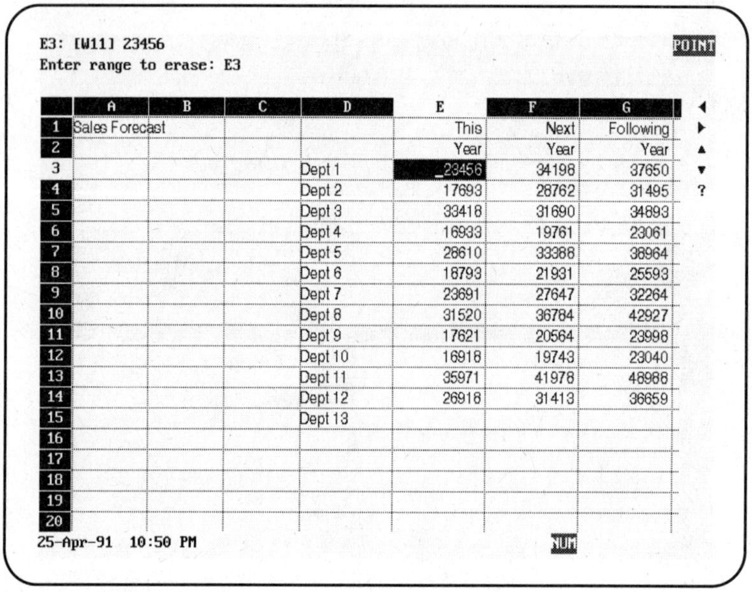

Fig. 4.13. The highlighted range and the anchor cleared.

Preselecting a Range

Before issuing a command, you can select the range to be affected by the command. This technique is called *preselecting a range*. Why preselect a range instead of selecting the range after you issue the command? When you preselect a range, you can issue several commands that affect the range. The range that you preselect remains selected. For example, to change the font of some numbers and then to outline the cells that contain the numbers, preselect the range, and perform both commands.

You can preselect a range in one of two ways. If you use the keyboard, move the cell pointer to the beginning of the range. Next press F4. The mode indicator changes from READY to POINT, and an anchored range address appears in the control panel. Using the arrow keys, select the range. Figure 4.14 shows the screen when you preselect the range C3..F4. After you select the desired range, press Enter to accept the range setting.

```
F4: (C0) 61478                                                    POINT
Range: C3..F4

         A          B         C        D        E        F       G        H      ◄
   1  All Departments                                                            ►
   2                          Qtr 1    Qtr 2    Qtr 3    Qtr 4                    ▲
   3             Sales       $96,487  $98,523  $92,874  $99,861                   ▼
   4             Expenses    $68,512  $63,521  $66,885  $61,478                   ?
   5             Profit      $27,975  $35,002  $25,989  $38,383
   6
   7
   8
   9
```

Fig. 4.14. *Preselecting the range C3..F4.*

If you use a mouse, move the mouse pointer to the corner cell of the range and click and hold down the left mouse button. 1-2-3 enters POINT mode. Drag the mouse to highlight the range and then release the left mouse button. You do not need to press Enter to complete the selection; releasing the mouse button completes the selection. After you select the range, you can begin issuing the commands to affect the preselected range.

Specifying a Range with Range Names

The final method for specifying a range at the prompt involves giving the range a name. Range names should be descriptive, can include up to 15 characters, and can be used as part of formulas and commands. When 1-2-3 expects a cell or range address, you can specify a range name. You can specify a range name in one of two ways. You can type the range name, or you can press Name (F3) and select the range name.

Cue:
You can use a range name any time 1-2-3 expects a range or cell address.

Using range names has a number of advantages. Range names are easier to remember than addresses. Using range names is at times faster than pointing to a range in another part of the worksheet. Range names also make formulas easier to understand. For example, if you see the range name

NOV_SALES_R1 in a formula, you may remember that the entry represents "November Sales for Region 1" (see fig. 4.15).

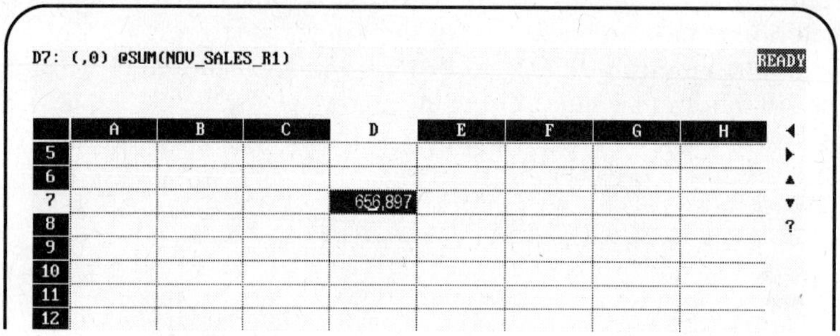

Fig. 4.15. *A formula that uses a range name.*

When you press Name (F3), the third line of the control panel lists, in alphabetical order, the first five range names. Use the mouse or direction keys to point to the correct range name and then either click the left mouse button or press Enter. If you have many range names, press Name (F3) again; 1-2-3 displays a full screen of range names (see fig. 4.16).

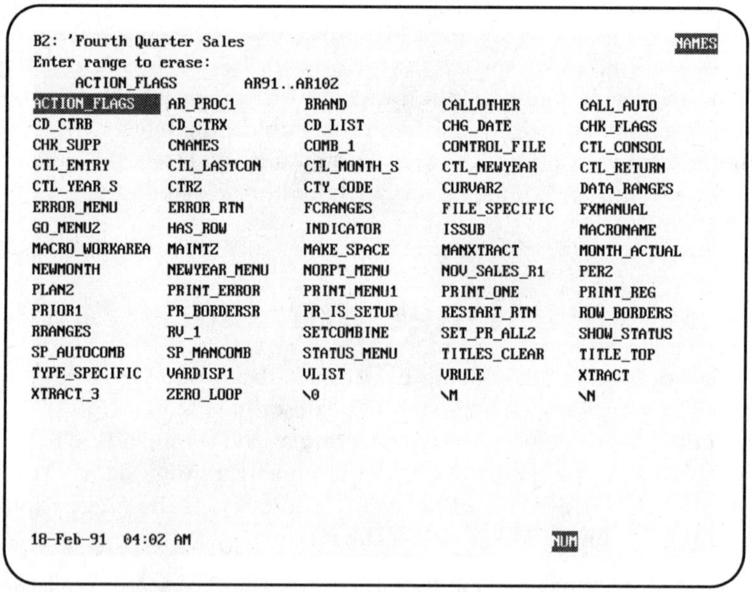

Fig. 4.16. *A full-screen listing of range names.*

If the prompt calls for a single cell address, such as with /Data Sort Primary-Key or GoTo (F5), 1-2-3 can find a range whether you type a range name or a cell address. If you type a range name that applies to a multiple-cell range, 1-2-3 uses the upper left corner of the range. If you type a non-existent range name, 1-2-3 displays a dialog box with an error message. To clear the error and try again, press Esc, Enter, or the right mouse button.

Cue:
You can use the Name (F3) key in commands, functions, and with the GoTo (F5) key.

Because a single cell is considered a valid range, you can name a single cell as a range. When 1-2-3 expects a cell address, you can type the address, point to the cell, type the single-cell range name, or press F3 for a list of range names.

Creating Range Names

To create range names, use the /Range Name Create or /Range Name Labels commands to assign names to individual cells or ranges. Follow these steps to create range names with the /Range Name Create command:

1. Move to the top left corner of the range you want to name.

2. Select /Range Name Create.

3. Type the name at the Enter name: prompt and then click the left mouse button or press Enter. 1-2-3 displays the Enter range: prompt.

If you type a new range name, 1-2-3 shows the current cell as an anchored range. Highlight the range or type the address or addresses of the cell or range; then click the left mouse button or press Enter.

If you type an existing range name, 1-2-3 highlights the existing range. Use the arrow keys to extend or contract the range. To specify a new range, press Backspace to cancel the existing range and cause the cell pointer to return to the cell it was in before you issued the command. Clicking the right mouse button or pressing Esc cancels the range but leaves the cell pointer in the upper left corner of the range (except for single-cell ranges). Then specify a new range. Click the left mouse button or press Enter to complete the operation.

Range names can include up to 15 characters and are not case-sensitive. Although you can type or refer to the name by using any combination of uppercase and lowercase letters, all range names are stored as uppercase letters.

Reminder:
Specify range names with upper- or lowercase letters.

The following list explains a few rules and precautions for naming ranges:

- Do not use spaces or special characters—except for the underscore character (_)—in range names. If you use special characters, such as numeric operators, you can confuse 1-2-3 when you use the name in formulas.

- Do not start the name with a number. You can use numbers in the rest of the range name, but because of a quirk in 1-2-3, you cannot type a range name that starts with a number as part of a formula.

- Do not use range names that also are cell addresses (such as P2), key names (such as GoTo), function names (such as @SUM), or advanced macro command names (such as BRANCH). If you use a cell address as a range name, when you type the range name, 1-2-3 uses the cell address instead.

Reminder:
Use /Range Name Labels to assign names to a group of one-cell ranges.

You also can create range names with the **/Range Name Labels** command. Use this command to assign range names to many individual cells at one time. You can use **/Range Name Labels** to assign range names to single-cell ranges only. When using **/Range Name Labels**, use labels already typed into the worksheet as range names for adjacent cells. In figure 4.17, for example, you can use the labels in cells B5..B8 to name the cells with sales data in C5..C8. Because you want to name the cells to the right of the labels, use **/Range Name Labels Right**. Specify a range of B5..B8 and click the left mouse button or press Enter. Now C5 has the range name DEPT_1; C6 has the name DEPT_2; and so on.

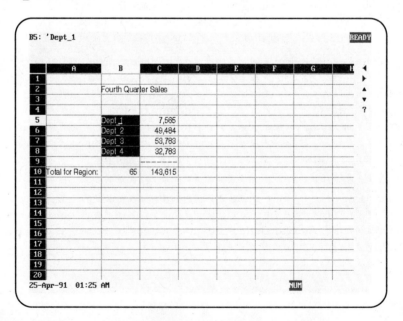

Fig. 4.17. *Labels that can be used for range names.*

The other options with /**Range Name Labels** are **Left**, **Down**, and **Up**. These commands only assign range names to cells with labels in the range you specify. If you specified a range of B2..B10 in figure 4.17, the blank cells in B3, B4, and B9 and the number in B10 are ignored. The first 15 characters in the label in B2 become the range name for C2: FOURTH QUARTER (note the trailing space in the name). You do no harm if you include blank cells or include numbers or formulas in a /**Range Name Labels** range. Do not, however, include other labels, or you end up with unwanted range names.

Listing All Range Names

You can use /**Range Name Table** to create a list of range names and addresses (see fig 4.18). This table is part of the documentation for the worksheet file and can be put in a worksheet separate from the actual data.

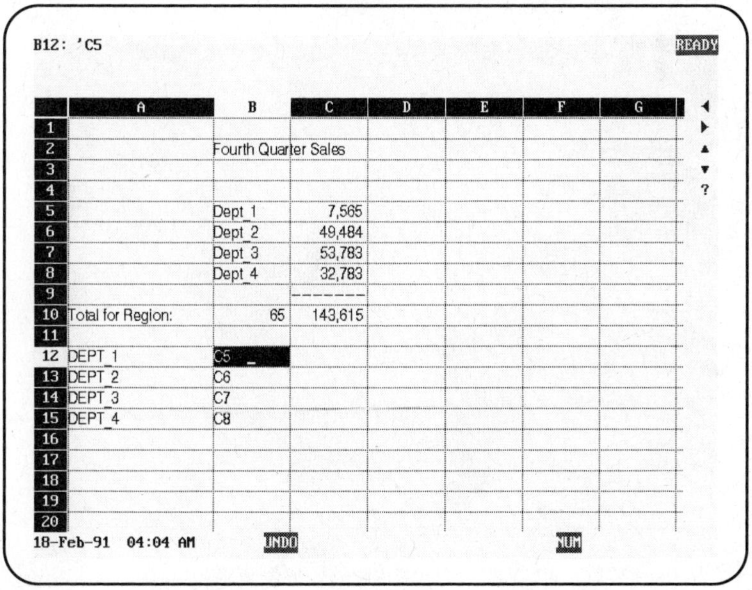

Fig. 4.18. A table of range names and addresses.

To delete an unwanted range name, use /**Range Name Delete**. Use caution when using the /**Range Name Reset** command, however. The command immediately deletes all the range names in the file.

Caution:
/Range Name Reset deletes all range names.

Setting Column Widths

Reminder:
The default
column width
of a worksheet
is 9 characters.

When you start a new worksheet, all columns are 9 characters wide. You can change this default column width and the width of each individual column to best accommodate your data. If columns are too narrow, numbers display as asterisks, and labels are truncated (if the adjacent cell to the right is used). If columns are too wide, you cannot see or print as much on-screen information. Figure 4.19 shows a worksheet with a default column width of 4 characters and an individual column width of 10 for column A. The number in cell J8 is too wide for the column and displays as a row of asterisks. The label in A5 is too long for the column width and is truncated by the number in B5. Any column width other than the default is displayed in the control panel, when a cell from that column is highlighted.

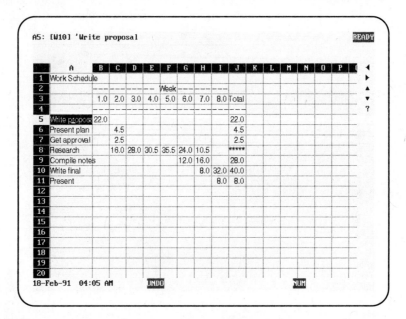

Fig. 4.19. *A worksheet with a global column width of 4 and an individual column width of 10 for column A.*

Whether a number can fit into a cell depends on both the column width and the format. In general, a number's width must be one character less than the column width. Some negative numbers display with parentheses, which take two extra characters. If a number displays as a row of asterisks, change either the column width, the format, or both. Use /Worksheet Global Column-Width to change the default column width for the entire worksheet. At the prompt, type a number between 1 and 240 and click the left mouse button within the control panel or press Enter.

When using the mouse to set the width of one column, move the mouse pointer to the top border of the worksheet and point to the vertical line that marks the right side of a particular column. When you hold down the left mouse button, the mouse pointer changes to a double-headed arrow pointing to the right and left, shown in figure 4.20. To increase the width of the column, move the mouse to the right while continuing to hold down the left mouse button. To decrease the width of the column, move the mouse to the left while continuing to hold down the left mouse button.

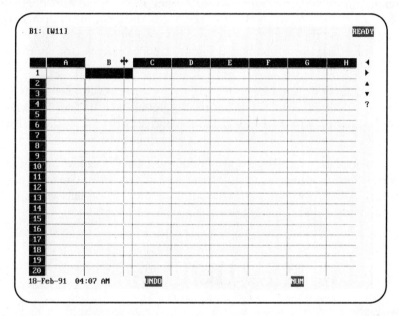

Fig. 4.20. A double-headed arrow appears in the top border when you change a column width with the mouse.

You also can set the width of a column with a 1-2-3 command or a Wysiwyg command. To set the width of one column, move the cell pointer to the column you want to change and select /Worksheet Column Set-Width. At the prompt, type a number between 1 and 240 and press Enter or click the left mouse button within the control panel. You also can use the Wysiwyg command **:**Worksheet Column Set-Width in the same manner. Each command has exactly the same effect on the column width.

To change column widths for more than one column at a time with the 1-2-3 menu, use /Worksheet Column Column-Range Set-Width. At the first prompt, highlight the range of columns to set; then type the column width and click the left mouse button within the control panel or press Enter. /Worksheet Column Column-Range Set-Width operates on a consecutive set of columns only. You also can select **:**Worksheet Column Set-Width from the Wysiwyg menu to change the column widths of a consecutive group of columns.

An individual column width overrides the global column width. If you change the global column width shown in figure 4.19, the width of column A does not change.

If you are not sure of the exact column width you want, use the left-arrow and right-arrow keys (or right and left mouse icons) instead of typing a number. Each time you press the left-arrow key, the column width decreases by one. Each time you press the right-arrow key, the column width increases by one. When the display looks the way you want, press Enter. This technique works for individual columns, column-ranges, and global column widths.

Use /Worksheet Column Reset-Width or :Worksheet Column Reset-Width to reset individual column widths to the global default. The /Worksheet Column Column-Range Reset-Width command or :Worksheet Column Reset resets a range of columns to the global default column width.

If the worksheet window is split when you change column widths, the column width applies only to the current window. When you clear a split window, 1-2-3 saves the column widths in the top or left window. All column widths in the bottom or right window are lost.

Setting Row Heights

The Wysiwyg features of Release 2.3 make it possible to view a variety of type fonts on screen (see fig. 4.21). However, some fonts are too large to fit in a normal size cell. 1-2-3 adjusts the height of a row to compensate for the size of the font. 1-2-3 also enables you to adjust the row height with the mouse. To adjust the height of a single row with the mouse, move the mouse pointer over to the left border of the worksheet and point to the horizontal line that marks the bottom of a particular row. When you hold down the left mouse button, a double-headed arrow (pointing up and down) appears, as shown in figure 4.22. To increase the row height, drag the mouse down. To decrease the row height, drag the mouse up.

You can adjust the height of a range of rows by selecting :Worksheet Row Set-Height. At the first prompt, highlight the range of rows to set; then type a number between 1 and 240 and click the left mouse button within the control panel or press Enter. You also can adjust the height of a single row with this method by selecting a single row as the range.

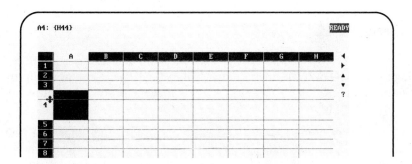

A3: [W13]   READY

	A	B	C	D	E	F	G	H	I	J	K	L	M
1	Work Schedule												
2						Week							
3		1.0	2.0	3.0	4.0	5.0	6.0	7.0	8.0	Total			
4													
5	Write proposal	22.0								22.0			
6	Present plan		4.5							4.5			
7	Get approval		2.5							2.5			
8	Research		16.0	28.0	30.5	35.5	24.0	10.5		144.5			
9	Compile notes						12.0	16.0		28.0			
10	Write final							8.0	32.0	40.0			
11	Present								8.0	8.0			
12													
13													
14													
15													
16													
17													
18													
19													

18-Feb-91 04:20 AM   UNDO   NUM

Fig. 4.21. *A variety of type fonts displayed on-screen.*

A4: {H44}   READY

	A	B	C	D	E	F	G	H
1								
2								
3								
4								
5								
6								
7								
8								

Fig. 4.22. *A double-headed arrow appears in the left border when you change a row height with the mouse.*

If you are not sure of the exact row height you want, use the up-arrow and down-arrow keys (or up and down mouse icons) instead of typing a number. Each time you press the up-arrow key, the row height decreases by one. Each time you press the down-arrow key, the row height increases by one. When the display looks the way you want, press Enter. This technique works for individual rows and row ranges.

After you set the height of a row or rows by using **:Worksheet Row Set-Height**, the height does not automatically adjust when you change the font size for this row. To make the row sizes automatically adjust again, select the command **:Worksheet Row Auto** and select the row(s) you want to reset.

Erasing and Deleting Rows and Columns

You can clear all or parts of your work in several ways. All data that you clear is removed from the worksheet in memory, but this action does not affect the files on disk until you use the /File commands explained in Chapter 7. You can clear part of your work in memory in two ways. If you erase the work, you remove all the contents of the cells. If you delete the work, you remove not only the contents but also all the deleted cells from the worksheet. The following sections show you how to erase contiguous ranges of data and how to delete entire rows and columns.

Erasing Ranges

Use the /**Range Erase** command to erase sections—either a single cell or a range of cells—of a file in memory. When you erase a range, only the contents are lost. Characteristics, such as format, protection status, and column width, remain.

After you select /**Range Erase**, 1-2-3 prompts you for the range you want eliminated. Highlight a range or type a range name and click the left mouse button within the control panel or press Enter. You also can press Name (F3) for a list of range names. To erase only the current cell, click the left mouse button within the control panel (or click twice on the cell) or press Enter.

Deleting Rows and Columns

After you erase a range, the blank cells remain. In contrast, when you delete rows or columns, 1-2-3 deletes the entire row or column and updates the addresses of the remaining worksheet to reflect the removal. To delete a row, move the cell pointer to the row you want to delete and use /**Worksheet Delete Row**. You then are prompted for the range of rows to delete. To delete one row, point to the cell pointer and click the left mouse button twice or press Enter. With the mouse or the direction keys, you can delete more than one row; highlight the rows you want to delete. Then click the left mouse button or press Enter. You only need to highlight one cell in each row—not the entire row (see fig. 4.23).

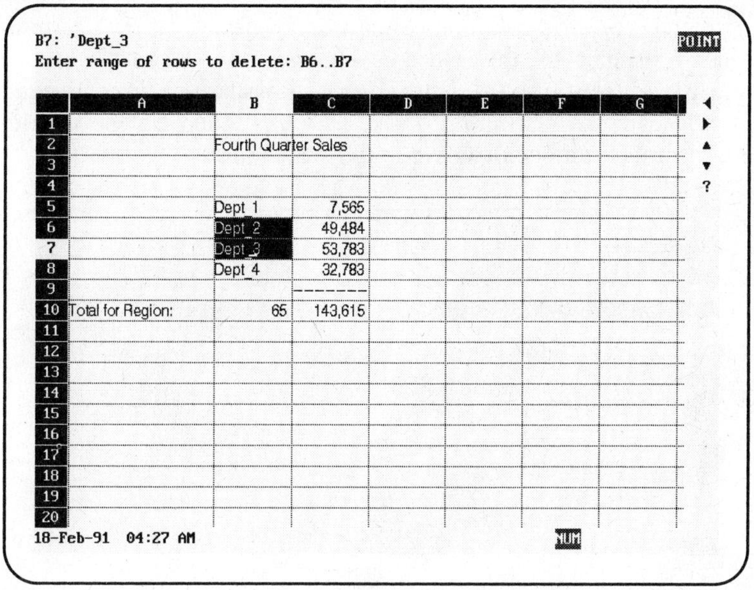

Fig. 4.23. One cell in each of two rows highlighted for deletion.

When you click the left mouse button or press Enter, the rows that contain highlighted cells are deleted. The rest of the worksheet then moves up (see fig. 4.24). 1-2-3 adjusts all addresses, range names, and formulas. Use the /Worksheet Delete Column command and follow the same procedure to delete columns.

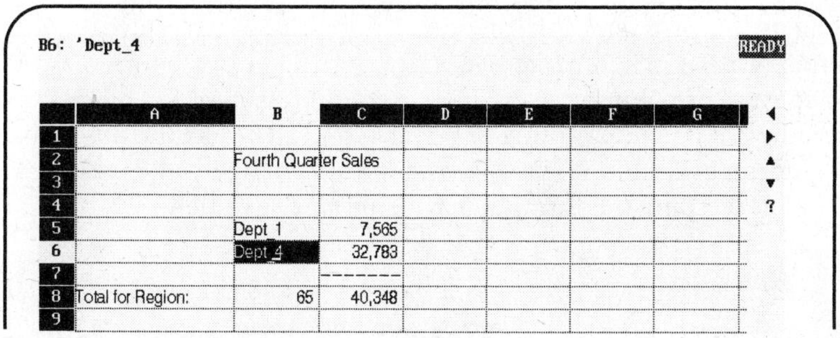

Fig. 4.24. The worksheet after rows are deleted..

Caution:
*When you delete
rows or columns,
ERR can occur.*

If you delete rows or columns that are a part of a range name or a range in a formula, 1-2-3 adjusts the range as long as you do not delete columns from the left or right side of the range or rows from the top or bottom of the range. If you delete these rows or columns, 1-2-3 cancels the range. When a range is cancelled, formulas that contain that range display ERR.

If the deleted rows or columns contain data referenced by a formula or formulas in other cells, the reference changes to ERR, and the formulas become invalid (see fig. 4.25). This action is a possible serious consequence of deleting rows and columns. These formulas need not be visible on-screen; formulas can be anywhere in the worksheet.

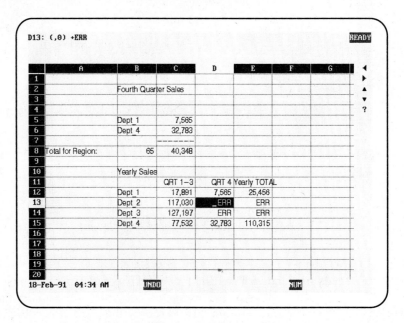

Fig. 4.25. ERR replacing cell addresses in formulas referencing deleted cells.

To remedy this problem, you can press Undo (Alt-F4) to restore the deleted columns or rows. Then make necessary changes to your formulas before deleting rows or columns again. If Undo (Alt-F4) is disabled, however, you must either retype the formula or retrieve from the disk the model before the changes were made. If you made significant changes since you last saved the model, retyping the formula may be more convenient.

Clearing the Entire Worksheet

You can clear a worksheet from memory with /Worksheet Erase Yes. This command also restores all the default global settings. The effect is the same if you first quit and then restart 1-2-3 from the operating system. Use this command if you want to begin working with a blank worksheet.

Remember to use /File Save before you use /Worksheet Erase. To reclaim a worksheet after /Worksheet Erase Yes is executed, use Undo (Alt-F4), if the Undo feature was active when the worksheet was erased.

Inserting Rows and Columns

In addition to deleting rows and columns, you also can insert rows and columns anywhere in the worksheet. Insert rows with /Worksheet Insert Row and columns with /Worksheet Insert Column. You can insert one or more rows or columns at one time. At the Enter column insert range: prompt, highlight the number of columns you want to insert and click the left mouse button or press Enter. At the Enter row insert range: prompt, highlight the number of rows you want to insert and click the left mouse button or press Enter.

When you insert columns, all columns including and to the right of the cell pointer move to the right. When you insert rows, all rows including and below the cell pointer are pushed down. All addresses in formulas and range names adjust automatically. Suppose that you want to insert a column between columns E and F in the worksheet in figure 4.26. Place your cell pointer in column F and use /Worksheet Insert Column. Figure 4.27 shows the result of this operation.

Reminder:
When you insert columns, all addresses in formulas and range names adjust automatically.

```
F4: "QTR 4                                                    POINT
Enter column insert range: F4..F4

          A         B        C        D        E        F        G        H
 1
 2   Department Totals: Personnel Expenses
 3
 4   Department Numbers   QTR 1    QTR 2    QTR 3    QTR 4    TOTAL
 5   Department 1        57,301   61,312   65,604   70,197   254,414
 6   Department 2        51,399   54,997   58,847   62,967   228,210
 7   Department 3        62,745   67,137   71,836   76,866   278,584
 8   Department 4        67,157   71,858   76,888   82,271   298,174
 9   Department 5        50,024   53,525   57,272   61,282   222,103
10   Department 6        59,708   63,887   68,359   73,145   265,099
11   Department 7        69,678   74,555   79,774   85,360   309,367
12   Department 8        63,203   67,627   72,361   77,427   280,618
13   Department 9        70,194   75,107   80,365   85,991   311,657
14   Department 10       49,451   52,912   56,616   60,580   219,559
15   Department 11       75,924   81,238   86,925   93,011   337,098
16   Department 12       44,294   47,394   50,712   54,262   196,662
17
18   TOTALS             721,078  771,549  825,559  883,359  3,201,545
19
20

18-Feb-91  05:02 AM                                          NUM
```

Fig. 4.26. The location of the column to be inserted is highlighted.

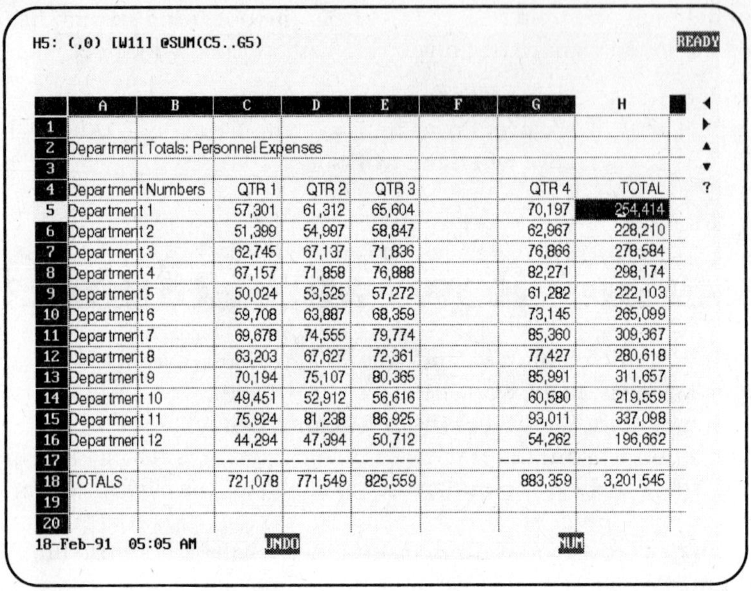

Fig. 4.27. *Cell addresses in formulas automatically adjusted after column insertion.*

Caution:
Inserting or deleting rows and columns can affect formulas and macros.

If you insert a row or column in the middle of a range, the range expands to accommodate the new rows or columns. In figure 4.26, the formula in G5 is @SUM(C5..F5). In figure 4.27, the formula is pushed to H5 to make room for the inserted column. The formula in H5 now reads @SUM(C5..G5) and includes the columns in the old range as well as the inserted column.

Using Window Options

You can change how you view the worksheet in a number of ways. You can change the display format to view more rows and columns at one time, and you can split the screen into two windows either vertically or horizontally. Using these options enables you to see different parts of your work at the same time.

Changing the Display Format

When working with large databases, reports, or tables of data, you cannot see all the data at one time. If your display hardware supports it, you can change the display to view more columns and rows of data at one time. The more data you can see at a time, the more easily you can compare different months or different departments.

In addition to the standard 80-character-by-25-line (80x25) display, many monitor and graphics card combinations give you a choice of other formats. You choose these display formats when you install 1-2-3 (see Appendix A). For example, if your system has a Hercules Monochrome Graphics Card, you can choose an 80x25 or 90x38 display. With an EGA card, you can choose an 80x25 or 80x43 display. With a VGA card, you can choose an 80x25, 80x43, or 80x50 display.

If you use a monochrome display adapter (no graphics), a Color/Graphics adapter, or an EGA adapter with only 64K of video memory, 1-2-3 displays data in the 80x25 format only.

You also can change how worksheets look on your display by changing worksheet colors, enlarging or reducing the size of cells so that a greater or lesser number of the cells appears on the display, adding grid lines and page breaks to worksheets, and changing how the cell pointer looks. You can even make 1-2-3 look just like it does when Wysiwyg is not loaded into memory. These Wysiwyg features are discussed in detail in Chapter 9.

Splitting the Screen

You can split the screen either horizontally or vertically into two windows by using /Worksheet Window Horizontal or /Worksheet Window Vertical. These commands—useful when creating large, single worksheets—enable you to see different parts of the worksheet at the same time.

Split the screen vertically when you want to see the TOTAL column to the right of the data, as in figure 4.28. Split the screen horizontally when you want to see the totals row at the bottom of the data. With a split screen, you can change data in one window and at the same time see how the totals change in the other window. This capability is well-suited for "what-if" analysis. A split screen also is helpful when you write macros. You can write the macro in one window and see the data that the macro alters in the other window. Macros are covered in Chapters 13 and 14.

The window splits at the position of the cell pointer, so be sure that you first move the cell pointer to the desired position before splitting the screen. When you split the screen vertically, the left window includes the columns to the immediate left of the cell pointer but does not include the cell pointer's column. (The cell pointer jumps to the left window when you execute the command.) In figure 4.28, the cell pointer was in column E when the window was split. Columns A-D (the columns to the left of the cell pointer) became the left window. The right window then was scrolled to display the TOTAL and VARIANCE in columns O and P. These two columns are always visible as you scroll the left window.

Reminder:
Move the cell pointer to the position where you want the screen to split.

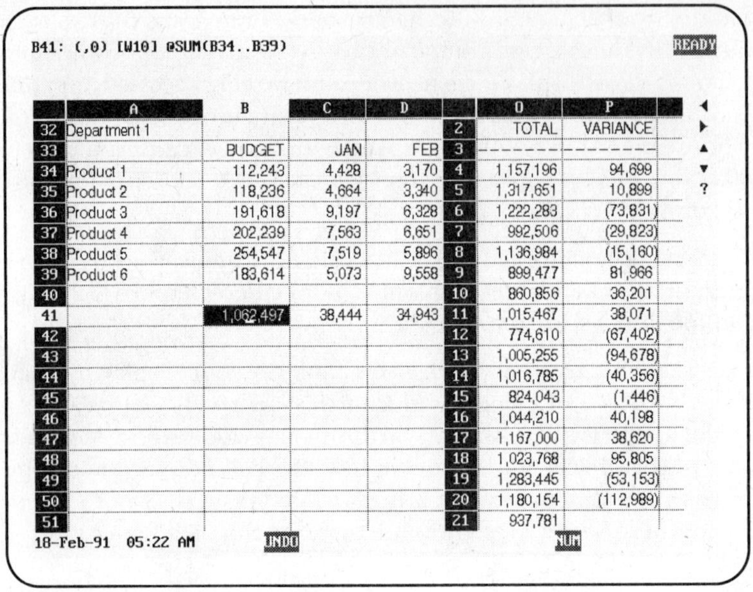

```
B41: (,0) [W10] @SUM(B34..B39)                                    READY
```

	A	B	C	D		O	P
32	Department 1				2	TOTAL	VARIANCE
33		BUDGET	JAN	FEB	3	--------	--------
34	Product 1	112,243	4,428	3,170	4	1,157,196	94,699
35	Product 2	118,236	4,664	3,340	5	1,317,651	10,899
36	Product 3	191,618	9,197	6,328	6	1,222,283	(73,831)
37	Product 4	202,239	7,563	6,651	7	992,506	(29,823)
38	Product 5	254,547	7,519	5,896	8	1,136,984	(15,160)
39	Product 6	183,614	5,073	9,558	9	899,477	81,966
40					10	860,856	36,201
41		1,062,497	38,444	34,943	11	1,015,467	38,071
42					12	774,610	(67,402)
43					13	1,005,255	(94,678)
44					14	1,016,785	(40,356)
45					15	824,043	(1,446)
46					16	1,044,210	40,198
47					17	1,167,000	38,620
48					18	1,023,768	95,805
49					19	1,283,445	(53,153)
50					20	1,180,154	(112,989)
51					21	937,781	

```
18-Feb-91  05:22 AM        UNDO                              NUM
```

Fig. 4.28. Data displayed in two vertical windows.

When you split the screen horizontally, the top window includes the rows above the cell pointer. (The cell pointer jumps to the top window when you execute the command.) To display rows 10-20 in the top window, scroll the display so that row 10 is at the top of the display and then move the cell pointer to row 21 and select /Worksheet Window Horizontal. Because a split screen has two borders, you cannot display as much data at one time as you can with a full screen.

As you move down the worksheet in figure 4.28, both windows scroll together. If you move the cell pointer below row 20, both windows scroll up so that you can see row 21. In this particular example, synchronized scrolling of data is what you want. No matter where the cell pointer is in the left window, you can see the total for this department in the right window.

Reminder:
When you want two windows to scroll separately, use /Worksheet Windows Unsync.

At other times, you want to see two unrelated views of the same worksheet. For example, when one window contains data and the other window contains macros, you want the two windows to scroll separately. Use /Worksheet Window Unsync to stop the synchronized scrolling and /Worksheet Window Sync to restore synchronized scrolling.

When the two windows display different types of data, you want unsynchronized scrolling. Notice that if you scroll down to row 50 in the left window in figure 4.28, you do not want to scroll down to row 50 in the right window.

To move between windows, use the mouse (click the left mouse button within the desired window) or use the Window (F6) key. To clear a split screen, use /Worksheet Window Clear. No matter what window is active, the cell pointer moves to the left or top window when you clear a split screen.

Freezing Titles On-Screen

Most worksheets are much larger than you can display on-screen at one time (see fig. 4.29). As you move the cell pointer, you scroll the display. New data appears at one edge of the display, and the data at the other edge scrolls out of sight. This scrolling can be a problem when titles at the top of the worksheet and descriptions at the left also scroll off the screen (see fig. 4.30) because you can no longer tell what month and what departments the worksheet contains.

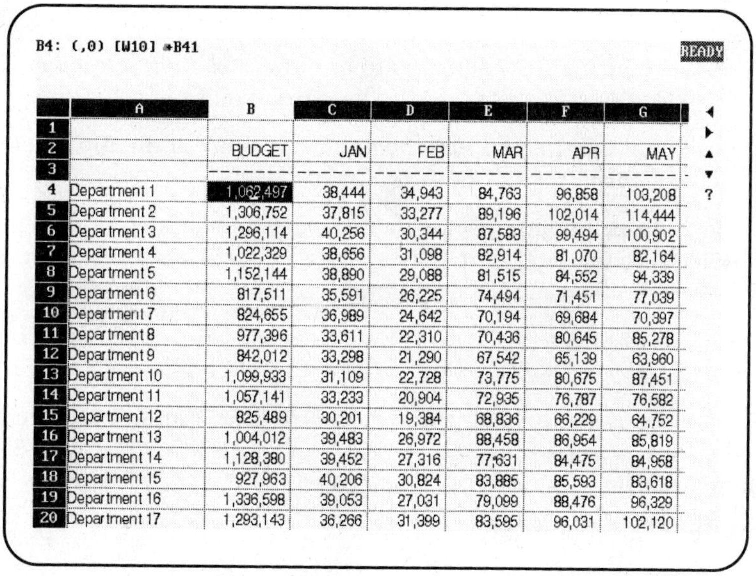

	A	B	C	D	E	F	G
1							
2		BUDGET	JAN	FEB	MAR	APR	MAY
3							
4	Department 1	1,062,497	38,444	34,943	84,763	96,858	103,208
5	Department 2	1,306,752	37,815	33,277	89,196	102,014	114,444
6	Department 3	1,296,114	40,256	30,344	87,583	99,494	100,902
7	Department 4	1,022,329	38,656	31,098	82,914	81,070	82,164
8	Department 5	1,152,144	38,890	29,088	81,515	84,552	94,339
9	Department 6	817,511	35,591	26,225	74,494	71,451	77,039
10	Department 7	824,655	36,989	24,642	70,194	69,684	70,397
11	Department 8	977,396	33,611	22,310	70,436	80,645	85,278
12	Department 9	842,012	33,298	21,290	67,542	65,139	63,960
13	Department 10	1,099,933	31,109	22,728	73,775	80,675	87,451
14	Department 11	1,057,141	33,233	20,904	72,935	76,787	76,582
15	Department 12	825,489	30,201	19,384	68,836	66,229	64,752
16	Department 13	1,004,012	39,483	26,972	88,458	86,954	85,819
17	Department 14	1,128,380	39,452	27,316	77,631	84,475	84,958
18	Department 15	927,963	40,206	30,824	83,885	85,593	83,618
19	Department 16	1,336,598	39,053	27,031	79,099	88,476	96,329
20	Department 17	1,293,143	36,266	31,399	83,595	96,031	102,120

B4: (,0) [W10] ◦B41   READY

Fig. 4.29. Part of the data visible in a worksheet.

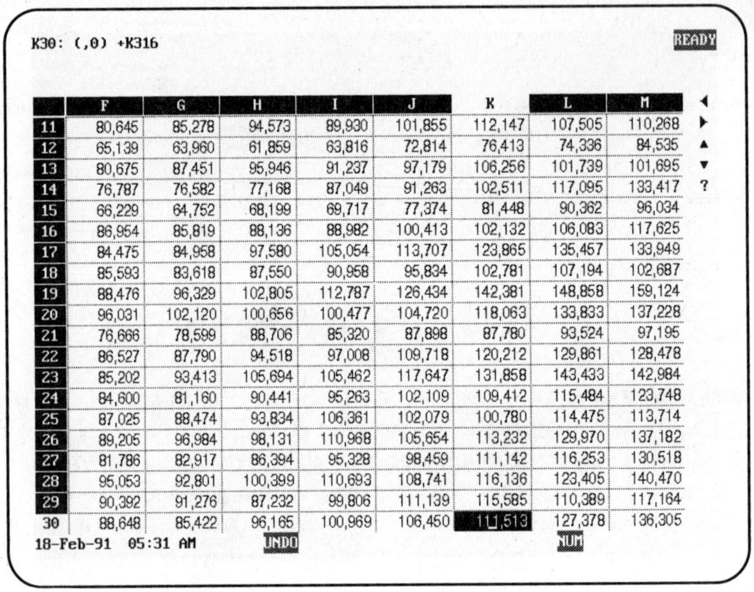

	F	G	H	I	J	K	L	M

K30: (,0) +K316   READY

	F	G	H	I	J	K	L	M
11	80,645	85,278	94,573	89,930	101,855	112,147	107,505	110,268
12	65,139	63,960	61,859	63,816	72,814	76,413	74,336	84,535
13	80,675	87,451	95,946	91,237	97,179	106,256	101,739	101,695
14	76,787	76,582	77,168	87,049	91,263	102,511	117,095	133,417
15	66,229	64,752	68,199	69,717	77,374	81,448	90,362	96,034
16	86,954	85,819	88,136	88,982	100,413	102,132	106,083	117,625
17	84,475	84,958	97,580	105,054	113,707	123,865	135,457	133,949
18	85,593	83,618	87,550	90,958	95,834	102,781	107,194	102,687
19	88,476	96,329	102,805	112,787	126,434	142,381	148,858	159,124
20	96,031	102,120	100,656	100,477	104,720	118,063	133,833	137,228
21	76,666	78,599	88,706	85,320	87,898	87,780	93,524	97,195
22	86,527	87,790	94,518	97,008	109,718	120,212	129,861	128,478
23	85,202	93,413	105,694	105,462	117,647	131,858	143,433	142,984
24	84,600	81,160	90,441	95,263	102,109	109,412	115,484	123,748
25	87,025	88,474	93,834	106,361	102,079	100,780	114,475	113,714
26	89,205	96,984	98,131	110,968	105,654	113,232	129,970	137,182
27	81,786	82,917	86,394	95,328	98,459	111,142	116,253	130,518
28	95,053	92,801	100,399	110,693	108,741	116,136	123,405	140,470
29	90,392	91,276	87,232	99,806	111,139	115,585	110,389	117,164
30	88,648	85,422	96,165	100,969	106,450	1□,513	127,378	136,305

18-Feb-91 05:31 AM   UNDO   NUM

Fig. 4.30. Titles scrolled off the screen.

Cue:

Use the /Worksheet Titles command to prevent titles from scrolling off the screen.

Use the /Worksheet Titles command to prevent titles from scrolling off the screen. To lock (or "freeze") titles, follow these steps:

1. Position the display so that the titles to lock are at the top and left of the display (see fig. 4.29).

2. Move the cell pointer to the first row below the titles and the first column to the right of the titles. In figure 4.29, the titles are in rows 2-3 and column A; the cell pointer is in B4.

3. Choose /Worksheet Titles Both to lock both horizontal and vertical titles.

After these titles are locked, the data below row 3 and to the right of column A can scroll off the screen, but the locked titles in rows 2-3 and column A remain on-screen (see fig. 4.31).

With locked titles, pressing Home moves the cell pointer to the position following the titles rather than to A1. Here, the Home position is B4 (see fig. 4.29). You cannot use the mouse or the direction keys to move into the titles area, but you can use the GoTo (F5) key. When you use GoTo to move to a cell in the titles area, the title rows and columns display twice (see fig. 4.32). This double set of titles can confuse you. You can move into the titles area in POINT mode (for example, when using the /Copy command) and see the same double display as in figure 4.32.

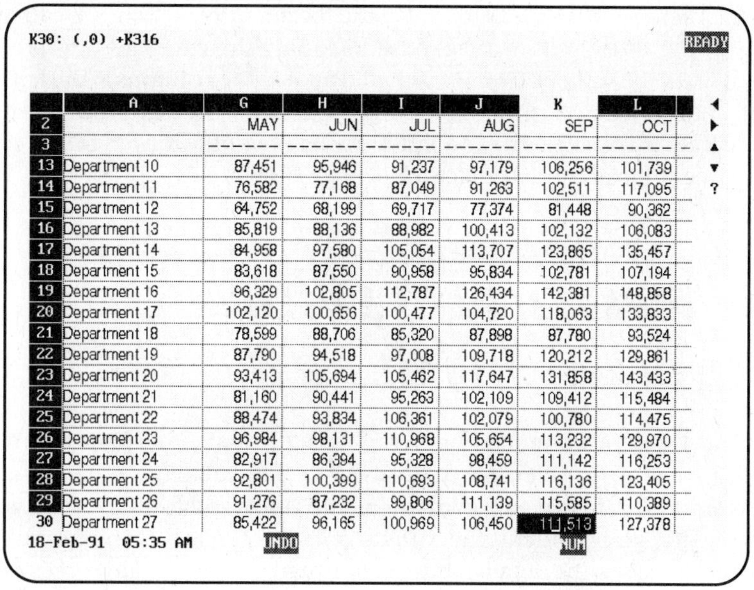

```
K30: (,0) +K316                                              READY

         A         G        H        I        J        K        L      ◄
  2                MAY      JUN      JUL      AUG      SEP      OCT     ►
  3              ------   ------   ------   ------   ------   ------    ▲
 13 Department 10  87,451   95,946   91,237   97,179  106,256  101,739  ▼
 14 Department 11  76,582   77,168   87,049   91,263  102,511  117,095  ?
 15 Department 12  64,752   68,199   69,717   77,374   81,448   90,362
 16 Department 13  85,819   88,136   88,982  100,413  102,132  106,083
 17 Department 14  84,958   97,580  105,054  113,707  123,865  135,457
 18 Department 15  83,618   87,550   90,958   95,834  102,781  107,194
 19 Department 16  96,329  102,805  112,787  126,434  142,381  148,858
 20 Department 17 102,120  100,656  100,477  104,720  118,063  133,833
 21 Department 18  78,599   88,706   85,320   87,898   87,780   93,524
 22 Department 19  87,790   94,518   97,008  109,718  120,212  129,861
 23 Department 20  93,413  105,694  105,462  117,647  131,858  143,433
 24 Department 21  81,160   90,441   95,263  102,109  109,412  115,484
 25 Department 22  88,474   93,834  106,361  102,079  100,780  114,475
 26 Department 23  96,984   98,131  110,968  105,654  113,232  129,970
 27 Department 24  82,917   86,394   95,328   98,459  111,142  116,253
 28 Department 25  92,801  100,399  110,693  108,741  116,136  123,405
 29 Department 26  91,276   87,232   99,806  111,139  115,585  110,389
 30 Department 27  85,422   96,165  100,969  106,450  111,513  127,378
18-Feb-91  05:35 AM    UNDO                        NUM
```

Fig. 4.31. *Locked titles on-screen (rows 2 and 3 and column A).*

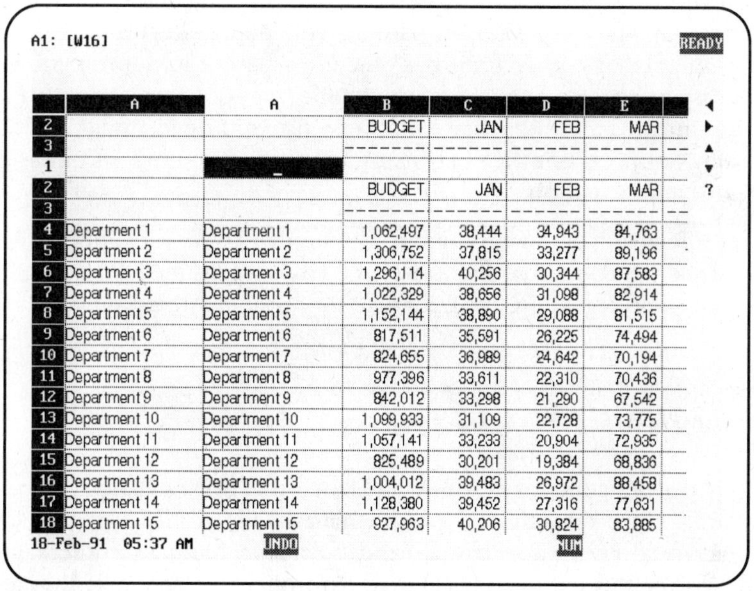

```
A1: [W16]                                                    READY

         A              A            B        C        D        E     ◄
  2                               BUDGET     JAN      FEB      MAR    ►
  3                               ------   ------   ------   ------   ▲
  1                                                                   ▼
  2                               BUDGET     JAN      FEB      MAR    ?
  3                               ------   ------   ------   ------
  4 Department 1   Department 1  1,062,497  38,444   34,943   84,763
  5 Department 2   Department 2  1,306,752  37,815   33,277   89,196
  6 Department 3   Department 3  1,296,114  40,256   30,344   87,583
  7 Department 4   Department 4  1,022,329  38,656   31,098   82,914
  8 Department 5   Department 5  1,152,144  38,890   29,088   81,515
  9 Department 6   Department 6    817,511  35,591   26,225   74,494
 10 Department 7   Department 7    824,655  36,989   24,642   70,194
 11 Department 8   Department 8    977,396  33,611   22,310   70,436
 12 Department 9   Department 9    842,012  33,298   21,290   67,542
 13 Department 10  Department 10 1,099,933  31,109   22,728   73,775
 14 Department 11  Department 11 1,057,141  33,233   20,904   72,935
 15 Department 12  Department 12   825,489  30,201   19,384   68,836
 16 Department 13  Department 13 1,004,012  39,483   26,972   88,458
 17 Department 14  Department 14 1,128,380  39,452   27,316   77,631
 18 Department 15  Department 15   927,963  40,206   30,824   83,885
18-Feb-91  05:37 AM    UNDO                        NUM
```

Fig. 4.32. *Double display of titles with the cell pointer in the titles area.*

Use /Worksheet Titles Clear to cancel the locked titles so that you can move freely in the titles area. You also can lock only the rows at the top of the screen with /Worksheet Titles Horizontal or only the columns at the left with /Worksheet Titles Vertical. To change the locked titles, you must use /Worksheet Titles Clear first and then specify the new locked titles. With a split screen, locking titles affects the current, or active, window.

Protecting and Hiding Worksheet Data

A typical 1-2-3 file contains numbers, labels, formulas, and macros. When you first build a worksheet file, you can lay the file out for an entire year. The budget model in figure 4.29 contains all the labels and formulas for a yearly budget. After you build this file, you do not want the labels and formulas to change. However, the detailed budget figures can change many times as you submit different versions for approval or submit the budget to different departments for revision.

1-2-3 includes a variety of features that protect data from accidental or deliberate change. For example, parts of a file may hold confidential data, such as salaries or cost factors. 1-2-3 includes a method of protection that enables unauthorized persons to use the file but not to see certain areas of the file. Unfortunately, this first line of defense, hiding formulas and other data, may not prevent others who know enough about 1-2-3 from finding this hidden information.

A more effective form of protection is, when you save files, to password-protect files that contain confidential data. This security measure completely prevents access to the file by users who do not know the password.

Protecting Cells from Change

Every worksheet contains formulas and labels that do not change over time. Other areas of the worksheet hold data that can change. You can protect the cells that you do not want changed and still allow changes to other cells by using two related commands: /Range Unprot marks the cells that allow changes; /Worksheet Global Protection Enable turns on protection for all other cells.

You must tell 1-2-3 to use the cell-protection feature. When you build a new worksheet, protection is disabled and all cells in the worksheet are accessible. To enable the protection feature, use /Worksheet Global Protection

Enable. After issuing this command, all cells in the worksheet are protected, and the symbol PR appears in the control panel for every cell. If you enable protection and try to change a protected cell, 1-2-3 displays an error message and does not make the change.

To unprotect the cells you want to change when worksheet protection is enabled, select /Range Unprot. At the Enter range to unprotect: prompt, highlight each range of cells. The letter U appears in the control panel for every unprotected cell. Cells that contain data and are unprotected normally display in a different color or intensity (colors can be changed through Wysiwyg's :Display Colors Unprot command) on color monitors and in boldface on monochrome monitors.

If you unprotect a range of cells, you can protect the range again with /Range Prot. You can protect or unprotect ranges with global protection either enabled or disabled. Typically, when you build a new worksheet, you leave global protection disabled. When you finish the worksheet, and you think that all the formulas and labels are correct, you can unprotect the data input areas and enable global protection.

If you need to change a protected cell, you unprotect, change, and then protect the cell again. You also can disable global protection, change the cell or cells, and then enable protection again. Because of this flexible feature of /Worksheet Global Protection, 1-2-3's protection features protect only against accidental change, not from deliberate alteration of the worksheet by unauthorized persons.

Caution:
Global protection does not stop 1-2-3 users from tampering with a file.

Using /Range Input

When you use /Worksheet Global Protection Enable, you restrict changes to individual cells that are unprotected. You can take one more step and restrict the cell pointer only to unprotected cells in a specified range by using the /Range Input command.

You use /Range Input with data entry areas or forms, such as the one in figure 4.33. The range J28..J33 is unprotected; the other cells are protected. Typically, you use /Range Input when you build worksheets for others to use to enter data. Here, you want those who enter the data to see the entire range I22..J33 but to be able to move the cell pointer only in the range J28..J33.

When you choose /Range Input, the Enter data-input range: prompt appears. You specify the input range and then click the left mouse button within the control panel or press Enter. In figure 4.33, the data-input range is I22..J33. 1-2-3 positions the display at the beginning of the data-input range and moves the cell pointer to the first unprotected cell in the range, in this case, J28.

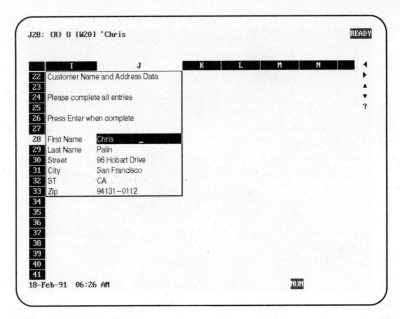

Fig. 4.33. *An input form used with /Range Input.*

When /**R**ange Input is active, you can move the cell pointer only to unprotected cells in the input range. If you press Home, the cell pointer moves to J28; press End to go to J33. If you are in J33 and click the down-triangle icon or press the down-arrow key, you "wrap" to J28. If you are in J29 and click the right-triangle, or press the right-arrow key, the cell pointer moves to J30 because no unprotected cells exist to the right of J29.

When /**R**ange Input is active, you can type entries and edit any unprotected cell, but you cannot execute commands. If you press the slash key, you enter the slash character into a cell. To deactivate /**R**ange Input, press Enter or Esc in READY mode. The cell pointer then returns to its former position.

/**R**ange Input is almost always executed by a macro as part of a data-entry system. The advanced macro command {FORM} is another way to create and use data-entry forms. The advanced macro commands are covered in Chapter 14.

Hiding Data

Occasionally, you want to do more than just stop others from changing data or formulas; you want to prevent others from even seeing the information. You can hide cells and columns so that the data is not easily visible. But if other users know enough about 1-2-3, you cannot prevent these users from seeing confidential data.

To hide a cell or range of cells, use /**R**ange Format **H**idden. Hidden cells display as blank cells in the worksheet. If you move the cell pointer to a hidden cell, and the cell is protected with global protection enabled, the cell contents do not display in the control panel. To display the cell contents again in the worksheet, use any other range format as described in Chapter 5. You also can use /**R**ange Format **R**eset to reset the cell or range of cells to the global format.

You cannot use the hidden format to hide data completely unless you protect all the cells in the file. If you can change the format or the protection status, you can see the contents of the cell. To completely hide columns, use /**W**orksheet **C**olumn **H**ide and highlight the columns you want to hide. You need to highlight only one cell in each column. A hidden column does not display in the window but retains its column letter. Figure 4.34 shows a worksheet with some columns about to be hidden. Figure 4.35 shows the worksheet after the columns are hidden. Note that in the column borders, column letters C, D, and E are skipped. The columns are still present, but the columns do not display, and you cannot move the cell pointer to those columns.

```
E3: (,0) 84763                                                    POINT
Specify column to hide: C3..E3

         A          B        C       D        E       F        G
 1
 2                 BUDGET    JAN     FEB      MAR    TOTAL  VARIANCE
 3  Department 1   144,214  38,444  34,943   84,763  158,150  13,936
 4  Department 2   164,942  37,815  33,277   89,196  160,288  (4,654)
 5  Department 3   163,010  40,256  30,344   87,583  158,183  (4,827)
 6  Department 4   156,855  38,656  31,098   82,914  152,668  (4,187)
 7  Department 5   154,556  38,890  29,088   81,515  149,493  (5,063)
 8  Department 6   128,374  35,591  26,225   74,494  136,310   7,936
 9  Department 7   114,947  36,989  24,642   70,194  131,825  16,878
10  Department 8   133,835  33,611  22,310   70,436  126,357  (7,478)
11  Department 9   119,778  33,298  21,290   67,542  122,130   2,352
12  Department 10  116,507  31,109  22,728   73,775  127,612  11,105
13  Department 11  116,584  33,233  20,904   72,935  127,072  10,488
14  Department 12  116,221  30,201  19,384   68,836  118,421   2,200
15
16
17
18
19
20
18-Feb-91  06:40 AM                                      NUM
```

Fig. 4.34. /*Worksheet Column Hide used to hide columns.*

When you print a range with hidden columns, the hidden columns do not print. Although you can change the appearance of the display and reports with hidden columns, this technique is not an effective way to hide sensitive information. When you are in POINT mode, 1-2-3 displays the hidden columns so that you can include cells in the hidden columns in the ranges.

Reminder:
Hidden columns do not print.

```
F3: (,0) @SUM(C3..E3)                                              READY
```

	A	B	F	G	H	I	J
1							
2		BUDGET	TOTAL	VARIANCE			
3	Department 1	144,214	158,150	13,936			
4	Department 2	164,942	160,288	(4,654)			
5	Department 3	163,010	158,183	(4,827)			
6	Department 4	156,855	152,668	(4,187)			
7	Department 5	154,556	149,493	(5,063)			
8	Department 6	128,374	136,310	7,936			
9	Department 7	114,947	131,825	16,878			
10	Department 8	133,835	126,357	(7,478)			
11	Department 9	119,778	122,130	2,352			
12	Department 10	116,507	127,612	11,105			
13	Department 11	116,584	127,072	10,488			
14	Department 12	116,221	118,421	2,200			
15							
16							
17							
18							
19							
20							

```
18-Feb-91  06:40 AM          UNDO                      NUM
```

Fig. 4.35. The worksheet with columns C through E hidden.

Saving a File with a Password To Prevent Access

Reminder:
Save the file with a password to prevent access.

To completely prevent access to a file, save the file with a password. Without the password, no one can read the file or get any information from the file. If you lose the password, you cannot access information in the file. You can learn more about password protection of files in Chapter 7.

Controlling Recalculation

The commands discussed thus far showed you how to view, clear, and protect data in worksheets and files. This section covers how you can control the way 1-2-3 updates the file while you are changing the file.

Whenever a value in a file changes, 1-2-3 recalculates all other cells that depend on the changed value. This feature is the essence of an electronic worksheet. 1-2-3 provides a number of recalculation options for different circumstances.

Understanding Recalculation Methods

Normally, 1-2-3 recalculates the file when any cell changes. This feature is called automatic recalculation. Some of the previous versions of 1-2-3 took a long time to recalculate large worksheets. With Release 2.3, however, recalculation is optimal.

Optimal recalculation means that the only cells recalculated are those cells that contain formulas that refer to the changed cell. If you change a cell in a large file, and the cell is used in only one formula, only that one formula is recalculated. Recalculation therefore is accelerated.

Because of this recalculation routine, recalculation is best left in the default automatic mode. However, you can tell 1-2-3 not to recalculate the worksheet when you make a change by using /Worksheet Global Recalculation Manual. To force a recalculation, press the Calc (F9) key. Until the recalculation is complete, the mode indicator is set to WAIT, and you cannot use 1-2-3. Automatic recalculation can slow a macro's execution. If you use macros, you may prefer to have the macro set the recalculation to manual while the macro executes and then reset recalculation to automatic before the macro ends. 1-2-3 makes special considerations for macros when recalculation is manual. These considerations are covered in Chapter 13.

During recalculation, 1-2-3 determines which formulas depend on which cells and sets up a recalculation order to ensure the correct answer. This process is the natural order of recalculation. Older spreadsheet programs, designed before 1-2-3, did not use this approach and sometimes required many successive recalculations before arriving at the right answers in all the cells.

Reminder:
The natural order of recalculation sets up a recalculation order to ensure the correct answer.

These early spreadsheet programs could only recalculate either columnwise or rowwise. Columnwise recalculation starts in cell A1 and calculates the cells down column A, then down column B, and so on. Rowwise recalculation starts in cell A1 and calculates the cells across row 1, then across row 2, and so on. Columnwise and Rowwise are options in the /Worksheet Global Recalculation menu, but as a rule, you should ignore these selections and leave recalculation on Natural.

Using Iteration To Solve Circular References

When a circular reference occurs, the natural order of recalculation does not ensure the correct answer for all cells. A circular reference is a formula that depends, either directly or indirectly, on its own value. Usually, a circular reference is an error that you should eliminate immediately. When 1-2-3 performs a recalculation and finds a circular reference, the CIRC indicator appears in the status line at the bottom of the display. Figure 4.36 shows a typical erroneous circular reference in which the @SUM function includes itself. In this example, the sum of cells B2, B3, and B4 (3300) is added to itself, totalling 6600.

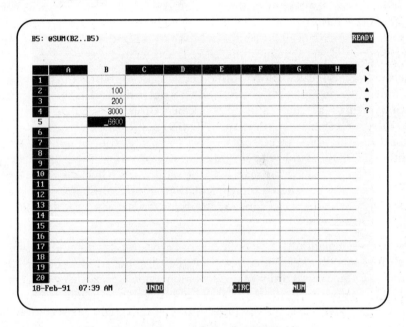

Fig. 4.36. *A circular reference that produces the CIRC indicator.*

Cue:
Use /Worksheet
Status to find a
circular reference.

If, when the CIRC indicator appears, you are unsure of the reason, use /Worksheet Status to display the Worksheet Status dialog box (see fig. 4.37). This display points out the cell that caused the circular reference, and you can fix the error. Occasionally, the source of the problem may not be obvious, and you may need to check all cells referenced by the formula cell.

Another aid for tracking down one or more circular references is the Auditor add-in. The Auditor add-in checks formulas in the worksheet. If you choose Circs from the Auditor menu, the Auditor displays a cell address for each circular reference. When you select a cell, the Auditor describes the path of the circular reference and displays the formulas involved. The Auditor also provides other useful data about formulas in the worksheet. Detailed information about the Auditor is given in Appendix B.

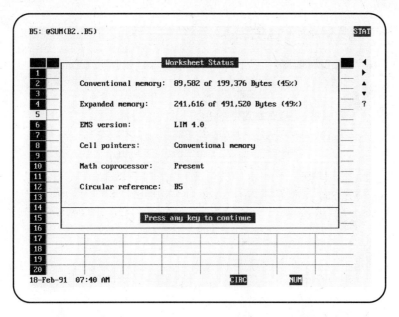

```
B5: @SUM(B2..B5)                                                    STAT

                        ┌──────────── Worksheet Status ────────────┐    ◄
  ┌──┬──┐               │                                           │    ►
  │ 1│  │               │                                           │    ▲
  │ 2│  │               │  Conventional memory:  89,582 of 199,376 Bytes (45%)  ▼
  │ 3│  │               │                                           │    ?
  │ 4│  │               │  Expanded memory:      241,616 of 491,520 Bytes (49%)
  │ 5│  │               │                                           │
  │ 6│  │               │  EMS version:          LIM 4.0            │
  │ 7│  │               │                                           │
  │ 8│  │               │  Cell pointers:        Conventional memory│
  │ 9│  │               │                                           │
  │10│  │               │  Math coprocessor:     Present            │
  │11│  │               │                                           │
  │12│  │               │  Circular reference:   B5                 │
  │13│  │               │                                           │
  │14│  │               │                                           │
  │15│  │               │        ┌───── Press any key to continue ─────┐
  │16│  │               └───────────────────────────────────────────┘
  │17│  │
  │18│  │
  │19│  │
  │20│  │
  18-Feb-91  07:40 AM                        CIRC          NUM
```

Fig. 4.37. The location of a circular reference displayed in the Worksheet Status dialog box.

In some special cases, you may want to create a circular reference. Figure 4.38 shows a worksheet with a deliberate circular reference. In this example, a company sets aside 10 percent of its net profit for employee bonuses. The bonuses, however, represent an expense that reduces net profit. The formula in C5 shows that the amount of bonuses is net profit in D5 times 0.1, or 10%. But net profit is profit before bonuses minus employee bonuses (B5–C5). The value of Employee Bonuses depends on the value of Net Profit and the value of Net Profit depends on the value of Employee Bonuses. In figure 4.38, C5 depends on D5, and D5 depends on C5.

Each time you recalculate the worksheet, the answers change by a smaller amount with a legitimate circular reference. Eventually, the changes become insignificant. This decrease is called convergence. Note that the erroneous circular reference in figure 4.36 never converges, and the @SUM grows bigger each time you recalculate.

The worksheet in figure 4.36 needs five recalculations before the changes become less than one dollar. After you establish this number, you can tell 1-2-3 to recalculate the worksheet five times every time it recalculates. Do this by selecting /**W**orksheet **G**lobal **R**ecalculation **I**teration. Press **5** and click the left mouse button in the control panel or press Enter. Usually, you can handle a converging circular reference with a macro.

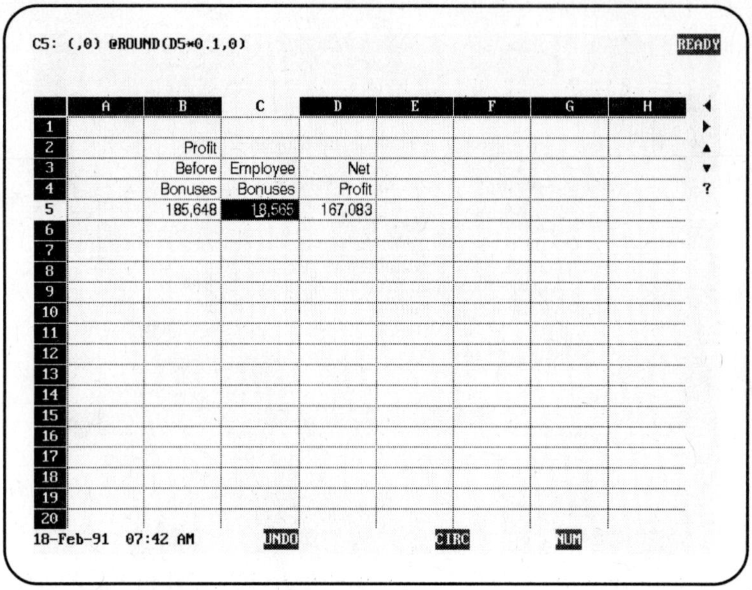

Fig. 4.38. A worksheet with a deliberate circular reference.

Use /**Worksheet Status** (see fig. 4.37) to see a mixture of information that includes the amount of memory available (conventional and expanded memory), the EMS (expanded memory specification) version used, the location of cell pointers in memory, whether or not a math coprocessor is present, and the cell location of a circular reference (if any). You use this status display mainly to check on the amount of memory available and to locate circular references. (If you need more help tracking down circular references, use the Auditor add-in.)

Moving the Contents of Cells

When you build worksheets, you often enter data and formulas in one part of the worksheet that you later want to move elsewhere. Use the /**Move** command to move the contents of a cell or range from one part of a worksheet to another.

Use /**Move** to move other data out of the way so that you can add to a list, a report, or a database. You also use /**Move** to rearrange a report so that it prints in the exact format you want. When you first start to lay out a report, you are often unsure of how you want the final design to look. After trial-and-error and moving the data around, you get the report format you want.

When you move a range, you also move the format and protection status. You do not, however, move the column width. The original cells still exist after you move the contents of those cells, but the cells are blank, and all protection and formatting is removed.

Moving the Contents of a Single Cell

Figure 4.39 shows three numbers in column B and the sum of the numbers in B5. These cells are formatted to display with commas and two decimal places. The numbers are unprotected. To move the sum in B5 to D6, move the cell pointer to B5 and start the /Move command. The Move what? prompt asks you to select the cells you want to move. To move just the B5 cell, click the left mouse button within the control panel (or click twice on the cell pointer) or press Enter. The next prompt, To where?, asks where you want the cells to go. Move the cell pointer to D6 and click the left mouse button within the control panel (or click twice on the cell pointer) or press Enter. The result is shown in figure 4.40. The exact formula that was in B5 now is moved to D6.

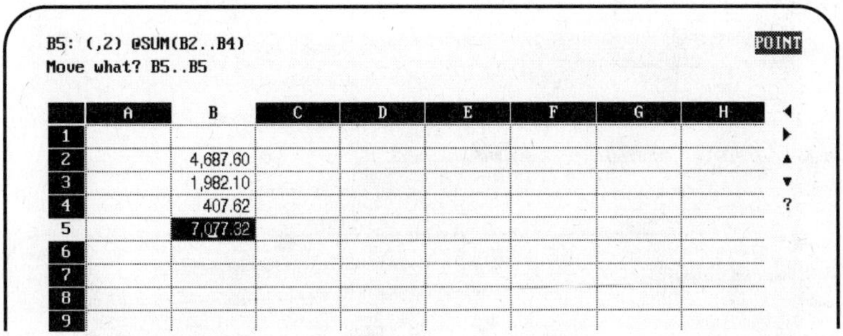

Fig. 4.39. *A formula to be moved.*

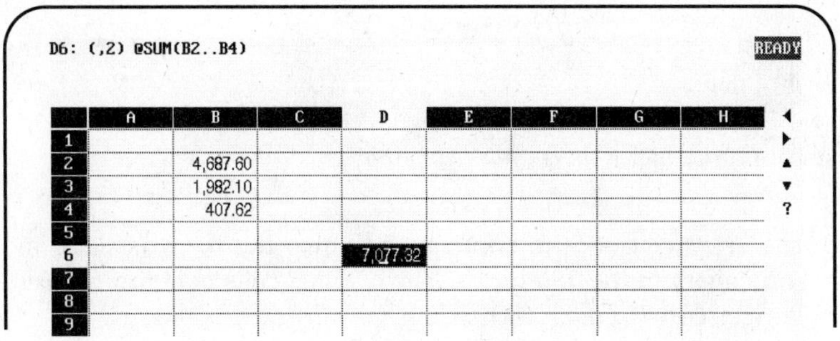

Fig. 4.40. *A formula after being moved.*

Moving the Contents of a Range

To move a range, move the cell pointer to the upper left corner of the range and start the /Move command. At the `Move what?` prompt, highlight the range of cells to move as in figure 4.41. This prompt starts with the address of the cell pointer as an anchored range. When you move the cell pointer, you highlight the range from the original location of the cell pointer to the corner you move to. Click the left mouse button or press Enter to lock in the `Move what?` range. At the `To where?` prompt, move the cell pointer to the upper left corner of the new location and click the left mouse button or press Enter. In figure 4.42, the range was moved to C1. Like all commands that prompt for ranges, you can type addresses, point and highlight, or use range names.

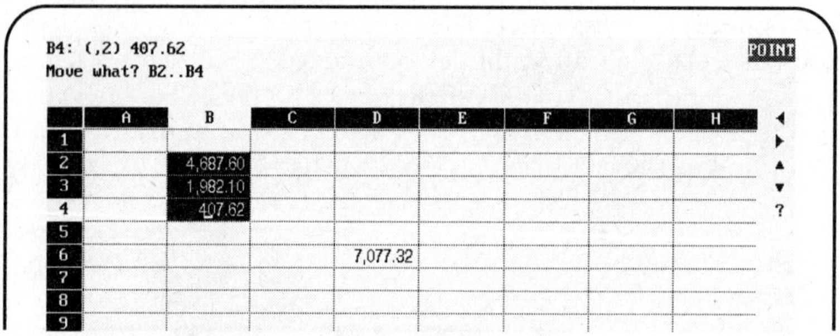

Fig. 4.41. *A range of numbers to be moved.*

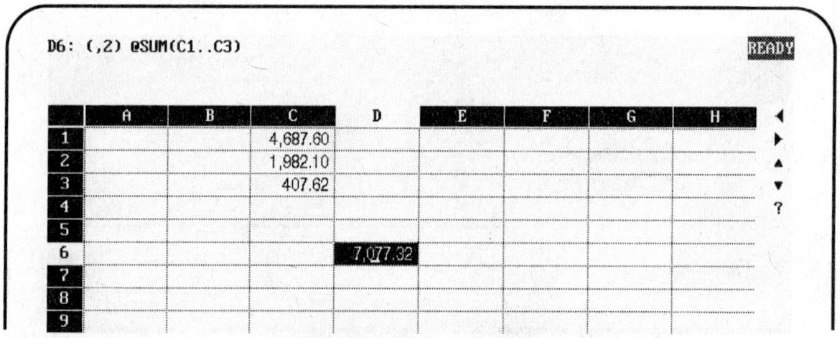

Fig. 4.42. *A range of numbers after being moved.*

In figure 4.41, not only the contents, but also the formats were moved (protection also is moved, if used). The original cells in column B remain, but no longer contain data, formatting, or unprotected status.

This self-adjusting capability is an important feature of /Move. The formula in D6 still shows the sum of the three numbers. When you move data, all formulas that refer to that data will adjust their cell references to refer to the new location. The formula in D6 has changed from @SUM(B2..B4) to @SUM(C1..C3). You can move ranges of any size.

If any formulas refer to cells in the destination range before the move, the references change to ERR. In figure 4.43, you want to replace the numbers in C1..C3 with the numbers in H1..H3. Figure 4.44 shows the result if you move H1..H3 to C1..C3. The formula in D6 changes from @SUM(C1..C3) to @SUM(ERR).

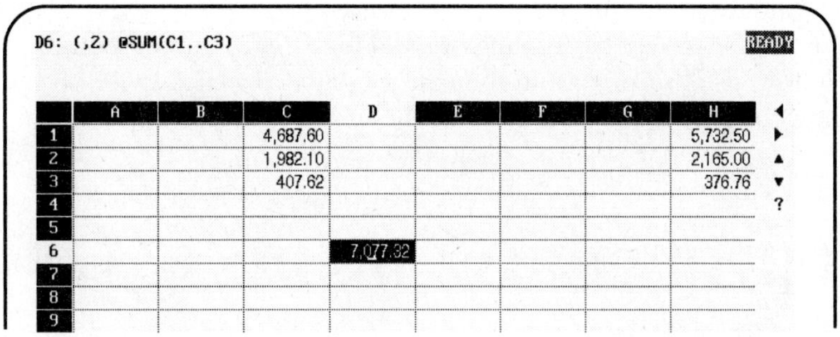

Caution:
The /Move range must fit in the rows and columns available.

Fig. 4.43. *The worksheet before data is moved into cells already used in a formula.*

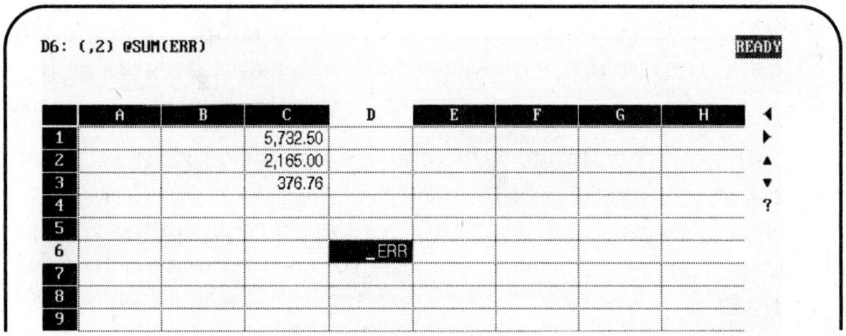

Fig. 4.44. *A formula changed to ERR when data is moved into cells already used in formulas.*

Unless you immediately press Alt-F4 to Undo the move (if the Undo feature is active), this change is permanent. Otherwise, you must re-enter the formula in D6. You can have hundreds of formulas throughout the file that refer to the cells C1..C3, and every one must be corrected. (You don't need to type every formula; you can use the /Copy command as explained in the next sections.) Because of this potentially undesirable result, be careful with /Move; you can destroy a worksheet if you use /Move incorrectly.

The correct way to replace the data in C1..C3 with the data in H1..H3 (see fig. 4.43) is to /Copy H1..H3 to C1..C3 and then use /Range Erase on H1..H3.

The cell pointer does not need to be at the top of the range when you start the /Move command. Sometimes, you can more easily start a move at the destination range. At the Move what? prompt, click the right mouse button or press Esc to unanchor the range. Move the cell pointer to the range you want to move; drag the mouse to highlight the range or press the period key to anchor the range and use the direction keys to highlight the range to move; and then click the left mouse button or press Enter. At the To where? prompt, 1-2-3 moves back to the original location of the cell pointer. Click the left mouse button within the control panel (or click twice on the cell pointer) or press Enter to complete the move operation.

Copying the Contents of Cells

/Move rearranges data in a file. /Copy, on the other hand, makes duplicate copies of a range in a worksheet. In a typical worksheet, most formulas are duplicated many times. Fortunately, if you need the same number, label, or formula in a number of places in a file, you can enter the information once and copy the repeating data many times. You probably will use /Copy more than any other 1-2-3 command. Copying can be simple or quite complicated. This section begins with simple examples and progresses to more complex examples.

Reminder:
When you copy, you lose the destination range's data and its format and protection status.

You can copy a cell or a range to another part of the worksheet. When you copy, you can make a single copy or many copies at the same time. When you copy a range, you also copy the format and protection status. You do not, however, copy the column width. The original cells remain unchanged after the copy process is complete. When you copy, the duplicate cells overwrite all information in the destination range. You lose the destination range's data, format, and protection status.

Copying the Contents of a Cell

The simplest example is to copy a label from one cell to another. Figure 4.45 shows the beginnings of a budget application. A repeating label in B6 separates the department detail from the totals in row 7. To copy this label from B6 to C6, move the cell pointer to B6 and select /Copy. At the prompt `Copy what?`, click the left mouse button within the control panel or press Enter to specify the one-cell range at C6. At `To where?`, move to C6 and click the left mouse button within the control panel or press Enter. The result is shown in figure 4.46. Unlike the /Move command, /Copy produces the label in both places.

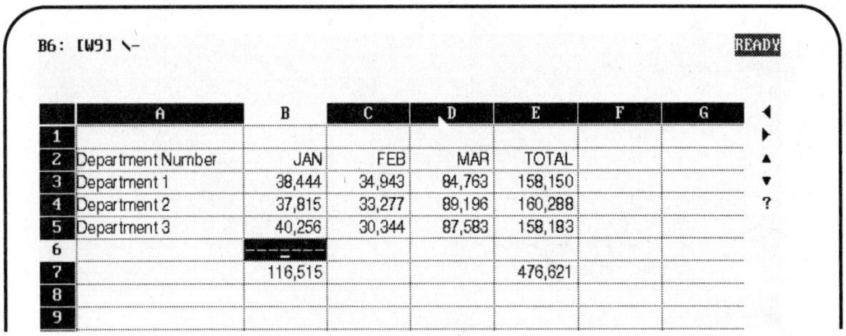

Fig. 4.45. A label to be copied.

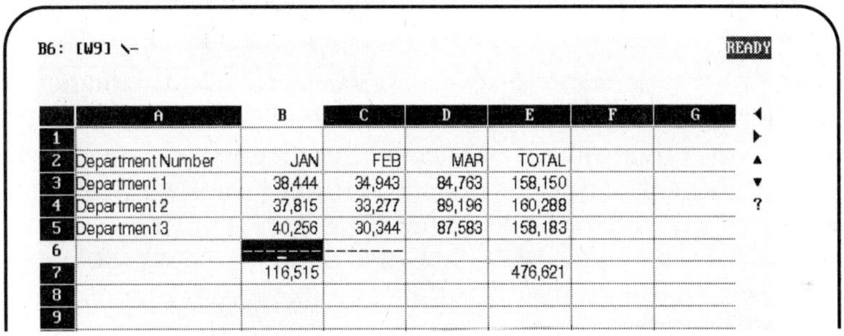

Fig. 4.46. A label that has been copied.

Copying a Formula with Relative Addressing

The real power of /Copy is disclosed when you copy a formula. The formula in B7 is `@SUM(B3..B5)`. When you copy B7 to C7, the formula in C7 is `@SUM(C3..C5)` (see fig. 4.47). This concept, called *relative addressing*, is one of the most important concepts in 1-2-3. When you copy a formula, 1-2-3 adjusts the new formula so that all the cell references are in the same relative location as they were to the original formula.

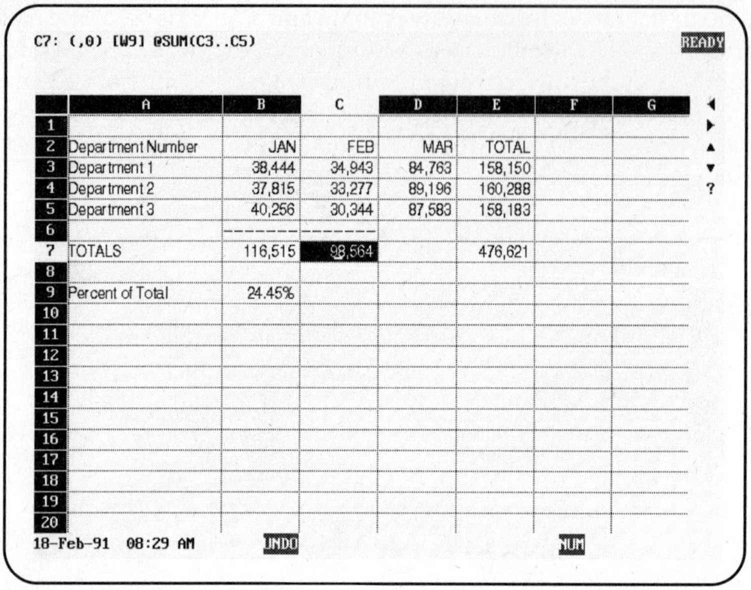

```
C7: (,0) [W9] @SUM(C3..C5)                                    READY
```

	A	B	C	D	E	F	G
1							
2	Department Number	JAN	FEB	MAR	TOTAL		
3	Department 1	38,444	34,943	84,763	158,150		
4	Department 2	37,815	33,277	89,196	160,288		
5	Department 3	40,256	30,344	87,583	158,183		
6		------					
7	TOTALS	116,515	98,564		476,621		
8							
9	Percent of Total	24.45%					

```
18-Feb-91  08:29 AM        UNDO                    NUM
```

Fig. 4.47. Cell addresses adjust automatically when a formula is copied.

The best way to understand relative addressing is to understand how 1-2-3 actually stores addresses in formulas. The formula in B7 is @SUM(B3..B5). In other words, this formula means "sum the contents of all the cells in the range from B3 to B5." But this definition is not how 1-2-3 really stores a formula. To 1-2-3, the formula is "sum the contents of all the cells in the range from the cell 4 rows above this cell to the cell 2 rows above this cell." When you copy this formula to C7, 1-2-3 uses the same relative formula but displays the formula as @SUM(C3..C5).

Usually, when you copy a formula, you want the addresses to adjust automatically. Sometimes, you do not want some addresses to adjust, or you want part of an address to adjust. These situations are examined separately.

Copying a Formula with Absolute Addressing

The formula in B9 in figure 4.48 is +B7/E7. This figure represents January's sales as a percent of the total. If you copy this formula to C9, you get +C7/F7. The value in C7, the sales for February, is correct. F7, however, is incorrect; F7 is a blank cell. When you copy the formula in B9, you want the address E7 to copy as an absolute address. This means that you do not want E7 to change after you copy it to C9.

To specify an absolute address, type a dollar sign ($) before each part of the address you want to remain "absolutely" the same. The formula in B9 should be +B7/$E$7. When you copy this formula to C9, the formula becomes +C7/$E$7. Instead of typing the dollar signs, you can press Abs (F4) after you type the address; the address changes to absolute. In this example, the complete formula becomes +C7/$E$7 (see fig. 4.48).

Cue:
Specify absolute addresses when you write the formula.

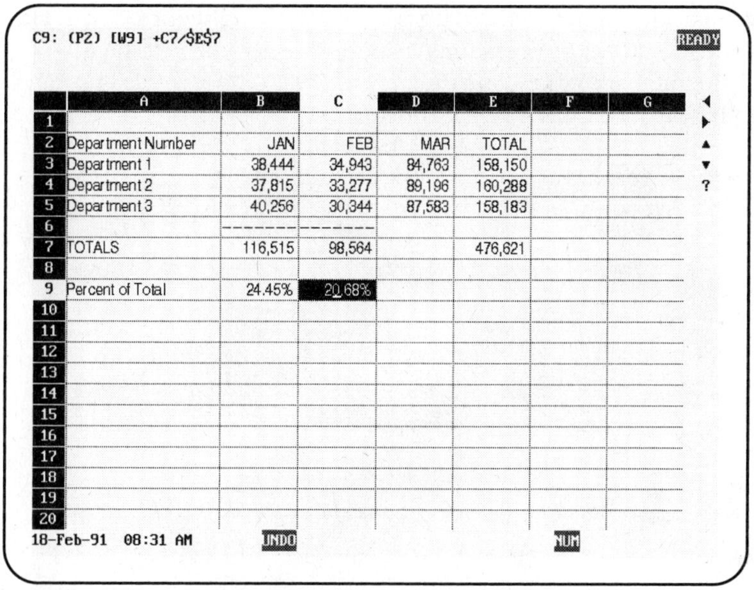

C9: (P2) [W9] +C7/$E$7   READY

	A	B	C	D	E	F	G
1							
2	Department Number	JAN	FEB	MAR	TOTAL		
3	Department 1	38,444	34,943	84,763	158,150		
4	Department 2	37,815	33,277	89,196	160,288		
5	Department 3	40,256	30,344	87,583	158,183		
6							
7	TOTALS	116,515	98,564		476,621		
8							
9	Percent of Total	24.45%	20.68%				
10							
11							
12							
13							
14							
15							
16							
17							
18							
19							
20							

18-Feb-91 08:31 AM   UNDO   NUM

Fig. 4.48. An absolute address ($E$7) that remains unchanged when copied.

You can enter dollar signs while pointing to addresses in a formula. As you point to a cell you want to include in a formula, press Abs (F4) to make the address absolute. If you make an error and forget to make an address absolute, just press Edit (F2) to go into EDIT mode, move the cursor in the control panel to the address you want to make absolute, and then press Abs (F4).

To change an absolute reference (with dollar signs) back to a relative reference, press Edit (F2), move the cursor to the reference, and then press Abs (F4) until you see no dollar signs. Click the left mouse button or press Enter to re-enter the formula.

Another kind of addressing is called *mixed addressing*. Mixed addressing, which combines relative addressing with absolute addressing, is covered later in this chapter.

Copying One Cell's Contents Several Times

In figure 4.47, one cell was copied one time. The idea, however, is to copy the formula in B7 to C7 and D7. You can replicate a cell's contents in one copy operation. The `Copy what?` range is still B7. At the `To where?` prompt, move the cell pointer to C7, drag the mouse to highlight D7, and click the left mouse button; or press the period to anchor the cell, highlight D7 by using the right-arrow key, and then press Enter. The formula in B7 is copied to both cells (see fig. 4.49).

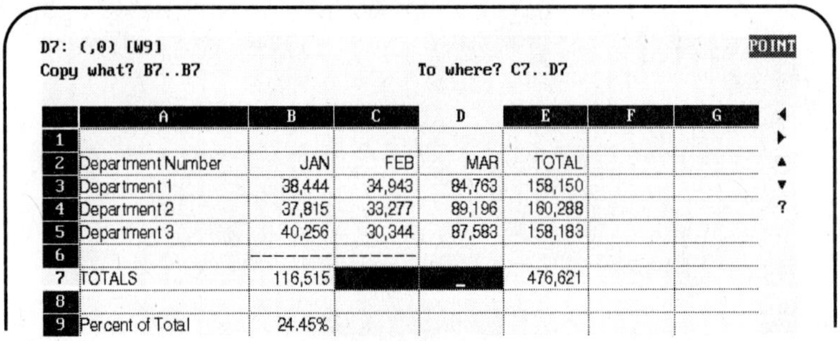

Fig. 4.49. A cell copied to two cells in one copy operation.

Copying One Cell's Contents to a Range of Cells

You can copy a single cell to a range in the worksheet. Figure 4.50 shows a simple price-forecasting model. The current prices are in column B. The formula in C3 increases the price by the percentage established in B1. To copy this formula through the table in the worksheet, copy from C3 to C3..G10. The result is displayed in figure 4.51.

When you copy a single cell, you cause no harm if you include the `Copy what?` cell in the `To where?` range, as in figure 4.50. As a general rule, the first cell in the `Copy what?` range can be the same cell as the first cell in the `To where?` range. In most other cases, an overlapping `Copy what?` and `To where?` range destroys the data before the copy process completes.

```
G10: (,2)                                                        POINT
Copy what? C3..C3                    To where? C3..G10
```

	A	B	C	D	E	F	G	H
1		8.50%						
2		1988	1989	1990	1991	1992	1993	
3	Product 1	138.60	150.38					
4	Product 2	48.90						
5	Product 3	467.83						
6	Product 4	309.30						
7	Product 5	37.03						
8	Product 6	59.50						
9	Product 7	549.00						
10	Product 8	678.50						
11								
12								
13								
14								
15								
16								
17								
18								
19								
20								

```
18-Feb-91  08:47 AM                              NUM
```

Fig. 4.50. A cell copied to a number of rows and columns in one copy operation.

```
C3: (,2) +$B$1*B3+B3                                             READY
```

	A	B	C	D	E	F	G	H
1		8.50%						
2		1988	1989	1990	1991	1992	1993	
3	Product 1	138.60	150.38	163.16	177.03	192.08	208.41	
4	Product 2	48.90	53.06	57.57	62.46	67.77	73.53	
5	Product 3	467.83	507.60	550.74	597.55	648.35	703.46	
6	Product 4	309.30	335.59	364.12	395.07	428.65	465.08	
7	Product 5	37.03	40.18	43.59	47.30	51.32	55.68	
8	Product 6	59.50	64.56	70.04	76.00	82.46	89.47	
9	Product 7	549.00	595.67	646.30	701.23	760.84	825.51	
10	Product 8	678.50	736.17	798.75	866.64	940.31	1,020.23	
11								
12								
13								
14								
15								
16								
17								
18								
19								
20								

```
18-Feb-91  08:48 AM       UNDO                    NUM
```

Fig. 4.51. The worksheet after the copy.

Copying the Contents of a Range

In previous examples, you copied one cell at a time. You can copy a row or a column of cells to a number of locations. In figure 4.52, suppose that you want to copy the label in C6 and the formula in C7 across the other columns. Copy from C6..C7 to D6..F6. Figure 4.52 shows the screen after the To where? range is highlighted. In this example, a range down one column is copied a number of times across a row. Note that the To where? range is only across row 6. This action highlights only the top cell where each copy goes. 1-2-3 remembers the size of each copy and the contents of the cells in the Copy what? range. 1-2-3 then fills in the lower cells of the copy accordingly. The result is shown in figure 4.53.

```
F6: [W9]                                                      POINT
Copy what? C6..C7                       To where? D6..F6

          A            B       C       D       E       F       G    ◄
  1                                                                  ►
  2  Department Number          JAN     FEB     MAR    TOTAL        ▲
  3  Department 1             38,444  34,943  84,763  158,150       ▼
  4  Department 2             37,815  33,277  89,196  160,288       ?
  5  Department 3             40,256  30,344  87,583  158,183
  6                          ------
  7  TOTALS                  116,515
  8
```

Fig. 4.52. *A range in a column copied a number of times across a row in one copy.*

```
C6: [W9] \-                                                   READY

          A            B       C       D       E       F       G    ◄
  1                                                                  ►
  2  Department Number          JAN     FEB     MAR    TOTAL        ▲
  3  Department 1             38,444  34,943  84,763  158,150       ▼
  4  Department 2             37,815  33,277  89,196  160,288       ?
  5  Department 3             40,256  30,344  87,583  158,183
  6                          ------
  7  TOTALS                  116,515  98,564 261,542  476,621
  8
```

Fig. 4.53. *The worksheet after two cells in a column are copied across three columns.*

You also can copy a range across one row, down a number of columns. In figure 4.54, you want to copy the TOTAL in F3 and the VARIANCE in G3 down the column. Copy from F3..G3 to F4..F6. Figure 4.54 shows the screen after the To where? range is highlighted. The result is shown in figure 4.55.

```
F6: (,0) [W9]                                          POINT
Copy what? F3..G3            To where? F4..F6
```

	A	B	C	D	E	F	G
1							
2	Department Number	BUDGET	JAN	FEB	MAR	TOTAL	VARIANCE
3	Department 1	144,214	38,444	34,943	84,763	158,150	13,936
4	Department 2	164,942	37,815	33,277	89,196		
5	Department 3	163,010	40,256	30,344	87,583		
6	TOTALS	472,166	116,515	98,564	261,542	—	
7							
8	Percent of Total						
9							

Fig. 4.54. *A range across a row copied a number of times down a column in one copy operation.*

```
F3: (,0) [W9] @SUM(C3..E3)                              READY
```

	A	B	C	D	E	F	G
1							
2	Department Number	BUDGET	JAN	FEB	MAR	TOTAL	VARIANCE
3	Department 1	144,214	38,444	34,943	84,763	158,150	13,936
4	Department 2	164,942	37,815	33,277	89,196	160,288	(4,654)
5	Department 3	163,010	40,256	30,344	87,583	158,183	(4,827)
6	TOTALS	472,166	116,515	98,564	261,542	476,621	4,455
7							
8	Percent of Total						
9							

Fig. 4.55. *The worksheet after two cells across a row are copied down two columns.*

Copying a range a number of times is useful; when you build worksheets, you can use this technique often. The technique, however, is limited. As a rule, if the Copy what? range is only one-cell wide in a dimension, you can copy it any number of times in that dimension. A single cell is part of one row and one column. You can copy a single cell across a row and down a column.

Cue:
If the Copy what? range is only one-cell wide in a dimension, you can copy it a number of times in that dimension.

Because the Copy what? range in figure 4.52 (C6..C7) occupies 2 rows, you can copy this range across columns. Generally, you cannot copy this range down rows. If you specified a To where? range in figure 4.52 of D6..F7, or even D6..F100, you get the same result as shown in figure 4.53. The rows are ignored in the To where? range because they are fixed in the Copy what? range. Generally, a two-dimensional range can be copied only once to a different area of the worksheet. For example, the range C3..G10 in figure 4.51 can be copied anywhere on the worksheet one time. If you highlight more than a single cell as the To where? range, 1-2-3 uses the upper left corner of the selected block of cells and ignores the rest.

Like all rules, the ones just stated have exceptions. You can copy cells such as C6..C7 down rows, if the copies are placed immediately below the cells to be copied. When you specify the Copy what? range, you need to include the cells you want to copy plus additional cells. The total number of cells you specify is equal to the number of cells copied times the number of copies. To copy two cells three times, specify six cells. For example, to copy C6..C7 three more times down the column, select /Copy. At the Copy what? prompt, specify six cells, C6..C11. At the To where? prompt specify C8—the cell right below C7. The result is three additional copies of C6..C7 in cells C8..C13. More than one copy of two or more cells in a row (for example C7..F7) can be made across columns in the same manner as long as you copy to the cells immediately to the right of the range.

A two-dimensional range also can be copied multiple times if the range to be copied to is immediately below or to the right of the range. For example, the range C3..G10 in figure 4.51 can be copied any number of times. To make two more copies, for example, select /Copy. At the Copy what? prompt, specify the range C3..G18. At the To where? prompt, specify cell C11 (or range C11 to G11), which is immediately below the copied range.

Copying with Mixed Addressing

Figure 4.56 shows a price-forecast worksheet similar to the one shown in figure 4.50, but this time with a different price increase percentage for each year. Now the formula in C3 is more complex. When you copy this formula down column C, you do not want the reference to C1 to change, but when you copy the formula across row 3, you want the reference to change for each column. The mixed reference is relative for the column and absolute for the row. The formula in C3 is +B3*(1+C$1). When you copy this formula down one row to C4, the formula becomes +B4*(1+C$1). The relative address B3 becomes B4, but the mixed address C$1 is unchanged. When you copy this formula to D3, the formula becomes +C3*(1+D$1). The relative address B3 becomes C3, and the mixed address becomes D$1. You can copy from C3 to C3..G10 and create the correct formula throughout the worksheet.

To make an address mixed without typing the dollar signs, use the Abs (F4) key. When you first press Abs (F4), the address becomes absolute. As you continue to press Abs (F4), the address cycles through all the possible mixed addresses and returns to relative. The complete list of relative, absolute, and mixed addresses is found in table 4.2. To obtain the address in figure 4.56, press Abs (F4) twice.

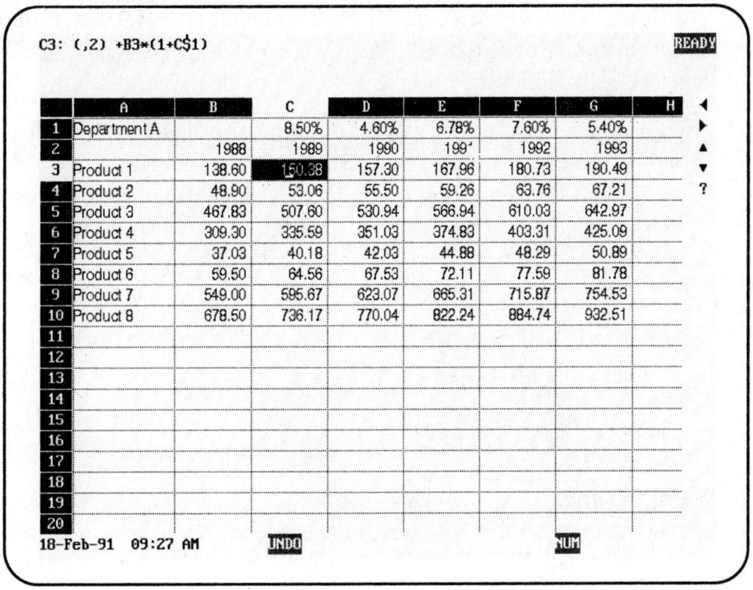

```
C3: (,2) +B3*(1+C$1)                                    READY

       A          B        C        D       E       F       G       H    ◄
 1  Department A          8.50%   4.60%   6.78%   7.60%   5.40%            ►
 2              1988     1989     1990    199'    1992    1993             ▲
 3  Product 1  138.60   150.38   157.30  167.96  180.73  190.49           ▼
 4  Product 2   48.90    53.06    55.50   59.26   63.76   67.21
 5  Product 3  467.83   507.60   530.94  566.94  610.03  642.97           ?
 6  Product 4  309.30   335.59   351.03  374.83  403.31  425.09
 7  Product 5   37.03    40.18    42.03   44.88   48.29   50.89
 8  Product 6   59.50    64.56    67.53   72.11   77.59   81.78
 9  Product 7  549.00   595.67   623.07  665.31  715.87  754.53
10  Product 8  678.50   736.17   770.04  822.24  884.74  932.51
11
12
13
14
15
16
17
18
19
20
 18-Feb-91  09:27 AM           UNDO                      NUM
```

Fig. 4.56. A mixed cell address in a formula used in a copy operation.

Table 4.2
Using Abs (F4) To Change Address Type

Number of Times Needed To Press Abs (F4)	*Result*	*Explanation*
1	$C$1	Absolute row and column
2	C$1	Absolute row
3	$C1	Absolute column
4	C1	Returned to relative

Using Range Names with /Copy

As with all commands that prompt you for a range, you can use range names
with the /Copy command. You can use range names for Copy what?, To

where?, or both. Type the range name or press the Name (F3) key and point to the range name. Unfortunately, 1-2-3 makes it impossible to use range names with mixed addresses.

To specify an absolute address, you must type the dollar sign before the range name. To use the range name SALES in a formula as an absolute address, type **$SALES**. You cannot use Abs (F4) with range names. You cannot specify a range name and make the range name a mixed address. You must use the actual cell addresses.

Using /Range Value To Convert Formulas to Values

/**R**ange Value is a special type of copy command. When you use /**R**ange Value on a cell that contains a label or a number, this command works exactly like /**C**opy. When you use /**R**ange Value on a cell that contains a formula, the current value, not the formula, is copied. You use /**R**ange Value to freeze the value of formulas so that they won't change. Figure 4.57 shows a model that forecasts profits for future years. You update the forecasts each quarter, but you want to keep track of the forecasts from the preceding quarter for comparison. You can achieve this type of comparison by converting the formula results in row 16 into values in row 18. When you use this command, the next quarter's changes do not affect row 18.

```
D16:  +D4-D8-D12                                                    READY
```

	A	B	C	D	E	F	G
1	Quarterly Sales Forecast for the Quarter Ending			Sep-91			
2		Actual	— — — —	— — — Projected		— — —	— —
3		1990	1991	1992	1993	1994	
4	Sales	37,845	46,015	54,334	66,040	81,128	
5	Growth rate	13.00%	9.00%	11.00%	14.00%		
6	Inflation rate	7.60%	8.33%	9.50%	7.76%		
7							
8	Fixed costs	16,945	18,789	20,785	24,311	27,161	
9	Growth rate	5.00%	3.00%	8.00%	6.00%		
10	Inflation rate	5.60%	7.40%	8.30%	5.40%		
11							
12	Variable costs	17,409	21,325	25,193	29,467	35,096	
13	Growth rate	16.00%	10.00%	8.00%	13.00%		
14	Inflation rate	5.60%	7.40%	8.30%	5.40%		
15							
16	Gross profit	3,491	5,901	8,356	12,262	18,871	
17							
18	Prior estimate						
19							
20	Change			8,356	12,262	18,871	

```
25-Apr-91  08:14 PM                                                 NUM
```

Fig. 4.57. A sales forecasting worksheet.

The profit figures shown in figure 4.57 are formulas. To obtain the previous estimate in row 18, use /**R**ange **V**alue from B16..F16 to B18. The previous estimate is a copy of the gross profit converted to numbers. The result is shown in figure 4.58. The numbers in row 18 are the current values of the formulas in row 16.

```
D18: 8356                                                          READY

        A           B        C        D        E        F        G
 1 Quarterly Sales Forecast for the Quarter Ending  Sep-91
 2              Actual -------------- Projected --------------
 3                1990     1991     1992     1993     1994
 4 Sales         37,845   46,015   54,334   66,040   81,128
 5 Growth rate   13.00%    9.00%   11.00%   14.00%
 6 Inflation rate 7.60%    8.33%    9.50%    7.76%
 7
 8 Fixed costs   16,945   18,789   20,785   24,311   27,161
 9 Growth rate    5.00%    3.00%    8.00%    6.00%
10 Inflation rate 5.60%    7.40%    8.30%    5.40%
11
12 Variable costs 17,409  21,325   25,193   29,467   35,096
13 Growth rate   16.00%   10.00%    8.00%   13.00%
14 Inflation rate 5.60%    7.40%    8.30%    5.40%
15
16 Gross profit   3,491    5,901    8,356   12,262   18,871
17
18 Prior estimate 3,491    5,901    8,356   12,262   18,871
19
20 Change                           0        0        0
25-Apr-91  08:12 PM                                          NUM
```

Fig. 4.58. The sales forecasting worksheet after the /Range Value operation that locked in the previous profit figures.

In figure 4.59, the various rates were updated, and 1-2-3 calculated new gross profits. Because the previous estimates in row 18 did not change, you can compare the newest estimate with the previous estimate and calculate the difference in row 20.

Formulas require more memory than numbers require; formulas also take time to recalculate. You can convert (to numbers) formulas that never change. For example, the years for projections in row 3 in figure 4.59 are formulas that add 1 to the preceding year. The formula in C3 is +B3+1. To convert these formulas to numbers, use /**R**ange **V**alue from C3..F3 to C3.

One danger you can encounter when using /**R**ange **V**alue occurs if you set /**W**orksheet **G**lobal **R**ecalculation to Manual. If you use /**R**ange **V**alue on a formula that is not current, you freeze the old value. This problem is not a major difficulty if the value is placed in a cell other than the cell that holds the formula. To correct this mistake, press Calc (F9) to update the formula

Cue:
Use /Range Value to convert formulas to numbers.

and then perform the /**Range** Value operation again. However, if you convert a formula that is not current to a number and copy the value to the cell that contains the formula, you lose the formula, and the resulting number is wrong, too. To correct this mistake, press Undo (Alt-F4). If Undo is not enabled, you must re-enter the formula in the cell. This procedure holds true both for ranges and for individual cells.

D16: +D4-D8-D12   READY

	A	B	C	D	E	F	G
1	Quarterly Sales Forecast for the Quarter Ending			Sep-91			
2		Actual		------ Projected ------			
3		1990	1991	19992	1993	1994	
4	Sales	37,845	46,015	54,534	64,492	77,836	
5	Growth rate	13.00%	8.30%	8.00%	12.00%		
6	Inflation rate	7.60%	9.43%	9.50%	7.76%		
7							
8	Fixed costs	16,945	18,789	21,087	25,701	28,985	
9	Growth rate	5.00%	4.50%	12.54%	7.00%		
10	Inflation rate	5.60%	7.40%	8.30%	5.40%		
11							
12	Variable costs	17,409	21,325	24,873	29,550	34,572	
13	Growth rate	16.00%	8.60%	9.70%	11.00%		
14	Inflation rate	5.60%	7.40%	8.30%	5.40%		
15							
16	Gross profit	3,491	5,901	8,574	9,241	14,279	
17							
18	Prior estimate	3,491	5,901	8,356	12,262	18,871	
19							
20	Change			218	(3,021)	(4,592)	

25-Apr-91   08:11 PM   NUM

Fig. 4.59. *The sales forecasting worksheet with new profit figures after the rates are updated.*

In figure 4.60, the CALC indicator shows that the worksheet is not current. If you use /**Range** Value on the formula in B5, you freeze an incorrect value. If your worksheet is set to manual recalculation and the CALC indicator is on, press Calc (F9) before you use /**Range** Value.

Using /Range Trans

Caution:
Make sure that the CALC indicator is off before you transpose a range.

/**Range** Trans (transpose) is another special type of copy command. /**Range** Trans converts rows to columns, columns to rows, and changes formulas to values at the same time. In figure 4.61, the range F12..N19 is the result of the command /**Range** Trans from A2..H10 to F12. The rows and columns are transposed, and the formulas in row 10 become numbers in column N.

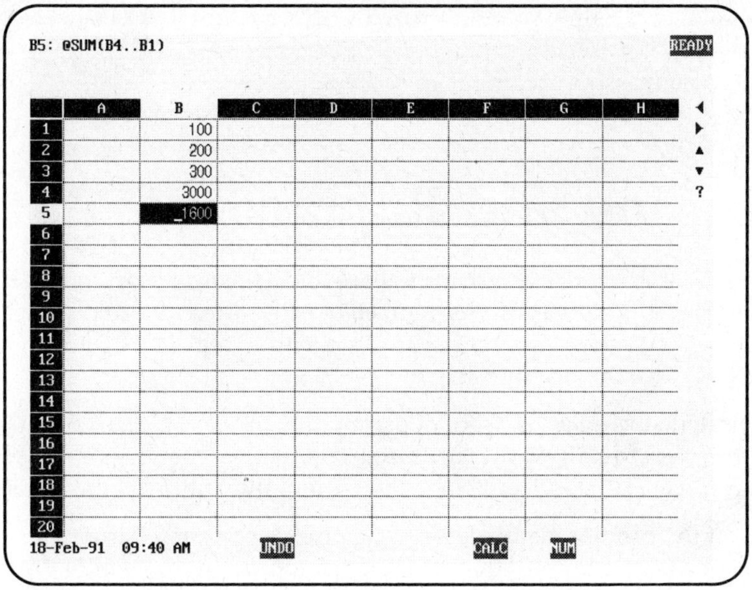

B5: @SUM(B4..B1) READY

	A	B	C	D	E	F	G	H
1		100						
2		200						
3		300						
4		3000						
5		1600						
6								
7								
8								
9								
10								
11								
12								
13								
14								
15								
16								
17								
18								
19								
20								

18-Feb-91 09:40 AM UNDO CALC NUM

Fig. 4.60. *An incorrect value can be locked in if* ***/Range Value*** *is issued while the CALC indicator is on.*

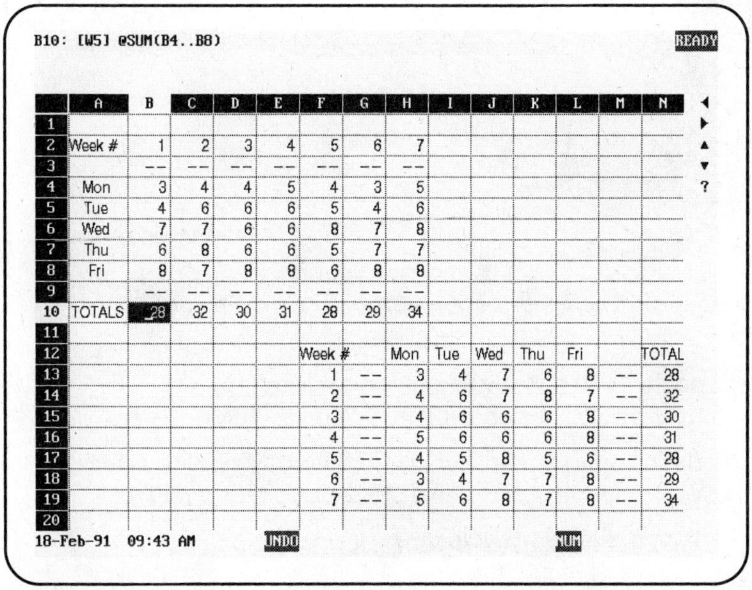

B10: [W5] @SUM(B4..B8) READY

	A	B	C	D	E	F	G	H	I	J	K	L	M	N
1														
2	Week #	1	2	3	4	5	6	7						
3		--	--	--	--	--	--	--						
4	Mon	3	4	4	5	4	3	5						
5	Tue	4	6	6	6	5	4	6						
6	Wed	7	7	6	6	8	7	8						
7	Thu	6	8	6	6	5	7	7						
8	Fri	8	7	8	8	6	8	8						
9		--	--	--	--	--	--	--						
10	TOTALS	28	32	30	31	28	29	34						
11														
12						Week #		Mon	Tue	Wed	Thu	Fri		TOTAL
13						1	--	3	4	7	6	8	--	28
14						2	--	4	6	7	8	7	--	32
15						3	--	4	6	6	6	8	--	30
16						4	--	5	6	6	6	8	--	31
17						5	--	4	5	8	5	6	--	28
18						6	--	3	4	7	7	8	--	29
19						7	--	5	6	8	7	8	--	34
20														

18-Feb-91 09:43 AM UNDO NUM

Fig. 4.61. *A table before and after* ***/Range Transpose*** *was used to transpose the rows and columns.*

As with /Range Value, you can freeze incorrect values if /Worksheet Global Recalculation is set to Manual. Make sure that the CALC indicator is off before you transpose a range.

Finding and Replacing Data

Caution:
Always save the file before you use /Range Search.

/Range Search searches a range of cells to find a string of characters in labels and formulas. This feature works much like the search-and-replace feature in many word processors. An incorrect search and replace can destroy a file, so always save the file to disk first.

Suppose that you have a list of department names as labels (see fig. 4.62), and you want to shorten the labels from "Department" to "Dept". To search and replace a label, select /Range Search and then follow these steps:

1. At the prompt, highlight the range that you want to search, A3..A10 (see fig. 4.62), and then click the left mouse button within the control panel or press Enter.

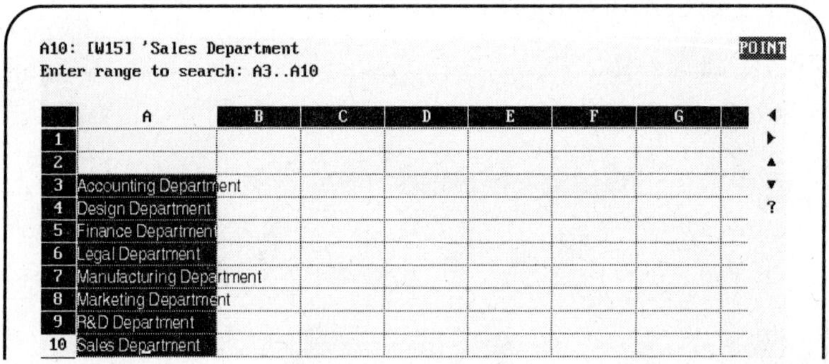

Fig. 4.62. A column of labels before a /Range Search operation.

2. Type the search string (**department**), and then click the left mouse button within the control panel or press Enter.

3. At the resulting menu, choose to search Formulas, Labels, or Both. In this example, select Labels to replace cells with labels.

4. At the Find or Replace menu, select Replace.

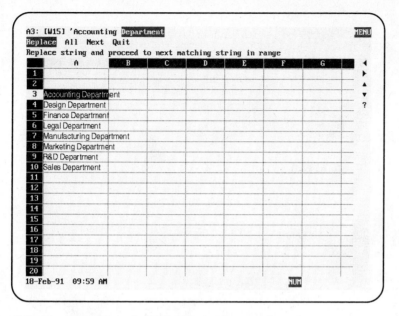

```
A3: [W15] 'Accounting Department                              MENU
Replace  All  Next  Quit
Replace string and proceed to next matching string in range
            A           B     C     D     E     F     G      ◄
  1                                                           ►
  2                                                           ▲
  3  Accounting Department                                    ▼
  4  Design Department                                        ?
  5  Finance Department
  6  Legal Department
  7  Manufacturing Department
  8  Marketing Department
  9  R&D Department
 10  Sales Department
 11
 12
 13
 14
 15
 16
 17
 18
 19
 20
18-Feb-91  09:59 AM                              NUM
```

Fig. 4.63. The /Range Search menu after Replace is selected.

5. Type the replacement string (**Dept**) and then click the left mouse button within the control panel or press Enter.

6. The cell pointer moves to the first cell with a matching string (A3) and gives you the following menu (see fig. 4.63):

   Replace All Next Quit

Select **R**eplace to replace Department with Dept in this one cell and move to the next matching cell. Choose **A**ll to replace Department with Dept in all cells in the range. Select **N**ext to skip—without changing—the current cell and move to the next matching cell. Choose **Q**uit to stop the search and replace and to return to READY mode. A good idea is to select **R**eplace for the first cell and ensure that the change is correct. If the change is correct, select **A**ll to replace the rest. If you make an error on the first **R**eplace, select **Q**uit and redo the command.

The result of the preceding series of steps is shown in figure 4.64. Case is not used with a search string (department matches Department, for example), but case is important in the replacement string (Dept).

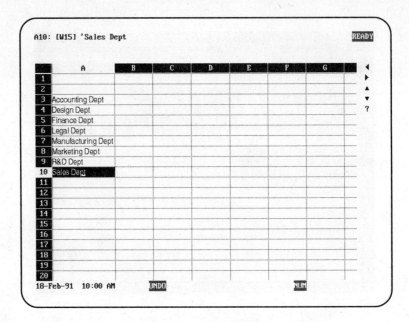

Fig. 4.64. The final result of the /Range Search operation.

If, instead of **Replace** (see step 4 of the preceding example), you select **Find**, the cell pointer moves to the first cell in the range with a matching string and a menu appears with the options **Next** or **Quit**. Select **Next** to find the next occurrence or **Quit** to return to READY mode. If no more matching strings are found, 1-2-3 stops with an error message. You also can use /**R**ange Search to modify formulas. If you have many formulas that round to two decimal places, such as @ROUND(A1*B1,2), you can change the formulas to round to four decimal places with a search string of **,2)** and a replace string of **,4)**. Use caution when you replace numbers in formulas. If you try to replace only the 2 character with a 4 in the last example, the formula @ROUND(A2*B2,2) becomes @ROUND(A4*B4,4).

If the number replacement makes a formula invalid, 1-2-3 cancels the replacement and returns to READY mode with the cell pointer at the cell that holds the formula that could not be replaced. At the end of a **R**eplace, the cell pointer is at the last cell replaced.

Accessing the Operating System

In this chapter, you learn how to use many different 1-2-3 commands to build and modify worksheet files. At times, however, you may need to perform a function 1-2-3 cannot handle, but a function that requires you to use the operating system or another program. For example, suppose that you want to save a file on a floppy disk, but you have no formatted disks available. Here, you want to use the DOS FORMAT command. While you are working in 1-2-3, you may be asked to print a copy of a letter you created with a word processor.

In these situations, you can save your files and use /Quit to exit 1-2-3. When you finish the other task, you can restart 1-2-3 and read in the files again. However, you are not forced to use /Quit; a faster way exists. Use the /System command to temporarily suspend 1-2-3 and access the operating system (DOS). When in the operating system, you can copy files, format floppy disks, execute other system functions—you can even execute another program, such as a word processor, if you have enough memory available. To return to 1-2-3, type **exit** and press Enter. You return to 1-2-3 with the same status you had when you left. The same worksheets and files are in memory, and the cell pointer is in the same place. Window settings and all other defaults remain undisturbed. If you don't have enough memory, 1-2-3 cannot invoke the operating system. You can recover some memory if you save and then erase your worksheet. However, to a large degree, clearing memory defeats the purpose of the /System command.

Always save your worksheet before you use /System. If you execute any program that remains in memory (memory-resident), you cannot re-enter 1-2-3. Examples of memory-resident programs include SideKick and SideKick Plus from Borland International, Lotus Magellan, the DOS MODE and PRINT commands, print spoolers, and many other programs. If you do not save your file and later find that you cannot re-enter 1-2-3, all your work is lost.

Caution:
Save your work before you use /System. You may not be able to return to 1-2-3.

If you use a DOS shell program, such as the DOS Shell (included with DOS 4.x and 5.0) or a graphical operating environment, such as Microsoft Windows, the /System command does not return you to the shell or environment. Instead, /System provides access to the DOS command line interface, often called the DOS prompt. If you are unfamiliar with the DOS prompt, avoid using the /System command.

Summary

In this chapter, you learned fundamental 1-2-3 and Wysiwyg commands. You learned how to use command menus, how to specify and name ranges, and how to save files. The chapter described the process of controlling how data is displayed on-screen, and you learned how to change column widths, split the screen into windows, and lock titles. The chapter presented methods to change the layout of your worksheets—by erasing ranges and by inserting and deleting rows and columns.

You also learned how to protect and hide data and files. Equally important, you learned the limitations of these techniques and how you can defeat the techniques. You learned how to use /Move and /Copy, two basic commands that enable you to rearrange data and build worksheets. You also learned how to use 1-2-3's search-and-replace feature to find or to change data. Finally, you learned how to suspend 1-2-3 and perform actions that cannot be done in 1-2-3 and then how to return to the program and to the worksheet in memory.

Learning all the commands in 1-2-3 is a formidable job. Fortunately, many commands perform specialized tasks. You can learn about the commands as you need to perform the tasks. The following chapters cover these more specialized commands.

5

Formatting Cell Contents

Using 1-2-3 to manipulate data is only the first step in using an electronic worksheet. Making the results clear and easy to understand can be as important as calculating the correct answer. In this chapter, you learn to use the tools that control how data within cells displays, or appears, on-screen. Changing how data displays is called *formatting*. 1-2-3 offers three types of formatting commands: the /Worksheet Global commands, which affect the display of an entire worksheet; the /Range commands, which affect the display of individual cells; and the Wysiwyg :Format commands, which enhance the appearance of data in the worksheet. You use these types of commands to customize the display of data.

When you format data, you change only the way the data looks on-screen; you do not change the value of the data. Formatting options also are available when you print reports. Chapter 8 covers these printing capabilities.

This chapter shows you how to do the following:

- Set worksheet global defaults

- Set range and worksheet global formats

- Change label alignment in the cell

- Use the /Format commands

- Justify long labels across columns

- Suppress the display of zeros within cells

Setting Worksheet Global Defaults

1-2-3 includes a number of overall settings that define how 1-2-3 operates or how the screen looks. These settings can be changed. You must select some settings with the Install program (see Appendix A). For example, the Install procedure enables you to specify the type of display and the printers you connect to your computer. You can change other settings as you work in 1-2-3. In 1-2-3, the main command to change these settings is /Worksheet Global Default. The menu that appears contains the following options:

Printer Directory Status Update Other Autoexec Quit

Select **Printer** to change the printer defaults, as described in Chapter 8. Select **Directory** to change the default directory (see Chapter 7). Select **Autoexec** to control autoexecutable macros (see Chapter 13).

Select **Other** from the /Worksheet Global Default menu for the following additional selections:

International Help Clock Undo Beep Add-In Expanded-Memory

The International option on the /Worksheet Global Default Other menu offers the following selections:

Punctuation Currency Date Time Negative Quit

The following sections of this chapter explain these selections in detail.

The **Help** option on the /Worksheet Global Default Other menu is a relatively obsolete command if you install 1-2-3 on a hard disk.

Select **Clock** from the /Worksheet Global Default Other menu to change the default date and time indicator at the lower left corner of the screen, as described in the command reference section of this book. Finally, Undo activates or deactivates the Undo feature (see Chapter 3).

Normally, 1-2-3 Release 2.3 beeps when you make an error. Select **Beep No** from the /Worksheet Global Default Other menu to turn off the beep; select **Beep Yes** to turn the beep back on. You may want to turn off the beep when you work in an area where the beep may disturb others, such as in a library. You also may want to turn off the beep when you demonstrate a 1-2-3 system to others so that pressing a key in error is not too obvious.

1-2-3 Release 2.3 includes five add-in programs: Wysiwyg, Macro Library Manager, Auditor, Viewer, and Tutorial. (These programs are covered in various sections throughout the book.) Select **Add-In Set** from the /**W**orksheet **G**lobal **D**efault **O**ther menu to have 1-2-3 load (attach) one of these—or any other add-in program you may use—automatically upon start-up. When you select Add-In Set, a menu appears with the numbers **1** through **8**. When you select a number, a list of add-ins appears on the third line of the control panel. After you select the add-in to attach, the following menu displays:

No-Key **7 8 9 10**

Select **7**, **8**, **9**, or **10** to invoke the add-in with Alt-F7, Alt-F8, Alt-F9 or Alt-F10, respectively. Select **No**-Key to invoke the add-in with the /**A**dd-In **I**nvoke command. After you decide how you want to invoke the add-in, a further menu gives you the option to automatically invoke the add-in when you start 1-2-3. If you choose **No**, you must invoke the add-in when you need to use it. If you select **Yes**, 1-2-3 invokes the add-in. If you no longer want an add-in to be attached automatically, select **Add-In Cancel** from the /**W**orksheet **G**lobal **D**efault **O**ther menu. A menu appears with the numbers **1** through **8**. Select the number of the add-in you want to cancel, and this add-in is no longer attached when 1-2-3 starts. Remember that attaching an add-in program to 1-2-3 uses memory and leaves less memory for building worksheets. Attaching an add-in also may cause a memory warning to occur if you are using 1-2-3's Undo feature.

If you have expanded memory in your computer and want to use it with 1-2-3, select **Expanded-Memory** on the /**W**orksheet **G**lobal **D**efault **O**ther menu to determine how 1-2-3 uses the additional memory. If your expanded memory meets any LIM (Lotus-Intel-Microsoft) standard, select **Expanded-Memory Standard**. This action enables 1-2-3 to store worksheet data in expanded memory. If your expanded memory meets the LIM 4.0 standard, select **Expanded-Memory Enhanced**. This selection enables you to build larger worksheets by storing worksheet data and cell pointers in expanded memory. A drawback to the Enhanced option is that this selection is slower than the Standard option. Standard can use up to 4M expanded memory for data; Enhanced can use up to 8M extra for cell pointers.

All setting changes you make are effective only until you use /**Q**uit to exit 1-2-3. The next time you start 1-2-3, these settings revert to their original values. To permanently update the changed settings, select /**W**orksheet **G**lobal **D**efault **U**pdate. This command updates a configuration file that 1-2-3 uses to determine the default settings.

Caution:
Update the global defaults, or all changes are lost when you exit 1-2-3.

If you don't want to use the command menus to change worksheet global defaults, you can use the Global Settings dialog box shown in figure 5.1. The

Global Settings dialog box appears when you select /Worksheet Global. To change settings with the keyboard, press F2 (Edit); to change settings with the mouse, click the left mouse button at any point in the dialog box. Highlighted letters appear in the dialog-box commands. A further selection, Default Settings..., appears at the bottom of the dialog box (see fig. 5.2). To change a default setting, select Default Settings...; the Default Settings dialog box appears as shown in figure 5.3.

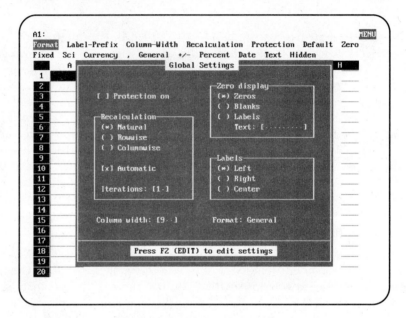

Fig. 5.1. *The Global Settings dialog box.*

To change a setting with the keyboard, press the appropriate highlighted letter and then make a further selection or enter text, as necessary. To change a setting with the mouse, click on the setting (and type in text, if necessary). For example, to show the current file name in place of the time and date at the bottom left corner of the screen, select **Clock** and then select **File name** or, from the keyboard, press **C F**. To perform this action with the mouse, click on the parenthesis ( ) in front of **File name**.

When you select certain options at the bottom of the screen, such as Printer... or International... (see fig. 5.3), another dialog box appears as shown in figure 5.4 (the ellipsis signifies this). Again, you change settings by selecting a command and then selecting the desired setting with the keyboard or by selecting the setting directly with the mouse.

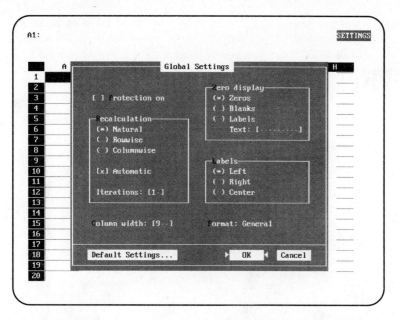

Fig. 5.2. *The* Default Settings... *option appears at the bottom of the Global Settings dialog box.*

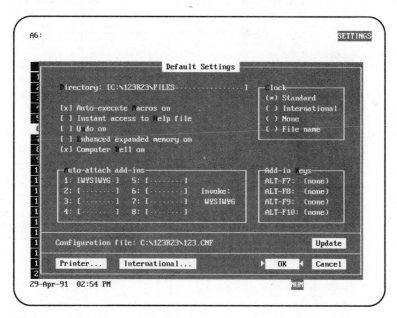

Fig. 5.3. *The Default Settings dialog box.*

When you finish changing the defaults, press Enter or click OK to save the settings for the current session. To make the settings permanent, select Update from the Default Settings dialog box. Press Esc or the right mouse button to clear the Global Settings dialog box from the screen.

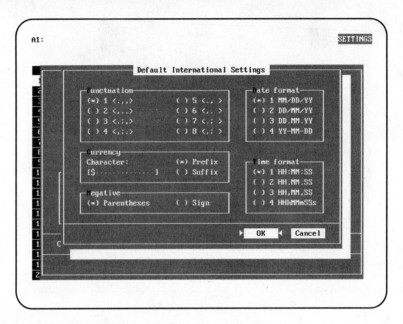

Fig. 5.4. The Default International Settings dialog box.

Reminder:
*Use /Worksheet
Status to check the
amount of available
memory.*

To see the current status of all these settings, use /Worksheet Global Default Status to show the dialog box, shown in figure 5.5.

Use /Worksheet Status to show a dialog box with a mixture of information that includes the conventional and expanded memory available, the EMS (or expanded memory specification) version, the location of cell pointer information, whether or not a math coprocessor is used, and—if any—the location of a circular reference (see fig. 5.6). The main use of this status dialog box is to check on the amount of memory available and to find circular references. (See Chapter 4 for more information on circular references.)

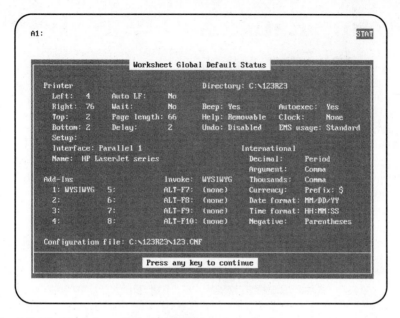

Fig. 5.5. *The Worksheet Global Default Status dialog box.*

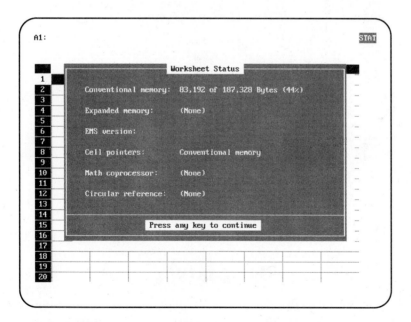

Fig. 5.6. *The Worksheet Status dialog box.*

Setting Range and Worksheet Global Formats

Data in a cell has two characteristics: contents and how the data is displayed on-screen. These two characteristics are related but are not the same. The contents of the current cell are shown in the control panel; the formatted display of the contents shows in the worksheet (see fig. 5.7). A cell may contain a formula, such as `+B8` in cell C8, but the current value of the formula is shown in the cell. The formula in C8 is shown on-screen as `1,234.30` in the worksheet. Other factors, such as column width and the Wysiwyg fonts used, affect the display, but cell format is the more important characteristic.

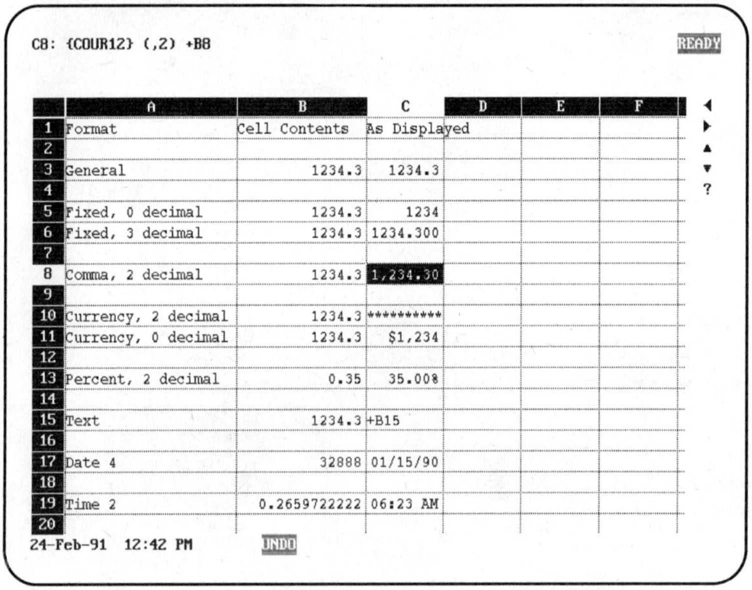

C8: {COUR12} (,2) +B8 READY

	A	B	C	D	E	F
1	Format	Cell Contents	As Displayed			
2						
3	General	1234.3	1234.3			
4						
5	Fixed, 0 decimal	1234.3	1234			
6	Fixed, 3 decimal	1234.3	1234.300			
7						
8	Comma, 2 decimal	1234.3	1,234.30			
9						
10	Currency, 2 decimal	1234.3	**********			
11	Currency, 0 decimal	1234.3	$1,234			
12						
13	Percent, 2 decimal	0.35	35.00%			
14						
15	Text	1234.3	+B15			
16						
17	Date 4	32888	01/15/90			
18						
19	Time 2	0.2659722222	06:23 AM			
20						

24-Feb-91 12:42 PM UNDO

Fig. 5.7. A worksheet displaying various formats.

The Available Formats

You can display data in a cell in several different formats. Table 5.1 lists the formats available from the 1-2-3 menu, and figure 5.7 shows some examples of the possible formats. Other formats are available from the Wysiwyg menu.

Most of the formats available from the 1-2-3 menu apply only to numeric data (numeric formulas and numbers). If you format a *label* as **Fixed** or **Currency**, for example, the format does not affect how the label looks on-screen. A few formats, such as **Hidden**, can apply to labels and string (text) formulas.

The formats available from the Wysiwyg menu apply equally to both numeric data and labels. For example, if you format a cell or a range of cells with a particular font, the contents, whether numbers or labels, appear in that font. No matter what format you use, numeric data is right-aligned. This result is true whether the data is entered directly or is the result of a numeric formula. The result of a string formula is always left-aligned, even if the formula refers to a label with another alignment.

You control the width of a cell by the column width setting (see Chapter 4). If the column is too narrow to display a numeric entry, asterisks fill the cell (see cell C10 in fig. 5.7). To show the data, you must change the format, the column width, or the Wysiwyg font (the font used in fig. 5.7 is 12-point Courier).

Table 5.1
Display Formats

Format	Example	Application
Fixed	1234.50	Numeric data
Sci	1.2345E+03	Numeric data
Currency	$1,234.50	Numeric data
, (Comma)	1,234.50	Numeric data
General	1234.5	Numeric data
+/–	+++++	Numeric data
Percent	35.4%	Numeric data
Date	10/10/90	Special date serial numbers
Time*	06:23 AM	Special time fractions
Text	+C6	All formulas
Hidden	No display	All data

*Time is an option on the Date menu

1-2-3 can display in text or graphics mode. If you use the 1-2-3 text display mode, the extreme right position of a cell is reserved for a percent sign or right parenthesis. Therefore, a number must fit into the cell, using one character less than the column width. If the column width is 9, the formatted number must fit into 8 positions, not counting a percent sign or right parenthesis. Negative numbers appear with a minus sign or parenthesis, which means that a negative number requires an extra character on the display. With a column width of 9, a negative number must fit into 7 positions. The 1-2-3 graphics display reserves a position on the extreme right for a right parenthesis but not a percent sign. However, the number of characters that appear in a column with a width of 9 depends on the font

Cue:
If numeric data displays as asterisks, change the format or change the column width.

that you use. For example, the 12-point nonproportional Courier font always displays nine characters, but the 12-point proportional Swiss font displays between 6 and 24 characters (depending on which characters are used).

The Contents versus the Format of a Cell

Remember that *formatting* changes only how data appears, not the data. For example, the number 1234 can appear as 1,234, $1,234.00, 123400%, and many other combinations. When you use the new Wysiwyg feature, you also can display the data in different fonts and colors. The number, no matter what display technique is used, always remains the same number.

Caution:
The number that displays in a cell may not be the exact value of the cell because of rounding errors.

Some formats show decimals as rounded to the next whole number. If you format 1234.5 in Fixed format with zero decimal places, the number displays as 1235, but the actual value of 1234.5 is used in formulas. In figure 5.8, the sales total in cell C8 looks like an addition error. Actually, the formula in cell C6 is +B6*1.1 (+B6 x 1.1), projecting 10 percent higher sales next year. The value of the formula in cell C6 is 95.7. The display, however, shows 96 formatted as Fixed with zero decimal places. The value of the formula in cell C7 is 83.6, but the display shows 84. The value of the sum in cell C8 is 179.3, but the display shows 179. The value appears as 96+84=179. This result is an apparent—but nonexistent—rounding error, produced by rounding the display.

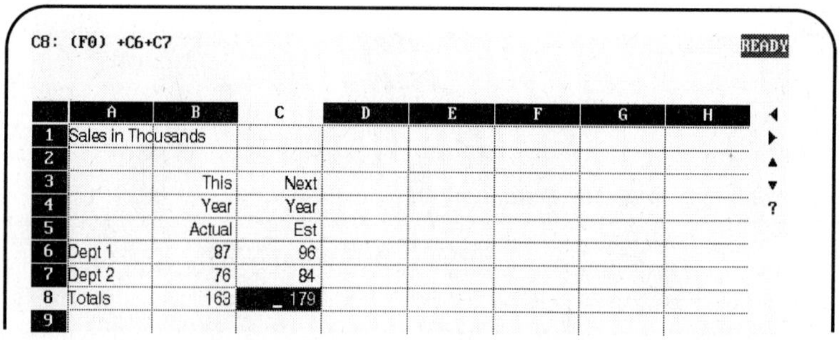

Fig. 5.8. An apparent rounding error caused by formatting.

Cue:
Use @ROUND to round the value in the cell.

To avoid rounding errors, you need to round the actual value of the formulas in figure 5.8. To round the value of a formula, use the @ROUND function (see Chapter 6).

Using the Format Commands of the 1-2-3 Main Menu

You change the format of a cell or range of cells with the /Range Format command of the 1-2-3 menu (see fig. 5.9). You then choose one of the formats from the menu. For comma format, press the comma key (,).

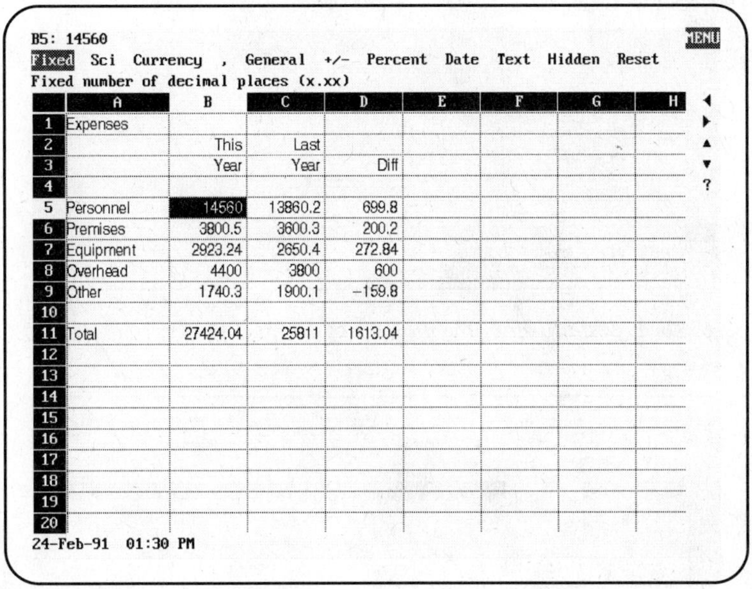

```
B5: 14560                                                      MENU
Fixed  Sci  Currency  ,  General  +/-  Percent  Date  Text  Hidden  Reset
Fixed number of decimal places (x.xx)
         A          B        C        D        E      F      G      H    ◄
  1  Expenses                                                             ►
  2                This     Last
  3                Year     Year     Diff                                 ▲
  4                                                                       ▼
  5  Personnel    14560   13860.2    699.8                                ?
  6  Premises     3800.5   3600.3    200.2
  7  Equipment   2923.24   2650.4   272.84
  8  Overhead      4400     3800      600
  9  Other        1740.3   1900.1   -159.8
 10
 11  Total      27424.04   25811   1613.04
 12
 13
 14
 15
 16
 17
 18
 19
 20
24-Feb-91  01:30 PM
```

Fig. 5.9. The /Range Format menu.

If you select Fixed, Sci, Currency, , (comma), or Percent, you are prompted for the number of decimal places (see fig. 5.10). When this prompt appears, 1-2-3 shows a default of two decimal places. To accept the default, press Enter. To change the number of decimal places, type a number between **0** and **15** and press Enter or click the left mouse button within the control panel. The Date and Time formats use additional menus, which are covered in a following section of this chapter. The Time format is an option on the Date menu.

After you select a format and the options you desire, the program prompts you for the range to format. Specify the range and press Enter or click the left mouse button. Figure 5.11 shows the result after you use /Range Format Fixed with two decimal places on the range **B5..B11**. An abbreviation of the format appears in the control panel when the current cell has a range format. In figure 5.11, (F2) in the control panel indicates that B5 was formatted as Fixed with two decimal places. If the cell has no format, no format indicator appears in the control panel.

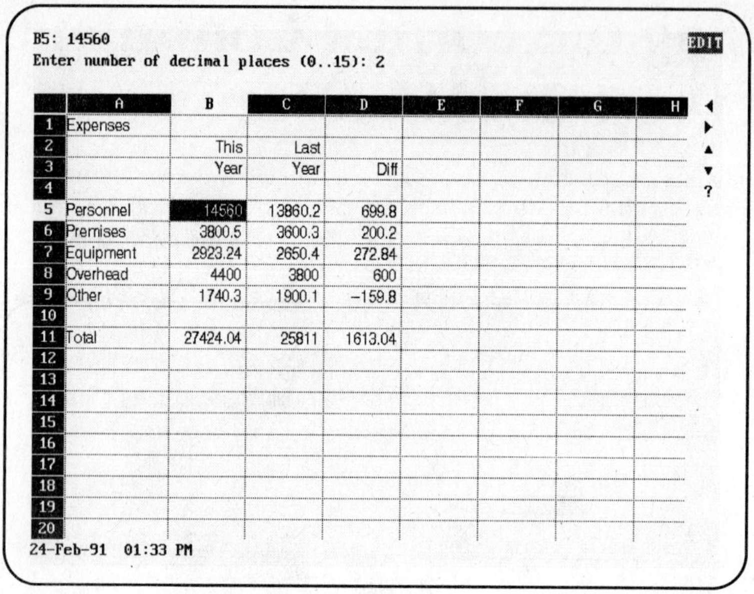

```
B5: 14560                                                          EDIT
Enter number of decimal places (0..15): 2
```

	A	B	C	D	E	F	G	H
1	Expenses							
2		This	Last					
3		Year	Year	Diff				
4								
5	Personnel	14560	13860.2	699.8				
6	Premises	3800.5	3600.3	200.2				
7	Equipment	2923.24	2650.4	272.84				
8	Overhead	4400	3800	600				
9	Other	1740.3	1900.1	−159.8				
10								
11	Total	27424.04	25811	1613.04				
12								
13								
14								
15								
16								
17								
18								
19								
20								

```
24-Feb-91  01:33 PM
```

Fig. 5.10. The prompt to enter the number of decimal places.

```
B5: (F2) 14560                                                    READY
```

	A	B	C	D	E	F	G	H
1	Expenses							
2		This	Last					
3		Year	Year	Diff				
4								
5	Personnel	14560.00	13860.2	699.8				
6	Premises	3800.50	3600.3	200.2				
7	Equipment	2923.24	2650.4	272.84				
8	Overhead	4400.00	3800	600				
9	Other	1740.30	1900.1	−159.8				
10								
11	Total	27424.04	25811	1613.04				
12								
13								
14								
15								
16								
17								
18								
19								
20								

```
24-Feb-91  01:35 PM        UNDO
```

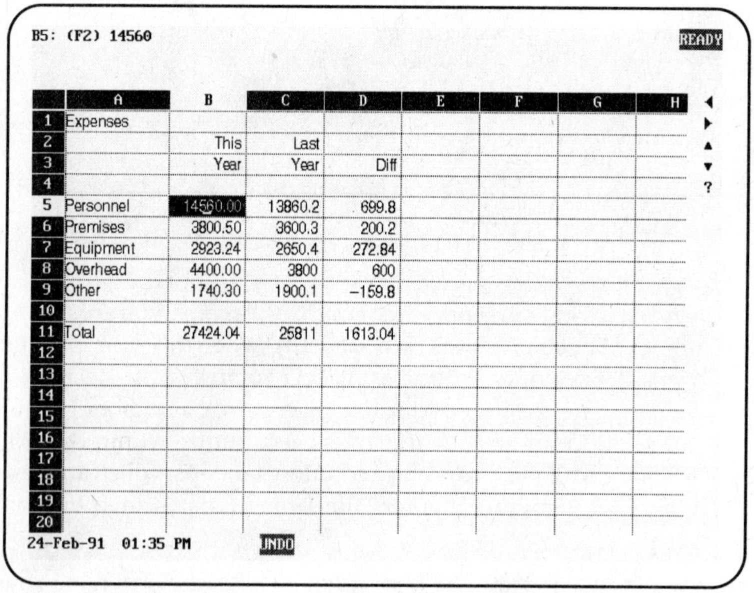

Fig. 5.11. A range formatted as Fixed with two decimal places.

When you start a new file, no cells have a range format. For example, in figure 5.10, no cells have a range format. In figure 5.11, only the cells in the range B5..B11 have a range format. When a cell lacks a range format, the cell takes the format specified as the default setting in /Worksheet Global Format.

When you start a new file, the global format default is **General**. To change the global format, use /Worksheet Global Format (see fig. 5.12), or use /Worksheet Global and edit the Global Settings dialog box (see fig. 5.13). To use the keyboard, press F2 (Edit) and then select Format; to use the mouse, click the left mouse button in the Global Settings dialog box and then click on Format. When the Global Settings Format dialog box is active, select a format by typing, by pointing to a highlighted letter, or by clicking the mouse on the appropriate parenthesis.

Reminder:
The default global format for a new worksheet is General.

Figure 5.14 shows the worksheet after changing to comma (,) format with two decimal places. Notice that the format in B5..B11 did not change. These cells have a range format; the global format affects only those cells with no range format.

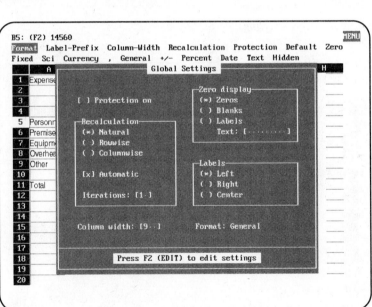

Fig. 5.12. *The Format option of the /Worksheet Global menu.*

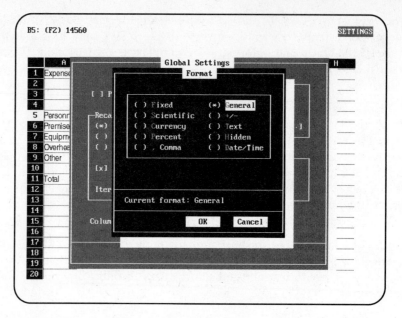

Fig. 5.13. The Global Settings Format dialog box.

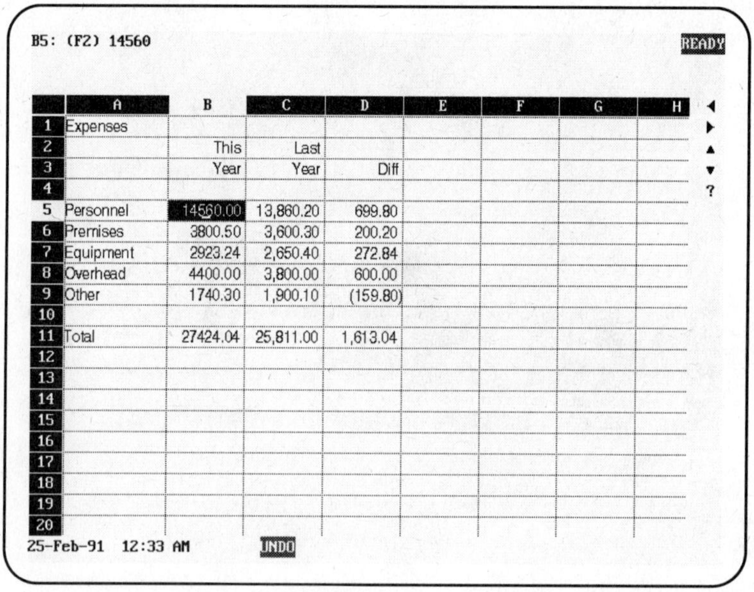

B5: (F2) 14560   READY

	A	B	C	D	E	F	G	H
1	Expenses							
2		This	Last					
3		Year	Year	Diff				
4								
5	Personnel	14560.00	13,860.20	699.80				
6	Premises	3800.50	3,600.30	200.20				
7	Equipment	2923.24	2,650.40	272.84				
8	Overhead	4400.00	3,800.00	600.00				
9	Other	1740.30	1,900.10	(159.80)				
10								
11	Total	27424.04	25,811.00	1,613.04				
12								
13								
14								
15								
16								
17								
18								
19								
20								

25-Feb-91 12:33 AM   UNDO

Fig. 5.14. The worksheet with a global format of comma (,) with two decimal places.

To alter a cell or range that already has a range format to the same format as the global format, remove range formatting with /**Range Format Reset**. Figure 5.15 shows the worksheet after /**Range Format Reset** is assigned to the range B5..B11. This range now displays with the global comma (,) format. To change a cell or range with a range format to a different range format, execute the /**Range Format** command again.

```
B5: 14560                                                    READY

        A           B        C        D        E     F     G     H
  1  Expenses
  2                   This    Last
  3                   Year    Year     Diff
  4
  5  Personnel      14,560.00 13,860.20  699.80
  6  Premises        3,800.50  3,600.30  200.20
  7  Equipment       2,923.24  2,650.40  272.84
  8  Overhead        4,400.00  3,800.00  600.00
  9  Other           1,740.30  1,900.10 (159.80)
 10
 11  Total          27,424.04 25,811.00 1,613.04
 12
 13
 14
 15
 16
 17
 18
 19
 20
25-Feb-91  12:34 AM         UNDO
```

Fig. 5.15. *The range B5..B11 takes on the global default of comma, two decimal places after using /Range Format Reset.*

Use the global format to change the worksheet to the format that you expect to use more than other formats. Then use /**Range Format** to format ranges you want to display with other formats. Most worksheets look better if you use a variety of formats to match the data. Figure 5.16 shows a worksheet with a global format of comma (,) as well as Currency, Percent, and Date range formats.

The following sections describe each 1-2-3 menu format. You can assign each format by using the /**Worksheet Global Format** or /**Range Format** menus.

```
F1: (D4) @DATE(91:5:16)                                    READY
```

	A	B	C	D	E	F	G
1	Expenses					05/16/91	
2		This	Last		%		
3		Year	Year	Diff	Diff		
4							
5	Personnel	$14,560.00	$13,860.20	$699.80	5.05%		
6	Premises	3,800.50	3,600.30	200.20	5.56%		
7	Equipment	2,923.24	2,650.40	272.84	10.29%		
8	Overhead	4,400.00	3,800.00	600.00	15.79%		
9	Other	1,740.30	1,900.10	(159.80)	−8.41%		
10							
11	Total	$27,424.04	$25,811.00	$1,613.04	6.25%		
12							
13							
14							
15							
16							
17							
18							
19							
20							

```
25-Feb-91  09:07 AM          UNDO
```

Fig. 5.16. *A worksheet with a global format of comma (,) and range formats of Currency, Percent, and Date.*

Fixed Format

Use the Fixed format when you want a column of numbers to align on the decimal point. 1-2-3 displays a fixed number of decimal places, from 0-15, that you specify. If a number uses more decimal digits than the number you specify in the format, the number is rounded on the display but not in the value used for calculation.

Reminder:
When a cell is filled with asterisks, the contents of the cell are wider than the cell.

The following listing shows several examples of Fixed format in cells that are formatted with a column width of 9 on the 1-2-3 text display (the same results occur on the 1-2-3 graphics display for monospace fonts, such as 12-point Courier):

Typed Entry	Cell Format	Display Result
123.46	(F0)	123
123.46	(F1)	123.5
−123.46	(F2)	−123.46
123.46	(F4)	123.4600
−123.46	(F4)	**********
12345678	(F2)	**********

In all cases, the full number in the cell is used in calculations. Negative numbers always show a leading minus sign. (Fn) appears in the control panel of cells that are formatted with /Range Format Fixed. n represents the number of decimal places.

Scientific Format

Use scientific (**Sci**) format to indicate very large or very small numbers. Very large and very small numbers usually have a few significant digits and many zeroes as place holders to tell you how large or small the number is.

A number in scientific notation consists of two parts: a *mantissa* and an *exponent*. The mantissa is a number from 1 to 10 that contains the significant digits. The exponent tells you how many places to move the decimal point to get the actual value of the number. You specify the number of decimal places in the mantissa from 0 to 15. If the number has more significant digits than the number you specify in the format, the number is rounded on the display.

1230000000000 displays as 1.23E+12 in scientific format with two decimal places. E+12 signifies that you must move the decimal point 12 places to the right to get the actual number. 0.000000000237 displays as 2.4E-10 in scientific format with one decimal place. E-10 means that you must move the decimal point 10 places to the left to get the actual number.

A number too large to display in a cell in **General** format appears in **Sci** format. (Sn) appears in the control panel of cells formatted with /Range Format Sci. n represents the number of decimal places.

The following listing shows several examples of **Sci** format in cells with a column width of 9 on the 1-2-3 text display (the same results occur on the 1-2-3 graphics display for monospace fonts, such as 12-point Courier):

Typed Entry	Cell Format	Display Result
1632116750000	(S2)	1.63E+12
1632116750000	(S0)	2E+12
–1632116750000	(S1)	-1.6E+12
–1632116750000	(S2)	**********
–.00000000012	(S0)	-1E-10

Currency Format

Currency format works much like comma format but includes a leading dollar sign. Because of the dollar sign, you need an extra position in the column width to display a number in Currency format. Negative numbers appear in parenthesis. The value –1234 displays as ($1,234) with 0 decimal places.

You can change the setting so that negative numbers appear with a leading minus sign by using /Worksheet Global Default Other International Negative Sign. Also, you can edit the Negative Sign setting in the Default International Settings dialog box, which appears when you issue the /Worksheet Global Default Other International command. The value –$1234 then appears as -$1,234. To return to parenthesis for negative numbers, use /Worksheet Global Default Other International Negative Parenthesis or edit the Negative Parenthesis setting in the Default International Settings dialog box. This default applies to 1-2-3 as a whole, not to single worksheets.

You can change the dollar sign, the default currency symbol, if you use a different currency. Use /Worksheet Global Default Other International Currency to specify a new currency symbol and whether the symbol is a prefix or a suffix. You also can issue the /Worksheet Global Default Other International command and edit the Currency command in the Default International Settings dialog box. This default applies to 1-2-3 as a whole, not to single worksheets.

For example, suppose that you create a file that uses Currency format for U.S. dollars, and you save the file. At a later date, you decide to create a file that uses the British pound (£). You can change the currency symbol to the British pound by issuing the /Worksheet Global Default Other International Currency command. When the prompt Enter currency sign:$ appears, you delete the dollar sign and substitute the British pound sign by pressing Alt-F1 (Compose) and then typing L=. Then press Enter and select Prefix.

You can accomplish the same result by issuing the /Worksheet Global Default Other International command and editing the Currency command of the Default International Settings dialog box that appears on-screen (see fig. 5.17). Press F2 (Edit) or click the left mouse button to highlight the caps for each command in the box. Select Currency Character and delete the dollar sign ($) that appears in the text box by pressing the backspace key. Then press Alt-F1 (Compose) and type L=. Because Prefix already is selected (indicated by the asterisk that precedes Prefix), you can end by clicking on OK with the left mouse button or by pressing Enter until the command line menu reappears.

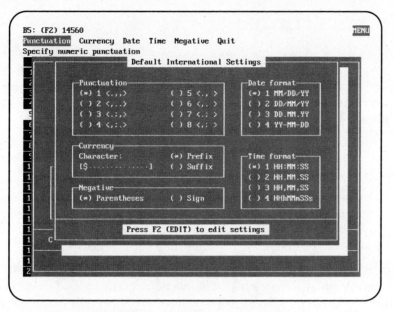

Fig. 5.17. The Default International Settings dialog box.

To clear the dialog boxes from the screen, select **Quit** and then **Quit** again. To make this change permanent, select **Worksheet Global Default Update** or select `Update` in the Default Settings dialog box (you must press F2 or click on the Default Settings dialog box to see the `Update` option). Retrieve another file; note that all cells formatted with **Currency** now show the pound as the currency symbol.

Caution: If you change the currency symbol, the change affects the current file and all subsequent files.

(`Cn`) appears in the control panel of cells formatted with **/Range Format Currency**. `n` represents the number of decimal places. The following listing shows several examples of Currency format in cells with a column width of 9 on the 1-2-3 text display (the same results occur on the 1-2-3 graphics display for monospace fonts, such as 12-point Courier):

Typed Entry	Cell Format	Display Result
123	`(C2)`	`$123.00`
(if /wgdoic)*	`£123.00`	
−123.124	`(C2)`	`($123.12)`
(if /wgdoins)*	`−$123.12`	
1234.12	`(C0)`	`$1,234`
−1234.12	`(C2)`	`*********`

*See text for an explanation of how to change the currency symbol and negative value display.

Comma Format

Like the Fixed format, the comma format (,) displays data with a fixed number of decimal places (from 0 to 15). Additionally, the comma format separates the thousands, millions, and so on, with commas. Positive numbers less than 1,000 display the same way in Fixed format and comma (,) format. The comma format is used most often for financial data.

If the number has more decimal digits than the number you specify in the format, the number is rounded on the display. The full value in the cell is used in calculations.

Cue:
Use comma format to make large numbers easier to read.

Use the comma (,) format instead of Fixed format for large numbers because you can more easily read 12,300,000.00 than 12300000.00. With comma format, negative numbers are handled in the same manner as Currency format. The value –1234 displays as (1,234) with 0 decimal places.

(,n) appears in the control panel of cells that are formatted with /**R**ange Format, (comma). n represents the number of decimal places. The following listing shows several examples of comma (,) format in cells with a column width of 9 on the 1-2-3 text display (the same results occur on the 1-2-3 graphics display for monospace fonts, such as 12-point Courier):

Typed Entry	Cell Format	Display Result
123.46	(,0)	123
1234.6	(,2)	1,234.60
–1234.6	(,0)	(1,235)
(if /wgdoins)	-1,235	
–1234	(,2)	**********

General Format

General format, the default for all new worksheets, displays only the number. If the number is negative, a minus sign precedes the number. Numbers that contain decimal digits can contain a decimal point. If the number contains too many digits to the right of the decimal point to fit in the column width, the decimal portion that does not fit in the cell is truncated. If the number is too large to display normally, 1-2-3 converts and then displays the number in Sci (or scientific) format. In a cell with a width of 9 characters, for example, 123400000 displays as 1.2E+08. In the same cell, a very small number, such as 0.0000000012, is truncated and shown as 0.000000. Negative numbers in Sci format display with a leading minus sign.

The following listing shows several examples of General format in cells with a column width of 9 on the 1-2-3 text display (the same results occur on the 1-2-3 graphics display for monospace fonts, such as 12-point Courier):

Typed Entry	Cell Format	Display Result
123.46	(G)	123.46
–123.36	(G)	-123.36
1.2345678912	(G)	1.234567
150000000	(G)	1.5E+08
–.00000002638	(G)	0.00000

(G) appears in the control panel of cells that are formatted with /Range Format General.

The +/– Format

Based on the number in the cell, the +/– format creates a horizontal bar chart. A positive number appears as a row of + signs; a negative number appears as a row of - signs; and a zero (or any other number less than 1 but greater than –1) appears as a period. The number of pluses or minuses can be no wider than the cell. (+) appears in the control panel of cells formatted with /Range Format +/–.

This format originally was devised to create imitation bar charts in spreadsheets that did not support graphing. The format has little use today.

The following listing shows several examples of +/– format in cells with a column width of 9 on the 1-2-3 text display (the same results occur on the 1-2-3 graphics display for monospace fonts, such as 12-point Courier):

Typed Entry	Cell Format	Display Result
6	(+)	++++++
4.9	(+)	++++
–3	(+)	- - -
0	(+)	.
17.2	(+)	**********
.95	(+)	.

Percent Format

Use the **Percent** format to show percentages. You specify the number of decimal places from 0 to 15. The number displayed is the value of the cell multiplied by 100, followed by a percent sign. If the number has more decimal digits than the number you specify in the format, the number is rounded on the display.

Note that the number of decimal places you specify is the number as a percent, not as a whole number. Only two decimal places are needed to display .2456 as a percent.

Reminder:
Enter percentages
as decimal
fractions.

The number displays as multiplied by 100, but the value of the cell is unchanged. To indicate 50% in a cell, you type **.5** and format for **Percent**. If you type **50** and format for **Percent** with zero decimal places, 5000% appears.

(Pn) appears in the control panel for cells formatted with **/Range Format Percent**. n represents the number of decimal places. The following listing shows several examples of **Percent** format in cells with a column width of 9 on the 1-2-3 text display (the same results occur on the 1-2-3 graphics display for monospace fonts, such as 12-point Courier):

Typed Entry	Cell Format	Display Result
.3	(P2)	30.00%
−.3528	(P2)	-35.28%
30	(P0)	3000%
30	(P4)	**********

Date and Time Formats

All the formats mentioned so far deal with regular numeric values. Use **Date** and **Time** formats when you deal with date and time calculations or time functions. These functions are covered in Chapter 6.

Select **/Range Format Date** or **/Worksheet Global Format Date** for the five **Date** format options or to select a **Time** format. The following line shows the menu for **/Range Format Date** or **/Worksheet Global Format Date**:

1 (DD-MM-YY) **2** (DD-MMM) **3** (MMM-YY) **4** (Long Int'l) **5** (Short Int'l) **Time**

Select **/Range Format Date Time** or **/Worksheet Global Format Date Time** for the four **Time** format options from the following menu:

1 (HH:MM:SS AM/PM) **2** (HH:MM AM/PM) **3** (Long Int'l) **4** (Short Int'l)

You also can use dialog boxes to set date and time formats. When you select /**W**orksheet **G**lobal, the Global Settings dialog box appears. Press F2 (Edit) or click the left mouse button to highlight a letter from each command in the dialog box. Select **F**ormat to activate the Format pop-up dialog box, shown in figure 5.18. Then select **D**ate/Time to activate the Date/Time Formats pop-up dialog box (see fig. 5.19). Finally, select the desired date or time format. End by pressing Enter or by clicking OK. To clear the Global Settings dialog box from the screen, press Esc or click the right mouse button.

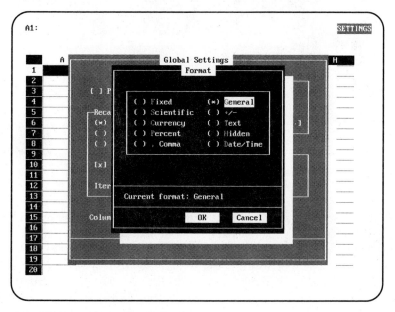

Fig. 5.18. The Format pop-up dialog box.

Date Formats

When you use date functions, 1-2-3 stores the date as a serial number that represents the number of days since January 1, 1900. The serial date number for January 1, 1900 is 1. The serial date number for January 1, 1992 is 33604. The latest date that 1-2-3 can handle is December 31, 2099, with a serial number of 73050. If the number is less than 1 or greater than 73050, the **D**ate format displays as asterisks. **D**ate formats ignore all fractions. 33604.99 with format D4 (long international) displays on-screen as 01/01/92. The fraction represents the time, a fractional portion of a 24-hour clock.

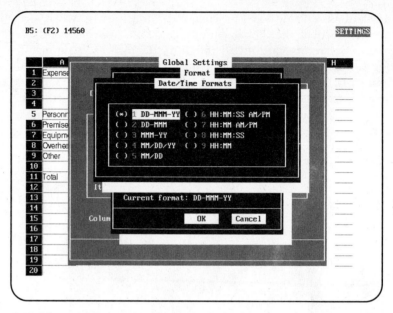

Fig. 5.19. *The Date/Time Formats pop-up dialog box.*

Don't be concerned about which serial date number refers to which date. Have 1-2-3 format the serial date number to appear as a textual date. Actually, all the date serial numbers, starting with March 1, 1900, are off by one day. The calendar inside 1-2-3 treats 1900 as a leap year, which is inaccurate. A date serial number of 60 is displayed as 02/29/00—a date that does not exist. Unless you compare dates before February 28, 1900 to dates after February 28, 1900, this error does not affect your worksheets. However, dates are off by one day if you export data to a database.

When you select /Range Format Date, the **Date** menu appears. Five **Date** formats can format serial numbers to look like dates. Table 5.2 lists these formats. Long international and short international each support four possible formats. The defaults are common formats that are used in the United States. If you prefer a format other than the international **Date** formats, use /Worksheet Global Default Other International Date and select from formats **A** through **D**. Also, you can select /Worksheet **Global** and use the Global Settings dialog box to change international date formats. Press F2 (Edit) or click anywhere in the box; select Default Settings...; select International...; select **Date** format (if you are using the keyboard); and then select international date format **1**, **2**, **3** or **4**. End by pressing Enter or by clicking OK. After the Default Settings dialog box appears, select Update to make the change permanent. End by pressing Enter or clicking OK. Press Esc or the right mouse button to clear the Global Settings dialog box from the screen.

Table 5.2
Date Formats

Menu Choice	Format	Description	Example
1	(D1)	Day-Month-Year DD-MMM-YY	01-Jan-92
2	(D2)	Day-Month DD-MMM	01-Jan
3	(D3)	Month-Year MMM-YY	Jan-92
4	(D4)	Long International*	
A		MM/DD/YY	01/15/92
B		DD/MM/YY	15/01/92
C		DD.MM.YY	15.01.92
D		YY-MM-DD	92-01-15
5	(D5)	Short International*	
A		MM/DD	01/15
B		DD/MM	15/01
C		DD.MM	15.01
D		MM-DD	01-15

*Use the /Worksheet Global Default Other International Date command to select one of the international formats (**A**, **B**, **C**, or **D**) or use the Global Settings dialog box as described in the text.

(Dn) appears in the control panel of cells formatted with /**R**ange **F**ormat **D**ate. n represents the Date format selection (1 to 5) in the Format Date menu.

The following list shows several examples of Date format in cells with a column width of 9 on the 1-2-3 text display (the same results occur on the 1-2-3 graphics display for monospace fonts, such as 12-point Courier):

Typed entry	Cell format	Display result	Cell contents
15	(D4)	01/15/00	**15**
33604	(D4)	01/01/92	**33604**
33604.4538	(D4)	01/01/92	**33604.4538**
–33604	any date	**********	**–33604**

You also enter dates into a worksheet by using one of the date functions: @DATE, @DATEVALUE, or @NOW. These functions are explained in Chapter 6.

Time Formats

1-2-3 maintains times in a special format called *time fractions*. You can format these time fractions to look like a time of the day. When you enter a time function, 1-2-3 stores the time as a decimal fraction, from 0 to 1, that represents the fraction of the 24-hour clock. The time fraction for 3 a.m. is 0.125; the time fraction for noon is 0.5; and the time fraction for 6 p.m. is 0.75. You can ignore the actual fraction and have 1-2-3 display the fraction in a time format.

When you select /**Range** Format Date Time, the **Time** menu appears. 1-2-3 includes four **Time** formats that show fractions as times. Table 5.3 lists these formats. Long international and short international each support four possible formats. The default settings are those most common in the United States. If you prefer one of the international time formats, use /**Worksheet Global Default Other International Time** and select from the formats **A** to **D**, which represent the four choices. Alternately, you can select /**Worksheet Global** and use the Global Settings dialog box to change international time formats. Press F2 (Edit) or click anywhere in the box with the mouse; select Default Settings...; select International...; select **Time** format (if you are using the keyboard); and then select international time format **1**, **2**, **3**, or **4**. End by pressing Enter or clicking OK. When the Default Settings dialog box appears, select Update to make the change permanent. End by pressing Enter or clicking OK. Press Esc or the right mouse button to clear the Global Settings dialog box from the screen.

If the number is greater than 1, Time formats ignore the integer portion. The value **33604.75** with format D7 (Time 2 or Lotus standard short form) displays as 06:00 PM. Negative numbers are not translated into time and are displayed as asterisks.

(Dn) appears in the control panel of cells formatted with /**Range Format Date Time**. n represents the Time format selection (**6** to **9**). 1-2-3 identifies **Time** formats in a confusing way. If you select **Date Time 1**, 1-2-3 displays (D6) in the control panel, not (T1). **Date Time 2** displays (D7), **Date Time 3** displays (D8), and **Date Time 4** displays (D9).

The following listing shows several examples of **Time** format in cells that use a column width of 9 on the 1-2-3 text display (the same results occur on the 1-2-3 graphics display for monospace fonts, such as 12-point Courier):

Typed Entry	*Cell Format*	*Display Result*	*Cell Contents*
2	(D7)	12:00 AM	2
.25	(D7)	06:00 AM	0.25
−.25	(D7)	**********	−0.25

Table 5.3
Time Formats

Menu Choice	Format	Description	Example
1	(D6)	Hour:Minute:Second	06:23:57 PM
		HH:MM:SS AM/PM	
2	(D7)	Hour:Minute	06:23 PM
		HH:MM AM/PM	
3	(D8)	Long International*	
A		HH:MM:SS	18:23:57
B		HH.MM.SS	18.23.57
C		HH,MM,SS	18,23,57
D		HHhMMmSSs	18h23m57s
4	(D9)	Short International*	
A		HH:MM	18:23
B		HH.MM	18.23
C		HH,MM	18,23
D		HHhMMm	18h23m

*Use the /Worksheet Global Default Other International Time command to select one of the international formats (**A**, **B**, **C**, or **D**) or use the Global Settings dialog box as described in the text.

You also enter times into a worksheet by using one of the time functions: @TIME, @TIMEVALUE, or @NOW. These functions are explained in Chapter 6.

Text Format

Use the **Text** format to display in a cell numeric and string formulas instead of their current values. Formulas display differently depending on 1-2-3's operating mode—text or graphics. In text mode, if a formula displayed in Text format is too long for the column width, the formula is truncated, or shortened; unlike long labels, formulas do not display to the right across blank cells. In graphics mode, formulas do display across blank cells. In either mode, numbers formatted for **Text** display in the **General** format.

The entries in figure 5.20 are formatted as **Text**. The labels are unaffected. The numbers in B3..B5 display in **General** format. The formula in B7 displays in place of the current value of the formula.

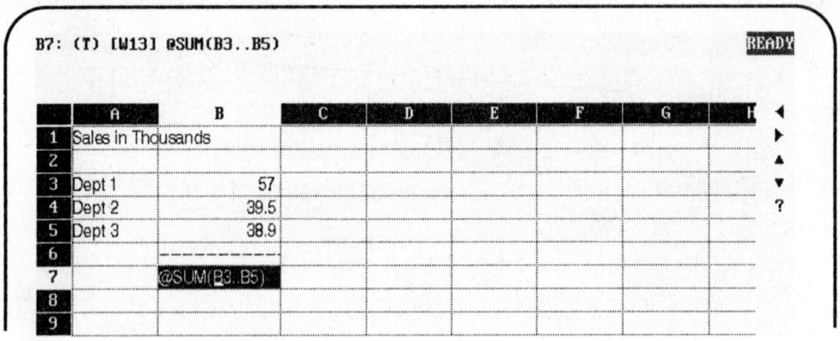

***Fig. 5.20.** A sample of Text format.*

Cue:
Use Text format to enter and debug complex formulas.

One use of the **Text** format is for criteria ranges with /**D**ata **Q**uery commands, which are covered in Chapter 12 (not needed as much with 1-2-3 Release 2.3 due to new, simplified criteria formulas). You also can use **T**ext format when you enter or debug complex formulas or when you want to see formulas with /**D**ata **T**able. You temporarily can change the format of a formula to **T**ext to see the formula in one cell as you build a similar formula in another cell. You may need to widen the column temporarily during this action.

(T) appears in the control panel for cells formatted with /**R**ange **F**ormat **T**ext.

Hidden Format

A cell formatted as **H**idden is displayed as blank, no matter what the cell contains. Use this format for intermediate calculations that you want to hide or to hide sensitive formulas. The contents of a hidden cell do not display in the control panel when you move the cell pointer to that cell, if the cell is protected and if global protection is enabled. In other cases, you can see the contents of the cell in the control panel. **H**idden format also is discussed in Chapter 4.

You cannot use **Hidden** format to completely hide data. If you can change the format or the protection status, you can see the contents of the cell. You can use /**Range** **Format** to change the format, and the contents of the cell become visible. You can change the protection status with /**Range** **Unprot**, and the contents of the cell become visible in the control panel.

Caution:
Don't rely on
Hidden formats to
hide sensitive
information.

The worksheet in figure 5.21 has global protection enabled. /**Range** **Prot** and /**Range** **Format** **Hidden** were used on Cell A1. The range C1..C5 is unprotected. The formula in C1 is +A1. This simple formula shows the value of the hidden cell. To determine the formula in A1, you need a macro. The CONTENTS command in cell C3 places the contents of A1 into C5 in **Text** format. See Chapter 14 for more about CONTENTS.

```
A1: (H) PR                                                    READY
      A       B            C          D      E      F     ◄
 1    _                  409.7721                        ►
 2                                                       ▲
 3           \A     {CONTENTS C5,A1,25,117)               ▼
 4                                                        ?
 5                  @SUM(M1..M15)*1.47469
 6
 7
 8
 9
```

Fig. 5.21. *The appearance of the worksheet changed by use of Hidden format.*

(H) appears in the control panel of cells formatted with /**Range** **Format** **Hidden**.

International Formats

You can change some **Date** and **Time** formats, as well as the characters 1-2-3 uses for currency, the decimal point, and the thousands separator. Because different countries use different formatting standards, these selections are called international formatting options. If you work with U.S. dollars in the United States, you can stay with the defaults and ignore these options. Use the /**Worksheet** **Global** **Default** **Other** **International** command to access the menu and change the defaults as shown:

Punctuation Currency Date Time Negative Quit

Then use /**Worksheet** **Global** **Default** **Update** to make the change permanent.

Select **Date** and **Time** to change the international **Date** and **Time** formats. Tables 5.2 and 5.3 list the format options. Select **Currency** to change the currency symbol from the dollar sign ($) to another symbol and specify whether the symbol is a prefix or suffix. You can use multiple characters and special Lotus International Character Set (LICS) characters. (For more on LICS characters, see Chapter 6 and Appendix C.)

Select **Punctuation** to change the characters used as a decimal point and as the thousands separator instead of a comma. Eight combinations are available. Select **Negative** to specify the way to show negative numbers in **Comma** and **Currency** formats. The default is the **Parenthesis** setting, which you can change to a minus sign.

If you do not want to change international formatting options through the 1-2-3 menus, you can change the options with the dialog boxes. When you select /Worksheet Global, the Global Settings dialog box appears. Press F2 (Edit) or click anywhere in the box; select `Default Settings...`; select `International...`; and the Default International Settings dialog box appears. Select **Punctuation**, **Currency**, **Negative**, **Date** format, or **Time** format to change settings. To exit from the dialog box press Enter or click OK. To make the settings permanent, select `Update` from the Default Settings dialog box. To clear the Global Settings dialog box, press Enter and then press Esc or click `OK` and then click the right mouse button.

Changing Label Prefixes

Most of the formats on the 1-2-3 menu apply to numeric data. Nearly all numeric data formats have one common denominator; the numbers are right-aligned in the cell. With labels or text entries, however, you can align the text in different ways. Label alignment is based on the label prefix, as shown in the following listing:

Prefix	Alignment
'	Left
"	Right
^	Center
\	Repeating
|	Nonprinting

Labels and label prefixes are covered in Chapter 3. If you want a repeating or a nonprinting label, you must type the label prefix. If you type a label with another prefix and you then want to change the alignment to repeating or nonprinting, you must edit the cell, delete the old prefix, and type the new prefix.

You can, however, change the label alignment of a cell or range to left, right, or center with the /Range Label or the :Text Align command (see Chapter 9). You also can change the default label prefix that 1-2-3 inserts when you enter a label and do not type a prefix.

When you enter a label without a label prefix, 1-2-3 automatically enters the default label prefix. With a new worksheet file, the default is left-aligned. You can change this default by using /Worksheet Global Label-Prefix, or by using /Worksheet Global and editing Labels in the Global Settings dialog box. Changing the default does not effect existing labels. To change the label prefix of existing labels, use /Range Label. Select Left, Right, or Center and then specify the range. These steps are usually faster than typing individual label prefixes as you enter labels.

Reminder:
When you enter a label without a label prefix, 1-2-3 enters the default label prefix.

Figure 5.22 shows left-aligned column headings that do not align with the data. Figure 5.23 shows the headings after /Range Label Right is selected. Right-alignment starts one position from the extreme right. Right-aligned labels match the alignment of numeric data.

```
B1: [W10] 'BUDGET                                                    READY

        A            B        C       D       E       F       G      ◄
  1                 BUDGET    JAN     FEB     MAR     APR     MAY     ►
  2     ----------- --------- ------- ------- ------- ------- ------- ▲
  3                 1,062,497  38,444  34,943  84,763  96,858 103,208 ▼
  4  Department 1   1,306,752  37,815  33,277  89,196 102,014 114,444 ?
  5  Department 2   1,296,114  40,256  30,344  87,583  99,494 100,902
  6  Department 3   1,022,329  38,656  31,098  82,914  81,070  82,164
  7  Department 4   1,152,144  38,890  29,088  81,515  84,552  94,339
  8  Department 5     817,511  35,591  26,225  74,494  71,451  77,039
  9  Department 6     824,655  36,989  24,642  70,194  69,684  70,397
 10  Department 7     977,396  33,611  22,310  70,436  80,645  85,278
 11  Department 8     842,012  33,298  21,290  67,542  65,139  63,960
 12  Department 9   1,099,933  31,109  22,728  73,775  80,675  87,451
 13  Department 10  1,057,141  33,233  20,904  72,935  76,787  76,582
 14  Department 11    825,489  30,201  19,384  68,836  66,229  64,752
 15  Department 12  1,004,012  39,483  26,972  88,458  86,954  85,819
 16  Department 13  1,128,380  39,452  27,316  77,631  84,475  84,958
 17  Department 14    927,963  40,206  30,824  83,885  85,593  83,618
 18  Department 15  1,336,598  39,053  27,031  79,099  88,476  96,329
 19  Department 16  1,293,143  36,266  31,399  83,595  96,031 102,120
 20  Department 17   924074   41130   30204   76311   76666   78599
25-Feb-91  03:29 AM      UNDO
```

Fig. 5.22. Left-aligned column headings.

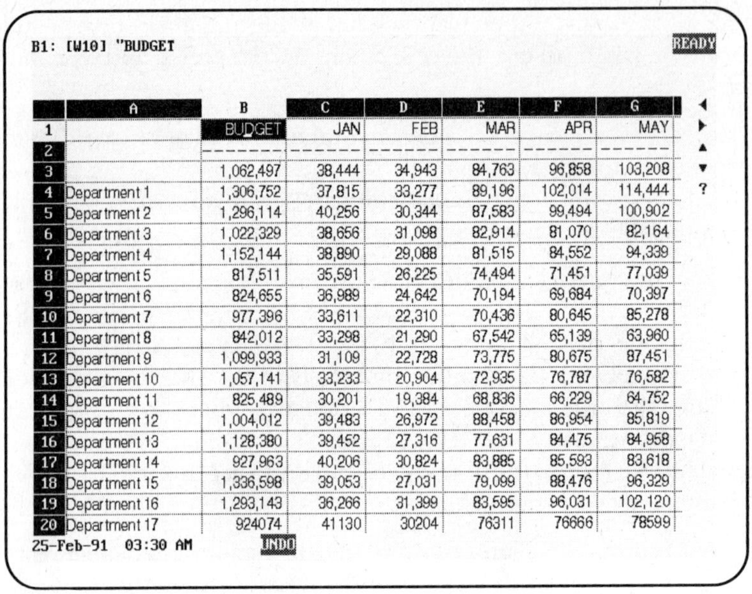

Fig. 5.23. *The column headings, right-aligned with the /Range Label Right command.*

Justifying Text

Occasionally, you want to include in a worksheet several lines, or even a paragraph, that explain a table, graph, or report. 1-2-3 includes word-wrap features that are similar to a word processor if you use the **:Text Edit** command from the Wysiwyg menu (see Chapter 9). Otherwise, everything you type (up to 240 characters) goes into one cell until you press Enter or click the left mouse button. You can type one line of text into each cell, but entering and editing paragraphs in this way is slow and imprecise. The result may appear similar to the ragged text in figure 5.24, and some of the text can run off the screen.

You can justify labels by using the **/Range Justify** command from the 1-2-3 menu; you also can use the **:Text Reformat** command (the preferred command for proportional fonts, such as Swiss and Dutch) from the Wysiwyg menu (see Chapter 9). You can type text into one cell or multiple cells down a column and use **/Range Justify** to arrange labels, as in figure 5.25. At the Enter justify range: prompt, highlight the rows that contain the labels and include additional rows (if needed) to make room for expansion of the labels area. Highlight across the columns to show how wide you want each label. When you press Enter or click the left mouse button, 1-2-3 rearranges the text to fit the area you highlighted (see fig. 5.25).

Labels are wrapped only at spaces. Where 1-2-3 breaks a label, the space is eliminated. Where 1-2-3 combines all or parts of two labels into one label, a space is added.

```
A1: [W16] '1-2-3 provides several ways to incorporate long notes or paragra READY

        A           B       C       D       E       F       G      ◄
 1  1-2-3 provides several ways to incorporate long notes or paragraphs   ►
 2  into a worksheet. This is an example of a long note                   ▲
 3  in a series of long labels in a single column. You do not get word wrap ▼
 4  like you do with a word processor, so you have to guess               ?
 5  about how long each label is and then press Enter. This method does work
 6  it is difficult to line up all the lines. Another way is to type the lab
 7  one or more cells and then use /Range Justify to justify the text. A mor
 8  way is to use :Text Edit from the WYSIWYG menu. This
 9  method does give you word wrap--just like a word processor.
10
11
12
13
14                BUDGET    JAN     FEB     MAR     APR     MAY
15              ---------  ------  ------  ------  ------  ------
16  Department 1 1,062,497  38,444  34,943  84,763  96,858 103,208
17  Department 2 1,306,752  37,815  33,277  89,196 102,014 114,444
18  Department 3 1,296,114  40,256  30,344  87,583  99,494 100,902
19  Department 4 1,022,329  38,656  31,098  82,914  81,070  82,164
20  Department 5 1,152,144  38,890  29,088  81,515  84,552  94,339
25-Feb-91  05:05 AM      UNDO
```

Fig. 5.24. A column of long labels for a note is difficult to line up correctly.

```
A1: [W16] '1-2-3 provides several ways to incorporate long notes or      READY

        A           B       C       D       E       F       G      ◄
 1  1-2-3 provides several ways to incorporate long notes or              ►
 2  paragraphs into a worksheet. This is an example of a long             ▲
 3  note in a series of long labels in a single column. You do            ▼
 4  not get word wrap with this method like you do with a word            ?
 5  processor, so you have to guess about how long each label is
 6  and then press Enter. This method does work, but it is
 7  difficult to line up all the lines. Another way is to type
 8  the label into one or more cells and then use /Range Justify
 9  to justify the text. A more elegant way is to use :Text Edit
10  from the WYSIWYG menu. This method does give you word
11  wrap--just like a word processor.
12
13
14                BUDGET    JAN     FEB     MAR     APR     MAY
15              ---------  ------  ------  ------  ------  ------
16  Department 1 1,062,497  38,444  34,943  84,763  96,858 103,208
17  Department 2 1,306,752  37,815  33,277  89,196 102,014 114,444
18  Department 3 1,296,114  40,256  30,344  87,583  99,494 100,902
19  Department 4 1,022,329  38,656  31,098  82,914  81,070  82,164
20  Department 5 1,152,144  38,890  29,088  81,515  84,552  94,339
25-Feb-91  05:05 AM      UNDO
```

Fig. 5.25. A series of long labels, after using the /Range Justify command.

If you add text in the middle of existing text, use **/Range Justify** again to rejustify the text. If you specify a one-row range, 1-2-3 justifies the entire "paragraph." Figure 5.26 shows the data in figure 5.25 after text is added and **/Range Justify** is selected for the range A1..F1. This practice, however, is very dangerous. 1-2-3 justifies the labels and uses rows as needed but moves all data in Column A down to make room. If fewer rows are needed, 1-2-3 moves up all data in Column A. In figure 5.26, the department numbers no longer align with each department's data.

```
A1: [W16] '1-2-3 provides several ways to incorporate long notes or          READY

          A            B       C       D       E       F       G
 1  1-2-3 provides several ways to incorporate long notes or
 2  paragraphs into a worksheet. This is an example of a long
 3  note in a series of long labels in a single column. You do
 4  not get word wrap with this method like you do with a word
 5  processor, so you have to guess about how long each label is
 6  and then press Enter. This method does work, but it is
 7  difficult to line up all the lines. Another way is to type
 8  the label into one or more cells and then use /Range Justify
 9  to justify the text. But you must be careful when you add
10  text and rejustify the paragraph. A more elegant way is to
11  use :Text Edit from the WYSIWYG menu. This method does give
12  you word wrap--just like a word processor.
13
14                   BUDGET     JAN     FEB     MAR     APR     MAY
15                 ---------  ------  ------  ------  ------  ------
16                 1,062,497  38,444  34,943  84,763  96,858 103,208
17  Department 1   1,306,752  37,815  33,277  89,196 102,014 114,444
18  Department 2   1,296,114  40,256  30,344  87,583  99,494 100,902
19  Department 3   1,022,329  38,656  31,098  82,914  81,070  82,164
20  Department 4   1,152,144  38,890  29,088  81,515  84,552  94,339
25-Feb-91  05:07 AM      UNDO
```

Fig. 5.26. *A one-row /Range Justify that pushes down the data below the paragraph.*

You cannot justify more than one column of labels at a time. When 1-2-3 reaches a blank or numeric cell in the first column, the justification process stops. All labels must be in the first column of the highlighted range. In figure 5.26, all the labels are in column A.

To summarize, follow these steps to justify labels with **/Range Justify**:

1. Move the cell pointer to the first cell in the range of text by using the cursor keys or mouse.

2. Select **/Range Justify**.

3. Highlight the rows that contain labels by using the direction keys or the mouse; allow enough extra rows for the labels to expand into when the labels are justified.

4. Again, by using the direction keys or mouse, highlight across the number of columns to show how wide each label can be. In figure 5.26, the text spans Columns A through F.

5. Press Enter or the left mouse button to complete the justification.

You can perform Steps 3 and 4 in either order.

Suppressing the Display of Zeros

You can use the /Worksheet Global Zero command to change the display of cells that contain the number zero or formulas that evaluate to zero. To hide the zeros completely, use /Worksheet Global Zero Yes. The zero cells appear to be blank.

This feature is useful with worksheets in which zeros represent missing or meaningless information. Making these cells appear blank often improves the appearance of the worksheet. However, blank cells also can cause confusion if you or other users are unsure whether the cell is blank because you forgot to enter the data.

You also can show a label of your choice instead of the zero or blank. Use /Worksheet Global Zero Label and type the label you want to appear in place of the zero. Common labels are None, Zero, and NA (not available). Figure 5.27 shows a worksheet with the /Worksheet Global Zero Label set to None.

Cue:
You can type a label you want to display instead of zero.

Use /Worksheet Global Zero No to cancel the option and display zeros as zeros. You also can use the Global Settings dialog box to change the way the number zero appears in the worksheet. Select /Worksheet Global to see the Global Settings dialog box. Press F2 (Edit) or click on the box with the left mouse button. Select Zero display (if you are using the keyboard) and then select Zeros, Blanks, or Labels. If you select Labels, type the text (**None**, **NA**, and so on) to replace the number zero in the worksheet. End by pressing Enter or clicking OK. Press Esc or click the right mouse button to clear the Global Settings dialog box from the screen.

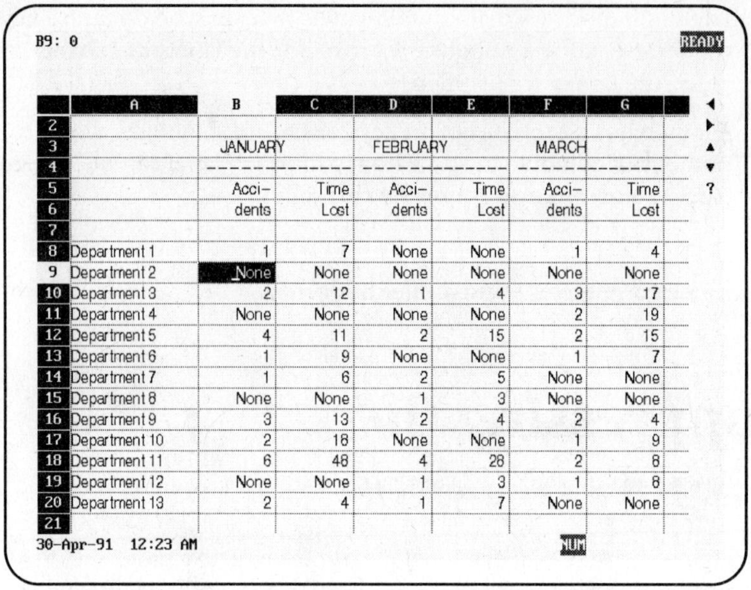

B9: 0 READY

	A	B	C	D	E	F	G
2							
3		JANUARY		FEBRUARY		MARCH	
4		-------	-------	-------	-------	-------	-------
5		Acci-	Time	Acci-	Time	Acci-	Time
6		dents	Lost	dents	Lost	dents	Lost
7							
8	Department 1	1	7	None	None	1	4
9	Department 2	None	None	None	None	None	None
10	Department 3	2	12	1	4	3	17
11	Department 4	None	None	None	None	2	19
12	Department 5	4	11	2	15	2	15
13	Department 6	1	9	None	None	1	7
14	Department 7	1	6	2	5	None	None
15	Department 8	None	None	1	3	None	None
16	Department 9	3	13	2	4	2	4
17	Department 10	2	18	None	None	1	9
18	Department 11	6	48	4	28	2	8
19	Department 12	None	None	1	3	1	8
20	Department 13	2	4	1	7	None	None
21							

30-Apr-91 12:23 AM NUM

Fig. 5.27. A worksheet with zero labels set to display as `None`.

Understanding the Wysiwyg :Format Commands

Cue:
:Format commands affect the way data is presented.

You change the format of a cell or range of cells with the **:Format** command on the Wysiwyg menu. The following list shows the commands found on the **:Format** menu:

Font **B**old **I**talics **U**nderline **C**olor **L**ines **S**hade **R**eset **Q**uit

These format commands affect how data is presented on the display and on printed reports. If you choose **B**old or **I**talics, you see two more choices: **S**et and **C**lear. Choose **S**et to add bold or italic to a range. When prompted for a range to format, specify the range and press Enter or click the left mouse button. Choose **C**lear to remove a format from a range. When prompted for a range to clear, specify the range and press Enter or click the left mouse button. The **F**ont, **U**nderline, **C**olor, **L**ines, and **S**hade formats (see Chapter 9) have additional menus. The **R**eset command removes all formatting from a range and restores the default font.

The name or an abbreviation of the format appears in the control panel when the current cell is formatted. One cell can contain several formats. In figure 5.28, `{Bold Italics U1}` displayed in the control panel indicates that cell A1 is formatted as Bold, Italics, and (single) Underline. If the cell has no format, no format indicator appears in the control panel. When you start a new file, no cells hold a format. When a cell has no format, the cell uses the default font.

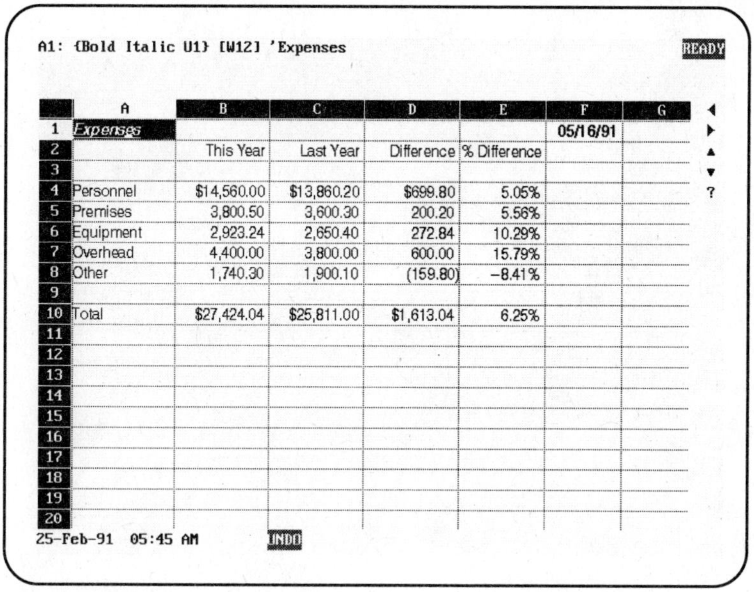

Fig. 5.28. A Wysiwyg format displayed in the control panel.

Chapter 9 describes the Wysiwyg formatting commands in detail.

Summary

In this chapter, you learned how to display numeric data in a variety of different formats and options, to display formulas as text, and to hide the contents of cells. You learned how to enter and format dates and times and how to change the International Date and Time formats. You learned how to change label alignment and justify blocks of text.

Additionally, you learned about the variety of formats available through the Wysiwyg menu that enhance the appearance of your worksheet data. You now can build and format worksheets and reports because you have the basic skills to use 1-2-3 constructively. The next chapter extends your skills to perform data analysis. Chapter 6 covers the extensive library of functions you can use to manipulate data beyond simple formulas and opens up the vast analytical power of 1-2-3.

Using Functions in
the Worksheet

1-2-3 provides a variety of ready-made formulas that you can use easily. These built-in functions enable you to take advantage of 1-2-3's analytical capability. You can use functions alone, in your own formulas, or in macros to calculate results and solve problems. This chapter describes the basic steps for using 1-2-3 functions and provides discussions and examples of specific functions.

This chapter presents you with many opportunities to use 1-2-3 functions, alone and in formulas. If you experience any difficulties, such as errors or unexpected answers, you may want to put the Auditor add-in to work. When you attach and invoke the Auditor add-in, you have a tool for tracking down errors that occur in formulas in a 1-2-3 worksheet.

The Auditor can do several things: track down circular references (as described in Chapter 5); execute a recalc-trace, which shows you the order in which 1-2-3 recalculates formulas in the worksheet; show you the cells that contain the data on which a particular formula depends; and show you the formulas that depend on data in a particular cell. For more information on the Auditor, as well as specific examples, see Appendix B.

1-2-3 provides functions in the following categories:

- Mathematical
- Date and Time
- Financial and Accounting
- Statistical
- Database
- Logical
- String
- Special

The six mathematical functions, three logarithmic functions, and eight trigonometric functions are useful in engineering and scientific applications. These functions also are convenient tools you can use to perform a variety of standard arithmetic operations, such as rounding values and calculating square roots.

The 11 date and time functions enable you to convert dates, such as November 26, 1991, and times, such as 6:00 p.m., to serial numbers. You can then use the serial numbers to perform date and time arithmetic. These functions are valuable tools to use when dates and times affect calculations and logic in your worksheets.

The 12 financial and accounting functions enable you to perform a variety of business-related calculations. These calculations include discounting cash flows, calculating depreciation, and analyzing the investment returns. This set of functions enables you to perform investment analysis, accounting functions, or depreciation calculations.

A set of seven statistical and seven database statistical functions enables you to perform all the standard statistical calculations on data in your worksheet or in a 1-2-3 database. You can find minimum and maximum values, calculate averages, and compute standard deviations and variances. In some cases, the database statistical functions are considered a separate function type; in practice, however, they are used as specialized versions of the statistical functions that apply only to 1-2-3 databases.

By using the nine logical functions, you can add standard Boolean logic to your worksheet and use the logic alone or with other worksheet formulas. Each of the logical functions enables you to test whether a condition—one that you have defined or one of 1-2-3's predefined conditions—is true or false. These logical tests are important for making functions that make decisions; the function or its result acts differently and depends on another condition in your worksheet.

The 19 string functions manipulate text. You can use string functions to repeat text characters—a handy trick for creating worksheet and row boundaries and visual borders—to convert letters in a string to upper- or lowercase, to change strings into numbers, and to change numbers into strings. String functions also can be used when you convert data for other programs, such as word processor mailing lists.

1-2-3's 12 special functions provide tools that deal with the worksheet itself. One special function, for example, returns information about specific cells. Other special functions count the number of rows or columns in a range.

Learning How To Enter a 1-2-3 Function

To enter a 1-2-3 function into a worksheet, follow these four steps:

1. Type the @ sign to tell 1-2-3 that you want to enter a function.

2. Type the function name.

3. Type within parentheses any information, or arguments, that the function needs.

4. Press Enter.

@AVG is a sample function. If you type the function **@AVG(1,2,3)**, 1-2-3 returns the calculated result 2, which is the average of the three numbers 1, 2, and 3.

All functions begin with and are identified by the @ character. By typing @, you tell 1-2-3 you are entering a function.

Reminder:
All functions
begin with @.

The next step is entering the name of the function. 1-2-3 helps you remember the name by using short abbreviations. These abbreviations assist you in identifying and remembering those functions you use most often. The function for calculating an average, a statistical function, is @AVG; the function for calculating the internal rate of return, a financial function, is @IRR; and the function for rounding numbers, a mathematical function, is @ROUND.

After typing @ and the function name, enter any of the arguments, or inputs, the function needs to perform its calculations. You place the arguments inside parentheses that immediately follow the function's name. If the function has multiple arguments, you separate them with commas or semicolons.

Entering functions is a straightforward procedure. Suppose, for example, that you want to calculate the average monthly revenue from four products. To calculate the result, type the following:

@AVG(1000,5000,6000,8000)

1-2-3 returns 5000, which is the average of the numbers entered as arguments. Notice that the function begins with the @ character, followed by the function name **AVG**, and that the function's arguments are included inside parentheses and separated by commas.

In the preceding example, the arguments use actual numeric values. You also can use cell addresses and range names as arguments. If you store the monthly revenue values of these products or the formulas that produce these revenue values in worksheet cells B1, B2, B3, and B4, for example, you can type the following function:

@AVG(B1,B2,B3,B4)

Alternatively, if you give the four cells that contain the revenue values or formulas each product's name or product number, you can type the following function:

@AVG(PART12,PART14,PART21,PART22)

Reminder:
Not all functions require arguments.

Some functions do not require arguments, or inputs; therefore, you do not use parentheses. The mathematical function, @PI, for example, returns π; and the mathematical function, @RAND, produces a random number.

Using Mathematical Functions

1-2-3 provides 17 mathematical functions that enable you to perform most common and some specialized mathematical operations. The operations you can perform include general, logarithmic, and trigonometric calculations.

General Mathematical Functions

1-2-3 enables six general mathematical functions: @ABS, @INT, @MOD, @ROUND, @RAND, and @SQRT. Table 6.1 summarizes these functions.

Table 6.1
General Mathematical Functions

Function	Description
@ABS(*number* or *cell_reference*)	Computes the absolute value of the argument
@INT(*number* or *cell_reference*)	Computes the integer portions of a specified number
@MOD(*number,divisor*)	Computes the remainder, or modulus, of a division operation
@ROUND(*number* or *cell reference,precision*)	Rounds a number to a specified precision
@RAND	Generates a random number
@SQRT(*number* or *cell_reference*)	Computes the square root of a number

@ABS—Computing Absolute Value

The @ABS function calculates the absolute value of a number. Use the following format for this function:

> @ABS(*number* or *cell_reference*)

The @ABS function has one argument, which can be a numeric value or a cell reference to a numeric value. The result of @ABS is the positive value of its argument. @ABS converts a negative value into its equivalent positive value. @ABS has no effect on positive values.

The @ABS function is useful when you want a calculation that produces a negative value in one area of your worksheet to produce a positive value in

Reminder:
The @ABS function calculates the absolute value of a number.

another area. Figure 6.1 shows how the @ABS function can be used for this purpose. Cell B8 contains the formula `@ABS(B15)`; this formula returns to cell B8 the absolute value of the value contained in cell B15. Although B15 contains `-33`, the formula in B8 returns `33`. The other cells in row 8 contain similar formulas.

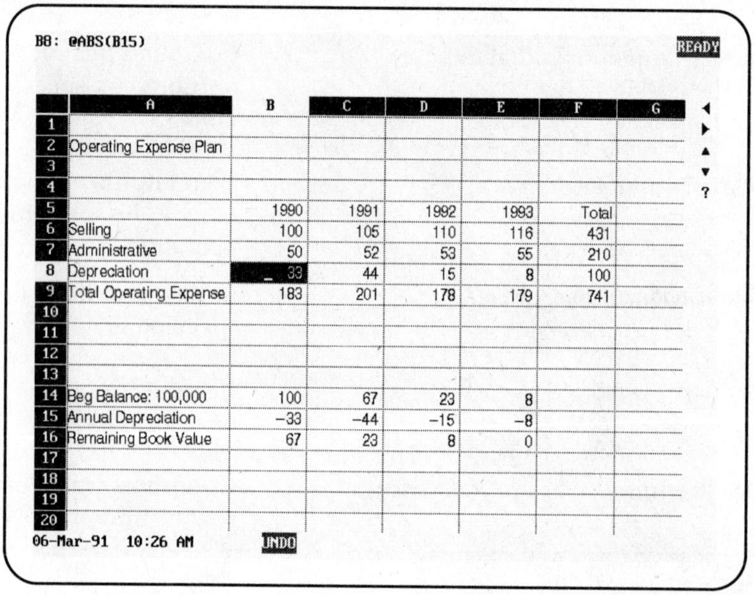

B8: @ABS(B15) READY

	A	B	C	D	E	F	G
1							
2	Operating Expense Plan						
3							
4							
5		1990	1991	1992	1993	Total	
6	Selling	100	105	110	116	431	
7	Administrative	50	52	53	55	210	
8	Depreciation	33	44	15	8	100	
9	Total Operating Expense	183	201	178	179	741	
10							
11							
12							
13							
14	Beg Balance: 100,000	100	67	23	8		
15	Annual Depreciation	-33	-44	-15	-8		
16	Remaining Book Value	67	23	8	0		
17							
18							
19							
20							

06-Mar-91 10:26 AM UNDO

***Fig. 6.1.** The @ABS function used to convert a negative number to its positive equivalent.*

You also can use @ABS in data-entry macros to ensure that an entered number results in a positive or negative number no matter which value was typed. Using @ABS also is essential in trigonometric calculations.

@INT—Computing the Integer

The @INT function converts a decimal number into an integer, or whole number. @INT creates an integer by truncating, or removing, the decimal portion of a number. @INT uses the following format:

> @INT(***number*** or *cell_reference*)

@INT has one argument, which can be a numeric value or a cell reference to a numeric value. The result of applying @INT to the values 3.1, 4.5, and 5.9 yields integer values of 3, 4, and 5, respectively.

@INT is useful for computations in which the decimal portion of a number is irrelevant or insignificant. Suppose, for example, that you have $1,000 to invest in XYZ company and that shares of XYZ sell for $17 each. You divide 1,000 by 17 to compute the total number that can be purchased: 58 shares. Because you cannot purchase a fractional share, you can use @INT to truncate the decimal portion (see fig. 6.2).

```
E6:  (G) @INT(E3/E4)                                            READY

        A       B       C       D       E       F       G        ◄
  1                                                              ►
  2                                                              ▲
  3   Available funds                    $1,000                  ▼
  4   Price per share                      $17                   ?
  5                                                 Function/formula
  6   Number of stocks purchased             58    @INT(E3/E4)
  7   Total purchase price                 $986    +E4*E6
  8
  9   Remaining funds by subtraction        $14    +E3-E7
 10   Remaining funds using @MOD            $14    @MOD(E3,E4)
 11
 12
 13
 14
 15
 16
 17
 18
 19
 20
 01-May-91  02:12 AM                               NUM
```

Fig. 6.2. The @INT function used to calculate the number of shares that can be purchased.

Remember the difference between the @ROUND and @INT functions: @ROUND with a positive precision argument rounds decimal numbers to the next integer; @INT removes the decimal portion and leaves only the integer.

@MOD—Finding the Modulus or Remainder

The @MOD function computes the remainder, or modulus, that results when one number is divided by another. @MOD uses two arguments that can be numeric values or cell references. The @MOD function uses the following syntax:

@MOD(*number,divisor*)

The *number* determines the positive or negative sign of the remainder, or modulus. The *divisor* cannot be zero, or @MOD returns ERR.

You can use the @INT function to calculate the number of shares of XYZ as shown in figure 6.2. Use @MOD, also shown in figure 6.2, to determine the remainder after the purchase.

@ROUND—Rounding Numbers

The @ROUND function rounds values to a precision you specify. The function uses two arguments: the value you want to round and the precision you want to use in the rounding. @ROUND uses the following format:

@ROUND(*number* or *cell_reference,precision*)

The *precision* argument determines the number of decimal places and can be a numeric value between –15 and +15. You use positive precision values to specify places to the right of the decimal place and negative values to specify places to the left of the decimal place. A precision value of 0 rounds decimal values to the nearest integer. Figure 6.3 shows how @ROUND is used to round results before totaling them.

Cue:
Round up to the nearest integer by adding 0.5 to the number you need to round.

The @ROUND function rounds a number according to the following standard rule: If the number is less than 0.5, it is rounded down to 0; if the number is 0.5 or more, it is rounded up to 1. The @ROUND function is useful for rounding a value being used inside other formulas or functions, such as @AVG or @SUM. If you need to round up to the nearest integer, add 0.5 to the number you want to round.

> **Note:** The @ROUND function and the /Range Format command perform differently. @ROUND changes the contents of a cell; /Range Format alters how the cell's contents are displayed.

Caution:
The formatted number you see may not be the number used in calculations.

In 1-2-3, the formatted number you see on-screen or on a printed report may not be the number used in calculations. This difference can cause errors in thousands of dollars in worksheets that calculate mortgage tables. To prevent errors, use @ROUND to round formula results or the numbers used in your formulas so that the calculated numbers are the same as those displayed.

```
D4: [W10] @ROUND(B4,C4)                                              READY

        A       B       C       D       E       F           G    ◄
  1                                                               ►
  2                                                               ▲
  3            Value  Precision  Result        Function          ▼
  4           123.456      2    123.46         @ROUND(B4,C4)      ?
  5           123.456      1    123.5          @ROUND(B5,C5)
  6           123.456      0    123            @ROUND(B6,C6)
  7           123.456     -1    120            @ROUND(B7,C7)
  8           123.456     -2    100            @ROUND(B8,C8)
  9           123.456     -3    0              @ROUND(B9,C9)
 10
 11   Use @ROUND to round values before totalling:
 12
 13
 14            Price   Percent Tax Amount
 15           $45.67    6.5%    $2.97         @ROUND(B15*C15,2)
 16           $43.89    6.5%    $2.95         @ROUND(B16*C16,2)
 17           $12.02    6.5%    $0.78         @ROUND(B17*C17,2)
 18                   Total Tax $6.60
 19
 20
06-Mar-91  11:01 AM      UNDO
```

Fig. 6.3. The @ROUND function used to round values.

@RAND—Producing Random Numbers

You use the @RAND function to generate random numbers. The function requires no arguments and uses the following syntax:

@RAND

@RAND returns a randomly generated number between 0 and 1 to a precision of 17 decimal places. If you want a random number greater than 1, multiply the @RAND function by the maximum random number you want. If you want a random number in a range of numbers, use a formula similar to the following:

+10+@RAND*20

Reminder:
Use @RAND for modeling problems that involve random occurrences.

In the preceding example, the random numbers generated will be between 10 and 30. Enclose random number calculations in an @INT function if you need random integers. New random numbers are generated each time you recalculate. To see the results from new random numbers, press Calc (F9).

@SQRT—Calculating the Square Root

The @SQRT function calculates the square root of a positive number. The function uses one argument: the number whose square root you want to find. @SQRT uses the following format:

@SQRT(*value* or *cell_reference*)

The value must be a nonnegative numeric value or a cell reference to such a value. If @SQRT is a negative value, then the function returns ERR. Figure 6.4 contains examples of the @SQRT function. The E6 cell shows how the @ABS function can change a negative number into a positive one before @SQRT finds the square root.

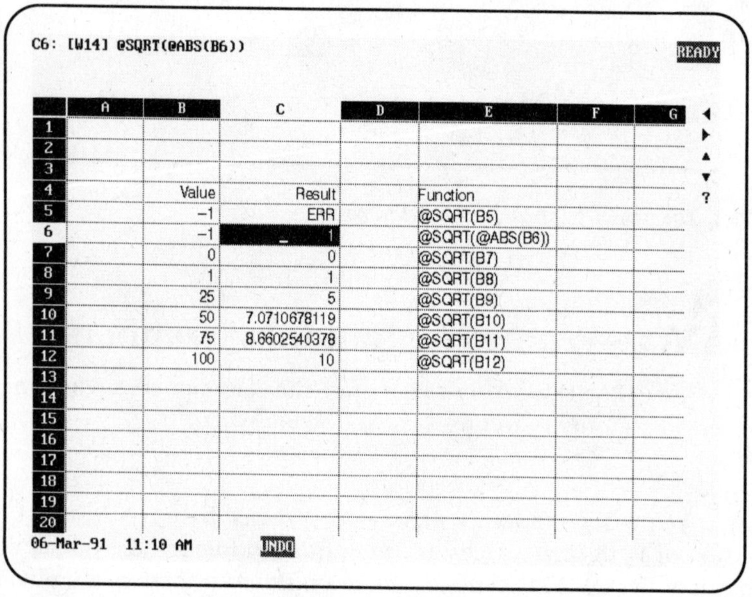

Fig. 6.4. The @SQRT function used to square numbers.

Logarithmic Functions

1-2-3 has three logarithmic functions: @LOG, @EXP, and @LN. Each function has one argument, which can be a numeric value or a cell reference to a numeric value. Figure 6.5 shows examples of @LOG, @EXP, and @LN. Table 6.2 lists the functions, their arguments, and the operations they perform.

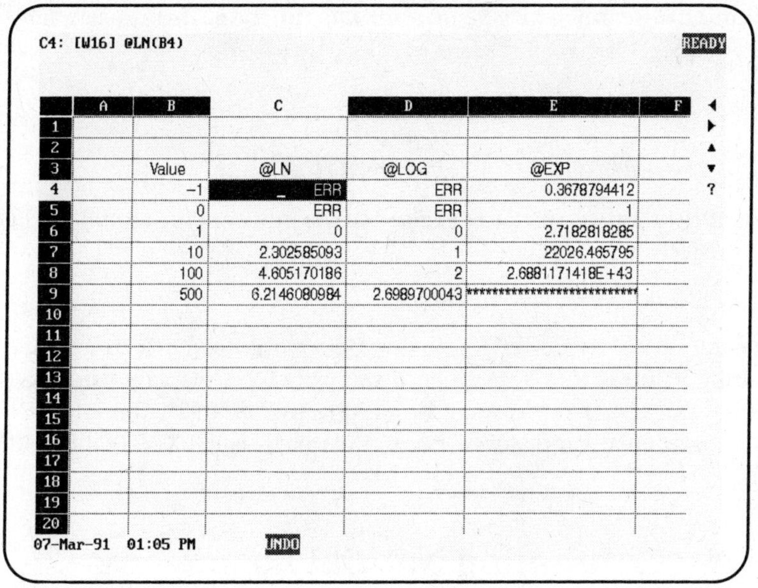

```
C4: [W16] @LN(B4)                                              READY

      A       B         C          D              E          F   ◄
 1                                                               ►
 2                                                               ▲
 3            Value     @LN        @LOG           @EXP           ▼
 4            -1        _   ERR    ERR            0.3678794412   ?
 5            0         ERR        ERR            1
 6            1         0          0              2.7182818285
 7            10        2.302585093 1             22026.465795
 8            100       4.605170186 2             2.6881171418E+43
 9            500       6.2146080984 2.6989700043 ***************************
10
11
12
13
14
15
16
17
18
19
20
07-Mar-91  01:05 PM        UNDO
```

Fig. 6.5. *Examples of the logarithmic functions @LN, @LOG, and @EXP.*

Table 6.2
Logarithmic Functions

Function	Description
@LOG(*number* or *cell_reference*)	Calculates the common, or base 10, logarithm of a specified number
@EXP(*number* or *cell_reference*)	Computes the number *e* raised to the power of the argument
@LN(*number* or *cell_reference*)	Calculates the natural logarithm of a specified number

@LOG—Computing Logarithms

The @LOG function computes the base 10 logarithm. @LOG uses the following format:

@LOG(*value* or *cell_reference*)

You cannot use a negative value with this function. If you use a negative value with @LOG, 1-2-3 returns ERR.

@EXP—Finding Powers of *e*

The @EXP function calculates *e* raised to the power of the argument. @EXP uses the following format:

@EXP(*value* or *cell_reference*)

You can quickly create very large numbers with the @EXP function. If the resulting value is too large to be displayed, 1-2-3 displays asterisks. The largest value 1-2-3 can display is @EXP(230.2585092); the largest value 1-2-3 can calculate and store—but not display—is @EXP(709.08953857).

@LN—Computing Natural Logarithms

The @LN function computes the natural, or base *e*, logarithm. @LN uses the following format:

@LN(*value* or *cell_reference*)

If you use a negative argument with @LN, 1-2-3 returns ERR.

Trigonometric Functions

1-2-3 provides eight trigonometric functions for engineering and scientific applications. Table 6.3 lists the functions, their arguments, and the operations they perform.

@PI—Computing Pi

The @PI function results in the value of π. The function uses no arguments. Its syntax is simply @PI.

Reminder:
@PI will return the value 3.141592653589794.

@PI returns the value 3.141592653589794 when formatted as Fixed with 15 decimal places (the maximum allowed in Release 2.3). Use @PI to calculate the area of circles and the volume of spheres. The @PI function also is needed to convert angle measurements in degrees to angle measurements in radians.

Table 6.3
Trigonometric Functions

Function	Description
@PI	Calculates the value of π
@COS(*angle*)	Calculates the cosine, given an angle in radians
@SIN(*angle*)	Calculates the sine, given an angle in radians
@TAN(*angle*)	Calculates the tangent, given an angle in radians
@ACOS(*angle*)	Calculates the arccosine, given an angle in radians
@ASIN(*angle*)	Calculates the arcsine, given an angle in radians
@ATAN(*angle*)	Calculates the arctangent, given an angle in radians
@ATAN2(*number1,number2*)	Calculates the four-quadrant arctangent

@COS, @SIN, and @TAN—Computing Trigonometric Functions

The @COS, @SIN, and @TAN functions calculate the cosine, sine, and tangent, respectively, for an angle. Each function uses one argument: an angle measured in radians. Use the following formats for the functions:

@COS(*angle*)

@SIN(*angle*)

@TAN(*angle*)

You must convert angle measurements into radians before you use these functions. Because 2*π radians are in 360 degrees, you can calculate radian angles by multiplying the number of degrees by @PI and dividing by 180, as shown in figure 6.6.

Also in figure 6.6, notice cells C7, C11, D9, and D13. The numbers returned are small, but not exactly zero, which they should be. Large numbers, therefore, are displayed in cells E7 and E11, which should be displaying ERR (due to division by zero), and small numbers are displayed in cells E9 and E13, which should be zero. These errors occur because of problems with 1-2-3's floating point driver. Keep this in mind when using these functions.

```
B5: (F3) (A5*@PI/180)                                              READY

      A        B          C              D              E           ◀
  1                                                                 ▶
  2   @PI=    3.141592                                              ▲
  3                                                                 ▼
  4   Degrees  Radians    @COS           @SIN           @TAN        ?
  5      0      0.000            1              0              0
  6     45      0.785    0.7071067812   0.7071067812            1
  7     90      1.571    6.125742275E−17          1    1.632455228E+16
  8    135      2.356   −0.7071067812   0.7071067812           −1
  9    180      3.142           −1      1.225148455E−16  −1.225148455E−16
 10    −45     −0.785    0.7071067812  −0.7071067812           −1
 11    −90     −1.571    6.125742275E−17         −1   −1.632455228E+16
 12   −135     −2.356   −0.7071067812  −0.7071067812            1
 13   −180     −3.142           −1     −1.225148455E−16  1.225148455E−16
 14
 15
 16
 17
 18
 19
 20
07−Mar−91  01:10 PM        UNDO
```

Fig. 6.6. Examples of the @PI, @COS, @SIN, and @TAN functions.

@ACOS, @ASIN, @ATAN, and @ATAN2— Computing Inverse Trigonometric Functions

The @ACOS, @ASIN, @ATAN, and @ATAN2 functions calculate the arc-cosine, the arcsine, the arctangent, and the four-quadrant arctangent, respectively. @ACOS computes the inverse of cosine. @ASIN computes the inverse of sine: a radian angle between $-\pi/2$ and $\pi/2$ (-90 and $+90$ degrees). @ATAN computes the inverse of tangent: a radian angle between $-\pi/2$ and $\pi/2$ (-90 and $+90$ degrees). @ATAN2 calculates the four-quadrant arctangent by using the ratio of its two arguments.

@ACOS and @ASIN each use one argument:

@ACOS(*angle*)

@ASIN(*angle*)

Because all cosine and sine values lie between –1 and 1, @ACOS and @ASIN work only with values between –1 and 1. Either function returns ERR if you use an argument outside this range. @ASIN returns angles between $-\pi/2$ and $+\pi/2$; whereas @ACOS returns angles between 0 and $\pi/2$. Figure 6.7 shows examples of the @ACOS, @ASIN, and @ATAN functions.

Reminder:
Because all cosine and sine values lie between –1 and 1, @COS and @SIN can be used only with values between –1 and 1.

```
C4: [W17] @ACOS(B4)                                                    READY

         A      B         C              D              E          F
   1
   2
   3          Value    @ACOS         @ASIN          @ATAN
   4              1         0     1.5707963268    0.7853981634
   5        0.70711  0.7853936113  0.7854027155    0.6154818545
   6              0  1.5707963268             0               0
   7       -0.70711  2.3561990423 -0.7854027155   -0.6154818545
   8             -1  3.1415926536 -1.5707963268   -0.7853981634
   9             10       ERR            ERR        1.4711276743
  10
  11
  12
  13
  14
  15
  16
  17
  18
  19
  20
07-Mar-91  01:13 PM        UNDO
```

Fig. 6.7. Examples of the @ACOS, @ASIN, and @ATAN functions.

Like @ACOS and @ASIN, the @ATAN function uses one argument. @ATAN can use any number and returns a value between $-\pi/2$ and $+\pi/2$. Use the following format for @ATAN:

    @ATAN(*angle*)

@ATAN2 computes the angle whose tangent is specified by the ratio *number2/number1*, which are the two arguments. One of the arguments must be a number other than zero. @ATAN2 returns radian angles between $-\pi$ and $+\pi$. Use the following format for @ATAN2:

    @ATAN2(*number1,number2*)

Using Date and Time Functions

1-2-3's date and time functions enable you to convert dates, such as November 26, 1991, and times, such as 6:00 p.m., to serial numbers. You then can use the serial numbers in date arithmetic and time arithmetic functions, which are valuable calculations when dates and times affect worksheet calculations and logic.

As you review the examples that show the mechanics of 1-2-3's date and time functions, you will develop a better appreciation of their potential contributions to your applications. The date and time functions available in 1-2-3 are summarized in table 6.4.

Table 6.4
Date and Time Functions

Function	Description
@DATE(*year,month,day*)	Calculates the serial number that represents the described date
@DATEVALUE(*date_string*)	Converts a date expressed as a quoted string into a serial number
@DAY(*date*)	Extracts the day number from a serial number
@MONTH(*date*)	Extracts the month number from a serial number
@YEAR(*date*)	Extracts the year number from a serial number
@NOW	Calculates the serial date and time from the current system date and time
@TODAY	Calculates the serial date from the current system data (displays as @INT(@NOW) in the control panel)

Function	Description
@TIME(*hour,minute,second*)	Calculates the serial number representing the described time
@TIMEVALUE(*time_string*)	Converts a time expressed as a string into a serial number
@SECOND(*time*)	Extracts the seconds from a serial number
@MINUTE(*time*)	Extracts the minute number from a serial number
@HOUR(*time*)	Extracts the hour number from a serial number

@DATE—Converting Date Values to Serial Numbers

The first step in using dates in arithmetic operations is converting the dates to serial numbers, which you then can use in addition, subtraction, multiplication, and division operations. Probably the most frequently used date function is @DATE. This function converts any date into a number that you can use in arithmetic operations and that 1-2-3 can display as a date. @DATE uses the following format:

@DATE(*year,month,day*)

You use numbers to identify a year, month, or day. You enter the date November 26, 1991, for example, which also can be expressed as 11-26-91, into the @DATE function in the following way:

@DATE(91,11,26)

The numbers you enter to represent the year, month, and day must comprise a valid date, or 1-2-3 will return ERR. 1-2-3 is programmed so that you can specify the *day* argument in February as 29 only during leap years, and you never can specify the day as 30 or 31 for February. When you specify the month as 1, which represents January, 30 and 31 are valid *day* arguments because January has 31 days.

Cue:
The year 2000 uses the number 100 when used with the @DATE function.

When you use the @DATE function, remember several guidelines. First, 1-2-3's internal calendar begins with the serial number 1, which is the first date that 1-2-3 recognizes, and that serial number represents January 1, 1900. A single day is represented by an increment of 1; thus, 1-2-3 represents January 2, 1900, as 2.

Second, although 1900 was not a leap year, 1-2-3 assigns the serial number 60 to the date February 29, 1900. Although this assignment generally should not be a problem, you may have difficulty if you transfer data between 1-2-3 and other programs. In that case, you may need to adjust your applications for this error yourself.

Figure 6.8 shows an example of the @DATE function being used to calculate the number of days a bill is overdue.

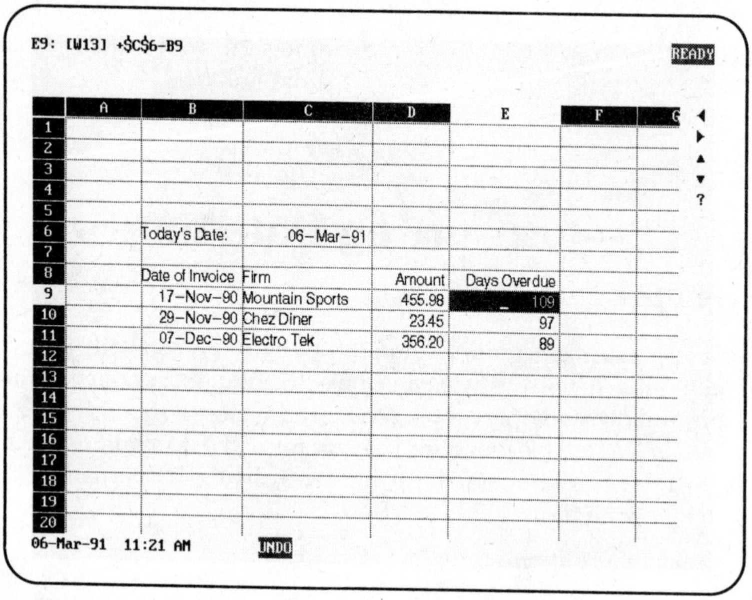

Fig. 6.8. The @DATE function used to calculate the number of days a bill is overdue.

Dates created or entered with the @DATE function appear on an unformatted worksheet as a number: the number of days since the beginning of the century. To make that serial number display as a text date, format the cell with the /Range Format Date command. When you format the dates, 1-2-3 uses the dates as serial numbers but displays them in reports and on-screen in the date format you selected. The /Range Format commands and the various Date and Time formats available are discussed in detail in Chapter 5.

@DATEVALUE—Changing Date Strings to Serial Numbers

@DATEVALUE computes the serial number for a text string typed into a referenced cell. The text string must use one of the formats recognized by 1-2-3. @DATEVALUE requires the following format:

@DATEVALUE(*date_string*)

The date string must look like one of the date formats you can select when you choose /**R**ange Format. If 1-2-3 cannot recognize the format, the function returns ERR.

Reminder:
If a string is unrecognizable, 1-2-3 returns the ERR value.

> *Note:* If you reset the default date format for 1-2-3 so that you can use international date formats, you must type one of the date formats for the country you selected.

Figure 6.9 shows @DATEVALUE converting the date strings in column B into serial numbers. Use /**R**ange Format Date to format a cell containing @DATEVALUE so that the cell displays the serial date number as a text date.

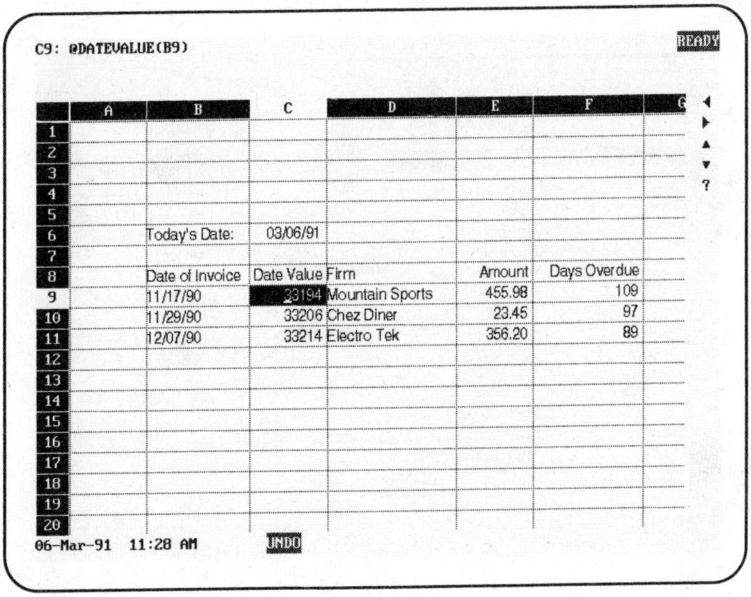

***Fig. 6.9.** The @DATEVALUE function used to convert date strings into serial date numbers.*

@DAY, @MONTH, and @YEAR—
Converting Serial Numbers to Dates

The @DAY, @MONTH, and @YEAR functions convert serial numbers into a numeric day, month, or year, respectively. These functions use the following respective formats:

@DAY(*date*)

@MONTH(*date*)

@YEAR(*date*)

Cue:
Add 1900 to the result of @YEAR to obtain a 4-digit year

The @DAY function accepts a valid serial number as its single argument and returns the day of the month, which is a number from 1 to 31. The @MONTH function accepts a valid date serial number as its single argument and returns the month of the year, which is a number from 1 to 12. The @YEAR function accepts a valid serial date number as its single argument and returns the number of the year, which is a number from 0 (1900) to 199 (2099).

Figure 6.10 illustrates the mechanics of these three date functions, which enable you to extract only the component of a date—year, month, or day—that you want to manipulate.

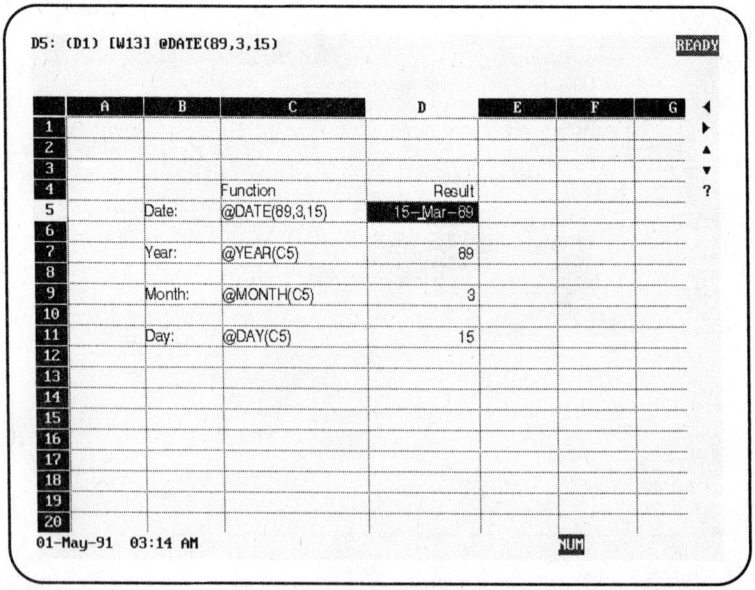

Fig. 6.10. *The @YEAR, @MONTH, and @DAY functions used to extract parts of date serial numbers.*

@NOW and @TODAY—Finding the Current Date and Time

1-2-3 provides two functions, @NOW and @TODAY, that extract information from the current system date and time. The @NOW function retrieves the current system date and the current system time. The portion to the left of the decimal point specifies the date; the portion to the right of the decimal point specifies the time. The @TODAY function is similar to @NOW except that @TODAY retrieves only the system date and not the system time (@TODAY displays as `@INT(@NOW)` in the control panel). These two functions provide a convenient tool for recording the dates and times in a printed worksheet. Neither function requires arguments.

Cue:
Add 1900 to the result of @YEAR to obtain a 4-digit year.

Use the @INT function to calculate the date or time portion of the @NOW function. Use the /**R**ange **V**alue command (or press F2 [Edit], F9 [Calc], and Enter) to freeze @NOW or @TODAY into an unchanging value. The easiest way to accomplish this task is to create a macro that enters @NOW into a cell, formats the cell, and freezes it with the /**R**ange **V**alue command (or the {EDIT}{CALC}~ sequence). Figure 6.11 illustrates the result of using both @functions. Column C shows the serial numbers, which represent the system date and time. Columns D and E show the results of the two functions formatted as dates and times, respectively.

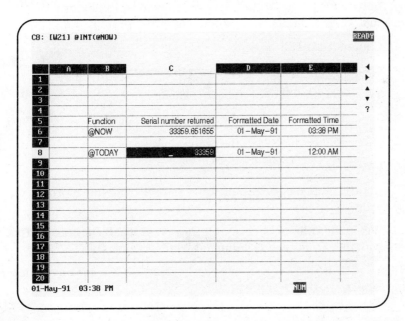

Fig. 6.11. *The @NOW and @TODAY functions used to insert the date and time on a worksheet.*

@TIME—Converting Time Values to Serial Numbers

1-2-3 expresses time as a decimal fraction of a full day. For example, 0.5 is equal to 12 hours, or 12:00 p.m. In addition, 1-2-3 works on international, or military, time. For example, 10:00 p.m. in U.S. time is 2200 in international time. Although 1-2-3's timekeeping system may seem awkward at first, you will soon become accustomed to it. The following time increment equivalents will help you understand the system:

Time Increment	Numeric Equivalent
1 hour	0.0416666667
1 minute	0.0006944444
1 second	0.0000115741

The @TIME function produces a decimal fraction for a specified time of day. @TIME uses the following format:

@TIME(*hour,minute,second*)

You can use @TIME to produce a range of times just as you use @DATE to generate a range of dates. One way to produce a range of times is to use the /Data Fill command. To produce a range of times from 8:00 a.m. to 5:00 p.m. in 15-minute increments, for example, follow these steps:

1. Choose /Data Fill.

2. Specify the range where you want the times to appear.

3. Type **@TIME(8,0,0)** as the Start value.

4. Type **@TIME(0,15,0)** as the Step value.

5. Type **@TIME(17,0,0)** as the Stop value.

6. Press Enter.

7. Choose /**R**ange Format **D**ate **T**ime and select the time format you want.

8. Widen the column, if necessary to prevent the display of asterisks, with the /**W**orksheet Column Set-Width command.

In figure 6.12, B6..B13 was selected as the range where the times appear in time format 7—HH:MM AM/PM.

```
B13: (D7) 0.40625                                         READY

       A       B         C         D         E         F         G    ◀
 1                                                                     ▶
 2                                                                     ▲
 3                                                                     ▼
 4                     Instrument           Reading difference         ?
 5           Time      Reading             at 15 min. intervals
 6         08:00 AM      354                      —
 7         08:15 AM      358                      4
 8         08:30 AM      363                      5
 9         08:45 AM      360                     −3
10         09:00 AM      359                     −1
11         09:15 AM      365                      6
12         09:30 AM      370                      5
13         09:45 AM      368                     −2
14
15
16
17
18
19
20
06-Mar-91  11:54 AM        UNDO                        NUM
```

Fig. 6.12. *An example of the @TIME function.*

The numeric arguments have some restrictions. First, *hour* must be between 0 and 23. Second, both *minute* and *second* must be between 0 and 59. Finally, although 1-2-3 accepts numeric arguments that contain integers and decimals, only the integer portion is used.

After 1-2-3 has interpreted a time as a fraction of a serial number, you can use the /Range Format Date Time and choose a format to display the time in a more recognizable way—10:42 p.m., for example. 1-2-3's time formats are discussed in the following section.

@TIMEVALUE—Converting Time Strings to Serial Values

Like @DATEVALUE and @DATE, the @TIMEVALUE function is a variation of @TIME. Like @TIME, @TIMEVALUE produces a serial number from the hour, minute, and second information you supply to the function. Unlike @TIME, however, @TIMEVALUE uses string arguments rather than numeric arguments. You type a time as text, and the @TIMEVALUE function converts the entry into a serial number. @TIMEVALUE requires the following format:

@TIMEVALUE(*time_string*)

The time string must appear in one of four time formats:

HH:MM:SS	AM/PM
HH:MM	AM/PM
HH:MM:SS	(24 hour)
HH:MM	(24 hour)

Reminder:
1-2-3 expresses time in fractions of serial numbers.

If the string conforms to one of the time formats, 1-2-3 displays the appropriate serial number fraction. If you then format the cell, 1-2-3 displays the appropriate time of day.

@SECOND, @MINUTE, and @HOUR—Converting Serial Numbers to Time Values

With the @SECOND, @MINUTE, and @HOUR functions, you can extract different units of time from the decimal portion of a serial date number. These functions use the following formats, respectively:

@SECOND(*time*)

@MINUTE(*time*)

@HOUR(*time*)

Figure 6.13 shows that these three functions are, in a sense, the inverse of the @TIME function, just as the @DAY, @MONTH, and @YEAR functions are the inverse of the @DATE function.

Using Financial and Accounting Functions

1-2-3 provides 11 financial and accounting functions that perform a variety of calculations for discounting cash flows, loan amortization, and asset depreciation. The 1-2-3 financial functions include two that calculate return on investment (@IRR and @RATE), one that calculates loan payment

(@PMT), two that calculate present value (@NPV and @PV), one that calculates future value (@FV), two that perform compound growth calculations (@TERM and @CTERM), and three that calculate asset depreciation (@SLN, @DDB, and @SYD). Table 6.5 summarizes the financial and accounting functions available in 1-2-3.

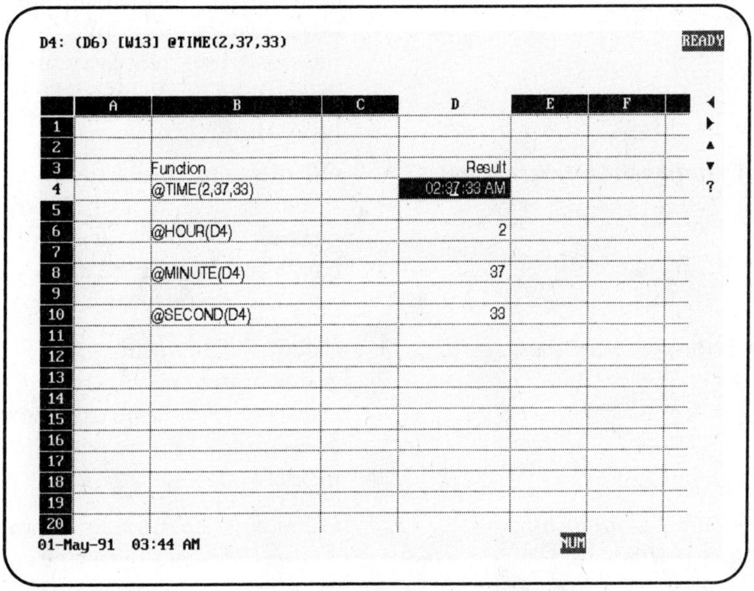

```
D4: (D6) [W13] @TIME(2,37,33)                                    READY

         A            B            C          D        E       F
    1
    2
    3              Function                          Result
    4              @TIME(2,37,33)                    02:37:33 AM
    5
    6              @HOUR(D4)                             2
    7
    8              @MINUTE(D4)                          37
    9
   10              @SECOND(D4)                          33
   11
   12
   13
   14
   15
   16
   17
   18
   19
   20
   01-May-91  03:44 AM                                     NUM
```

Fig. 6.13. *The @SECOND, @MINUTE, and @HOUR functions compared to the @TIME function.*

Table 6.5
Financial and Accounting Functions

Function	Description
@IRR(*guess,cashflows*)	Calculates the internal rate of return on an investment
@RATE(*future_value, present_value,term*)	Calculates the periodic return required to increase the present-value investment to the size of the future value in the length of time indicated (term)
@PMT(*principal,interest,term*)	Calculates the loan payment amount

continues

Table 6.5 *(continued)*

Function	Description
@NPV(*interest,cashflows*)	Calculates the present value (today's value) of a stream of cash flows of uneven amounts, but at evenly spaced time periods when the payments are discounted by the periodic interest rate
@PV(*payment,interest,term*)	Calculates the present value (today's value) of a stream of periodic cash flows of even payments discounted at a periodic interest rate
@FV(*payment,interest,term*)	Calculates the future value (value at the end of payments) of a stream of periodic cash flows compounded at the periodic interest rate
@TERM(*payment,interest, future_value*)	Calculates the number of times an equal payment must be made in order to accumulate the future value when payments are compounded at the periodic interest rate
@CTERM(*interest,future value, present_value*)	Calculates the number of periods required for the present value amount to grow to a future value amount given a periodic interest rate
@SLN(*cost,salvage,life*)	Calculates straight-line depreciation
@DDB(*cost,salvage,life,period*)	Calculates 200 percent declining-balance depreciation
@SYD(*cost,salvage,life,period*)	Calculates sum-of-the-years'-digits depreciation

@IRR—Calculating Internal Rate of Return

The @IRR function calculates the internal rate of return on an investment. @IRR uses the following format:

@IRR(*guess,cashflows*)

The *guess* argument typically should be a guess at the interest rate and entered as a decimal between 0 and 1. The first cash flow typically is a negative amount, the amount initially invested at time 0 or at the start of the investment. 1-2-3 uses the *guess* argument as the initial interest rate in the following formula, and tests whether the result equals 0:

Reminder:
A time string must conform to one of four time formats.

$$0 = \sum_{n=0}^{n} \frac{C_n}{(1+IRR)^n}$$

where

C_n = Cash flow at *n*th period

i = Discount rate

If the result does not equal 0, 1-2-3 substitutes different interest rates in an attempt to make the equation true, where the left side of the equation, 0, equals the right side of the equation. Notice that the right side of the equation is the formula for calculating the profit measure, or *net present value*.

You should start the calculation with a guessed interest rate that is as close as possible. From this guess, 1-2-3 attempts to converge to a correct interest rate, with .0000001 precision within 30 iterations. If the program cannot do so, the @IRR function returns ERR. If ERR occurs, try another guess.

The initial cash flow at time 0 is negative because it flows from your initial investment. Cash flows in the range after that may be negative payments by you or positive payments to you. Cash flows occur at the end of equally spaced periods with the initial payment by you being at time 0. 1-2-3 ignores empty cells in the range of cash flows and treats cells containing labels as zero.

Figure 6.14 shows the @IRR function calculating the internal rate of return on an investment with uneven cash flows. Notice that during some time periods the investor had to inject additional cash into the investment. Notice also that multiplying the monthly amount by 12 converts the monthly internal rate of return to an annual rate.

```
G6: (P2) @IRR(G5,D5..D13)*12                                    READY

        A           B         C    D    E    F     G        H          ◄
 1                                                                      ►
 2                                                                      ▲
 3                                                                      ▼
 4  Period      Description          Amount              Formula        ?
 5  -           Initial Investment   ($54,000)  Guess:   0.01
 6  Feb         Feb 28               $0         IRR      30.07%  @IRR(G5,D5..D13)*12
 7  Mar         Mar 30               $0
 8  Apr         Apr 30               ($1,200)
 9  May         May 31               $2,500
10  Jun         Jun 30               ($2,000)
11  Jul         Jul 31               $1,500
12  Aug         Aug 31               $0
13  Sep         Sep 30 Sold          $65,000
14
15
16
17
18
19
20
06-Mar-91   12:54 PM      UNDO                           NUM
```

Fig. 6.14. The internal rate of return calculated with the @IRR function.

Although the internal-rate-of-return method is used widely as a measure of profitability, you should be aware that the IRR method has several draw-backs when used to analyze investments. The problem is with the internal-rate-of-return method itself, not the @IRR function.

Cue:
The guess argument should be a percent between 0 and 1.

One problem is evident when you use the internal-rate-of-return measure on an investment that has multiple internal rates of return. In theory, for example, the formula for calculating the internal rate of return for an investment with cash flows over 10 years is a 10th-root polynomial equation with up to 10 correct solutions. In practice, an investment has as many correct internal rates of return as there are sign changes in the cash flows.

A sign change occurs when the cash flow changes from positive to negative, or vice versa, between periods. Even if the @IRR function returns an internal rate of return with your first guess, therefore, try other guesses to see whether another correct internal-rate-of-return answer is evident; you probably should not use the measure when it delivers multiple solutions.

A serious problem with the @IRR method is that it tends to overestimate a positive rate of return from the investment and neglects to account for additional outside investments that must be injected into the investment over its life span. The overestimate on return occurs because the @IRR method assumes that positive cash flows are reinvested at the same rate of return earned by the total investment. Actually, it is rare that a small return can be reinvested at the same high rate as that of a large investment. This limitation is especially true in the analysis of large fixed assets and land investments.

An alternative and more accurate method of evaluating investments is calculating your investment's net present value. You use 1-2-3's @NPV function to perform net present value analysis, which is discussed later in this chapter.

@RATE—Calculating Compound Growth Rate

The @RATE function calculates the compound growth rate for an initial investment that grows to a specified future value over a specified number of periods. The rate is the periodic interest rate and not necessarily an annual rate. @RATE uses the following format:

@RATE(*future_value,present_value,term*)

For the @RATE calculation, the formula is rearranged to compute the interest rate in terms of the initial investment, the future value, and the number of periods.

The actual formula for calculating the interest rate is the following:

Interest rate = (*future value/present value*)$^{1/\text{term}}$ − 1

You can use @RATE to determine, for example, the yield of a zero-coupon bond sold at a discount of its face value. Suppose that for $350 you can purchase a zero-coupon bond with a $1,000 face value maturing in 10 years. What is the implied annual interest rate? The answer, shown in figure 6.15, is 11.07 percent.

Cue:
Use the @RATE function to determine the yield of a zero-coupon bond.

The @RATE function also is useful in forecasting applications that calculate the compound growth rate between current and projected future revenues and earnings.

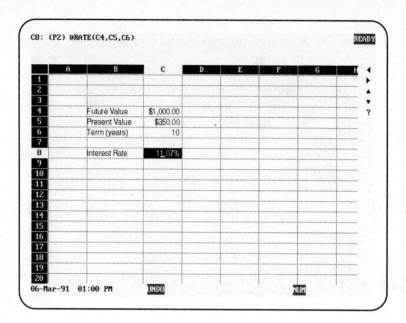

Fig. 6.15. The @RATE function used to calculate the zero-coupon bond yield.

@PMT—Calculating Loan Payment Amounts

You use the @PMT function to calculate the periodic payments necessary to pay the entire principal on an amortizing loan. To use @PMT you must know the loan amount, which is the principal, the periodic interest rate, and the term in the following format:

@PMT(*principal,interest,term*)

@PMT assumes that payments are to be made at the end of each period as an ordinary annuity. The function uses the following formula to make the payment calculation:

$$\text{Payment} = \text{principal} * \text{periodic interest} / 1 - (\text{periodic interest} + 1)^{-\text{term}}$$

Figure 6.16 shows the @PMT function being used to calculate the monthly car payment on a $12,000 car loan. The loan is repaid over 48 months, and the loan rate is 1 percent: 12 percent divided by 12 periods per year.

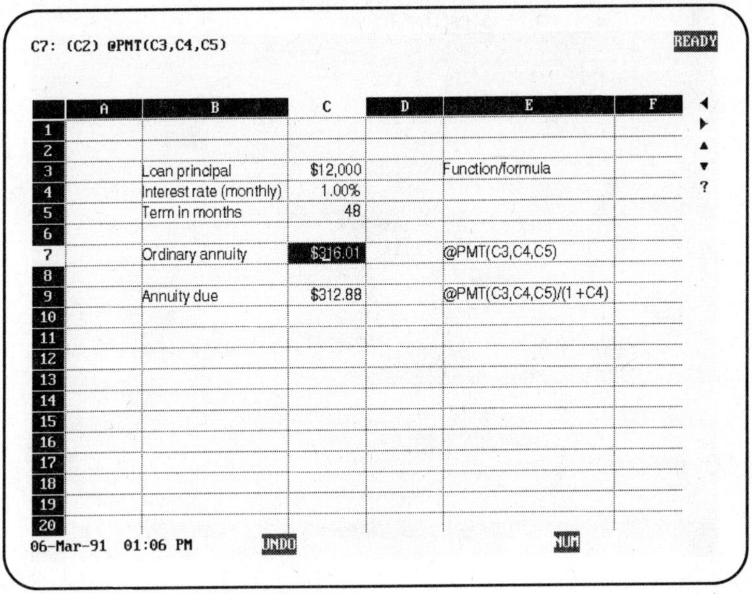

Fig. 6.16. The @PMT function used to calculate loan payment.

You can modify the calculated result of the @PMT function if payments are to be made at the beginning of the period as an annuity due. The modified format for the @PMT function is:

@PMT(*principal*,*interest*,*term*)/(1+*interest*)

Whether you calculate ordinary annuities or annuities due, you must remember two important guidelines. First, calibrate the interest rate as the rate-per-payment period. Second, express the loan term in payment periods. If you make monthly payments, you accordingly should enter the interest rate as the monthly interest rate and enter the term as the number of months you will be making payments. If you make annual payments, you alternatively should enter the interest rate as the annual interest rate and the term as the number of years you will be making payments.

@NPV—Calculating Net Present Value

The @NPV function closely resembles the @PV function except that @NPV can calculate the present value of a varying, or changing, stream of cash flows. @NPV uses the following format:

@NPV(*interest*,*cashflows*)

Cue:
The @NPV function closely resembles the @PV function.

The @NPV function calculates the following formula:

$$NPV = \sum_{n=1}^{N} \frac{C_n}{(1+i)^n}$$

where

C_n = Cash flow at nth period

i = Discount rate

Figure 6.17 shows how you can use @NPV to calculate the present value of a stream of varying cash flows.

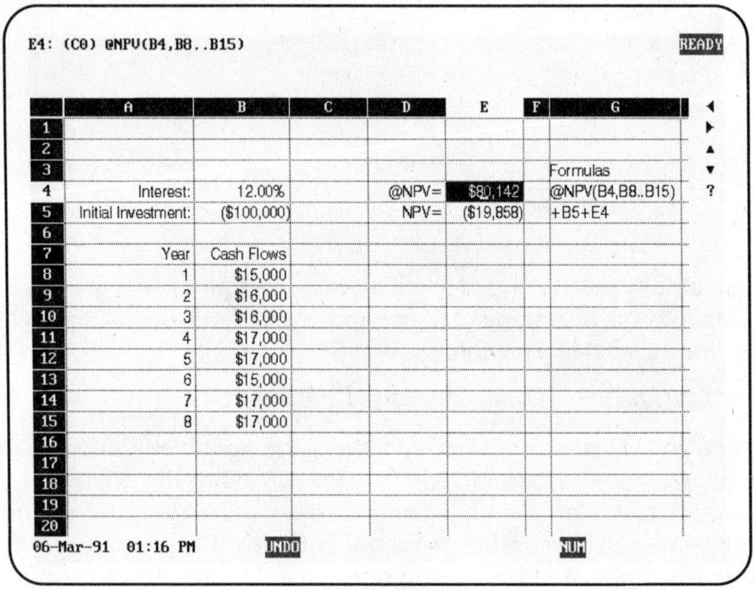

```
E4: (C0) @NPV(B4,B8..B15)                                    READY

        A           B         C      D      E    F    G         ◄
   1                                                            ►
   2                                                            ▲
   3                                                  Formulas   ▼
   4       Interest:   12.00%            @NPV=  $80,142  @NPV(B4,B8..B15)  ?
   5  Initial Investment: ($100,000)     NPV=  ($19,858) +B5+E4
   6
   7           Year   Cash Flows
   8             1      $15,000
   9             2      $16,000
  10             3      $16,000
  11             4      $17,000
  12             5      $17,000
  13             6      $15,000
  14             7      $17,000
  15             8      $17,000
  16
  17
  18
  19
  20
06-Mar-91  01:16 PM         UNDO                    NUM
```

Fig. 6.17. The @NPV function used to calculate the present value of varying cash flows.

The @NPV function assumes that the first cash flow occurs at the end of the first period; the function, therefore, actually is a flexible present value function. Anytime you use the @PV function, you also can use the @NPV function to obtain the same result.

Accountants and financial analysts use the term *net present value* to refer to a measure of an investment's profitability, by using the following formula:

$$NPV = \sum_{n=0}^{N} \frac{C_n}{(1+i)^n}$$

where

C_n = Cash flow at nth period

i = Discount rate

To calculate the actual profitability measure, or net present value, you must subtract the initial investment from the result of the @NPV function. When you construct a formula that uses the @NPV function in this way, you essentially are testing whether the investment meets, exceeds, or falls short of the interest rate specified in the @NPV function. Such a formula would be as follows:

Cue:
To calculate the net present value, subtract the initial investment.

+INITL_AMOUNT+@NPV(*rate,cashflows*)

The value in the cell named INITL_AMOUNT is negative because the amount is money you invested, or paid out. If the calculated result of the preceding formula is a positive amount, the investment produces a return that exceeds the interest rate specified in the @NPV function. If the calculated result equals zero, the investment produces a return that equals the interest rate specified in the @NPV function. Finally, if the calculated result is a negative amount, the investment produces a return that falls short of the interest rate specified in the @NPV function.

@PV—Calculating Present Value of an Annuity

The @PV function closely resembles the @NPV function because @PV calculates the present value of a stream of cash flows. The difference is that @PV calculates the present value of a stream of equal cash flows occurring at the end of the period. This stream of equal cash flows is called an ordinary annuity, or payments in arrears. The @PV function uses the following format:

@PV(*payment,interest,term*)

The @PV function uses the following formula:

$$PV = payment * \frac{1-(1+interest)^{-term}}{interest}$$

Figure 6.18 shows the result of using @PV to calculate the present value of 24 payments of $1,000 each.

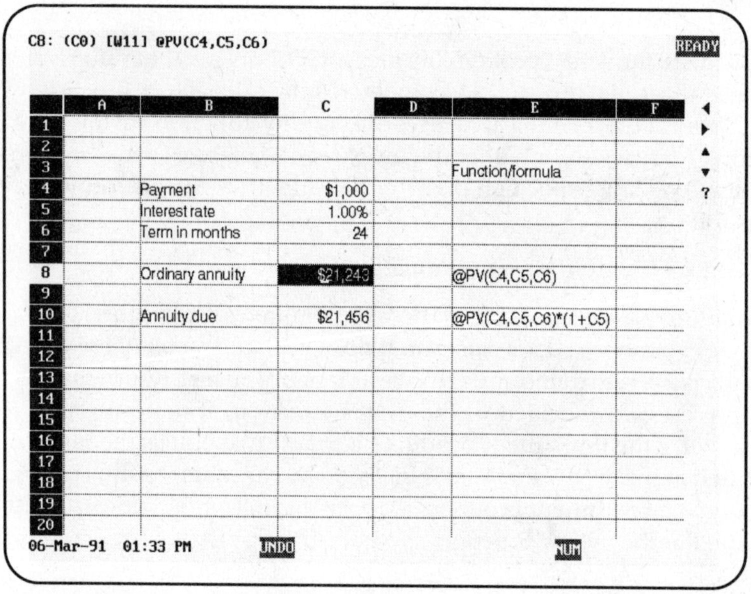

Fig. 6.18. *The @PV function used to calculate the present value of 24 payments of $1,000 each.*

Remember that the @PV function assumes that the equal-amount cash flows, or payments, occur at the *end* of the period. If the cash flows occur at the *beginning* of the period as an annuity due or payments in advance, you use the following formula:

$$@PV(payment,interest,term)*(1+interest)$$

@FV—Calculating Future Value

The @FV function calculates what a current amount will grow to, based on an interest rate and number of years you specify. The function is helpful for estimating the future balances of current savings and investments. The @FV function requires the following format:

@FV(*payment,interest,term*)

The function uses the following formula:

$$PV = payment * \frac{1-(1+interest)^{-term}}{interest}$$

Suppose that you want to use the @FV function to calculate the estimated size of your vacation savings 24 months from now. Figure 6.19 shows such a calculation assuming monthly contributions of $1,000 and annual interest rates of 12 percent.

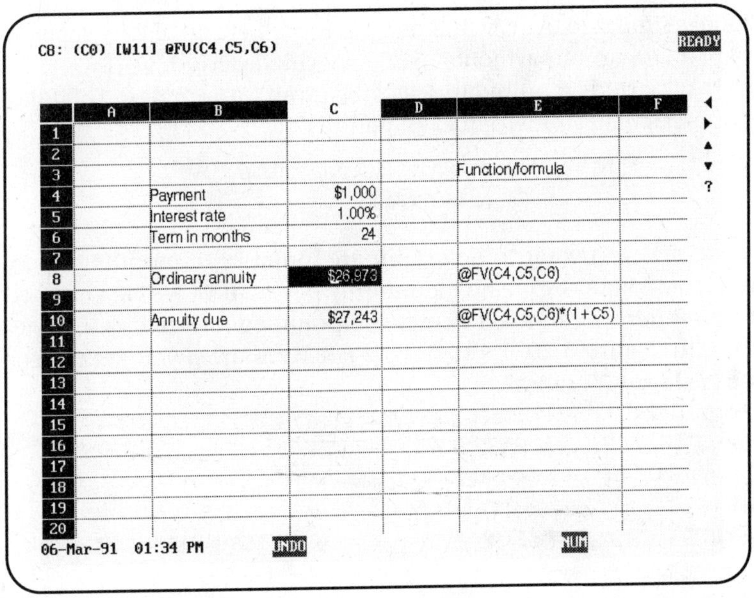

Fig. 6.19. *The @FV function used to calculate vacation savings.*

To calculate the future value of an annuity due, use a formula similar to the one that calculates the present value of an annuity due:

Future Value of
an Annuity Due = @FV(*payment,interest,term*)*(1+*interest*)

In addition to calculating the future value of a stream of periodic cash-flow payments by using the @FV function, you also may want to calculate the future value of amounts you already set aside. The following formula calculates the future value of a present value:

Future value = present value * (1 + interest)^{term}

@TERM—Calculating the Term of an Investment

The @TERM function calculates the number of periods required to accumulate a specified future value by making equal payments into an interest-bearing account at the end of each period. This number of periods is the term for an ordinary annuity. The @TERM function uses the following formula:

$$@TERM(payment,interest,future\_value)$$

@TERM is similar to @FV, with one exception. Instead of finding the future value of a stream of payments over a specified period, @TERM finds the number of periods required to reach the given future value. The following equation calculates the number of periods:

$$Term = \frac{@LN(1+(interest*future\ value)/payment)}{@LN(1+interest)}$$

Reminder:
The @TERM function finds the number of periods required to reach the given future value.

Suppose that you want to determine the number of months required to accumulate $5,000 by making a monthly payment of $50 into an account that pays 8 percent annual interest compounded monthly as 0.67 percent per month. Figure 6.20 shows how @TERM can help you get the answer, which is almost 77 months.

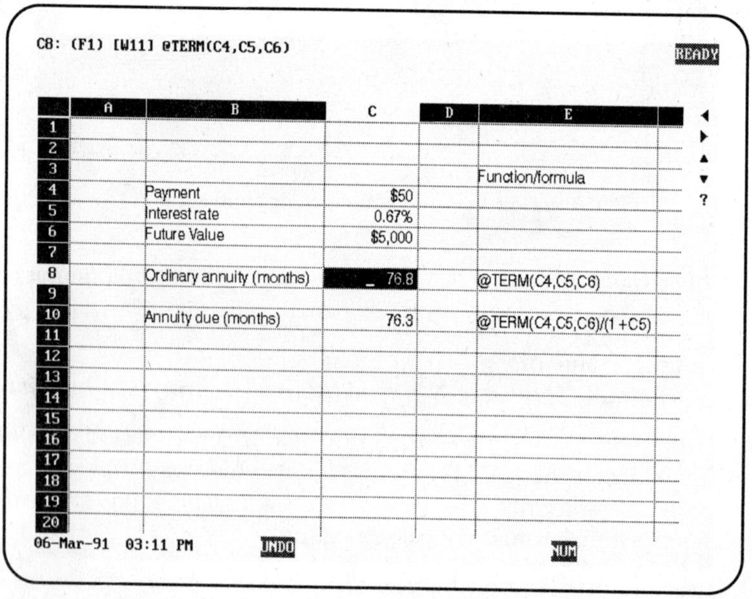

```
C8: (F1) [W11] @TERM(C4,C5,C6)                              READY

        A            B              C      D          E         ◄
   1                                                            ►
   2                                                            ▲
   3                                            Function/formula ▼
   4              Payment             $50                        ?
   5              Interest rate      0.67%
   6              Future Value      $5,000
   7
   8              Ordinary annuity (months)  76.8   @TERM(C4,C5,C6)
   9
  10              Annuity due (months)       76.3   @TERM(C4,C5,C6)/(1+C5)
  11
  12
  13
  14
  15
  16
  17
  18
  19
  20
  06-Mar-91  03:11 PM        UNDO                    NUM
```

Fig. 6.20. The @TERM function used to calculate the number of months to reach a specified future value.

To calculate the term for an annuity due, in which payments are made at the beginning of the period, use the following equation:

Term for an
annuity due = @TERM(*payment,interest,future_value*/(1+*interest*))

@CTERM—Calculating the Term of a Compounding Investment

The @CTERM function calculates the number of periods required for an initial investment that earns a specified interest rate to grow to a specified future value. The @TERM function calculates the number of periods needed for a series of payments to grow to a future value, but the @CTERM function calculates the number of periods needed for the present value of a single initial amount to grow to a future value. The @CTERM function uses the following format:

@CTERM(*interest,future_value, present_value*)

The @CTERM function uses the following formula:

$$\text{Term} = \frac{@LN(\text{future value/present value})}{@LN(1+\text{interest})}$$

@CTERM is useful in determining the term an investment needs to achieve a specified future value. Suppose, for example, that you want to determine how many years are necessary for $2,000 invested in an IRA at 10 percent interest to grow to $10,000. Figure 6.21 shows how to use the @CTERM function to determine the answer, which is just past 16 years and 10 months.

@SLN—Calculating Straight-Line Depreciation

The @SLN function calculates straight-line depreciation given the asset's cost, salvage value, and depreciable life. The @SLN function uses the following format:

@SLN(*cost,salvage,life*)

The following formula calculates @SLN:

SLN = (cost–salvage)/life

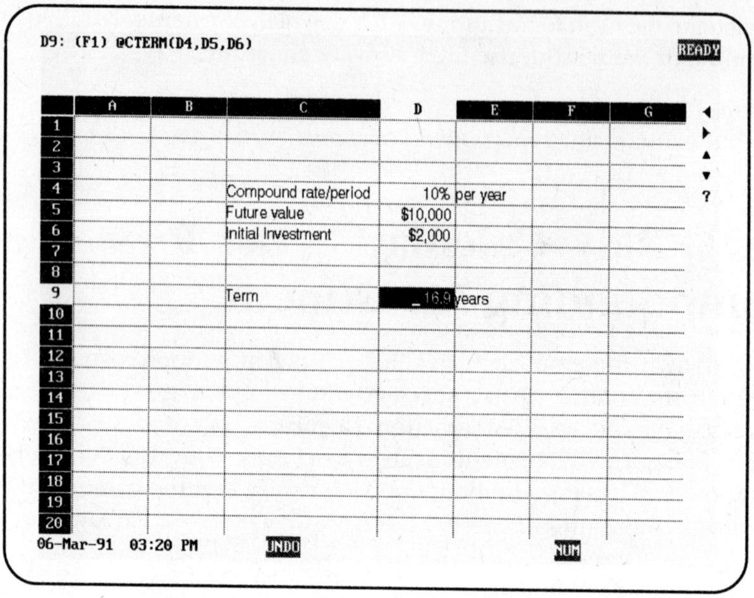

Fig. 6.21. The @CTERM function used to calculate the number of years for $2,000 to grow to $10,000 at 10 percent.

@SLN conveniently calculates straight-line depreciation for an asset. Suppose, for example, that you purchased a machine for $5,000 that has a useful life of three years and a salvage value of 10 percent of the purchase price ($500) at the end of the machine's useful life. Figure 6.22 shows how to use @SLN to determine the straight-line depreciation for the machine, which is $1,500 per year.

@DDB—Calculating Double Declining-Balance Depreciation

The @DDB function calculates depreciation by using the double declining-balance method where depreciation ends when the book value equals the salvage value. The double declining-balance method accelerates depreciation so that greater depreciation expense occurs in the earlier periods rather than in the later periods. Book value in any period is the purchase price less the total depreciation in all prior periods. @DDB uses the following format:

@DDB(*cost,salvage,life,period*)

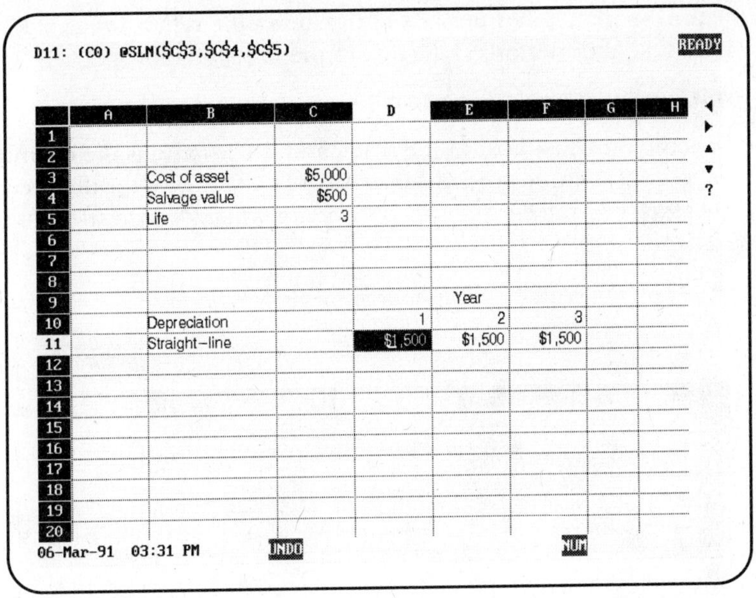

Fig. 6.22. The @SLN function used to calculate straight-line depreciation.

The double declining-balance depreciation in any period usually is the following:

> book value*2/n

In this formula, the book value is the book value in the period, and *n* is the depreciable life of the asset. 1-2-3, however, adjusts the result of this formula in later periods to ensure that total depreciation does not exceed the purchase price minus the salvage value.

Figure 6.23 shows how the @DDB function can calculate depreciation on an asset purchased for $5,000 with a depreciable life of three years and an estimated salvage value of $500.

When you use the double declining-balance depreciation method for an asset with a small salvage value, the asset will not be depreciated fully in the final year.

@SYD—Calculating Sum-of-the-Years'-Digits Depreciation

The @SYD function calculates depreciation by the sum-of-the-years'-digits method. Similar to double declining balance, this method accelerates depreciation so that earlier periods of the item's life reflect greater depreciation than do later periods. @SYD uses the following format:

@SYD(*cost,salvage,life,period*)

The *cost* is the purchase cost of the asset, and the *salvage* is the estimated value of the asset at the end of the depreciable life. The *life* is the depreciable life of the asset, and the *period* is the period for which depreciation is to be computed.

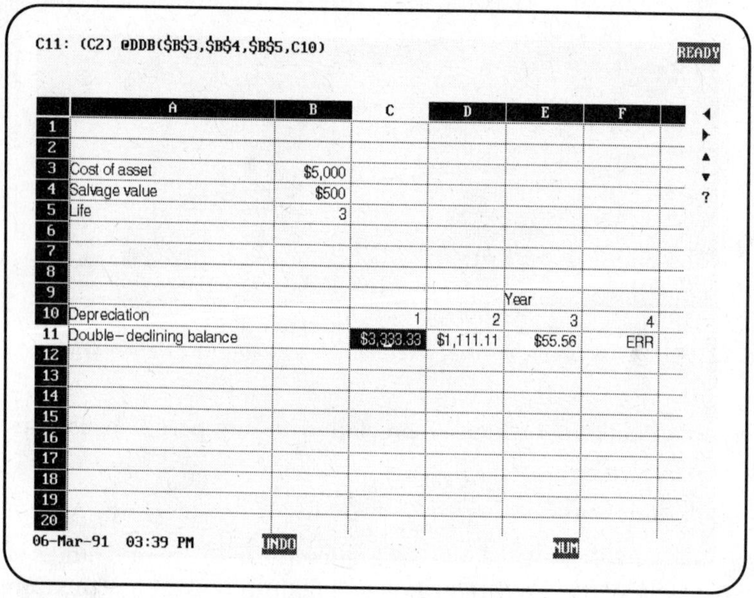

Fig. 6.23. *The @DDB function used to calculate double declining-balance depreciation.*

@SYD calculates depreciation with the following formula:

$$SYD = \frac{(cost\_salvage)^*(life\_period+1)}{life^*(life+1)/2}$$

The expression (life_period+1) in the numerator shows the life of the depreciation in the first period decreased by 1 in each subsequent period. This expression reflects the declining pattern of depreciation over time. The expression in the denominator, life*(life+1)/2, is equal to the sum of the digits, as in the following expression:

1 + 2 +...+ life

The name *sum-of-the-years'-digits* originated from this formula. Figure 6.24 shows how the @SYD function can calculate depreciation for an asset costing $5,000 with a depreciable life of three years and an estimated salvage value of $500.

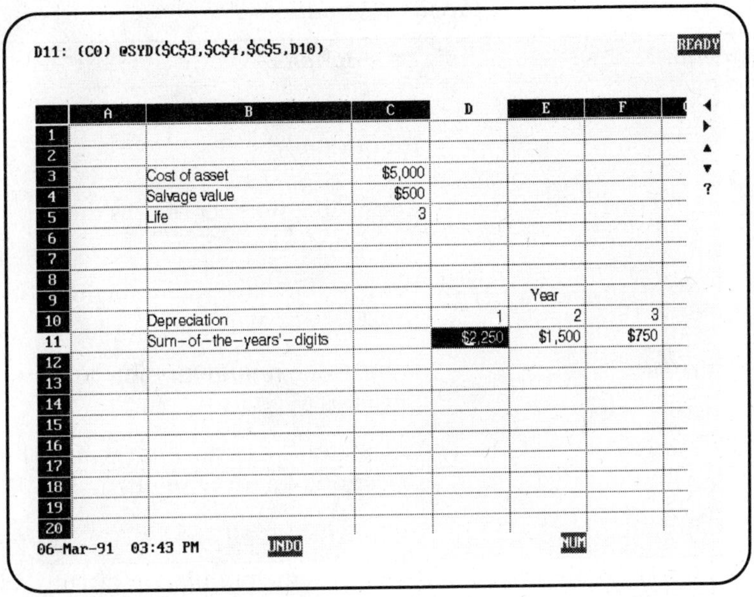

Fig. 6.24. *The @SYD function used to calculate sum-of-the-year's-digits depreciation.*

Using Statistical Functions

1-2-3 provides seven statistical functions: @AVG, @COUNT, @MAX, @MIN, @STD, @SUM, and @VAR. Additional statistical functions, which are used specifically for databases, are described later in this chapter. Table 6.6 lists the functions, their arguments, and the statistical operations they perform.

Every statistical function uses the *list* argument. This argument can include values or cell addresses individually specified, a range of cells, or multiple ranges of cells. 1-2-3 considers each of the following formats, for example, or any combination, as valid list arguments:

Reminder:
Every statistical function uses the list argument.

> @SUM(1,2,3,4)
>
> @SUM(B1,B2,B3,B4)
>
> @SUM(B1..B4)
>
> @SUM(B1..B2,B3..B4)

Although the preceding examples use the @SUM function, which totals the values included as arguments, the principles that these examples illustrate apply equally to each of the statistical functions.

Table 6.6
Statistical Functions

Function	Description
@AVG(*list*)	Calculates the arithmetic mean of a list of values
@COUNT(*list*)	Counts the number of cells that contain entries
@MAX(*list*)	Returns the maximum value in a list of values
@MIN(*list*)	Returns the minimum value in a list of values
@STD(*list*)	Calculates the population standard deviation of a list of values
@SUM(*list*)	Sums a list of values
@VAR(*list*)	Calculates the population variance of a list of values

Some statistical functions perform differently when you specify cells individually instead of as ranges. The functions that perform differently in this case include @AVG, @MAX, @MIN, @STD, and @VAR. When you specify a range of cells, 1-2-3 ignores empty cells within the specified range. When you specify cells individually, however, 1-2-3 takes empty cells into consideration for the particular functions mentioned.

Suppose, for example, that you are looking for the minimum value in a range that includes an empty cell and cells containing the entries 1, 2, and 3. In this case, 1-2-3 returns the value 1 as the minimum value. Suppose, however, that you instead specify individually a cell that is empty and cells that contain the entries 1, 2, and 3; in this case, 1-2-3 returns the value 0 as the minimum.

1-2-3 assumes that if you actually specify an individual cell, even an empty cell, you must want it included in the calculation.

When you specify cells, remember that 1-2-3 treats cells as zeros when they contain labels, such as when the cell is included as part of a range or when you individually specify the cell.

@AVG—Computing the Arithmetic Mean

To calculate the average of a set of values, you add all the values and then divide the sum by the number of values. The @AVG function essentially produces the same result as if you divided @SUM(*list*) by @COUNT(*list*), both of which are described later in this section. The @AVG function is a helpful tool for calculating the arithmetic mean, which is a commonly used measure of a set of values' averages. Use the following format for @AVG:

@AVG(*list*)

The *list* argument can be values, cell addresses, cell names, cell ranges, range names, or a combination of these. Figure 6.25 shows an example of the @AVG function calculating the mean price per share of an imaginary company. In the figure, the function's argument is D5..D16. If cells D5..D6 and D12..D13 are empty and are included in the *list* argument only as part of a range, these cells are ignored in the average calculation.

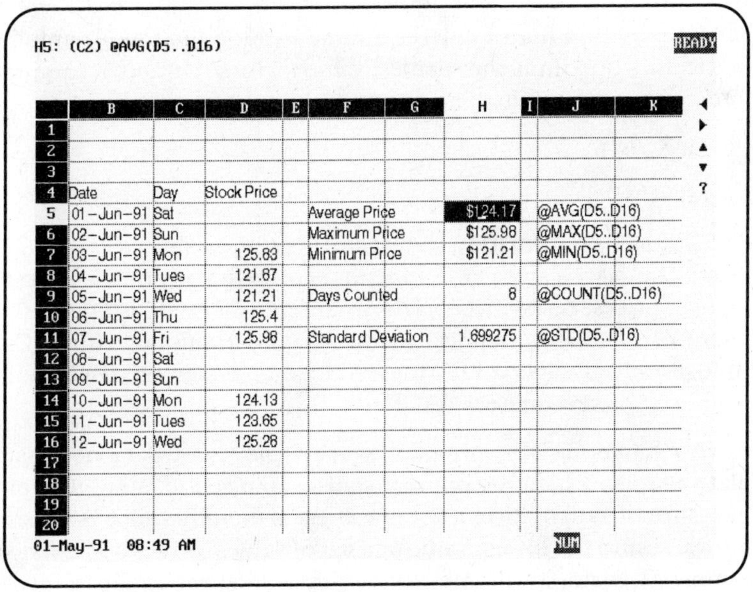
H5: (C2) @AVG(D5..D16) READY

	B	C	D	E	F	G	H	I	J	K
1										
2										
3										
4	Date	Day	Stock Price							
5	01-Jun-91	Sat			Average Price		$124.17		@AVG(D5..D16)	
6	02-Jun-91	Sun			Maximum Price		$125.98		@MAX(D5..D16)	
7	03-Jun-91	Mon	125.83		Minimum Price		$121.21		@MIN(D5..D16)	
8	04-Jun-91	Tues	121.87							
9	05-Jun-91	Wed	121.21		Days Counted		8		@COUNT(D5..D16)	
10	06-Jun-91	Thu	125.4							
11	07-Jun-91	Fri	125.98		Standard Deviation		1.699275		@STD(D5..D16)	
12	08-Jun-91	Sat								
13	09-Jun-91	Sun								
14	10-Jun-91	Mon	124.13							
15	11-Jun-91	Tues	123.65							
16	12-Jun-91	Wed	125.28							
17										
18										
19										
20										

01-May-91 08:49 AM NUM

Fig. 6.25. *The @AVG, @COUNT, @MAX, @MIN, and @STD functions.*

@COUNT—Counting Cell Entries

The @COUNT function totals the number of cells that contain entries of any kind, including labels, label-prefix characters, or the values ERR and NA. Use the following format for @COUNT:

> @COUNT(*list*)

The *list* argument can be values, cell addresses, cell names, cell ranges, range names, or a combination of these. You can use @COUNT to show the number of share prices included in the @AVG calculation made, for example, in figure 6.25. Figure 6.25 shows this calculation being made in cell H9.

Include only ranges as the argument in the @COUNT function. If you individually specify a cell, 1-2-3 counts that cell as having an entry, even if the cell is empty. If you absolutely must individually specify a cell, but you want it counted only if actually containing an entry, you must use the @@ function. The @@ function is described with 1-2-3's other special functions later in this chapter.

@MAX and @MIN—Finding Maximum and Minimum Values

Reminder:
The @MAX function finds the largest value included in your list.

The @MAX function finds the largest value included in the *list* argument; the @MIN function finds the smallest value included in the *list* argument. The functions use the following formats:

> @MAX(*list*)

> @MIN(*list*)

Figure 6.25 shows information concerning prices per share of an imaginary company. The @MAX and @MIN functions can help you find the lowest and the highest prices, respectively. The argument of @MAX is D5..D16. The argument of @MIN is identical to the @MAX argument. Although the example shows only eight values, these functions can return a list containing several dozen or several hundred items.

These two functions also provide the two pieces of data necessary to calculate a range, which is a popular statistical measure. A range, which is one measure of variability in a list of values, is the difference between the highest value and the lowest value in a list of values. A range as a statistical measurement is not the same thing as a worksheet range, which is a rectangular block of cells.

@STD—Calculating the Standard Deviation

The @STD function calculates the standard deviation of a population. Use the following format for this function:

@STD(*list*)

The standard deviation essentially is a measure of how individual values vary from the mean or average of the other values in the list. A smaller standard deviation indicates that values are grouped closely around the mean; a larger standard deviation indicates that values are widely dispersed from the mean. A standard deviation of 0 indicates, therefore, no dispersion, which means that every value in the list of values is the same. Figure 6.25 shows the @STD function used to calculate the standard deviation of the stock price values.

The precise definition of the standard deviation formula is shown by the formula 1-2-3 uses to calculate it:

$$\text{STD} = \sqrt{\frac{\sum_{n=1}^{N}(X_n-avg)^2}{N}} \qquad \text{STDS} = \sqrt{\frac{\sum_{n=1}^{N}(X_n-avg)^2}{N-1}}$$

where

N = Number of items in list

X_n = The *n*th item in list

avg = Arithmetic mean of list

@SUM—Totaling Values

The @SUM function provides a convenient way to add a list of values. Of the statistical functions that 1-2-3 provides, you probably will use @SUM the most often. @SUM uses the following format:

@SUM(*list*)

Figure 6.26 shows tax subtotals in column E. You may calculate the total tax by using the following formula:

$$+E5+E6+E7+E8+E9+E10+E11$$

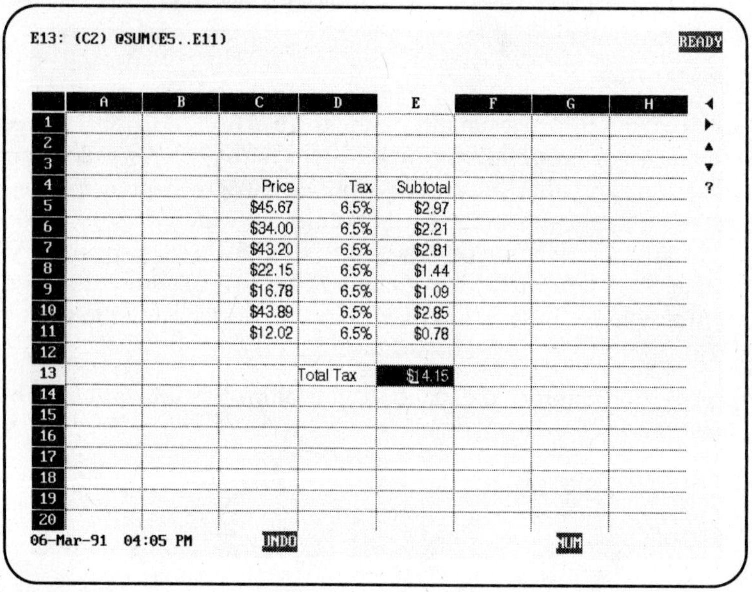

```
E13: (C2) @SUM(E5..E11)                                    READY

         A       B       C       D        E      F      G      H      ◄
  1                                                                    ►
  2                                                                    ▲
  3                                                                    ▼
  4                        Price     Tax   Subtotal                    ?
  5                       $45.67    6.5%     $2.97
  6                       $34.00    6.5%     $2.21
  7                       $43.20    6.5%     $2.81
  8                       $22.15    6.5%     $1.44
  9                       $16.78    6.5%     $1.09
 10                       $43.89    6.5%     $2.85
 11                       $12.02    6.5%     $0.78
 12
 13                              Total Tax  $14.15
 14
 15
 16
 17
 18
 19
 20
06-Mar-91  04:05 PM          UNDO                       NUM
```

Fig. 6.26. The @SUM function used to calculate the subtotals in column E.

This method of calculating the total tax, however, is inefficient and prone to error. A better way to total the column is to use the @SUM function over the range of the subtotals (see fig. 6.26).

When you add a range of cells with @SUM, you can insert more cells or delete cells from the middle of the range, and 1-2-3 continues to calculate accurate results. You can, however, accidentally insert a row at one end of an @SUM range. Then, new data entered at that spot appears to be included in the @SUM but is not. To prevent such an occurrence, include a placeholder, which is a blank or text-filled cell, at the top or bottom of the range of cells being summed. If filled with text, the cell will not affect the total. If you regularly use this technique, rows or columns inserted above or below the first and last number will still be inside the placeholders that mark the end points of the range being summed.

@SUM can be used (as can the other statistical functions) on a range that covers several rows and columns. Operations such as @SUM(A1..F10), therefore, are valid.

@VAR—Calculating the Variance

The variance, like the standard deviation, is a measure of dispersion about, or around, an average. The @VAR function calculates the variance of a population. This function uses the following format:

@VAR(*list*)

Calculating a statistical variance is an intermediate step in calculating the standard deviation described in the discussion of the @STD function. By comparing the following two formulas, you can see that the standard deviation is simply the square root of the variance:

$$ VAR = \frac{\sum\limits_{n=1}^{N}(X_n - avg)^2}{N} \qquad VARS = \frac{\sum\limits_{n=1}^{N}(X_n - avg)^2}{N-1} $$

where

N = Number of items in list

X_n = The nth item in list

avg = Arithmetic mean of list

Using Database Functions

1-2-3's database functions are similar to the worksheet functions but are modified to manipulate database fields. Like the standard functions, the database functions perform calculations in one simple statement that may otherwise require several statements. This efficiency and ease of application make these functions excellent tools. The database functions are described in table 6.7.

Cue:
Use the database functions to summarize your database selectively.

Table 6.7
Database Functions

Function	Description
@DCOUNT	Gives the number of items in a list that match the selected criteria
@DSUM	Sums the values of items in a list that match the selected criteria
@DMIN	Gives the minimum value of items in a list that match the selected criteria
@DMAX	Gives the maximum value of items in a list that match the selected criteria
@DSTD	Gives the standard deviation of items in a list that match the selected criteria
@DVAR	Gives the variance of items in a list that match the selected criteria
@DAVG	Gives the arithmetic mean of items in a list that match the selected criteria

The general format of these functions follows:

@DSUM(*input_range,offset,criteria_range*)

Cue:
Remember that all the database functions consider that the first column in a database has an offset of zero.

The *input_range* and *criteria_range* arguments are the same as those used by the /**Data Query** command. The *input_range* specifies the database or part of a database to be scanned, and the *criteria_range* specifies which records are to be selected. The *offset* argument indicates which field to select from the database records; the offset value must be zero or a positive integer. A value of zero indicates the first column in the data table and a one indicates the second column.

Suppose that you want to compute the mean, variance, and standard deviation of the average interest rates offered by money market funds for a given week. Figure 6.27 shows a money market database and the results of the various database functions. The functions to find the count, sum, maximum, and minimum rates of return also are included. The database formulas from column E also are repeated in column F with /**Range Format Text** applied.

```
D5: [W10] @IF(B5>4,"Valid","Not Valid")                              READY

     A      B      C      D      E              F                    G    ◄
                                                                          ►
 1                                                                        ▲
 2                                                                        ▼
 3                                                                        ?
 4          Value  Result        Formula
 5              5  Valid _        @IF(B5>4,"Valid","Not Valid")
 6              3  Not Valid      @IF(B6>4,"Valid","Not Valid")
 7
 8       Wrench    OK             @IF(B8="Wrench","OK","Wrench only")
 9       Hammer    Wrench only    @IF(B9="Wrench","OK","Wrench only")
10
11    12-Dec-91   Past Dec       @IF(B11>=@DATE(91,12,1),"Past Dec","Before Dec")
12    12-Nov-91   Before Dec     @IF(B12>=@DATE(91,12,1),"Past Dec","Before Dec")
13
14
15
16
17
18
19
20
06-Mar-91  07:07 PM      UNDO                              NUM
```

Fig. 6.27. *Database functions used with the money market database.*

Figure 6.27 shows that the week's mean return for 17 different money market funds is an annual percentage rate of 7.7 (cell E5) and a variance of .057 (cell E6). One standard deviation below a mean of 7.7 is 7.5. One standard deviation above a mean of 7.7 is 7.9.

The result of the @DMIN function (cell E9) shows that Summit Cash Reserves returns the lowest rate at 7.3 percent. This value is almost two standard deviations below the mean. That figure, two standard deviations below the mean, is computed as follows:

Two Std. Devs. below mean $7.7 - (2 \times .238) = 7.2$

Because approximately 95 percent of the population falls within plus or minus two standard deviations of the mean, Summit Cash Reserves is close to being in the lowest 2.5 percent of the population of money market funds for that week; 5 percent is divided by 2 because the population is assumed to be normal.

The Shearson T-Fund conversely returns 8.2 percent, the highest rate. The @DMAX function has determined the highest rate, in cell B16, to be about two standard deviations above the mean, the highest 2.5 percent of the population.

By defining the proper criteria, you can analyze any portion of the database. How do the statistics change if funds returning less than 7.5 percent are excluded from the statistics? Figure 6.28 gives the answer.

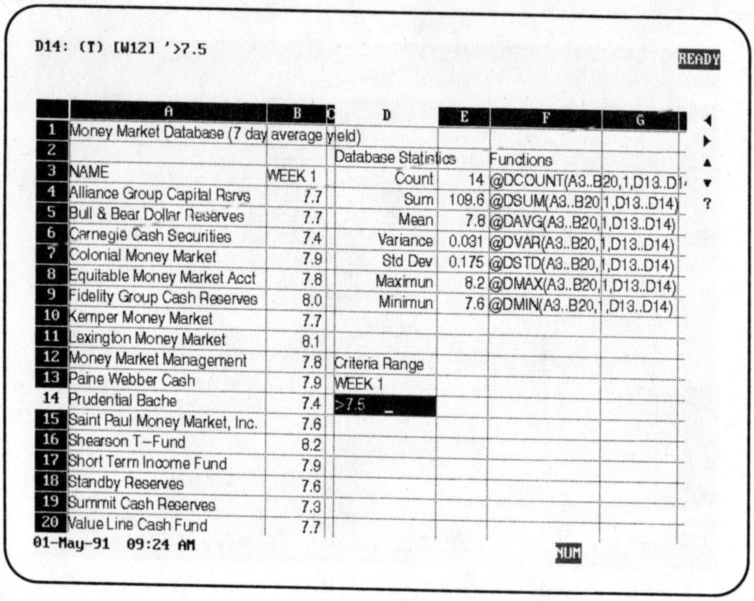

D14: (T) [W12] '>7.5 READY

	A	B	C	D	E	F	G
1	Money Market Database (7 day average yield)						
2				Database Statistics		Functions	
3	NAME	WEEK 1		Count	14	@DCOUNT(A3..B20,1,D13..D1	
4	Alliance Group Capital Rsrvs	7.7		Sum	109.6	@DSUM(A3..B20,1,D13..D14)	
5	Bull & Bear Dollar Reserves	7.7		Mean	7.8	@DAVG(A3..B20,1,D13..D14)	
6	Carnegie Cash Securities	7.4		Variance	0.031	@DVAR(A3..B20,1,D13..D14)	
7	Colonial Money Market	7.9		Std Dev	0.175	@DSTD(A3..B20,1,D13..D14)	
8	Equitable Money Market Acct	7.8		Maximun	8.2	@DMAX(A3..B20,1,D13..D14)	
9	Fidelity Group Cash Reserves	8.0		Minimun	7.6	@DMIN(A3..B20,1,D13..D14)	
10	Kemper Money Market	7.7					
11	Lexington Money Market	8.1					
12	Money Market Management	7.8		Criteria Range			
13	Paine Webber Cash	7.9		WEEK 1			
14	Prudential Bache	7.4		>7.5			
15	Saint Paul Money Market, Inc.	7.6					
16	Shearson T–Fund	8.2					
17	Short Term Income Fund	7.9					
18	Standby Reserves	7.6					
19	Summit Cash Reserves	7.3					
20	Value Line Cash Fund	7.7					

01-May-91 09:24 AM NUM

***Fig. 6.28.** Money fund analysis with funds earning less than 7.5 percent excluded.*

The database functions can tell you much about the database and about interpreting the values in the database. If you add a few more weeks' data to the database, as shown in figure 6.29, the database functions also can analyze all or part of the larger database.

You can use the preceding methods to interpret the statistics in figure 6.29. You must, however, adjust the input, or database, range address and the offset used in the database formulas to access the data from the third week. The input range is now A3..D20, and the offset must be adjusted to 3. Although the figure shows `Week 3` in cell E13 for clarity, any database field name can be used when the criteria range uses a formula instead of a value.

Using Logical Functions

Cue:
Logical functions add Boolean logic to your worksheet.

The logical functions enable you to use Boolean logic within your worksheets. Most logical functions test whether a condition is true or false. For most logical functions, both the test and what the function returns based on the test are built into the function.

The @ISSTRING function, for example, tests whether the argument is a string and returns a 1 if the test is true and a 0 if the test is false. For @IF, one of the logical functions, you describe the test and what the function result should be based on the test. @IF tests a condition and returns one value or label if the test is true and another value or label if the test is false.

The nine logical functions that 1-2-3 provides are summarized in table 6.8. In the text that follows, the logical functions are described in order of complexity.

```
F9: (F1) [W8] @DMIN(A3..D20,3,E13..E14)                        READY
```

	A	B	C	D	E	F	G
1	Money Market Database (7 day average yield)						
2					Database Statistics		
3	NAME	WEEK 1	WEEK 2	WEEK 3	Count	17	
4	Alliance Group Capital Reserves	7.7	7.8	7.9	Sum	133.5	
5	Bull & Bear Dollar Reserves	7.7	7.8	7.8	Mean	7.9	
6	Carnegie Cash Securities	7.4	7.5	7.5	Variance	0.058	
7	Colonial Money Market	7.9	7.9	7.9	Std Dev	0.240	
8	Equitable Money Market Account	7.8	7.9	7.9	Maximun	8.3	
9	Fidelity Group Cash Reserves	8.0	8.1	8.1	Minimun	7.4	
10	Kemper Money Market	7.7	7.8	7.8			
11	Lexington Money Market	8.1	8.2	8.2			
12	Money Market Management	7.8	7.9	7.9	Criteria Range		
13	Paine Webber Cash	7.9	8.0	8.0	WEEK 3		
14	Prudential Bache	7.4	7.5	7.5	>7		
15	Saint Paul Money Market, Inc.	7.6	7.7	7.7			
16	Shearson T-Fund	8.2	8.3	8.3			
17	Short Term Income Fund	7.9	8.0	8.1			
18	Standby Reserves	7.6	7.7	7.8			
19	Summit Cash Reserves	7.3	7.4	7.4			
20	Value Line Cash Fund	7.7	7.7	7.7			

```
01-May-91  09:26 AM                                            NUM
```

Fig. 6.29. Additional money fund data.

Table 6.8
Logical Functions

Function	Description
@IF(*test,true_result, false_result*)	Tests the condition and returns one result if the condition is true and another result if the condition is false
@ISERR(*cell_reference*)	Tests whether the argument results in ERR
@ISNA(*cell_reference*)	Tests whether the argument results in NA

continues

Table 6.8 *(continued)*

Function	Description
@TRUE	Equals 1, the logical value for true
@FALSE	Equals 0, the logical value for false
@ISNUMBER(*cell_reference*)	Tests whether the argument is a number
@ISSTRING(*cell_reference*)	Tests whether the argument is a string
@ISAAF(*name*)	Tests whether the argument is a defined add-in function
@ISAPP(*name*)	Tests whether the argument is an attached add-in program

@IF—Creating Conditional Tests

Cue:
The @IF function enables you to add decision-making logic to your worksheets.

The @IF function represents a powerful tool that you can use to manipulate text within your worksheets and to affect calculations. You can use the @IF statement, for example, to test the condition *The inventory on-hand is below 1,000 units* and then return one value or string if the statement is *true* or another value or string if the statement is *false*. The @IF function uses the following format:

> @IF(*test,true_result,false_result*)

Figure 6.30 shows several examples of the @IF function in action. To show clearly the functions, their arguments, and their results, the first column displays the value; the second column shows the calculated results of the function; and the third column shows the formula.

The first two @IF functions check whether the contents of cell B6 or B7 are greater than 4. The second two @IF functions check whether a cell contains the text string Wrench. The third example checks whether the dates in B12 and B13 are after December 1, 1990.

The @IF function can use six operators when testing conditions. These operators are summarized as follows:

Operator	Description
<	Less than
<=	Less than or equal to
=	Equal to
>=	Greater than or equal to
>	Greater than
<>	Not equal to

```
D5: [W10] @IF(B5>4,"Valid","Not Valid")                                    READY

     A     B     C     D      E                    F                   G      ◄
  1                                                                           ►
  2                                                                           ▲
  3                                                                           ▼
  4        Value  Result       Formula                                       ?
  5            5  Valid         @IF(B5>4,"Valid","Not Valid")
  6            3  Not Valid     @IF(B6>4,"Valid","Not Valid")
  7
  8        Wrench OK            @IF(B8="Wrench","OK","Wrench only")
  9        Hammer Wrench only   @IF(B9="Wrench","OK","Wrench only")
 10
 11     12-Dec-91 Past Dec      @IF(B11>=@DATE(91,12,1),"Past Dec","Before Dec")
 12     12-Nov-91 Before Dec    @IF(B12>=@DATE(91,12,1),"Past Dec","Before Dec")
 13
 14
 15
 16
 17
 18
 19
 20
06-Mar-91  07:07 PM      UNDO                        NUM
```

Fig. 6.30. Examples of the @IF function using strings and values.

As figure 6.30 shows, the @IF function is a powerful tool that enables you to add decision-making logic to your worksheets. The logic test can be based on strings or numeric comparison, and the function can return string or numeric values. You can further expand the power of @IF by using compound tests.

You also can perform complex conditional tests by using @IF functions with logical operators that enable you to test multiple conditions in one @IF function. These complex operators are summarized as follows:

Operator	Description
#AND#	Used to test two conditions, both of which must be true for the entire test to be true
#NOT#	Used to test that a condition is not true
#OR#	Used to test two conditions; if either condition is true, the entire test condition is true

Testing whether data entries are in the correct range of numbers is a simple but valuable use for complex @IF functions. Consider the following formula:

@IF(B5>=5#AND#B5<=20,"","Enter a number between 5 and 20.")

This formula checks whether the value entered in cell B5 is within the range of 5 to 20. If the entry is within the range, quotation marks appear with nothing between them. If the entry is not within the range, the following message appears in quotation marks in the cell containing the @IF function:

```
Enter a number between 5 and 20.
```

You also can specify within an @IF function the true or false result as another @IF function. Putting @IF functions inside other @IF functions is a common and important logical tool. This technique, called *nesting IF statements*, enables you to construct sophisticated logical tests and operations in your 1-2-3 worksheets.

@ISERR and @ISNA—Trapping Errors in Conditional Tests

The @ISERR function tests whether the argument equals ERR. If the test is true, the function returns the value 1; if the test is false, the function returns the value 0. @ISERR uses the following format:

@ISERR(*cell_reference*)

Reminder:
To trap errors produced in one location that can cause more drastic results in other locations, use @ISERR.

This function is helpful because you can use it to trap errors produced in one location that can cause more drastic results in other locations. Figure 6.31 shows how to use @ISERR to trap a possible division-by-zero error or a serious data-entry error that would cause an error to appear on-screen or in the printout. When you use this function as part of the @IF function shown in figure 6.31, the letters NA appear on-screen in place of ERR.

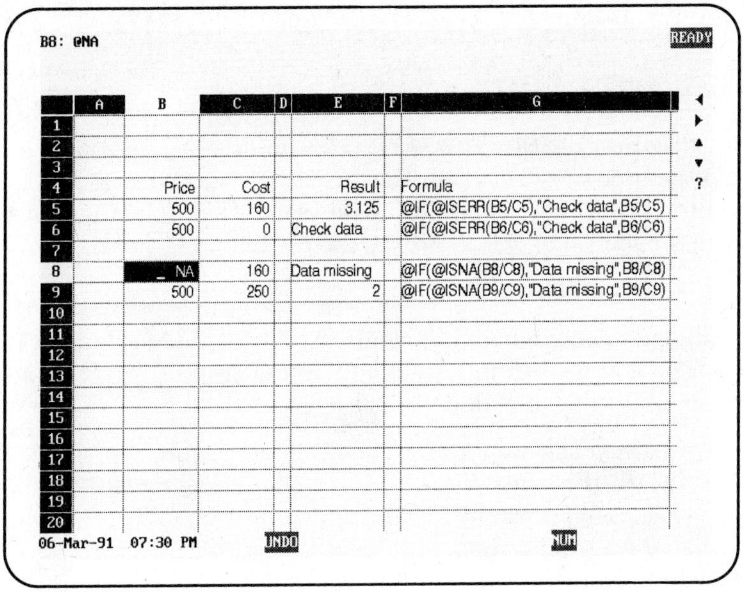

Fig. 6.31. The @ISERR and @ISNA functions used to test for errors.

The @ISNA function works similarly to @ISERR. @ISNA tests whether the argument you include is equal to NA. If the test is true, the function returns the value 1; if the test is false, the function returns the value 0. The @ISNA function uses the following format:

@ISNA(*cell_reference*)

You can use the @ISNA function to trap NA values in worksheets in which you have been using the @NA function. The @NA function, which represents "Not Available," is discussed in the "Using Special Functions" section, later in this chapter.

@TRUE and @FALSE— Checking for Errors

You use the @TRUE and @FALSE functions to check for errors. Neither function requires arguments, but both are useful for providing documentation for formulas and advanced macro commands. The @TRUE function returns the value 1, the Boolean logical value for true. The @FALSE function returns the value 0, the Boolean logical value for false.

@ISSTRING and @ISNUMBER— Checking the Cell's Aspect

@ISSTRING and @ISNUMBER are two functions that help you determine the type of value stored in a cell. They often are used with @IF to check for data-entry errors, numbers entered in the place of text or text entered in the place of numbers. For @ISNUMBER, use the following format:

@ISNUMBER(*cell_reference*)

If the argument is a number, the numeric value of the function is 1 (true). If the argument is a string, including the null string (" ") (nothing), the numeric value of the function is 0 (false).

You alternatively may want to use the @ISSTRING function. @ISSTRING works in nearly the same way as @ISNUMBER. The @ISSTRING function, however, determines whether a cell entry is a string value. The format of @ISSTRING is the following:

@ISSTRING(*cell_reference*)

If the argument for @ISSTRING is a string, the value of the function is 1 (true). If the argument is a number or a blank, however, the value of the function is 0 (false).

@ISNUMBER tests for a number, NA, or ERR, although the function cannot distinguish between numbers and blank cells. In many applications, however, @ISNUMBER provides sufficient testing of values, especially when you are certain that a cell is not blank. @ISSTRING can test for a string, although the function cannot distinguish between strings and blank cells. In many applications, however, @ISSTRING provides sufficient testing of strings, especially when you are certain that a cell is not blank.

You additionally can use the @CELL and @CELLPOINTER functions within formulas or macros to test whether a cell's content is a number, is a text string, or is blank. The functions are covered later in this chapter.

@ISAAF and @ISAPP—Checking for Add-Ins

Two functions check the status of add-in functions and programs. The @ISAAF function checks the status of an add-in function and discriminates between add-in functions and built-in functions. The format for @ISAAF is the following:

@ISAAF(*name*)

The argument *name* is the description of the add-in function for which you are testing. You can enter *name* as a literal string, a string formula, or a reference to a cell that contains a label. Do not include the initial @ sign in the argument. To test for an add-in function, such as @D360, use the following formula:

@ISAAF("D360")

If the formula returns 1, the function is available; if 0 returns, the function is not available. @ISAAF also returns 0 if the function is a built-in function.

The @ISAPP function checks whether a particular add-in program has been installed or attached with the Add-in manager. The format of the @ISAPP function is as follows:

@ISAPP(*name*)

If *name* is an attached add-in function, @ISAPP returns 1 (true); if *name* is not an attached add-in function or if it is a dynamic driver add-in, @ISAPP returns 0 (false).

You can enter name as a literal string, a string formula, or a reference to a cell that contains a label. To check the status of an add-in program, such as Wysiwyg, use the following formula:

@ISAPP("Wysiwyg")

If the formula returns 1, Wysiwyg is available; if it returns 0, Wysiwyg is not available.

Using String Functions

1-2-3 offers a variety of functions that provide significant power to manipulate literal text strings.

Strings are labels or portions of labels. More specifically, strings are data consisting of characters—alphabetic, numeric, blank, and special—enclosed in quotation marks, such as "total." The functions specifically designated as string functions are one category of 1-2-3 functions that use the power and flexibility of strings. Logical, error-trapping, and special functions use strings and values. The string functions, however, are specifically designed to manipulate strings. Table 6.9 summarizes the string functions available in 1-2-3.

Table 6.9
String Functions

Function	Description
@FIND(*search_string, string,start_number*)	Locates the start position of one string within another string
@MID(*string, start_number,number)*	Extracts a string of a specified number of characters from the middle of another string, beginning at the starting position
@LEFT(*string,number*)	Extracts the left-most specified number of characters from the string
@RIGHT(*string,number*)	Extracts the right-most specified number of characters from the string
@REPLACE(*original_ string,start_number, n,new_string)*	Replaces a number of characters in the original string with new string characters, starting at the character identified by the start position
@LENGTH(*string*)	Returns the number of characters in the string
@EXACT(*string1,string2*)	Returns 1 (true) if string1 and string2 are exact matches; otherwise, returns 0 (false)
@LOWER(*string*)	Converts all characters in the string to lowercase
@UPPER(*string*)	Converts all characters in the string to uppercase
@PROPER(*string*)	Converts the first character in each word in the string to uppercase and converts the remaining characters to lowercase
@REPEAT(*string,number*)	Copies the string the specified number of times in a cell
@TRIM(*string*)	Removes blank spaces from the string
@N(*range*)	Returns as a value the contents of the cell in the upper left corner of a range of values

Function	Description
@S(*range*)	Returns as a label the contents of the cell in the upper left corner of a range of values
@STRING(*numeric_value, decimal_places*)	Converts a value to a string showing the specified number of decimal places
@VALUE(*string*)	Converts a string to a value
@CLEAN(*string*)	Removes nonprintable characters from the string
@CHAR(*number*)	Converts a code number into an ASCII/LICS character
@CODE(*string*)	Converts the first character in the string into an ASCII/LICS code

You can link strings to other strings by using the concatenation operator (&). The discussion of the individual string functions in this section shows several examples of the use of the concatenation operator. You cannot link strings to cells that contain numeric values or that are empty. If you try, 1-2-3 returns ERR. Use @STRING if you want to concatenate a number with text.

Reminder:
You can link strings to other strings using the concatenation operator (&).

Avoid mixing data types in string functions. Some functions produce strings, for example, but other functions produce numeric results. If a function's result is not of the data type you need, use the @STRING and @VALUE functions to convert a numeric value to a string value or a string value to a numeric value.

The numbering scheme for positioning characters in a string begins with zero and continues to the number corresponding to the last character in the label. The prefix ' (apostrophe) before a label is not counted for numeric positioning. Negative position numbers are not allowed.

@FIND—Locating One String within Another

The @FIND function locates the starting position of one string within another string. You can use @FIND, for example, to determine at what position the blank space occurs within the string "Jim Johnson." The position number of the blank space then can be used with the @LEFT and @RIGHT functions to separate "Jim" and "Johnson" into two separate cells

Reminder:
@FIND performs only exact searches; upper- and lowercase are significant.

for use in a mailing list database. Although this example shows a search for the single blank-space character, @FIND also can find the location of multiple-character strings, such as "Calif," within longer strings.

The @FIND function uses the following format:

@FIND(*search_string,string,start_number*)

The *search_string* argument is the string you want to locate. In this example, the search string is " ". The string being searched is "Jim Johnson." And *start_number* is the position number in the string where you want to start the search. If you want to start at the first character and search through the contents of cell A6 for a blank space, use the following statement:

@FIND(" ",A6,0)

With "Jim Johnson" as the string, the @FIND function returns the value 4. In figure 6.32, @FIND locates the last name Lange, starting at the ninth character in cell B13. Note that the first position in a string is 0.

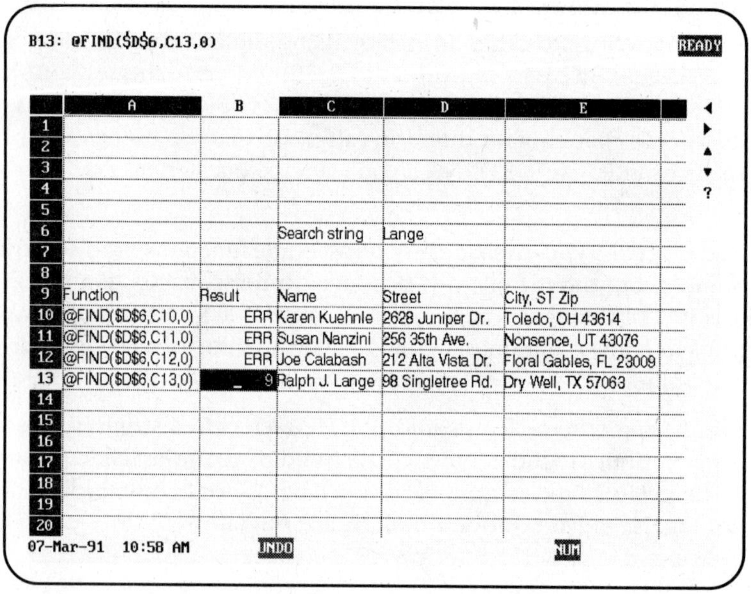

Fig. 6.32. The @FIND function used to find the text string in D6.

You can search for a second occurrence of the search string by adding 1 to the result of the first @FIND function. This move starts the next @FIND at the character location after the blank space that already was found. This formula searches for the character position of the second blank space:

@FIND(" ",A6,@FIND(" ",A6,0)+1)

When @FIND cannot find a match, the result is ERR.

@MID—Extracting One String from Another

@FIND helps you locate one string within another, and the @MID function enables you to extract one string from within another. @MID uses the following format:

@MID(*string,start_number,number*)

The *start_number* argument is a number representing the character position in the string where you want to begin extracting characters. The *number* argument, which indicates the length of the string, is the number of characters to extract. To extract the first name from a label containing the full name "Page Davidson," for example, use the following statement:

@MID("Page Davidson",0,4)

This function extracts the string starting in position 0, the first character, and continues for a length of four characters through the string "Page."

Now suppose that you want to extract the first and last names from a column of full names, and you want to put those two extracted names in separate columns. To accomplish both tasks, use the @MID and @FIND functions. Because you know that a blank space separates the first and last names, you can use @FIND to locate the position of the blank space in each full name. By using this character position, you can create the functions to extract the first and last names.

Cue:
Use @MID with @FIND to extract first and last names from a list of full names.

If cell C9 contains the full name "Karen Kuehnle," as shown in figure 6.33, place the following function in cell A9:

@MID(C9,0,@FIND(" ",C9,0))

The value of this function appear as "Karen" because @FIND(" ",C9,0) returns a value of 5 for the *number* argument. Next place the following function statement in cell B9, as shown in figure 6.33:

@MID(C9,@FIND(" ",C9,0)+1,99)

Here the @FIND function indicates that the start position is one character beyond the blank space and that the length of the string to be extracted is 99 characters. Although a length of 99 is greater than you need, no ERR results for this excess. The string that 1-2-3 extracts is "Kuehnle."

If you use this type of formula to convert a long string in a database into shorter strings, you may want to convert the string formulas—first and last names—into values before using the database. To make these conversions, use the /**R**ange Value command to copy the string formulas onto themselves. This technique replaces the formulas with the formula results.

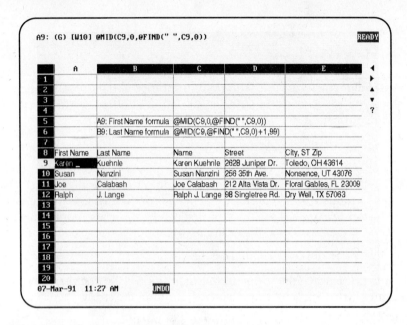

Fig. 6.33. *The @MID and @FIND functions used to locate and extract first and last names.*

@LEFT and @RIGHT—Extracting Strings from Left and Right

The @LEFT and @RIGHT functions are variations of @MID and are used to extract one string of characters from another by beginning at the left most and right most positions in the string. These functions require the following formats:

@LEFT(*string,number*)

@RIGHT(*string,number*)

Cue:
Use @RIGHT to extract the ZIP code from an address.

The *number* argument is the number of characters to be extracted. If, for example, you want to extract the ZIP code from the *string* "Cincinnati, Ohio 45243," use the following function statement:

@RIGHT("Cincinnati, Ohio 45243",5)

@LEFT works the same way as @RIGHT, except that @LEFT extracts from the beginning of a string. Use the following statement, for example, to extract the city in the preceding example:

@LEFT("Cincinnati, Ohio 45243",10)

You usually should use @FIND(",","Cincinnati, Ohio 45243",0), instead of 10, for the length in the function to extract the city from the address. To replace the @LEFT or @RIGHT functions with their results, copy the formulas onto themselves with the /**R**ange **V**alue command.

Figure 6.34 shows a mailing list database in which the original entries contain the city, state, and ZIP code in a single cell. The @FIND, @MID, @LEFT, and @RIGHT functions separate the long strings into separate cells.

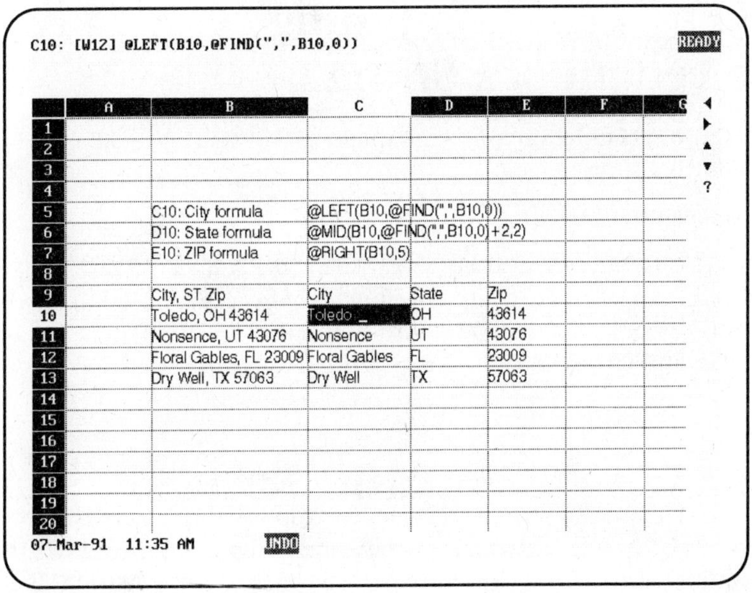

Fig. 6.34. *The @FIND, @MID, @LEFT, and @RIGHT functions used to separate long strings.*

@REPLACE—Replacing a String within a String

The @REPLACE function replaces one group of characters in a string with another group of characters. @REPLACE is a valuable tool for correcting a frequently incorrect text entry without retyping it. Use the following format for @REPLACE:

@REPLACE(*original_string,start_number,n,new_string*)

Cue:
If you start n=0, you insert new characters without replacing existing characters.

The *start_number* argument indicates the position at which 1-2-3 begins removing characters in the original string. The *n* argument shows how many characters to remove, and *new_string* contains the new characters to replace the removed ones. @REPLACE numbers the character positions in a string by starting with zero and continuing to the end of the string up to 239 characters.

@LENGTH—Computing the Length of a String

The @LENGTH function calculates the length of a string. @LENGTH uses the following format:

> @LENGTH(*string*)

@LENGTH frequently is used to calculate the length of a string being extracted from another string. This function also can be used to check for data entry errors. The function returns ERR as the length of numeric values, formulas, and empty cells.

@EXACT—Comparing Strings

The @EXACT function compares two strings and returns the value 1 (true) for strings that are exactly the same or the value 0 (false) for strings that are different. @EXACT uses the following format:

> @EXACT(*string1,string2*)

The @EXACT function's method of comparison is similar to the = operator in formulas, except that the = operator checks for a match regardless of uppercase, lowercase, or accented letters. @EXACT checks for an exact match that distinguishes among uppercase, lowercase, and accented letters. If, for example, cell B9 holds the string "wrench" and cell D9 holds the string "Wrench," the logical value of B9=D9 is 1 because the two strings are an approximate match. But the value of @EXACT(B9,D9) is 0 because the two strings are not an exact match; their cases are different.

Cue:
Use the @S function to ensure that the argument of @EXACT is a string.

The *string1* and *string2* arguments can be text, the result of text formulas, or references to cells containing text or text formulas. The examples in figure 6.35 demonstrate the use of @EXACT. Notice in the fourth and fifth examples that @EXACT cannot compare nonstring arguments. If either argument is a nonstring value of any type, including numbers, 1-2-3 returns ERR. You can use the @S function, explained later in this chapter, to ensure that the arguments used within @EXACT have string values.

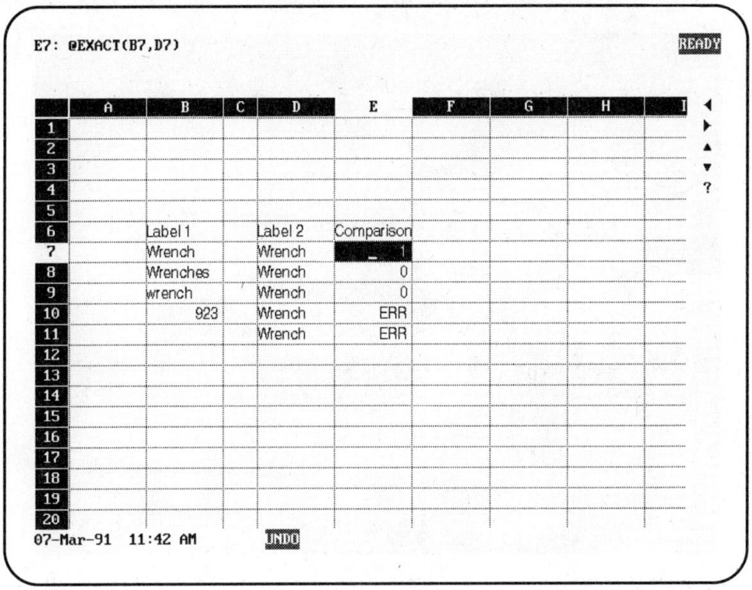

```
E7: @EXACT(B7,D7)                                          READY
```

Fig. 6.35. *Strings compared with the @EXACT function.*

@LOWER, @UPPER, and @PROPER— Converting the Case of Strings

1-2-3 offers three different functions for converting the case of a string value (see fig. 6.36):

@LOWER(*string*)   Converts all letters in a string to lowercase

@UPPER(*string*)   Converts all letters in a string to uppercase

@PROPER(*string*)   Capitalizes the first letter in each word of a label and converts the remaining letters in each word to lowercase

These three functions work with string values or references to strings. If a cell contains a number or a null string (" "), 1-2-3 returns ERR for each of these functions. You can use the @S function, explained later in this chapter, to ensure that the arguments of these functions have string values.

You can use @LOWER, @UPPER, or @PROPER to modify the contents of a database so that all entries in a field appear with the same capitalization. This technique produces reports that appear consistent.

```
D9: [W18] @LOWER(D6)                                           READY

        A          B         C            D            E      F      G   ◄
  1                                                                       ►
  2                                                                       ▲
  3                                                                       ▼
  4                                                                       ?
  5
  6                              Data:  jonathan Jone3
  7
  8              Function              Result
  9              @LOWER(D6)            jonathan jones
 10
 11              @UPPER(D6)            JONATHAN JONES
 12
 13              @PROPER(D6)           Jonathan Jones
 14
 15
 16
 17
 18
 19
 20
07-Mar-91  11:55 AM           UNDO
```

Fig. 6.36. The @LOWER, @UPPER, and @PROPER functions used to convert the case of alphanumeric strings.

If you select ASCII sort order in the Install program, capitalization also affects sorting order. In this case, uppercase and lowercase letters do not sort together. To ensure that data with different capitalization sorts together, create a column by using one of these functions that references the data and then sort on this new column. (The default collating sequence sorts upper- and lowercase together.)

@REPEAT—Repeating Strings within a Cell

The @REPEAT function repeats strings a specified number of times, as the backslash (\) repeats strings to fill a cell. But @REPEAT has some distinct advantages over the backslash. With @REPEAT, you can repeat the string the precise number of times you want. If the result is wider than the cell width, the result is displayed in empty adjacent cells to the right. @REPEAT uses the following format:

@REPEAT(*string,number*)

The *number* argument indicates the number of times you want to repeat a *string* in a cell. If you want to repeat the string "-**-" three times, for example, you can enter @REPEAT("-**-",3). The resulting string will be "-**—**—**-." This string follows 1-2-3's rule for long labels: the string is displayed beyond the right boundary of the column, if no entry is in the cell to the right. When you use the backslash to repeat a string, however, 1-2-3 fills the column to the exact column width. The string is limited to 240 characters.

Reminder:
@REPEAT copies strings beyond the current column width.

@TRIM—Removing Blank Spaces from a String

The @TRIM function eliminates unwanted blank spaces from the beginning, end, or middle of a string. If multiple adjacent spaces are within a string, they are reduced to a single space. Use the following format for @TRIM:

@TRIM(*string*)

@TRIM is useful for trimming spaces from data as it is entered into a macro or for trimming unwanted spaces from data in a database. Such spaces in a database can cause the sort order to be different from what you expect. Figure 6.38, which illustrates the @CLEAN function, described later in this chapter, also illustrates the use of @TRIM to remove extra space characters.

@N and @S—Testing for Strings and Values

The @N and @S functions convert cell contents into numeric values or string values. These functions are important when you use other functions that operate on numeric values only or functions that operate on string values only. When you are in doubt as to whether a cell contains a numeric or text value, use @N or @S to force the contents into becoming a number or text.

@N converts the contents of a cell to a number. If the cell is blank or contains a label, @N returns the value 0. @N always will have a numeric value.

@S converts the contents of a cell to text. If the cell contains a string or a formula that evaluates to a string, @S returns this string. If the cell contains a number or is empty, @S returns the empty string (').

The @N and @S functions have the following respective formats:

> @N(*range*)

> @S(*range*)

The argument must be a range or a single-cell reference. If you use a single-cell reference, 1-2-3 adjusts the argument to range format and returns the numeric or string value of the single cell. If the argument is a multicell range, @N or @S returns the numeric or string value of the upperleft corner of the range.

@STRING—Converting Values to Strings

The @STRING function enables you to convert a number to its text-string equivalent so that you can work with the number as text. For example, @STRING can override 1-2-3's automatic right-justification of numbers and display a number justified to the left. You also can use @STRING to convert a number to text and then concatenate the result into a text sentence.

Use the following format for @STRING:

> @STRING(*numeric_value,decimal_places*)

1-2-3 uses the Fixed format for the @STRING function. The *decimal_places* argument represents the number of decimal places to be included in the string. 1-2-3 rounds the resulting textual number to match the number of decimal places you specify. @STRING ignores all numeric formats you placed on the cell and operates on the numeric contents of the cell only. Figure 6.37 shows examples of values being used as strings.

@VALUE—Converting Strings to Values

The @VALUE function converts a number that is a string into a numeric value that can be used in calculations. The string must be text or a label that is made up of numbers only. The string argument within @VALUE must contain only numbers; the string cannot contain alphabetical characters. One valuable feature of @VALUE is that it converts text fractions into decimal numbers. The function is useful, therefore, in converting stock data from database or wire services into numbers that you can analyze and graph. @VALUE requires the following format:

@VALUE(*string*)

```
D6: [W14] +"There are "&@STRING(B6,0)&" left."                          READY
```

	A	B	C	D	E
1					
2					
3		Cell contents		Result	Function/formula
4	Values	45		45.00	@STRING(B4,2)
5		53.25		You owe $53.25.	+"You owe $"&@STRING(B5,2)&"."
6		6		There are 6 left.	+"There are "&@STRING(B6,0)&" left."
7					
8	Labels	22 1/2		22.5	@VALUE(B8)
9		22 3/8		22.375	@VALUE(B9)
10		22.5%		0.225	@VALUE(B10)
11					
12					
13					
14					
15					
16					
17					
18					
19					
20					

```
07-Mar-91  12:08 PM        UNDO
```

Fig. 6.37. *The @STRING and @VALUE functions used to convert strings and values.*

@CLEAN—Removing Nonprintable Characters from Strings

Sometimes when you import strings with /File Import, particularly when you use a modem, the strings will contain nonprintable characters. The @CLEAN function removes the nonprintable characters from the strings (see fig. 6.38). @CLEAN uses the following format:

@CLEAN(*string*)

Cue:
@CLEAN removes nonprintable characters from data imported into your worksheet.

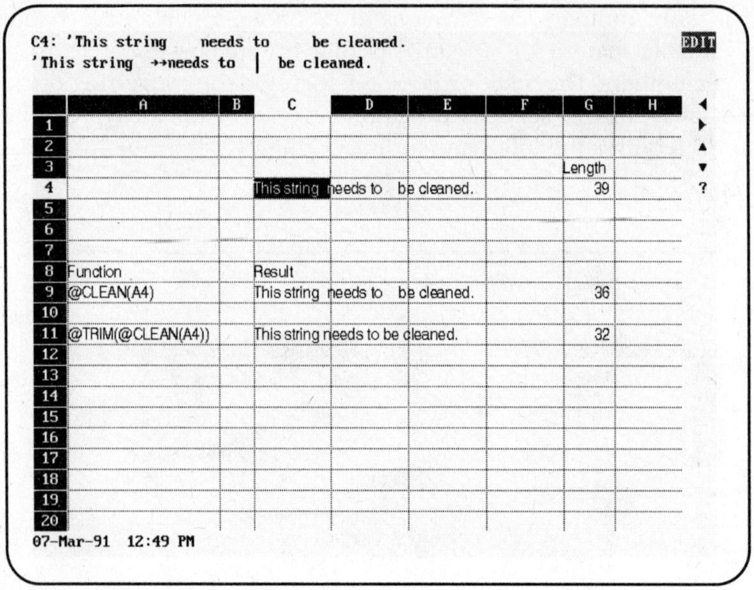

```
C4: 'This string    needs to    be cleaned.                              EDIT
'This string  ++needs to  |  be cleaned.
```

	A	B	C	D	E	F	G	H
1								
2								
3							Length	
4			This string	needs to	be cleaned.		39	
5								
6								
7								
8	Function		Result					
9	@CLEAN(A4)		This string	needs to	be cleaned.		36	
10								
11	@TRIM(@CLEAN(A4))		This string needs to be cleaned.				32	
12								
13								
14								
15								
16								
17								
18								
19								
20								

```
07-Mar-91  12:49 PM
```

Fig. 6.38. The @CLEAN function used to remove nonprintable characters.

The argument used with @CLEAN must be a string value or a cell reference to a cell that contains a string value. 1-2-3 does not accept a cell entry containing @CLEAN with a range argument specified.

Using Functions with Character Sets

1-2-3 offers several special functions for working with the Lotus International Character Set (LICS). LICS is a character set that enables you to display foreign language characters and mathematical symbols. The ASCII code number for a given character may not correspond to its LICS code number.

The complete set of LICS characters, listed in Appendix C of this book, includes everything from the copyright sign © to the lowercase e with the grave accent (è).

@CHAR—Displaying ASCII/LICS Characters

The @CHAR function produces on-screen the ASCII/LICS equivalent of a number between 1 and 255 that specifies that character. @CHAR uses the following format (see fig. 6.39):

@CHAR(*number*)

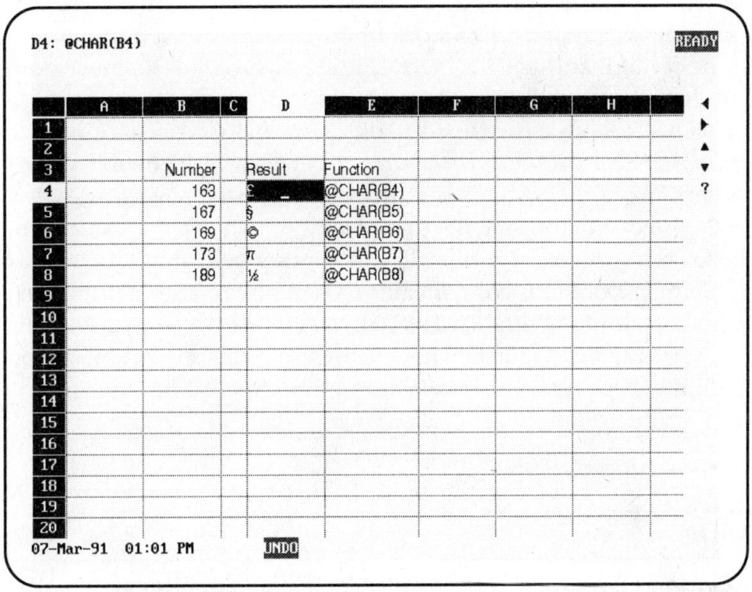

Fig. 6.39. Examples of the @CHAR function.

@CODE—Computing the LICS Code

The @CODE function performs the opposite of @CHAR. @CHAR takes a number and returns an LICS character, and @CODE examines an LICS character and returns a number. @CODE uses the following format:

@CODE(*string*)

Reminder:
Upper- and
lowercase
characters have
different LICS
codes.

Suppose that you want to find the LICS code for the letter A. You enter @CODE("A") in a cell, and 1-2-3 returns the number 65. If you enter @CODE("Aardvark"), 1-2-3 still returns 65, the code of the first character in the string.

Using Special Functions

The special functions are listed in a separate category in this book, because they provide information about cell or range contents or about worksheet location. @CELL and @CELLPOINTER are two of 1-2-3's most powerful special functions and have many different capabilities. @CELL and @CELLPOINTER can return up to 10 different characteristics of a cell. These characteristics are known as *attributes*. @NA and @ERR enable you to trap errors that may otherwise appear in your worksheet. With @ROWS and @COLS, you can determine the size of a range. The @@ function enables you to reference indirectly one cell with another cell within the worksheet. The @? function helps you locate an unknown add-in function in a worksheet formula. With @CHOOSE, @HLOOKUP, @VLOOKUP, and @INDEX, you can use specified keys in the functions' arguments to look up values in tables or lists. Table 6.10 lists 1-2-3's special functions.

Table 6.10
Special Functions

Function	Description
@@(*cell_reference*)	Returns the contents of the cell referenced by the cell address in the argument
@?	Indicates the location of an unknown add-in function used in a worksheet formula
@CELL(*attribute,range*)	Returns the attribute designated for the cell in the upper left corner of the range
@CELLPOINTER(*attribute*)	Returns the attribute designated for the current cell
@CHOOSE(*offset,list*)	Locates in a list the entry that is offset a specified amount from the front of the list
@COLS(*range*)	Computes the number of columns in a range

Function	Description
@ROWS(*range*)	Computes the number of rows in a range
@ERR	Displays ERR in the cell
@NA	Displays NA in the cell
@HLOOKUP (*key,range, row_offset*)	Locates the specified key in a lookup table and returns a value from that row of the range
@VLOOKUP (*key,range, column_offset*)	Locates the specified key in a lookup table and returns a value from that column of the range
@INDEX (*range,column_offset, row-offset*)	Returns the contents of a cell specified by the intersection of a row offset and column offset of a range

@@—Referencing Cells Indirectly

The @@ function provides a way of indirectly referencing one cell through the contents of another cell. @@ uses the following format:

> @@(*cell_reference*)

Cue:
@ @ provides a way of indirectly referencing one cell by way of another cell.

Simple examples show how the @@ function works. If cell A1 contains the label 'A2, and cell A2 contains the number 5, then the function @@(A1) returns the value 5. If the label in cell A1 is changed to 'B10, and cell B10 contains the label hi there, the function @@(A1) returns the string value "hi there."

The argument of the @@ function must be a cell reference of a cell containing an address. This address is an indirect address. Similarly, the cell referenced by the argument of the @@ function must contain a string value that evaluates a cell reference. This cell can contain a label, a string formula, or a reference to another cell, but the resulting string value is a cell reference.

The @@ function primarily is useful in cases in which several formulas have the same argument, and the argument must be changed from time to time during the course of the application. 1-2-3 enables you to specify the argument of each formula through a common indirect address, as shown in figure 6.40.

```
F5: (C2) [W11] @PMT(10000,@@(D5)/12,5*12)                        READY
```

	A	B	C	D	E	F	G	H	I	J
1										
2										
3										
4		Interest Rates		Reference Cell		Result		Functions		
5		9.0%		B6		$212.47		@PMT(10000,@@(D5)/12,5*12)		
6		10.0%				$9,413.07		@PV(200,@@(D5)/12,5*12)		
7		11.0%				$15,487.41		@FV(200,@@(D5)/12,5*12)		
8		12.0%				42.0		@TERM(200,@@(D5)/12,10000)		
9		13.0%				61.6		@CTERM(@@(D5)/12,10000,6000)		
10		14.0%								
11		15.0%								
12										
13										
14										
15										
16										
17										
18										
19										
20										

```
07-Mar-91  02:00 PM              UNDO
```

Fig. 6.40. The @@ function used to reference indirectly one cell through another cell.

In figure 6.40, column F contains a variety of financial functions, all of which use the @@ function to reference 1 of 6 interest rates in column B indirectly through cell D5. When you are ready to change the cell being referenced, you change only the label in cell D5, rather than editing all six formulas in column F.

@?—Indicating a Missing Add-In Function

If you use add-in functions with 1-2-3, you must attach the appropriate add-in before retrieving a worksheet. If you do not attach the add-in before you retrieve the worksheet, 1-2-3 substitutes the function name with @? and interprets the function as NA. You cannot enter @? directly into a worksheet.

@CELL and @CELLPOINTER— Checking Cell Attributes

The @CELL and @CELLPOINTER functions provide an efficient way to determine the nature of a cell, because these functions return a variety of different cell characteristics, such as a cell's contents, address, or width. @CELL and @CELLPOINTER are used primarily in macros and advanced macro command programs (see Chapters 13 and 14). Use the following formats for @CELL and @CELLPOINTER:

Cue:
@CELL and @CELLPOINTER provide an efficient way to determine the nature of a cell.

@CELL(*attribute,range*)

@CELLPOINTER(*attribute*)

Because you want to examine a cell's attributes, both functions have *attribute* as a string argument. @CELL, however, also requires the specification of a range; @CELLPOINTER works with the current cell.

The following examples illustrate how the @CELL function can be used to examine some cell attributes:

- CELL("address",SALES)

  If the range named SALES is C187..E187, 1-2-3 returns the absolute address $C$187. This statement is convenient for listing the upper left corner of a range's address in the worksheet.

- CELL("prefix",C195..C195)

  If cell C195 contains the label 'Chicago, 1-2-3 returns ' (indicating left alignment). If, however, cell C195 is blank, 1-2-3 returns nothing; in other words, the current cell appears blank.

- CELL("format",A10)

  1-2-3 returns the format of cell A10 as a text string by using the same notation as in the worksheet. For example, a Currency format with two decimal places appears as C2.

- CELL("width",B12..B12)

  1-2-3 returns the width of column B.

The *attribute* argument is text and must be enclosed in quotation marks.

If a range of cells is specified, the returned value refers to the top-left cell in the range. The full set of attributes that can be examined with @CELL and @CELLPOINTER follows:

Attribute	What the Function Returns
"address"	The absolute cell address
"col"	Column letter, as a value from 1 to 256 (A=1; IV=256)
"contents"	Cell contents
"filename"	Name of file that contains the cell
"format"	Fixed decimal, F0 to F15 Scientific, S0 to S15 Currency, C0 to C15 Comma, ,0 to ,15 G for General, label, or blank + for +/– Percent, P0 to P15 Date/Time, D1 to D9 Text, T Hidden, H
"prefix"	Same as label prefixes; blank if no label
"protect"	1 if protected; 0 if not
"row"	Row number, 1 to 8192
"type"	b is blank; v is value; and l is label
"width"	Column width

Figure 6.41 illustrates the use of the @CELLPOINTER function. The @CELLPOINTER function works well within @IF functions to test whether data entered into a cell is numeric or text. @CELL and @CELLPOINTER frequently are used within macros to examine the current contents or format of cells. {IF} macros then can use the results to change the worksheet accordingly.

The difference between @CELL and @CELLPOINTER is important. The @CELL function examines the string attribute of a cell you designate in a range format, such as A1..A1. If you use a single-cell range format, such as A1, 1-2-3 changes to the range format (A1..A1) and returns the attribute of the single-cell range. If you define a range larger than a single cell, 1-2-3 evaluates the cell in the upper left corner of the range.

```
B3: 123                                                        READY

       A        B        C    D        E            F        G        ◄
  1                                                                    ►
  2                     Result        Formula                          ▲
  3           _ 123    $B$3          @CELLPOINTER("address")           ▼
  4                         3        @CELLPOINTER("row")               ?
  5                         2        @CELLPOINTER("column")
  6                       123        @CELLPOINTER("contents")
  7                     v            @CELLPOINTER("type")
  8                                  @CELLPOINTER("prefix")
  9                         1        @CELLPOINTER("protect")
 10                         9        @CELLPOINTER("width")
 11                     G            @CELLPOINTER("format")
 12
 13
 14
 15
 16
 17
 18
 19
 20
07-Mar-91  02:22 PM        UNDO
```

Fig. 6.41. The @CELLPOINTER function used to determine cell attributes.

The @CELLPOINTER function operates on the current cell, the cell in which
the cell pointer was positioned when the worksheet was last recalculated.
The result remains the same until you enter a value, press Calc (F9) if your
worksheet is in automatic recalculation mode, or until you press Calc (F9)
in manual recalculation mode.

Suppose, for example, that you enter @**CELLPOINTER("address")** in cell
B22. The value displayed in that cell is the absolute address $B$22. If
recalculation is set to automatic, this same address remains displayed until
you make an entry elsewhere in the worksheet or move the cell pointer to
a new location and press Calc (F9). The address that appears in cell B22 then
changes to reflect the new position of the cell pointer. If recalculation is set
to manual, the address changes only if you move the cell pointer to a new
location and press Calc (F9).

@CHOOSE—Selecting an Item from a List

The @CHOOSE function selects an item from a list according to the item's
position in the list. The format of the function is the following:

Reminder:
@CHOOSE selects
an item from a list.

@CHOOSE(*offset,list*)

The function selects the item in the specified position, or *offset*, in the *list*. Positions in the list are numbered starting with 0. The first position is 0, for example; the second is 1; and the third is 2.

Figure 6.42 shows examples of the @CHOOSE function. Notice, in the second example, how the @INT function is combined with a formula to designate the offset for the @CHOOSE function. This method is useful if you need to choose from a list but are given numerical inputs that span a range.

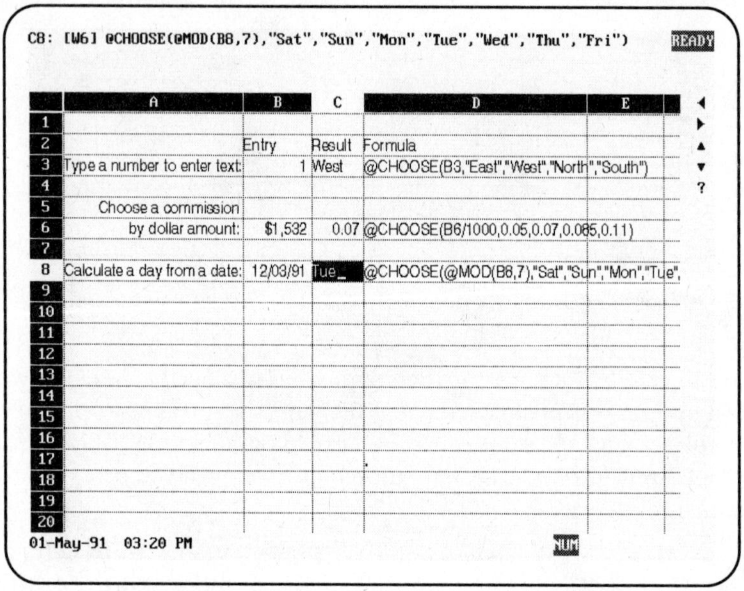

Fig. 6.42. The @CHOOSE function used to select an item from a list.

@COLS and @ROWS—Finding the Dimensions of Ranges

The @COLS and @ROWS functions describe the dimensions of ranges. Use the following formats for these functions:

@COLS(*range*)

@ROWS(*range*)

Suppose that you want to determine the number of columns in a range called PRICE_TABLES, which has the cell coordinates D4..G50, and to display that value in the current cell. To calculate the number of columns, you enter **@COLS(PRICE_TABLES)**. Similarly, you can enter **@ROWS(PRICE_TABLES)** to display the number of rows in the range.

@COLS and @ROWS are useful functions to use within macros to determine the size of a range. After the size of a range is determined, you can use {FOR} loops to step the macro through all the cells within the range.

If you specify a single cell, such as **C3**, as the argument for the @COLS or @ROWS function, 1-2-3 changes the argument to range format (**C3..C3**) and returns the value 1 for the function.

@ERR and @NA—Trapping Errors

When you create templates for other users, you may want to use @NA or @ERR to screen out unacceptable values for cell entries. Suppose, for example, that you are developing a checkbook-balancing macro in which checks with values less than or equal to zero are unacceptable. One way to indicate the unacceptability of these checks is to use @ERR to signal that fact. You can use the following version of the @IF function:

@IF(B9<=0,@ERR,B9)

In plain English, this statement says, "If the amount in cell B9 is less than or equal to zero, then display ERR on the screen; otherwise, use the amount." Notice that the @ERR function controls the display in almost the same way that @NA does in a previous example. A better technique, however, is to display a message to the user that indicates the specific error, which the following function provides:

@IF(B9<=0,"Enter positive amounts",B9)

This function then displays the message, Enter positive amounts, to indicate an amount error. 1-2-3 also uses ERR as a signal for unacceptable numbers—division by zero or mistakenly deleted cells, for example. ERR often displays temporarily when you reorganize the cells in a worksheet. If ERR persists, you may need to do some careful analysis to determine the reason.

1-2-3 displays ERR, as it does for NA, in any cells that depend on a cell with an ERR value. Sometimes the ERR cascades through other dependent cells. Use Undo (Alt-F4) to return the worksheet to its state before the change.

@HLOOKUP and @VLOOKUP—
Looking Up Entries in a Table

The @HLOOKUP and @VLOOKUP functions retrieve a string or value from a table based on a specified key used to find the information. The operation and format of the two functions are essentially the same, except that @HLOOKUP looks through horizontal tables—hence, the H in the function name—and @VLOOKUP looks through vertical tables—the source of the V in the function name. These functions use the following formats, respectively:

@HLOOKUP(*key,range,row_offset*)

@VLOOKUP(*key,range,column_offset*)

Cue:
When you use numeric keys, make sure that the key values ascend in order.

When you use numeric keys, the key values must ascend in order; otherwise, 1-2-3 produces incorrect results. If the keys are strings, the keys can be listed in any order. With numeric keys, @HLOOKUP and @VLOOKUP actually are searching for the largest value that is less than or equal to the key. Therefore, if either function cannot find a value that is equal, the function selects the largest value that is less than the numeric key.

The *range* argument is the area of the entire lookup table. Offset specifies which row or column contains the data you want. The *offset* argument always is a number in ascending order ranging from 0 to the highest number of columns or rows in the lookup table. Number 0 marks the column or row containing key data. The next column or row is 1, and the next is 2. When you specify an offset number, it cannot be negative or exceed the correct number of columns or rows.

Figure 6.43 shows a table for @HLOOKUP. This function is useful for finding a value you otherwise would need to find manually in a table, such as tax amounts, shipping zones, or interest charges.

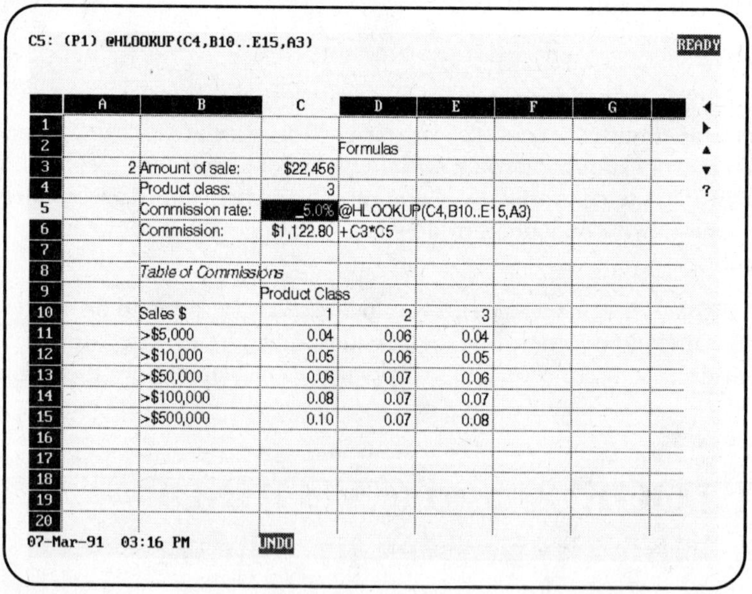

C5: (P1) @HLOOKUP(C4,B10..E15,A3) READY

	A	B	C	D	E	F	G
1							
2				Formulas			
3	2	Amount of sale:	$22,456				
4		Product class:	3				
5		Commission rate:	5.0%	@HLOOKUP(C4,B10..E15,A3)			
6		Commission:	$1,122.80	+C3*C5			
7							
8		*Table of Commissions*					
9			Product Class				
10		Sales $	1	2	3		
11		>$5,000	0.04	0.06	0.04		
12		>$10,000	0.05	0.06	0.05		
13		>$50,000	0.06	0.07	0.06		
14		>$100,000	0.08	0.07	0.07		
15		>$500,000	0.10	0.07	0.08		
16							
17							
18							
19							
20							

07-Mar-91 03:16 PM UNDO

Fig. 6.43. *The @HLOOKUP function used to retrieve strings and values from tables.*

Avoid three common errors when you use @HLOOKUP and @VLOOKUP. First, when you use a string as the key argument, the LOOKUP function returns an error if the function cannot find the string in the lookup table. If either function with a string key returns ERR, check that you have not misspelled the string in the function or in the lookup table.

A second error is failing to include the columns or rows that contain key strings or values in the range of the lookup table; the result is an ERR condition. Figure 6.44 uses cell addresses to specify the table so that you can easily understand the examples. However, you probably will want to name your lookup tables with the /**Range Name Create** command; yet naming them can make spotting missing rows or columns more difficult.

A third error is placing the key strings or values in the wrong column. The key strings or values belong in the first column or row, and the column or row numbering starts at 0. Therefore, the first offset is 0 containing the key; the second is 1; and the third is 2.

A lookup using an offset of zero returns the position of the match. An @VLOOKUP function with an offset of zero, for example, returns the row offset, and an @HLOOKUP function returns the column offset to the match.

@INDEX—Retrieving Data from Specified Locations

@INDEX, a data-management function, is similar to the table-lookup functions described earlier. However, @INDEX has some unique features. @INDEX uses the following format:

@INDEX(*range,column_offset,row_offset*)

Like @HLOOKUP and @VLOOKUP, @INDEX finds a value within a table. Unlike the lookup functions, however, @INDEX does not compare a key value against values in the first row or column of the table. @INDEX instead requires you to indicate the *column_offset* and *row_offset* of the range from which you want to retrieve data. For example, the following function, shown in figure 6.44, returns the value 3317:

@INDEX(C10..G14,C5,C6)

Cell C5 contains the column offset, and cell C6 contains the row offset. Notice that the number 0 corresponds to the first column, and 1 corresponds to the second column. The same numbering scheme applies to rows. Using 3 for the *column_offset* argument and 2 for the *row_offset* argument indicates that you want an item from the fourth column, third row.

```
C7: @INDEX(C10..G14,C5,C6)                                    READY
```

	A	B	C	D	E	F	G	H
1								
2								
3								
4				Formula				
5		Column	3					
6		Row	2					
7		Lookup value	3317	@INDEX(C10..G14,C5,C6)				
8								
9		Row/Column	0	1	2	3	4	
10		0	8936	5886	4703	5063	8506	
11		1	4095	7285	9231	9431	7005	
12		2	1393	2625	7221	3317	4382	
13		3	7183	1185	3477	7681	5173	
14		4	9234	4563	5678	6214	1286	
15								
16								
17								
18								
19								
20								

```
07-Mar-91  03:30 PM        UNDO
```

Fig. 6.44. *An example of the @INDEX function.*

Reminder:

With the @INDEX function, you cannot use column or row numbers that fall outside the relevant range.

With the @INDEX function, you cannot use column or row numbers that are outside the range. Using negative numbers or numbers too large for the range causes 1-2-3 to return ERR. Using the @INDEX function is useful when you know the exact position of a data item in a range of cells and you want to locate the item quickly. @INDEX works well for rate quotation systems, for example. Figure 6.45 shows an example of a system for quoting magazine advertising rates. The following function is used:

@INDEX(B8..G12,C3,C4)

Notice that the range is extended to include column B and row 8. This adjustment compensates for the fact that the column and row offsets begin at zero. When **1** and **3** are entered in cells C3 and C4, respectively, the rate is $2,085, which is the amount in the cell in the first column and third row of the rate matrix.

```
C5: (C0) @INDEX(B8..G12,C3,C4)                                    READY
```

	A	B	C	D	E	F	G	H
1		Advertising Rate Card						
2								
3		No Times	1					
4		Size	3					
5		Rate	$2,085					
6								
7			(1)	(2)	(3)	(4)	(5)	
8			1 X	3 X	6 X	9 X	12 X	
9	(1)	1/2 page	1500	1275	1084	921	783	
10	(2)	3/4 page	1835	1560	1326	1127	958	
11	(3)	1 page	2085	1772	1506	1280	1088	
12	(4)	2 pages	3210	2658	2260	1921	1633	
13								
14								
15								
16								
17								
18								
19								
20								

```
07-Mar-91  04:03 PM        UNDO
```

Fig. 6.45. The @INDEX function used for advertising rate quotations.

Summary

This chapter described the functions that 1-2-3 provides to make formula and worksheet construction easier and more error-free. After you become proficient in the use of the functions, you regularly can incorporate them into your worksheet models and use this chapter as a reference for the formats and the types of arguments the functions require.

In the next chapter, you learn how to save, retrieve, and manage files with 1-2-3.

7

Managing Files

The commands available when you select /File from 1-2-3's main menu provide a wide range of file management, modification, and protection functions. Some commands, such as /File Erase and /File List, are similar to operating system commands. Other commands relate to specific 1-2-3 tasks and applications. Through the /File menu, you can, for example, combine data from several files or extract data from one file to place in another file. You also can give a file "reservation" status so that only one user can update and write information to the file. In addition to the /File menu, 1-2-3 Release 2.3 provides another file management tool—Viewer, an add-in program that enables you to see or retrieve the contents of on-disk worksheet files and to create links. This chapter covers the /File commands and Viewer and offers advice for efficient 1-2-3 file management.

This chapter shows you how to perform the following tasks:

- Manage a file in memory
- Name files
- Change directories
- Save files to disk
- Retrieve files from disk
- Erase files from memory
- Extract and combine data
- Protect files
- Erase files from disk

- List different types of files

- Use the Viewer file management add-in

- Transfer files between different programs

- Use 1-2-3 in a multiuser environment

To work with 1-2-3's worksheet file management commands, select the **File** option on the 1-2-3 main menu. From this menu option, you can retrieve files, combine information into the current file, create files, and perform other operations. A brief description of these commands follows. The rest of this chapter covers the /File commands in detail.

When you first start 1-2-3, your worksheet is blank. To build a new worksheet, use the blank one. To start with an existing file, use /**File Retrieve**. The /**File Retrieve** command replaces the blank worksheet (the current file) in memory with a file that you previously created.

To combine information into the current file, use /**File Combine** or /**File Import**. With Combine, you can read all or part of a 1-2-3 worksheet file and combine the data into the current file. With Import, you can read a text file and combine the data into the current file.

To save a file, use /**File Save** or /**File Xtract**. /**File Save** saves the file in memory onto the disk. /**File Xtract** saves part of a file as a new file.

You usually work with data files in one directory at a time on your disk. To change the default data directory, use /**File Directory**. To see a list of all or some of the files in the current directory, use /**File List**. To save a list of files as a table in a worksheet, use /**File Admin Table**. To erase unneeded files from your disk to make room for other files, use /**File Erase**.

If you work with shared files in a network or other multiuser environment, you can use /**File Admin Reservation** to control write-access to files. If some of your files use formulas that refer to cells in shared files, use /**File Admin Link-Refresh** to update these formulas.

Managing a File in Memory

Reminder:
In 1-2-3, a file is a disk-based file.

In 1-2-3 Release 2.3, the word *file* refers to a disk-based file that stores computer information magnetically for the long term. When you build or change worksheets in memory, the information is lost unless you first save the new changes to a disk-based file. Reading a file from disk produces in the computer's memory an exact copy of the disk file. The file still exists, unchanged, on disk.

When you save a file, you store on the disk an exact copy of the file that is in the computer's memory. The file still exists, unchanged, in memory. To manage files on disk, you must understand how to manage files in memory.

The computer's memory is your work area. When you use the /Quit command to leave 1-2-3 or the /Worksheet Erase command, you lose the file in memory. When you use /File Retrieve, you replace the current file in memory with another file from the disk. If you save a file before removing the file from memory, you can read the file again from disk. If you change a file and do not save the file to disk, you lose the changes if you erase the file or replace the file in memory.

Naming Files

The exact rules for file names depend on the operating system you use. In this book, the assumption is that you use a version of MS-DOS or PC DOS. File names consist of a one- to eight-character name plus an optional file extension of one to three characters. The extension usually identifies the type of file. An example of a file name is BUDGET.WK1. Usually, you choose the file name, and 1-2-3 supplies the extension.

A file name in DOS can contain letters, numbers, and the following characters:

> ~ ! @ $ % ^ & ( ) - _ { } # '

Spaces are not allowed. All letters convert automatically to uppercase. A file name should include only letters, numbers, the hyphen (-), and the underline character (_). Other characters may work for now, but some may not work in a future version of DOS or in other operating systems. For example, the characters # and ' work with current versions of DOS but not with OS/2. Whether or not you plan to switch to OS/2, a future release of DOS may make these two characters invalid in file names.

Reminder:
A file name should include only letters, numbers, the hyphen, and the underline character.

The standard extension for 1-2-3 Release 2.3 worksheet files is WK1. When you type a file name, type the one- to eight-character part of the name. 1-2-3 adds the extension for you. 1-2-3 Release 2.3 uses the following extensions:

Extension	Description
WK1	For worksheet files
BAK	For backup worksheet files
FMT	For Wysiwyg format files

Extension	Description
PRN	For print-image text files with no special characters
ENC	For encoded print-image files with graphics and/or formatting characters specific to one printer
PIC	For files in Lotus graph-image format
ADN	For add-in programs
MLB	For Macro Library files

You can override these standard extensions and type your own. In addition, 1-2-3 can read worksheets that have the following extensions:

Extension	Description
WKS	For 1-2-3 Release 1A worksheet files
WRK	For Symphony Releases 1 and 1.01 worksheet files
WR1	For Symphony Releases 1.1, 1.2, and 2 worksheet files

When you execute most file commands, 1-2-3 expects that you want to see the existing files that have WK* extensions and lists these files in the control panel. The asterisk (*) means "any character;" WK*, therefore, designates such extensions as WK1 and WKS. If you create a file whose extension does not start with WK, 1-2-3 does not list that file name as a default.

To read a file that uses a nonstandard extension, type the complete file name and extension. You may want to save a file with a nonstandard extension so that the file does not show up when 1-2-3 lists the worksheet files. For example, you may want to use a nonstandard extension with a file that is part of a macro-controlled system in which macros retrieve or open the file. Keeping the macro file hidden prevents you from accidentally retrieving the file outside of the macro. The nonstandard extension "hides" the file from any list of worksheet files. To retrieve the file outside of the macro environment, perhaps to change the file, type the complete file name and extension.

To change the file list's default extension from WK* to another extension, use /**File List Other** and specify the new default extension. To list only Release 2.3, 2.2, 2.01, and 2.0 worksheets, type ***.WK1**. To list all 1-2-3 and Symphony worksheet files, type ***.W***.

You need not accept the default WK1 extension when you save a file. You can type any extension you want.

Changing Directories

A hard disk is logically separated into several directories (also called *subdirectories*). The set of directories leading from the root to the directory that contains the file you want is called the *path*, or *directory path*. When you perform file operations in 1-2-3, you usually deal with one directory at a time.

To select the default directory when you start 1-2-3, use /Worksheet Global **Default Directory**. Then press Esc and type the path to the directory that contains the files you use most often (or edit the current path name) and press Enter. Figure 7.1 shows the sample path name C:\123R23\FILES. To make the name of the path permanent, use /Worksheet Global Default **Update**.

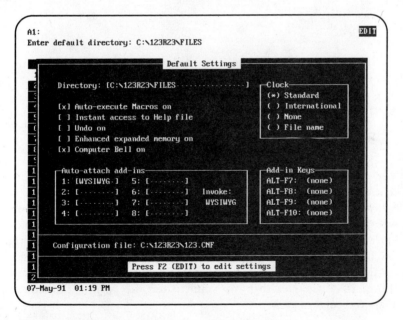

Fig. 7.1. The sample default directory C:\123R23\FILES.

To select the default directory with the dialog boxes, select /Worksheet **Global**. At the Global Settings dialog box, press F2 (Edit) or click on the box with the left mouse button. Then select Default Settings.... From the Default Settings dialog box that appears, select Directory. Press Esc and type the path to the directory that holds the files you use most often (or edit the current path name) and press Enter. Figure 7.2 shows the current path name C:\123R23\FILES. To save the name of the path permanently, select Update, and the Global Settings dialog box returns to the screen. To return to 1-2-3, select OK at the Global Settings dialog box and then press Esc or click the right mouse button.

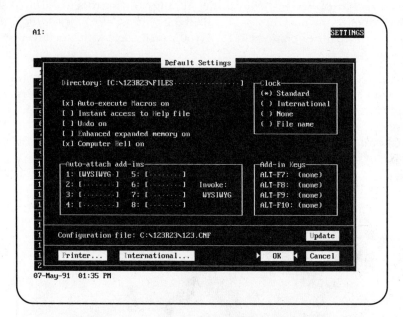

***Fig.* 7.2.** *The current directory displayed in the Default Settings dialog box.*

To change the current directory (for the current session only), use /File Directory. 1-2-3 displays the current directory path (see fig. 7.3). You can ignore the current path and type a new path. As you type a character, the old path clears. To edit the current path, use the End, Home, left-arrow, right-arrow, Del, and Backspace keys. Type the directory path you want to use and press Enter. When you perform all other file commands, such as /File Retrieve, 1-2-3 assumes that you want to use the current directory and displays the current path.

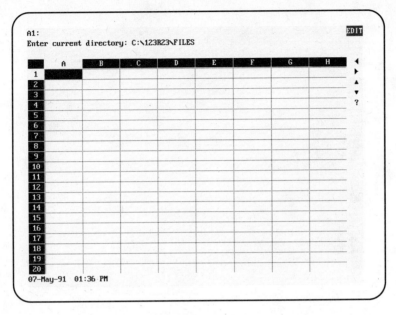

A1:
Enter current directory: C:\123R23\FILES

07-May-91 01:36 PM

Fig. 7.3. The current directory, following a prompt for a directory path.

Saving Files

The /File Save command enables you to store on disk a magnetic copy of the file in memory, including all the formats, names, and settings.

When you save a file for the first time, the file is unnamed. 1-2-3 supplies a list of the worksheet files (in the current directory) on the disk (see fig. 7.4). You can either select a directory entry or type a new file name. Always try to choose a meaningful name for the file. Figure 7.5 shows the control panel after you type the letters **BUD** as the first three characters of the file name BUDGET. After you type the file name, press Enter. 1-2-3 automatically supplies the WK1 extension if you do not supply a different extension.

When you save a file that was previously saved, the file is already named. 1-2-3 supplies this name as the default. Figure 7.6 shows the control panel that appears when you save the file BUDGET, which you previously saved. To save the file under the same name, press Enter. To save the file under a different name, ignore the old name, type the new name, and press Enter. To save the file under a name similar to the old name, press the space bar and Backspace. Use the arrows, Backspace, and Del keys to erase part of the old name; then type any additional characters.

```
List  ◄  ►  ▲  ▼  ?  ..  A:  B:  C:  D:                          FILES
Enter name of file to save: C:\123R23\FILES\*.wk1
BOSTON.WK1      CAMBRIDG.WK1    LONDON.WK1      MONTREAL.WK1   NEW_YORK.WK1
           A           B        C         D         E        F        G
    1  Department 1   QTR 1    QTR 2     QTR 3     QTR 4   TOTALS
    2             ------   ------    ------    ------   ------
    3  Product 1    4,428    3,170     7,035     9,829   24,462
    4  Product 2    4,664    3,340     7,410    10,354   25,768
    5  Product 3    9,197    6,328    13,623    17,181   46,329
    6  Product 4    7,563    6,651    15,779    21,130   51,123
    7  Product 5    7,519    5,896    15,208    20,245   48,868
    8  Product 6    5,073    9,558    25,708    18,119   58,458
    9             ------   ------    ------    ------   ------
   10            38,444   34,943    84,763    96,858  255,008
   11
   12
   13
   14
   15
   16
   17
   18
   19
   20
03-May-91  11:14 AM                                         NUM
```

Fig. 7.4. *The /File Save prompt.*

```
A1: [W14] 'Department 1                                          EDIT
Enter name of file to save: C:\123R23\FILES\BUD

           A           B        C         D         E        F        G      ◄
    1  Department 1   QTR 1    QTR 2     QTR 3     QTR 4   TOTALS              ►
    2             ------   ------    ------    ------   ------               ▲
    3  Product 1    4,428    3,170     7,035     9,829   24,462              ▼
    4  Product 2    4,664    3,340     7,410    10,354   25,768              ?
    5  Product 3    9,197    6,328    13,623    17,181   46,329
    6  Product 4    7,563    6,651    15,779    21,130   51,123
    7  Product 5    7,519    5,896    15,208    20,245   48,868
    8  Product 6    5,073    9,558    25,708    18,119   58,458
    9             ------   ------    ------    ------   ------
   10            38,444   34,943    84,763    96,858  255,008
   11
   12
   13
   14
   15
   16
   17
   18
   19
   20
12-Mar-91  02:01 PM
```

Fig. 7.5. *A new file name entered at the /File Save prompt.*

```
A1: [W14] 'Department 1                                    EDIT
Enter name of file to save: C:\123R23\FILES\BUDGET.WK1
```

	A	B	C	D	E	F	G	
1	Department 1	QTR 1	QTR 2	QTR 3	QTR 4	TOTALS		◄
2		------	------	------	------	------		►
3	Product 1	4,428	3,170	7,035	9,829	24,462		▲
4	Product 2	4,664	3,340	7,410	10,354	25,768		▼
5	Product 3	9,197	6,328	13,623	17,181	46,329		?
6	Product 4	7,563	6,651	15,779	21,130	51,123		
7	Product 5	7,519	5,896	15,208	20,245	48,868		
8	Product 6	5,073	9,558	25,708	18,119	58,458		
9		------	------	------	------	------		
10		38,444	34,943	84,763	96,858	255,008		
11								
12								
13								
14								
15								
16								
17								
18								
19								
20								

```
07-May-91  01:37 PM
```

Fig. 7.6. The default file name supplied by 1-2-3 for a file previously saved under that name.

For example, suppose that you build and then want to save a worksheet for the first time. You type **BUDGET**, and press Enter. Suppose that you subsequently add to the worksheet and then want to save the file again, under the name BUDGET1. If you don't want the default file name BUDGET.WK1, press the space bar and then use the left-arrow key to move the cursor after the T in BUDGET, type **1**, and then press Enter. Renaming different versions of the same worksheet is a good way to keep several backup copies accessible while you build a new worksheet. If you make a catastrophic error which you don't discover until after you saved the file, you can use a previous version of the file to correct the mistake.

Cue:
Save different versions of your files under different names.

If another file exists in the same directory and under the same file name that you chose, 1-2-3 warns you and at the same time gives you three options: Cancel, **R**eplace, and **B**ackup (see fig. 7.7). If you do not want to write over the old file on disk, select **C**ancel to cancel the command and start over. You then can save your file under a different name.

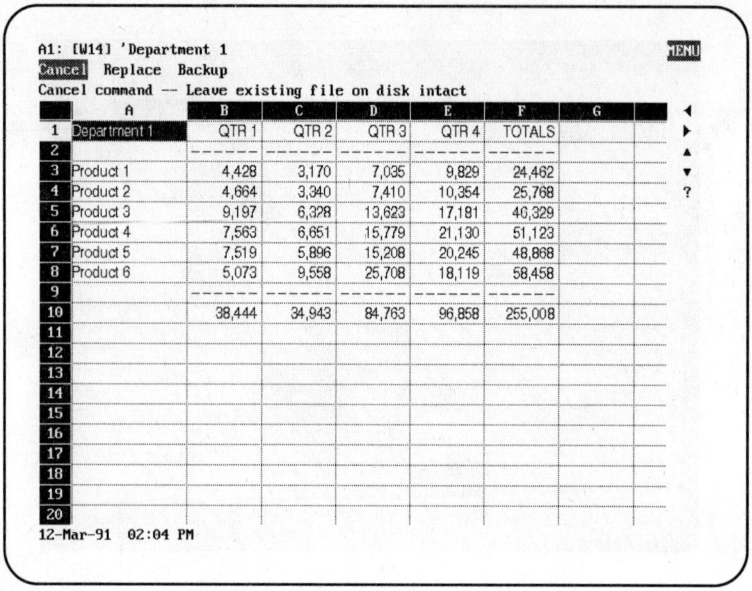

```
A1: [W14] 'Department 1                                            MENU
Cancel  Replace  Backup
Cancel command -- Leave existing file on disk intact
            A        B       C       D       E       F       G
  1 Department 1    QTR 1   QTR 2   QTR 3   QTR 4   TOTALS
  2              ------- ------- ------- ------- -------
  3 Product 1      4,428   3,170   7,035   9,829  24,462
  4 Product 2      4,664   3,340   7,410  10,354  25,768
  5 Product 3      9,197   6,328  13,623  17,181  46,329
  6 Product 4      7,563   6,651  15,779  21,130  51,123
  7 Product 5      7,519   5,896  15,208  20,245  48,868
  8 Product 6      5,073   9,558  25,708  18,119  58,458
  9              ------- ------- ------- ------- -------
 10             38,444  34,943  84,763  96,858 255,008
 11
 12
 13
 14
 15
 16
 17
 18
 19
 20
12-Mar-91  02:04 PM
```

Fig. 7.7. *The menu that appears when you try to save a file under a name that already exists in the current directory.*

To write over the old file, select **R**eplace. The old file with the same name is lost permanently. When you choose **R**eplace, 1-2-3 first deletes the old file from the disk. If you get a `Disk full` message while saving a file, you must save the file on another disk or erase some existing files to make room to save the file. If you do not successfully save the file, both the new version in memory and the old version on disk are lost.

To save your file under the same name, but still keep the old file on disk, choose **B**ackup. **B**ackup renames the old file with a BAK extension and then saves the new file under the same file name, with a WK1 extension. This command enables you to have both files on disk.

You can use the **B**ackup option to save only one file as a backup. If you save the file again and choose **B**ackup, 1-2-3 deletes the current backup file, renames the WK1 file with a BAK extension, and saves the new file (the worksheet in memory) under a WK1 extension. To keep the old file with a BAK extension, you must copy the file to a different disk or directory, or you must rename the file.

Retrieving Files from Disk

/**File** **R**etrieve enables you to read a file from disk into memory. This command replaces the current file in memory with the new file. If you just started 1-2-3, or if nothing but a blank worksheet is in memory, this command brings a new file into memory. If you have a current file in memory, and you changed the file since you last saved the file to disk, these changes are lost if you use /**File** **R**etrieve to retrieve another file. 1-2-3 Release 2.3 warns you if you are about to replace a file you changed, as shown in figure 7.8. Be sure that you save the current file before you retrieve a new file.

Caution:
/*File* *Retrieve*
replaces the current
file; if you made
changes to this file
since the last /*File*
Save, the changes
are lost.

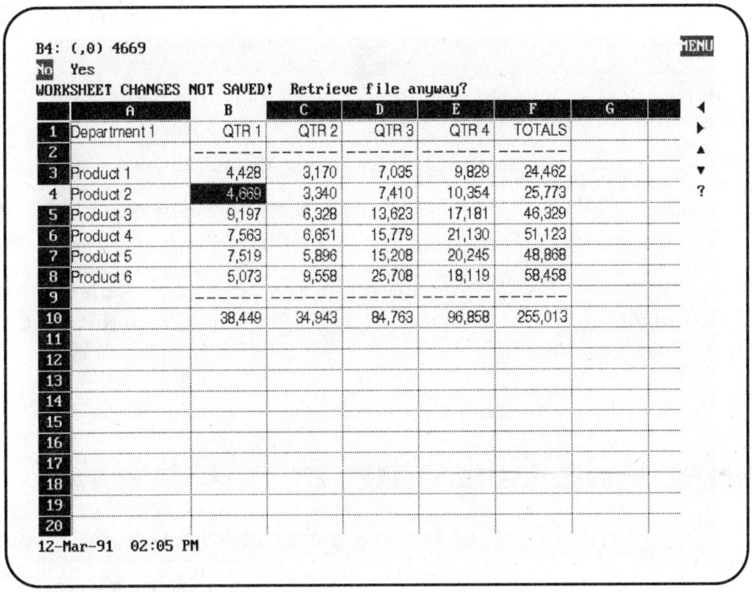

Fig. 7.8. The prompt to warn you that changes were made to the current file since the file was last saved.

At the 1-2-3 prompt that requests the file name, /**File** **R**etrieve lists the files on disk. You can either type the file name or point to the file from the list in the control panel. If many files exist in the directory, press Name (F3) or click on List with the mouse for a full-screen display of file names (see fig. 7.9). 1-2-3 lists the files in alphabetical order as you read the file names from left to right. Point to the desired file and then press Enter or click the left mouse button.

Cue:
Press Name (F3)
for a full-screen list
of file names.

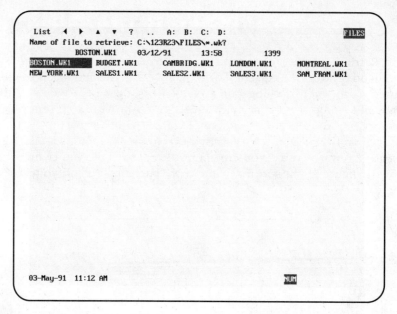

Fig. 7.9. A full-screen list of file names, produced by pressing Name (F3).

Besides reading the WK1 file into memory, 1-2-3 also reads formatting information into memory from the Wysiwyg format file with the same name (with the extension FMT).

Using Wild Cards for File Retrieval

When 1-2-3 prompts for a file name, you can add the asterisk (*) and the question mark (?) as wild cards in the file name. Wild cards are characters that enable you to make one file name match several files. Although you can use wild cards with many /**File** commands, you probably use these special characters most often with /**File Retrieve**.

The ? matches any one character in the name (or no character if the ? is the last character in the file name's main part or extension). The * matches any number of characters (or no character).

When you use wild cards in response to a file name prompt, 1-2-3 lists only those files whose names match the wild-card pattern; 1-2-3 does not actually execute the command (unless you use /File List). For example, if you use wild cards after you select /File Retrieve, /File Combine, or /File Import, 1-2-3 does not try to read a file, but lists only the files in the current directory that match the wild-card pattern. When the files matching the wild-card pattern are displayed, you can select the desired file.

Suppose that you type **SALES?** at the prompt shown in figure 7.9. 1-2-3 lists all file names that start with SALES, followed by a single character, such as SALES1, SALES2, and SALES3. If you type **B***, 1-2-3 lists all file names that start with B, followed by any number of characters, such as BOSTON and BUDGET.

Reminder:
When you use wild cards in response to a file name prompt, 1-2-3 lists only the files whose names match the wild-card pattern.

Retrieving Files from Subdirectories

When 1-2-3 prompts you for a file name and shows a default, the program also shows the complete path, such as C:\123R23\FILES*.WK1.

To change the current directory, use /File Directory. To retrieve or save a file in another directory without changing the current directory, press Esc twice to clear the old path, and then type a new path. You also can edit the existing path in the prompt.

When 1-2-3 lists the files in the current directory, the program lists all the subdirectories below the current directory, placing a backslash (\) after each directory's name. To read a file in one of the subdirectories, point to the subdirectory name and press Enter or click the left mouse button. 1-2-3 then lists the files and all subdirectories in *that* subdirectory. To list the files in the parent directory (the directory above the one displayed), press Backspace; 1-2-3 lists the files and subdirectories in the parent directory. In this manner, you can move up and down the directory structure until you find the desired file.

Reminder:
Press Backspace to list a parent directory; select a subdirectory to list the files in that subdirectory.

To learn more about directories, you can refer to Que Corporation's many books that cover this subject. If you are unfamiliar with DOS, try *MS-DOS 5 QuickStart*, Second Edition. If you need to learn more about DOS or OS/2 file and directory management, consult *Using MS-DOS 5*; *Que's MS-DOS 5 User's Guide*, Special Edition; *Using Your Hard Disk*; or *Using OS/2*. If you are upgrading to DOS 5, consult *Upgrading to MS-DOS 5*.

Retrieving a File Automatically

Usually, when you start 1-2-3, a blank worksheet appears. However, if you are in the default directory and you save a file under the name AUTO123, 1-2-3 retrieves this file automatically when 1-2-3 starts. This capability is useful if you work with macro-driven worksheet files. You can use the AUTO123 file to provide the first menu of a macro-driven system or a menu of other files to retrieve.

Erasing a File in Memory

To build a new worksheet file, you can clear the work area with /Worksheet Erase. This command clears the file in memory. If you changed the files since you last used the save feature, you lose all changes. However, here, 1-2-3 asks you to confirm **No** or **Yes** before you clear the work area. To save the changes in memory, choose **No** and save the file; then execute /Worksheet Erase again and select **Yes**. You do not have to use this command when retrieving an existing file, because the original file is erased when another file is retrieved.

Extracting and Combining Data

You can take data from part of a file and then use the data to create another, smaller file. For example, suppose that you create a large budget file that contains information from many departments. For each department, you can create an input file that contains only the data for that department.

You also can reverse the procedure; suppose that you have many departmental input files that you want to combine into one file for company-wide analysis and reporting.

1-2-3 provides the /File Xtract command so that you can save a part of the current file as a new file. 1-2-3 also offers the /File Combine command so that you can combine data from another file into the current file.

Extracting Information

The /File **X**tract command enables you to save, as a separate file, a range in the current file. This command can save part of a file before you make a change, break a large file into smaller files (so that you can read the files in another computer with less memory), or create a partial file for others to use.

The extracted range can be a single cell or a range of cells. The extracted file contains the following: all range names of the original file; the contents of the cells in the range, including the cells' formats and protection status; and all file settings, such as column widths, window options, print ranges, and graph options of the original file.

To extract part of a worksheet, select /File **X**tract and then select either **F**ormulas or **V**alues. When you select **F**ormulas, all cells in the extract range of the current file that hold formulas copy into the extracted file as formulas. When you select **V**alues, the formulas of all cells in the extract range of the current file are converted to the formulas' current values, and these values copy into the extracted file. 1-2-3, acting as if you are saving a file for the first time, asks for a file name. Type a file name and press Enter or click the left mouse button. Next, specify the range to extract and press Enter or click the left mouse button within the control panel. For the range, you can type addresses, highlight the range, type a range name, or press Name (F3) and point to a range name. If another file exists with the same name, you see the **C**ancel **R**eplace **B**ackup menu (see fig. 7.7).

Caution:
*Use /**F**ile **X**tract to extract a range of data to a new file, but do not use range names or other settings outside the extracted range.*

The extracted range can start anywhere in the current file (see fig. 7.10). The upper left corner of the extracted range becomes cell A1 in the new file (see fig. 7.11). All range names adjust to their new positions.

Compare the range name table in the file SALES (see fig. 7.12) with the range name table in the file XVALUES (see fig. 7.13). The XVALUES file was created with /**F**ile **X**tract **V**alues from the range F1..F9 in the SALES file, and a range name table was added to the extracted file.

In the original file (shown in fig. 7.12), GRAND_TOT refers to F9. In the new file (shown in fig. 7.13), GRAND_TOT refers to A9. All other range names also are adjusted. Be aware that range names to the left or above the upper left of the extract range "wrap" to the end of the worksheet, as shown in the range name table in figure 7.13. Most of these range names refer to blank cells and have no real meaning in this worksheet. The only meaningful range names are those completely within the extract range—in this example, TOTALS and GRAND_TOT.

```
F11: (P2) [W9] +E11/D11                                    POINT
Enter extract range: B5..F11
```

	A	B	C	D	E	F	G
1							
2		Recap of Expenses for Eastern Region					
3							
4			This Year	Last Year	Diff	%Diff	
5		Personnel	459,628	413,892	45,736	11.05%	
6		Premises	154,938	148,927	6,011	4.04%	
7		Travel	92,451	97,356	(4,905)	−5.04%	
8		Supplies	15,730	16,910	(1,180)	−6.98%	
9		Data Processing	36,564	32,649	3,915	11.99%	
10		Overhead	47,601	51,864	(4,263)	−8.22%	
11		TOTALS	806,912	761,598	45,314	5.95%	
12							
13							
14							
15							
16							
17							
18							
19							
20							

```
12-Mar-91  02:18 PM
```

Fig. 7.10. *A highlighted range to be extracted.*

```
A1: [W17] 'Personnel                                       READY
```

	A	B	C	D	E	F	G
1	Personnel _	459,628	413,892	45,736	11.05%		
2	Premises	154,938	148,927	6,011	4.04%		
3	Travel	92,451	97,356	(4,905)	−5.04%		
4	Supplies	15,730	16,910	(1,180)	−6.98%		
5	Data Processing	36,564	32,649	3,915	11.99%		
6	Overhead	47,601	51,864	(4,263)	−8.22%		
7	TOTALS	806,912	761,598	45,314	5.95%		
8							
9							
10							
11							
12							
13							
14							
15							
16							
17							
18							
19							
20							

```
12-Mar-91  02:19 PM        UNDO
```

Fig. 7.11. *The extracted range, which starts in cell A1 of the new file.*

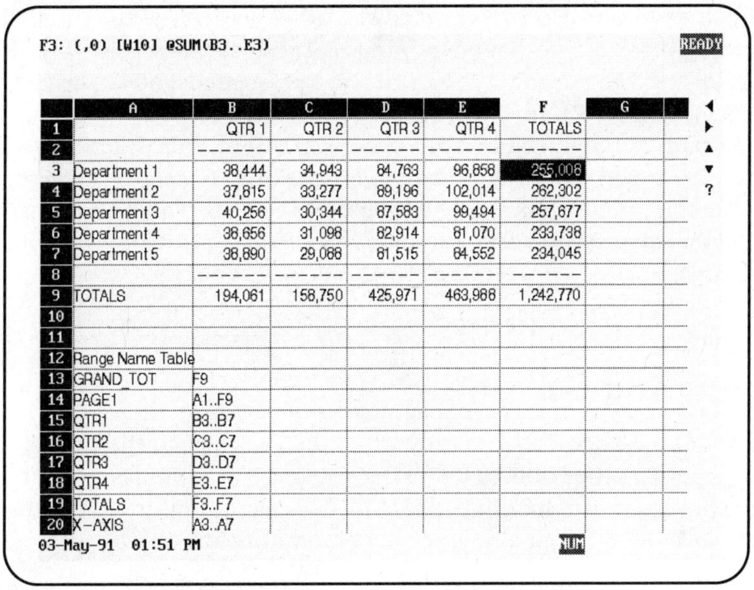

F3: (,0) [W10] @SUM(B3..E3)   READY

	A	B	C	D	E	F	G
1		QTR 1	QTR 2	QTR 3	QTR 4	TOTALS	
2		------	------	------	------	------	
3	Department 1	38,444	34,943	84,763	96,858	255,008	
4	Department 2	37,815	33,277	89,196	102,014	262,302	
5	Department 3	40,256	30,344	87,583	99,494	257,677	
6	Department 4	38,656	31,096	82,914	61,070	233,738	
7	Department 5	38,890	29,088	81,515	84,552	234,045	
8		------	------	------	------	------	
9	TOTALS	194,061	158,750	425,971	463,988	1,242,770	
10							
11							
12	Range Name Table						
13	GRAND TOT	F9					
14	PAGE1	A1..F9					
15	QTR1	B3..B7					
16	QTR2	C3..C7					
17	QTR3	D3..D7					
18	QTR4	E3..E7					
19	TOTALS	F3..F7					
20	X−AXIS	A3..A7					

03-May-91 01:51 PM   NUM

Fig. 7.12. *The SALES file with a range name table.*

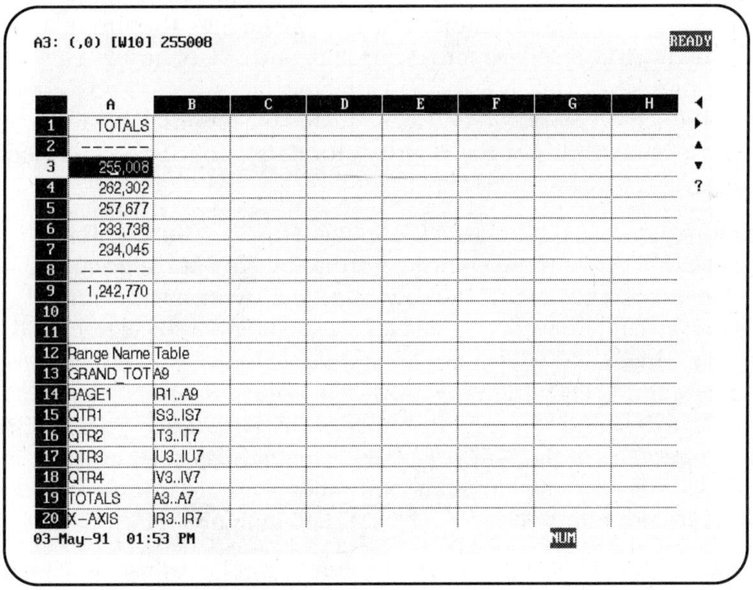

A3: (,0) [W10] 255008   READY

	A	B	C	D	E	F	G	H
1	TOTALS							
2	------							
3	255,008							
4	262,302							
5	257,677							
6	233,738							
7	234,045							
8	------							
9	1,242,770							
10								
11								
12	Range Name Table							
13	GRAND TOT	A9						
14	PAGE1	IR1..A9						
15	QTR1	IS3..IS7						
16	QTR2	IT3..IT7						
17	QTR3	IU3..IU7						
18	QTR4	IV3..IV7						
19	TOTALS	A3..A7						
20	X−AXIS	IR3..IR7						

03-May-91 01:53 PM   NUM

Fig. 7.13. *The extracted file XVALUES (created by /File Xtract Values) with a range name table.*

The extracted file also preserves all the other settings of the original file, including print, graph, and data ranges. These settings adjust, as do the range names. For example, the print range (named PAGE1) in SALES is A1..F9 (see fig. 7.12). In XVALUES, the print range is IR1..A9 (see fig. 7.13). The /Graph X range (named X-AXIS) is A3..A7 in SALES and IR3..IR7 in XVALUES. As with range names, do not use /Print, /Graph, or /Data settings in an extract file unless the entire setting range is within the range you originally extracted. In this example, the /Print and /Graph settings are meaningless.

Extracting Formulas

Caution:
Extract formulas only if those formulas refer solely to cells in the extract range.

You should extract formulas only when the formulas in the extract range refer solely to other cells in the extract range. The formulas in figure 7.12 were converted to values in figure 7.13. This fact is important because the formulas in F3..F7 sum a range that you did not extract.

Figure 7.14 shows the XFORMULA file created with /File Xtract Formulas from the range F1..F9 in the SALES file in figure 7.12. This range is the same range extracted with /File Xtract Values in figure 7.13. In the SALES file, the formula in F3 is @SUM(E3..B3). In figure 7.14, this formula becomes @SUM(IS3..IV3). This result is *relative addressing*. The formula is summing cells from four cells to the left through one cell to the left. This relative addressing carries through to the extracted file just as if you copied or moved the cells in a worksheet. The extracted file retains the column width, the cell formats (but not the Wysiwyg formats), and the values from the original file.

Occasionally, you need to extract formulas. Suppose, for example, that you want to extract part of the worksheet from the file SALES, discussed in the preceding section. Figure 7.15 shows the SALES worksheet, with a horizontal window that shows the details for Department 1. To extract and then place the range A21..F30 in a separate file, use the /File Xtract Formulas command and specify the range A21..F30. You can name this extract file XSALES1 to remind yourself that this file is an extract from SALES for Department 1 (see fig. 7.16). Because all formulas refer to cells in the extracted range, the formulas are still valid. The values in figure 7.16 are identical to the values in the range A21..F30 in figure 7.15.

Cue:
Even absolute cell references adjust with /File Xtract.

When you extract formulas, even absolute formulas adjust. The resulting formulas are still absolute but have new addresses. If the formulas in F3 in figure 7.11 were @SUM($B$3..$E$3), the formulas in A3 in figure 7.13 become @SUM($IS$3..$IV$3).

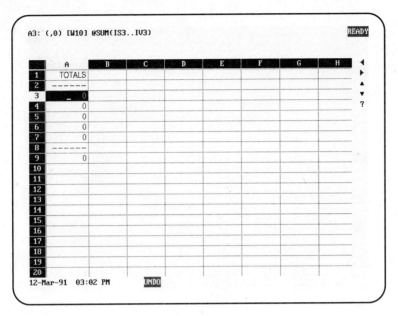

Fig. 7.14. *Meaningless results, produced by using /File Xtract Formulas on a range that does not include the referenced cells.*

```
F30: (,0) [W10] @SUM(F23..F28)                              READY
```

	A	B	C	D	E	F	G
1		QTR 1	QTR 2	QTR 3	QTR 4	TOTALS	
2		------	------	------	------	------	
3	Department 1	38,444	34,943	84,763	96,858	255,008	
4	Department 2	37,815	33,277	89,196	102,014	262,302	
5	Department 3	40,256	30,344	87,583	99,494	257,677	
6	Department 4	38,656	31,098	82,914	81,070	233,738	
7	Department 5	38,890	29,088	81,515	84,552	234,045	
8		------	------	------	------	------	
9		194,061	158,750	425,971	463,988	1,242,770	

	A	B	C	D	E	F	G
21	Department 1	QTR 1	QTR 2	QTR 3	QTR 4	TOTALS	
22		------	------	------	------	------	
23	Product 1	4,428	3,170	7,035	9,829	24,462	
24	Product 2	4,664	3,340	7,410	10,354	25,768	
25	Product 3	9,197	6,328	13,623	17,181	46,329	
26	Product 4	7,563	6,651	15,779	21,130	51,123	
27	Product 5	7,519	5,896	15,208	20,245	48,868	
28	Product 6	5,073	9,558	25,708	18,119	58,458	
29		------	------	------	------	------	
30		38,444	34,943	84,763	96,858	255,008	

```
12-Mar-91  03:04 PM          UNDO
```

Fig. 7.15. *The original SALES file, with the detail for Department 1 displayed in a separate window.*

```
F10: (,0) [W10] @SUM(F3..F8)                                    READY
```

	A	B	C	D	E	F	G
1	Department 1	QTR 1	QTR 2	QTR 3	QTR 4	TOTALS	
2		------	------	------	------	------	
3	Product 1	4,428	3,170	7,035	9,829	24,462	
4	Product 2	4,664	3,340	7,410	10,354	25,768	
5	Product 3	9,197	6,328	13,623	17,181	46,329	
6	Product 4	7,563	6,651	15,779	21,130	51,123	
7	Product 5	7,519	5,896	15,208	20,245	48,868	
8	Product 6	5,073	9,558	25,708	18,119	58,458	
9		------	------	------	------	------	
10		38,444	34,943	84,763	96,858	255,008	
11							
12							
13							
14							
15							
16							
17							
18							
19							
20							

```
12-Mar-91  03:07 PM          UNDO
```

Fig. 7.16. The XSALES1 file extracted from the SALES file by using /File Xtract Formulas.

Extracting Values

Caution:
If the CALC indicator is on, press Calc (F9) to calculate the worksheet.

When you extract values, you obtain the current value of all formulas in the extract range. If recalculation is set to manual and the CALC indicator is on, press Calc (F9) to calculate the worksheet before you extract a range; otherwise, you may inadvertently extract old values.

Combining Information from Other Files

Cue:
/File Combine does not read the formatting information into memory from any corresponding format file.

You can combine information from one or more files into the current file. Depending on your needs, you can perform this action either with formulas or with the /File Combine command. (The /File Combine command does not include information from the corresponding Wysiwyg format file.) A formula can include references to cells in other files, as in figure 7.17. The formula in B3 of the file LSALES refers to the total sales for Department 1 in B10 of the file XSALES1. Chapter 3 describes linked worksheets and formulas.

```
B3: (,0) +<<XSALES1.WK1>>B10                                    READY
```

	A	B	C	D	E	F	G
1		QTR 1	QTR 2	QTR 3	QTR 4	TOTALS	
2		------	------	------	------	------	
3	Department 1	38,444	34,943	84,763	96,858	255,008	
4	Department 2	37,815	33,277	89,196	102,014	262,302	
5	Department 3	40,256	30,344	87,583	99,494	257,677	
6	Department 4	38,656	31,098	82,914	81,070	233,738	
7	Department 5	38,890	29,088	81,515	84,552	234,045	
8		------	------	------	------	------	
9		194,061	158,750	425,971	463,988	1,242,770	
10							
11							
12							
13							
14							
15							
16							
17							
18							
19							
20							

Fig. 7.17. *A worksheet with references to cells in other files.*

In certain situations, you do not want to use linked files for consolidations. If you use formulas that link many external files, then each time you read in the consolidation file, 1-2-3 must read parts of each linked file to update the linked formulas. This process can become time-consuming.

You may not want to update the consolidation automatically every time you read in the file. You may want to update the consolidation only once a month, for example, when all new detail data becomes available. At other times, you may use the consolidation file for "what if" analysis by using the previous month's data. To gain manual control over when and how you update a file with data from other files, use /File Combine. This command combines the cell contents of all or part of another file into the current file, starting at the location of the cell pointer.

Reminder:
When you want manual control over when and how you update a file with data from other files, use /File Combine.

The /File Combine command offers three options: Copy, Add, and Subtract. Copy enables you to replace data in the current file with data from an external file. With Add, you sum the values of the cells in the external file with the values of the cells in the current file. Subtract enables you to subtract the data in the external file from the data in the current file.

You can use any of the /File Combine options with either an entire file or a range. After selecting Copy, Add, or Subtract, the menu choices you see are Entire-File and Named/Specified-Range. The range can be a single cell or a range of cells. You can specify range addresses but use range names if possible. You easily can make an error if you specify range addresses because, when you execute the command, you cannot see the external file from where the data is coming.

When you use the /File Combine options, 1-2-3 ignores blank cells in the external file. Cells with data in the external file update the corresponding cells in the current file.

Using /File Combine Copy

In the section "Extracting Information," /File Xtract was used with a consolidated file to create separate files for the individual departments. In this section, the process is reversed. You use /File Combine Copy to update the consolidated file from the individual departmental files.

The following examples are typical of how to use /File Xtract and /File Combine. Start with the consolidated file, and each month (or other time period) extract the departmental files for input and then combine the files for consolidated analysis and reporting.

You use /File Combine Copy, for example, if you need to update the SALES file with new data contained in another file—the file XSALES2, for example (see fig. 7.18).

Making sure that the receiving worksheet is in memory, move the cell pointer to the upper left corner of the range to receive the combined data—here, B34 (see fig. 7.19)—and execute /File Combine Copy. You have a choice of combining the whole file or only a range. For example, to include only the values in the range B3..E5 in XSALES2, select Named/Specified-Range; then specify the range B3..E5 and press Enter or click the left mouse button within the control panel. Finally, specify the external file—here, XSALES2—where the range B3..E5 originates. Figure 7.20 shows how the data in figure 7.19 was replaced by the data in figure 7.18.

In this example, the old data and the new data have a known format, with no blank cells. Each cell in the external file replaces the data in the current file. However, if blank cells exist in the external file, these cells are ignored, and the corresponding cell in the current file does not change; the corresponding cell is not blanked out.

```
B7: (,0) @SUM(B3..B5)                                    READY
```

	A	B	C	D	E	F	G
1	Department 2	QTR 1	QTR 2	QTR 3	QTR 4	TOTALS	
2		------	------	------	------	------	
3	Product 1	11,276	17,947	37,865	34,280	101,368	
4	Product 2	8,797	12,639	29,815	34,639	85,890	
5	Product 3	17,742	21,698	56,419	56,493	152,352	
6		------	------	------	------	------	
7		37,815	52,284	124,099	125,412	339,610	
8							
9							
10							
11	NOTES:						
12	Sales forecasts were increased based on the success of						
13	the new marketing campaign and the fact that we increased						
14	our distributor base by 30%.						
15							
16							
17							
18							
19							
20							

Fig. 7.18. *The XSALES2 file, to be combined into the SALES file.*

```
B34: (,0) 11276                                          READY
```

	A	B	C	D	E	F	G
31							
32	Department 2	QTR 1	QTR 2	QTR 3	QTR 4	TOTALS	
33		------	------	------	------	------	
34	Product 1	11,276	10,842	21,629	26,590	70,337	
35	Product 2	8,797	6,719	16,590	22,648	54,754	
36	Product 3	17,742	15,716	50,977	52,776	137,211	
37		------	------	------	------	------	
38		37,815	33,277	69,196	102,014	262,302	
39							
40							
41							
42							
43							
44							
45							
46							
47							
48							
49							
50							

```
03-May-91  02:27 PM                                      NUM
```

Fig. 7.19. *The SALES file before the incorporation of new data.*

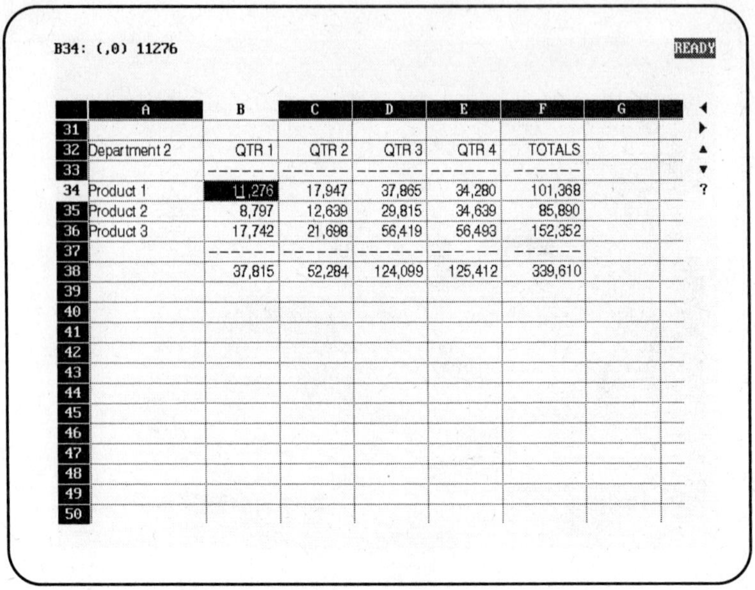

B34: (,0) 11276   READY

	A	B	C	D	E	F	G
31							
32	Department 2	QTR 1	QTR 2	QTR 3	QTR 4	TOTALS	
33		-------	-------	-------	-------	-------	
34	Product 1	11,276	17,947	37,865	34,280	101,368	
35	Product 2	8,797	12,639	29,815	34,639	85,890	
36	Product 3	17,742	21,698	56,419	56,493	152,352	
37		-------	-------	-------	-------	-------	
38		37,815	52,284	124,099	125,412	339,610	
39							
40							
41							
42							
43							
44							
45							
46							
47							
48							
49							
50							

Fig. 7.20. *The SALES file after the incorporation of new data.*

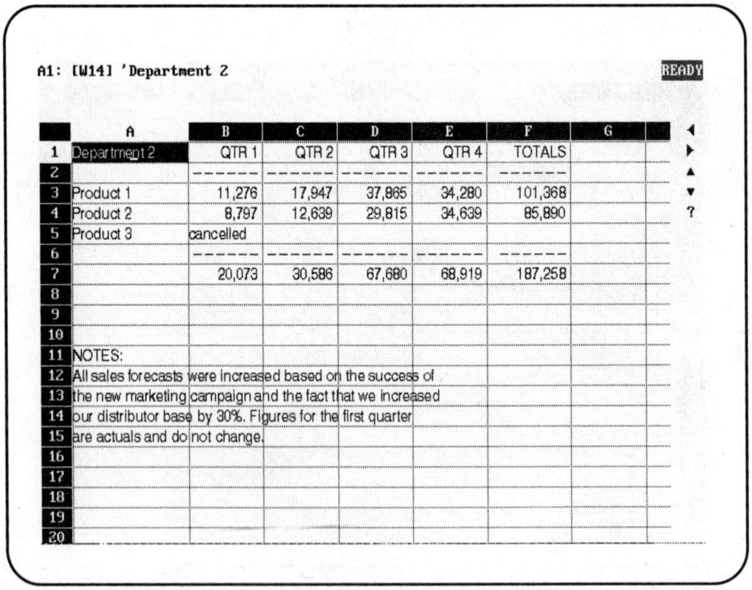

A1: [W14] 'Department 2   READY

	A	B	C	D	E	F	G
1	Department 2	QTR 1	QTR 2	QTR 3	QTR 4	TOTALS	
2		-------	-------	-------	-------	-------	
3	Product 1	11,276	17,947	37,865	34,280	101,368	
4	Product 2	8,797	12,639	29,815	34,639	85,890	
5	Product 3	cancelled					
6							
7		20,073	30,586	67,680	68,919	187,258	
8							
9							
10							
11	NOTES:						
12	All sales forecasts were increased based on the success of						
13	the new marketing campaign and the fact that we increased						
14	our distributor base by 30%. Figures for the first quarter						
15	are actuals and do not change.						
16							
17							
18							
19							
20							

Fig. 7.21. *An input worksheet with blank cells, to be incorporated into the SALES file shown in figure 7.20.*

```
B34: (,0) 11276                                                    READY

         A          B        C         D        E         F        G      ◄
                                                                          ►
  31                                                                      ▲
  32  Department 2   QTR 1    QTR 2     QTR 3    QTR 4    TOTALS           ▼
  33               --------  --------  -------  -------  --------         ?
  34  Product 1      11,276   17,947    37,865   34,280   101,368
  35  Product 2       8,797   12,639    29,815   34,639    85,890
  36  Product 3    cancelled  21,698    56,419   56,493   134,610
  37               --------  --------  -------  -------  --------
  38               20,073    52,284   124,099  125,412   321,868
  39
  40
  41
  42
  43
  44
  45
  46
  47
          POINTE3: [W11] 23456
          Enter range to erase: E3..E3
```

Fig. 7.22. Incorrect results in the SALES file, produced because the blank cells did not update the file.

Figure 7.21 is a variation of the input file shown in figure 7.18. In figure 7.21, Product 3 is canceled, and the sales data erased. If you repeat the /File Combine Copy command to update the file in figure 7.20 with the data shown in figure 7.21, you get the results shown in figure 7.22. Notice that the old sales figures for Product 3 are not erased and that the totals for the department are wrong. To avoid this error, erase the range in the current file before you incorporate the new data. In this example, erase B34..E36.

In these examples, only numbers and not formulas are combined. You can combine formulas if you also combine the data referenced in those formulas. From figures 7.18 and 7.21, you can incorporate B3..F7 and include the TOTALS formulas in row 7 and column F. Because you also combine the data for these formulas, the formulas are correct in figures 7.20 and 7.22.

Be careful when you use /File Combine Copy with formulas. Formulas— even absolute formulas—adjust automatically to their new location after the execution of /File Combine Copy. In figures 7.18 and 7.21, for example, the formula for the total for QTR 1 in cell B7 is @SUM(B3..B5). If you combine this formula into SALES in figures 7.19 and 7.22, the formula adjusts to @SUM (B34..B36) in cell B38. If the formula in cell B7 is @SUM($B$3..$B$5), the formula adjusts, after the execution of /File Combine, to @SUM($B$34..$B$36) in cell B38.

Caution:
Make sure that the CALC indicator is off before you save a file that might be used for a /File Combine Add or Subtract.

If you combine the formulas without the data, the formulas are meaningless, and you get incorrect results. Figure 7.23 shows the master consolidation for the SALES file. Because the detail exists in another worksheet, you may decide to combine only the totals from B7..E7 in figure 7.21 directly into B4..E4. The formula in B7 in figure 7.21 is @SUM(B3..B5). In figure 7.23, the formula adjusts to @SUM(B8192..B2), which is clearly wrong. This formula makes the figures for Department 2 wrong and causes a circular reference. To get what you want here, use /File Combine Add, as described in the text that follows.

Using /File Combine Add and /File Combine Subtract

/File Combine Add works somewhat like /File Combine Copy but differs in some important ways. /File Combine Subtract is identical to /File Combine Add except that you subtract instead of add. With this exception, all that follows about /File Combine Add also applies to /File Combine Subtract.

Instead of replacing the contents of cells in the current file, /File Combine Add adds the values of the cells in the external file to the values of cells in the current file that contain numbers or are blank. In other words, this command adds a number or a formula result to a number or a blank cell. If the cell in the current file contains a formula, the formula is unchanged by /File Combine Add.

To update the totals correctly for Department 2 in figure 7.23, move the cell pointer to B4 and use /Range Erase to erase B4..E4. Then use /File Combine Add Named/Specified-Range to add B7..E7 from file XSALES2 in figure 7.21. The result is shown in figure 7.24.

/File Combine Add adds to the current file the current value of all formulas in the external file. Because you erased the range B4..E4 in SALES in figure 7.23, these blank cells are treated as zeros.

If you specify a /File Combine Add range of B7..F7 instead of B7..E7, you may see the same result. The total in F7 in figure 7.21 is not added to the contents of F4 in figure 7.23 because F4 contains the formula @SUM(E4..B4). This formula remains @SUM(E4..B4) after the /File Combine Add because this command does not affect formulas in the current file.

B4: (,0) @SUM(B8192..B2)   READY

	A	B	C	D	E	F	G
1		QTR 1	QTR 2	QTR 3	QTR 4	TOTALS	
2							
3	Department 1	38,444	34,943	84,763	96,858	255,008	
4	Department 2	3,238,234	3,233,252	8,266,422	8,863,148	23,601,056	
5	Department 3	40,256	30,344	87,583	99,494	257,677	
6	Department 4	38,656	31,098	82,914	81,070	233,738	
7	Department 5	38,890	29,088	81,515	84,552	234,045	
8							
9		3,394,480	3,358,725	8,603,197	9,225,122	24,581,524	
10							
11							
12	Range Name Table						
13	GRAND_TOT	F9					
14	PAGE1	A1..F29					
15	QTR1	B3..B7					
16	QTR2	C3..C7					
17	QTR3	D3..D7					
18	QTR4	E3..E7					
19	TOTALS	F3..F7					
20							

CIRC

Fig. 7.23. *An erroneous formula in the SALES file, caused when /File Combine Copy was used with formulas.*

B4: (,0) 20073   READY

	A	B	C	D	E	F	G
1		QTR 1	QTR 2	QTR 3	QTR 4	TOTALS	
2							
3	Department 1	38,444	34,943	84,763	96,858	255,008	
4	Department 2	20,073	30,586	67,680	68,919	187,258	
5	Department 3	40,256	30,344	87,583	99,494	257,677	
6	Department 4	38,656	31,098	82,914	81,070	233,738	
7	Department 5	38,890	29,088	81,515	84,552	234,045	
8							
9		176,319	156,059	404,455	430,893	1,167,726	
10							
11							
12	Range Name Table						
13	GRAND_TOT	F9					
14	PAGE1	A1..F29					
15	QTR1	B3..B7					
16	QTR2	C3..C7					
17	QTR3	D3..D7					
18	QTR4	E3..E7					
19	TOTALS	F3..F7					
20							

Fig. 7.24. *The SALES file, after updating with /File Combine.*

Be aware that with /File Combine Add, you may add incorrect formula results. Because /File Combine Add converts formulas in the external file to their current values before the command adds the values to the external file, these values must be current to get the correct result. If XSALES2 in figure 7.21 was set to manual calculation and the CALC indicator was on when you last saved the file, incorrect data may have been added during the execution of the /File Combine command. You can do nothing about this problem when you issue the /File Combine Add command. You must press Calc (F9) to calculate before you save the external file.

Another way to use /File Combine Add is to sum the values from two or more files into one consolidation. If you want only the single row of totals in B9..F9 in figure 7.24, you can add the totals from all the input worksheets directly. First, use /Range Erase to erase A3..F7, because you want to omit department totals in this example. Make sure that F9 contains @SUM(B9..E9). Then move the cell pointer to B9 and use /Range Erase on B9..E9. Finally, use /File Combine Add to add the totals from each input file (XSALES1, XSALES2, and so on). This process accumulates the totals from each department.

If you have a separate file for credits or returns, you can use /File Combine Subtract to subtract these returns. If the returns are entered as negative numbers, however, use /File Combine Add to add the negative numbers and correctly decrease the sales totals.

Protecting Files

1-2-3 Release 2.3 offers a variety of file protection methods. You can password-protect a file, or you can ensure protection for files that you access in a multiuser or networking environment. The following sections describe the file protection methods available in Release 2.3.

Using Passwords for File Protection

Caution:
If you forget the password, you cannot access a password-protected file.

You can protect worksheet files by using passwords. After you password-protect a file, no one can read the file without first issuing the password. This restriction applies to /File Retrieve, /File Combine, and the Translate option on the Lotus 1-2-3 Access menu. Also, you cannot have linking formulas that refer to password-protected files.

You password-protect a file when you specify the file name during a /File Save or a /File Xtract action. Type the file name, press the space bar, type **p** (see fig. 7.25), and then press Enter or click the left mouse button within the control panel. 1-2-3 prompts you to type a password of 1 to 15 characters. Remember that *a password cannot contain spaces*. For additional security, square blocks appear on the screen in place of the characters you type.

```
B4: (,0) 20073                                                    EDIT
Enter name of file to save: C:\123R23\FILES\SALES P
```

	A	B	C	D	E	F	G
1		QTR 1	QTR 2	QTR 3	QTR 4	TOTALS	
2		------	------	------	------	------	
3	Department 1	38,444	34,943	84,763	96,858	255,008	
4	Department 2	20,073	30,586	67,680	68,919	187,258	
5	Department 3	40,256	30,344	87,583	99,494	257,677	
6	Department 4	38,656	31,098	82,914	81,070	233,738	
7	Department 5	38,890	29,088	81,515	84,552	234,045	
8		------	------	------	------	------	
9		176,319	156,059	404,455	430,893	1,167,726	
10							
11							
12	Range Name Table						
13	GRAND_TOT	F9					
14	PAGE1	A1..F29					
15	QTR1	B3..B7					
16	QTR2	C3..C7					
17	QTR3	D3..D7					
18	QTR4	E3..E7					
19	TOTALS	F3..F7					
20							

```
07-May-91  01:38 PM
```

Fig. 7.25. *The file name followed by the letter P, which tells 1-2-3 to password-protect the file.*

After you type the password, press Enter; you are prompted to type the password again. Type the password again (see fig. 7.26, which shows square blocks where characters were typed) and press Enter. If both passwords are identical, the file is saved in a special format that—without the password—neither you nor anyone else can access. If the two passwords do not match, 1-2-3 displays the error message `Passwords do not match`, and you must restart the /File Save command.

Passwords are case-sensitive. If a password includes a lowercase letter, that letter does not match the corresponding uppercase letter. When you assign a password, check the Caps Lock indicator so that you know how you are entering the characters.

```
B4: (,0) 20073                                                    EDIT
Enter password: ■■■■■■           Verify password: ■■■■■■
```

	A	B	C	D	E	F	G	
1		QTR 1	QTR 2	QTR 3	QTR 4	TOTALS		◄
2								►
3	Department 1	38,444	34,943	84,763	96,858	255,008		▲
4	Department 2	20,073	30,586	67,680	68,919	187,258		▼
5	Department 3	40,256	30,344	87,583	99,494	257,677		?
6	Department 4	38,656	31,098	82,914	81,070	233,738		
7	Department 5	38,890	29,088	81,515	84,552	234,045		
8								
9		176,319	156,059	404,455	430,893	1,167,726		
10								
11								
12	Range Name Table							
13	GRAND_TOT	F9						
14	PAGE1	A1..F29						
15	QTR1	B3..B7						
16	QTR2	C3..C7						
17	QTR3	D3..D7						
18	QTR4	E3..E7						
19	TOTALS	F3..F7						
20								

```
12-Mar-91  03:36 PM
```

Fig. 7.26. The control panel after you typed the password twice.

When you use /**File Retrieve** or /**File Combine** with a password-protected file, 1-2-3 prompts you for the password. Only those who type the password correctly can access the file.

When you save a file that you previously saved with a password, 1-2-3 displays the message [PASSWORD PROTECTED] after the file name (see fig. 7.27). To save the file with the same password, just press Enter. To delete the password, press Backspace once to clear the [PASSWORD PROTECTED] message and then press Enter. To change the password, press Backspace once to clear the [PASSWORD PROTECTED] message; then press the space bar once, type **p**, and press Enter. Finally, assign a new password.

Using File Reservation for Protecting Files

This method of file protection is intended for multiuser or networking environments. To ensure that network users who share your data files do not write over your work, 1-2-3 provides controls called reservations. A *reservation* guarantees that network users can make changes and then save a file, using the same file name.

```
B4: (,0) 20073                                                    EDIT
Enter name of file to save: C:\123R23\FIGS\SALES.wk1 [PASSWORD PROTECTED]
```

	A	B	C	D	E	F	G
1		QTR 1	QTR 2	QTR 3	QTR 4	TOTALS	
2							
3	Department 1	38,444	34,943	84,763	96,858	255,008	
4	Department 2	20,073	30,586	67,680	68,919	187,258	
5	Department 3	40,256	30,344	87,583	99,494	257,677	
6	Department 4	38,656	31,098	82,914	81,070	233,738	
7	Department 5	38,890	29,088	81,515	84,552	234,045	
8							
9		176,319	156,059	404,455	430,893	1,167,726	
10							
11							
12	Range Name Table						
13	GRAND_TOT	F9					
14	PAGE1	A1..F29					
15	QTR1	B3..B7					
16	QTR2	C3..C7					
17	QTR3	D3..D7					
18	QTR4	E3..E7					
19	TOTALS	F3..F7					
20							

```
12-Mar-91  03:37 PM
```

Fig. 7.27. *A password-protected file that is about to be saved again.*

To obtain a file reservation, you need to access the /**F**ile **A**dmin **R**eservation command. After you activate this command, you can make all the changes you desire, even when others use the same file at the same time.

Using /Worksheet Global Protection for File Protection

This method of protection is used to protect the worksheet data. You can read a file protected with /**W**orksheet **G**lobal **P**rotection into memory, but you can make no changes to data in protected cells. Check whether the cell pointer is on a protected cell by looking at the control panel where 1-2-3 displays PR to indicate that global protection is on.

Erasing Files

Each time you save a file under a different file name, you use more space on your disk. Eventually, you run out of disk space if you do not occasionally erase unneeded files from the disk. Even if you still have disk space left, you may have a harder time finding needed files if the disk contains many obsolete files. Before you erase any old files, you may want to save these files to a floppy disk because you may someday need the information in the worksheets these files contain.

To erase an unneeded file from disk, use /File Erase. This command removes the file from disk and frees up the disk space for other files. If you made no subsequent saves to the disk, a deleted file may be recovered by using DOS 5.0's UNDELETE command or a special utility program. However, after a file is written to the disk, new data may replace the deleted file's space on the disk. You also can use DOS's ERASE or DEL command to erase files on disk. Within 1-2-3, you can erase only one file at a time.

When you select /File Erase, you see the menu shown in figure 7.28. You can use this menu to select the type of file you want to erase. If you select **Worksheet**, 1-2-3 lists all files in the current directory that have WK? extensions. If you select **Print** from the /File Erase menu, 1-2-3 lists all files in the current directory that have PRN extensions. Selecting **Graph** produces a list of all files found in the current directory that have PIC extensions. Selecting **Other** from the /File Erase menu produces a list of *all* files in the current directory.

To list another set of files, choose any option in figure 7.28; then type the file specification. To list all worksheet files that start with BUDGET, type **BUDGET*.WK?**; to list all backup files, type ***.BAK**. When the file you want to erase is listed, highlight the file name and press Enter or click the left mouse button. Press **Yes** to confirm that you want to erase the file. 1-2-3 erases the file.

When you select a file to erase, 1-2-3 also erases the corresponding Wysiwyg format file (the file with the extension FMT) or Allways format file (with the extension ALL), if one exists.

Creating Lists and Tables of Files

If you work with many files, you may forget the names of certain files or the times the files were last updated. 1-2-3 provides commands to help you keep track of the files on your disk. You can either list the files or save a table of files in your worksheet.

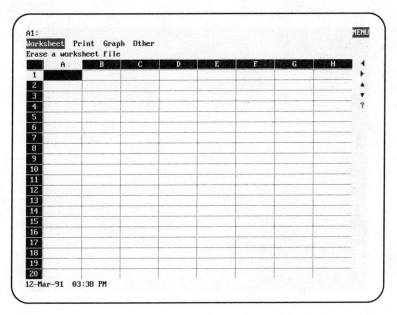

Fig. 7.28. *The /File Erase menu.*

To see a list of files, use /File List. The menu shown in figure 7.29 appears. The Worksheet, Print, Graph, and Other options provide the same lists that are provided with the /File Erase menu described previously. Choose Linked from the /File List menu to list all files referenced in formulas in the current file.

To save a file list in your worksheet as a table, use /File Admin Table. You get the same menu as in figure 7.29. If you choose Worksheet, the prompt Enter directory: appears with the current directory path name. To specify a new directory, press Esc or the right mouse button and enter the new directory path name or edit the current directory path name. When you press Enter (or click the left mouse button within the control panel), the prompt Enter range for table: appears. Specify the range and press Enter. A table appears, like the table in figure 7.30. You may need to change the column widths to see all the information.

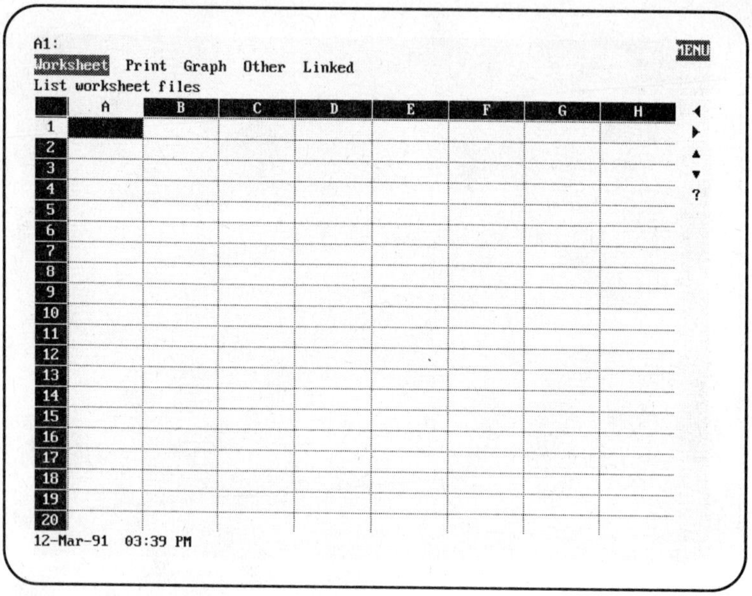

Fig. 7.29. The /File List or /File Admin Table menu.

The first column lists the file name. The second column lists the date of the last save. You must format these cells as a date. The third column lists the time of the last save. You must format these cells as a Time; 1-2-3 does not format the cells for you. The fourth column lists the size, in bytes, of the file. You get these first four columns by choosing any of the /File Admin Table options. When you choose Linked, the file name includes the complete path. The list is constructed beginning in the upper left corner of a cell or range you specify in the worksheet.

Using the Viewer Add-In

Cue:
Use the Viewer
add-in to view the
contents of files.

1-2-3 Release 2.3 includes an add-in program called Viewer that enables you to see the contents of worksheet files on disk, to retrieve them, and to create linked files. Viewer appears similar to Lotus Magellan, the file management program. To attach Viewer, select /Add-In Attach and then choose VIEWER.ADN from the list of add-in programs. Assign a function key (or no key) to the add-in and then select Invoke. When you choose Viewer, the menu shown in figure 7.31 appears.

```
A1: [W14] 'BOSTON.WK1                                              READY

         A            B          C          D       E      F      G    ◄
  1  BOSTON.WK1    10-Mar-91   01:58:28 PM   1399                      ►
  2  BUDGET.WK1    10-Mar-91   02:02:07 PM   2441                      ▲
  3  CAMBRIDG.WK1  10-Mar-91   01:57:12 PM   1399                      ▼
  4  DALLAS.WK1    11-Mar-91   02:18:29 PM   2278                      ?
  5  LONDON.WK1    11-Mar-91   01:58:21 PM   1399
  6  MONTREAL.WK1  12-Mar-91   02:06:20 PM   1399
  7  NEW_YORK.WK1  12-Mar-91   01:59:02 PM   1399
  8  SALES1.WK1    12-Mar-91   02:06:24 PM   1399
  9  SALES2.WK1    12-Mar-91   02:06:28 PM   1399
 10  SALES3.WK1    12-Mar-91   02:07:03 PM   1399
 11  SAN_FRAN.WK1  12-Mar-91   01:59:07 PM   1399
 12
 13
 14
 15
 16
 17
 18
 19
 20
 12-Mar-91  03:44 PM       UNDO
```

Fig. 7.30. *A table of active files.*

Select **R**etrieve to view a worksheet before loading the worksheet into main memory, as shown in figure 7.32. On the left side of the split screen, 1-2-3 shows file names with WK1, WKS, WR1, and WRK extensions; on the right side, 1-2-3 shows file contents. You use the arrow keys to navigate through the files in a directory, through directories on the hard disk, and through other disks. When you determine the file you want to retrieve, highlight the file name and press Enter. You also can double-click the left mouse button on the desired file name. The worksheet appears on-screen.

Link enables you to link cells from the file in memory to cells from a file on the disk. For more information about using this option, see Chapter 3.

Browse enables you to view the contents of any file on the disk. This command is useful for viewing text files. When you select **B**rowse, a split screen similar to the one for **R**etrieve appears with files on the left side and file contents on the right. You navigate through the hard disk with the arrow keys. If you see a file you want to examine in detail, press the right-arrow key to move into the right window. To move back to the left window, press the left-arrow key. Press Esc or click the right mouse button to quit browsing and to return to the Viewer menu; press Enter to quit browsing and return to READY mode.

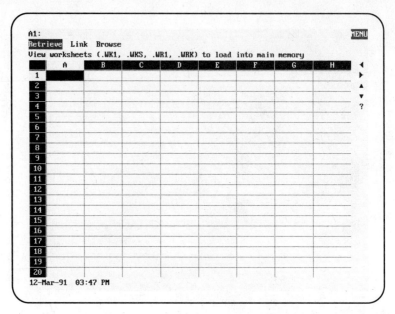

Fig. 7.31. *The Viewer menu.*

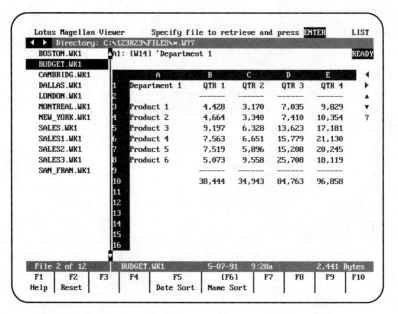

Fig. 7.32. *The Viewer screen, from which you can display worksheet file contents and retrieve the desired file.*

For all the Viewer menu choices, you can sort files by date by pressing F5, sort by name by pressing F6, change the current Viewer directory to match the current 1-2-3 directory by pressing F2, and obtain help by pressing F1.

Transferring Files

1-2-3 supplies several ways to pass data between itself and other programs. The simplest file format is straight text, also called an ASCII file. Most programs, including spreadsheets, word processors, and database management systems, can create text files. To create a text file in 1-2-3, use /Print File, which Chapter 8 covers in detail. To read a text file into a worksheet, use /File Import.

Transferring Files with /File Import

/File Import is a special type of /File Combine. You combine the information into the current worksheet, starting at the position of the cell pointer. All existing data in these cells is overwritten. When you execute the /File Import command, 1-2-3 lists all files found in the current directory that end with PRN extensions. To list files that use another extension—TXT, for example—type the appropriate characters, such as ***.TXT**, and press Enter.

Caution:
When you use /File Import, existing data in the worksheet is overwritten.

Importing Unstructured Text Files

The typical text file holds lines of data, and each line ends with a carriage return. Except for the carriage returns, these text files have no structure. You combine these files by using /File Import Text. Figure 7.33 shows the result of importing a typical text file into a worksheet; the data came from a mainframe or minicomputer personnel program. Each line in the text file becomes a long label in a cell. All the data is in column A. If you import a list of names, or if you only want to see the data, you are finished. Usually, however, you want to work with the data in separate cells. You want numbers as numbers and dates as dates, not labels. To make this data usable, use the /Data Parse command. See Chapter 12 for a complete discussion of the /Data Parse command.

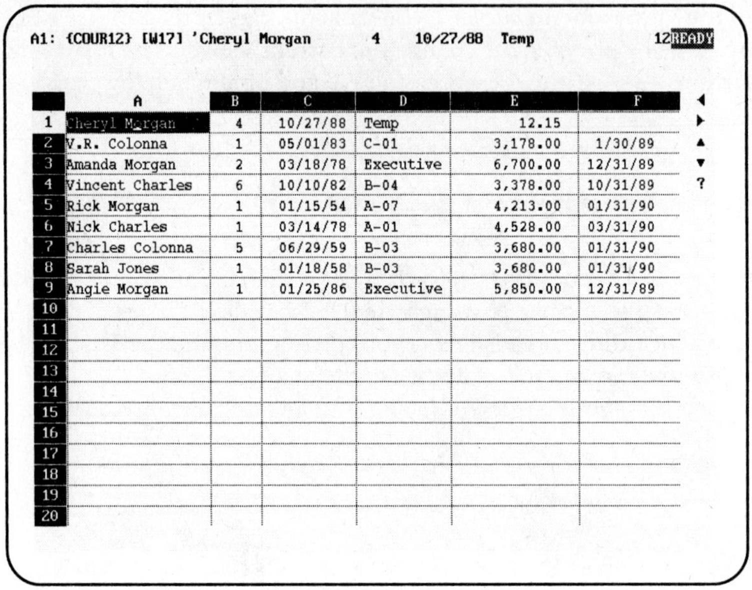

A1: {COUR12} [W17] 'Cheryl Morgan 4 10/27/88 Temp 12 READY

	A	B	C	D	E	F
1	Cheryl Morgan	4	10/27/88	Temp	12.15	
2	V.R. Colonna	1	05/01/83	C-01	3,178.00	1/30/89
3	Amanda Morgan	2	03/18/78	Executive	6,700.00	12/31/89
4	Vincent Charles	6	10/10/82	B-04	3,378.00	10/31/89
5	Rick Morgan	1	01/15/54	A-07	4,213.00	01/31/90
6	Nick Charles	1	03/14/78	A-01	4,528.00	03/31/90
7	Charles Colonna	5	06/29/59	B-03	3,680.00	01/31/90
8	Sarah Jones	1	01/18/58	B-03	3,680.00	01/31/90
9	Angie Morgan	1	01/25/86	Executive	5,850.00	12/31/89

Fig. 7.33. *An unstructured text file imported with /File Import Text as long labels.*

Importing Delimited Files

Some ASCII files are in a special format that enables you to import these files into separate cells, without parsing. This special format is called the delimited format. A delimiter is embedded between each field, and labels are enclosed in quotation marks. A delimiter can be a space, comma, colon, or semicolon. Labels not enclosed in quotation marks are ignored, and only the numbers are imported.

To import a delimited file, use /**F**ile **I**mport **N**umbers. Despite the name, this command really means "file import delimited." Figure 7.34 shows an example of a delimited file. Figure 7.35 shows the results after the /File Import Numbers command is executed.

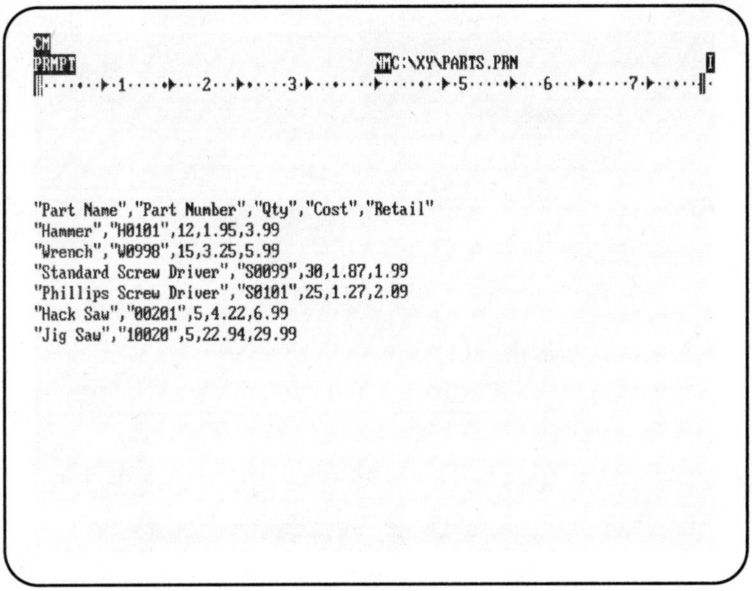

```
CM
PRMPT                        C:\XY\PARTS.PRN                              I
  ····▶·1···▶··2···▶·3▶··········▶·5···▶··6··▶▶····7·▶····




    "Part Name","Part Number","Qty","Cost","Retail"
    "Hammer","H0101",12,1.95,3.99
    "Wrench","W0998",15,3.25,5.99
    "Standard Screw Driver","S0099",30,1.87,1.99
    "Phillips Screw Driver","S0101",25,1.27,2.09
    "Hack Saw","00201",5,4.22,6.99
    "Jig Saw","10020",5,22.94,29.99
```

Fig. 7.34. A delimited ASCII file.

Transferring Files with the Translate Utility

Translate is not part of the 1-2-3 worksheet program but is a separate program. Type **trans** from the operating system prompt to execute Translate or choose **T**ranslate from the Lotus 1-2-3 Access menu.

You use Translate to convert files that you want to be read by a different program. You can convert files to 1-2-3 Release 2.3 *from* the following programs:

- dBASE II, III, and III Plus
- Enable 2.0
- Multiplan in the SYLK format
- SuperCalc4
- Visicalc
- Products that use the DIF format

You can convert files from 1-2-3 Release 2.3 *to* the following programs:

- 1-2-3 Release 1A
- Symphony Release 1.0
- dBASE II, III, and III Plus
- Enable 2.0
- Multiplan in the SYLK format
- SuperCalc4
- Products that use the DIF format

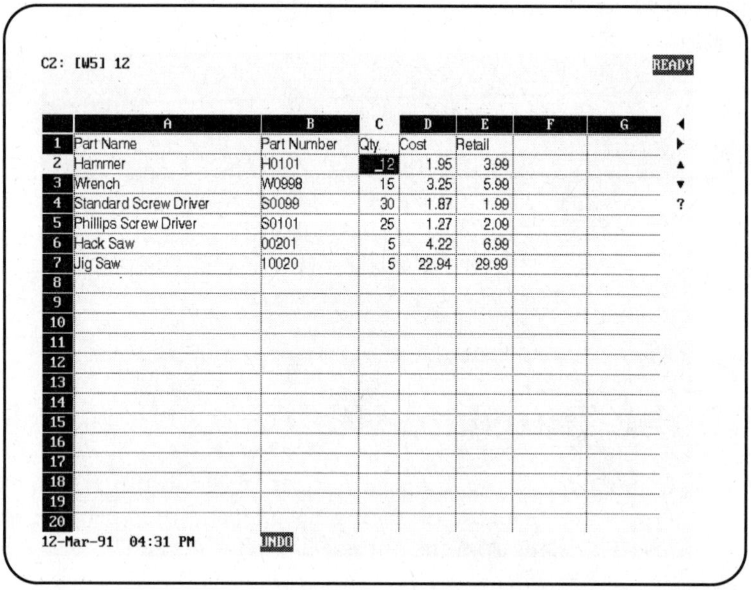

C2: [W5] 12   READY

	A	B	C	D	E	F	G
1	Part Name	Part Number	Qty	Cost	Retail		
2	Hammer	H0101	12	1.95	3.99		
3	Wrench	W0998	15	3.25	5.99		
4	Standard Screw Driver	S0099	30	1.87	1.99		
5	Phillips Screw Driver	S0101	25	1.27	2.09		
6	Hack Saw	00201	5	4.22	6.99		
7	Jig Saw	10020	5	22.94	29.99		

12-Mar-91 04:31 PM   UNDO

Fig. 7.35. The delimited ASCII file after the execution of /File Import Numbers.

When you convert 1-2-3 Release 2.3 files to Releases 1A, 2, 2.01, or 2.2 of 1-2-3, or to Symphony, you lose some information if you used any features unique to Release 2.3.

To use Translate, first select the format or program that you want to translate *from*; then choose the format or program that you want to translate *to* (see figs. 7.36 and 7.37). Finally, choose the file to be translated. Type the file name of the output file you want to create with Translate and press Enter.

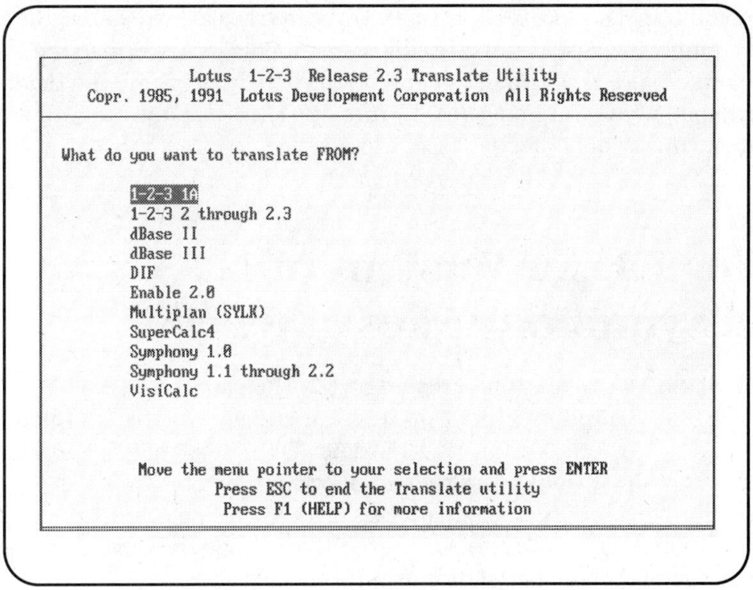

```
                 Lotus  1-2-3  Release 2.3 Translate Utility
        Copr. 1985, 1991  Lotus Development Corporation  All Rights Reserved


What do you want to translate FROM?

            1-2-3 1A
            1-2-3 2 through 2.3
            dBase II
            dBase III
            DIF
            Enable 2.0
            Multiplan (SYLK)
            SuperCalc4
            Symphony 1.0
            Symphony 1.1 through 2.2
            VisiCalc




            Move the menu pointer to your selection and press ENTER
                 Press ESC to end the Translate utility
                  Press F1 (HELP) for more information
```

*Fig. 7.36. The programs Translate enables you to convert **from**.*

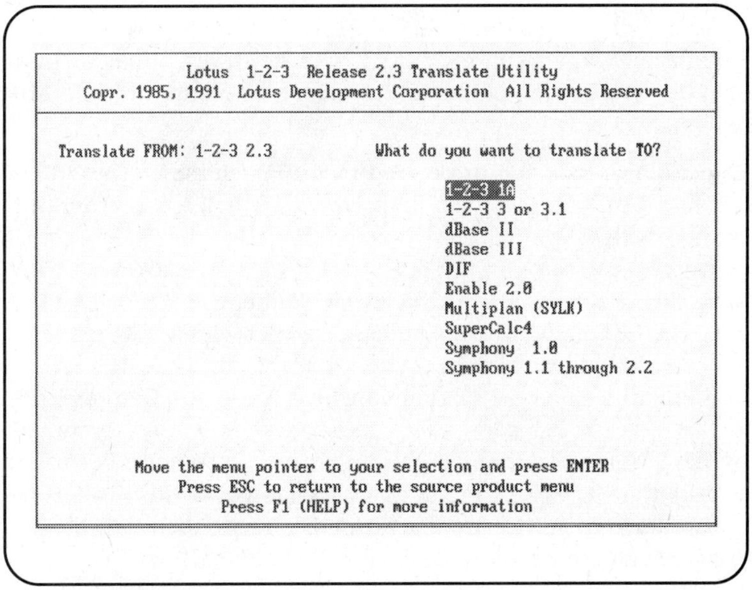

```
                 Lotus  1-2-3  Release 2.3 Translate Utility
        Copr. 1985, 1991  Lotus Development Corporation  All Rights Reserved


Translate FROM: 1-2-3 2.3          What do you want to translate TO?

                                   1-2-3 1A
                                   1-2-3 3 or 3.1
                                   dBase II
                                   dBase III
                                   DIF
                                   Enable 2.0
                                   Multiplan (SYLK)
                                   SuperCalc4
                                   Symphony  1.0
                                   Symphony 1.1 through 2.2




            Move the menu pointer to your selection and press ENTER
               Press ESC to return to the source product menu
                  Press F1 (HELP) for more information
```

*Fig. 7.37. The programs Translate enables you to convert **to**.*

When you translate to dBASE format, you can translate the entire file or a named range. Because the file usually contains data in addition to the Input range, make sure that you use /**R**ange **N**ame **C**reate to name the database Input range. When you translate a file into dBASE format, the range or entire file must consist only of a database Input range.

Using Earlier Versions of 1-2-3 and Symphony Files in Release 2.3

1-2-3 Release 2.3 can read files created by 1-2-3 Releases 1A, 2, 2.01, 2.2, and all releases of Symphony. Use /**F**ile **R**etrieve and specify the complete file name and extension; do not use Translate. The Translate menu seems to give the option of translating files to 1-2-3 Release 2.3 format from the formats for Releases 1A, 2, 2.01, and 2.2 of 1-2-3 and Releases 1.0, 1.1, 1.2, or 2.0 of Symphony. If you choose one of these formats, however, a message appears to tell you file translation is unnecessary.

1-2-3 Release 2.3 can write files in 1-2-3 Release 2, 2.01, or 2.2 format if you used no features unique to Release 2.3. Just use /**F**ile **S**ave. Symphony 1.1, 1.2, and 2 also can read these files.

If a Release 2.3 file is linked to other worksheets, ERR appears in each cell in the worksheet when you execute a /**F**ile **R**etrieve command in 1-2-3 Release 2.01 or 2 but not Release 2.2, which also supports the linking feature.

To create a Release 2.3 file to be read by 1-2-3 Release 1A or Symphony Releases 1 or 1.01, you must use Translate. 1-2-3 Release 2.3 cannot read files created with 1-2-3 Release 3 or 3.1 that use the WK3 extension. However, if a file created in 1-2-3 Release 3 or 3.1 is saved with a WK1 extension, 1-2-3 Release 2.3 can read the file. Remember, however, that you cannot save a file created in 1-2-3 Release 3 or 3.1 with a WK1 extension if that file contains multiple worksheets or if the file is sealed. The new functions in Release 3 or 3.1 or functions that contain new arguments are treated like Release 2.3 add-in functions—new functions, or functions holding new arguments, evaluate to NA in the worksheet. Formats and settings added by Release 3 or 3.1, as well as notes, are lost. Labels larger than 240 characters are truncated. Formulas larger than 240 characters remain in the cell but cannot be edited in Release 2.3.

Using 1-2-3 in a Multiuser or Networking Environment

When you use 1-2-3 in a network or in another multiuser environment, be aware that two or more people can try to access or update the same file simultaneously. The network administrator sets up shared disks so that some files can be shared and some files cannot. You do not need to worry about the files on a network server that you alone can read. Different programs handle the problems of multiple access in different ways. With a database management system—such as dBASE III Plus—the database program controls access so that many users can access the database at the same time. With most programs, such as word processors, the network administrator must ensure that these files are identified as nonsharable or that only one person can access any one file at a time. If you work with a word processing file, no others can read the file until you close that file. Then the file becomes available to others to read or to change.

Reminder:
Only the user who has the file reservation can save changes to a file.

As discussed previously in this chapter, 1-2-3 uses reservations to handle file sharing tasks. The reservation system avoids multiple updates of the same file. When you read a file that no one else is using, 1-2-3 gives you a reservation for that file. When you have the reservation, you can update and then save the file under the same name.

1-2-3 displays the WAIT indicator when you try to read a file from a disk while a second user is trying to read the same file or when you try to read a file while another user is saving the same file on disk. The WAIT indicator remains on-screen until the first user completes the reading or saving process. The WAIT indicator should never display for very long. You can use Ctrl-Break to interrupt the wait cycle and to return you to the point you were at before you tried to read or save the file. An error message appears if 1-2-3 cannot read or save the file within one wait cycle.

File Sharing Guidelines

If you create or save a shared file and then release the reservation or decide to end 1-2-3, another user may get the file's reservation and make new changes. Such a file change and save procedure by another user alters the file before you can read the file into memory again. To determine when the last changes were saved to a file, use the /File List command, which was covered in a previous section of this chapter.

Descriptions of /File Admin Commands

The /File Admin commands control reservations for sharing worksheet files and for creating tables of information about files. This section describes the commands you use to perform these tasks.

/File Admin Reservation

To avoid concurrent updates of the same shared file, 1-2-3 provides the reservation command. Only one user at a time can have a file's reservation. The reservation status is either available or unavailable. Before reading a file into memory, 1-2-3 checks the reservation status and acts accordingly.

If the reservation is available, 1-2-3 reads the file and the reservation into memory. If the reservation is not available, 1-2-3 displays a **Yes/No** prompt, asking to read the file into memory without a reservation. If you choose **Yes**, you can access the file in read-only status—or you can look at the file, but all changes made are not saved to the file with the original file name.

The RO status indicator at the bottom of the screen warns that you cannot save the file under the current name. To save the file, you must use a different name. When the reservation for the original file becomes available, do not copy your file over the original file. This action may inadvertently write over another user's work.

Network users can assign a file read-only status, or a network file may be in a read-only network directory. If either condition is present, you cannot obtain a reservation for a file of this type, even when no other user has the reservation. In this network situation, the network commands take precedence over 1-2-3's reservation status.

If you have the reservation for a file, you keep this reservation until you remove the file (under the same name) from your worksheet. You can remove the file with /Quit, /Worksheet Erase, or /File Retrieve. You also can release the reservation with /File Save, provided that you save the file under a different name. You can release the reservation with /File Admin Reservation Release. Although the file is still in memory, you cannot save a file after issuing the /File Admin Reservation Release command.

/File Admin Table

1-2-3 uses the /File Admin Table command to create a table of information about files on disk or about files linked to the current file. As described previously in this chapter, the /File Admin Table command lists varied information about the files, depending on the type of file you select. Make sure that the designated location in the worksheet is blank because 1-2-3 writes over the existing data to create the table.

Caution:
1-2-3 writes over existing data to create a table with /File Admin Table.

/File Admin Link-Refresh

When a file contains references to other files, 1-2-3 updates these formulas when you read the file and use /File Admin Link-Refresh to update the formulas. See Chapter 3 for more information about linking files and using /File Admin Link-Refresh.

Summary

In this chapter, you learned how to manage files on disk, how to save and read whole files, and how to extract and combine partial files. You learned how to combine text files and how to translate files to other formats. You learned the different methods of protecting files in a single-user computer and in a multiuser or networking environment. You also learned how to use lists and tables of files to help keep track of your files on-disk and in memory. Finally, you learned the special considerations for using 1-2-3 on a network.

In the following chapter, you learn how to print reports using 1-2-3's /Print commands.

Part II

Creating 1-2-3 Reports and Graphs

Includes

Printing Reports

Using Wysiwyg To Enhance and Print Reports

Creating and Printing Graphs

Enhancing and Printing Graphs in Wysiwyg

8

Printing Reports

The 1-2-3 program is a powerful tool for developing information presented in column-and-row format. You can enter and edit your worksheet and database files on-screen as well as store the input on disk. But to make full use of the data, you often need it in printed form such as a target production schedule, a summary report to your supervisor, or a detailed reorder list to central stores.

1-2-3 Release 2.3 gives you two methods for printing worksheet data. You can use the /Print command from the main 1-2-3 menu, or you can use the :Print command from the Wysiwyg menu. This chapter covers the /Print command from the main 1-2-3 menu; Chapter 9 covers the :Print command from Release 2.3's Wysiwyg menu. See "Printing with /Print versus :Print" in this chapter to learn how the two commands are different and when you may want to use one or the other.

By using 1-2-3's /Print or :Print command, you can access many levels of print options to meet your printing needs. For example, you can write directly from 1-2-3 to the printer by using the /Print Printer command, or you can use the alternative /Print File command to create a print (PRN) file. Also, you can produce a printout of the file from within 1-2-3 or from DOS, or you can incorporate the file into a word processing file.

This chapter shows you how to complete the following tasks by using the /Print command from the main 1-2-3 menu:

- Choose between /Print **P**rinter, /Print **F**ile, /Print **E**ncoded, and /Print **B**ackground by using default settings

- Print single or multiple pages

- Exclude segments within a designated print range

- Control paper movement

- Change the default settings

- Test the print format of large print ranges

- Print worksheet contents cell by cell

- Prepare output for acceptance by other programs

Because you must use the PrintGraph program or the Wysiwyg menu to print graphs, printing graphs is not covered in this chapter. See Chapter 10 for a complete discussion of the PrintGraph program. See Chapters 9 and 11 for a discussion of how to print graphs by using the Wysiwyg menu.

Printing with /Print versus :Print

When the Wysiwyg add-in is attached, you can print worksheet data by using either the /Print command or the :Print command.

If the Wysiwyg add-in is not attached, you can use only the /Print command from the 1-2-3 main menu. Many of the options provided by the two commands are similar. You can, for example, enter page headers or footers through either command, and you can change the size of margins with both. Both commands, however, work independently; setting margins with the /Print command does not automatically transfer the same margin settings to the :Print command.

What are the differences between /Print and :Print? /Print is the command carried over from Releases 2.01 and 2.2 of 1-2-3; /Print gives you the basic print capabilities available in these two releases. :Print, as explained in Chapter 9, enables you to preview every page of the printout before you print so that you can check the format and layout on-screen before issuing the command to start printing. Also, you must use :Print if you want the printout to show any of the format or graph enhancements made through the Wysiwyg menu. For example, if you add lines, boxes, and shading to the worksheet through the Wysiwyg menu, these enhancements do not appear on a document printed with the /Print command. Also, :Print enables you to control which pages to print and which page numbers to use in the header or footer. /Print does not have these capabilities.

When should you use /Print versus :Print? If the Wysiwyg add-in is not attached, you must use /Print to print your reports. If Wysiwyg is attached, you can use either command. You certainly would use :Print when you want to produce a report, handout, transparency, or other document that should match the quality of documents produced with desktop publishing software. Experienced 1-2-3 Release 2.01 and 2.2 users also may choose to use the /Print commands because these users work with macros containing commands from the standard /Print menu. You also should use /Print when you want to print cell formulas rather than the numbers displayed by the formulas. Finally, /Print enables you to remove temporarily page breaks, headers, and footers with one command—/Print [**P,F,E**] Options Other Unformatted—so that these elements are not printed. :Print has no single command equivalent that works the same. Even if you don't need high-quality printed pages, the Wysiwyg :Print command gives you better quality printed text than /Print.

Reminder:
You can use the
:Print commands
only if Wysiwyg is
attached.

Getting Started from the /Print Menu

You must start any /Print command sequence from the 1-2-3 command menu. After choosing /Print, you must select one of the first three options: **Printer, File,** or **Encoded** (see fig. 8.1). You use the next option, **Back-ground,** when you want to continue working in 1-2-3 while the print range is printing.

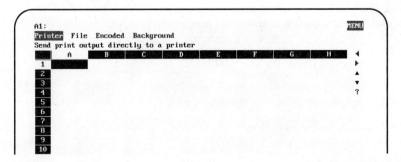

Fig. 8.1. *The initial print decision: print to the printer or to a disk file.*

To send the report directly to the current printer, choose **Printer**.

Cue:
Choose /Print File
to create a file to be
incorporated into a
word processing
file.

To create a text file on disk, select **File**. A text file can contain data but no graphs or special printer codes. Later, you can print the text file from the operating system prompt, or you can incorporate the text file into a word processing file.

To create a disk file that includes instructions on printing, choose **Encoded**. An encoded file can contain data and printer codes for 1-2-3 print options, such as margins and setup strings. An encoded file can be printed from the operating system prompt, but such a file is not suitable for transferring data to another program.

If you choose **File** or **Encoded**, you must respond to the prompt for a file name by typing a name that contains up to eight characters. You need not add a file extension because 1-2-3 automatically assigns the PRN (print file) or ENC (encoded file) extension. You can specify a different extension if you want. You use an encoded file for printing at another time or from another computer while preserving all the special print options available in 1-2-3's /Print menu. When you create an encoded file, be sure that the selected printer is the same as the one you use to print the file. An encoded file contains printer codes that control special printer features, such as fonts and line spacing. Because these codes are printer-specific, an encoded file created for one printer may not print correctly on another printer.

The printer control codes embedded in the encoded file ensure that the final output looks the same as output printed directly from 1-2-3.

To print an encoded file, you use the operating system COPY command with the **/B** option. Consider the following example:

        COPY C:\123R23\SALES.ENC/B PRN

This command prints the file SALES.ENC, located in directory C:/123R23, on the printer connected to the default printer port. If you need to specify a specific printer port, you can use LPT1, LPT2, COM1, or COM2 instead of PRN.

In addition to printing an encoded file from DOS, you also can print a PRN file created with the **/Print File** command. Consider the following example:

        PRINT C:\123R23\SALES.PRN LPT1

The command prints the file SALES.PRN, located in the directory C:\123R23, on the printer connected to the port LPT1.

After you select **Printer**, **File**, or **Encoded**, the second line of the control panel displays a menu with eight options and the Print Settings dialog box appears on-screen (see fig. 8.2).

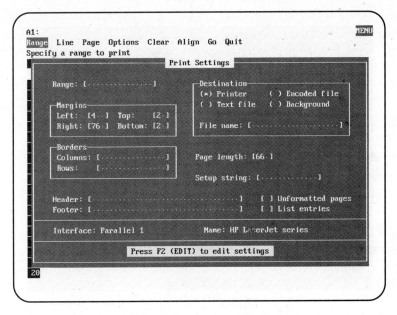

Fig. 8.2. The /Print [P, F, E] menu and the Print Settings dialog box.

The /Print [**P,F,E**] menu offers the following choices:

Selection	Description
Range	Indicates the section(s) of the worksheet to be printed
Line	Advances the paper in the printer by one line
Page	Advances the paper in the printer to the top of the next page
Options	Changes default print settings and offers a number of print enhancements
Clear	Erases some or all of the previously entered print settings
Align	Signals that the paper in the printer is set to the beginning of a page
Go	Starts printing
Quit	Exits from the /**P**rint menu and closes the current print job

In 1-2-3, the most frequently used (or least dangerous) commands are usually on the left side of a menu. In any print command sequence, you start with /Print; branch to **Printer**, **File**, or **Encoded**; and then proceed to the next menu. Regardless of which branch you select, you must specify a **Range** to print, choose **Align**, select **Go** to begin printing, and then select **Quit** or press Esc twice to return to the worksheet. All other selections are optional.

Although selecting **Align** is not essential, it is recommended. **Align** ensures that printing begins at the top of all succeeding pages after the first page. Make sure in particular that you reposition the printer paper and use the **Align** command when you have canceled a print job.

You use **Page** to move the paper to the top of the next page. **Page** also can be used to eject a blank page, making it easier for you to tear off the last page of the report.

Before you learn which print commands to use for performing specific tasks or operations, you need a general understanding of 1-2-3's default print settings. These settings are discussed in the next section.

Understanding the Print Default Settings

To minimize the keystrokes necessary for a print operation, 1-2-3 makes certain assumptions about how you want the copy printed. The usual print operation produces 72 characters per line and 56 lines per page on 8 1/2-by-11-inch continuous-feed paper and uses the first parallel printer installed to print a report. You should know the current settings for your 1-2-3 program.

Current Printer Status

Cue:
Use /Worksheet
Global Default
Printer to check
current default print
settings.

You should check the global default settings before you print a report. To do so, issue the /Worksheet **G**lobal **D**efault **P**rinter command. The Default Printer Settings dialog box appears (see fig. 8.3). You use /Worksheet **G**lobal **D**efault **P**rinter to change a setting for the current work session and /Worksheet **G**lobal **D**efault **U**pdate to make the change remain in effect every time you reload 1-2-3.

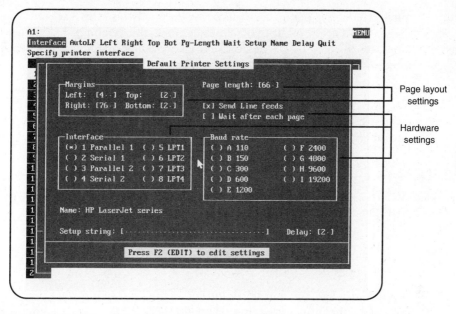

Fig. 8.3. The /Worksheet Global Default menu and the Default Printer Settings dialog box.

The following sections discuss the settings in the Default Printer Settings dialog box: page layout settings are indicated in the **Margins** and **Page length** sections; hardware specific information is displayed in the following sections:

Interface

Send Line feeds

Name

Wait after each page

Baud rate

The **S**etup string entry shows any setup strings in effect. Finally, **D**elay indicates the amount of time (in minutes) 1-2-3 waits before generating a printer error.

Page Layout Options

For page layout, you must consider the length and width of the printer paper, the number of lines that print on one page (lines per inch), and the pitch (characters per inch). Because 1-2-3 initially assumes 8 1/2-by-11-inch paper and a printer output of 6 lines per inch, the default page length is 66 lines. Because of 1-2-3's default settings (two-line margins at the top and bottom), however, all 66 lines are not used.

Every line ordinarily contains 10 or 12 characters per inch, although you can vary the pitch by using setup strings (discussed later in this chapter). Look at figure 8.4. The following five menu options determine default page-layout characteristics:

Option	Message
Left	Enter left margin (0..240):4
Right	Enter right margin (0..240):76
Top	Enter top margin (0..32):2
Bot	Enter bottom margin (0..32):2
Pg-Length	Enter lines per page (1..100):66

In each message, the number at the end of the prompt indicates the default value, and the numbers enclosed in parentheses indicate the minimum and maximum values you can select.

To calculate the width of the report, subtract the current left-margin setting (4) from the current right-margin setting (76). The report is printed with 72 characters per line.

To calculate the length of the worksheet, you need to subtract not only the lines for top and bottom margins but also the lines that 1-2-3 automatically reserves for a header and a footer. If you are using all default settings, for example, the actual number of lines (or rows) from the worksheet that are printed is 56. 1-2-3 assigns two lines each for the top and bottom margins and reserves three lines each for a header and a footer (although only one line can be used for each). The six header and footer lines are reserved even if you do not enter a header or footer. Because the default page length is 66, you subtract four lines for top and bottom margins and the six lines reserved for a header and footer to get 56 printed lines. (To learn how to enter headers and footers, see "Creating Headers and Footers" in this chapter.)

Global Default Hardware-Specific Options

If you want to change the print settings shown in the default printer status report, invoke the /Worksheet Global Default Printer command. Notice that the first two options in the menu shown in figure 8.3 (Interface and AutoLF) correspond to the Interface and Send Line feeds settings in the Default Printer Settings dialog box.

Use the Interface option to specify one of the following eight possible connections between the computer and the printer:

1 First parallel port (the default)

2 First serial port

3 Second parallel port

4 Second serial port

5 DOS Device LPT1

6 DOS Device LPT2

7 DOS Device LPT3

8 DOS Device LPT4

Choices 5 through 8 are usually applicable only if the workstation is part of a local area network. If you select either serial port option (2 or 4), another menu appears. From this menu, you must specify one of the following baud rates (data transmission speed). For example, a 1200 baud rate roughly equals 120 characters per second.

1 110 baud

2 150 baud

3 300 baud

4 600 baud

5 1200 baud

6 2400 baud

7 4800 baud

8 9600 baud

9 19200 baud

Check the printer manual for information about the type of interface and baud rate, if applicable. Most printers manufactured today have baud rates above 600. If your printer does, you want to take advantage of the higher speed by selecting a higher baud rate, typically 1200 or 2400. The baud rate settings you specify are indicated in the **B**aud rate section of the dialog box.

The AutoLF option specifies the printer's end-of-line procedure. **Yes** signals the printer to advance a line automatically when it receives a carriage return; **No** means that the printer does not advance a line. With most printers, leave AutoLF in its **No** default setting. If the reports are double-spaced, select **Yes**. An × in the brackets to the left of Send Line feeds in the dialog box indicates that **No** is selected; brackets with a blank space indicate **Yes** has been chosen.

Reminder:
Set AutoLF to Yes for double-spaced reports.

Other Default Options: Wait, Setup, Name, and Delay

There are five final options on the /Worksheet Global Default Printer menu. Wait controls the way paper is fed to the printer; Setup controls the size and style of type; Name enables you to change between two installed printers; and Delay enables you to set the amount of time before issuing a printer error message. The final option, Quit, enables you to leave the menu and return to the READY mode.

If you are using continuous-feed paper, a laser printer, or automatic sheet feeder that can feed single sheets, leave the Wait option set to No (the default). If you are using single sheets of paper (such as for a manual-feed plotter), select Yes to change the default setting; printing pauses at the end of each page so that you can insert a new sheet of paper. After you insert the page, press Enter to continue printing.

The default setting for Setup is no setup string. This setting means that no special printer-control codes, such as condensed print, eight lines per inch instead of six, or boldface type, are in effect. (For examples of setup strings, see "Changing the Print Options" in this chapter.)

The menu that appears after you select Name depends on which printers you selected when you installed 1-2-3. For example, you may have installed your 1-2-3 program to print on two different printers: the EPSON printer you have at home and the Toshiba printer at work. In this case, selecting Name produces a menu with options 1 (the EPSON) and 2 (the Toshiba).

Remember that if you use the /Worksheet Global Default Printer command to change print settings, the new settings remain in effect for the current work session only. To have the settings remain the default when you start 1-2-3, use the /Worksheet Global Default Update command after you have made the changes you want.

The last item in the Default Printer Settings dialog box—Delay—shows the number of minutes 1-2-3 waits before interpreting a delay as an error. Use Delay, for example, to give the printer the time it needs to complete a printer check or to print a sample.

Printing a Draft-Quality Report

1-2-3's /Print menu is designed for the simplest to the most complex worksheet printing needs. If you want to print a report quickly that does not require changing any default print settings (such as those for paper size) or adding special enhancements (such as headers, footers, or different sizes and styles of type), you can print a report with default settings. If you want to dress up the report or have special requirements for paper size, margins, or page length, you need to use the commands available in the /Print or :Print menu system. To illustrate printing techniques, this chapter uses the large worksheet in figure 8.4, which occupies the range A1..S38.

This section shows you how to print draft-quality reports quickly by using a minimum of commands. Later in the chapter, you learn how to use those commands that enhance reports, change type size and style, and automatically repeat border titles. You also learn how to produce printouts of complete formulas rather than their resulting values.

Printing a Screenful of Data

Before you print any portion of a 1-2-3 worksheet, decide whether the output must be of report quality (suitable for official distribution or filing) or whether all you need is a screen print (hard copy of the screen's contents).

You can, for example, retrieve the Regional Income file and then press Print Screen (or Shift-PrtSc) for a screen print (see fig. 8.5). The resultant screen print captures everything on-screen, even such unwanted items as the contents of the highlighted cell A1 and the mode indicator. Such quick printouts may be adequate for interoffice memos and, because they capture the date-and-time indicator, for documenting model construction.

Cue:
Pressing Print Screen (or Shift-PrtSc) prints whatever is on-screen.

	A B	C	D	E	F	G	H	I
1	REGIONAL INCOME REPORT	Jan	Feb	Mar	1st Q	Apr	May	Jun
2	11–Mar–91							
3								
4	Sales							
5	Northeast	$31,336	$34,370	$37,404	$103,110	$40,438	$43,472	$46,506
6	Southeast	30,572	33,606	36,640	100,818	39,674	42,708	45,742
7	Central	131,685	134,719	137,753	404,157	140,787	143,821	146,855
8	Northwest	94,473	97,507	100,541	292,521	103,575	106,609	109,843
9	Southwest	126,739	129,773	132,807	389,319	135,841	138,875	141,909
10								
11	Total Sales	414,805	429,975	445,145	1,289,925	460,315	475,485	490,655
12								
13	Cost of Goods Sold							
14	Northeast	10,341	11,274	12,207	33,822	13,140	14,073	15,006
15	Southeast	6,546	7,479	8,412	22,437	9,345	10,278	11,211
16	Central	65,843	66,776	67,709	200,328	68,642	69,575	70,508
17	Northwest	63,967	64,900	65,833	194,700	66,766	67,899	68,832
18	Southwest	72,314	73,247	74,180	219,741	75,113	76,046	76,979
19								
20	Total Cost of Goods Sold	219,011	223,676	228,341	671,028	233,006	237,671	242,336
21								
22	Operating Expenses							
23	Northeast	21,529	23,470	25,411	70,410	27,352	29,293	31,234
24	Southeast	15,946	17,887	19,828	53,661	21,769	23,710	25,651
25	Central	27,554	29,495	31,436	88,485	33,377	35,318	37,259
26	Northwest	16,130	18,071	20,012	54,213	21,953	23,894	25,835
27	Southwest	32,361	34,302	36,243	102,906	38,184	40,125	42,066
28								
29	Total Operating Expenses	113,520	123,225	132,930	369,675	142,635	152,340	162,045
30								
31	Net Income							
32	Northeast	(534)	(374)	(214)	(1,122)	(54)	106	266
33	Southeast	8,080	8,240	8,400	24,720	8,560	8,720	8,880
34	Central	38,288	38,448	38,608	115,344	38,768	38,928	39,088
35	Northwest	14,376	14,536	14,696	43,608	14,856	15,016	15,176
36	Southwest	22,064	22,224	22,384	66,672	22,544	22,704	22,864
37								
38	Total Net Income	$82,808	$83,074	$83,874	$249,222	$84,674	$85,474	$86,274

Fig. 8.4. The Regional Income Report worksheet.

```
A1: [W3] 'REGIONAL INCOME REPORT                                      READY


      A        B          C         D         E         F
 1  REGIONAL INCOME REPORT    Jan       Feb       Mar       1st Q
 2            11-Mar-91
 3
 4  Sales
 5       Northeast        $31,336   $34,370   $37,404   $103,110
 6       Southeast         30,572    33,606    36,640    100,818
 7       Central          131,685   134,719   137,753   404,157
 8       Northwest         94,473    97,507   100,541   292,521
 9       Southwest        126,739   129,773   132,807   389,319
10
11  Total Sales          414,805   429,975   445,145 1,289,925
12
13  Cost of Goods Sold
14       Northeast         10,341    11,274    12,207    33,822
15       Southeast          6,546     7,479     8,412    22,437
16       Central           65,843    66,776    67,709   200,328
17       Northwest         63,967    64,900    65,833   194,700
18       Southwest         72,314    73,247    74,180   219,741
19
20  Total Cost of Goods Sold 219,011 223,676  228,341   671,028
11-Mar-91   11:55 AM
```

Fig. 8.5. The result of using Print Screen (or Shift-PrtSc).

J 2nd Q	K Jul	L Aug	M Sep	N 3rd Q	O Oct	P Nov	Q Dec	R 4th Q	S TOTAL
$130,416	$49,540	$52,574	$55,608	$157,722	$58,642	$61,876	$64,710	$185,028	$576,276
128,124	48,776	51,810	54,844	155,430	57,878	60,912	63,946	182,736	567,108
431,463	149,889	152,923	155,957	458,769	158,991	162,025	165,059	486,075	1,780,464
319,827	112,677	115,711	118,745	347,133	121,779	124,813	127,847	374,439	1,333,920
416,625	144,943	147,977	151,011	443,931	154,045	157,079	160,113	471,237	1,721,112
1,426,455	505,825	520,995	536,165	1,562,985	551,335	566,505	581,675	1,699,515	5,978,880
42,219	15,939	16,872	17,805	50,616	18,738	19,671	20,604	59,013	185,670
30,834	12,144	13,077	14,010	39,231	14,943	15,876	16,809	47,628	140,130
208,725	71,441	72,374	73,307	217,122	74,240	75,173	76,106	225,519	851,894
203,097	69,565	70,498	71,431	211,494	72,364	73,297	74,230	219,891	829,182
228,138	77,912	78,845	79,778	236,535	80,711	81,644	82,577	244,932	929,346
713,013	247,001	251,666	256,331	754,998	260,996	265,661	270,326	796,983	2,936,022
87,879	33,175	35,116	37,057	105,348	38,996	40,939	42,880	122,817	386,454
71,130	27,592	29,533	31,474	88,599	33,415	35,356	37,297	106,068	319,458
105,954	39,200	41,141	43,082	123,423	45,023	46,964	48,905	140,892	458,754
71,682	27,776	29,717	31,658	89,151	33,599	35,540	37,481	106,620	321,866
120,375	44,007	45,948	47,889	137,844	49,830	51,771	53,712	155,313	516,438
457,020	171,750	181,455	191,160	544,365	200,865	210,570	220,275	631,710	2,002,770
318	426	586	746	1,758	906	1,066	1,226	3,198	4,152
26,160	9,040	9,200	9,360	27,600	9,520	9,680	9,840	29,040	107,520
116,784	39,248	39,408	39,568	118,224	39,728	39,888	40,048	119,664	470,016
45,048	15,336	15,496	15,656	46,488	15,816	15,976	16,136	47,928	183,072
68,112	23,024	23,184	23,344	69,552	23,504	23,664	23,824	70,992	275,328
$256,422	$87,074	$87,874	$88,674	$263,622	$89,474	$90,274	$91,074	$270,822	$1,040,088

Printing Draft-Quality Reports on One Page or Less

If you don't change any of the default print settings, and no other print settings have been entered during the current worksheet session, you can print a page or less by using the following steps:

1. Choose to print to the printer or file.

2. Highlight the worksheet area you want printed.

3. Choose the command to begin printing.

Two other steps may be necessary if another person uses the copy of 1-2-3 and has possibly changed either the default print settings or has entered new settings during the current worksheet session. First, you can check the print settings by selecting /**P**rint **P**rinter. A quick review of the Default Printer Settings dialog box indicates whether the printer and page layout settings are the ones you need. Second, you can clear any special settings that may have been entered. To do so, select /**Print Printer Clear** to erase all settings or to erase only the range, borders, or format setting.

If you are certain that all default settings are correct and no other settings have been entered, you can print a report of a page or less easily by completing the following sequence of operations. First, check that the printer is on-line and that the paper is positioned where you want the data to print. Next choose /**Print Printer**. The following menu appears:

Range Line Page Options Clear Align Go Quit

Indicate what part of the worksheet you want to print by selecting **Range** and highlighting the area. Suppose that you want to print the first-quarter sales data from the regional sales part of the Regional Income Report (see fig. 8.5). To print this area, you specify the range A1..F11.

You can use the PgUp, PgDn, and End keys to designate ranges when you print. If you want to designate a range that includes the entire active area of the worksheet, anchor the left corner of the print range, press the End key, and then press the Home key.

In 1-2-3 Release 2.3, you can prespecify a range and avoid having to highlight it manually when you want to print the range during a work session. To prespecify a range, place the cell pointer in a corner of the range and press F4 to anchor the pointer. If you are using the mouse, click and drag the mouse to highlight the range. Without a mouse, use the arrow keys or the PgUp and PgDn keys to highlight the range. After you have prespecified a range, you can use /**Print Printer** (or **File** or **Encoded**) **Range** to highlight the range automatically.

Cue:
Use Ctrl-Break to stop printing at any time.

After you highlight the range you want to print, select **Align Go** (see fig. 8.6). If you accidentally press Enter after you already have used the **Go** option, the file prints a second time. If this happens, you can stop printing by pressing Ctrl-Break.

```
REGIONAL INCOME REPORT        Jan      Feb      Mar     1st Q
              11-Mar-91

Sales
     Northeast           $31,336  $34,370  $37,404  $103,110
     Southeast            30,572   33,606   36,640   100,818
     Central             131,685  134,719  137,753   404,157
     Northwest            94,473   97,507  100,541   292,521
     Southwest           126,739  129,773  132,807   389,319

Total Sales              414,805  429,975  445,145 1,289,925
```

Fig. 8.6. The result of printing one page with default settings.

Printing Reports Longer Than One Page

If the area of your worksheet has more rows and columns than can be printed on one page, you can use the basic steps discussed in the preceding section for printing reports on a page or less. Setting the print range, however, so that a new page begins exactly where you want it to begin can sometimes be a bit tricky. Also, if you want to print a section of a large worksheet like the Regional Income Report in figure 8.5, you may need to use the /Print Printer Options Borders command so that labels are repeated on each page.

Cue:
If your worksheet is more than one page, use the /Print Printer Options Borders command to repeat the borders.

To ensure that information is printed on the pages as you want, remember that 1-2-3 treats numeric and text data differently when splitting data from one page to the next. Complete numbers print because numbers can span only one cell. On the other hand, text, such as long labels that span several cells, may be split in awkward places from one page to the next.

Suppose that you want to print six month's worth of data from the Regional Income worksheet in figure 8.4. Suppose also that you want to print the report on 8 1/2-by-11-inch paper, the default paper size. To print the report on this size paper with the default margin settings and a pitch of 10 characters per inch, you need to print on two pages.

To print eight columns of data from the Regional Income Report, first check that the printer is on-line and that the paper is positioned where you want the printing to begin. Then choose the /Print Printer command.

Because you want the labels in A6 through A38 in figure 8.4 to print on both pages, you must use the Options Borders command. When you select Options Borders, 1-2-3 asks whether the labels you want repeated are located down a column or across a row. For the sample report, choose Columns. (To print a report on two or more pages and repeat labels displayed across a row, select Rows after choosing Options Borders.)

After you choose Columns, the prompt Enter range for border columns: appears. If the cell pointer is located in the column or columns where the labels appear, press Enter; if not, move the cell pointer to the column and press Enter. To return to the main /Print Printer menu, select Quit.

After you have indicated which column or row of labels you want repeated on each page, you should not include those labels in the actual print range. 1-2-3 automatically places those labels in the first column or row on every page. To print the January-through-June data from the Regional Income Report, highlight the range C1..J38. Notice that this range does not include A1..B38, which is the range that contains the labels.

Keep the following cautions in mind when using the /Print Printer Options Borders command. First, be sure to highlight all columns across which labels extend. Highlighting only the A column, for example, when labels extend into column B, results in only part of the label printing. Second, if you are working in Wysiwyg graphics mode, switch to text mode to see exactly how many columns the labels cover. Because of the differing font sizes in Wysiwyg graphics mode, labels may appear to fit in a narrower range than what they actually do in text mode.

Cue:
If you use Ctrl-Break to cancel a print job, use /Print Printer Align before you restart printing.

Next, select Align, Go, and Quit. Choosing Align ensures that printing begins at the top of all succeeding pages after the first. Make sure in particular that you reposition the printer paper and use the Align command when you have canceled a print job. The printed pages of the Regional Income Report are shown in figures 8.7 and 8.8. Notice that the column descriptions print on both pages.

REGIONAL INCOME REPORT 11-Mar-91	Jan	Feb	Mar	1st Q
Sales				
Northeast	$31,336	$34,370	$37,404	$103,110
Southeast	30,572	33,606	36,640	100,818
Central	131,685	134,719	137,753	404,157
Northwest	94,473	97,507	100,541	292,521
Southwest	126,739	129,773	132,807	389,319
Total Sales	414,805	429,975	445,145	1,289,925
Cost of Goods Sold				
Northeast	10,341	11,274	12,207	33,822
Southeast	6,546	7,479	8,412	22,437
Central	65,843	66,776	67,709	200,328
Northwest	63,967	64,900	65,833	194,700
Southwest	72,314	73,247	74,180	219,741
Total Cost of Goods Sold	219,011	223,676	228,341	671,028
Operating Expenses				
Northeast	21,529	23,470	25,411	70,410
Southeast	15,946	17,887	19,828	53,661
Central	27,554	29,495	31,436	88,485
Northwest	16,130	18,071	20,012	54,213
Southwest	32,361	34,302	36,243	102,906
Total Operating Expenses	113,520	123,225	132,930	369,675
Net Income				
Northeast	(534)	(374)	(214)	(1,122)
Southeast	8,080	8,240	8,400	24,720
Central	38,288	38,448	38,608	115,344
Northwest	14,376	14,536	14,696	43,608
Southwest	22,064	22,224	22,384	66,672
Total Net Income	$82,808	$83,074	$83,874	$249,222

Fig. 8.7. The first page of a report printed on two pages.

```
REGIONAL INCOME REPORT        Apr      May      Jun      2nd Q
           11-Mar-91

Sales
      Northeast            $40,438  $43,472  $46,506   $130,416
      Southeast            39,674   42,708   45,742    128,124
      Central             140,787  143,821  146,855    431,463
      Northwest           103,575  106,609  109,643    319,827
      Southwest           135,841  138,875  141,909    416,625

Total Sales               460,315  475,485  490,655  1,426,455

Cost of Goods Sold
      Northeast            13,140   14,073   15,006     42,219
      Southeast             9,345   10,278   11,211     30,834
      Central              68,642   69,575   70,508    208,725
      Northwest            66,766   67,699   68,632    203,097
      Southwest            75,113   76,046   76,979    228,138

Total Cost of Goods Sold  233,006  237,671  242,336    713,013

Operating Expenses
      Northeast            27,352   29,293   31,234     87,879
      Southeast            21,769   23,710   25,651     71,130
      Central              33,377   35,318   37,259    105,954
      Northwest            21,953   23,894   25,835     71,682
      Southwest            38,184   40,125   42,066    120,375

Total Operating Expenses  142,635  152,340  162,045    457,020

Net Income
      Northeast              (54)      106      266        318
      Southeast             8,560    8,720    8,880     26,160
      Central              38,768   38,928   39,088    116,784
      Northwest            14,856   15,016   15,176     45,048
      Southwest            22,544   22,704   22,864     68,112

Total Net Income          $84,674  $85,474  $86,274   $256,422
```

Fig. 8.8. The second page of a report printed on two pages.

Hiding Segments within the Designated Print Range

Because the /Print commands require you to specify a range to print, you may print only rectangular blocks from the worksheet. You may, however, suppress the display of cell contents within the range, eliminate one or more rows, hide one or more columns, or remove from view a segment that spans only part of a row or column. The results of each of the following illustrations print on one page, using default settings.

Excluding Rows

To exclude rows from printing, you must mark the rows for omission. Do this by typing a double vertical bar (||) in the blank leftmost cell of the print range of each row you want to omit. Only one of these vertical bars appears on-screen, and neither appears on the printout. A row marked in this way does not print, but the suppressed data remains in the worksheet and is used in any applicable calculations.

Suppose that you want to print the first-quarter data of the Net Income section from the Regional Income Report. When the /Print Printer Range command prompts you for a range to print, specify A31..F38. Next, cancel the column borders setting by selecting /Print Printer Clear Borders. (All data fits on one page, so you don't need to use column borders.) Finally, use /Print Printer Options Borders Rows and highlight A1..A2 so that the report title, date, month headings, and quarter headings are printed. The printout of the contents of rows 31 through 38 is shown in figure 8.9.

```
REGIONAL INCOME REPORT        Jan       Feb       Mar      1st Q
              11-Mar-91
Net Income
       Northeast               (534)     (374)     (214)    (1,122)
       Southeast              8,080     8,240     8,400     24,720
       Central              38,288    38,448    38,608    115,344
       Northwest            14,376    14,536    14,696     43,608
       Southwest            22,064    22,224    22,384     66,672

Total Net Income          $82,808   $83,074   $83,874   $249,222
```

Fig. 8.9. A printout of net income for the first quarter.

Cue:
If necessary, insert a new column A to provide blank cells for the nonprinting symbol.

Now suppose that you don't want the printout to show the data for the Northeast region (row 32). Do not use a worksheet command to delete the row. Instead, omit the row from printing by typing a double vertical bar in the leftmost cell of the row to be omitted. Because the leftmost cell is not blank, however, you need to make an adjustment. The simplest method is to insert a new column A and narrow it to a one-column width. Then type || in cell A32.

When you execute the Print command, be sure to specify the expanded range A31..G38 (not A31..F38 or B31..G38). Figure 8.10 shows the resulting printout.

```
REGIONAL INCOME REPORT    1st Q     2nd Q     3rd Q     4th Q
           11-Mar-91

Net Income
     Southeast            24,720    26,160    27,600    29,040
     Central             115,344   116,784   118,224   119,664
     Northwest            43,608    45,048    46,488    47,928
     Southwest            66,672    68,112    69,552    70,992

Total Net Income        $249,222  $256,422  $263,622  $270,822
```

Fig. 8.10. The row containing Northeast regional data is omitted.

To restore the worksheet after you have finished printing, delete column A to remove the vertical bars.

Excluding Columns

As you learn in Chapter 4, you can use 1-2-3's /Worksheet Column Hide command to mark columns you don't want to display on-screen. If these marked columns are included in a print range, they do not appear on the printout if you use the /Print [**P**, **F**, **E**] Options Other As-Displayed command. Hidden columns do not print if you are printing cell formulas by using the /Print [**P**, **F**, **E**] Options Other Cell-Formulas command.

Cue:
Use /Worksheet Column Hide to hide columns you don't want to print.

Suppose that you are working with the Regional Income Report model and you want to print only the data for each quarter contained in columns F, J, N, and R. Invoke the /Worksheet Column Hide command; specify columns C, D, E, G, H, I, K, L, M, O, P, and Q; and set your print range to A1..R38. The resulting printout is shown in figure 8.11.

To restore the columns, select /Worksheet Column Display. When the hidden columns (marked with an asterisk) reappear on-screen, you can specify which column or columns to show.

Excluding Ranges

If you want to hide only a partial row, a partial column, or an area that partially spans one or more rows and columns, use the /Range Format Hidden command to mark the ranges.

```
REGIONAL INCOME REPORT      1st Q     2nd Q     3rd Q     4th Q
            11-Mar-91

Sales
      Northeast           $103,110  $130,416  $157,722  $185,028
      Southeast            100,818   128,124   155,430   182,736
      Central              404,157   431,463   458,769   486,075
      Northwest            292,521   319,827   347,133   374,439
      Southwest            389,319   416,625   443,931   471,237

Total Sales             1,289,925 1,426,455 1,562,985 1,699,515

Cost of Goods Sold
      Northeast            33,822    42,219    50,616    59,013
      Southeast            22,437    30,834    39,231    47,628
      Central             200,328   208,725   217,122   225,519
      Northwest           194,700   203,097   211,494   219,891
      Southwest           219,741   228,138   236,535   244,932

Total Cost of Goods Sold  671,028   713,013   754,998   796,983

Operating Expenses
      Northeast            70,410    87,879   105,348   122,817
      Southeast            53,661    71,130    88,599   106,068
      Central              88,485   105,954   123,423   140,892
      Northwest            54,213    71,682    89,151   106,620
      Southwest           102,906   120,375   137,844   155,313

Total Operating Expenses  369,675   457,020   544,365   631,710

Net Income
      Northeast           (1,122)       318     1,758     3,198
      Southeast            24,720    26,160    27,600    29,040
      Central             115,344   116,784   118,224   119,664
      Northwest            43,608    45,048    46,488    47,928
      Southwest            66,672    68,112    69,552    70,992

Total Net Income        $249,222  $256,422  $263,622  $270,822
```

Fig. 8.11. The printout after hiding unwanted columns.

Perhaps your worksheet includes documentation you want to save on disk but omit from the printout. For example, you may want to omit the date in the second row of the Regional Income Report worksheet. To omit the date, issue the /Range Format Hidden command and specify cell B2. Then clear the borders with /Print Printer Clear Borders and print the range A1..F11 (see fig. 8.12).

After you finish printing, select /Range Format Reset and then select B2 to restore the date.

```
┌─────────────────────────────────────────────────────────────┐
│                                                               │
│    REGIONAL INCOME REPORT     Jan       Feb       Mar         │
│                                                               │
│    Sales                                                      │
│        Northeast           $31,336   $34,370   $37,404        │
│        Southeast            30,572    33,606    36,640        │
│        Central             131,685   134,719   137,753        │
│        Northwest            94,473    97,507   100,541        │
│        Southwest           126,739   129,773   132,807        │
│                                                               │
│    Total Sales             414,805   429,975   445,145        │
│                                                               │
└─────────────────────────────────────────────────────────────┘
```

Fig. 8.12. *The printout after hiding cell B2.*

If you find yourself repeating print operations (hiding the same columns, suppressing and then restoring the same information, and so on), remember that you can save time and minimize frustration by developing and using print macros (see Chapter 13).

Cue:
Use print macros for repeated print operations.

Controlling Paper Movement

Unless you specify otherwise, the top of a page initially is marked by the print head's position when you turn on the printer and load 1-2-3. If you print a range containing fewer lines than the default page length, the paper does not advance to the top of the next page; the next print operation begins wherever the preceding operation ended. If you print a range containing more lines than the default page length, 1-2-3 inserts page breaks between pages, but the paper does not advance to the top of the next page after the last page has printed.

If you don't want to accept 1-2-3's automatic paper-movement controls, you can change the controls from the keyboard. You can specify the top of a page in any paper position, advance the paper by line or by page, and insert page breaks exactly where you want them.

Using Line, Page, and Align

If you are using continuous-feed paper, position the paper so that the print head is at the top of the page and then turn on the printer. Do not advance the paper manually. Because 1-2-3 coordinates a line counter with the current page-length setting, any lines you advance manually are not counted, and page breaks may crop up in strange places.

If you want to advance the paper one line at a time (to separate several small printed ranges that fit on one page, for example), invoke the **/Print Printer Line** command. This command makes the printer skip a line.

If you want to advance to a new page after printing less than a full page, select the **/Print Printer Page** command. When you issue this command, the printer skips to a new page. (The following section shows how you can embed a page-break symbol in the print range to instruct 1-2-3 to advance to the top of the next page.)

In many cases, a faster way to advance the paper is to take the printer off-line, adjust the paper manually, put the printer on-line, and then issue the **/Print Printer Align** command. In fact, whether you adjust the paper off-line in this manner or on-line with the paper-control commands, you should invoke **Align**. Note that **Align** also resets the page counter, which you may not want to do if you are numbering pages in a header or footer (see the section on "Creating Headers and Footers" in this chapter).

Reminder:
To print a footer on the last page of the printout, invoke /Print Printer Page.

When you begin a print job at the top of a page, you should make it a practice to select **Align** before selecting **Go**.

To print an existing footer on the last page, use the **Page** command at the end of the printing session. If you select the **Quit** command from the **/Print Printer** menu without issuing the **Page** command, this final footer does not print. You can reissue the **/Print Printer** command and select **Page** to print the footer.

Setting Page Breaks within the Worksheet

Look again at figure 8.4, which shows the entire Regional Income Report worksheet. Suppose that you want to print three months of data (January to March) for the Sales, Cost of Goods Sold, and Operating Expenses sections of the worksheet. To make sure that each section begins printing on a new page, you can insert a page break into the worksheet by using a command or by typing a special symbol.

To enter a page break by using 1-2-3's commands, first move the cell pointer to column A and then to one row above the row at which you want the page break to occur. Then select the **/Worksheet Page** command; this command inserts a new blank row containing a page-break symbol (|::).

For example, to insert a page break just above the first separating line in the Cost of Goods Sold section, place the cell pointer on A12 and then execute the command. Figure 8.13 shows the inserted row with the double-colon page-break symbol. To remove the inserted row and the page-break symbol after you finish printing, use the **/Worksheet Delete Row** command.

A12: [W3] |::   READY

	A B C	D	E	F	G	H
1	REGIONAL INCOME REPORT	Jan	Feb	Mar	1st Q	Apr
2	11–Mar–91					
3						
4	Sales					
5	Northeast	$31,336	$34,370	$37,404	$103,110	$40,438
6	Southeast	30,572	33,606	36,640	100,818	39,674
7	Central	131,685	134,719	137,753	404,157	140,787
8	Northwest	94,473	97,507	100,541	292,521	103,575
9	Southwest	126,739	129,773	132,807	389,319	135,841
10						
11	Total Sales	414,805	429,975	445,145	1,289,925	460,315
12	|::					
13	Cost of Goods Sold					
14	Northeast	10,341	11,274	12,207	33,822	13,140
15	Southeast	6,546	7,479	8,412	22,437	9,345
16	Central	65,843	66,776	67,709	200,328	68,642
17	Northwest	63,967	64,900	65,833	194,700	66,766
18	Southwest	72,314	73,247	74,180	219,741	75,113
19						
20	Total Cost of Goods Sold	219,011	223,676	228,341	671,028	233,006

29-Apr-91 08:10 AM

Fig. 8.13. Inserting a page-break symbol in the worksheet.

As an alternative, insert a blank row into the worksheet where you want a page break and then type a page-break symbol (|::) into a blank cell in the leftmost column of the print range in that row. The contents of cells in any row marked by the page-break symbol do not print.

Be careful when you alter a worksheet. You may cause a macro to fail or cause an error by inserting rows, or you accidentally may delete the wrong row after you finish printing. You may be able to avoid these problems by typing the page-break symbol into the leftmost column in the print range of a blank row in the worksheet. Check first to ensure that the row is blank and then use the End and arrow keys to scan across the row.

Caution: *Inserting a blank row for a page-break symbol may affect macros or cause problems.*

Changing the Print Options

You can use the /**W**orksheet **G**lobal **D**efault **P**rinter command to change the default print settings. The new default settings remain in effect for all print operations performed in the current work session. If you want the new settings to remain in effect when you load 1-2-3, select /**W**orksheet **G**lobal **D**efault **U**pdate.

You can change print settings also by using the selections on the /Print Printer Options menu shown in figure 8.14. As shown in the figure, Release 2.3 displays the current print settings in the Print Settings dialog box. The Margins, Setup, and Pg-Length options override the /Worksheet Global Default Printer settings for margins, setup strings, and page length. The Header, Footer, and Borders options are unique to this menu; they are provided to help you improve the readability of your reports.

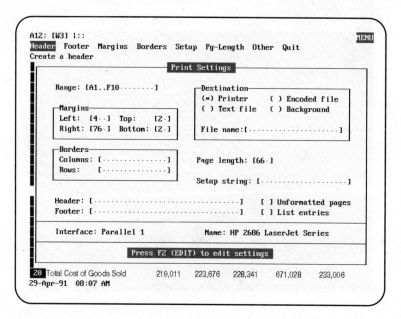

Fig. 8.14. *The /Print Printer Options menu and Print Settings dialog box.*

The print settings you use for your worksheet are saved with the file when you execute /File Save. When you retrieve the file, the settings are still in effect for that file.

Creating Headers and Footers

1-2-3 reserves three lines in a document for a header and an additional three lines for a footer. You can either retain the six lines (regardless of whether you use them) or eliminate all six lines by selecting Other Unformatted from the /Print Printer Options menu.

Technically, the Header and Footer options of the /Print Printer Options menu enable you to specify up to 240 characters of text within one line in each of three positions: left, right, and center. From a practical standpoint, however, the overall header or footer line cannot exceed the number of characters printed per inch, multiplied by the width of the paper in inches, minus the right and left margins.

The header text, which is printed on the first line after any blank top margin lines, is followed by two blank header lines (for spacing). The footer text line is printed above the specified bottom-margin blank lines and below two blank footer lines (for spacing).

Although you can enter text from the keyboard, 1-2-3 provides special characters for controlling page numbers, entering the current date, and positioning text within a header or footer. These special characters include the following:

Cue:
You can use special characters in the header and footer to enter page numbers, enter the date, and position the text.

Character	*Function*
#	Automatically prints page numbers, starting with 1
@	Automatically includes (in the form 29-Jun-91) the date you entered when you started your computer
|	Automatically separates text: absence of a | mark left-justifies all text; the first | mark centers text that follows; the second | mark right-justifies remaining text

To illustrate, reprint the range A1..F11 after adding a header that includes all the preceding special characters. To add the header, select /**Print Printer Range**, specify the range A1..F11, and then select **Options Header**. At the prompt `Enter Header:`, type the following:

@|YOUR FIRM NAME|#

Next, select **Quit** from the /**Print Printer Options** menu; signal the top of the page to the printer, if necessary, by selecting **Align**; and then select **Go**. The header line shown in figure 8.15 improves the report's appearance.

```
   11-Mar-91                  YOUR FIRM NAME                    5


   REGIONAL INCOME REPORT       Jan      Feb      Mar     1st Q

   Sales
       Northeast            $31,336  $34,370  $37,404  $103,110
       Southeast             30,572   33,606   36,640   100,818
       Central              131,685  134,719  137,753   404,157
       Northwest             94,473   97,507  100,541   292,521
       Southwest            126,739  129,773  132,807   389,319

   Total Sales              414,805  429,975  445,145 1,289,925
```

Fig. 8.15. *The result of specifying a header.*

When the print range exceeds a single-page output, the header is printed on each succeeding page, and the page number increases by one. If you have used the special page-number character (#) and want to print the report a second time before you leave the /Print Printer menu, you can reset the page counter and set the top of the form by selecting Align before you select Go.

If you have specified a header line, but the centered or right-justified (or both) text doesn't print, make sure that the right-margin setting is appropriate for the current pitch and paper width. To change the header, select /Print Printer Options Header. When the prompt and your header appear, edit the header by using the Backspace and right- and left-arrow keys. To enter a new header, press Esc when the original header is displayed and type the new one. To delete the header completely, press Esc and then press Enter. (You can delete a header or footer without removing other specified options.)

Reminder:
You can include the contents of a cell in a header or footer.

In Release 2.3, you can include the contents of a worksheet cell in a header or footer. Instead of typing the header or footer text, type \ followed by the address of the cell that contains the label. For example, if a title is in cell A1, you can enter \A1 as the header.

Using Setup Strings

Cue:
For special printing effects within a print range, embed setup strings in the worksheet.

Setup strings are optional printer codes you can use to change the size or style of type when you are printing from the /Print menu. If you need to change the size or style of type very often in a report, you can use the :Format command from the Wysiwyg menu. This method provides a much easier way than using the setup string option. Chapter 9 covers the Wysiwyg commands that enable you to change the size or style of type. If you need to change type size or style, use the Wysiwyg options rather than /Print Printer Options Setup.

To pass setup strings temporarily to the printer, use one of two methods. Either select /Print Printer Options Setup and specify the appropriate ASCII code, or embed the code in the worksheet. (Remember that you can establish a permanent or default setup string that is used when 1-2-3 is loaded. To do so, use the /Worksheet Global Default Printer Update command.)

To illustrate setup strings, you can print portions of the working-capital accounts information in the Regional Income Report worksheet. The examples assume that you are using an HP LaserJet printer.

To use the first method, send a setup string (the decimal code for ASCII must not exceed 39 characters) by executing a 1-2-3 command. Assume that the print range is C1..J11 and that columns A1..B1 are established as a border at the left side of every printed page.

Access the /Print **P**rinter **O**ptions menu, select **S**etup, type \027(s16.66H to indicate the line printer font, the smallest type size on an HP LaserJet printer, and then press Enter. At this point, if you were to quit the **O**ptions menu and issue a **G**o command, the first printed page would contain only January-through-1st Q amounts in small print.

Because you want the January-through-2nd Q amounts to fit on the page, you must establish margins that coincide with print pitch. Select **M**argins **R**ight from the /Print **P**rinter **O**ptions menu. Then enter **136** (8 1/2 inches multiplied by 16 characters per inch). Figure 8.16 shows page 1 of the resulting printout.

REGIONAL INCOME REPORT	Jan	Feb	Mar	1st Q	Apr	May	Jun	2nd Q
Sales								
Northeast	$31,336	$34,370	$37,404	$103,110	$40,438	$43,472	$46,506	$130,416
Southeast	30,572	33,606	36,640	100,818	39,674	42,708	45,742	128,124
Central	131,685	134,719	137,753	404,157	140,787	143,821	146,855	431,463
Northwest	94,473	97,507	100,541	292,521	103,575	106,609	109,643	319,827
Southwest	126,739	129,773	132,807	389,319	135,841	138,875	141,909	416,625
Total Sales	414,805	429,975	445,145	1,289,925	460,315	475,485	490,655	1,426,455

Fig. 8.16. The result of specifying a setup string for the line printer font from the /Print menu.

To remove the temporary setup string, select **S**etup from the /Print **P**rinter **O**ptions menu, press Esc, and then press Enter. Exit the /Print **P**rinter **O**ptions menu by selecting **Q**uit or by pressing Esc. You use this method when you want all output from the current print operation to reflect the default font setting. In the preceding illustration, for example, the contents in the entire print range, as well as the column borders, are printed in the line printer font.

Reminder:
You can type setup strings within the worksheet.

If you want only a portion within a print range to reflect a special printing characteristic, you can embed a setup string in the worksheet instead of invoking several separate print commands. In blank rows preceding and following the area that requires special treatment, type a double vertical bar (||\?) and the appropriate ASCII code (or codes) separated by backslashes. (Insert a blank row, if necessary, making sure that it does not disturb any formulas in the worksheet.) The first vertical bar does not appear in the worksheet, and neither the bars nor the print codes print. If you must embed a code in a row that contains data, that data does not print.

If you want to print the Total Sales in bold and everything else in normal type, you first select /Print **P**rinter **C**lear **A**ll to restore all print settings to default values. Insert a blank row at row 10 and then enter ||\027(s3B in the first cell of the blank row (A11) directly above the Total Sales row to turn on bold on an HP LaserJet printer. Enter ||\027(s0B in the first cell of the row following Total Sales (A13) to turn off bold print. If you specify A1..F12 as the print range, the printed output is similar to that shown in figure 8.17.

```
┌─────────────────────────────────────────────────────────────┐
│ REGIONAL INCOME REPORT      Jan       Feb       Mar           │
│          11-Mar-91                                            │
│                                                               │
│ Sales                                                         │
│     Northeast           $31,336   $34,370   $37,404           │
│     Southeast            30,572    33,606    36,640           │
│     Central             131,685   134,719   137,753           │
│     Northwest            94,473    97,507   100,541           │
│     Southwest           126,739   129,773   132,807           │
│                                                               │
│ Total Sales             414,805   429,975   445,145           │
└─────────────────────────────────────────────────────────────┘
```

Fig. 8.17. The result of embedding a setup string for bold print in the worksheet.

Reminder:
Do not include spaces in setup strings.

You can combine more than one print characteristic in a setup string if the combined setup code does not exceed the 39-character limit and the printer supports the combination. Check the printer manual for information about the compatibility of codes. A setup string contains the print-enhancement codes found in the printer manual. If the manual says, for example, to use ESC E to turn on emphasized mode, look up the decimal equivalent for ESC (27) and follow the digits with uppercase E (\027E). Do not include spaces in a setup string.

Changing the Page Layout

To change the page layout temporarily, use the /Print Printer Options menu. If you want to change the margins, select the Margins option and then select Left, Right, Top, Bottom, or None from the menu.

Before making any changes, review the "Understanding the Print Default Settings" section at the beginning of this chapter. Keep in mind general layout considerations such as the number of lines per page, the number of characters per inch, and so on.

Be sure that you set left and right margins consistent with the width of the paper and the established pitch (characters per inch). The right margin must be greater than the left margin. Also make sure that settings for the top and bottom margins are consistent with the paper's length and the established number of lines per inch.

The specified page length must not be less than the top margin plus the header lines plus one line of data plus the footer lines plus the bottom margin, unless you use the /Print Printer Options Other Unformatted command to suppress all formatting. To maximize the output on every printed page of a large worksheet, you can combine the Unformatted option with setup strings that condense print and increase the number of lines per inch.

Cue:
*Use the **None** margin option to eliminate margins when you print to a disk file.*

Printing a Listing of Cell Contents

You can spend hours developing and debugging a model worksheet and much additional time entering and verifying data. You should safeguard your work not only by making backup copies of your important files but also by printing the cell contents of important worksheets. Be aware, however, that this print job can take a while if you have a large worksheet.

You produce printed documentation of cell contents by selecting Other from the /Print Printer Options menu and then selecting either Cell-Formulas or As-Displayed. Choosing Cell-Formulas produces a listing that shows (with one cell per line) the width of the cell (if different from the default), the cell format, cell-protection status, and the contents of cells in the print range. (The report does not show all of the cells in the range. Blank cells are not printed.) Selecting As-Displayed restores the default instructions to print the range as it appears on-screen.

Cue:
*Choose **Cell-Formulas** to print a listing of formulas in cells.*

You can produce a cell-by-cell listing of only the first six columns and the first 11 rows of the Regional Income Report worksheet, for example, by selecting /Print Printer Range, specifying the range A1..F11, and then selecting Options Other Cell-Formulas. Return to the main /Print Printer menu by choosing Quit. Then select Align and Go. Figure 8.18 shows the resulting one-cell-per-line listing.

Notice that within the specified print range, the contents of each cell in the first row are listed before the next row is presented. Information enclosed in parentheses indicates a range format established independently of the global format in effect. For example, the (,0) in cell F11 indicates that the cell is formatted (with a /Range Format command) in comma format (,) with zero decimal places.

Information enclosed in brackets indicates a column width set independently of the global column width in effect. For example, the [W10] in cell B5 indicates that column B is set specifically to be 10 characters wide. Cell content is printed after the column-width and format information.

```
A1:  [W3] 'REGIONAL INCOME REPORT
D1:  ^Jan
E1:  ^Feb
F1:  ^Mar
B2:  (H) [W10] @DATE(91,3,11)
C2:  (D1) [W10] @DATE(91,3,11)
A4:  [W3] 'Sales
B5:  [W10] 'Northeast
D5:  (C0) 31336
E5:  (C0) 34370
F5:  (C0) 37404
B6:  [W10] 'Southeast
D6:  (,0) 30572
E6:  (,0) 33606
F6:  (,0) 36640
B7:  [W10] 'Central
D7:  (,0) 131685
E7:  (,0) 134719
F7:  (,0) 137753
B8:  [W10] 'Northwest
D8:  (,0) 94473
E8:  (,0) 97507
F8:  (,0) 100541
B9:  [W10] 'Southwest
D9:  (,0) 126739
E9:  (,0) 129773
F9:  (,0) 132807
A11: [W3] 'Total Sales
D11: (,0) @SUM(D9..D5)
E11: (,0) @SUM(E9..E5)
F11: (,0) @SUM(F9..F5)
```

Fig. 8.18. A listing produced by using the Cell-Formulas option.

If you need more extensive documentation and analysis, you should use the Auditor add-in discussed in Appendix B.

Clearing the Print Options

Selecting /Print Printer Clear enables you to eliminate all or a portion of the print options you chose earlier. The Clear options include the following:

All   Range   Borders   Format

You can clear every print option, including the print range, by selecting **All**, or you can be more specific by using the following other choices:

Cue:
Reset every print option with /Print Printer Clear All.

Selection	Description
Range	Removes the previous print-range specification
Borders	Cancels columns and rows specified as borders
Format	Eliminates margins, page-length, and setup string settings

Remember that you can automate many routine print operations by setting up the print macros discussed in Chapter 13. **/Print Printer Clear All** is usually the first instruction in this type of macro.

Preparing Output for Other Programs

Many word processing and other software packages accept ASCII text files. You can maximize your chances of successfully exporting 1-2-3 files to other programs if you use some **/Print** commands to eliminate unwanted specifications for page layout and page breaks.

To create a print (PRN) file, select **/Print File**, specify a file name, and then specify the range to print. Next, choose **Options Margins Left** and set the left margin to 0. After setting the left margin to 0, set the right margin to 240. Finally, choose **Options Other Unformatted.** Selecting **Unformatted** removes all headers, footers, and page breaks from a print operation.

Cue:
*In most cases, choose **U**nformatted when printing to a file.*

To create the PRN file on disk, quit the **Options** menu, select **Go**, and then choose **Quit** from the **/Print File** menu. Follow the instructions in the word processing or other software package to import the specially prepared 1-2-3 disk files. Many software packages can import 1-2-3 data directly from a worksheet file instead of requiring you to print to a file first.

To restore the default printing of headers, footers, and page breaks, invoke the **/Print Printer Options Other Formatted** command.

Printing in the Background

Release 2.3 enables you to print reports and continue working in 1-2-3 while waiting for your report to finish printing. With Releases 2.01 and 2.2, you had to wait, sometimes many minutes, for a report to print before you could return to the program and continue working in the worksheet.

When you enter a special command at the operating system prompt, background printing creates or uses an existing encoded file and prints that file through a utility print program stored in your computer's memory. Background printing enables you to begin printing directly from the operating system prompt or to begin printing from the /Print command in 1-2-3.

To begin printing from the operating system prompt, enter the following:

> [*path*]BPRINT[*argument1...argument2...argument3*]

[*path*] specifies the drive in which the BPrint program (BPRINT.EXE) is stored.

BPRINT is the command for the background printing program.

Arguments: You can use the following arguments to specify items such as the printer port and names of all files you want to print. You also can use arguments to pause, continue, or stop printing. BPrint arguments do not need to follow a particular order.

filename	Specifies the files or files you want to print. These files include encoded files (ENC) or text files.
–p=*number*	Specifies the parallel printer port, followed by the equal sign (=) and then a 1 indicating port 1 (the default) or a 2 indicating port 2
	After you specify a particular port, you cannot change that port without first clearing the BPrint program from memory and starting BPrint with the different port.
–s=*number*	Specifies the serial printer port, followed by the equal sign (=) and number 1 or 2
–pa	Instructs the BPrint program to pause printing
–r	Restarts printing after printing is paused with the –pa argument
–c *filename*	Cancels printing of the file you enter after –c. This argument does not cancel printing currently in process.
–t	Stops all printing currently in process and waiting in queue to print

For example, to print the encoded file Q1BUDGET.ENC in the directory \123R23\BUDGET from serial port 2, you enter the following command and arguments:

BPRINT −s=2 C:\123R23\BUDGET\Q1BUDGET.ENC

To start background printing by using /**P**rint **B**ackground, follow these steps:

1. Load the background printing program into your computer's memory by entering the following at the operating system prompt:

    [*path*]BPRINT [−s=*number*] or [−p=*number*]

    If you are printing from a port other than the default Parallel 1 port, you must specify the port.

2. Start the 1-2-3 program.

3. When you are ready to print, select /**P**rint **B**ackground.

4. Specify a name for the encoded file that 1-2-3 creates for the background printing operation. You also can use an existing encoded file. If you use an existing file, however, remember that new settings overwrite the existing file.

5. Specify the print range and any other print settings you want to include (for example, margin settings, borders, headers, and so on).

6. Select **A**lign and then **G**o.

7. Select **Q**uit to exit the menu and start printing in the background.

To pause, continue, or stop the print job in process, choose /**S**ystem from the main 1-2-3 menu and enter BPrint with the appropriate argument. Remember to save the worksheet file you are working on before using the /**S**ystem command. You can return to 1-2-3 and your worksheet by typing **exit** at the system prompt.

Because the BPrint program is a terminate-and-stay resident program (TSR), keep the following tips and cautions in mind when using Bprint:

• If you are running other TSR programs, begin BPrint after having begun the others to avoid BPrint conflicting with others. If you are working in 1-2-3 and want to use BPrint by leaving 1-2-3 temporarily and returning to the system prompt, save your 1-2-3 worksheet file before leaving 1-2-3.

• BPrint does not work if you have loaded the DOS program PRINT.COM.

- If you are working on a network, you must start the networking program before starting BPrint. Finally, using BPrint with Windows requires that you use the PIF file that starts 1-2-3 to run BPrint. See your Windows documentation for information about creating a PIF file.

Because 1-2-3 Release 2.3's background printing program requires extra memory in addition to the main 1-2-3 program, you may need to activate BPrint only when you are ready to print rather than keeping BPrint in memory the entire time you are working on a worksheet.

Summary

This chapter showed you how to create printed reports from your 1-2-3 worksheets. You learned how to print by using the default settings and how to change the defaults. To customize your reports and make them more readable, you can break the worksheet into pages; change the margins and page length; and provide headers, footers, and borders on the printout. You also discovered how to take full advantage of your printer's capabilities by sending setup strings to the printer.

Successfully printing large worksheets with a variety of options generally takes practice and some study of the printer manual. Use this chapter as a reference as you continue to experiment. The next chapter shows you how to use Wysiwyg to create, enhance, and print more professional-looking reports.

Using Wysiwyg
To Enhance and
Print Reports

The Wysiwyg add-in feature offers Release 2.3 users a graphical interface. In Wysiwyg (a name based on the acronym *WYSIWYG*, or what-you-see-is-what-you-get), the screen reflects all formatting, and the worksheet prints almost exactly as you see on-screen, if you use a monitor that can display the graphical elements provided by Wysiwyg. With Wysiwyg, you also can use a mouse to move the cell pointer, to size rows and columns, to access the 1-2-3 main menu, and to select ranges.

A major benefit of 1-2-3 Release 2.3 is the capability to access the 1-2-3 main menu without having to turn off the Wysiwyg screen (as you must do in Allways of 1-2-3 Release 2.2).

Although not a full-featured desktop publishing program, Wysiwyg may be all you need for many desktop publishing tasks that involve 1-2-3 reports and graphs. Using this add-in, you can produce printed 1-2-3 reports that incorporate a variety of type fonts, lines, shadings, and other formatting features. Compare a report printed from the 1-2-3 /Print command (see fig. 9.1) with the same report formatted and printed with Wysiwyg (see fig. 9.2). The difference in presentation quality is dramatic.

```
LaserPro Corporation
Balance Sheet
July 1, 1991


ASSETS

                                This Year    Last Year    Change

Current Assets
Cash                               247,886      126,473       96%
Accounts Receivable                863,652      524,570       65%
Inventory                           79,071       53,790       47%
Prepaid Expenses                     9,257       11,718      -21%
Investments                        108,577       31,934      240%
Total Current Assets            $1,308,443     $748,485       75%

Fixed Assets
Machinery and Equipment            209,906      158,730       32%
Vehicles                           429,505      243,793       76%
Office Furniture                    50,240       36,406       38%
(Accumulated Depreciation)        (101,098)     (64,394)      57%
Total Fixed Assets                 588,553      374,535       57%
                                $1,177,106     $749,070       57%

LIABILITIES AND SHAREHOLDERS' EQUITY

                                This Year    Last Year    Change

Current Liabilities
Accounts Payable Trade             426,041      332,845       28%
Notes Payable                       45,327       23,486       93%
Accrued Liabilities                 34,614       26,026       33%
Income Taxes Payable                88,645       51,840       71%
Total Current Liabilities          594,627      434,197       37%

Noncurrent Liabilities
Long-term Debt                     488,822      349,253       40%
Deferred Federal Tax               147,844       92,101       61%
Total Noncurrent Liabilities       636,666      441,354       44%
Shareholders' Equity
Common Stock                         1,000        1,000        0%
Opening Retained earnings          246,469       82,531      199%
Profit (Loss) for the Period       418,234      163,938      155%
Total Shareholders' Equity         665,703      247,469      169%
                                $1,896,996   $1,123,020       69%
```

Fig. 9.1. A report printed with the 1-2-3 /Print command.

LaserPro Corporation
Balance Sheet
July 1, 1991

ASSETS

	This Year	Last Year	Change
Current Assets			
Cash	247,886	126,473	96%
Accounts Receivable	863,652	524,570	65%
Inventory	79,071	53,790	47%
Prepaid Expenses	9,257	11,718	−21%
Investments	108,577	31,934	240%
Total Current Assets	$1,308,443	$748,485	75%
Fixed Assets			
Machinery and Equipment	209,906	158,730	32%
Vehicles	429,505	243,793	76%
Office Furniture	50,240	36,406	38%
(Accumulated Depreciation)	(101,098)	(64,394)	57%
Total Fixed Assets	588,553	374,535	57%
	$1,177,106	$749,070	57%

LIABILITIES AND SHAREHOLDERS' EQUITY

	This Year	Last Year	Change
Current Liabilities			
Accounts Payable Trade	426,041	332,845	28%
Notes Payable	45,327	23,486	93%
Accrued Liabilities	34,614	26,026	33%
Income Taxes Payable	88,645	51,840	71%
Total Current Liabilities	594,627	434,197	37%
Noncurrent Liabilities			
Long−term Debt	488,822	349,253	40%
Deferred Federal Tax	147,844	92,101	61%
Total Noncurrent Liabilities	636,666	441,354	44%
Shareholders' Equity			
Common Stock	1,000	1,000	0%
Opening Retained earnings	246,469	82,531	199%
Profit (Loss) for the Period	418,234	163,938	155%
Total Shareholders' Equity	665,703	247,469	169%
	$1,896,996	$1,123,020	69%

Fig. 9.2. The report formatted and printed with Wysiwyg.

In addition to providing enhanced text formatting, Wysiwyg enables you to embed 1-2-3 graphs into your printouts and to use a graphics editor to embellish your graphs. The graphing aspects of Wysiwyg are covered in Chapter 11. This chapter focuses on Wysiwyg's formatting and printing features. You learn the following in this chapter:

- How to load Wysiwyg

- How 1-2-3 and Wysiwyg work together

- How to change the screen's appearance

- How to format worksheets with fonts and other print attributes

- How to manage formats

- How to use Wysiwyg's text commands

- How to print in Wysiwyg, including how to fine-tune the page layout and how to add titles and borders

Loading Wysiwyg

Before you can use Wysiwyg, you must first load the add-in into memory. To load Wysiwyg, press Alt-F10 (or select /Add-In from the 1-2-3 main menu) to display the Add-In menu; then select **Attach**. Select WYSIWYG.ADN from the list that appears on-screen. You then are asked to select a function key for invoking the Wysiwyg menu:

No-Key **7 8 9 10**

If you select **No-Key**, you can display the Wysiwyg menu by pressing the colon (:) key or by using the mouse. If you select one of the remaining four options (**7**, **8**, **9**, **10**), you can display the Wysiwyg menu by pressing the Alt key and the function key of the number selected from the menu or by pressing the colon (:) key or mouse. If you select **10**, for example, you can display the Wysiwyg menu by pressing Alt-F10. Choose **Q**uit to exit the Add-In menu.

Because you may want to use Wysiwyg each time you use 1-2-3, you should change the default settings so that the add-in is loaded automatically after 1-2-3 is loaded. To do so, select /**W**orksheet **G**lobal **D**efault **O**ther **A**dd-In **S**et. When you choose this command, 1-2-3 displays the numbers 1 through 8 in the control panel and the Default Settings dialog box shown in figure 9.3.

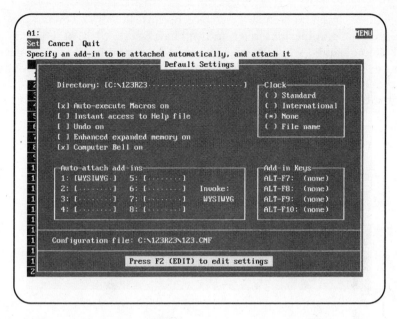

Fig. 9.3. *The Default Settings dialog box.*

Select the first number that does not display an add-in in the brackets within the Auto-attach add-ins section of the Default Settings dialog box. For example, if all the brackets are empty, as in figure 9.3, select 1. After you select none of the eight numbers, select WYSIWYG.ADN from the list of add-ins presented in the control panel. Next, 1-2-3 asks you to select No-Key or a function key so that you can display the Wysiwyg menu with the Alt and function key in addition to displaying the menu with the colon (:) key or mouse. In response to the question Automatically invoke this add-in whenever you start 1-2-3? select **Yes** so that the Wysiwyg add-in is attached and displayed each time you start 1-2-3. Finally, if you want the changed settings permanently saved in 1-2-3's configuration file, select **Update** from the /Worksheet Global Default menu.

Understanding How 1-2-3 and Wysiwyg Work Together

1-2-3 Release 2.3 and Wysiwyg are closely integrated—more closely than Allways is integrated into Release 2.2. You do not need to switch between the graphical and the standard interface, because Release 2.3 enables you to work in the graphical interface and still have access to all of the standard 1-2-3 commands. When Wysiwyg is loaded, your screen looks similar to figure 9.4. Because you are in READY mode, you can move the cell pointer, make cell entries, or bring up the 1-2-3 main menu by pressing the slash key. But with the Wysiwyg add-in attached, you can do much more.

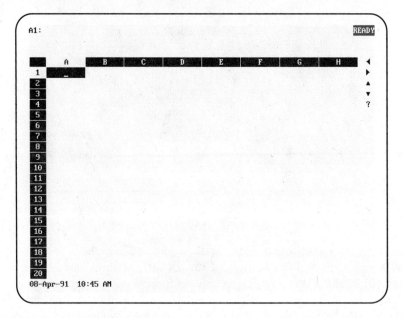

Fig. 9.4. The worksheet screen when Wysiwyg is loaded.

Understanding the Wysiwyg Menu

When you are in Wysiwyg, two menus are available. As always, pressing the slash key displays the standard 1-2-3 menu. To display the Wysiwyg menu, press the colon (:) key. The Esc key backs you out of whatever menu is currently displayed.

Another way to display the menus is with the mouse. A menu automatically appears when you place the mouse pointer in the control panel. The particular menu displayed depends on which menu you previously used.

The Wysiwyg menu offers the following choices:

Worksheet Format Graph Print Display Special Text Named-Style Quit

Although some Wysiwyg option names are similar to the option names on your standard 1-2-3 menu, the submenus' contents and functions are quite different. The following is a summary of each Wysiwyg main menu option.

Selection	Description
Worksheet	Sets column widths, row heights, and page breaks
Format	Adds boldface, lines, shading, fonts, and so on
Graph	Inserts a graph into a worksheet range; enhances the graph
Print	Prints the formatted worksheet or graph; specifies page layout
Display	Alters the screen characteristics (for example, colors)
Special	Copies, moves, imports, and exports formats
Text	Edits, aligns, and reformats a range of text
Named-Style	Assigns names to commonly used format combinations
Quit	Returns to READY mode

Note that both the 1-2-3 and Wysiwyg menus offer a **Print** option. How do you know when you should use /**Print** (1-2-3) or **:Print** (Wysiwyg)? Use **:Print** if you previously used any of Wysiwyg's **:Format** commands to enhance the worksheet or if you inserted a graph into a worksheet range. Use /**Print** if you haven't used Wysiwyg formatting commands on the worksheet or graph that you want to print.

Cue:
Use :Print if you previously used :Format commands to enhance the worksheet.

Wysiwyg menus work the same way as 1-2-3 menus: select a command by typing the first letter of the command, by highlighting the command name and pressing Enter, or by clicking the left mouse button on the menu option. Most of the Wysiwyg commands are explained in detail in this chapter. The **:Graph** commands are covered in Chapter 11.

Saving Your Wysiwyg Formatting

Wysiwyg stores enhanced formatting information in its own file, separate from the worksheet file. The Wysiwyg file has the same first name as your 1-2-3 file but bears the extension FMT. For example, if Wysiwyg is loaded

Reminder:
Wysiwyg stores formatting information in a FMT file.

and you save a worksheet file called BUDGET.WK1, Wysiwyg automatically saves an associated BUDGET.FMT file. This file contains all the formatting enhancements selected with Wysiwyg. When you want to copy a worksheet (WK1) file and its FMT file to another disk or directory, you must copy both. If the FMT file is not on the same disk or directory containing the WK1 file, none of the Wysiwyg settings connected to the worksheet are attached when you retrieve the worksheet file.

Caution:
If Wysiwyg is detached before you save the worksheet, the FMT file is not updated.

Wysiwyg saves enhanced formatting information only when you use the 1-2-3 /File Save command to save the current 1-2-3 worksheet. If you press Alt-F10 (or select /Add-In) and select **D**etach, Wysiwyg is erased immediately from memory, and therefore no enhanced formatting can be saved. If Wysiwyg is detached before you save the worksheet, your FMT file is not updated, and you may lose an extensive amount of formatting work.

Do not modify the structure of a Wysiwyg-formatted worksheet when the add-in is not attached. If you delete, insert, or move anything, the formatting does not match up with the proper cells the next time you attach Wysiwyg.

Understanding the Wysiwyg Screen

The 1-2-3 and Wysiwyg screens are similar in structure. Figure 9.5 points out the different areas of the Wysiwyg screen. You see the worksheet frame (column letters and row numbers), the date-and-time indicator at the bottom left corner of the screen, and the READY mode indicator in the upper right corner. As with the 1-2-3 screen, the top three lines make up the Wysiwyg screen's control panel. The only difference is that Wysiwyg format abbreviations are indicated between the current cell address and the cell contents. For example, {Bold} indicates boldface.

The right side of the Wysiwyg screen displays an *icon panel* for use with the mouse. The mouse icons also are displayed on the standard 1-2-3 screen, and the mouse can be used in the same way it is used with the Wysiwyg screen. Table 9.1 describes the function of each of these symbols. To select an icon, place the mouse pointer on the icon and click the left mouse button. Click and hold down the button to scroll continuously.

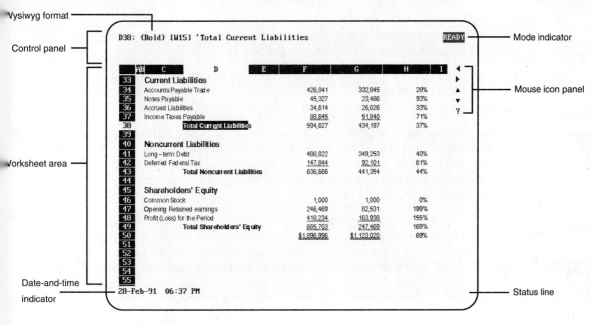

Fig. 9.5. *The Wysiwyg screen.*

Table 9.1
The Mouse Icon Panel

Symbol	Function
◄	Moves the cell pointer one cell to the left
►	Moves the cell pointer one cell to the right
▲	Moves the cell pointer up one cell
▼	Moves the cell pointer down one cell
?	Displays Help

Specifying Cell Ranges in Wysiwyg

Many Wysiwyg commands require you to specify a range. You can specify a range by using any of the following techniques:

- Typing the cell references or range name
- Pressing Name (F3) and choosing the name from a list

- Using the arrow keys to highlight the range

- Using the mouse to highlight the range

To highlight a range with the mouse, click the left mouse button on the upper left corner of the range, hold the button down, drag the mouse to the lower right corner of the range, and release the mouse button.

In Release 2.3, you can specify a single range before you invoke one or more commands. The preselected range applies to all commands until you change the range specification. Prespecifying a range saves time when you want a series of commands (for example, Wysiwyg commands for shading, lines, and bold) to apply to the same range.

Cue:
You can prespecify a range that applies automatically to a series of commands.

To select a range when you are in READY mode, place the cell pointer in the upper left corner of the range, press F4 to anchor, and then move to the lower right corner of the range. If you use a mouse, highlight the range with the click-and-drag technique. After the range is selected, you can invoke the Wysiwyg menu and select as many commands as you like. Wysiwyg automatically uses the highlighted range and does not prompt you for one.

Setting Display Characteristics

Although a major advantage provided by Wysiwyg is the capability to produce professional printed documents, you also can change the screen display to suit your needs. First, you can make the screen look similar to the way text, numbers, and graphics appear when printed. You also can change the screen to create computer slide presentations or change the screen to make creating and changing a worksheet application easier.

With Wysiwyg, you can change many of the characteristics of the screen. Among other things, you can set the screen colors, display the worksheet in graphics mode ("what-you-see-is-what-you-get") or in text mode (like the display in 1-2-3), display grid lines between worksheet columns and rows, change the brightness of the screen, and specify a cell pointer style.

In addition, you can change the size of the characters on the screen. You can reduce the characters so that you can see more of the worksheet at the same time or magnify them to see small fonts more clearly. The **:Display** commands do not affect the report printout; they change how the worksheet looks on-screen. When you select **:Display**, the following menu of options appears:

Mode Zoom Colors Options Font-Directory Rows Default Quit

The following sections describe each of these options.

Mode

With the **:Display Mode** command, you can choose between the **Graphics** and **Text** options and between **B&W** (black and white, or monochrome) and **Color**. In graphics mode, formatting shows on-screen close to how the final printout looks. You must use a graphics monitor to select graphics mode. Only in graphics mode can you change the color of various screen elements (worksheet background, text, cell pointer, frame, grid, and so on). You cannot see formatting on-screen in text mode, although the control panel displays the formatting instructions for the current cell if Wysiwyg is in memory.

If you use a color monitor, you may want to use **B&W** mode to see how the worksheet looks when printed on a black-and-white printer.

Zoom

The **:Display Zoom** command enables you to choose from **Tiny**, **Small**, **Normal**, **Large**, **Huge**, and **Manual**. Selecting **Tiny**, **Small**, **Normal**, **Large**, or **Huge** adjusts the character display; selecting **Manual** enables you to change the size within a range of 25 to 400 percent of the normal size. The magnification percentage appears in the corner of the worksheet frame. Figure 9.6 shows **Tiny** magnification; figure 9.7 shows **Huge**. The zoom feature does not work in text mode.

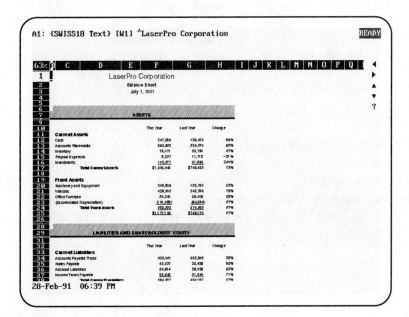

Fig. 9.6. *A worksheet zoomed to the Tiny magnification size.*

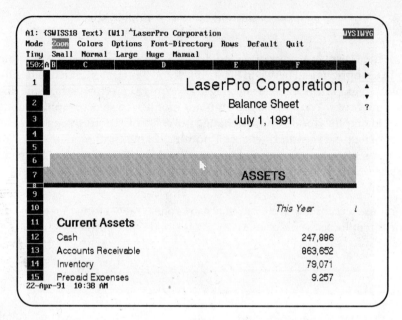

Fig. 9.7. A worksheet zoomed to the Huge magnification size.

Colors

The Colors option of the **:D**isplay command enables you to select the colors for different parts of the screen: background, text (the characters), unprotected cells, cell pointer, grid lines, worksheet frame, negative numbers, lines, and drop shadows. Wysiwyg can use the following eight colors: black, white, red, green, dark blue, cyan, yellow, and magenta. On a monochrome monitor, you can switch the background from white to black if you prefer a dark background on your screen.

Reminder:
The screen colors you select do not affect the printed report.

For the most part, the screen colors you select do not affect the printed report. If you use a color printer, however, the negative values, lines, and drop shadows print in the color you specify.

The **R**eplace option on the **:D**isplay Colors menu enables you to define the palette setting for each color. To change the shade of a color, choose **:D**isplay Colors Replace, select the color, and enter a number between 0 and 63. To make the color-change permanent, use the **:D**isplay Default Update command.

Options

With the **:Display Options** command, you can set options for the following screen aspects: **Frame**, **Grid**, **Page-Breaks**, **Cell-Pointer**, **Intensity**, and **Adapter**. Each of these options is described in the following sections.

Frame

The **Frame** option of the **:Display Options** command controls how the worksheet borders (column letters and row numbers) are displayed. The default frame display is **Enhanced**—rectangles enclose each column letter and row number. **Relief** displays a bright, sculpted worksheet frame. The **1-2-3** frame is similar to the one you see in 1-2-3 without Wysiwyg attached.

The **Special** option displays measurements in the worksheet frame instead of the standard column letters and row numbers. You can display **Characters**, **Inches**, **Metric** (centimeters), or **Points/Picas**. The **Inches** frame is shown in figure 9.8. Because the use of 1-2-3 depends heavily on cell coordinates, you probably do not want to work with a **Special** frame setting all the time. These settings are most useful when you are laying out and balancing elements on your screen—for example, when setting up tables, positioning graphics, centering text, or outlining sections of your worksheet.

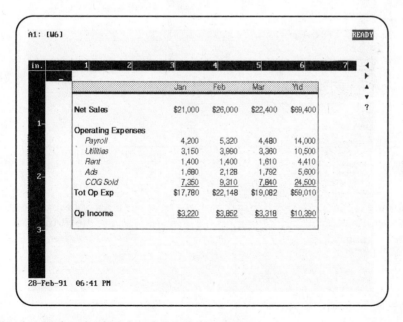

Fig. 9.8. *Inches displayed in the worksheet frame.*

The final **Frame** option, None, turns off the display of the frame. You may want to use this option in macros when you do not need to see column letters and row numbers on the screen—for example, when an information screen is displayed.

Grid

Cue:
When grid lines are displayed, you can easily determine cell coordinates on the screen.

The Grid option on the **:Display Options** menu enables you to display dotted lines between columns and rows, as shown in figure 9.9. With grid lines displayed, your electronic worksheet more closely resembles an accountant's ledger paper. You can use this option to easily determine the cell coordinates of the cells displayed on the screen. Many of the figures in this book were created with the grid lines displayed.

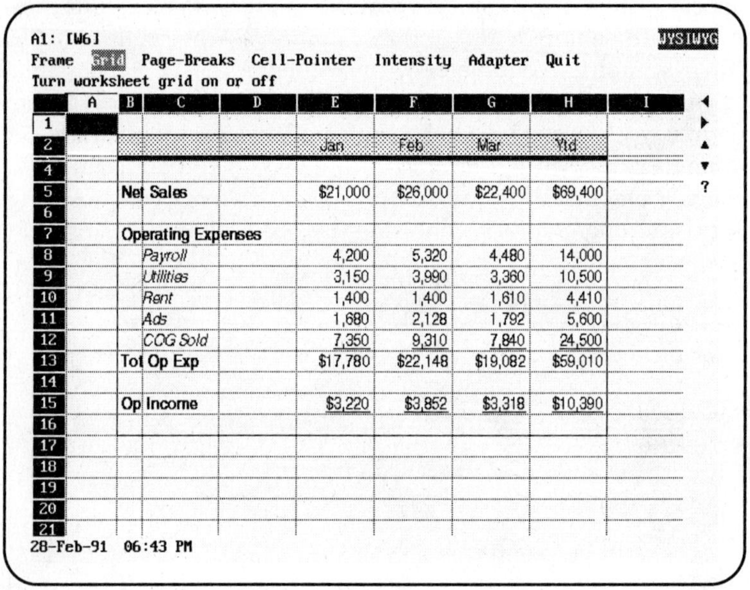

Fig. 9.9. Grid lines.

Turning on the grid with **:Display Options Grid Yes** does not mean that the grid appears on your printed report. To print the grid, use the **:Print Settings Grid** command.

Page-Breaks

With the **Page-Breaks** option of the **:D**isplay **O**ptions command, you control whether the dashed print borders are displayed on the screen. These borders normally display when you define your print range with **:P**rint **Range Set** and when you insert page breaks with **:W**orksheet **P**age. To turn off their display, choose **No** for the **Page-Breaks** option. Regardless of whether the page breaks are displayed, they are used when you print the report.

Cell-Pointer

The Cell-Pointer option controls the style of your cell pointer: **Solid** or **Outline**. The cell pointer can be displayed as a solid rectangular bar (the default) or as an outline around the cell. This option also controls how ranges are highlighted. With the Outline style, the highlighted range is not truly highlighted: actually, the range is enclosed in an outline border. Unless you choose background, grid, and cell-pointer colors that are distinguishably different, the cell pointer is more difficult to see in Outline style, especially when the grid is turned on.

Cue:
Make the cell pointer solid if you turn on the grid or change colors.

Intensity

The **:D**isplay **O**ptions **Intensity** command provides two intensity settings: **Normal** (the default) and **High**. For a brighter screen, change the screen intensity to **High**.

Adapter

The **A**dapter option of the **:D**isplay **O**ptions command enables you to reset your 1-2-3 program for a different monitor without quitting 1-2-3 and changing your monitor setting through 1-2-3's Install program. Specifically, Adapter gives you eleven options:

    Auto **1** **2** **3** **4** **5** **6** **7** **8** **9** **Blink**

Auto is the default monitor setting for which your program is installed. Options **1** through **9** provide all the monitor settings available in the 1-2-3

Install program. The **Blink** option turns on or off the blinking cursor displayed in the cell pointer, in the edit line of the control panel, and in a line of text when you are using the Wysiwyg **:Text** command.

Font-Directory

Use the **:Display** Font-Directory command to indicate the directory in which your screen and print fonts are located. When the Install program creates the Bitstream soft fonts, the files are stored in the WYSIWYG directory, which is a subdirectory of the directory that contains the 1-2-3 program files. If you move these fonts to another directory or want to use fonts located in another directory, enter the path with the Font-Directory option.

Rows

The **:Display** Rows command enables you to specify how many worksheet rows are displayed on the screen. Enter a value between 16 and 60. This option applies only when the screen is in graphics mode (**:Display** Mode Graphics).

Default

Reminder:
To save the
:Display settings
permanently,
choose :Display
Default Update.

The settings you change on the **:Display** menu are temporary. They are valid for the current 1-2-3 session only and are lost when you quit the program. To save the **:Display** settings permanently, choose **:Display** Default Update. Your current settings are then active every time you use 1-2-3 and Wysiwyg. To cancel your current display settings and return them to their default values, choose **:Display** Default Restore.

Formatting with Wysiwyg

The heart of Wysiwyg's power is the capability to add professional formatting touches. The 1-2-3 formats—numeric display and label alignment—carry through automatically to Wysiwyg. Wysiwyg's formats determine printed typeface, character size, boldfacing, and other stylistic features, such as lines, shading, and drop shadows.

Wysiwyg's additional formats provide many ways to enhance the appearance of printed text. To assign a Wysiwyg format to a cell or range, use the Wysiwyg :Format command. To determine the format of a cell, move the cell pointer to the cell. The format displays at the top of the screen, next to the current cell address. If you use Wysiwyg in graphics mode (the default), you actually can see the formatting on the screen. See the previous section "Setting Display Characteristics" in this chapter for information about changing the display mode.

Understanding Fonts

Most of Wysiwyg's formatting effects result from the use of different fonts. In Wysiwyg, a font is a particular typeface—for example, Dutch—in a particular point size. A point, a printer's unit of measure, is 1/72 inch (an inch contains 72 points). The larger the point size, the larger the type. The font selection depends on your printer. Wysiwyg can use any font that your printer is capable of printing.

Wysiwyg comes with four soft fonts from Bitstream: Swiss, Dutch, Courier, and XSymbol. A soft font is a file on disk that specifies to a printer how to make a font. Soft fonts are sent to the printer's memory before the document is printed so that the printer can use the information to print the document. If you print your documents on a dot-matrix printer, Wysiwyg uses your printer's graphics mode to produce these fonts. If you use a laser printer, these four fonts are downloaded to your printer when you use them. Your printer, however, may lack sufficient memory for many different fonts or larger point sizes.

If your printer provides additional fonts, these fonts also are available to Wysiwyg. The Hewlett-Packard LaserJet II and III printers come with two built-in fonts (Courier and Line Printer), for example, and you can buy dozens of cartridges to access additional fonts. Each worksheet can use up to eight different fonts. These eight fonts are stored in a font set. The font list displayed in figure 9.10 is the default font set, composed primarily of Swiss and Dutch fonts. Figure 9.11 shows examples of the default fonts.

Reminder:
For worksheet text, Wysiwyg can use any additional laser printer fonts you have.

Using Fonts

With Wysiwyg, you can format each cell or range of cells with a different font. You can use up to eight fonts for a single worksheet, but by default, all cells are assigned to font 1.

You assign a font to a cell or range by using the Wysiwyg :Format Font command. A description of each font (typeface and point size) appears in a box below the menu (see fig. 9.10). Highlight the desired font number on the menu and press Enter or click on the number. (Alternatively, you can type the number.) Wysiwyg then prompts you for a range, unless you already selected a range. When you supply the range and press Enter, the selected font is applied to the specified range. If necessary, Wysiwyg adjusts the height of the row to conform to the tallest point size used (see fig. 9.11).

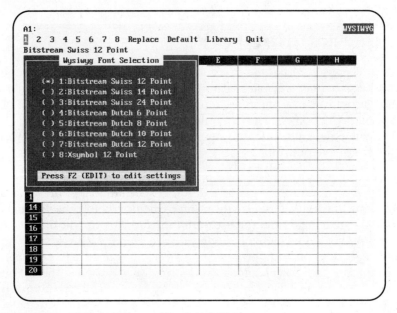

Fig. 9.10. The default font set offered with Wysiwyg.

If you change the font size of a paragraph of text, you may find that the text occupies more or fewer columns than the original text occupied. To respace the text, use the :Text Reformat command. This command is similar to 1-2-3's /Range Justify command, which word-wraps text within the range you define. (See "Reformatting Paragraphs" in a later section in this chapter.)

Replacing Fonts

Reminder:
You cannot have more than eight fonts in the font list.

If a font you want to use is not in the default font set shown in figure 9.10, you can substitute that font for any of the default fonts. Because you are limited to eight fonts per worksheet, you must replace one of the existing fonts in the list; the list cannot hold more than eight fonts.

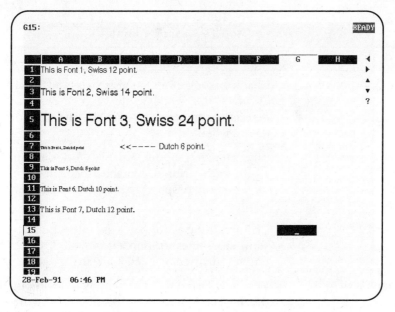

Fig. 9.11. Examples of the default fonts.

To replace one of the fonts in the current set with a font not currently shown, select **:**Format **F**ont **R**eplace. Choose the number associated with the font you want to replace (choose a font you don't need in the current worksheet). The following menu appears:

> **S**wiss **D**utch **C**ourier **X**Symbol **O**ther

The soft fonts included with Wysiwyg represent four of the most common types of fonts: proportional sans serif (Swiss), proportional serif (Dutch), fixed-space (Courier), and special-effects characters (XSymbol). Table 9.2 defines some of these terms.

The XSymbol font contains special characters, such as arrows and circled numbers. Figure 9.12 shows different letters and numbers formatted with the XSymbol font. For example, if you enter a lowercase **a** into a cell and format the cell to **X**Symbol font, a right-pointing arrow is displayed. These special characters are sometimes referred to as *dingbats*.

Reminder:
The XSymbol font contains special characters, such as arrows and circled numbers.

The **O**ther option on the **:**Format **F**ont **R**eplace menu enables you to select from a list of other typefaces. For example, if you use an HP LaserJet II or III, you can select the printer's built-in Line Printer font or a font cartridge. Note that your printer may not have the capability to use all typefaces on the list. If you select a font your printer cannot use, Wysiwyg substitutes a similar typeface.

Table 9.2
Terms Used To Describe Fonts

Term	*Definition*
Proportional	Characterizing a font (such as Swiss and Dutch) in which the actual width of each character determines how much space the character occupies when printed
Fixed-space	Characterizing a font (such as Courier) in which each printed character occupies the same amount of space, regardless of character width
Serif	Characterizing a font (such as Dutch) that has short cross-lines, or decorative "tails," at the ends of many characters' main strokes.
Sans serif	Characterizing a font (such as Swiss) without the short cross-lines or decorative "tails" at the ends of many characters' main strokes

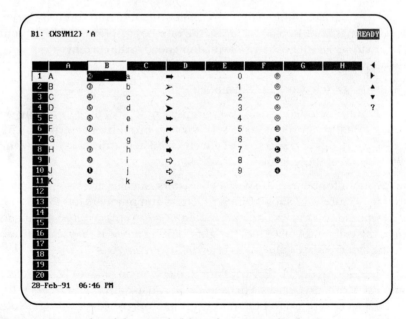

Fig. 9.12. Examples of the XSymbol font characters (dingbats).

After you select the typeface, indicate a type size. Although the screen prompts you to enter a size between 3 and 72 points, not all point sizes are available. For example, the Line Printer font comes in only one size: 8 point. If you select a point size that is not available in a certain typeface, Wysiwyg substitutes a similar typeface in the size you specified (for example, Courier 10 point in place of a nonexistent Line Printer 10 point). If you generated the Basic font set when you installed 1-2-3 Release 2.3, the following high-resolution type sizes are available for each typeface: 4, 6, 8, 10, 12, 14, 18, and 24. The Medium font set contains all the sizes in the Basic set and 9-, 11-, 16-, 20-, and 36-point fonts. The Extended set has all the fonts available with the Medium font set and adds 5-, 7-, 13-, 30-, 48- 60-, and 72- point fonts. To generate a more complete font set, you can run the Install program again.

After you enter the font size, the new font is listed in the font set and can be used immediately or at a later time. To use the newly added font, select the number from the **:**Format Font menu, highlight the range to which you want to apply the font, and press Enter.

When you replace fonts, any worksheet cells formatted with that particular font number automatically change. Suppose that you use **:**Format Font **R**eplace to replace Bitstream Swiss 12 Point with Bitstream Courier 10 Point. All worksheet cells previously formatted as Bitstream Swiss 12 Point are reformatted as Bitstream Courier 10 Point.

As mentioned previously, font 1 is assigned automatically to all cells. Thus, when you replace font 1 with a different font, all cells—except for the ones assigned to other font numbers—automatically change to the new font 1. You do not need to choose **:**Format Font **1** and highlight a range.

Reminder:
Font 1 is assigned automatically to all cells.

Creating Font Libraries

When you use **:**Format Font **R**eplace to customize the font list for the current worksheet, you may want to save the font set for use with another worksheet file. The font set can be named and saved in a font library to be used over again in any other worksheet. Create font libraries for combinations of fonts you are likely to use in other worksheets. Creating a font library saves you from using the **:**Format Font **R**eplace command in each worksheet.

Cue:
Save in a font library those font sets you are likely to use with other worksheets.

To save the current font set in a library, select **:**Format Font **L**ibrary **S**ave. Wysiwyg prompts you to enter a file name. Type a file name of up to eight characters and press Enter. The file is saved with the extension AFS.

When you want to use a font library, select **:**Format Font **L**ibrary **R**etrieve. Wysiwyg displays a list of library files with the AFS extension. Highlight the name of the library you want to use; then press Enter. The eight fonts saved in this library are displayed in the font box, and you can use any of these fonts on the current worksheet.

Cue:
*Make your most
frequently used font
library the default.*

If you know you want to use the fonts stored in another file, but you haven't saved the fonts to a library, you still can use those fonts in the current file. Use the **:Special Import Fonts** command as described in the "Importing Formats" section of this chapter. If you frequently retrieve the same font library, make that library the default font set. To do so, retrieve the font library and select **:Format Font Default Update**.

Reminder:
*Your laser printer
may lack adequate
memory to
download soft fonts
of large point sizes.*

Some laser printers have a restricted amount of memory. In general, the larger the point size of a font, the more memory the font takes in the printer's memory. When you download soft fonts to a laser printer, the printer stores the fonts in its memory for use during the printing process. If you get an out-of-memory message when you print, your printer lacks the needed memory to support the downloaded font set. Try replacing the large fonts with smaller fonts or using an internal or cartridge font.

Changing Formatting Attributes

Font formats are only one type of formatting you can apply to a cell or a range. You also can apply boldface, italic, and underline attributes. In addition, you can change the color of a range of cells; if you use a color printer, you can print in different colors. Figure 9.13 shows examples of these formatting attributes. The headings (for example, `Operating Expenses`) appear in boldface; the other labels (for example, `Payroll`) are italicized; and the last number preceding the total is underlined.

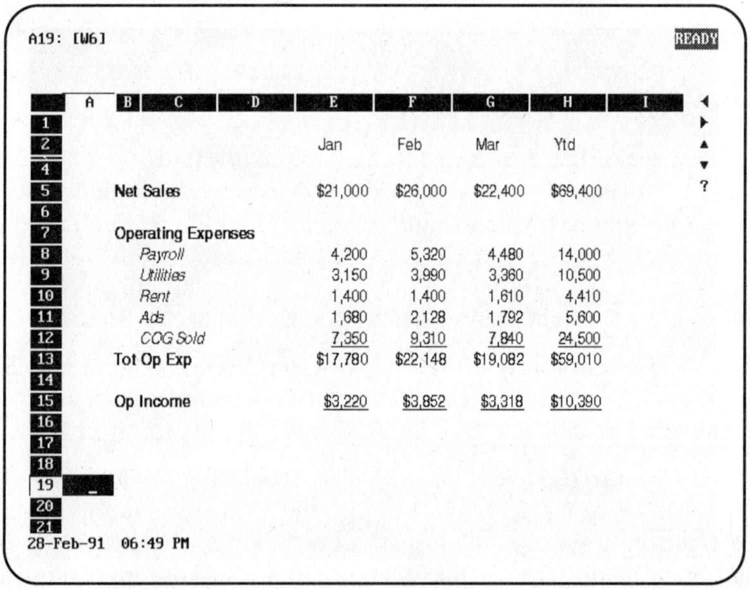

Fig. 9.13. A worksheet formatted with boldface, italic, and single underlines.

You can use bold or italic formatting to enhance column headings, totals, or other ranges you want to emphasize. To boldface a range, select **:Format Bold Set** and indicate the range to which you want to apply the attribute. Use **:Format Italics Set** to italicize a range. Boldfaced text appears heavier on the screen; italicized text slants to the right. The first line of the control panel indicates the attribute with {Bold} or {Italic}.

To apply two or more formatting attributes to a range, preselect the range by using the F4 key or mouse and then selecting each of the appropriate Wysiwyg commands to apply the formatting attribute. Preselecting the range enables you to set the range once rather than each time you add a formatting attribute.

Use the Wysiwyg **:Format Underline** command instead of the 1-2-3 repeating label to create underlines. In 1-2-3, you enter \- to create a single underline and \= to produce a double underline. This method has several disadvantages. First, you must enter these labels into blank cells, consuming valuable worksheet space. Second, the underlines are not solid and do not look professional.

Cue:
Use Wysiwyg to create professional-looking underlines in your worksheet.

Wysiwyg solves these problems by offering true underlining—the same as is available in word processing. You do not use blank rows for the underlines; underlines are solid and appear directly underneath existing cell entries, not in separate cells.

The Underline option on the **:Format** menu offers three types of underlining: Single, Double, and Wide. The Single underline option can be used at the bottom of a column of numbers, above a total. This option underlines only the characters in the cell, not the full width of the cell. If the single underline is not long enough, use the **:Format Lines Bottom** command (see "Drawing Lines and Boxes" later in this chapter for details). You probably will use the Single option only when the last number in the column is the longest number. The Double option is ideal for double-underlining grand totals. To get a thicker line, use the Wide underline option. You can cancel boldfacing and underlining by using the **:Format Bold Clear** and **:Format Underline Clear** commands, or you can clear all Wysiwyg format attributes by using **:Format Reset**

If you use a color printer, such as the HP PaintJet, you may want to enhance your printouts by using different colors. You can print up to seven different colors if your printer has the capability. To change the color of a range, select **:Format Color**. The following menu appears:

Reminder:
You can print up to seven different colors if your printer has the capability.

> Text Background Negative Reverse Quit

The **Text** option defines the color of the characters in the range; whereas **Background** refers to the color behind the characters. You can select from the following colors in the resulting menu:

> **Normal Red Green Dark-Blue Cyan Yellow Magenta**

Use the **Reverse** option of the **:Format Color** command to switch the text and background colors for a range. The **Negative** option enables you to display negative values in red.

Drawing Lines and Boxes

You also can make your worksheet look more professional by adding horizontal or vertical lines and creating boxes. Figure 9.14 shows how lines can enhance a worksheet.

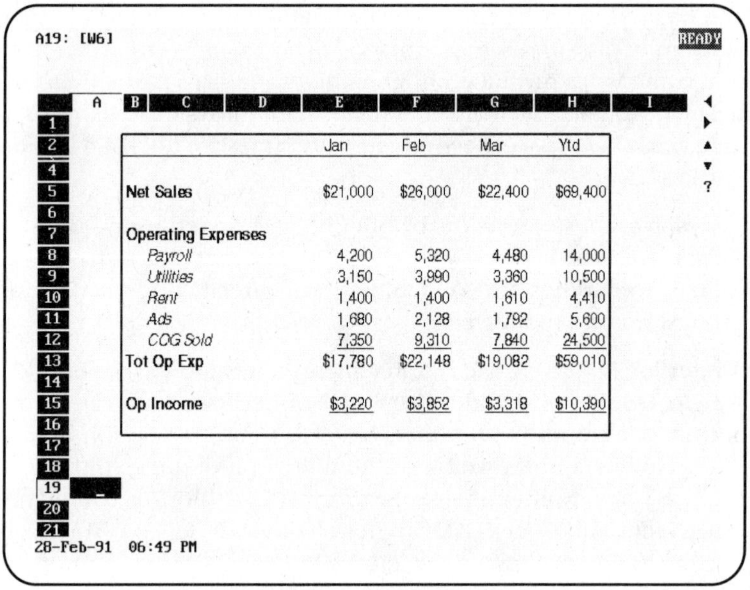

Fig. 9.14. Lines created with the :Format Lines command.

Reminder:
Use :Format Lines to draw a box around a range of cells.

The **:Format Lines** command enables you to place lines around any part of a cell or range, using the options Outline, Left, Right, Top, Bottom, and All. With the **Outline** option, you can draw lines around the entire range, forming a single box. Figure 9.14 shows an outline border surrounding a range of cells. The **Left**, **Right**, **Top**, and **Bottom** options enable you to draw a line along the appropriate side of each selected cell in the range. Using the **All** option, you can draw lines around each cell in the range, to box each cell. Choosing this option is the equivalent of choosing **Left**, **Right**, **Top**, and **Bottom** for each cell in the range.

If you select one of these options on the Lines menu, a single, thin line is drawn in the specified range. However, Wysiwyg offers two other line styles: **Double** and **Wide**. To draw a double line, choose **:Format Lines Double** and then select the line location (**Outline**, **Left**, **Right**, **Top**, **Bottom**, or **All**). The **:Format Lines Wide** command creates a thicker line. If you need even thicker lines, you can use the **:Format Shade Solid** formatting option. (See the next section for details.)

The final option on the **:Format Lines** menu, **Shadow**, enables you to create a special three-dimensional effect called a drop shadow, shown in figure 9.15. You can create a drop shadow in two steps. First, draw a box around the range, using the **:Format Lines Outline** command. Second, use **:Format Lines Shadow** on the same range. Use **:Format Lines Clear** to cancel your line drawing from a range.

Cue:
To create a drop shadow, use :Format Lines Outline and :Format Lines Shadow.

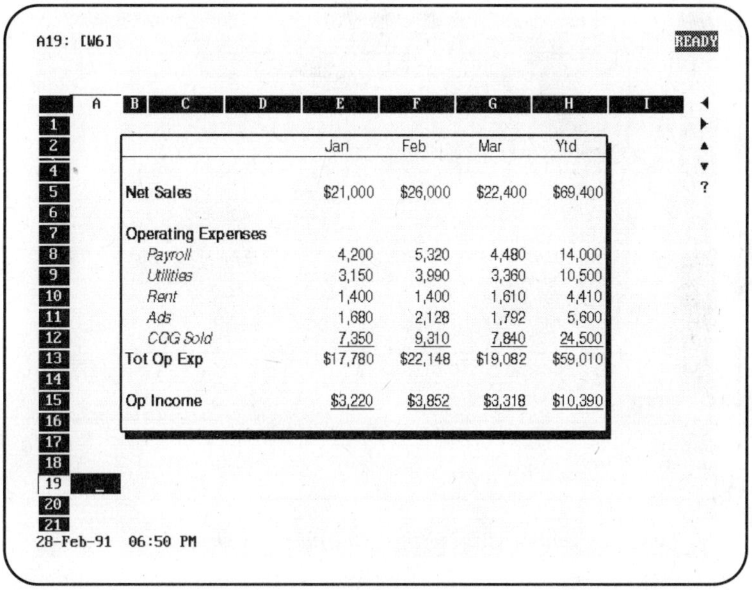

Fig. 9.15. *A box with a drop shadow.*

Adding Shades

The **:Format Shade** command enables you to highlight important areas on the printed worksheet. The column headings in figure 9.16 stand out because of the background shading. Shades can be Light (as in fig. 9.16), Dark, or Solid (black). The Dark shade appears darker on-screen than on paper—you should encounter no problem reading text in a dark-shaded area on a printed report. Using the Solid shade on blank cells, you can create thick horizontal and vertical lines. The thick line under the column headings in figure 9.16, for example, is the result of using the Solid shade on a narrow row. The row is reduced in height by using the :Worksheet Row command. (The next section explains how to adjust row heights.) You cannot see the cell contents if you assign Solid to cells that contain data. To create a border around a shaded area, use :Format Lines Outline. To remove shading, select :Format Shade Clear.

A19: [W6]   READY

	A	B	C	D	E	F	G	H	I
1									
2					Jan	Feb	Mar	Ytd	
4									
5		Net Sales			$21,000	$26,000	$22,400	$69,400	
6									
7		Operating Expenses							
8		Payroll			4,200	5,320	4,480	14,000	
9		Utilities			3,150	3,990	3,360	10,500	
10		Rent			1,400	1,400	1,610	4,410	
11		Ads			1,680	2,128	1,792	5,600	
12		COG Sold			7,350	9,310	7,840	24,500	
13		Tot Op Exp			$17,780	$22,148	$19,082	$59,010	
14									
15		Op Income			$3,220	$3,852	$3,318	$10,390	
16									
17									
18									
19									
20									
21									

28-Feb-91   06:50 PM

Fig. 9.16. Headings emphasized with light and solid shades.

Using Formatting Sequences

Reminder:
Formatting
sequences enable
you to apply formats
to single words in a
cell

The options on the :Format menu enable you to format cells and ranges. To format individual characters within a cell, you can use formatting sequences. With formatting sequences, you can bold or italicize a single word in a cell, for example. Formatting sequences are codes you enter as you are typing or editing text in the control panel. The codes appear in the control panel, but when you press Enter, they are replaced with the actual formatting.

The code to insert when you begin entering a formatting sequence is Ctrl-A (for attribute). A solid triangle symbol appears. You then type the one-character or two-character code for the attribute. Table 9.3 lists these codes. Be sure that you type the exact upper- or lowercase characters listed in the table. To end the formatting sequence, press Ctrl-N (an upside down solid triangle appears).

Table 9.3
Character Codes for Attributes

Code	Description	Code	Description	Code	Description
b	Bold	1c	Default color	1F	Font 1
i	Italic	2c	Red	2F	Font 2
u	Superscript	3c	Green	3F	Font 3
d	Subscript	4c	Dark blue	4F	Font 4
o	Outline	5c	Cyan	5F	Font 5
f	Flashing	6c	Yellow	6F	Font 6
x	Flip x-axis	7c	Magenta	7F	Font 7
y	Flip y-axis	8c	Reverse colors	8F	Font 8
1_	Single underline				
2_	Double underline				
3_	Wide underline				
4_	Box around characters				
5_	Strike-through characters				

To specify multiple attributes, press Ctrl-A and the first attribute code, followed by Ctrl-A and the second code, and so on. For example, to boldface and italicize a word, press Ctrl-A and type **b** and then press Ctrl-A and type **i**. At the end of the word, press Ctrl-N to cancel all formatting sequences. To cancel just one of the attributes, press Ctrl-E followed by the attribute code you want to discontinue (for example, **i** for italic).

Adjusting Column Widths and Row Heights

When you start changing fonts, you may discover a need to adjust column widths. If you use a larger font size, the labels may truncate, and the values may display asterisks. The menus in both 1-2-3 and Wysiwyg offer options for adjusting column widths; you can use either menu.

The :Worksheet Column Set-Width command is the exact equivalent of the /Worksheet Column Column-Range Set-Width command. Before you indicate the column width, you are prompted to select the range of columns whose width you want to change. As in 1-2-3, you can adjust the column width in Wysiwyg by using the left- and right- arrow keys to change the width one character at a time.

Wysiwyg does not offer a way to change column widths globally; to do that you must use 1-2-3's /Worksheet Global Column-Width command.

Reminder:
You can use the
mouse to adjust
column widths.

Wysiwyg offers yet another way to adjust column widths: with the mouse. Place the mouse pointer on the vertical line to the right of the column letter and then press and hold down the left mouse button. As shown in figure 9.17, the mouse pointer turns into a cross with left- and right-pointing arrows, and vertical dotted lines define the column width. Keeping the mouse button pressed down, move the mouse pointer to the left or right until the column is the proper width. Then release the mouse button.

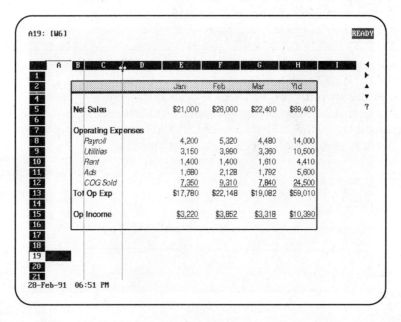

***Fig. 9.17.** Adjusting a column's width with the mouse.*

You can adjust only one column at a time with the mouse. Also, the mouse technique works if the worksheet frame is displayed with any of the four options—1-2-3, **E**nhanced, **R**elief, or **S**pecial. (The worksheet frame display is changed with the **:D**isplay **O**ptions **F**rame command.)

By default, the height of the rows in Wysiwyg adjusts to accommodate the largest font in the row. The row height is approximately 20 percent greater than the font size. For example, if the font size is 10 points, the row height is 12 points. The **:W**orksheet **R**ow **S**et-Height command enables you to set the height of a single row or a range of rows. This command essentially "freezes" the row to the height you specify. Until changed again, the row height remains frozen Returning the row-height setting to automatic with **:W**orksheet **R**ow **A**uto also changes the row height.

Reminder:
Wysiwyg row height adjusts to accommodate the largest font in the row.

To enter a row height, either type the new point size when prompted or press the up- and down- arrow keys to adjust the height of the row one point size at a time. (When specifying the number of points for the row height, remember that one inch equals 72 points.) The current row height is displayed when you select **:W**orksheet **R**ow **S**et-Height.

Reminder:
One inch equals 72 points.

Another way to adjust row heights is with the mouse. Place the mouse pointer on the horizontal line underneath the row number and then press and hold down the left mouse button. The mouse pointer turns into a cross with up- and down-pointing arrows, and horizontal dotted lines define the row height. Keeping the mouse button pressed down, move the mouse pointer up or down until the row is the proper height. Then release the mouse button.

Managing Your Formats

Because formatting is really the heart of Wysiwyg, the program offers several commands for dealing with the formats assigned to your cells. You can copy and move formats—not the cell contents, but the formats associated with the cell. You can assign a name to the set of formatting instructions in a cell and then apply this format to any range. Also, you can save all the formats associated with the file and apply them to another file.

Copying and Moving Formats

If one cell or range should be formatted the same way as another cell or range, you can use the **:S**pecial **C**opy command to copy the formatting instructions. For example, if you formatted a range to 14-point Swiss, in boldface with shading and an outline, you save a great deal of time by copying the format to another range rather than using four separate **:F**ormat commands. The command copies formats only, not cell contents. 1-2-3's

/Copy command copies cell contents and formats (assuming that Wysiwyg is attached). The formatting that can be copied with :Special Copy includes the font, boldfacing, italic, underline, shading, color, and lines. You should find that Wysiwyg's :Special Copy command saves you time in formatting.

Cue:
Use :Special Copy to format ranges quickly.

When you invoke Wysiwyg's :Special Copy command, you are asked to enter the range to copy attributes from (the cell or cells that contain the formatting) and the range to copy the attributes to (the target cell or cells).

The :Special Move command moves formats from the source range to the target range and resets all source-range formats to the defaults. The source range is set to font 1, and all special formatting (boldfacing, italic, underline, shading, lines, and colors) is cleared. Like :Special Copy, this command does not affect the cell contents of the source or the target range.

Because the command resets your source-range formats, use :Special Move with care. If you accidentally use :Special Move on a cell or part of a range in which you want to keep current format settings, you need to reset all formats after using the command. In some cases, using :Special Copy and then resetting source-range formats as necessary with :Format may be a safer method.

Like :Special Move, 1-2-3's /Move command reverts the source range to the default format settings. However, /Move moves the cell contents in addition to the format.

Using Named Styles

Reminder:
Create named styles for the formats you use frequently.

Another way to apply a format from one cell to another is by creating and using named styles. You may want to create named styles for the formats you use frequently. Suppose, for example, that your worksheet contains 10 subheadings, and you want all 10 to be in 14-point Swiss bold with a heavy shade. To ease the formatting process and to ensure consistency, you can name this particular formatting style SUB and then apply this style to all the subheadings.

Another advantage to using named styles is that you can make format changes rapidly. If you decide to change your subheadings to have a light rather than a heavy shade, you need only change the format of one cell.

To define a style, format a cell with the attributes you want and then select :Named-Style Define. As the menu indicates, you can define up to eight different styles per file. At first, all eight styles have the name Normal. As you define styles, the names you specify (instead of Normal) appear next to the number. Choose any number.

The definition process entails specifying the cell that contains the formats, assigning a name up to six characters long, and giving a brief description of the style. After the style is defined, the style name appears in the :Named-Style menu.

To apply a format style to a cell or range, choose :Named-Style and then select the desired style from the menu of eight style names. Indicate the range by typing the cell coordinates or a range name or by using the arrow keys or mouse in POINT mode. When a cell is formatted with a named style, the style name appears inside the format braces. For example, if you created the style SUB, discussed previously, the formatting instructions are {SUB: SWISS14 Bold S2}. *SWISS14 Bold S2* are the format codes associated with the style (14-point Swiss bold with a dark shade).

One reason to use named styles is that they make global formatting changes easy. Changing the format of an existing style requires two simple steps. First, go to any cell formatted with the style you want to change and modify the format. At this point, the cell is no longer associated with the named style. You just need to redefine the style. Thus, the second step is to use the :Named-Style Define command and to assign the same style number and name to the cell. Change the description if necessary. Now all cells with that style name reflect the format change. When you change the format of a cell that was formatted with a named style, the cell is no longer associated with the style name.

Reminder:
Using named styles makes global formatting changes easier.

Importing Formats

Wysiwyg offers the :Special Import command to apply the formats contained in another format file on disk to the current worksheet. You can import the following types of formatting: the font set, graphs, named styles, or all formatting.

:Special Import is similar to 1-2-3's /File Combine Copy, but the Wysiwyg command imports only formatting and printing instructions, not the data. If a series of files have identical structures (for example, a series of budget worksheets), you can eliminate the need to format each worksheet: just import all the formatting. If you want only to import named styles, fonts, or graphics from another file, you can restrict your copying to just these settings.

To import formats from another file, select :Special Import and choose one of the following:

Selection	Description
All	Copies individual cell formats, the font set, named styles, graphics, print range, orientation, bin, settings, and layout
Named-Styles	Replaces the styles in the current file with the styles in the specified format file
Fonts	Replaces the font set in the current file with the font set in the specified format file (similar to :Format Font Library Retrieve)
Graphs	Places graphs in the same location and with the same enhancements as in the specified format file)

You are prompted to enter the name of the format file from which you want to import. You can import from Wysiwyg, Impress, or Allways format files. By default, Wysiwyg displays a list of files that have the FMT extension (either Wysiwyg FMT files or Impress FMT files). You can import from an Allways file by including the ALL extension when you type the file name.

The :Special Import All command completely strips all formatting from the current worksheet and replaces the formats with imported ones. The imported formats appear in the same locations in the current worksheet as they appear in the imported worksheet. If the two worksheets are not organized identically, formats can appear in unexpected cells. You may be able to fix minor problems by using :Special Move to move imported cell formats that do not match up exactly with the current file.

Caution:
When you use :Special Import All, your current worksheet must be organized like the worksheet from which you are importing formats.

Exporting Formats

When you use the /File Save command with Wysiwyg attached, two files are stored: the 1-2-3 worksheet file (WK1 extension) and the Wysiwyg format file (FMT extension). To save the format file only, use the :Special Export option. This command creates a file on disk that contains the current file's formatting, graphing, and printing instructions. The exported file can be a Wysiwyg FMT file, an Impress FMT file, or an Allways ALL file. The file contains individual cell formats; the current font set; named styles; graphic placement and enhancements (but not the actual graphs); and the print range, settings, orientation, and layout.

One possible use of the **:S**pecial Export command is to create a format file that can be used in Impress or Allways. Be aware that if the file contains formatting commands unavailable in Allways, these particular formats are not saved in the ALL file. For example, because Allways lacks a double or wide line feature, these formats are not stored in the ALL file.

Reminder:
Formatting commands unavailable in Allways are not saved in the ALL file.

Using Wysiwyg Text Commands

By using Wysiwyg's **:T**ext commands, you can manipulate the labels in your worksheet in several different ways. With the **:T**ext Align command, you can align a label over a defined worksheet range. This option is great for centering a title over a worksheet table. With the **:T**ext Edit command, you can type text directly into the worksheet, and the words wrap just like in a word processor. You can even change the format of individual characters. For example, you can underline or italicize a single word. The **:T**ext Reformat command adjusts a column of long labels so that they fit into a designated range. Use this command after you edit or change the font of a range and when some or all of the lines in the text block are no longer the correct width.

All the **:T**ext commands require that you define a text range. After you manipulate a text range, the code {Text} appears in the control panel.

Typing or Correcting Text

Many people love 1-2-3 so much that they even use the program to type short letters and memos. However, typing and editing in a spreadsheet program are far more cumbersome than typing and editing in a word processor—that is, until Wysiwyg came along. Now you can type directly into the worksheet, and Wysiwyg word-wraps when you get to the end of the line. You have a cursor that you can position on any character in the text range, and you then can edit the characters—insert, delete, overtype, or format them.

Cue:
*Use **:T**ext Edit to type word-wrapped paragraphs.*

In addition to typing letters and memos, you can use **:T**ext Edit to type a paragraph or two of descriptive information about the purpose of a worksheet. You also can use the **:T**ext Edit command to modify existing worksheet labels or to type new text. When you select **:Text Edit**, you are prompted for a text range. Be sure that you include the complete width and length of the range you want to edit. To insert text, you need to include blank rows or columns, or both, in your text range. Otherwise, you encounter the error message `Text input range full`. Press Esc once to clear the error and to return to READY mode. Then redefine your text range.

As shown in figure 9.18, several important changes occur when you are in the text editor. First, the cell pointer and mouse pointer disappear and a small vertical-line cursor appears within the **:Text Edit** range. The arrow keys move the cursor within the defined text range. Second, the mode indicator displays TEXT. Third, after you start typing or moving the cursor, the control panel displays the following information: the cell the current line of text was typed into, the cursor's row and column number position, and the line's alignment (Left-Aligned, Centered, and so on). The row number corresponds to the row in the defined text range, not the actual worksheet row. For example, if worksheet row 13 is the first row in the current text range, the row number is 1. The column number refers to the number of characters over from the beginning of the line.

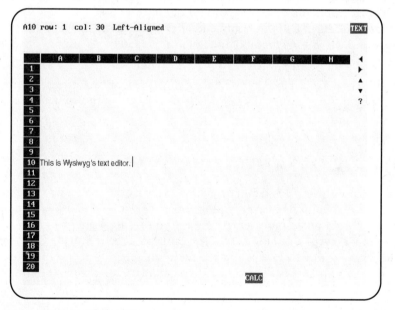

Fig. 9.18. Wysiwyg's text editor.

As you type new text, the words wrap to the next line. When you want to start a new paragraph, take one of three actions, depending on how you want the text to look:

- Press Enter twice, leaving a blank line between paragraphs.

- Press Enter once and press the space bar one or more times at the beginning of the paragraph.

- Press Ctrl-Enter to insert a paragraph symbol.

The preceding rules come into play when you reformat the text. (See "Reformatting Paragraphs" for additional information.) Table 9.4 lists the cursor-movement and editing keys you can use in **:**Text Edit. Many of these keys are similar to the ones you can use in 1-2-3's EDIT mode.

Table 9.4
Cursor-Movement and Editing Keys Available in :Text Edit

Key	Description
↑	Character above
↓	Character below
→	One character to the right
←	One character to the left
Ctrl-←	Beginning of the preceding word
Ctrl-→	End of the next word
PgDn	Next screen
PgUp	Preceding screen
Home	Beginning of line
Home, Home	Beginning of paragraph
End	End of line
End, End	End of paragraph
Backspace	Deletes character to the left of cursor
Del	Deletes character to the right of cursor
Ins	Toggles between insert mode (the default) and overtype mode
Enter	Begins a new line
Ctrl-Enter	Begins a new paragraph
F3	Displays a format menu
Esc	Returns to READY mode

When you finish typing and editing the text, press Esc to exit the text editor. In READY mode, you can see that each line of text actually is entered into cells in the first column of the text range. You can change easily from READY mode to **:Text Edit** mode by moving the mouse pointer within a text range and double-clicking the left mouse button.

Formatting Characters

Previously in this chapter, you learned how to use formatting sequences to assign attributes to individual characters in a cell. You press Ctrl-A and a code, and then you press Ctrl-N to end the attribute. The text editor offers an easier way to format characters: the F3 key. You don't need to remember codes because pressing F3 displays the following menu:

Font Bold Italics Underline Color + – Outline Normal

Cue:

In the text editor, use F3 to format individual characters.

To add formatting attributes, you must first give the **:Text Edit** command and define the text range. Be sure that you include the entire width of the long labels, not just the column they are typed into. Place the cursor just to the left of the first character you want to format and press F3 to display the menu of attributes.

The first five attributes (**Font**, **Bold**, **Italic**, **Underline**, and **Color**) already should be familiar to you. The latter four attributes are unique to the F3 key in **:Text Edit** mode. The **+** option superscripts the text; the **–** option subscripts the text; **Outline** traces the outside of the letter forms, leaving the inside hollow; and the **Normal** option removes formatting. Examples of the superscript (**+**), subscript (**–**), and **Outline** attributes are shown in figure 9.19.

If superscripted or subscripted text is cut off at the top or bottom, you can increase the row height. You first must escape out of text-editing mode and issue the **:Worksheet Row Set-Height** command.

After you select the attribute you want, everything from the right of the cursor through the end of the line appears with this attribute. Your next step is to indicate where you want the attribute to stop (for example, at the end of a word). Place the cursor to the right of the final character you want to format and press F3. Choose **Normal** or select a different font.

Because some of the attributes change the size of characters, you may notice that your paragraphs are no longer neatly aligned after you format. When this misalignment happens, use the **:Text Reformat** command to adjust the paragraphs. If you prespecify the text range, as described in "Specifying Cell Ranges in Wysiwyg" in this chapter, you do not have to do so when you need to reformat paragraphs. (See "Reformatting Paragraphs" for additional information on reformatting.)

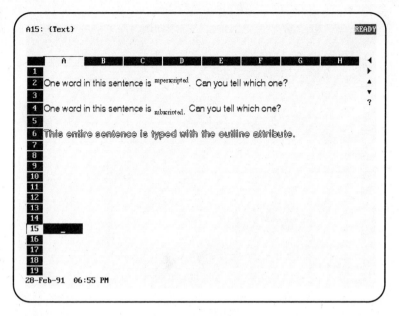

Fig. 9.19. *Some of the format attributes that can be added to individual characters in the text editor.*

Character formatting is not limited to existing text; you also can apply attributes as you type new text in **:Text Edit** mode. Press F3 and select the format before you begin typing. Type the text, and when you want to discontinue this attribute, press F3 and choose **Normal**.

Aligning Labels

Wysiwyg's **:Text Align** command is an enhanced version of 1-2-3's /Range Label command. 1-2-3's command aligns a label within the current column width. A label that exceeds the column width aligns on the left. Wysiwyg's command aligns a label within a specified range. Thus, you can center a label across a range of cells so that the label is centered over the worksheet. Figure 9.20 shows titles entered into A1..A3 and centered over the range A1..H3.

Cue:
Use :Text Align to center a title over a worksheet.

After you choose **:Text Align**, Wysiwyg offers four choices: **Left, Right, Center,** and **Even. Left** is the default alignment. **Right** aligns the label on the right edge of the rightmost cell in the text range; **Center** aligns the text in the middle of the range; and **Even** stretches the text between the left and the right edge of the text range (spaces are inserted between words to create the smooth margins). Figure 9.21 shows examples of each type of alignment.

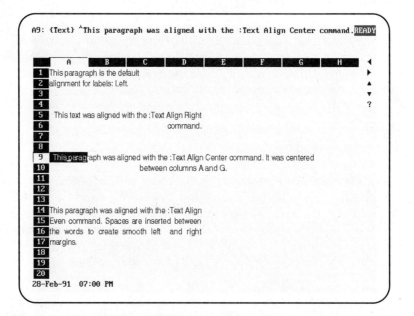

Fig. 9.20. *A report heading centered with :Text Align.*

```
A9: {Text} ^This paragraph was aligned with the :Text Align Center command. READY
```

	A	B	C	D	E	F	G	H
1	This paragraph is the default
2	alignment for labels: Left.
3	
4	
5	This text was aligned with the :Text Align Right
6	command.
7	
8	
9	This paragraph was aligned with the :Text Align Center command. It was centered
10	between columns A and G.
11	
12	
13	
14	This paragraph was aligned with the :Text Align
15	Even command. Spaces are inserted between
16	the words to create smooth left and right
17	margins.
18	
19	
20	

```
28-Feb-91  07:00 PM
```

Fig. 9.21. *The four types of alignment: Left, Right, Center, and Even.*

After you make your alignment selection, you are prompted for a text range. Highlight the rows for which you want to change the alignment. To align the text in the current range, you need only to highlight the first column of the range. For example, the text range for the even-aligned paragraph in figure 9.21 is A14..A18. To align the text in a wider range, highlight the entire width of the text range.

Wysiwyg uses the following symbols to identify each type of alignment:

Symbol	Description
'	Left
"	Right
^	Center
|	Even

Notice that these symbols correspond to the label-alignment symbols inserted with the /Range Label command. The symbols have different functions, however, when the cell shows the {Text} attribute. You can insert these symbols when in 1-2-3's EDIT mode, as long as the cell shows the {Text} attribute. When you edit in Wysiwyg's text editor, the control panel displays the alignment of the current line (Left-Aligned, Centered, and so on).

Reformatting Paragraphs

One of the advantages of using the text editor is that you easily can correct typing mistakes, reword a passage, or insert additional text. After you start editing and formatting, however, you may notice that your paragraphs are no longer properly aligned. For example, some lines may be too short. The first paragraph in figure 9.22 shows that words were deleted. The second paragraph illustrates how the text readjusts after the Text Reformat command is issued.

Reminder:
Use Text Reformat to realign paragraphs after editing and formatting them.

:Text Reformat is similar to 1-2-3's /Range Justify command, and in many cases, the two can be used interchangeably. The main difference between the two features is that /Range Justify ignores Wysiwyg alignment commands and consequently left-aligns all the labels during the reformat process. :Text Reformat, on the other hand, retains the alignment commands during reformatting.

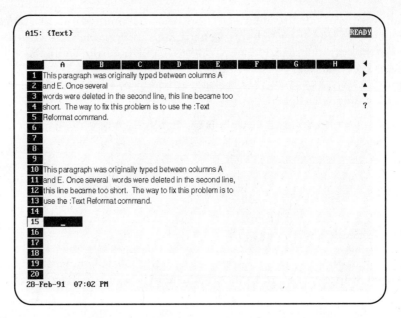

A15: {Text}   READY

	A	B	C	D	E	F	G	H
1	This paragraph was originally typed between columns A
2	and E. Once several
3	words were deleted in the second line, this line became too
4	short. The way to fix this problem is to use the :Text
5	Reformat command.
6	
7	
8	
9	
10	This paragraph was originally typed between columns A
11	and E. Once several words were deleted in the second line,
12	this line became too short. The way to fix this problem is to
13	use the :Text Reformat command.
14	
15	
16	
17	
18	
19	
20	

28-Feb-91 07:02 PM

Fig. 9.22. *Using the :Text Reformat command.*

To invoke the **:Text Reformat** command, you must be in READY mode. (If you are in the text editor, press Esc.) If you have prespecified the text range, the range you last indicated in the **:Text Edit** command is highlighted for you. If this range is acceptable, press Enter, and the text readjusts. To indicate a different range, press Esc or Backspace and then highlight the width and length of the range you want.

:Text Reformat rearranges the text within each paragraph and, when necessary, brings text up from subsequent lines to fit into the reformat range you specified. This command does not combine text from separate paragraphs, assuming that you followed the paragraph rules defined in the "Typing or Correcting Text" section.

Cue:
:Text Reformat also can be used to align text into a different number of columns.

Another reason to use the **:Text Reformat** command is to align the text into a different number of columns. Suppose, for example, that the range currently spans four columns, and you want the range to go across six. To make longer lines of text, include these extra columns in your reformat range.

Making lines of text shorter is another story, however. If your reformat range contains fewer columns than your text range, nothing happens when you reformat—the command is ignored. Wysiwyg does not reformat because all columns in your text range contain the {Text} attribute. For example, in figure 9.23, all cells in the range A1..G3 have the {Text} attribute. You must remove this attribute from the extra columns before you can reformat. Thus, to reformat the range in figure 9.23 to columns A through E, you must clear the {Text} attribute from columns F and G. Use **:Text Clear** to eliminate the attribute. If you find the multiple steps too awkward, you can use the **/Range Justify** command, which doesn't require the extra step.

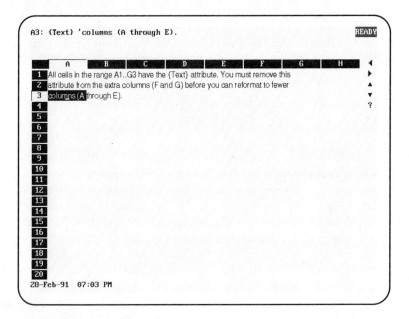

Fig. 9.23. *Reformatting a text range to fewer columns.*

Another consideration when reformatting to fewer columns is that your new text range becomes longer than the current range. Therefore, you must include additional blank rows at the bottom of the range, or the message Text input range full appears. When this message appears, press Esc to clear the error message, reissue the **:Text Reformat** command, and include a longer range.

Setting and Clearing Text Attributes

The **:Text** menu offers two more options: **Set** and **Clear**. The **Set** option assigns the {Text} attribute to a cell or a range. Because the **:Text Align**, **Edit**, and **Reformat** commands assign the {Text} attribute, you probably do need to use this option often. Use **:Text Set** if you accidentally clear the {Text} attribute from a cell (for example, with the **:Text Clear** or **:Format Reset** commands).

Another reason to define a text range with **:Text Set** is so that you can use the mouse to invoke the text editor. If you have a mouse, you don't need to use the **:Text Edit** command. After a text range is defined (with **:Text Set** or any of the other **Text** commands), you can place the mouse pointer anywhere in the text and click the left mouse button twice. Your cursor then moves to the beginning of the text range in the row in which the mouse pointer was clicked. The right mouse button cancels **:Text Edit** mode and returns you to READY mode.

As mentioned previously, use the **:Text Clear** command to eliminate the {Text} attribute from cells you don't want included in the reformat range.

Printing with Wysiwyg

The following sections examine each of the options available with the Wysiwyg **:Print** command. The **:Print** menu displays a full-screen dialog box as shown in figure 9.24. You can immediately see what your current print settings are. Notice that each corner of the dialog box contains a different category of print information. The upper left corner displays the configuration; the margins are in the upper right corner; the print range and print settings are in the lower left corner; the layout and units are on the lower right side of the screen. Because your worksheet is hidden when the dialog box is displayed, the **Info** command on the **:Print** menu enables you to temporarily hide the dialog box. Choose **Info** again to redisplay the Wysiwyg Print Settings dialog box. You also can use the F6 key to toggle the dialog box on and off.

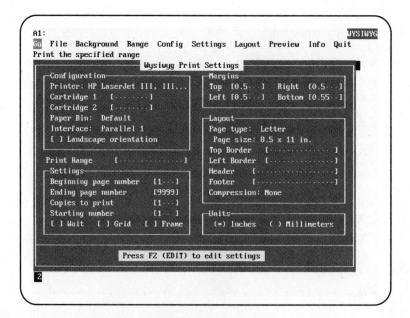

Fig. 9.24. The Wysiwyg Print Settings dialog box.

In the following sections, you learn how to configure your printer, specify a print range, preview the report on the screen, lay out a page, set page breaks, specify print settings, and print to an encoded file.

Configuring Your Printer

Before you print, select **:Print Config** and check the dialog box to make sure that Wysiwyg is set up to work with your printer. Figure 9.24 displays the configuration for an HP LaserJet Series II printer.

Not all the options on the **:Print Config** menu apply to all printers. For example, an Epson RX-80 does not have cartridges or bins, nor can the printer work with the landscape orientation. The following listing describes the **:Print Config** options:

Selection	Description
Printer	The printer to be used. When multiple printers are selected in the Install program, you can use the **Printer** option to specify the printer you want to use.
Interface	The printer port to which your printer is attached (Parallel 1, Serial 1, Parallel 2, Serial 2, or one of the following output devices: LPT1, LPT2, LPT3, or LPT4)
1st-Cart	Your primary printer cartridge. Some printers have separate cartridges or cards you can buy to get additional fonts for your printer. The HP LaserJet, for example, offers a "B" cartridge that includes 14-point Helvetica and 8-point and 10-point Times Roman.
2nd-Cart	Your secondary cartridge
Orientation	The orientation of the page to be printed: **Portrait** (vertical) or **Landscape** (horizontal). This setting is saved in the current worksheet's format file.
Bin	The feeding method, if your printer offers more than one way to feed paper. Your printer may provide multiple paper trays and a way to feed paper manually. To feed paper manually, select **Manual**. (If you feed paper manually, you also may want to select **:Print Settings Wait** to pause between pages.) This setting is saved in the current worksheet's format file.
Quit	Leaves the **:Print Config** menu

Cue:
*Specify landscape orientation from the **:Print Config** menu.*

Specifying a Print Range

Reminder:
Print ranges entered in 1-2-3 are not transferred to Wysiwyg.

Wysiwyg's **:Print Range Set** command is the equivalent of 1-2-3's /Print Printer Range command. A print range entered in 1-2-3, however, is not transferred to Wysiwyg. You must set the print range in Wysiwyg before you print.

To specify a Wysiwyg print range, select **:Print Range Set** and indicate the range just as you do in 1-2-3: highlight the range with the direction keys or the mouse, type the range, or use a range name. To use a range name, type the range name or press F3 to choose from a list of names when prompted for the print range.

After you define the Wysiwyg print range, dashed borders appear around the area. To see these lines, select **Quit** from the **:Print** menu, choose **Info** to display the worksheet, or press F6. If the print area is large, dashed lines appear around each page. To change the location on the worksheet where the pages break, you can insert your own breaks.

To print a Wysiwyg graph, you first must define its range with **:Graph Add**, as explained in Chapter 11. Be sure that you include the entire graph range in the print range.

You also can select the range to print before choosing **:Print Range**. To preselect the range, place the cell pointer in the top left cell in the range, press F4, and extend the highlight to the lower right corner of the desired range. Click and drag the mouse to highlight the range. Then, when you use **:Print Range Set**, Wysiwyg highlights the selected range.

To print the range, assuming that the print configuration is defined properly, select **Go** from the **:Print** menu. If the selected range exceeds both the width and length of the page, Wysiwyg (like 1-2-3) prints the left part of the range from top to bottom and then prints the right parts of the range from top to bottom until the entire range is printed. The dashed lines on the screen show you where the page breaks occur.

Reminder:
Your laser printer may not have enough memory to print graphics at a high resolution.

Laser printers have varying amounts of memory. Your laser printer may not have enough memory to accept downloaded fonts with large point sizes or several different fonts on a page. If you get an out-of-memory message when you print, specify smaller font sizes, make fewer font selections, or use an internal or cartridge font.

Inserting Page Breaks

After you choose a print range, you see dashed lines around each page. If you don't like the location of the page breaks, use **:Worksheet Page** to set new page breaks before you print. You can specify the row or column on which you want Wysiwyg to start a new page.

To set a horizontal page break, position the pointer on the first row of the new page, select **:W**orksheet **P**age **R**ow, and select **Q**uit to return to Ready mode. As shown in figure 9.25, a dashed line appears above the specified row to indicate the new page break.

```
A20: {MPage} [W2]                                                    READY

     A     B      C      D      E      F      G      H       I     ◀
13                                                                   ▶
14  Liabilities                                                      ▲
15     Accounts Payable                       125,000               ▼
16     Line of Credit                               0               ?
17
18     Net Working Capital                   $549,339
19  - - - - - - - - - - - - - - - - - - - - - - - - - -
20  ■
21
22  SALES                      Oct     Nov     Dec
23
24
25  Profit Center 1          $27,832 $23,864 $26,125
26  Profit Center 2           13,489  21,444  20,140
27  Profit Center 3          126,811 124,382 123,618
28  Profit Center 4           94,285  92,447  89,010
29
30  Total Sales             $262,417 $262,137 $258,893
31
32
28-Feb-91  07:07 PM
```

Fig. 9.25. *A worksheet with a page break added at row 19.*

1-2-3 also offers an option for inserting horizontal page breaks: **/W**orksheet **P**age. /Worksheet Page is different from **:W**orksheet **P**age in two ways. First, when you use **/W**orksheet **P**age, the row below the page break must be blank; second, the cell pointer must be positioned in the first column of your print range. Feel free to use 1-2-3's or Wysiwyg's page-break option; both types of breaks are honored when you print in Wysiwyg.

To tell Wysiwyg at which column to start a new page, position the pointer on the first column of the new page, choose **:W**orksheet **P**age Column, and select **Q**uit to return to Ready mode. A dashed line appears to the left of the specified column to indicate the new page break.

To remove a page break you inserted in Wysiwyg, place the cell pointer on the first row or column of the page and select **:W**orksheet **P**age **D**elete. The dashed page-break line immediately disappears.

Setting Up the Page

Reminder:
All headers, footers, margins, and borders specified in 1-2-3 must be respecified in Wysiwyg.

Use the **:Print Layout** command to fine-tune the page layout. Figure 9.26 shows the **:Print Layout** menu and the Wysiwyg Print Settings dialog box. All the Layout settings are located in the right side of the screen. Notice that many of the options are similar to those offered in 1-2-3's **/Print Printer Options** menu. However, the headers, footers, margins, and borders you enter in 1-2-3 do not transfer into Wysiwyg. If you defined headers and footers in 1-2-3, you must use the Wysiwyg **:Print Layout** command to set them up again. The following sections explain how to use the various options on the Layout menu.

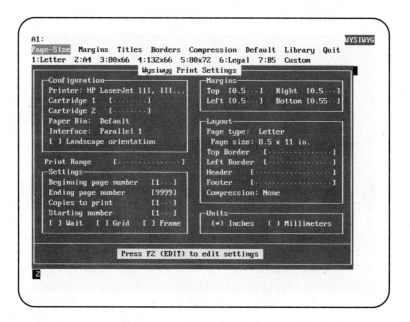

Fig. 9.26. The :Print Layout menu and Wysiwyg Print Settings dialog box.

Defining the Page Layout

The default page size is standard letter size (8 1/2 inches by 11 inches). Using **:Print Layout Page-Size**, you can choose from several different sizes. If your paper size does not fall in any of the predefined dimensions, you can choose **Custom**. The Custom option enables you to define the page width and page length as any size you need. You can enter the size in either inches or millimeters. The current unit of measurement appears in the top right corner of the Layout screen. To change to a different unit of measurement, follow the number by **mm** (millimeters) or **in** (inches).

Wysiwyg's **Margins** option is similar to 1-2-3's, with several important differences. In 1-2-3, the right and left margins are entered in terms of characters, and the top and bottom margins are entered in terms of lines. In Wysiwyg, all margins are entered in inches, millimeters, or centimeters. (If you enter a number in centimeters [for example, **1cm**], Wysiwyg converts the number to millimeters [10mm].) In 1-2-3, the right margin is the number of characters from the left edge of the page. In Wysiwyg, the right margin is the space between the printed worksheet and the right edge of the page.

Remember that page orientation (**Landscape** and **Portrait**) is on the **:Print Config Orientation** menu. (You may expect page orientation to be on the Layout menu, but it is not.)

Printing Titles and Borders

Wysiwyg's **:Print Layout Titles** command is the equivalent of 1-2-3's **/Print Printer Options Header** and **Footer** commands. A header is a one-line title at the top of every page; a footer is a line that prints at the bottom of each page. You do not see these titles on-screen with Wysiwyg unless you preview the range with **:Print Preview**. (See the section "Previewing on Your Screen.")

As with 1-2-3, in Wysiwyg you can include special characters in a header or footer. Including the @ symbol prints the current day's date in that position; including the **#** symbol prints the page number. Including vertical bar characters (|) separates the text into left-justified, centered, and right-justified sections.

If you type a header as @|**Projection**|**Page #**, the printed header for page 1 appears (see fig. 9.27).

In your Wysiwyg headers and footers, you can enter formatting sequences to assign an attribute to all or part of the text. See "Formatting Sequences," previously covered in this chapter, for details.

Wysiwyg reserves three lines on the printout for each header and footer. Remember to figure in these extra lines when you calculate how many lines of text fit on a printed page. Unlike 1-2-3, Wysiwyg does not reserve lines for titles if you did not enter any titles. To cancel headers or footers, use the **:Print Layout Titles Clear** command.

Reminder:
Figure in three lines for each header and footer when estimating page line length.

The **Layout** menu's **Borders** option is the same as 1-2-3's **/Print Printer Options Borders** command. This command specifies a worksheet range (rows or columns) to be printed on every page of a multipage printout. Suppose that you wanted to print 12 months of data from the balance sheet shown in figure 9.27 and could not fit all 12 months on one page. You would need several pages to print the report, with the leftmost column as the first column on each page so that you know what each row of data signifies. Using the **B**orders option, you can specify the columns to print at the left side of each page when the worksheet is wide. You also can specify the rows to print at the top of each page if the worksheet is long.

```
04–Mar–91                         Projection                          Page 1



                        CASH FLOW PROJECTOR

BALANCES IN WORKING CAPITAL ACCOUNTS                    December


Assets
   Cash                                        $17,365
   Accounts Receivable                         493,151
   Inventory                                   163,833

Liabilities
   Accounts Payable                            125,000
   Line of Credit                                    0

   Net Working Capital                        $549,339



SALES                        Oct      Nov      Dec


Profit Center 1           $27,832  $23,864  $26,125
Profit Center 2            13,489   21,444   20,140
Profit Center 3           126,811  124,382  123,618
Profit Center 4            94,285   92,447   89,010

Total Sales              $262,417 $262,137 $258,893
```

Fig. 9.27. *A printed worksheet with a header.*

To repeat a column or row of text on other pages of the report, follow these steps:

1. Use the Wysiwyg **:P**rint **R**ange **S**et command to specify a range that includes the entire report except for the border columns and rows.

2. Select **:P**rint **L**ayout **B**orders **L**eft and highlight any cell in the border column and/or select **B**orders **T**op and highlight any cell in the border row. If you designed the border with multiple rows or columns, press the period (.) key to anchor the highlight and extend the highlight over the additional rows or columns (or highlight them with the mouse). Press Enter.

3. Print the report using **:P**rint **G**o or select **:P**rint **B**ackground.

The border columns and rows should print on each page. Make sure that the border range is not included in the print range, or the border range is printed twice on the first page. To cancel borders, use the **:P**rint Layout **B**orders **C**lear command.

Compressing the Print

The **C**ompression option on the **L**ayout menu offers an ideal way to fit a large worksheet on one page. Rather than guess at the font size needed to print a report on a single page, you can use the **:P**rint Layout **C**ompression **A**utomatic command. Wysiwyg then determines how much the font size needs to be reduced. Wysiwyg calculated that the worksheet in figure 9.28 needed to be reduced 38 percent. A worksheet cannot be reduced to less than 15 percent of its original size. (15 percent is so tiny that you can barely read the data.) If your print range is too large for the maximum-allowed reduction, the worksheet prints on multiple pages.

Cue:
Use the **:P**rint *Layout* **C**ompression *command to fit a large worksheet on one page.*

Compressed type does not look different on the screen, although the dashed lines around the print range accurately reflects the page breaks. All manual page breaks that you entered with **:W**orksheet **P**age or /**W**orksheet **P**age are still in effect. If you don't want these page breaks in the compressed printout, delete them before printing. To get an idea of what the page looks like with the compressed print, use the **:P**rint **P**review command.

The **C**ompression command also offers a **M**anual option, by which you can enter your own reduction or enlargement percentage. To reduce the type, enter a number greater than or equal to 15 but less than 100. To spread the type across and down the page, enter a number greater than 100.

To remove the automatic or manual compression factors you previously entered, use the **:P**rint Layout **C**ompression **N**one command.

Saving Layout Settings

The **L**ayout **D**efault and **L**ayout **L**ibrary commands from the **:P**rint menu enable you to modify all the layout settings at the same time. To return all the layout settings to the default values, choose **:P**rint Layout **D**efault **R**estore. To change the default settings permanently to those currently displayed, use **:P**rint Layout **D**efault **U**pdate. Use the latter command if you discover that you constantly change the layout settings to the same values. This way, all new worksheets that you create adopt the layout values you normally use.

Cue:
Use **:P**rint *Layout* **D**efault *to change the layout settings permanently.*

REGIONAL INCOME REPORT	Jan	Feb	Mar	Apr	May
Sales					
Northeast	$31,336	$34,370	$37,404	$40,438	$43,472
Southeast	30,572	33,606	36,640	39,674	42,708
Central	131,685	134,719	137,753	140,787	143,821
Northwest	94,473	97,507	100,541	103,575	106,609
Southwest	126,739	129,773	132,807	135,841	138,875
Total Sales	414,805	429,975	445,145	460,315	475,485
Cost of Goods Sold					
Northeast	10,341	11,274	12,207	13,140	14,073
Southeast	6,546	7,479	8,412	9,345	10,278
Central	65,843	66,776	67,709	68,642	69,575
Northwest	63,967	64,900	65,833	66,766	67,699
Southwest	72,314	73,247	74,180	75,113	76,046
Total Cost of Goods Sold	219,011	223,676	228,341	233,006	237,671
Operating Expenses					
Northeast	21,529	23,470	25,411	27,352	29,293
Southeast	15,946	17,887	19,828	21,769	23,710
Central	27,554	29,495	31,436	33,377	35,318
Northwest	16,130	18,071	20,012	21,953	23,894
Southwest	32,361	34,302	36,243	38,184	40,125
Total Operating Expenses	113,520	123,225	132,930	142,635	152,340
Net Income					
Northeast	(534)	(374)	(214)	(54)	106
Southeast	8,080	8,240	8,400	8,560	8,720
Central	38,288	38,448	38,608	38,768	38,928
Northwest	14,376	14,536	14,696	14,856	15,016
Southwest	22,064	22,224	22,384	22,544	22,704
Total Net Income	82,808	83,074	83,874	84,674	85,474

REGIONAL RATIO ANALYSIS	Jan	Feb	Mar	Apr	May
Gross Profit on Sales					
Northeast	67.0%	67.2%	67.4%	67.5%	67.6%
Southeast	78.6%	77.7%	77.0%	76.4%	75.9%
Central	50.0%	50.4%	50.8%	51.2%	51.6%
Northwest	32.3%	33.4%	34.5%	35.5%	36.5%
Southwest	42.9%	43.6%	44.1%	44.7%	45.2%
Total	47.2%	48.0%	48.7%	49.4%	50.0%
Return on Sales					
Northeast	−1.7%	−1.1%	−0.6%	−0.1%	0.2%
Southeast	26.4%	24.5%	22.9%	21.6%	20.4%
Central	29.1%	28.5%	28.0%	27.5%	27.1%
Northwest	15.2%	14.9%	14.6%	14.3%	14.1%
Southwest	17.4%	17.1%	16.9%	16.6%	16.3%
Total	20.0%	19.3%	18.8%	18.4%	18.0%

Fig. 9.28. *Automatic compression.*

Jun	Jul	Aug	Sep	Oct	Nov	Dec	TOTAL
$46,506	$49,540	$52,574	$55,608	$58,642	$61,676	$64,710	$576,276
45,742	48,776	51,810	54,844	57,878	60,912	63,946	567,108
146,855	149,889	152,923	155,957	158,991	162,025	165,059	1,780,464
109,643	112,677	115,711	118,745	121,779	124,813	127,847	1,333,920
141,909	144,943	147,977	151,011	154,045	157,079	160,113	1,721,112
490,655	505,825	520,995	536,165	551,335	566,505	581,675	5,978,880
15,006	15,939	16,872	17,805	18,738	19,671	20,604	185,670
11,211	12,144	13,077	14,010	14,943	15,876	16,809	140,130
70,508	71,441	72,374	73,307	74,240	75,173	76,106	851,694
68,632	69,565	70,498	71,431	72,364	73,297	74,230	829,182
76,979	77,912	78,845	79,778	80,711	81,644	82,577	929,346
242,336	247,001	251,666	256,331	260,996	265,661	270,326	2,936,022
31,234	33,175	35,116	37,057	38,998	40,939	42,880	386,454
25,651	27,592	29,533	31,474	33,415	35,356	37,297	319,458
37,259	39,200	41,141	43,082	45,023	46,964	48,905	458,754
25,835	27,776	29,717	31,658	33,599	35,540	37,481	321,666
42,066	44,007	45,948	47,889	49,830	51,771	53,712	516,438
162,045	171,750	181,455	191,160	200,865	210,570	220,275	2,002,770
266	426	586	746	906	1,066	1,226	4,152
8,880	9,040	9,200	9,360	9,520	9,680	9,840	107,520
39,088	39,248	39,408	39,568	39,728	39,888	40,048	470,016
15,176	15,336	15,496	15,656	15,816	15,976	16,136	183,072
22,864	23,024	23,184	23,344	23,504	23,664	23,824	275,328
86,274	87,074	87,874	88,674	89,474	90,274	91,074	$1,040,088

Jun	Jul	Aug	Sep	Oct	Nov	Dec	TOTAL
67.7%	67.8%	67.9%	68.0%	68.0%	68.1%	68.2%	67.8%
75.5%	75.1%	74.8%	74.5%	74.2%	73.9%	73.7%	75.3%
52.0%	52.3%	52.7%	53.0%	53.3%	53.6%	53.9%	52.2%
37.4%	38.3%	39.1%	39.8%	40.6%	41.3%	41.9%	37.8%
45.8%	46.2%	46.7%	47.2%	47.6%	48.0%	48.4%	46.0%
50.6%	51.2%	51.7%	52.2%	52.7%	53.1%	53.5%	50.9%
0.6%	0.9%	1.1%	1.3%	1.5%	1.7%	1.9%	0.7%
19.4%	18.5%	17.8%	17.1%	16.4%	15.9%	15.4%	19.0%
26.6%	26.2%	25.8%	25.4%	25.0%	24.6%	24.3%	26.4%
13.8%	13.6%	13.4%	13.2%	13.0%	12.8%	12.6%	13.7%
16.1%	15.9%	15.7%	15.5%	15.3%	15.1%	14.9%	16.0%
17.6%	17.2%	16.9%	16.5%	16.2%	15.9%	15.7%	17.4%

Use :**Print Layout Library** to save a disk file of your layout settings. If you need certain combinations of layout settings for different types of worksheets, you can save each group of settings and then retrieve them to use later with any worksheet. To save the current page-layout settings in a library, use :**Print Layout Library Save** and specify a file name. The file is given the extension ALS. When you want to use the settings with another worksheet, use :**Print Layout Library Retrieve**. You can delete an unneeded library file by using :**Print Layout Library Erase**.

Specifying Print Settings

Use the :**Print Settings** command to control page numbering, ranges of pages to print, the number of copies to print, print pausing, and the printing of the worksheet grid or frame. The :**Print Settings** menu offers the options listed in the following chart.

Selection	Description
Begin and End	Prints the specified page numbers. Normally, Wysiwyg prints the entire range specified with :**Print Range Set**. To print only selected pages in the range (for example, only the pages that changed from a previous printing), set the **Begin** and **End** options accordingly.
Start-Number	Specifies the first page number to be printed in a title. The page number is inserted where the # symbol appears in the header or footer. If you are printing your document from several different worksheets, for example, use this option to specify the first page number of each subdocument so that the page numbers are continuous. The default setting is 1.
Copies	Prints the specified number of copies.
Wait	Pauses the printer between pages. The default setting is **No**. To feed individual sheets into the printer, select **Yes** to pause the printer before each new page. Use this option if you previously selected the **Manual** option for :**Print Config Bin**. If you set **Wait** to **Yes**, the message `Press a key when ready to print (ESC to cancel)` appears at the bottom of the screen.
Grid	Produces a printout that looks like ledger paper, with dotted lines that enclose every cell on your printout.

Selection	Description
	This option prints grid lines through the entire print-out. To enclose only part of your printout in a grid, use **:Format Lines All** and specify a range.
Frame	Prints the column letters at the top of each page, and the row numbers to the left of the print range if the **Frame** setting is on. Use this option for draft copies.
Reset	Restores the Wysiwyg default print settings for the document.
Quit	Leaves the **:Print Settings** menu.

Previewing on Your Screen

The **:Print Preview** option gives you an idea of what your worksheet looks like before you commit the worksheet to paper. This option displays your print range, one page at a time; press any key to display subsequent pages and to return to the **:Print** menu. Although you probably cannot read every character on the screen, you can get a feel of your overall page layout and page breaks. Figure 9.29 displays an example of a previewed page.

Cue:
Preview your report on-screen before printing.

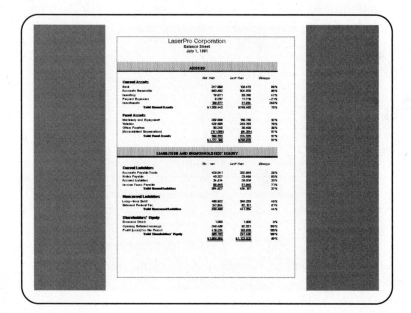

***Fig. 9.29.** A previewed page.*

Printing to a File

You can create an encoded file to print the worksheet on a remote printer if the computer connected to this printer doesn't have 1-2-3 and Wysiwyg. The print file you create contains all the necessary data and formatting instructions so that you can print the worksheet from DOS. Before you print to a file, make sure that the following conditions are met:

- The final destination printer is selected under **:Print Config Printer**.

- The fonts you selected for your worksheet are available on the final destination printer.

- The print range is selected.

To create the encoded file, select **:Print File**. You are prompted for a file name. Wysiwyg supplies the extension ENC (for encoded) if you don't provide an extension. To print the file, type the following DOS command:

COPY filename/B device

Reminder:
Include the /B switch, or DOS may interpret certain binary codes as end-of-file markers and prematurely end the printout.

The argument *filename* is the full name of your file (for example, ASSET.ENC), and *device* is the name of the DOS port or logical device to which your printer is connected. Parallel port 1, for example, has the device name LPT1:. Be sure that you include the /B switch, or DOS may interpret certain binary codes in the file as end-of-file markers and terminate the printout prematurely. The DOS command to print ASSET.ENC to a printer connected to the first parallel port is as follows:

COPY ASSET.ENC/B LPT1:

Summary

In this chapter, you learned how to use Wysiwyg to enhance your 1-2-3 worksheets. Wysiwyg's extensive formatting capability is this add-in's feature attraction. You can emphasize important areas of the worksheet by changing fonts, or by adding lines, colors, bold, italic, and shading. By using Wysiwyg's formatting options, you can create attractive, professional-looking reports.

Although formatting is key in Wysiwyg, you can do much more than formatting with the add-in. The text editor is another powerful feature. This simple word processor enables you to type, edit, format, and align text. Graph enhancement is yet another capability of Wysiwyg. This subject is covered in Chapter 11.

10

Creating and Printing Graphs

Keeping detailed worksheets that show real or projected data is worthless if the data cannot be readily understood. 1-2-3 business graphics can help make your data clear. Spotting a trend or analyzing data often is easier with a graph than with a sea of numbers.

The program offers seven types of basic business graphs and sophisticated options for enhancing the graphs' appearance. The real strength of 1-2-3's graphics feature, however, lies in its integration with the worksheet.

This chapter shows you how to do the following:

- Create graphs from worksheet data

- Use 1-2-3's automatic graphing capability

- Add descriptive labels and numbers to a graph

- Save graphs and graph settings for later use

- Select an appropriate graph type

- Use the PrintGraph program to print graphs created in 1-2-3

In this chapter, you learn how to apply most of 1-2-3's graph options to a line graph. Then you learn how to construct all the other types of 1-2-3 graphs.

Working with Wysiwyg

Graphing commands are available on the main 1-2-3 menu and the Wysiwyg menu. The options on the :Graph menu, however, are primarily for enhancing graphs created with 1-2-3's /Graph menu.

Wysiwyg contains a built-in graph editor that you can use to annotate your graphs. The following list describes a few tasks you can accomplish with your graphs in Wysiwyg:

- Insert a graph in any worksheet range
- Type text anywhere on the graph
- Draw arrows, lines, circles, and other shapes
- Print graphs and worksheet data on the same page

Although the Wysiwyg commands are not covered in this chapter, pertinent :Graph commands are listed when appropriate. Chapter 11 contains a thorough explanation of the :Graph commands available in Release 2.3.

Determining Hardware and Software Needs

Before creating your first graph, you must determine whether your hardware supports viewing and printing graphs and whether your 1-2-3 software is correctly installed. You also should be familiar with the various graph types so that you know which type of graph is best suited for presenting specific numeric data.

Reminder:
To view a graph on-screen, you need graphics-capable video hardware.

To view a graph on-screen, you need graphics-capable video display hardware (almost all systems have such hardware). Without graphics capability, you can construct, save, and print 1-2-3 graphs, but you cannot view graphs on-screen.

To print a graph, you need a graphics printer or plotter supported by 1-2-3. Graph printing is described at the end of this chapter.

Understanding Graphs

To understand 1-2-3's graphics, you need to be familiar with a few terms concerning graph plotting. The two basic terms—*x-axis* and *y-axis*—are illustrated in figure 10.1.

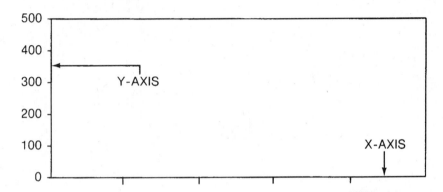

Fig. 10.1. *The x- and y-axes of a graph.*

All graphs (except pie graphs) have two axes: the y-axis and the x-axis. By default, the y-axis is positioned along the vertical left edge, and the x-axis is positioned at the horizontal bottom edge. You can, however, reverse the locations of the x- and y-axes by using the /Graph Type Features Horizontal command. See the section "Using /Graph Type Features Options" in this chapter. 1-2-3 provides tick marks for both axes. The program also scales the numbers on the y-axis, based on the minimum and maximum figures included in the plotted data range(s).

Every point plotted on a graph has a unique *x,y* location. The *x* represents the horizontal position, corresponding to the category associated with the data point (for example, Gross Sales, Expenses, or January). The *y* represents the vertical position, corresponding to the second value associated with the data point (for example, Dollars or Percent Profit). In figure 10.2, for example, the *x* variable is Month, and the *y* variable is a dollar value.

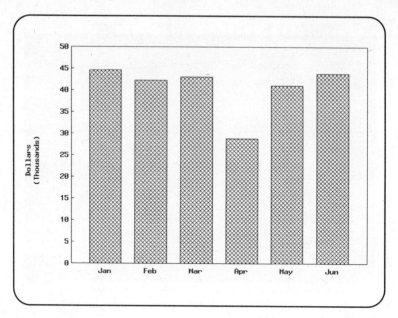

Fig. 10.2. A basic bar graph in which the x *variable is Month, and the* y *variable is a dollar value.*

The intersection of the y-axis and the x-axis is the *origin*. Notice that the origin of the axes in figure 10.2 is zero for *x* and *y* (0,0). Although graphs can be plotted with a nonzero origin, use a zero origin in your graphs to minimize misinterpretation of results and to make graphs easier to compare. Later in this chapter, you learn how to change the upper and lower limits of the scale initially set by 1-2-3.

Creating Simple Graphs

To create a graph, you first must load 1-2-3 and retrieve the file that contains the data you want to graph. Many of the examples in this chapter are based on the Sales Data worksheet shown in figure 10.3.

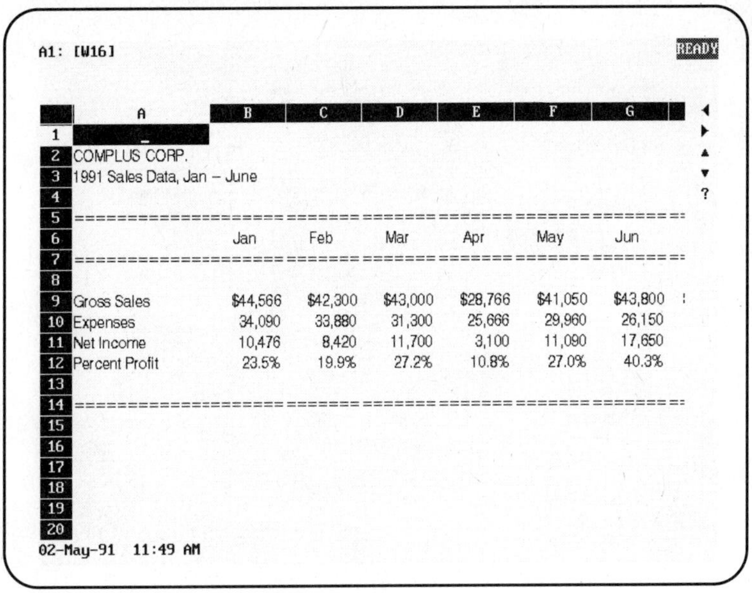

A1: [W16]   READY

	A	B	C	D	E	F	G	
1								
2	COMPLUS CORP.							
3	1991 Sales Data, Jan – June							
4								
5	========= ======== ======== ======= ======= ======= ======= ======== ==							
6		Jan	Feb	Mar	Apr	May	Jun	
7	========= ======== ======== ======= ======= ======= ======= ======== ==							
8								
9	Gross Sales	$44,566	$42,300	$43,000	$28,766	$41,050	$43,800	!
10	Expenses	34,090	33,880	31,300	25,666	29,960	26,150	
11	Net Income	10,476	8,420	11,700	3,100	11,090	17,650	
12	Percent Profit	23.5%	19.9%	27.2%	10.8%	27.0%	40.3%	
13								
14	========= ======== ======== ======= ======= ======= ======= ======== ==							
15								
16								
17								
18								
19								
20								

02-May-91 11:49 AM

Fig. 10.3. *A sample sales data worksheet.*

To graph information from the Sales Data worksheet, you need to know which numeric data you can plot and which data (numeric or label) you can use to enhance the graph. In figure 10.3, time period labels are listed across row 6. Category labels are located in column A. The numeric entries in rows 9 and 10 and the formula results in rows 11 and 12 are suitable for graphing as data points.

To begin the graphing process, select /Graph from the 1-2-3 command menu. This action displays the following menu:

Type **X A B C D E F R**eset **V**iew **S**ave **O**ptions **N**ame **G**roup **Q**uit

When you select /Graph, the Graph Settings dialog box is displayed (see fig. 10.4). The Graph Settings dialog box displays a full screen of information identifying the type of graph, ranges, orientation, and position of a graph's zero line (x- or y-axis). The dialog box also shows information about display settings such as grid lines, frame, and color.

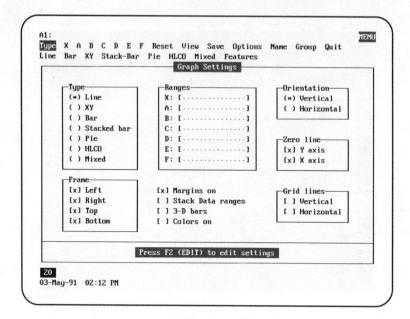

Fig. 10.4. The Graph Settings dialog box.

Only two items from the main /**Graph** menu are required. You must indicate which **Type** of graph you want, unless you are using **Line**, which is the default. You also must set one of the ranges between A and F from the choices **X**, **A**, **B**, **C**, **D**, **E**, and **F**. After you have specified the two required items, you can select **View** to display the graph.

Labels along the x-axis (the horizontal axis) use the range **X**. Units of time (for example, months or years) usually are displayed on this axis. Data ranges **A**, **B**, **C**, **D**, **E**, and **F** are plotted along the y-axis (the vertical axis). You can plot as many as six sets of data. The result is a basic graph that depicts relationships between numbers or trends across time.

Look at the sample worksheet in figure 10.3. To create a basic graph, suitable for a quick on-screen look at the data, issue the following command sequences. After each range specification (lines 2 and 3), press Enter.

> /**Graph Type Bar**
>
> **A B9..G9** (Gross Sales, data range A)
>
> **B B10..G10** (Expenses, data range B)
>
> **View**

The resulting graph is shown in figure 10.5. In this graph, the six sets of bars represent monthly data. The bars are graphed in order from left to right, starting with the January data. Within each set of bars, the left-hand bar represents the Gross Sales figure, and the right-hand bar represents the corresponding Expenses figure. This minimal graph shows a fairly steady sales rate over the six-month period, except for the fourth month, which has significantly lower sales. Expenses remain relatively constant.

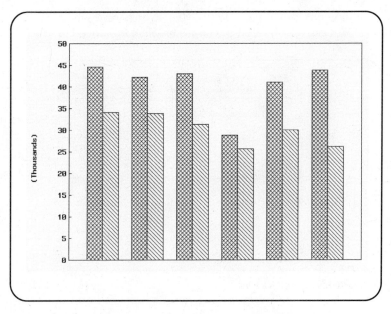

Fig. 10.5. A basic bar graph.

The graph in figure 10.5 is not, however, something you want to show to your boss. 1-2-3 offers numerous options that enable you to improve the appearance of your graphs and produce final-quality output suitable for business presentations. To convert the graph in figure 10.5 to presentation quality, press any key to return to the Graph menu. Then select the following commands from the /Graph menu. (These options are explained in detail later in this chapter.)

Reminder:
To return to the Graph menu from the View option, press any key.

> **X   B6..G6** (press Enter)
>
> **Options Titles First COMPLUS CORP.** (press Enter)
>
> **Titles Second 1991 Sales Data, Jan - June** (press Enter)
>
> **Titles X-Axis East Coast Operations** (press Enter)
>
> **Titles Y-Axis Dollars** (press Enter)
>
> **Legend A Gross Sales** (press Enter)

> **Legend B Expenses** (press Enter)
>
> **Grid Horizontal**
>
> **Scale Y-Scale Format Currency 0** (press Enter)
>
> **Quit Quit View**

The resulting graph is shown in figure 10.6. Even people who are unfamiliar with the data can understand the contents of an enhanced graph.

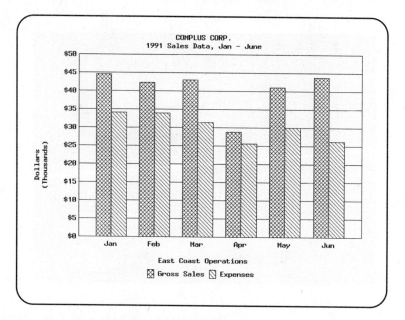

Fig. 10.6. The enhanced presentation-quality graph.

Selecting a Graph Type

Selecting one of the seven available graph types is easy. When you select Type from the /Graph menu, the following menu appears:

> **Line Bar XY Stack-Bar Pie HLCO Mixed Features**

By selecting one of the first seven options (graph types), you specify that graph type and restore the /Graph menu to the control panel. If you select Features, you access another menu with options for enhancing graphs (discussed later in this chapter).

Of the seven 1-2-3 graph types, all but the pie graph display x- and y-axes. The line, bar, stacked-bar, HLCO (high-low-close-open), and mixed graphs display numbers (centered on the tick marks) along the y-axis. The x-axis of these graph types can display user-defined labels centered on the tick marks. The XY graph displays numbers on both axes.

Specifying Data Ranges

You cannot type data directly on a 1-2-3 graph, except through Wysiwyg. The data to be graphed must be present in the current worksheet—as values or as the result of formula calculations. Do not confuse the process of specifying data points, which are always numeric, with that of typing descriptions, such as titles. (The process for typing descriptions is illustrated later in this chapter.)

You must specify which data in the currently displayed worksheet should be graphed. A graph data range consists of one or more rectangular ranges of numbers. If the range contains labels or blank cells, these cells are given a value of zero. If the data is in adjacent rows or columns, you can use 1-2-3's automatic graph feature (/**Graph Group**—discussed later in this section) to assign the data ranges. Otherwise, you must assign the data ranges by entering coordinates or highlighting the range.

Reminder:
Specify worksheet data to be graphed by entering or highlighting data ranges.

To specify a graph data range, first select **A**, **B**, **C**, **D**, **E**, or **F** from the /**Graph** menu and then specify the range just as you do any other 1-2-3 range—by entering cell addresses or a range name or by using the mouse or direction keys in POINT mode.

The **X** data range option is used for numeric data only with XY graphs. For the other graph types, this option can be used to specify x-axis labels.

Before you start building a graph, read the following general statements about the choice(s) for each graph type:

Graph type	*Option(s)*
Line	Enter as many as six sets of data in ranges **A**, **B**, **C**, **D**, **E**, and **F**. 1-2-3 creates one graph line for each range; each point on a line represents one value in the range. The data points in each data range are marked by a unique symbol and/or color when graphed (see table 10.1).

Graph type	Option(s)
Bar	Enter as many as six data ranges: **A**, **B**, **C**, **D**, **E**, and **F**. 1-2-3 creates one set of bars for each range; each bar in a set represents one value in the range. The bars for multiple data ranges appear within each x-axis group on the graph in alphabetical order from left to right. On a monochrome monitor, the bars for each data range are displayed with a unique cross-hatching. On a color monitor, the default display is the same as that on a monochrome monitor. When you select **/Graph Options Color**, the bars are displayed with a unique color (limited by the maximum number of colors possible on your hardware). Cross-hatching and screen colors are summarized in table 10.1.
XY	Choose **X** from the **/Graph** menu and select the data range that contains the independent variable (the x-axis variable). Enter as many as six dependent variable ranges (**A**, **B**, **C**, **D**, **E**, and **F**). 1-2-3 creates one set of points for each dependent variable range. The data points for each data range are marked by a unique symbol when graphed. The symbols are the same as the Line symbols shown in table 10.1.
Stack-Bar	Follow the bar graph instructions. In a stacked-bar graph, multiple data ranges are stacked on top of each other, with the **A** range on the bottom.
Pie	Enter only one data series by selecting **A** from the **/Graph** menu. For each value in the **A** range, 1-2-3 creates a pie slice. The **X** range describes each pie slice. (To crosshatch and explode slices of the pie, select a **B** range, as explained later in this chapter.)
HLCO	The **A**, **B**, **C**, and **D** ranges respectively specify the high, low, closing, and opening values of the data being tracked. The **E** range is used for the bars in the lower portion of the graph, and the **F** range is used for the single graph line. (See the section on HLCO graphs later in this chapter.)

Graph type	Option(s)
Mixed	Mixed graphs contain a bar graph and a line graph. The **A**, **B**, and **C** ranges are used for the bar portion of the graph, and the **D**, **E**, and **F** ranges are used for the line portion.

As you build your graphs, refer to the preceding comments about graph types and to the information in table 10.1.

Table 10.1
Graph Symbols, Cross-Hatching, and Colors

Data Range	Line Graph Symbols	Bar Graph Cross-hatching	On-Screen Color* Text Mode	Wysiwyg Graphics Mode
A	□	▨	Yellow	Blue
B	+	▨	Magenta	Green
C	◇	▨	Blue	Light Blue
D	△	▨	Red	Red
E	×	▨	Light Blue	Magenta
F	▽	▨	Green	Yellow

The symbols, cross-hatching, and color combinations in this table are those displayed on a VGA monitor (other monitors may display different results).

This table shows each data range with the corresponding default assignments for line symbols, bar cross-hatching, and color.

Specifying Data Ranges with /Graph Group

When your data ranges for 1-2-3 graphs are in adjacent worksheet rows or columns, you can use /Graph Group to save a significant number of keystrokes. The **Group** option enables you to specify all graph data ranges, **X** and **A** through **F**, in one operation. The procedure is as follows:

1. Select /Graph Group.

2. Indicate the rectangular range to be divided into data ranges. You can enter cell addresses and a range name or use the mouse or direction keys in POINT mode. This range should not include the data range descriptions.

Reminder:
Use /Graph Group to save keystrokes when the X and A-F data ranges are in adjacent rows or columns.

Note: If you have prespecified the range, you need to press Enter after selecting /Graph Group.

3. Select **Columnwise** or **Rowwise** to indicate whether the data ranges are located in columns or rows.

Consider the small worksheet shown in figure 10.7. To graph this data as rows in a bar graph, you first set **Type** to **Bar**. In this figure, /Graph Group has been selected, and POINT mode is being used to indicate the range B2..D5. When prompted, choose **Rowwise** followed by **View**, and the graph in figure 10.8 appears.

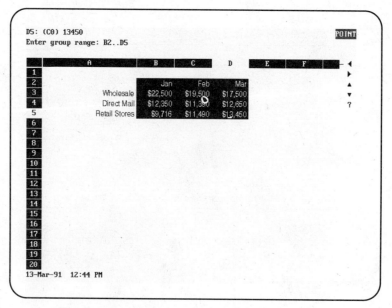

Fig. 10.7. A /Graph Group range selected for graphing.

The following data range assignments are made by 1-2-3:

  X B2..D2

  A B3..D3

  B B4..D4

  C B5..D5

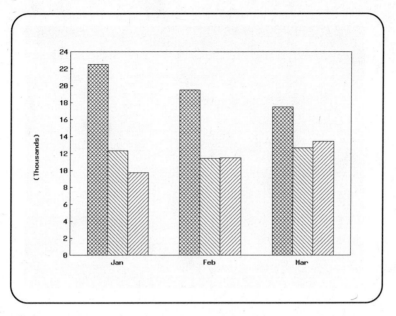

Fig. 10.8. *A graph created from the data in figure 10.7, with Rowwise orientation.*

You can graph the same data as columns with the following command sequence:

> **Group A3..D5**
>
> **Columnwise**
>
> **View**

The result is shown in figure 10.9.

Constructing the Default Line Graph

After you specify the type of graph you want for your data and the location of that data, producing a graph is easy. By using the sales data shown in figure 10.10, you easily can create a line graph of the January through June amounts.

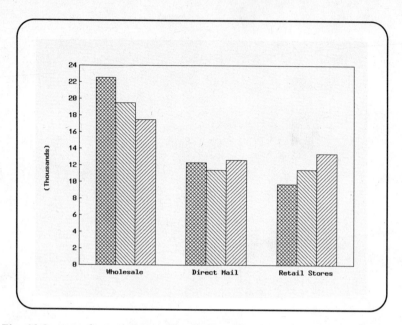

Fig. 10.9. *A graph created from the data in figure 10.8, with Columnwise orientation.*

A1: [W16]   READY

	A	B	C	D	E	F	G
1							
2	COMPLUS CORP.						
3	1991 Sales Data, Jan – June						
4							
5	==========	=======	=======	=======	=======	=======	==
6		Jan	Feb	Mar	Apr	May	Jun
7	==========	=======	=======	=======	=======	=======	==
8							
9	Gross Sales	$44,566	$42,300	$43,000	$28,766	$41,050	$43,800
10	Expenses	34,090	33,880	31,300	25,666	29,960	26,150
11	Net Income	10,476	8,420	11,700	3,100	11,090	17,650
12	Percent Profit	23.5%	19.9%	27.2%	10.8%	27.0%	40.3%
13							
14	==========	=======	=======	=======	=======	=======	==
15							
16							
17							
18							
19							
20							

02-May-91 11:49 AM

Fig. 10.10. *A sample sales data worksheet.*

From 1-2-3's command menu, select /Graph. Ordinarily, the next step is to select **Type**. If you want to create a line graph, however, you don't have to make a selection, because **Line** is the default graph type.

The next step is to specify the data range(s). To enter the first data range (the Gross Sales amounts in row 9), choose **A** from the /Graph menu and then respond to the prompt by typing **B9..G9**. Alternatively, you can use the mouse or direction keys in POINT mode to specify the range or enter the range name if one has been assigned. You also can enter the data range on the **Graph Settings** dialog box by using the direction keys or mouse to highlight the **A** option under **Ranges** and typing the cell references for the range.

By specifying the type of graph and the location of data to plot, you have completed the minimum requirements for creating a graph. If you choose **View**, you see a graph similar to the one shown in figure 10.11.

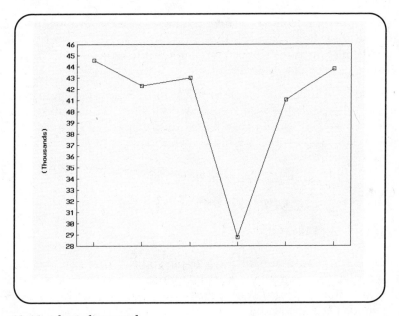

Fig. 10.11. *A basic line graph.*

Although *you* know what this graph represents, the graph means little to anyone else. The six data points corresponding to the January through June figures have been plotted, but the points have not been labeled to indicate what they represent, nor have the graph axes been labeled (the Thousands indicator appears on the y-axis). Notice also that the y-axis origin on this initial graph is not zero, which makes the April decrease seem larger than it really is. The text that follows teaches you how to enhance this basic graph.

Enhancing the Appearance of a Basic Graph

Many of 1-2-3's graph features apply equally to all seven graph types. Most of the 1-2-3 features for enhancing a graph's appearance are accessed through **Options** on the /Graph menu. When you select /Graph **Options**, the following menu appears:

Legend Format Titles Grid Scale Color B&W Data-Labels Quit

As you work with this menu to add enhancements to your graphs, check the results frequently. To see the most recent version of your graph, press F10 (Graph); you do not need to return to the main /Graph menu to select View. Press any key to exit the graph display and restore the /Graph menu to the screen.

To display the graph you are changing alongside, below, or above the graph data, use the **:Graph** command from the Wysiwyg menu. After you have entered data ranges to create a graph, follow the directions in Chapter 11 for adding a graph to your worksheet.

After you have added the graph to your worksheet, you can return to the /Graph **Options** menu, enhance the graph, and then select **:Graph Compute** to display the new elements added to your graph. See Chapter 11 for a complete discussion of displaying graphs within your worksheet.

Adding Descriptive Labels and Numbers

To add descriptive information to a graph, you use the **Titles**, **Data-Labels**, and **Legend** options from the /Graph **Options** menu. The specific settings for these options are displayed in the Graph Legends and Titles dialog box (see fig. 10.12). For all graph types except XY, you can use the **X** data range option. You also can add descriptive information to a graph by using the **:Graph Edit** options from the Wysiwyg menu. See Chapter 11 for a complete discussion of the **:Graph Edit** features. The text that follows discusses options from the /Graph **Options** menu.

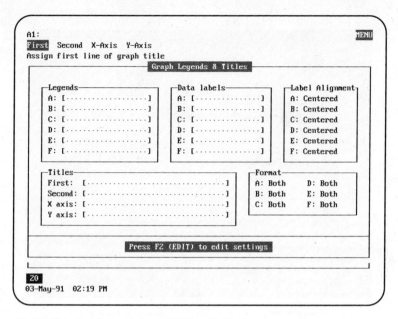

Fig. 10.12. *The Graph Legends and Titles dialog box.*

Using the Titles Option

If you select /Graph Options Titles, the following options are displayed in the control panel:

First Second **X-Axis Y-Axis**

The **First** and **Second** options are used to enter titles to be centered above the graph. The first title is in larger type above the second title. After selecting **First** or **Second** from the /Graph Options Titles menu, you can type the desired title in response to the prompt or enter a backslash followed by the address of the worksheet cell containing a label, number, or formula to be used as the title. When you use a backslash to display formula data in a title, the formula information is updated in the graph every time the worksheet formula is recalculated.

The **X-Axis** and **Y-Axis** options are for labeling the graph axes. **X-Axis** centers a horizontal label below the x-axis. **Y-Axis** places a vertical label just to the left of the y-axis. You can type the labels or enter a cell address or range name preceded by a backslash.

Figure 10.13 shows the positions of the various titles as they appear on a graph.

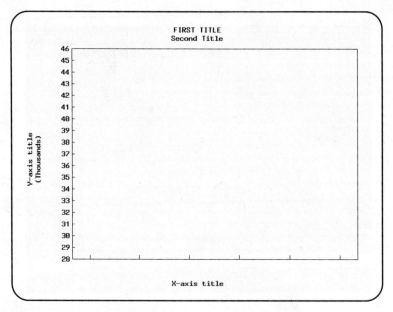

***Fig. 10.13.** Graph positions of the four types of titles.*

Reminder:
You can enter up to four titles by using cell references or typing new descriptions.

To enhance the basic line graph of the sales data amounts shown in figure 10.8, you can enter four titles by using cell references for two of the titles and by typing new descriptions for the others.

Select /**Graph Options Titles First**. When 1-2-3 prompts you for a title, type **A2** to reference the cell that contains COMPLUS CORP. (the first title) and press Enter. The /**Graph Options** menu (not the Titles menu) reappears. Select **Titles Second**, type **A3**, and press enter to use the label in cell A3 as the second title centered above the graph.

To label the x-axis, select **Titles X-Axis**, type **MONTH**, and press Enter. To Enter the fourth title (for the y-axis), select **Titles Y-Axis**, type **Dollars**, and press Enter. Then check the graph by pressing F10 (Graph). Your graph should look like the enhanced graph shown in figure 10.14.

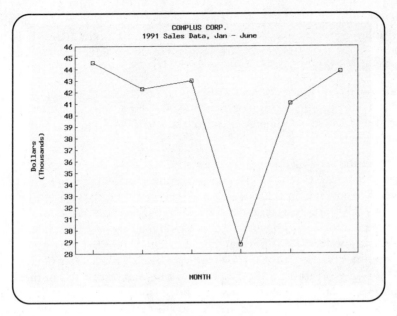

Fig. 10.14. *The line graph enhanced with titles.*

To edit a title, use the command sequence you used for creating the title. The existing text, cell reference, or range name appears in the control panel, ready for editing; to eliminate the title, press Esc and then Enter.

Entering Data Labels within a Graph

You may want to use labels on the graph to explain each of the data points. You can add these labels by selecting Data-Labels from the /Graph Options menu and then selecting options from the following menu:

   A B C D E F Group Quit

From this menu, select the data range to which you are assigning data labels. Select Group if the data labels for multiple ranges are in adjacent columns or rows. You cannot type the data labels directly, except with Wysiwyg; instead, you need to specify a worksheet range that contains the labels. You can specify the range by typing cell addresses, by using POINT mode, or by entering a range name. After you specify the data label range, the following menu appears:

   Center Left Above Right Below

Cue:
Use /Graph Options Data-Labels to place descriptive labels within a graph.

The selection you make from this menu determines where each data label is displayed in relation to the corresponding data point. The labels (or values) in the data label range are assigned to data points in the order that the labels appear in the worksheet.

Continue to enhance your sample line graph by entering as data labels the Jan-Jun headings from row 6 of the worksheet. First, select /**Graph Options Data-Labels** and then select **A** to assign labels to the **A** range (the only range on the graph).

To enter the six abbreviated monthly headings from the worksheet, highlight or type **B6..G6** in response to the prompt for a label range and press Enter. Then to specify a position for the labels, select **Above** from the next menu. Each set of data labels can have only one position. For example, you cannot position one cell within a data-label range above its associated data point and another cell within that same data-label range below its associated data point. You can, however, display data labels for up to six data ranges and vary the position of the labels from one data range to another. For example, the labels for the A range may be positioned above the data points and the labels for the B range may be positioned below the data points.

Press F10 (Graph) to display the graph on-screen. Your graph should appear similar to the one shown in figure 10.15.

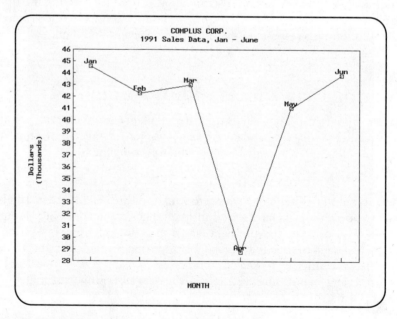

Fig. 10.15. *The line graph with data labels added.*

If you graph more than one data series, attach the data labels to the data range that includes the largest numeric values. Then select **Above** to position the data labels above the data points. These steps place the data labels as high as possible in the graph, where they do not obscure the data points.

You also can use the data label text as the plotted points, by following these steps:

1. Select **/Graph Options Format A Neither**, which results in neither lines nor symbols being plotted for the **A** data range.

2. Select **Quit** to return to the **/Graph Options** menu.

3. Select **Data-Labels A Center** to center the labels over the positions where the data points would have appeared.

By using this technique with a dummy data range, you can place labels anywhere on the graph. (Wysiwyg offers a more direct way to place text on your graphs; see Chapter 11 for details.)

To edit the range or position of the data labels, use the same command sequence you used to create the labels. Enter a different data-label range or specify a different position.

To remove data labels from a data range, follow the same steps used when first creating the labels, but this time specify an empty cell as the data-label range. You cannot eliminate the existing range by pressing Esc, as you did to eliminate an unwanted title. You also can remove data labels by resetting the data range with **/Graph Reset Options**. Be careful, because this method removes the data labels, the data range, and any other associated options.

Reminder:
You cannot use Data-Labels with a pie graph.
Caution:
/Graph Reset Options clears all settings for graph options.

Entering Labels below the X-Axis

Instead of placing descriptive information within a graph, you may prefer to enter label information along the x-axis. With all graph types except pie and XY, the /Graph menu's **X** option can be used to position labels below the x-axis.

To enter the January through June labels from the worksheet in figure 10.3 below the x-axis, select **/Graph X** and enter the range that contains the data labels (**B6..G6**). Then select **View**. Your graph should appear as in figure 10.16. Compare this graph to the graph in figure 10.15.

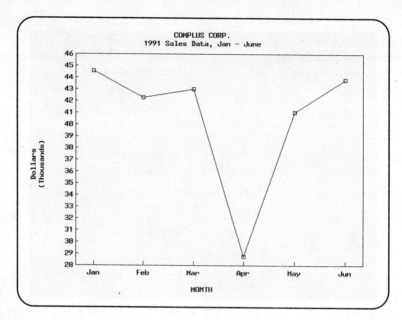

Fig. 10.16. The line graph with an X range specified.

The cells you specify for the **X** range or for a data-label range can contain labels or values. If you use values, they are displayed on the graph in the same format as in the worksheet.

Leave the **X** labels in place for now. To eliminate the x-axis labels later, select /Graph **Reset X**.

Using the Legend Option

A *legend* is a key or label on the graph that explains the meaning of one or more symbols, colors, or hatch patterns. Legends are particularly useful on graphs that include multiple data ranges.

When a graph contains more than one data range, you need to distinguish between the different ranges. If you are using a color monitor and select /Graph **Options Color**, 1-2-3 differentiates data ranges with color. If the **B&W** (black and white) option is in effect, data ranges are marked with different symbols in line graphs (unless you select /Graph **Options Format Lines**) and with different hatching patterns in bar-type graphs. (Refer to table 10.1 for a summary of the assignments specific to each data range.)

To add legends to a graph, select /**Graph Options Legend**. The following menu appears:

A B C D E F Range

Select the data range to which you are assigning a legend. In response to the prompt, type the text for the legend or enter a backslash followed by the address or range name of the worksheet cell containing the legend text. Select **Range** to specify a worksheet range containing legend text for all the data ranges. Using a range name for the cell containing the legend text is preferable because this method ensures that the legend does not change if the cell data moves.

To see the use of legends, you can add a second data range to the Sales Data line graph and then add legends to identify the two data ranges. Suppose that you want the graph to reflect two items: Gross Sales and Expenses.

To add the second data range, select /**Graph**, choose **B**, and enter the range **B10..G10** for the Expenses data. Next, select **Options Legend**, choose **A** to specify the legend for the first data range and enter **Gross Sales**. You also can reference the worksheet cell by typing **A9**. The program returns to the /**Graph Options** menu. To specify the legend for the second data range, again select **Legend**, choose **B**, and enter **Expenses** or **A10**. Finally, press F10 (Graph) to display the graph. The modified graph should appear similar to the one shown in figure 10.17.

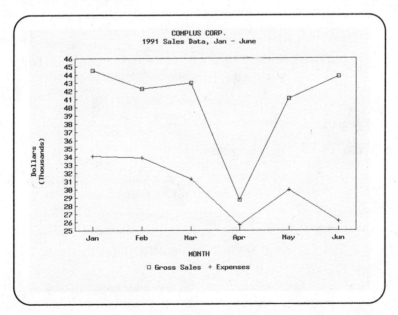

Fig. 10.17. A graph with two data ranges and a legend.

To edit a legend, use the same command sequence you used to create the legend. The existing text, cell reference, or range name appears in the control panel, ready for you to edit. To eliminate a legend, press Esc and then Enter.

Legends are appropriate only for graphs with two or more data series. You cannot use the Legend option for pie graphs, which have only one data series.

Altering the Default Graph Display

The graph enhancements discussed so far involve making additions to a basic, simple graph. Other enhancements are possible by modifying the default settings 1-2-3 uses to create a simple graph. In this section, you learn to enhance the basic line graph by changing some of 1-2-3's defaults.

Selecting the Format for Data in Graphs

The /Graph Options Format command enables you to specify the format of the lines in line, XY, mixed, and HLCO graphs. (The option affects only the line portions of mixed and HLCO graphs.) When you select /Graph Options Format, the following menu appears:

Graph **A B C D E F** Quit

Select the data range whose format you want to specify or select Graph to set the format for all data ranges. The following menu appears:

Lines Symbols Both Neither Area

These commands have the following effects:

Selection	Description
Lines	The data points are connected by lines, but no symbols are displayed.
Symbols	A symbol is displayed at each data point, but the symbols are not connected by lines.
Both	Symbols and connecting lines are displayed. This is the default setting.
Neither	Neither symbols nor lines are displayed. (This option is used with centered data labels.)

Selection	Description
Area	The space between the indicated line and the line below it (or the x-axis) is filled with a color or hatch pattern. If **Area** format is specified for more than one data range, the lines are stacked. Negative values in the line are treated as zeros, and the **Area** option does not display negative values.

Experiment with these settings to see the effect each creates. For example, selecting /**Graph Options Format Graph Area** results in the sample graph shown in figure 10.18.

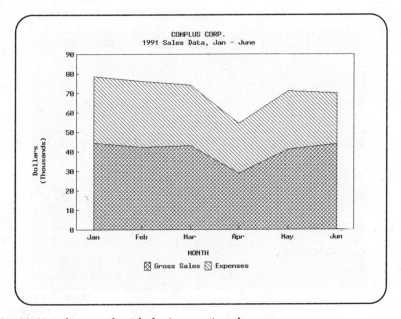

Fig. 10.18. *A line graph with the Area option chosen.*

To return your graph to the standard format showing lines and symbols, select /**Graph Options Format Graph**.

Setting a Background Grid

Grid lines can help make your data-point values easier to read. 1-2-3 enables you to specify horizontal and /or vertical grid lines for all graph types except pie graphs. Horizontal grid lines are shown in figure 10.19.

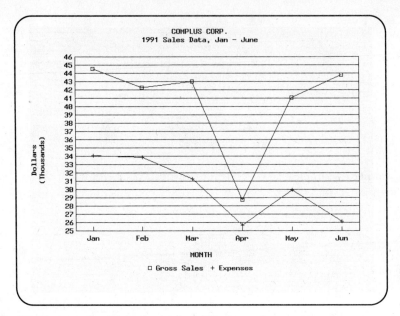

Fig. 10.19. A graph with horizontal grid lines.

Selecting **/Graph Options Grid** produces the following menu:

Horizontal Vertical Both Clear

The options on this menu have the following effects:

Selection	Description
Horizontal	Draws a series of horizontal lines across the graph, spaced according to the tick marks on the y-axis
Vertical	Draws a series of vertical lines across the graph, spaced according to the tick marks on the x-axis
Both	Draws horizontal and vertical lines
Clear	Clears all grid lines from the graph

To add horizontal lines to the sample graph, select **/Graph Options Grid Horizontal** and press F10 (Graph). The graph should look like the one shown in figure 10.19.

Experiment with different grids, repeating the command sequence and specifying other options. Besides the types of grids you can display with /Graph Options Grid, you can create a grid by using the Wysiwyg **:F**ormat Lines or **:G**raph Edit commands (see Chapter 11). To eliminate a grid display, select /Graph Options Grid Clear.

Reminder:
Use the Clear option to remove a grid.

Modifying the Graph Axes

The Scale option takes you to a series of menus that enable you to control various aspects of how the graph's axes are displayed. The Scale option affects all graph types except pie graphs. When you select /Graph Options Scale, the following menu appears:

Reminder:
Scale options do not apply to pie graphs.

> **Y**-Scale **X**-Scale **Skip**

The specific settings for all three options are displayed in the Graph Scale Settings dialog box (see fig. 10.20). If you choose Skip, you can specify that you want the graph to display only every *n*th data point in the **X** range. The *n* variable can range from 0 to 8192, although you usually use low values such as 2 or 5.

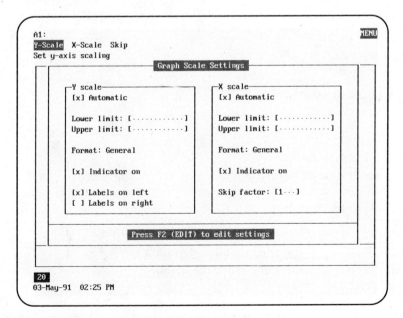

Fig. 10.20. *The Graph Scale Settings dialog box.*

Cue:
Use /Graph Options Scale Skip when you have too many x-axis values to display together.

If you select /**Graph Options Scale Skip** and enter a value of 2, the resulting graph looks similar to the one shown in figure 10.21. Notice that only January, March, and May are displayed on the x-axis scale; February, April, and June have been skipped. In this case, using **Skip** does not improve the graph's appearance. If label text is short and you don't have too many data points, 1-2-3 can fit text neatly on one horizontal line or stagger labels on two horizontal lines. If many of the data points and labels are very long, however, they look too crowded. Using **Skip** then makes the x-axis more legible.

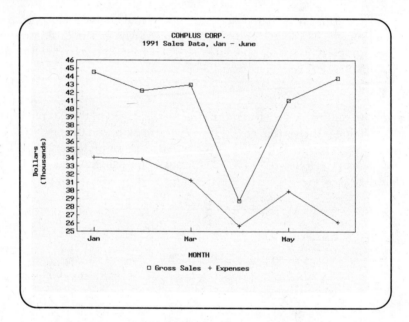

Fig. 10.21. The graph with Skip set to 2.

The other two options on this menu are for selecting which axis to change: the y-axis or the x-axis. When you select the **Y-Scale** option, the following menu is displayed:

> **Automatic Manual Lower Upper Format Indicator Display Quit**

When you select the **X-Scale** option, all options but the **Display** option are available, as indicated in the following menu:

> **Automatic Manual Lower Upper Format Indicator Quit**

Display is available with the **Y-Scale** option so that you can display y-axis labels on the left side of the graph, right side, both sides, or neither side.

Remember that any changes made from this menu apply only to the specific graph axis selected in the preceding step.

Minimum and Maximum Axis Values

When you create a graph with 1-2-3, the program sets the scale, or minimum-maximum range, of the y-axis based on the smallest and largest numbers in the data range(s) plotted. For XY graphs, 1-2-3 also establishes the x-axis scale based on minimum and maximum values in the **X** data range.

To set your own scale, first select **Manual** from the /**Graph** Options [**Y-Scale**, **X**-Scale] menu, choose **Lower**, and enter the minimum axis value. Finally, select **Upper** and enter the maximum axis value. Selecting **Automatic** returns 1-2-3 to the default automatic scaling.

Although you can change the minimum and maximum axis values, you cannot determine the size of the tick mark increment; 1-2-3 sets this increment. Also, you can set an axis range too small to include all the data points. If the range is too small, some data points are not plotted. 1-2-3 does not warn you when this happens.

To change the y-axis origin on the sample graph, select /**Graph** **O**ptions **G**rid **C**lear to get rid of the grid lines (if you have not done so already). Next, select **S**cale **Y**-Scale **M**anual. Select **L**ower, enter **0**, select **U**pper, and enter **50000**. Finally, press F10 (Graph) to display the graph shown in figure 10.22.

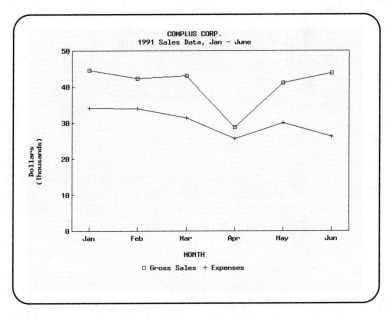

***Fig. 10.22.** The graph with y-axis scale set from 0 to 50000.*

Notice how the perspective of the graph has changed. Earlier, with automatic scaling, the y-axis range was from 25000 to 46000. The April dip in sales appeared more severe than it actually was. By setting the scale, so that the y-axis origin is at 0, you change the visual impression of the graph to more accurately reflect the actual figures.

Axis Number Format

1-2-3 defaults to General format for displaying the axis scale values; the same format is the default for the screen display of worksheet values. You can display axis scale values in any of 1-2-3's numeric formats. Select Format from the /Graph Options Scale [Y-Scale, X-Scale] menu, and the following menu appears:

Fixed Sci Currency , General +/– Percent Date Text Hidden

Making a format choice is like selecting a format for a worksheet range with /Range Format. This process includes specifying the number of decimal places and the particular format desired. Note that /Graph Options Scale [Y, X] Format differs from /Graph Options Format, which controls the way lines are displayed.

For the sample graph, a currency format is appropriate for the y-axis. Select /Graph Options Scale Y-Scale Format Currency and enter 0 for the number of decimal places. Pressing F10 (Graph) displays the graph as shown in figure 10.23.

Axis Scale Indicator

When axis scale values are a multiple of 10, 1-2-3 displays a scale indicator, such as Thousands or Millions, between the y-axis and the y-axis title. You can suppress display of the scale indicator. After selecting Indicator from the /Graph Options Scale [Y, X] menu, you have two choices. No suppresses display of the scale indicator. Yes displays the appropriate indicator.

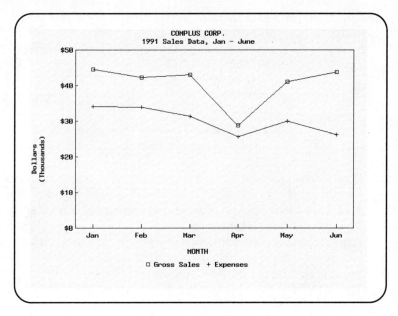

Fig. 10.23. The graph with y-axis scale values in Currency format.

Using /Graph Type Features Options

The Features option, the last option available on the /Graph Type menu, provides five different ways to change the appearance of your graph. Selecting /Graph Type Features results in the following menu:

    Vertical   Horizontal   Stacked   Frame   3D-Effect   Quit

These options have the following effects:

Selection	Description
Vertical	Displays the graph upright (the default setting)
Horizontal	Reverses the x- and y-axes (An example is given in the section of this chapter that discusses bar graphs.)
Stacked	Can be used with line, bar, mixed, and XY graphs that have two or more data ranges; all the values in the data range are stacked on top of each other rather than being plotted relative to the x-axis.

Selection	Description
Frame	Enables you to frame all sides, no sides, or three sides of your graph; Frame also controls the display of the x-axis or y-axis line and controls the size of margins surrounding the graph.
3D-Effect	Enables you to create a three-dimensional display of bar and stacked-bar graphs

Figure 10.24 shows an example of a graph created without the Stacked option. The graph shows Gross Sales plotted as range **A** and Expenses plotted as range **B**, with Stacked (the default) turned off. After displaying this graph, return to the /Graph menu, select Type Features Stacked Yes, and redisplay the graph. The graph then should appear as shown in figure 10.25. Note that the **B** range, Expenses, is stacked on, or added to, the **A** range. Continue to enhance the graph by selecting **Options Format Graph Area**. The result is shown in figure 10.26.

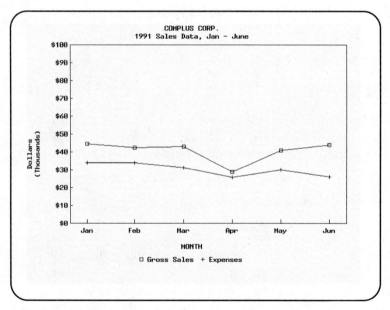

Fig. 10.24. *Gross Sales and Expenses plotted on a nonstacked graph.*

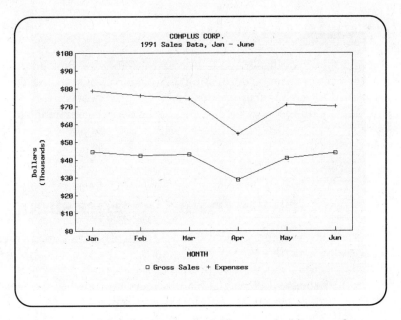

Fig. 10.25. *Gross Sales and Expenses plotted as a stacked line graph.*

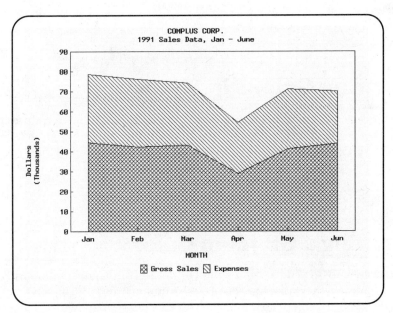

Fig. 10.26. *Using /Graph Options Format Graph Area to fill a stacked line graph.*

Viewing Graphs

Several options are available in 1-2-3 Release 2.3 for viewing a graph on-screen. You can view a graph by pressing F10 (Graph) or by selecting /Graph View so that a full-screen version of the graph is displayed, or you can display a graph directly on the worksheet by using the :Graph commands in the Wysiwyg menu. You also can control whether the graph is displayed in black-and-white or in color.

Viewing Graphs from the Worksheet

With a worksheet on-screen, you can view a graph in two ways. You can press Graph (F10) or issue the /Graph View command. If a graph is currently defined, 1-2-3 clears the screen and displays the graph. If no graph is defined, 1-2-3 beeps and displays a blank screen. Pressing Esc or any key except Shift, Ctrl, or Alt returns your worksheet to the screen.

Cue:
Use Graph (F10) to toggle between graph display and worksheet display.

After you have defined a graph, you can use Graph (F10) to alternate quickly between the worksheet and the graph. This technique can be used for what-if scenarios; as you modify worksheet data, you quickly can see the effects of the changes graphically.

Viewing Graphs in Wysiwyg

Wysiwyg offers yet another way to view your graphs. After defining the graph with 1-2-3's /Graph commands, you can insert the graph into a worksheet range with Wysiwyg's :Graph Add command. This command enables you to simultaneously view your worksheet data and its accompanying graph. See Chapter 11 for details.

Viewing a Graph in Color

The Color and B&W (black-and-white) options of the /Graph Options menu determine whether graphs are displayed in monochrome or color. For color display, you need a color monitor; you can select B&W with a color or monochrome monitor.

When a graph is displayed in color, each data range is displayed in a different color. When displayed in monochrome, data ranges are differentiated by symbols or cross-hatching patterns. Some of 1-2-3's cross-hatching patterns are shown in the bar graph in figure 10.27.

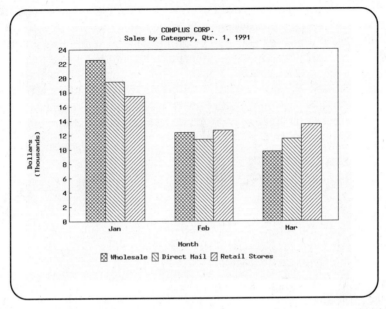

Fig. 10.27. *Some of 1-2-3's cross-hatching patterns.*

The cross-hatching or colors assigned to data ranges **A**, **B**, **C**, **D**, **E**, and **F** do not apply to pie graphs. Pie graphs, unlike other types of graphs, have only one possible data range—**A**. Coding specified for the **B** data range determines the color or cross-hatching assigned to each section of the pie. (See the discussion on pie graphs later in this chapter.)

You can view (but not print) your graphs in color. Restore the **B&W** setting by selecting **/Graph Options B&W** before you save the graph to be printed. Otherwise, the data ranges in the graph print in solid black. To print your graph in color and retain the hatching patterns, save the graph in black and white and then set the graph's colors by using the Range-Colors option in the PrintGraph program. See "Choosing Colors" later in this chapter.

Saving Graphs and Graph Settings

You have learned how to create a basic graph and how to use options to enhance the display of that graph. This section shows you how to use the /Graph Save command to save the graph so that you can print the graph with the PrintGraph program or use the file with another program, such as Freelance Plus. With the /Graph Name command, you can save the settings for one or more graphs with the worksheet so that you can view or modify them later. Saving graph settings with /Graph Name also enables you to add graphs to the worksheet with the Wysiwyg :Graph Add command.

Saving Graphs on Disk for Printing

Suppose that you have constructed a graph you want to store for subsequent printing with the PrintGraph program or another graphics program. After verifying that the graph appears in the form you want to print, save the graph to a PIC file by using the /Graph Save command.

When you save a graph with /Graph Save, you then are prompted for the graph file name to save. You can use the cursor-movement keys to highlight an existing name or type a name as long as eight characters. 1-2-3 supplies the PIC extension. If a file by the same name exists in the current directory, a Cancel/Replace menu appears, similar to that which appears when you try to save a worksheet file under an existing name. To overwrite the contents of the existing file, select Replace. Otherwise, select Cancel.

If you have set up subdirectories for disk storage, you can store the graph to a subdirectory other than the current one without first having to issue a /File Directory command to change directories. To store the graph, select /Graph Save. Press Esc twice to remove existing directory information. Then type the name of the new subdirectory in which you want to store this particular graph, followed by the file name for the graph.

Remember the following points:

- /Graph Save stores only an image of the current graph, locking in all data and enhancements, for printing the graph with the PrintGraph program or another graphics program such as Freelance Plus. At print time you cannot access the print file to make changes.

- You cannot recall the graph to screen unless you have named the graph and saved the worksheet or unless the graph is the last active graph on the current worksheet. Naming graphs is described in the next section.

Saving Graph Settings

Although using 1-2-3 to construct a graph from existing data in a worksheet is easy, having to rebuild the graph when you want to print or display the graph on-screen can be tedious. Saved graphs can be recalled and modified only by using the :Graph menu in Wysiwyg and cannot be changed by options in the /Graph menu. You can, however, save and recall the settings for one or more graphs and use /Graph options to modify these settings. The settings are not saved in a separate file but are kept as part of the worksheet.

To save the current graph settings, issue the /Graph Name command to access the following menu:

Use Create Delete Reset Table

These commands perform the following actions:

Selection	Description
Use	Displays a list of named graphs; the one you select becomes the current graph.
Create	Saves the current graph setting under a specified name
Delete	Deletes a single named graph
Reset	Deletes *all* named graphs (Use caution with this option, as 1-2-3 does not enable you to verify this selection.)
Table	Creates a listing of all named graphs in the current worksheet

To use the Table option, move the cell pointer to the cell in which you want the listing to appear and press Enter. The listing occupies three columns. For each named graph, the listing gives the name, graph type, and the first graph title. This list overwrites any existing worksheet data.

Reminder:
Use Create before you reset or change settings for the next graph.

When designing multiple graphs, be sure to use the Create option before you reset or change any settings for the next graph. If you forget, you may end up changing the preceding graph's settings. If you want to save the graph name in your worksheet file, be sure to save the worksheet even if the actual data has not changed.

Resetting the Current Graph

Throughout this chapter, instructions for editing or removing options are given at the end of each new topic. These instructions are important because 1-2-3 continues to use an enhancement in the next version of the same graph, or in a new graph, unless you take specific actions to remove that enhancement. For example, you can build a series of different bar graphs by specifying the graph type (with the Type option) for only the first graph. For example, after you specified the titles in the sample Sales Data graph, you did not have to specify them again for the subsequent versions of the graph.

Reminder:
To speed up the process when making substantial changes in a graph, use /Graph Reset.

To make changes to only a few items in a graph's design, you can do so from the /Graph Options menu. If the next graph you construct is substantially different from the current one, however, you may want to use the /Graph Reset command. Be careful when using /Graph Reset because selecting the wrong option from the Graph Reset menu accidentally can clear many settings you may want to keep.

Developing Alternative Graph Types

You can use 1-2-3 to build seven types of graphs: line, bar, XY, stacked-bar, mixed, HLCO, and pie. In some cases, more than one graph type can accomplish the desired presentation. Choosing the best graph for a given application sometimes can be a matter of personal preference.

At other times, however, only one graph type will do the job. For example, HLCO graphs are specialized for presenting certain types of stock market information. Before you work through the remainder of this chapter, take a moment to review the primary uses of each graph type. Then you can go on to learn how to construct each type of graph.

Selecting an Appropriate Graph Type

A brief summary of each graph type and its major uses follows. This list is not exhaustive, of course. Your creativity and ingenuity are the only limiting factors when applying 1-2-3's graph types to your data.

Graph Type	Purpose
Line	Shows the trend of numeric data across time
Bar	Compares related data at one point in time or shows the trend of numeric data across time
XY	Shows the relationship between one numeric independent variable and one or more numeric dependent variables
Stack-Bar	Shows two or more data ranges in terms of the proportion of the total contributed by each data point
Pie	Graphs a data series, showing the percentage of the total each data point contributes (Do not use this type of graph if your data includes negative numbers.)
HLCO	Shows fluctuations in a stock's high-low-close-open prices over time. Other types of data with high/low values (such as test scores and temperatures) also can be plotted as HLCO.
Mixed	Combines, in one graph, data best shown in bar format and data best shown in line format

Building All Graph Types

Throughout this chapter, examples of line graphs have been used to illustrate most of 1-2-3's graph enhancements. Most of the options described also can be used for all of the other graph types. This section focuses briefly on each of the graph types, giving an example and discussing any enhancements that apply particularly to that graph type. In this section, each of the example graphs is based on the worksheet shown in figure 10.28.

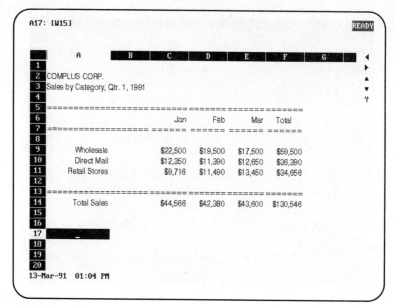

Fig. 10.28. A worksheet showing sales by category.

Line Graphs

To create a line graph that shows the steady increase in retail store sales during the first quarter, select **/Graph Reset Graph** to reset any existing graph settings. Because **Line** is the default graph type, you do not need to specify the type of graph. Use the following command sequence to select the **A** data range:

/Graph **A** C11..E11 (press Enter)

Next, select the **X** data range:

X C6..E6 (press Enter)

Finally, enter the graph titles:

Options Titles First \A2 (press Enter)

Titles Second \A11 (press Enter)

When you press F10 (Graph), the graph shown in figure 10.29 appears.

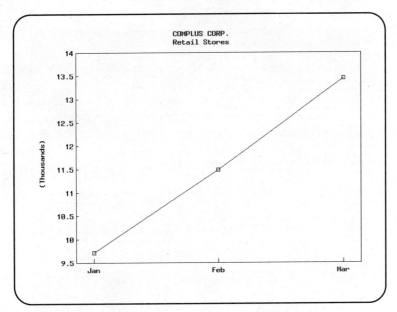

Fig. 10.29. *A line graph depicting first quarter retail store sales.*

Bar Graphs

A bar graph is appropriate for data that shows each month's sales by category because the differences in sales figures can be shown clearly by the different bar heights.

Reminder:
A bar graph can be displayed vertically or horizontally.

Select /**Graph Reset Graph** to reset any existing graph settings. Next, use the following command sequence to select the graph type and the data ranges:

> **Type Bar**
>
> **A   C9..E9** (press Enter)
>
> **B   C10..E10** (press Enter)
>
> **C   C11..E11** (press Enter)

Then select an **X** data range and specify a range for data legends:

> **X   C6..E6** (press Enter)
>
> **Options Legend Range A9..A11** (press Enter)

Finally, specify graph titles and a y-axis title:

> **Titles First \A2** (press Enter)

Titles Second \A3 (press Enter)

Titles Y-Axis Dollars (press Enter)

The resulting graph, shown in figure 10.30, shows that Wholesale sales have been decreasing; Direct Mail sales have been holding steady; and Retail Store sales have been increasing. In this graph, each of the three bars on the x-axis represents sales from a certain category for that month. In each set of bars, the left bar represents data range A; the center bar represents data range B; and the right bar represents data range C. Monthly headings are centered under the x-axis tick marks.

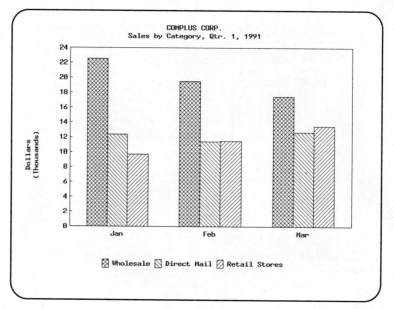

Fig. 10.30. *Data from figure 10.28 set in bar graph format.*

Because you need this graph for later examples, assign the graph a name by selecting /Graph Name Create and entering **Q1SALES**. Then you can modify the graph as instructed in the next examples and recall the graph in its original form when needed.

To display this graph horizontally, select **Type Features Horizontal** from the /Graph menu. The graph now is displayed as shown in figure 10.31. Horizontal display can be used with other graph types (except pie) but seems particularly appropriate for bar graphs. Selecting between **Vertical** and **Horizontal** is usually a matter of personal preference.

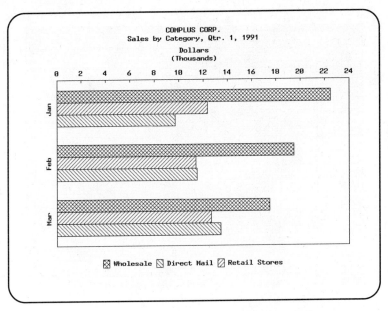

Fig. 10.31. The graph from figure 10.30 configured horizontally.

Stack-Bar Graphs

You may want to experiment with different graph types when you plot multiple time-series data. If the data ranges combine in a way that produces a meaningful figure (for example, the total monthly sales for COMPLUS Corp.), try using the **Stack-Bar** graph type. The bars are plotted in the order **A** through **F**, with the **A** data range closest to the x-axis. After creating the graph in figure 10.30, for example, you can create the stacked-bar graph shown in figure 10.32 by selecting **Type Features Vertical** from the /Graph menu to return to vertical graph display. Then select **Type Stack-Bar** and select **View** to display the graph on-screen.

All the options you set to produce the bar graph in figure 10.28 are carried over to the new stacked-bar graph. 1-2-3 also adjusts the upper and lower limits of the y-axis. In a stacked-bar graph, the lower limit always must be zero.

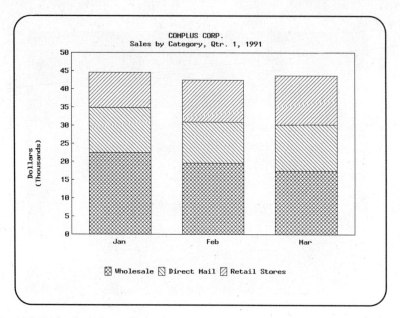

Fig. 10.32. The data from the worksheet in figure 10.28 displayed as a stacked-bar graph.

Mixed Graphs

A mixed graph is nothing more than a combination of the line and bar types. Data ranges **A**, **B**, and **C** are plotted as bars, and ranges **D**, **E**, and **F** are plotted as lines. Otherwise, all graph options and restrictions apply.

To modify the graph in figure 10.28 as a mixed graph that displays individual sales categories as bars and total sales as a line, recall the settings (remember, you saved them as a named graph). Select /Graph Name Use, highlight **Q1SALES**, and press Enter. The graph is displayed as shown in figure 10.28. Return to the /Graph menu, select **Type Mixed**, and redisplay the graph.

The graph didn't change because only the *bar* ranges (**A**, **B**, and **C**), have been assigned. If no *line* ranges are assigned, a mixed graph is displayed as a bar graph. The converse also is true; if line ranges but no bar ranges are assigned, a mixed graph is displayed as a line graph.

You can complete the mixed graph by entering the following commands from the /Graph menu:

D   C14..E14 (press Enter)

Options Legend D   \A14 (press Enter)

Quit View

The result is the graph shown in figure 10.33. The message of this graph is that, although individual sales categories are changing, Total Sales are remaining relatively constant.

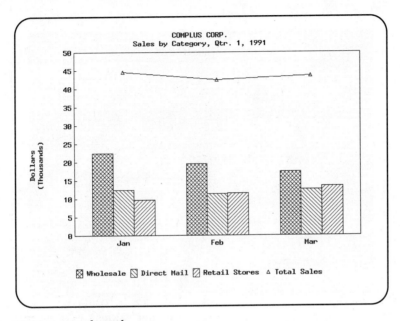

Fig. 10.33. *A mixed graph.*

Pie Graphs

You use a pie graph only for plotting a data range that contains just positive numbers. Many of the /Graph menu options, including all of those dealing with the x- and y-axes, do not apply to pie graphs.

To construct a pie graph from the data shown in figure 10.28 and to graph the percentage of Total Sales for the quarter from each category, select /Graph Reset Graph. Next, select Type Pie and specify **F9..F11** as data range A. When you display the graph, it appears as shown in figure 10.34.

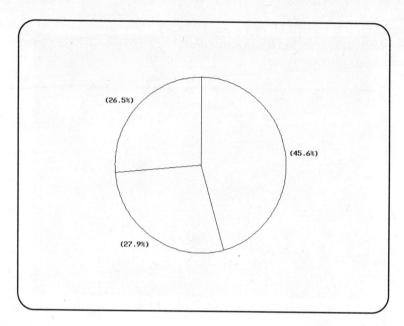

Fig. 10.34. *An unenhanced pie graph.*

Cue:
*Use the **B** data range to specify colors or cross-hatching patterns for the slices of a pie graph.*

1-2-3 calculates and displays parenthetically the percentage of the whole represented by each pie slice. These percentage values can be suppressed by using a **C** range.

You can enhance this basic pie graph by adding titles and an **X** range of descriptive labels. For example, you can use the labels in column A as the **X** range by entering the following command sequence:

    X   A9..A11 (press Enter)

    Options Titles First \A2 (press Enter)

    Titles Second Total Sales by Category (press Enter)

    Quit View

The resulting graph is shown in figure 10.35.

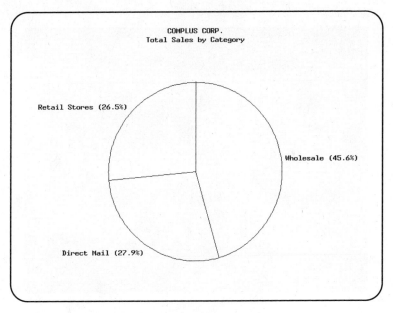

Fig. 10.35. A pie graph enhanced with titles and labels.

1-2-3 provides eight different cross-hatching patterns for monochrome display of graphs, eight colors for EGA color display, and four colors for CGA color display.

Figure 10.36 shows the pie graph cross-hatching associated with each code number when displayed using the black-and-white option /**Graph** Options **B&W**.

1-2-3 displays the pie slices in different colors or cross-hatching patterns, depending on whether **Options B&W** or **Options Color** (from the /**Graph** menu) is in effect. You can modify the assignment of colors or cross-hatching or even explode individual pie slices for emphasis by using the **B** data range to enter codes for each pie slice. The **B** range can be any range of your worksheet that has the same number of cells as the **A** data range being plotted as a pie graph. The codes for color or cross-hatching (depending on whether the graph is displayed in black-and-white or color) are as follows:

0	An unshaded pie slice with an outer border
1-7	A specified cross-hatching or color
Negative value	Unshaded with an outer border

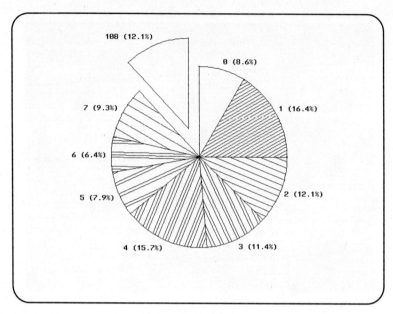

Fig. 10.36. The pie graph cross-hatching patterns associated with the code numbers shown.

Adding **100** to the preceding codes results in an exploded pie slice. Suppose that you want to add cross-hatching or exploding codes to the Sales by Category worksheet graph. Although you can place the **B** range anywhere in the worksheet, place it adjacent to the **A** range for this example. In cells G9..G11, enter the values **4**, **105**, and **6**, in that order. Then, from the /Graph menu, specify those three cells as the **B** range. Selecting View displays the graph shown in figure 10.37.

XY Graphs

The XY graph, often called a *scatter plot*, is a unique variation of a line graph. In an XY graph, a data point's position on the x-axis is determined by a numeric value instead of a category. Two or more different data items from the same data range can have the same **X** value. Rather than showing time-series data, XY graphs illustrate the relationships between different attributes of data items—age, income, educational achievements, salary, and so on. You must think of one data item (**X**) as the *independent variable* and consider the other item (**Y**) to be the *dependent variable*—dependent on **X**.

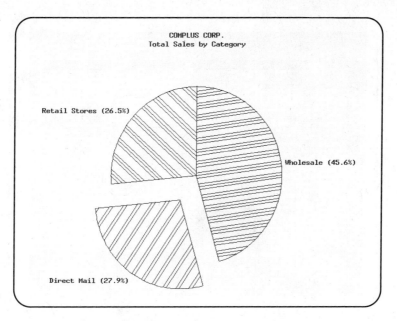

Fig. 10.37. A pie graph with an exploded slice.

Use the /**Graph** menu's **X** data range option to specify the range containing the independent variable and one or more of the **A** through **F** options to enter the dependent variable(s).

To create a graph that shows the relationship between the amount spent on advertising each month and the sales generated, you can use the data in figure 10.38, which shows COMPLUS Corp.'s advertising budget and sales by month for an entire year. Note that a line graph would be appropriate for plotting Sales as a function of Month. For Sales vs. Advertising Budget, however, you must use an XY graph.

To create the XY graph, enter the following commands:

/**Graph** Type **XY**

X   **C6..C17** (press Enter)

A   **D6..D17** (press Enter)

The resulting graph is shown in figure 10.39.

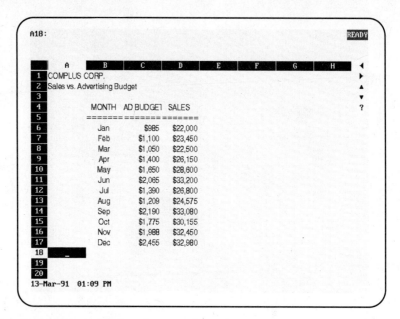

Fig. 10.38. Data to be plotted on an XY graph.

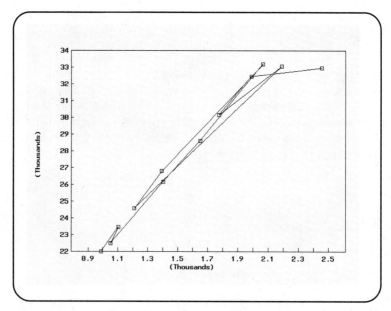

Fig. 10.39. The basic XY graph with the default format of Both.

Notice that the data points are connected by lines, making the graph difficult to interpret. This problem results because 1-2-3 orders the data points from right to left, based on the values in the **X** range (smallest to largest), and the points are connected in the order they appear in your worksheet. For some data, you can avoid this problem by sorting your data first. For XY graphs, you usually select **/Graph Options Format Graph Symbols**. Setting the **Format** for the graph to **Symbols** plots each data point as a symbol without lines connecting the symbols. Use the following commands to change the format to symbols and to add some other enhancements:

Cue:
To create a scatter plot, use an XY graph with Format set to Symbols.

/Graph Options Format Graph Symbols

Quit

Titles First \A1 (press Enter)

Titles Second \A2 (press Enter)

Titles X-Axis \C4 (press Enter)

Titles Y-Axis \D4 (press Enter)

The resulting graph is shown in figure 10.40.

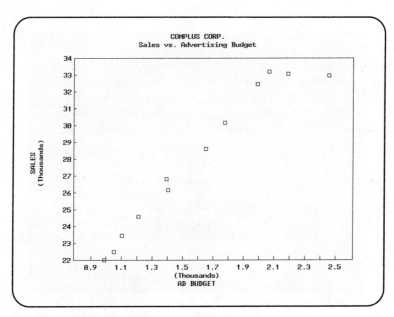

Fig. 10.40. *The XY graph with Format set to Symbols.*

This graph clearly shows a trend between advertising expenditures and sales. As the advertising budget goes up, so do sales. Note, however, that the plot flattens out at the top, suggesting that when advertising expenditures increase beyond $2,000 per month, they are not having any additional effect on sales.

HLCO Graphs

Reminder:
Use an HLCO graph type to plot stock market information.

HLCO stands for high-low-close-open. This graph is a special type used in graphing data on the price of a stock over time. The meanings of the values are as follows:

High   The stock's highest price in the given time period

Low   The stock's lowest price in the given time period

Close   The stock's price at the end, or close, of the time period

Open   The stock's price at the start, or open, of the time period

While HLCO graphs are specialized for stock market information, they also can be used to track other kinds of fluctuating data over time, such as daily temperature or currency exchange rates.

Each set of data—four figures representing high, low, close, and open values—is represented on the graph as one vertical line. The vertical extent of the line (the length) is from the low value to the high value. The close value is represented by a tick mark extending right from the line, and the open value by a tick mark extending left. The total number of lines on the graph depends on the number of time periods included.

Data ranges for an HLCO graph are assigned as follows:

Range	Values or elements
A	The high values
B	The low values
C	The closing values
D	The opening values

You can specify only some of these ranges, and only the corresponding part of the graph is plotted. The minimum requirements are that the **A** and **B** ranges must be specified. The graph in figure 10.41, for example, shows an HLCO plot of common stock data for a fictional company. Data ranges **A** through **D** were assigned.

Graph enhancements, such as an **X** range, titles, and axis labels, are added, as with the other graph types. Stock market figures often are downloaded from on-line information services as text labels in the form '45 3/8. To change these labels to values that can be used in an HLCO graph, use the @VALUE function, as described in Chapter 6.

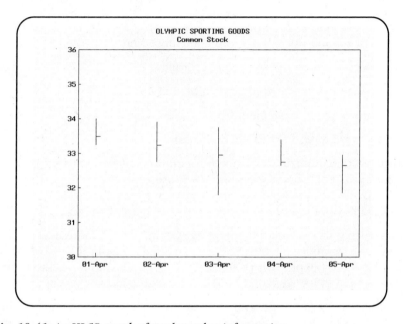

Fig. 10.41. *An HLCO graph of stock market information.*

Using the PrintGraph Program

You can use the PrintGraph program provided with 1-2-3 Release 2.3 to print the graphs you saved as graph (PIC) files, or you can use Wysiwyg to print graphs. Wysiwyg provides many options not available in PrintGraph. With Wysiwyg, you can customize and improve the quality of your printed graphs, and you can print worksheet data and graphs together. See Chapters 9 and 11 for a complete description of Wysiwyg.

You can use the PrintGraph program for quick printouts of graphs; you also can choose from a variety of optional print settings for enhancing the appearance of graphs. The next few sections of this chapter show you how to do all of the following:

- Access the PrintGraph program

- Use the status report

- Print a graph using PrintGraph default settings

- Select or alter hardware-related settings

- Change graph size, font, and color settings

- Control paper movement from the keyboard

- Establish temporary PrintGraph settings

To access PrintGraph directly from the operating system, type **pgraph** at the operating system prompt (from the 1-2-3 directory). If you use a driver set other than the default 1-2-3 set, you also must type the name of that driver set (**pgraph hp**, for example) to reach the PrintGraph menu.

Rather than starting from the operating system, you are more likely to use PrintGraph immediately after you have created a graph. If you originally accessed 1-2-3 by typing **lotus**, select /Quit Yes from within 1-2-3 to return to the Lotus 1-2-3 Access menu. Then select **PrintGraph**.

Caution:
Save your worksheet before you use the 1-2-3 /System command.

If you have sufficient RAM, you also can use the /System command from within 1-2-3 to access the operating system and then type **pgraph** at the operating system prompt. Rather than having to reload 1-2-3 after you leave PrintGraph, you can return directly to 1-2-3 by typing **exit** at the system prompt. Be careful; before you use the /System command, save your worksheet. Also, use the /Worksheet Status command to check remaining internal memory (RAM) before you attempt to use /System—you must have at least 256K of remaining RAM to run PrintGraph and 1-2-3 simultaneously without overwriting your worksheet.

Producing Basic Printed Graphs

When you select **PrintGraph** from the Lotus 1-2-3 Access menu or type **pgraph** at the operating system prompt, the following menu appears:

Image-Select Settings Go Align Page Exit

Printing a graph can be a simple procedure if you use PrintGraph's default print settings. Before beginning to use PrintGraph, you must select a printer (within the PrintGraph program) and check to make sure that other hardware settings, such as the printer interface and location of graph and font files, are correct. If the correct hardware configuration has been specified, you can produce a half-size, block-font, black-and-white graph on 8 1/2-by-11-inch continuous-feed paper by marking a graph for printing and then printing it. You choose Image-Select to mark a graph for printing and select Go to print the graph.

Suppose that you want to print the line graph saved in the WCLINE.PIC file. Make sure that the current printer and interface specifications accurately reflect your hardware and that the printer is on-line and positioned at the top of a page. Then you can print the default graph by issuing the following command sequences:

> Image-Select WCLINE
>
> (Highlight the file name WCLINE, press the space bar to indicate which file you want to print, and press Enter.)
>
> Go

Figure 10.42 shows the printout of the graph. This graph is centered upright (zero degrees rotation) on the paper and fills about half of an 8 1/2-by-11-inch page. The titles are printed in the default BLOCK1 font.

To enhance this default graph, you can use any or all of PrintGraph's many special features. These special capabilities include the enlargement, reduction, and rotation of graph printouts and the use of several additional colors and font types. With Release 2.3, you can use Wysiwyg to enhance your graph with additional formatting options.

To illustrate PrintGraph's Size and Font options, issue the following command sequences:

> Image-Select WCLINE (press Enter)
>
> Settings Image Size Full Quit
>
> Font 1 ITALIC1 (Highlight ITALIC1, press space bar, and press Enter)
>
> Font 2 ROMAN1 (Highlight ROMAN1, press space bar, and press Enter)
>
> Quit Quit Align Go

Reminder:
Printing a graph can be as easy as selecting the image to be printed and then choosing Go.

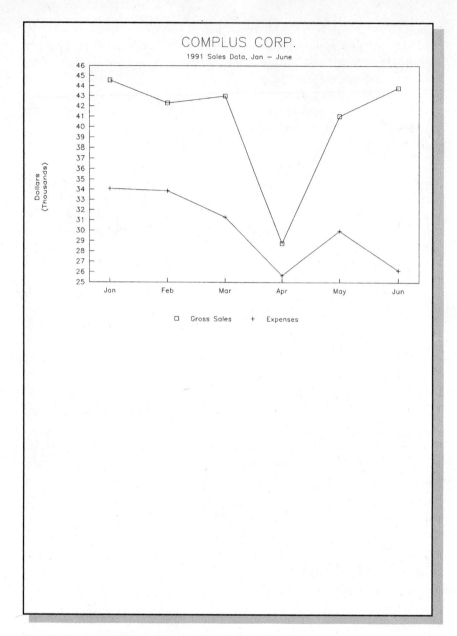

Fig. 10.42. *A sample graph printed with default settings.*

The resulting graph is printed in landscape format (90 degrees rotation) and almost fills an 8 1/2-by-11-inch page (see fig. 10.43). The top center title is printed in italic font; the other titles are printed in Roman font.

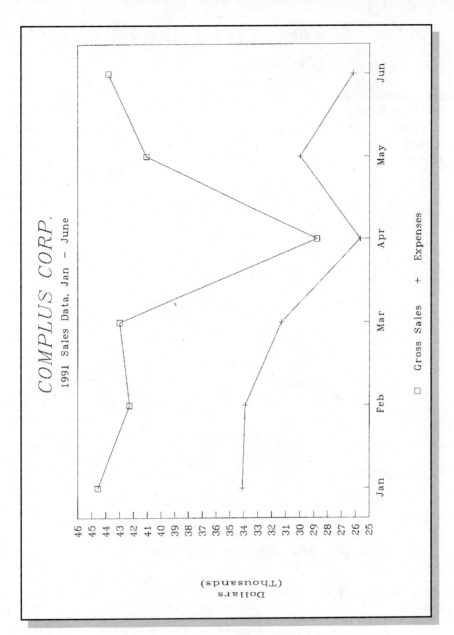

Fig. 10.43. *A sample graph printed with font and size changes.*

Comparing On-Screen Graphs to Printed Graphs

As you create and prepare to print graphs, note that a printed graph looks different from its on-screen display. If you compare figure 10.44 (which captures the on-screen display of a stacked-bar graph) with figure 10.45 (which shows the same graph printed), one difference is immediately apparent.

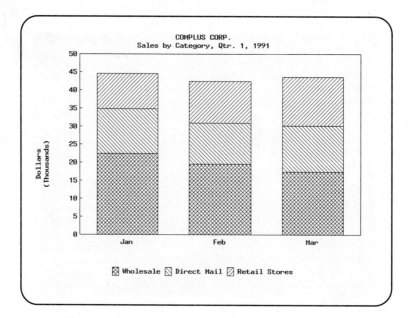

Fig. 10.44. The screen display of a sample stacked-bar graph.

The two top center titles in the on-screen version appear to be the same size, but, in the printed graph, the first title has been changed to a larger point size.

You also may find a difference in the truncating of legends on-screen versus printed output. Release 2.3 wraps legends to a second line on-screen and in the printout if too many legends exist to fit on one line.

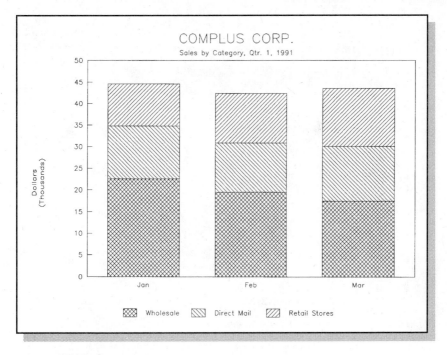

Fig. 10.45. *The printed stacked-bar graph from figure 10.44.*

Using the PrintGraph Menu and Status Screen

The PrintGraph program is entirely menu-driven. The menu screens provide instructions for printing graph (PIC) files and information about current print conditions. The screen displayed when you enter the PrintGraph program is similar to that shown in figure 10.46.

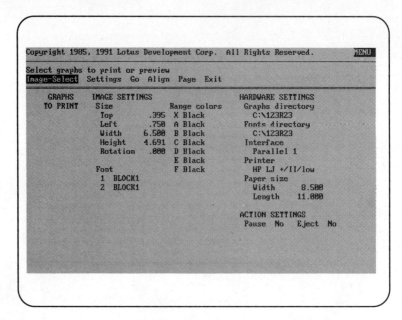

Fig. 10.46. The main Print Graph screen.

The first three text lines, which display a copyright message and two levels of current menu options, always remain on-screen. In the area below the double solid line, option selections are updated continually. (The status section of the screen disappears temporarily when you select a printer, graphs to print, or a font style.)

Cue:
*Check the
PrintGraph status
screen before
printing any graphs.*

Before you select the Go command to begin printing a graph, get in the habit of checking the status report. Figure 10.46 shows the Settings displayed in the status report. These settings are organized in four areas: GRAPHS TO PRINT, IMAGE SETTINGS, HARDWARE SETTINGS, and ACTION SETTINGS. Each of these areas is directly related to the Image-Select or Settings option on the PrintGraph menu.

For example, graphs you select for printing appear in a list under GRAPHS TO PRINT on the left side of the status report. (In fig. 10.46, no graphs have been selected for printing.) To make changes in the other three status areas, you first select Settings from the main PrintGraph menu. When you select Settings, the following menu appears:

Image Hardware Action Save Reset Quit

If you choose Image, you can change the size, font, and color of the graph; the revisions are displayed in the status report's IMAGE SETTINGS area. The

Settings shown in figure 10.46 produce a black-and-white, half-size graph in which all titles, labels, and legends are printed in block style.

To alter the paper size, printer, or disk-drive specifications displayed in the `HARDWARE SETTINGS` area, you select Hardware. The instructions in figure 10.46 tell PrintGraph to look for PIC files in the C:\123R23 subdirectory, to look for font program files in the C:\123R23 directory, to print on standard-size paper, and to use a LaserJet printer.

If you want the printer to pause before printing each page and want the paper to eject automatically, select Action from the Settings menu. Then update the `ACTION SETTINGS` section of the status report by changing the Pause and Eject options from No to Yes. These settings are appropriate for single sheet printers but may not be appropriate for continuous-feed paper. The following sections discuss how to make changes in each of these settings.

Cue:
To give you a chance to change PrintGraph Settings between graphs, change the Pause and Eject options to Yes.

Establishing the Physical Print Environment

The physical print environment includes disk drives that contain your graph files, printer type and name, paper size, and printer actions to control print delay and paper movement.

In figure 10.46, current physical-environment settings are displayed under `HARDWARE SETTINGS` and `ACTION SETTINGS`. For example, the `HARDWARE SETTINGS` information shows that the files to be graphed are located in the subdirectory C:\123R23; the `ACTION SETTINGS` show that the printer will not pause between printing two or more selected graph images.

Before you select any graphs for printing and before you select options that affect the printed image, you should understand each Hardware and Action option of the Settings menu.

When you select Settings Hardware, you see the following menu:

    Graphs-Directory Fonts-Directory Interface Printer Size-Paper Quit

The Graphs-Directory and Fonts-Directory options pertain to disk-drive specifications; Interface and Printer determine the current printer name and type; and Size-Paper enables you to specify paper length and width in inches.

Changing the Graphs Directory

In figure 10.46, the current graphs directory is C:\123R23. This listing means that you store your PIC files in a directory named 123R23. You can change this directory; for example, to print PIC files from a floppy disk, insert the floppy disk in drive A and select **Settings Hardware Graphs-Directory** from the main PrintGraph menu. At the prompt `Enter directory containing graph (PIC) files:`, type the new drive or directory (**A:** in this example). You don't have to erase the preceding setting by pressing Esc or the Backspace key. The setting is updated in the upper right corner of the status report as you type (see fig. 10.47).

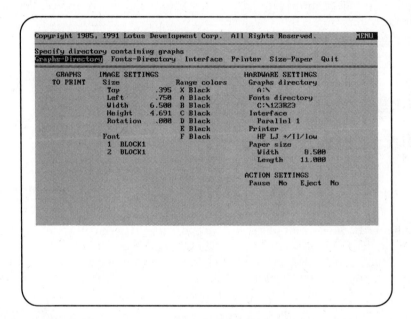

Fig. 10.47. *The status screen showing a revised graphs directory.*

To restore C:\123R23 as the current graphs directory, select **Settings Hardware Graphs-Directory** again and type **C:\123R23**.

Changing the Fonts Directory

When you print a graph, you use PrintGraph's font files, which contain program instructions for font styles. These files are located in the same directory containing the PrintGraph program. (Available font styles are discussed in this chapter's "Selecting Fonts" section.) As figure 10.46 shows, the location of the fonts directory in this example is C:\123R23.

To change this directory, use the **Settings Hardware Fonts-Directory** command. For example, if you have installed 1-2-3 in a directory other than the default directory (C:\123R23), you need to change the font's directory. To change the directory to C:\LOTUS, for example, select **Settings Hardware Fonts-Directory** and type **C:\LOTUS**. You also may change the directory if you moved the files to another directory or renamed the directory.

Setting the Type and Name of the Current Printer

In addition to setting the graphs and fonts directories, you must specify the printer or plotter you will use to print the selected graph images. Use two **Settings Hardware** menu options: **Interface** and **Printer**. Interface sets the type of connection to a graphics printer; **Printer** establishes a specific type of printer.

You can direct the graph output to one of two parallel printers, one of two serial printers, or one of four DOS devices (usually set up as part of a local area network). To determine whether a printer is parallel or serial, consult your printer manual.

Selecting **Settings Hardware Interface** produces eight menu choices, labeled 1 through 8, which represent the physical connections between your computer and your printer:

1 Parallel 1

2 Serial 1

3 Parallel 2

4 Serial 2

5 DOS Device LPT1

6 DOS Device LPT2

7 DOS Device LPT3

8 DOS Device LPT4

In figure 10.48, option 3 (Parallel 2) is highlighted in the menu. (The default setting is Parallel 1.)

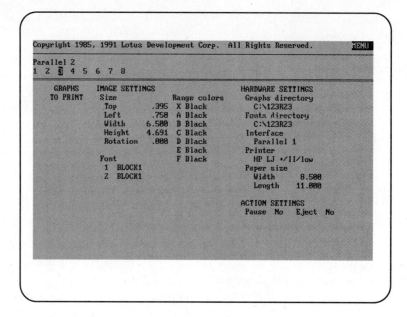

Fig. 10.48. The Settings Hardware Interface menu.

If you specify a serial interface, you also must select a baud rate. Baud rates determine the speed at which data is transferred. Because each printer has specific requirements, consult your printer manual for the appropriate rate. Many serial printers accept more than one baud rate. A general guideline is to choose the fastest rate your printer will accept without corrupting the data. A baud rate of 1200 is normally a safe choice.

After you have specified the appropriate interface, PrintGraph again displays the Hardware menu so that you can name the printer attached to the designated interface.

To select a printer, you must have installed one or more graphics printers when you installed 1-2-3. If you installed three printers (a LaserJet, an Epson, and a Toshiba, for example) to run with 1-2-3, a list of these printers is displayed when you select **Printer** from the Settings Hardware menu (see fig. 10.49).

Cue:
Use a low-density option for faster, draft-quality printing.

Notice that the list includes six options. Some printer selections enable you to print at high or low density (dark or light print). If you use a high-density option, the printed graph will be of high quality, but printing will take more time.

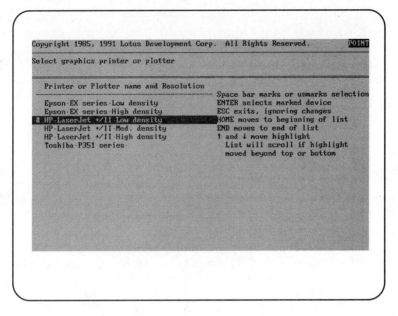

```
Copyright 1985, 1991 Lotus Development Corp.  All Rights Reserved.        POINT

Select graphics printer or plotter


  Printer or Plotter name and Resolution
  ------------------------------------------  Space bar marks or unmarks selection
    Epson-EX series-Low density                ENTER selects marked device
    Epson-EX series-High density               ESC exits, ignoring changes
  # HP-LaserJet +/II-Low density               HOME moves to beginning of list
    HP-LaserJet +/II-Med. density              END moves to end of list
    HP-LaserJet +/II-High density              ↑ and ↓ move highlight
    Toshiba-P351 series·                         List will scroll if highlight
                                                 moved beyond top or bottom
```

Fig. 10.49. The Settings Hardware Printer display.

Instructions for selecting an option appear on-screen, and a pound sign (#) marks the current printer. To mark or unmark a selection, press the space bar. The highlighted line # HP LaserJet +/II Low density indicates that the current printer is an HP LaserJet II and that you have chosen to print at low density. To select another printer, press the space bar to remove the # from the LascrJet +/II listing; then reposition the highlight and mark the new device by pressing Enter.

Changing the Paper Size

Along with selecting your printer, you should set the paper size. The default paper size is 8 1/2 by 11 inches, but you can print your graph on different sized paper by selecting Settings Hardware Size-Paper. When you select Size-Paper, the following options are displayed:

Length Width Quit

Select **Length** or **Width** and specify the appropriate number of inches. To adjust the paper size to the 14-inch paper used in wide-carriage printers, for example, select **Settings Hardware Size-Paper Width** and type **14**. Remember that this command changes the size of the paper, not the size of the graph. (Changing the size of a graph is discussed in the "Adjusting Size and Orientation" section of this chapter.) Be sure to select a paper size that can accommodate the specified graph size.

Pausing the Printer between Graphs

If you have selected more than one PIC file for a print operation, you can make the printer pause between printing the specified graphs. If you are using a manual sheet-fed printer, for example, you can pause to change the paper. You may want to stop printing temporarily so that you can change the hardware settings, directing the output to a different printer. (You cannot change the font, color, and size options during the pause.)

To pause the printing operation, select **Settings Action Pause Yes** before you select **Go** from the main PrintGraph menu. After each graph has been printed, the printer pauses and beeps. To resume printing, press the space bar. To restore the default setting so that all currently specified graphs print nonstop, choose **Settings Action Pause No**.

Ejecting the Paper To Start a New Page

Another **Action** option that applies to batching several graphs in one print operation is Eject. When you select **Settings Action Eject Yes**, continuous-feed paper advances to the top of a new page before the next graph is printed. Use the alternative default setting, **Eject No**, to print two (or more) half-size (or smaller) graphs on a page.

Do not confuse the **Settings Action Eject Yes** command with the PrintGraph menu's **Page** command. (The **Page** option is described in the "Completing the Print Cycle" section of this chapter.) Both commands advance the paper to the top of a new page. **Settings Action Eject Yes** is appropriate when you use a **Go** command to print more than one selected graph; the paper advances after each graph has been printed. You select **Page** from the PrintGraph menu, on the other hand, to advance the paper one page at a time before or after a printing session.

Controlling the Appearance of Printed Graphs

You have learned about the physical print environment needed to produce a graph: printer type and name, disk-drive location of required files, and paper size and movement. Now that you are familiar with the mechanics of producing a graph, you can learn about options that affect the printed graph's appearance. These options are displayed in the status screen under IMAGE SETTINGS.

If you select Settings Image from the PrintGraph menu, you see the following menu:

> Size Font Range-Colors Quit

Use these options to change the size of a graph, to specify one or two print styles in a single graph, and to select colors. (You use the 1-2-3 /Graph or :Graph commands to enter graph enhancements, such as titles, legends, and labels.)

Adjusting Size and Orientation

The Size option adjusts the size, position, and angle of graphs on the printed page. You determine the size of the graph by specifying the desired width and height; you set the graph's position on the page by specifying the top and left margins. You also can rotate the graph a specified number of degrees on the page.

When you select Settings Image Size, you see the menu shown in figure 10.50. The default Half option produces a graph that fills half of a standard-size 8 1/2-by-11-inch page. Figure 10.50 also shows the following default assignments:

Top	.395	(inches)
Left	.750	(inches)
Width	6.500	(inches)
Height	4.691	(inches)
Rotation	.000	(degrees)

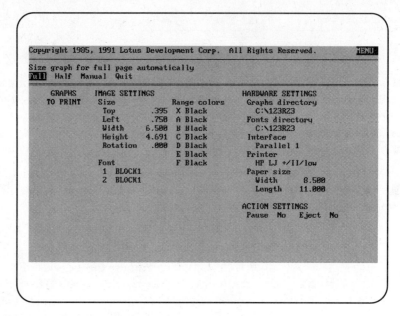

Fig. 10.50. The Settings Image Size menu.

Because these Settings are the default, you don't have to use the Size option to print a graph with these dimensions centered upright at the top of the page on a standard-size page.

Width refers to the horizontal graph dimension produced on a page. The width of the half-size graph shown in figure 10.40 is the x-axis. In a zero-rotation graph, the ratio of x-axis size (width) to y-axis size is 1.386 to 1.

The Full option determines a combination of the width, height, top, left, and rotation settings to produce a graph that fills an 8 1/2-by-11-inch page. The top of this horizontal graph (90 degrees rotation) lies along the left edge of the paper. The automatic assignments for a full-size graph include the following:

Top	.250	(inches)
Left	.500	(inches)
Width	6.852	(inches)
Height	9.445	(inches)
Rotation	90.000	(degrees)

The width of the full-size graph shown in figure 10.41 is the y-axis, which has been changed to 6.852 inches. In a graph rotated 90 degrees, the ratio of x-axis size (height) to y-axis size is 1.378 to 1.

To change any or all of the Size settings, select Manual from the Settings Image Size menu. Then select one or more of the following options:

Top Left Width Height Rotation Quit

To position a printed graph at a location other than the automatic distances from the edges of the paper, change the margin settings. To center a half-size graph at the top of 11-by-14-inch paper, for example, specify a different left margin by selecting Settings Image Size Manual Left and typing **3.75** as the revised number of inches. When you press Enter, the updated left margin is displayed in the status screen.

To calculate the correct margin so that your graph is centered on the page, subtract the width of the graph (6.5 inches) from the width of the paper (14 inches) and divide this number (7.5 inches) in half. Therefore, 3.75 inches is the correct width for the margin.

When you change the Width and Height Settings, maintain the basic x- to y-axis ratio of approximately 1.38 to 1. Suppose that you want to produce an upright (zero rotation) graph that is only 3 inches high. The x-axis dimension should exceed the y-axis dimension, and at zero rotation, the x-axis is the width. Multiply the desired height of 3 inches by 1.38 to calculate the proportionate width (4.14 inches) of the graph.

Cue:
The x- to y-axis ratio should remain at 1.38 to 1 for every combination of width and height setting.

Be sure that the combined dimensions (margin, width, and height) do not exceed the size of the paper. If a graph exceeds the physical bounds of the paper, 1-2-3 prints as much of the graph as possible and then truncates the rest.

Although you can set rotation anywhere between 0 and 360 degrees, you will use 3 Settings (0, 90, or 270) for most graphs. To print an upright graph, use 0; to position the graph's center titles along the left edge of the paper, use 90; use 270 to position the graph's center titles along the right edge of the paper.

Selecting Fonts

You can use different typefaces, or *fonts*, in a printed graph. For example, you can print a graph's top title in one typeface (Font 1) and then select a different font (Font 2) for the remaining titles, data labels, x-labels, and legends. To use only one print style, your Font 1 choice is used for all descriptions.

Cue:
Select Font 1 to print the top title in one typeface; select Font 2 for the remaining text.

When you select Settings Image Font 1, you see the options shown in figure 10.51. BLOCK1 is the default font. The number after the font name indicates the density (darkness) of the printed characters. Notice that four of the fonts enable alternative print density specifications. If you choose BLOCK2, for example, the printed characters are darker than those produced by choosing BLOCK1. Figure 10.52 shows a sample of each font style.

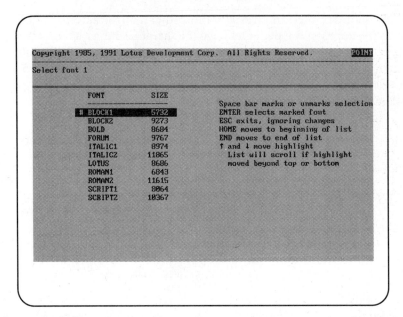

Fig. 10.51. The Settings Image Font options.

Cue:
Print the graph at the faster, low-density setting to check font appearance.

Two of these fonts (italic and script) may be difficult to read, especially on half-size graphs produced on a nonletter-quality printer. Before you print a final-quality draft in darker density, print the graph at the lower density so that you can determine whether the font and size settings are correct. When printing the final output, use a high-density printer selection to improve the readability of the font.

Choosing Colors

If you have a color printing device, you can use the PrintGraph program to assign colors to all parts of a graph. Select **Settings Image Range-Colors** to display the following menu:

    X A B C D E F Quit

This is BLOCK 1 type
This is BLOCK 2 type
This is BOLD type
This is FORUM type
This is ITALIC 1 type
This is ITALIC 2 type
This is the LOTUS type
This is ROMAN 1 type
This is ROMAN 2 type
This is SCRIPT 2 type

Fig. 10.52. *Samples of fonts available in PrintGraph.*

Reminder:
Use the A through F settings to assign a different color to each data range.

For all graph types except pie, use the **X** option to assign a color to the edges of the graph, any background grid, and all displayed options other than legends and data labels. Use **A**, **B**, **C**, **D**, **E**, and **F** to assign a different color to every data range used. The color set for an individual data range also is used for any data label or legend assigned to that data range.

You use a different method to determine the print colors for a pie graph. Because you create a pie graph by using only data in the **A** range, and because each slice of the pie is assigned a **B** range cross-hatching code, you must use the appropriate cross-hatching codes to determine which colors will print. First, associate each code with the following Settings Image Range-Colors menu options:

Range-Colors option	B-range cross-hatching option
X	Code ending in 1 (101 or 1)
A	Code ending in 2
B	Code ending in 3
C	Code ending in 4
D	Code ending in 5
E	Code ending in 6
F	Code ending in 7

When you select an option from the Settings Image Range-Colors menu, a menu of colors is displayed. The number of colors displayed depends on the capabilities of the current printer (named in the HARDWARE SETTINGS area of the PrintGraph status report). If your printer does not support color printing, only the **B**lack option appears. To choose a color for each range, highlight that color and press Enter. In figure 10.53, the assigned colors are listed in the IMAGE SETTINGS section of the PrintGraph status screen.

If you know that you will print a specific graph in color, select /Graph **O**ptions **C**olor before you store that graph as a PIC file. If you store the graph in black and white and then print the graph in color, the cross-hatching and the colors assigned to the ranges print.

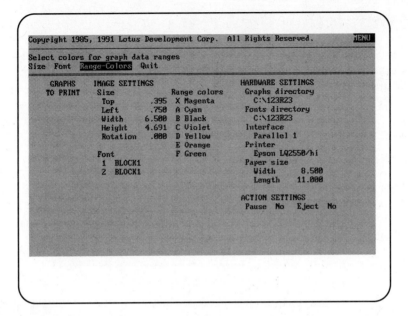

Fig. 10.53. *A sample status screen after selecting colors.*

Saving and Resetting PrintGraph Settings

After you have established current Hardware, Action, and Image Settings and completed the current printing operation, you select one of two options from the Settings menu: Save or Reset. Both of these options apply to the entire group of current Settings.

If you choose Save, the current options are stored in a file named PGRAPH.CNF; this file is read when PrintGraph is loaded. Select Reset to restore all Hardware, Action, and Image Settings to PrintGraph's default settings or to the options saved during the current session—whichever occurred most recently. Image-Selected graphs are not reset.

Completing the Print Cycle

After you have accepted the default options or selected other Hardware, Action, and Image options, access the main PrintGraph menu to complete the printing operation. From this menu, you select the graph(s) to be printed, adjust the paper alignment, and select Go.

Previewing a Graph

To preview a graph, select Image-Select from the main PrintGraph menu. The menus and the status report area disappear temporarily; in their place on-screen you see a list of the PIC files in the current graphs directory (see fig. 10.54).

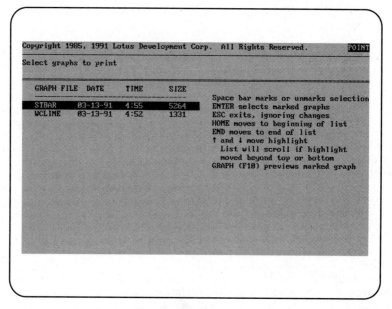

Fig. 10.54. *A list of PIC files displayed after choosing Image-Select.*

Cue:

Press the Graph (F10) key from within PrintGraph to preview the graph on-screen before printing.

Instructions for selecting graphs are displayed on-screen. The last item on the list of instructions indicates that pressing the Graph (F10) key displays the highlighted graph on-screen. To verify that the graph shown is the one you want to print, use the Graph (F10) key to preview the graph. Size and font options are not displayed in this preview, and you cannot see rotation or half-size results. The preview does give a good idea of what the printed graph looks like—in some cases, a better idea than /Graph View. For example, legend titles that are too wide to print appear complete when viewed on-screen with /Graph View but not with the Graph (F10) key.

Selecting a Graph

Selecting graphs you want to print is easy. Select Image-Select and then mark the file you want to print. To mark the files for printing, use the cursor-movement keys to position the highlight bar on the graph you want to select. Then press the space bar to mark the file with a # symbol. The space bar acts as a toggle key; use the same action to remove any unwanted marks. If necessary, continue to mark additional graphs. (In fig. 10.55, two graphs have been marked for printing.) After you press Enter to accept the currently marked graphs for printing, the updated status report is displayed again.

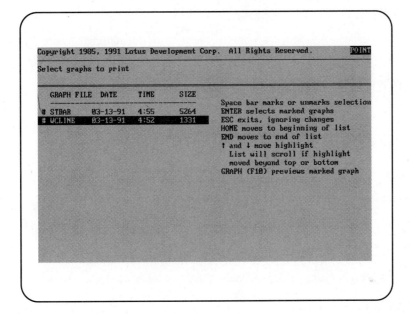

Fig. 10.55. *PIC files marked for printing.*

Controlling Paper Movement

The main PrintGraph menu's Align option sets the program's built-in, top-of-page marker. When you choose Align, PrintGraph assumes that the paper in the printer is aligned correctly at the top of the page. Using the page-length information you provided when you installed the graphics device, PrintGraph then inserts a form feed at the end of every page. Regularly selecting Align before selecting Go is a good practice.

Reminder:
To ensure that the graph lines up properly on the printed page, select Align before selecting Go.

The **P**age option advances the paper one page at a time. At the end of a printing session, this option advances continuous-feed paper to help you remove the printed output. While you are using the PrintGraph program, control the movement of paper from the keyboard, not from the printer. Although many printers have controls that enable you to scroll the paper one line at a time, PrintGraph does not recognize these controls. For example, if you scroll the paper three lines but do not realign it, PrintGraph is three spaces off when you issue the next form-feed command.

Printing the Graph

To print a graph, select **G**o from the main PrintGraph menu. After you select **G**o, the screen's menu area displays messages indicating that picture and font files are loading. Then the graphs are printed. Printing a graph takes much longer than printing a similar-sized worksheet range, especially if you are printing in high-density mode.

Cue:
To stop PrintGraph while printing is in progress, press Ctrl-Break.

To interrupt the process of printing a graph or series of graphs, use the Ctrl-Break key combination. Then press Esc to access the PrintGraph menu.

Exiting the PrintGraph Program

To leave the PrintGraph program, choose **E**xit from the main PrintGraph menu. The next screen to appear depends on the method you used to access PrintGraph. If you entered PrintGraph from the Lotus 1-2-3 Access Menu, the Access menu reappears. Select **E**xit to restore the operating system prompt or select another Access menu option. If you entered PrintGraph by typing **pgraph** from the operating system prompt, the operating system prompt is restored.

To enter 1-2-3 after you have exited PrintGraph and restored the operating system prompt, remember how you originally accessed the operating system prompt (before you typed **pgraph**). If you were using 1-2-3 and selected /**S**ystem to reach the operating system prompt, type **exit** and press Enter to return to the 1-2-3 worksheet. If you were not using 1-2-3 before the PrintGraph session, type **123**, or type **lotus** and then select **1-2-3** from the Lotus 1-2-3 Access menu.

Summary

You have learned a great deal about 1-2-3 graphs from this chapter: how to create and enhance all seven graph types and how to store graphs for recall in the worksheet and for use by other programs. You also were introduced to 1-2-3's many options for enhancing and modifying graphs. This chapter discussed how you can print graphs with the PrintGraph program provided with Release 2.3. Chapter 11 shows you how to use the Wysiwyg :Graph commands to display, modify, and print high-quality graphs.

11

Enhancing and Printing Graphs in Wysiwyg

I n the preceding chapter, you learn how to create and print business graphs with 1-2-3's /Graph commands and the PrintGraph program. As you see in this chapter, Wysiwyg offers its own set of graphing commands. However, the Wysiwyg **:Graph** commands are not for *creating* graphs; they enable you to embellish graphs you have created in 1-2-3 and other graphic programs. You can print these enhanced graphs with worksheet data on the same page by using the Wysiwyg **:Print** commands. (You can even create your own drawings with the Wysiwyg **:Graph** commands.) A graphics editor enables you to add geometric shapes, rotate and flip objects, and perform other advanced drawing tasks. The following topics are covered in this chapter:

Cue:
Release 2.2 users should turn to Appendix D for information on the Allways add-in.

- Including your 1-2-3 charts in a Wysiwyg-formatted report

- Changing a chart's position on the page

- Adjusting graph settings

- Adding, modifying, and rearranging text and geometric shapes

- Transforming the size and rotation of objects

- Printing graphs with Wysiwyg

499

Adding a Graph

Before you can use any of the :Graph commands in the Wysiwyg menu, you must add the graph to the worksheet with the :Graph Add command. By using this command, you define the worksheet range into which you want the graph to appear—you actually see the graph in the worksheet. After you select :Graph Add, you see the following choices:

Option	Description
Current	Inserts the current 1-2-3 graph (the one you see when you press F10)
Named	Inserts a 1-2-3 graph that you have named with the /Graph Name Create command
PIC	Inserts a 1-2-3 graph created with the /Graph Save command (in any version of 1-2-3 or Symphony). This file has the extension PIC.
Metafile	Inserts a graphic that was saved in metafile format. This file, which could have been created in 1-2-3 Release 3 or 3.1 or an external graphics program, has the extension CGM.
Blank	Inserts an empty placeholder. Use this option if you have not created the graph but want to reserve space for it. Also use this option if you want to create your own freehand drawing.

Cue:
*Insert a **B**lank placeholder when creating a graphic drawing.*

Choose the Current option only if the worksheet contains a single graph or if you want the current graph to be repeated in two or more places on the worksheet. If you want to add two or more different graphs to the worksheet, name each graph with the /Graph Name command and then add each graph by using the :Graph Add Named command.

Adding a graph or a drawing to your worksheet with :Graph Add involves the following steps:

- Selecting a named graph or graphics file

- Highlighting the range where you want to place the graph in the worksheet

Cue:
Use :Graph View to see a PIC or Metafile graph before you add it.

Selecting a graph or drawing: The :Graph Add options you select determine which information you are prompted for. If you select Named, for example, you must select the name of the graph. If you select PIC or Metafile, a list of PIC or CGM files in the current directory appears; select one of the names or choose a different directory. If you cannot remember which PIC or Metafile graph you want, cancel the :Graph Add command (press Esc until you are back in READY mode). Then choose :Graph View to display the graphs so that you can choose the correct one.

Highlighting the range: Next, specify the range over which you want to paste the graph. The size and shape of the range you specify determines the size and shape of the printed graph. The graph is scaled automatically (down or up) to fit the specified range.

To display and print the graph in the middle of a worksheet, before you add the graph, be sure to insert blank rows or columns where you want the graph to appear. If you don't add these blank rows or columns, the graph overlays worksheet data. Generally, the graph range includes only blank cells; be sure to insert enough rows and columns to make the graph the size you want.

For example, suppose that you want to paste the current 1-2-3 bar graph into the middle of a worksheet and then print the worksheet and graph. Figure 11.1 shows the Wysiwyg screen with the 1-2-3 graph added. Notice that the graph appears in the worksheet. This graph was added to the worksheet by choosing **:G**raph **A**dd **C**urrent and selecting the range B15..E26.

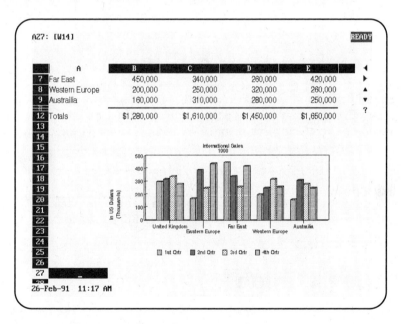

Fig. 11.1. *A graph inserted into a worksheet range.*

If you discover that you added the wrong graph, or you later create a graph you want to put in the same perfectly sized graph range, you can replace the existing graph with another. You do not have to remove one graph before adding another in the same location. To replace a graph with another in the exact location of the original graph, follow these steps:

Reminder:
You don't have to remove one graph before adding another graph in the same location.

1. Select **:Graph Settings Graph**.

2. Move the cell pointer to one cell in the graph range and press Enter.

   If your cell pointer is not near the graph, you can press **Name** (F3) and select the graph name from a list.

3. Answer the questions about the replacement graph: Indicate the type of graphic (**Current**, **Named**, **PIC**, **Metafile**, or **Blank**) and specify the name, if prompted.

4. Select **Quit**.

Remember that the new graph retains any enhancements (such as annotations) which are part of the original graph. If you don't want these enhancements in the new graph, don't use the **:Graph Settings Graph** command. Instead, use **:Graph Remove** to delete the initial graph and then insert the new graph with **:Graph Add**.

Repositioning a Graph

After adding a graph, you may realize that the range isn't appropriate for your graph, or you may want to position the graph in a different area of the worksheet. The **:Graph** menu offers several commands for changing a graph's position. You can move, remove, or resize the graph.

Reminder:
Use :Graph Goto to move to a specific graph.

If your worksheet is large or contains many graphs, you can use the **:Graph Goto** command to move the cell pointer to a specific graph before you reposition the graph. After you choose **:Graph Goto**, select the name of the graph from the list or press **Name** (F3) to see a full-screen list.

Moving a Graph

Reminder:
:Graph Move moves a graph from one location in the worksheet to a new location without changing the size and shape of the graph.

To move a graph from one worksheet location to another, use the **:Graph Move** command. This command retains the graph's original size and shape (that is, the number of rows and columns), changing only the graph's position in the worksheet. When prompted for which graph to move, either place the cell pointer anywhere in the graph or press **Name** (F3) to select the name of the graph from a list. After you press Enter, you are prompted for the target location. Place the cell pointer in the upper left corner of the target range and press Enter. (You don't have to highlight the entire range.) The graph moves to its new location, retaining its original size and shape. If the new location has different row heights or column widths, the moved graph's size and shape are slightly different than the size and shape of the graph before being moved.

Resizing a Graph

If the range you highlight is too large or too small for the graph, you can resize an existing graph by using the **:Graph Settings Range** command.

Reminder:
Use :Graph
Settings Range to
resize a graph.

After you select the graph to resize, the current graph range is highlighted on-screen. Type the new range or move the cell pointer to highlight a larger or smaller area. If you want to specify a new range entirely different from the existing one, press Esc or Backspace to cancel the old range before you specify the new one.

Removing a Graph

To erase a graph from the worksheet report, use **:Graph Remove**. A 1-2-3 prompt asks which graph you want to remove. Either move the cell pointer to the graph range or press Name (F3) and then highlight the name of the graph you want to remove. When you press Enter, the graph disappears. **:Graph Remove** does not delete the graph name or the graph's settings.

Specifying Graph Settings

In the previous sections, you looked at two of the options on the **:Graph Settings** menu (Graph and Range). These two settings enable you to replace and resize a graph. The three other options that the **:Graph Settings** menu offers are discussed in this section. Each of these options can be applied to individual graphs; each can be applied to several graphs simultaneously. To use the options on more than one graph, specify a range that covers all of the graphs you want the **:Graph Settings** commands to affect.

The **:Graph Settings Display** command controls whether you see the graphs you add in the worksheet. By default, all graphs are displayed. When a graph is on-screen, the process of redrawing the screen can be slow (depending on your computer's speed). If you set the **Display** option to **No**, Wysiwyg displays a shaded rectangle in the graph range (see fig. 11.2). When you print, the graph replaces this rectangle. Clearly, you want to see the graph

Cue:
Turn off the :Graph
Settings Display
setting to speed up
screen redrawing.

as you edit and enhance it; after you finish working on the graph, however, you may want to turn off its display so that you don't have to wait for the screen to redraw the graphic.

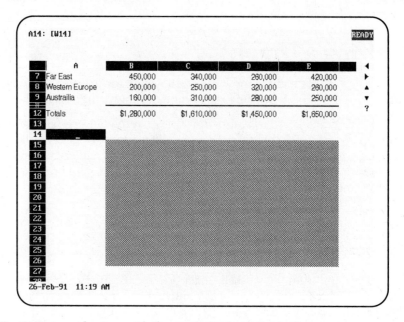

Fig. 11.2. *A graph range with the graph display turned off.*

The **:Graph Settings Sync** command controls whether the graph is synchronized with your worksheet data. By default, when you change a number in the worksheet, the graph redraws to reflect the new values. This synchronization enables you to play what-if games with your worksheet: type different values, and the picture changes instantly.

Because redrawing the screen takes time, you may want to unsynchronize the graph and data. To do so, choose **:Graph Settings Sync No** and point to a cell in the graph. Now, when your data changes, the graph remains static. To update the graph, choose **:Graph Compute** or turn on synchronization with **:Graph Settings Sync Yes**. The **:Graph Compute** command redraws all graphs in the file; **:Graph Settings Sync Yes** turns on synchronization for the specified graphics only.

Cue:
To view the contents of the cells underneath the graph, turn off the :Graph Settings Opaque option.

The **:Graph Settings Opaque** command controls whether the graph hides any data typed in cells within the graph range. By default, the graph is opaque, and underlying data is hidden. To view the contents of the cells through the graph, choose **:Graph Settings Opaque No**. Turning off the **Opaque** setting is useful if you have entered, in a cell in the graph range, text that you want to appear as a note or label on the graph.

Using the Graphics Editor

Included in Wysiwyg is a graphics editor that enables you to add and manipulate graphic objects. With this text editor, you can add text, arrows, boxes, and other geometric shapes. After adding these special objects, you can modify, rearrange, duplicate, and transform them.

You can place a graph in the graphics editing window in one of two ways. You can choose **:Graph Edit** and then choose which graph you want to edit by placing the cell pointer anywhere in that graph's range and then pressing Enter. You also can place the mouse pointer on the graphic and double-click the left mouse button.

Cue:
To place a graph in the graphics editing window, double-click the mouse on the graph.

Figure 11.3 shows the graphics editing window with a graph in place. Working in the graphics editing window is like being in a different world. You see only the graphic—not the worksheet. This arrangement enables you to concentrate on the task at hand: enhancing the graphic. Furthermore, the editing menu always remains at the top of the screen and is active at all times; you cannot press Esc or click the right mouse button to clear the menu. The only way to exit the graphics editor is to choose the **Quit** menu option or press Ctrl-Break.

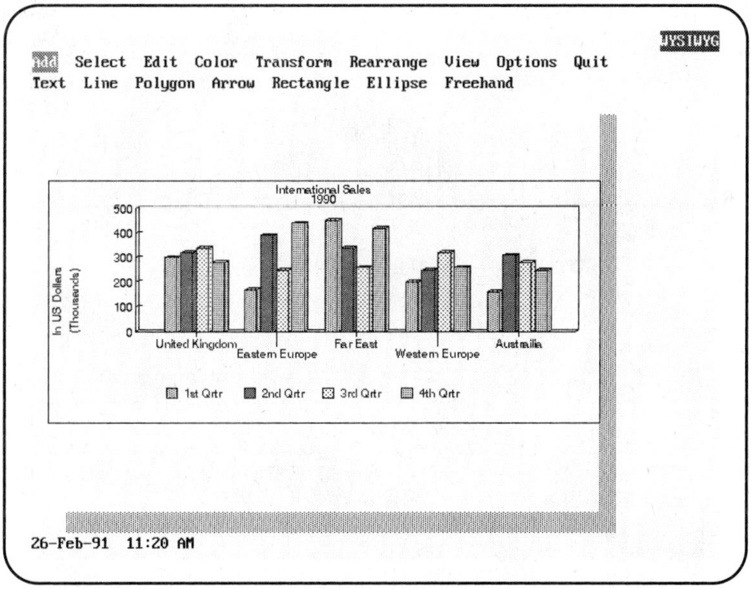

Fig. 11.3. The graphics editing window.

Caution:
The Undo command (Alt-F4) does not work in the graphics editing window.

The Undo command does not work on individual options in the :Graph Edit menu. To undo all the additions and modifications made in the current graph-editing session, select **Quit** from the :Graph Edit menu, press Undo (Alt-F4), and choose **Yes**. Remember that Undo will work only if the 1-2-3 configuration file is set to enable Undo automatically, or if you have enabled Undo by selecting /Worksheet Global Default Other Undo Enable.

Adding Objects

Wysiwyg enables you to add the following types of objects to your graphic: text, lines, polygons, arrows, rectangles, and ellipses. You also can draw freehand. The objects Wysiwyg provides are designed to help you annotate your charts. For example, you can add a brief explanation of why a data point is unusually high or low. Figure 11.4 shows how text, an arrow, and an ellipse are used to point out a value on the graph.

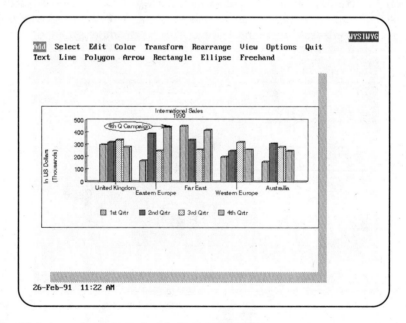

Fig. 11.4. A graph annotated with the graphics editor.

To create an object for your chart, choose **Add** from the :Graph Edit menu and then select the type of object you want to add. The following sections describe how to add each type of object.

Adding Text

The **:Graph Edit Add Text** command enables you to insert titles or comments anywhere on the graph. Instead of typing text directly on the graph, you add the text in two steps, as follows:

1. Select **Add Text** from the **:Graph Edit** menu, type the text at the `Text:` prompt at the top of the screen, and press Enter.

2. 1-2-3 displays the text on the graph and prompts you to move the text to the area on the graph where you want the text displayed. Use the mouse or arrow keys to position the text in its final location.

Cue:
Use the mouse to quickly position the text you add to a graph.

Normally, using the mouse to position the text is easier and quicker than using the arrow keys, which cause the text to move in tiny increments. If you cannot see the text when it is first displayed on the graph, press one of the arrow keys or move the mouse to an open area on the graph.

To confirm the target location for the text, either click the left mouse button or press Enter. Small filled-in squares, called *selection indicators*, surround the text. These boxes mean that the object is selected and that you can perform another operation on it (such as move it, change its font, and so on). To change the font, use the **:Graph Edit Edit Font** command. To change the content of the text, use the **:Graph Edit Edit Text** command. These editing options are discussed in the "Editing Objects" section later in this chapter.

The text you add can include formatting sequences (bold, italic, outline, and fonts, for example). Chapter 10 describes how to format text.

Adding Lines and Arrows

The processes you follow to draw lines and arrows are identical. The only difference is the end result: the arrow has an arrowhead at the end of the line. To draw a line or arrow, select **Line** or **Arrow** from the **:Graph Edit Add** menu and then follow these basic steps:

1. When 1-2-3 prompts you with `Move to the first point:`, use the mouse or the arrow keys to move the pointer on the graph to one end of the line you want to draw.

2. Press the left mouse button or the space bar to anchor this point.

3. When 1-2-3 prompts you with `Stretch to the next point:`, use the mouse or the arrow keys to move the pointer to the other end of the line.

4. Click the left mouse button twice or press Enter to complete the line.

The line or arrow is drawn on-screen, and the selection indicator appears in the center of the line. If you are adding an arrow, the arrowhead appears at the last point you indicated. To switch the direction of the arrow, use the Edit Arrowheads option of the **:Graph Edit** menu. To change the line width, use the Edit Width option of the **:Graph Edit** menu. For more information on these options, see "Editing Objects" later in this chapter.

To connect several lines, repeat steps 2 and 3 of the preceding procedure at each line-ending. When you finish drawing a line, click the left mouse button twice or press Enter.

When drawing horizontal, vertical, or diagonal lines, you may notice that drawing straight lines is difficult; the lines are somewhat jagged. To prevent this jagged look, press and hold down the Shift key before you anchor the last point. The line segment snaps to 45-degree angles, enabling you to draw perfectly straight lines.

Adding Polygons

A polygon is a multisided object—the object can have as many connecting lines as you want. You don't need to connect the last side to the first—Wysiwyg does the job for you. The steps for creating a polygon are similar to the steps for creating lines and arrows. You create a polygon as follows:

1. Choose **:Graph Edit Add Polygon**.

2. When 1-2-3 prompts you to move to the `Move to the first point:`, use the mouse or the arrow keys to move the pointer to the first point of the polygon.

3. Press the left mouse button or the space bar to anchor this point.

4. When 1-2-3 prompts you for the `Stretch to the next point:`, use the mouse or the arrow keys to move the pointer to the opposite end of the first line.

5. Press the left mouse button or the space bar to anchor this point.

6. Repeat steps 3 and 4 for each side of the polygon.

7. Click the left mouse button twice or press Enter to complete the polygon.

Adding Rectangles and Ellipses

Use the rectangle and ellipse objects to enclose text and other objects on your graphic (see fig. 11.5).

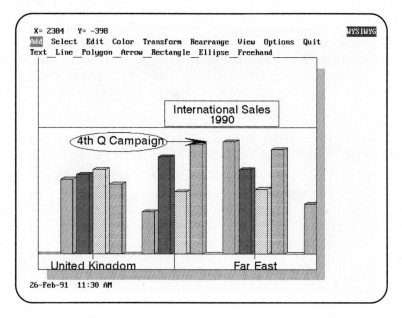

Fig. 11.5. Text enclosed in a rectangle and an ellipse.

If you are drawing rectangles and ellipses with a mouse, use the click-and-drag method to define the shape. Click and hold down the left mouse button in any corner of the object. Then drag the mouse to create the object in the desired size. Whether you are creating a rectangle or an ellipse, a rectangle (called the *bounding box*—the broken-lined box) appears on-screen while you are drawing the graphic. As soon as you release the mouse button, the appropriate shape is created on the graph.

To draw rectangles and ellipses from the keyboard, follow these steps:

1. Choose **Add Rectangle** or **Add Ellipse** from the **:Graph Edit** menu.

2. Place the cursor on any corner of the area in which you want the rectangle or ellipse to be located.

3. Press the space bar to anchor the corner.

4. Use the arrow keys to stretch the bounding box to the size you want. (The bounding box appears regardless of whether you are drawing a rectangle or an ellipse.)

5. Press Enter.

Reminder:
Use the click-and-drag method to define the shape and size of rectangles and ellipses.

In the middle of each side of the rectangle or ellipse are selection indicators. These indicators show that the object is still selected; they indicate that you can make changes to the object without reselecting it. To change the type of line (solid, dashed, or dotted) used in the rectangle or ellipse, use the :Graph Edit Edit Line-Style command. The Line-Style option is discussed later in this chapter in the "Editing Objects" section.

Cue:
To create a perfect circle or square, press and hold down the Shift key before you set the size.

To create a circle when you have chosen Ellipse or a square when you have chosen Rectangle from the :Graph Edit Add menu, press and hold down the Shift key before you set the object's size. Although the object may not appear perfectly circular or square on-screen, it prints accurately.

Adding Objects Freehand

Caution:
Unless you have artistic ability, freehand drawing looks like scribbling.

Using the Freehand option of the :Graph Edit Add menu is similar to having someone give you a pencil and let you draw on the screen. Unless you have artistic ability, freehand drawing looks more like freehand scribbling (see fig. 11.6). You may want to leave this option to the professionals.

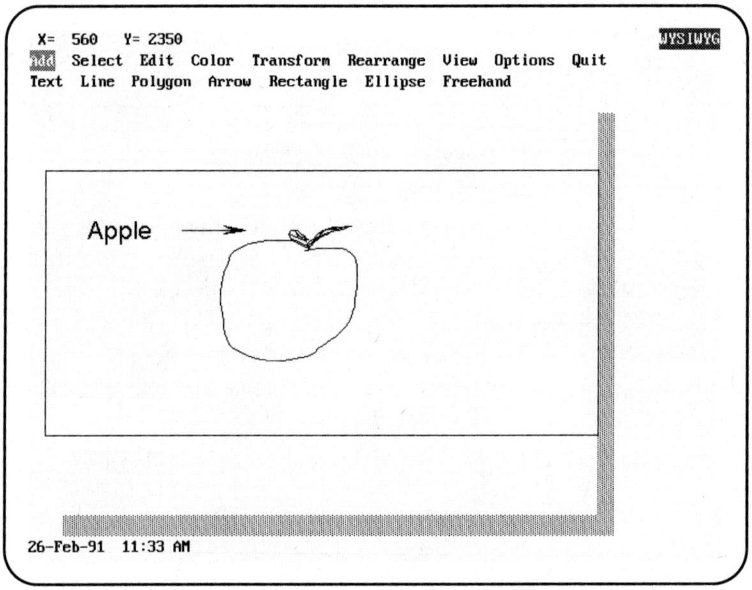

Fig. 11.6. Freehand drawing.

Although you can use the arrow keys to draw freehand, the easist way to draw is by using the mouse. Place the cursor where you want to begin drawing, click and hold down the left mouse button, and move the mouse to draw. Release the mouse button when you finish drawing a segment of the graphic. Each segment of the freehand drawing displays a selection indicator. To change the type of line (solid, dashed, or dotted), use the **:Graph Edit Edit Line-Style** command. The Line-Style option is discussed in "Editing Objects," later in this chapter.

Selecting Objects

After adding objects to a graphic, you can change them by using the mouse or the **:Graph Edit Select** command. For example, you can change the line-style and font, and you can move, delete, or copy the objects. Regardless of what operation you perform on the object, you must select the object or objects you want to change. An object you just added is selected automatically. Selection indicators appear on an object after that object is selected.

Several selection techniques are available to mouse users (see the following section, "Selecting with the Mouse"). Keyboard users use the **:Graph Edit Select** menu to select objects (see the "Selecting with the Menu" section).

Normally, you select the object or objects you want to change before you issue a command. If no object is selected, you are prompted to point to an object.

Reminder:
Select the object before issuing a command.

Selecting with the Mouse

Mouse users can select a single object by clicking on it. (You can select an object only when the main **:Graph Edit** menu is displayed.) Check to make sure that the selection indicators are around the object you want to change. If two objects are close together, you may have to click several times to select the correct object.

Sometimes you may want to select more than one object. For example, you may want to change the font of all the text you have added. To select multiple objects, press and hold down the Shift key as you click the left mouse button on each object. If you accidentally select the wrong object, press and hold down the Shift key while you click on the object again.

Cue:
To select several objects, press and hold down the Shift key as you click the mouse button on each.

Alternatively, you can select several objects with a mouse by pressing and holding down the left mouse button when the pointer is outside any of the objects. A hand with a pointing index finger appears on-screen. Move the mouse so that the selection box includes all the objects you want to select and then release the mouse button.

Selecting with the Menu

To select a single object from the keyboard, choose the **:Graph Edit** menu's **Select** menu option and then choose **One**. Wysiwyg displays the prompt Point to desired object:. Use the arrow keys to move the cursor to the object and then press Enter. The selection indicators appear on the object.

Another way to select an object is with the **:Graph Edit Select Cycle** option. This option cycles through all the objects, one by one, so that you can select one or more objects. Each time you press an arrow key, a different object displays small boxes that look like selection indicators, except that these boxes are hollow. When an object you want to select (or deselect) displays the hollow selection boxes, press the space bar. Continue pressing the arrow keys and space bar until you have selected all the objects you want. When you are finished, press Enter. Mouse users who are having trouble selecting an object that is close to another object may want to use the **:Graph Edit Select Cycle** option.

The **:Graph Edit Select** menu offers several other ways to select objects. The **All** option selects all objects you have added except the graphic itself. The **None** option deselects everything—the objects and the graphic. **Graph** selects only the underlying graphic. The **More/Less** option enables you to select an additional object or deselect one of the currently selected objects: selecting the object you point to if that object is not selected or removing an object that already is selected.

Editing Objects

As this chapter's "Adding Objects" section mentions, the graphics editor provides ways to fine-tune the objects you add. Following is a list of the features you can change on your objects:

- Text content, alignment, and font
- Position of the arrowhead on an arrow
- Line-style and width
- Sharpness of angles

The following sections examine each of the options on the **:Graph Edit Edit** menu. Remember to select the object or objects you want to edit before you issue the command.

Editing Text

The Text option on the **:Graph Edit Edit** menu enables you to edit text you have added with the **:Graph Add Text** command. You cannot edit text that was added with the /Graph commands (titles and legends, for example) or that was part of the PIC or Metafile graphic you inserted. When you choose **:Graph Edit Edit Text**, a copy of the text appears at the top of the screen. To correct or insert text, use the editing keys you normally use in EDIT mode. (See Chapter 3 for a list of editing keys.) Press Enter when you are finished—the text is corrected.

Cue:
To correct a typing mistake, use :Graph Edit Edit Text.

Centering Text

The Centering option of the **:Graph Edit Edit** menu aligns text in relation to the text's center point. If you choose **Left** from the **:Graph Edit Edit Centering** menu, the left edge of the text is aligned with the text's original center point. If you choose **Center**, the center of the text is aligned with the text's center point. If you choose **Right**, the text is aligned to the right of the center point.

Because of the way text is aligned, the Centering command is not particularly useful. You may find that positioning text is easier with the **:Graph Edit Rearrange Move** command.

Changing Fonts

To change the font (typeface and size) of the text you have added with the **:Graph Edit Add Text** command, use the Edit Font option of the **:Graph Edit Edit** command.

When you choose **:Graph Edit Edit Font**, a list displays the eight fonts currently available in the worksheet. Choose the appropriate font number to change all the selected text. If the font you want to use is not listed, exit the graphics editor by choosing **Quit**. Then use the **:Format Font Replace** command to replace one of the existing eight fonts with the font you want to use.

Reminder:
Use the :Format Font Replace command to use a different font.

Changing Line-Style

By using the **:Graph Edit Edit Line-Style** command, you can display different types of lines in your objects. Figure 11.7 shows examples of each of the
six line styles. Solid is the default. You can change the line styles of lines,
arrows, rectangles, polygons, ellipses, and freehand drawings. You also can
hide a line with the **Hidden** option.

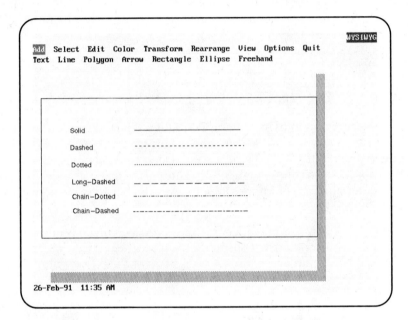

Fig. 11.7. Examples of the six line styles.

Changing Line Width

By default, Wysiwyg lines are quite thin. Use the **:Graph Edit Edit Width**
command to change the width of lines in arrows, rectangles, polygons,
ellipses, lines, and freehand drawings. Only the lines in selected object(s)
are affected. Figure 11.8 shows examples of the five line widths.

Changing Arrowheads

When you draw arrows with the **:Graph Edit Add Arrow** command, the
arrowhead points from the line ending (the last point you indicated). Using
the **Edit Arrowhead** option of the **:Graph Edit** command, you can adjust
arrowhead positioning. The following options are available:

Option	Description
Switch	Moves the arrowhead to the opposite end of the line
One	Adds an arrowhead to a line (use this option to turn a line into an arrow)
Two	Adds an arrowhead to each end of the line
None	Removes all arrowheads (use this option to turn an arrow into a line)

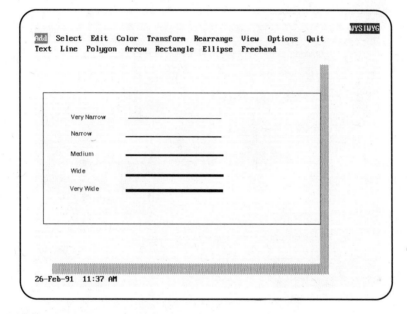

Fig. 11.8. *Examples of the five line widths.*

Smoothing Angles

By using the **:Graph Edit Edit S**moothing command, you can create smooth curves from sharp angles. You can smooth squares, rectangles, polygons, freehand drawings, and line segments that are connected together. The **Edit** **S**moothing menu displays the following options:

Option	Description
None	Returns a smoothed object to its original angles
Tight	Slightly smoothes or rounds the object's angles
Medium	Provides the maximum smoothing available; smoothes the angles to a greater degree than the **Tight** option

Figure 11.9 shows a rectangle with **None**, **Tight**, and **Medium** smoothing.

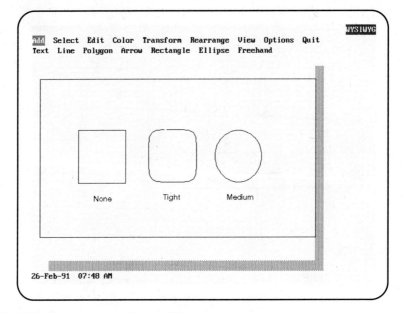

Fig. 11.9. *The three types of smoothing.*

Adding Patterns and Colors

The Color option on the **:Graph Edit** menu enables you to assign colors or patterns to the following areas of your graphic:

Area	Description
Lines	Lines, arrows, and object outlines
Inside	The space inside the rectangle, ellipse, or polygon
Text	Text added with **:Graph Edit Add Text** (not legends or titles entered with **/Graph** commands)

Area	Description
Map	Enables you to change the color or gray shading for as many as eight different elements on a graphic
Background	In the defined graphic range, the area behind the graphic (where the titles, legends, and scale appear)

Note: The options listed do not apply to the underlying 1-2-3 graph.

To change the colors or patterns of any elements in the 1-2-3 graph, you can use color mapping (discussed later in this section). Remember that you must select **/Graph Options Color** to see the different colors in your graph. Refer to Chapter 10 for more information about the **/Graph** commands.

To change a color, first select the object(s) you want to modify and then choose **Color** from the **:Graph Edit** menu. Next, select one of the four areas in which you want to change the color (**Lines**, **Inside**, **Text**, or **Background**). If you select the **Lines** or **Text** option, choose from a menu of the following colors:

Black	**Dark-Blue**
White	**Cyan**
Red	**Yellow**
Green	**Magenta**

If you select the **Inside** or **Background** option of **:Graph Edit Color**, a color palette appears on-screen. If you have a monochrome monitor, the palette displays different patterns in shades of gray. Either type the number shown next to the color/pattern you want or use the arrow keys to move the box to the color/pattern and press Enter. If you have a mouse, you can point to the color/pattern and click the left mouse button.

The **:Graph Edit Color Map** command enables you to change the fill colors and patterns of the underlying graphic. Suppose, for example, that the bars in a bar graph are a shade of green you don't like. You can use color mapping to adjust the shade, or you can use a different pattern. You cannot use this option to change the color of lines or text.

You can change the graphic with as many as eight colors; the **:Graph Edit Color Map** menu indicates the eight choices with the numbers 1 through 8. Each number corresponds to the specific data range set for your graph; select **1** for the color of the X range, **2** for the color of the A range, **3** for the color of the B range, and so on.

Cue:
*Use the **:Graph Edit Color Map** command to change the fill colors and patterns of the underlying graphic.*

After you choose the color number, the color palette displays with the current color/pattern boxed. To select the color/pattern with which you want to replace the current one, either type the number shown next to the color/pattern you want or use the arrow keys to move the box to the color/pattern and then press Enter. With a mouse, just point to the color/pattern and click the left mouse button.

For example, suppose that you want to change the color of the A range. From the **:Graph Edit Color Map** menu, select **2**; the color palette displays a box around one of the colored squares. To choose a different color or pattern, use the arrow keys to move the box to another colored square. When you press Enter, the original A-range color changes to the color or pattern you just selected.

Changing the colors in a Metafile-format graphic is a trial-and-error process. You must check the color palette for each of the numbers (1 through 8) until you find the color you want to change. For example, suppose that a Metafile-format graphic contains a shade of yellow you detest, and that you want to replace it with a shade of teal. From the **:Graph Edit Color Map** menu, choose **1**. If the boxed shade in the color palette is yellow, you are in luck— you found the correct color number; now you can highlight the teal shade you want to replace it with. If color **1** is not yellow, press Esc and continue choosing options on the Color Map menu until you see yellow boxed on the color palette.

Cue:
To see how colors translate into gray shades, use the :Display Mode B&W command.

If you have a color monitor but plan to print the graph on a black-and-white printer, you may want to view the graph in black and white before you print. Viewing the graph in black and white enables you to see how the colors translate into gray shades. Use the **:Display Mode B&W** command to change to a black-and-white display.

Changing the Display of the Graphic Editing Window

The **:Graph Edit Options** and **:Graph Edit View** menus provide ways to change the graphic editing window's display. The **:Graph Edit Options** menu offers the following options: Grid, Cursor, and Font-Magnification. The **:Graph Edit View** menu enables you to size and reposition the contents of the editing window. The **:Graph Edit View** menu offers the following options: Full, In, Pan, +, –, Up, Down, Left, and Right.

Using the :Graph Edit Options Menu

The **:Graph Edit Options** menu's **Grid** option enables you to display dotted lines to define the cells in the underlying worksheet. Grid lines can help you line up the objects you create with worksheet cells. The cell outlines (not the cell coordinates) are displayed. Alternatively, you can press F4 to toggle the display of grid lines in the graphics editor.

Cue:
Use the :Graph Edit Options Grid command to toggle the display of grid lines.

The **Cursor** option of the **:Graph Edit Options** menu enables you to define the size of the cursor as **Small** or **Big**. By default, the graph editor's cursor is a small cross. A big cursor also is a cross, but its lines extend across the entire editing window. Figure 11.10 shows a rectangle being drawn with a big cursor. With a big cursor, lining up one edge of an object with another is easy.

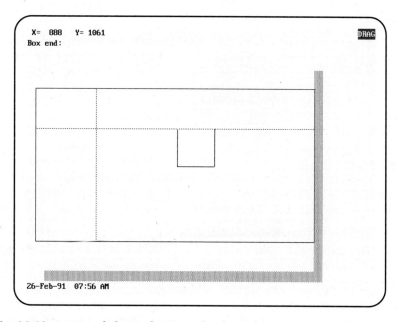

Fig. 11.10. *A rectangle being drawn with a big cursor.*

By using the Font-Magnification option of the **:Graph Edit Options** menu, you can scale the size of all text up or down. This option applies to text inserted with **:Graph Edit Add Text** as well as the text in the underlying graphic (titles and legends). If all your titles and legends are too large, for example, you can use Font-Magnification to reduce them all simultaneously.

Cue:
To scale the size of all text use :Graph Edit Options Font-Magnification.

The font-magnification value is a percentage between 0 and 1,000 (the default value is 100). To scale down sizes, enter a value of less than 100. For example, to reduce the text to 80 percent of its current size, type **80**. To magnify the text, enter a value greater than 100. For example, to double the size of the text, enter **200**. To display the text at its original point size—rather than at the size Wysiwyg scaled the text when you added the graphic—enter a font-magnification value of **0**.

Using the :Graph Edit View Menu

The :Graph Edit View menu enables you to size and reposition the contents of the graphics editing window. You can use the menu options to zoom in on an area you are modifying. None of the :Graph Edit View menu options changes the size of the graphic.

The Full option of the :Graph Edit View menu restores the graphic to its normal full size after you have resized or repositioned it with the other View options.

The :Graph Edit View menu's In option enables you to zoom in on a selected area of the graphic. Figure 11.11 shows a zoomed-in graphics window. When you select **In**, the prompt `Move to the first corner:` appears. To indicate the area you want to zoom in on, draw a box around the range. With a mouse, use the click-and-drag technique to stretch the box around the area. From the keyboard, use the arrow keys to position the cursor on the first corner, press Enter, use the arrow keys to stretch the box so that the area is surrounded, and press Enter again.

For mouse users, a second zooming method is available. From the :Graph Edit menu, press and hold down Ctrl while clicking-and-dragging a box around the area. To unzoom, press and hold down Ctrl and click anywhere in the graphic.

After you zoom in on an area, you may want to zoom in even further or move the graphic slightly in one direction. The remaining :Graph Edit View options enable you to make these adjustments.

Use the View Pan option of the :Graph Edit menu to simultaneously zoom, unzoom, and move the display. When you choose View Pan, the following message explains what to do:

```
Use cursor keys to move view, +/- to zoom, Enter to  leave
```

Thus, you can press + to zoom and the arrow keys to display a different part of the graphic. When you are satisfied with the window's contents, press Enter. To restore the screen to its original size and arrangement, choose

View **F**ull from the **:G**raph **E**dit menu. Use the **+** option to zoom in further than the view currently displayed. Each time you choose **+**, you zoom in. From the normal full size, you can zoom five times. You don't even need to access the **:G**raph **E**dit **V**iew menu to use the **+** option; you can press **+** from the **:G**raph **E**dit menu.

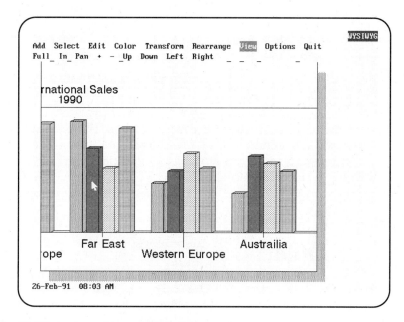

Fig. 11.11. *A zoomed-in graphics window.*

The **U**p, **D**own, **L**eft, and **R**ight options on the **:G**raph **E**dit **V**iew menu enable you to see parts of a zoomed graphic that are not currently in the window. Each of these options moves the display one-half screen in the specified direction. To move the display up or down when you are at the main graphics editing menu, press the up- or down-arrow key. To move left or right, hold down the Ctrl key and press the left- or right-arrow key.

Rearranging Objects

The **R**earrange option on the **:G**raph **E**dit menu enables you to delete, copy, and move the objects you added to your graphic with **:G**raph **E**dit **A**dd. See "Selecting Objects" earlier in this chapter for details on selecting objects with the mouse or the **S**elect menu.

Deleting and Restoring Objects

The **Rearrange Delete** option of the **:Graph Edit** menu removes the selected object(s) from the graphic. Although Wysiwyg does not ask you to confirm your intention to delete, you can use the **:Graph Edit Rearrange Restore** command to retrieve the last deleted object or group of objects. Suppose that you select three objects at the same time and then choose **Rearrange Delete** from the **:Graph Edit** menu. All three objects are deleted. If you choose **Rearrange Restore**, all three objects are retrieved to their original locations. If you select and delete a line and then select and delete a rectangle, you cannot restore the deleted line; you can retrieve only the deleted rectangle.

As an alternative to using the **Rearrange Delete** command from the **:Graph Edit** menu, you can select the object(s) you want to delete and press Del. Press Ins to restore the most recently deleted object or group of objects. Make sure that no object is selected when you press Ins to restore a deleted object; if you press Ins when an object is selected, that object is copied.

Moving Objects

To reposition an object, use the **:Graph Edit Rearrange Move** command option. If you haven't already selected the objects you want to move, you are asked to do so. Either use the arrow keys to move the cursor to the object and then press Enter or click the mouse on the object. (You must click directly on or very close to the outline of the rectangle, ellipse, or polygon. If you click too far inside the object, you cancel the command.) After you make your selection, a copy of the object is displayed inside a dotted rectangle (the bounding box). The hand that appears inside the bounding box indicates that you are moving the object. Use the mouse or the arrow keys to move the bounding box to the target location and click the left mouse button or press Enter. Figure 11.12 shows a rectangle being moved.

If you have a mouse, you do not have to use the **Rearrange Move** option of the **:Graph Edit** menu; from the main graphics editing menu, you can use the click-and-drag technique to reposition an object.

Copying Objects

After creating an object, you may want to clone it. Using the **Rearrange Copy** command from the **:Graph Edit** menu ensures that two or more objects are the exact same size, with the exact same options. For example, if you create a shaded rectangle with wide lines, the copy of the rectangle also is shaded and has wide lines. When you copy an object, the following options are copied with the object:

- Edit options (**T**ext, **F**ont, **L**ine-Style, **W**idth, **A**rrowheads, **S**moothing)

- Color settings

- Transform options (**S**ize, **R**otate, **Q**uarter-Turn, **X**-Flip, **Y**-Flip, **H**orizontal, **V**ertical); for more information, see "Transforming Objects" later in this chapter

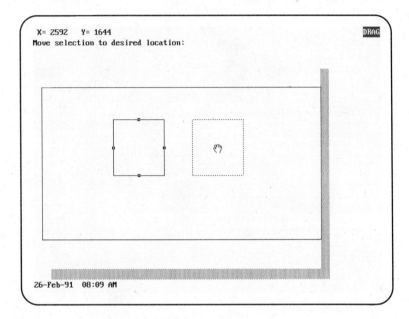

Fig. 11.12. *A rectangle being moved.*

If an object is selected when you choose the **:Graph Edit Rearrange Copy** command, a duplicate is placed slightly to the right and below the original object. If no object is selected when you choose **:Graph Edit Rearrange Copy**, you are prompted to select the objects to copy. The **Copy** command does not prompt you for a target location; you must use the **:Graph Edit Rearrange Move** command to put the object in place. Thus, copying is a two-step process.

Instead of using the **:Graph Edit Rearrange Copy** command, you can select the object and press the Ins key. Like the **:Graph Edit Rearrange Copy** command, Ins places the duplicated object next to the original; you must use the **:Graph Edit Rearrange Move** command to put the object into position. If no object is selected when you press Ins, the last deleted object is restored.

Cue:
To copy an object, select it and press Ins.

Moving an Object to the Back or Front

A colored or shaded object positioned on top of an existing object can obscure the objects it covers. Suppose that you add some text, draw an ellipse around the text, and then add a pattern to the ellipse. After adding the pattern, you cannot see the text because the ellipse is on top of the text (see fig. 11.13). To see the text, you need to bring the text in front of the ellipse or place the ellipse in back of the text; either select the ellipse and choose **Rearrange Back** from the **:Graph Edit** menu or select the text and choose **Rearrange Front**. In figure 11.13, the ellipse on the right shows how the text reappears after the ellipse is moved to the back.

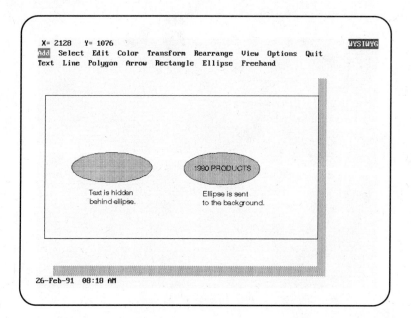

Fig. 11.13. Hidden text redisplayed with the :Graph Edit Rearrange Back command.

Objects that seem to have disappeared mysteriously may be hidden by an overlaying object. To find such missing objects, use the **Rearrange Front** and **Rearrange Back** options of the **:Graph Edit** menu.

Locking an Object

After an object is the perfect size, in the perfect location, with the perfect options, you may want to prevent accidental changes. To protect your perfect object, use the **Rearrange Lock** option of the **:Graph Edit** menu. When you lock an object, you cannot delete it, move it, transform it, color it, or edit it. You can copy it, however; the duplicate is not locked. Later, if you need to a change the locked object, use the **Rearrange Unlock** option of the **:Graph Edit** menu.

Cue:
To prevent an object from being changed, use :Graph Edit Rearrange Lock.

Transforming Objects

With the options on the **:Graph Edit Transform** menu, you can perform plastic surgery on basic geometric shapes. The shape in figure 11.14 (originally a basic rectangle) was transformed with several of the **:Graph Edit Transform** options. If you aren't happy with the transformed object, you can use **:Graph Edit Transform Clear** to clear all transformations made to the selected object.

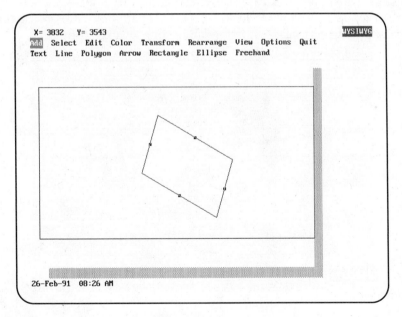

***Fig. 11.14.** A transformed rectangle.*

Sizing an Object

Reminder:
Use **:Graph Edit Transform Size** to change the height and width of any added objects.

You can change the size (height and width) of any added objects except text. (To change the text size, specify a different font with the **:Graph Edit Edit Font** command.) When you choose the **:Graph Edit Transform Size** command, the selected object is surrounded by a bounding box. The box's upper left corner is anchored; the cursor is in the box's lower right corner. To control the size of the object, press the arrow keys or move the mouse until the bounding box is the size you want. Then press Enter or click the left mouse button to change the object's size.

Another way to adjust an object's size is to use the **:Graph Edit** command's **Transform Horizontal** or **Transform Vertical** options. These options also change the angles of the objects. See "Adjusting the Slant" later in this chapter for additional information.

Rotating an Object

Cue:
To rotate an object, use **:Graph Edit Transform Quarter-Turn** or **Rotate**.

The **:Graph Edit Transform** menu offers two ways to rotate an object. The Quarter-Turn option rotates the selected object(s) in 90-degree increments. The turns are made counterclockwise. Figure 11.15 shows two objects (the ellipse and the text below it) before and after a Quarter-Turn.

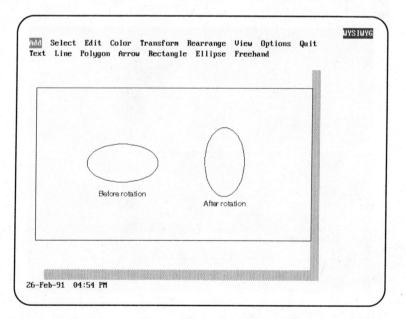

Fig. 11.15. Objects before and after a Quarter-Turn rotation.

If you want to rotate an object in increments other than 90 degrees, use the **Transform R**otate option of the **:G**raph **E**dit command; you can rotate the selected object(s) to any angle. An axis extends from the center of the object to outside the bounding box. Think of this axis as a handle that pulls the object in the direction you press the arrow keys or move the mouse. A copy of the object rotates while the original object remains intact. As soon as you press Enter or click the left mouse button, the rotated copy is replaced by the original.

Some printers can print text that has been rotated in 90-degree increments only. The HP LaserJet Series II and III and PostScript printers can print text at any angle.

Flipping an Object

Imagine that the selected object is a pancake and that the **X**-Flip and **Y**-Flip options of the **:G**raph **E**dit **T**ransform command are spatulas. **X**-Flip flips the object over, positioning the original upper left corner in the upper right corner. **Y**-Flip turns the object upside down, positioning the upper left corner in the lower left corner. If you choose the wrong flip direction, you can reverse the action by choosing the same direction again. For example, if you choose **X**-Flip and don't like the results, flip the object back to its original position by choosing **X**-Flip again.

You do not notice any effect when you flip lines, rectangles, or ellipses that are in a 90-degree angle position, because the objects flip to their original position.

Adjusting the Slant

The **Transform H**orizontal and **Transform V**ertical options of the **:G**raph **E**dit command enable you to change the slant (angles) and size of the selected object(s). You can even flip the object in the same step. The rectangle in figure 11.16 is being transformed horizontally. The upper line is anchored. As you press the arrow keys or move the mouse, you see the bounding box stretch freely in the direction you move the cursor. To flip the object, position the bounding box above the selected object. When the bounding box is the size and shape you want, press Enter or click the left mouse button. The object is moved into the position of the bounding box.

Cue:
Use :Graph Edit Transform Horizontal or Transform Vertical to change the angles and size of an object.

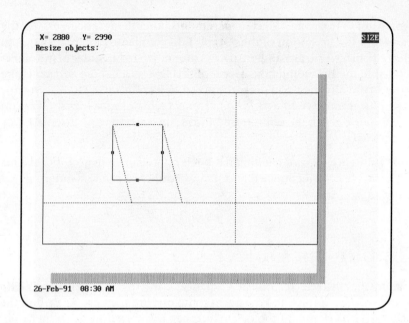

Fig. 11.16. A rectangle transformed horizontally.

When you transform an object vertically, the left side of the object is anchored. To flip the object, position the bounding box to the left of the selected object.

Printing Graphs in Wysiwyg

Unlike printing graphs with PrintGraph in 1-2-3 Release 2.01, printing graphs with 1-2-3 Release 2.3's Wysiwyg menu does not require special graph printing commands. When you position a graph on the worksheet with :Graph Add, you can print the graph using the same Wysiwyg :Print commands used for printing text.

To print a graph either by itself or with text above, below, or next to a graph, select :Print and follow the steps covered in Chapter 9 for printing Wysiwyg text. Briefly, these steps include the following:

1. Set the printing range. If you want to print a graph by itself, position the graph in a blank area of the worksheet, making sure that you size the graph on-screen to the size you want printed. You may find that using the :Display Options Frame Special command helps you determine the inches, meters, or point/picas measurements of the graph.

2. Change whatever **:Print Config** or **:Print Settings** options you need
    to. If you want to print the graph sideways, for example, select
    :Print Config Orientation Landscape. If you want to print multiple
    copies of the graph, select **:Print Settings Copies**.

3. Change the **:Print Layout** settings. For example, adjust margins or
    add titles to your printout.

4. Use the **:Print Preview** command to see how your graph will appear
    on the page.

5. Select **:Print Go** to initiate printing your graph.

Whether you want to print a graph by itself or print a graph along with
worksheet data or text, 1-2-3 Release 2.3's Wysiwyg **:Print** menu is easy to
use and contains all the settings for producing professional, high-quality
printouts. See Chapter 9 for a detailed discussion of all **:Print** commands.

Summary

This chapter showed you how to use Wysiwyg's graphing commands and
options to enhance and print graphs. At the simplest level, you can insert a
graph so that you can include it with a Wysiwyg-formatted report. Then you
can make annotations to the 1-2-3 graph to point out key data values. At
another level, you can use the graphics editor to create drawings that
include text and geometric objects.

Part III

Customizing 1-2-3

Includes

Managing Data

Using Macros

Introducing the Advanced Macro Commands

12

Managing Data

In addition to the electronic spreadsheet and business graphics, 1-2-3 has a third capability: data management. You perform data management tasks in 1-2-3 by using a database. A 1-2-3 database is easy to create because you enter it directly into the cells of the worksheet. You don't need any special commands to set up the database, change its design, or enter records. In fact, you can create it by using the entry and editing techniques you have learned in this book. If you have a great deal of data in one database, you also can use worksheet windows and the mouse or arrow keys to scroll through the database.

As you create a database, 1-2-3 places all of the information you enter into computer memory (RAM). Because 1-2-3 uses RAM, you have faster access to the contents of the database than if it were stored on floppy disks or even on your hard disk. If you have expanded memory (more than 640K of RAM), 1-2-3 also uses that memory.

To enhance the use of the database, 1-2-3 includes /**Data** commands that you use to look at or change entries in the database. This chapter covers all /**Data** command options. The menu displayed when you select /**Data** contains the following options:

    Fill Table Sort Query Distribution Matrix Regression Parse

You use the **S**ort and **Q**uery options to manipulate records in the database: to sort, select, and modify the records. You use the other options to create or analyze data.

This chapter shows you how to do the following:

- Design a 1-2-3 database.

- Create and maintain records in a database.

- Sort and search for database records.

- Fill a range with numbers.

- Create a table of values for a single formula.

- Graph a distribution curve.

- Perform matrix math.

- Analyze data statistically.

- Load data from ASCII files and other programs.

Defining a Database

A *database* is a collection of related data organized for a particular task. For example, you can use a database to track personnel changes in a company, update inventory counts, or maintain sales expenses. A database can contain any kind of information.

In 1-2-3, the word *database* means a range of cells that spans at least one column and two or more rows. This definition is the same as the definition of any other range of cells; 1-2-3 has certain requirements for the design of the database, however.

Each 1-2-3 database consists of a series of fields and records. A *field* is a column that contains one type of information. For example, an address database can contain the following fields:

Name

Address

City

State

ZIP

Phone

A *record* is a single row of cells that contain entries for each field in the database. For example, the address for one company makes up one record in the database. Please note, therefore, that the data in the database must be organized as horizontal rows in the worksheet. Each column contains the same type of information for each entry in the database.

Reminder:
A field is a column with one type of information, and a record is a row of cells.

Designing a 1-2-3 Database

Figure 12.1 shows the general organization of a 1-2-3 database. Labels, or *field names*, define the contents of each field (column) in the database. The cells under each field name contain the specific entries for that field. For example, cell A4 in figure 12.1 contains the entry A1 Computing for the field COMPANY. The other fields in the database are ADDRESS, CITY, STATE, ZIP, and PHONE. All of the information for the A1 Computing company (that is, its name, address, and telephone number) makes up one record in this database.

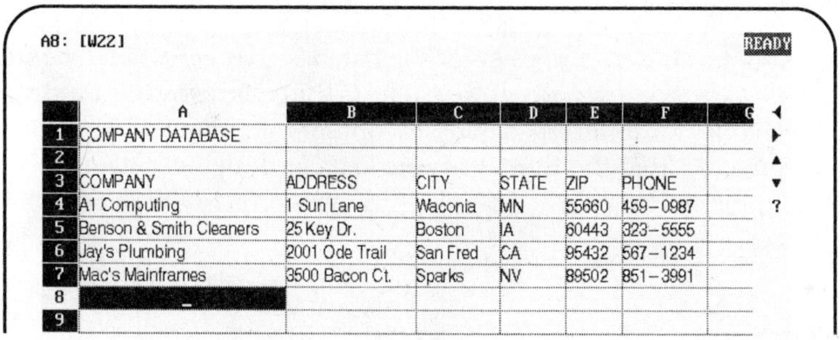

Fig. 12.1. *The organization of a sample 1-2-3 database.*

Theoretically, the maximum number of records available in a 1-2-3 database corresponds to the maximum number of rows in the worksheet (8,192 rows minus 1 row for the field names). Realistically, however, the number of records in a specific database is limited by the amount of available memory: conventional memory (RAM), expanded memory, and disk storage.

A typical computer system with 640K of conventional memory can store in a single 1-2-3 Release 2.3 database only about 2,000 records of the type shown in figure 12.1. For a larger database, you need to add expanded memory to your computer.

If you store your database on floppy disks, you are limited by the capacity of the disk, which is between 360K and 1.44M, depending on the disk's size (5 1/4-inch or 3 1/2-inch) and density (low or high). Therefore, when you design a database, you must consider not only how much RAM you need but also how you will store the data in the database you create.

Creating a Database

Caution:
Locate your
database where it
won't be affected by
inserted columns,
deleted rows, or
changed column
widths.

You can create a database as a new worksheet file or as part of an existing worksheet. If you decide to build a database as part of an existing worksheet, choose a worksheet area that you do not need for anything else. This area should be large enough to accommodate the number of records you plan to enter now and in the future. If you add the database to the side of a worksheet, be careful about inserting or deleting worksheet rows that also may affect the database. If you add a database below an existing worksheet, be careful not to disturb predetermined column widths in the worksheet portion when you adjust the column widths of the database fields. The best idea is to create a separate worksheet file for each database.

After you determine where to enter the database, you create it by entering field names across a row and entering data in the cells below the field names. The mechanics of entering database contents are simple. You must be aware, however, that the format of your data and the field names you use directly influence how well 1-2-3 can locate records in the database.

Entering Field Names

1-2-3 locates data in a database by using the field names. To help you determine which field names to include, you may want to write down the output you expect from the database. You also need to consider any source documents already in use that will provide input to the database.

If you use the contents of a report or form as a guide for your database, you can speed data entry by setting up the fields in the same order used by the corresponding report or form.

Reminder:
Keep all field names
unique.

Keep in mind that all field names must be unique; any repetition of names confuses 1-2-3 when you search or sort the database. The field names also must be labels, even if they are the numeric labels '1, '2, and so on. You can enter as many as 256 fields (the number of columns in 1-2-3) for a database.

Although you can enter more than one row for the field names, 1-2-3 uses only the labels in the bottom row as the field names. For example, if you type **STREET** in cell B2 and **ADDRESS** in B3, the field name is ADDRESS, not STREET ADDRESS.

Note also that if a field with numeric entries precedes a field that contains labels, the data in the two fields may run together because numbers are right-justified in the column, and labels are left-justified. To improve the look of the database, insert blank columns or widen the width of the right-hand column to add extra space between fields.

After you have entered field names and added spacing columns, you are ready to enter records.

Entering Data

A common error when users enter data is that they do not think about how they will ask 1-2-3 to find data after it has been entered. For example, suppose that the ORDERDATE field in your database contains the last date an order was made. You enter dates for the ORDERDATE field as labels, in the general form MMM-DD-YYYY (such as JAN-01-1991). Although you can search for an ORDERDATE that matches a specific date, you may not be able to perform a mathematical search for all ORDERDATEs within a specified period of time or before a certain date. To get maximum flexibility from the /Data commands, use @DATE to enter dates (see Chapter 6 for more information on functions).

Another factor to consider when you enter data is the level of detail you need for each item of information. For example, suppose that you want to use the area code to sort all records which contain telephone numbers. You should enter telephone numbers as two separate fields: area code (XXX) and the base number (XXX-XXXX).

You also should determine whether to enter the data as a label or a number. For example, you want to enter ZIP codes in a ZIP field as labels, because some codes begin with a leading zero. If you enter the code as a number, 1-2-3 drops the zero and the ZIP code is no longer correct.

To change the display of data on the screen, you use the /Range Format and /Worksheet Column Set-Width options. In figure 12.1, notice that the column widths on the worksheet vary from 6 to 22 characters.

After you have planned your database, you build it. To understand how the process works, create a Company database on a blank worksheet. Enter the field names across a single row (A3..F3 in fig. 12.1).

To enter the first record, move the cursor to the row directly below the field-name row and enter the data across the row.

Type the following entries in these cells:

A4:	**A1 Computing**
B4:	**'1 Sun Lane**
C4:	**Waconia**
D4:	**MN**
E4:	**'55660**
F4:	**'459-0987**

Notice that the contents of the ADDRESS, PHONE, and ZIP fields are identified explicitly as labels (designated by the label character [']—a leading apostrophe). Because the data for these fields begins with a number, you must type the ' label prefix character before you enter the data.

Throughout this chapter, this sample company database is used to illustrate the results of using various /Data commands. In this book, the fields fit in a single screen display. In real applications, however, you would track many more data items.

Modifying a Database

After you enter the data in the database, you use many standard 1-2-3 commands to maintain the accuracy of the database. To add records, you first insert a row with the /Worksheet Insert Row command. Then fill the different fields in the rows with appropriate data. Figure 12.2 shows a record being inserted in the middle of a database. Another way to add records is to enter them at the end of the database and then use the /Data Sort command, described in the next section, to rearrange their physical order.

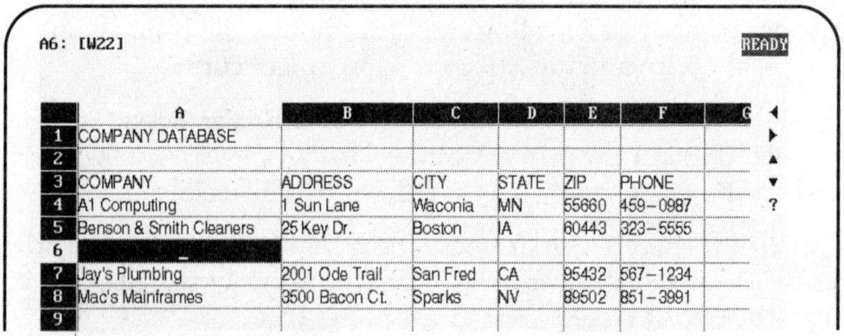

Fig. 12.2. Inserting a record (row) in the database.

To delete records, you move the cell pointer to the row or rows to be deleted and select the /Worksheet Delete Row command. If Undo (Alt-F4) is not active, be extremely careful when you select the records to delete.

To modify records, you can edit the entry by using the Edit key (F2), or you can retype the entry. See Chapter 3 for details about editing the contents of cells.

To add a new field to a database, place the cell pointer in the column that will contain the new field and select the /**W**orksheet **I**nsert **C**olumn command. Then fill the field with values for each record. For example, to insert an AREA field in column F of the sample database, place the cell pointer anywhere in column F and issue the /**W**orksheet **I**nsert **C**olumn command. Then type the new field name, **AREA**, in cell F3 (see fig. 12.3).

Reminder:
Add new fields to your database with /Worksheet Insert Column.

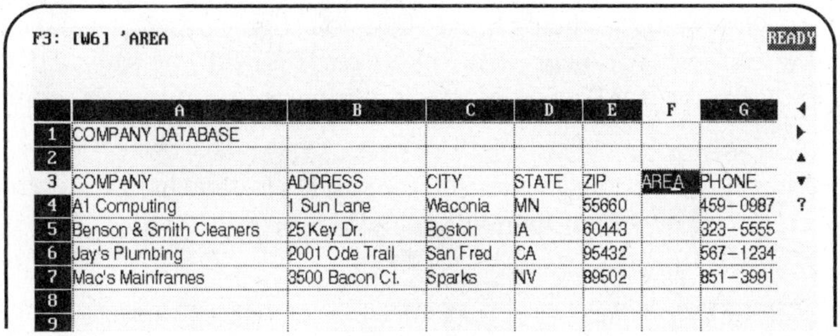

F3: [W6] 'AREA READY

	A	B	C	D	E	F	G
1	COMPANY DATABASE						
2							
3	COMPANY	ADDRESS	CITY	STATE	ZIP	AREA	PHONE
4	A1 Computing	1 Sun Lane	Waconia	MN	55660		459-0987
5	Benson & Smith Cleaners	25 Key Dr.	Boston	IA	60443		323-5555
6	Jay's Plumbing	2001 Ode Trail	San Fred	CA	95432		567-1234
7	Mac's Mainframes	3500 Bacon Ct.	Sparks	NV	89502		851-3991
8							
9							

Fig. 12.3. *Inserting a column for a new field.*

To delete a field, place the cell pointer anywhere in the column you want to remove and select the /**W**orksheet **D**elete **C**olumn command.

Sorting Database Records

One of the many database-management functions you may want to do with your new 1-2-3 database is to change the order of the records. Suppose, for example, that you entered records in alphabetical order, but you now need a list of the records in ZIP-code sorted order. To sort records, you use the /**D**ata **S**ort command.

When you select /**D**ata **S**ort, the Sort Settings dialog box and a menu with the following options displays:

Data-Range **P**rimary-Key **S**econdary-Key **R**eset **G**o **Q**uit

The first step in sorting the database is to specify a **D**ata-Range. This range includes all records to sort and all the fields in each record. If you do not include all fields when sorting, you destroy the integrity of your database because parts of one record end up with parts of other records.

Caution:
Do not include the field-name row in the range to sort.

In figure 12.3, the database covers the range from A4..G7. Notice that the **Data-Range** must not include the field-name row. (If you are not sure how to designate ranges or how to name them, refer to Chapter 4.)

The **Data-Range** does not necessarily have to include the entire database. If some records in the database already have the organization you want, or if you do not want to sort all the records, you can sort just a portion of the database.

After choosing the **Data-Range**, you must specify the keys for the sort. The *key* is the field 1-2-3 uses to determine the order of the records. For example, ZIP could be the primary, or first, key to use when sorting. If two records have the same value in their primary key, you then can select a secondary key. For example, you may want to sort records with the same ZIP code alphabetically, by NAME. You must set a **Primary-Key**, but the **Secondary-Key** is optional.

After you specify the range to sort and the sort key(s), you have to determine the sort order. The sort order is either ascending (0-9 and A-Z) or descending (Z-A and 9-0).

> **Caution:** Use /File Save before performing the sort so that you can retrieve the original database if you want to restore the order of the records. Another way to restore the original order is to number the records before sorting them. (See "Restoring the Presorted Order," later in this chapter for more information.)

After you save the database, select /Data /Sort Go to sort the records.

Using the One-Key Sort

Cue:
When using the mouse in 1-2-3, use either the left or right mouse button to select a field. The default is the left button.

You can use the sorting capability in 1-2-3 to reorder records in the sample database alphabetically on the STATE field. If you have not already specified the **Data-Range** (to sort by ZIP, as in fig. 12.4, for example), select **Data-Range** and highlight A4..G7. To enter the data range in the Sort Settings dialog box, click anywhere in the box (or press F2) and then click once in the **Data-Range** field. 1-2-3 highlights the **Data-Range** option and places the cursor in the field. Type the range.

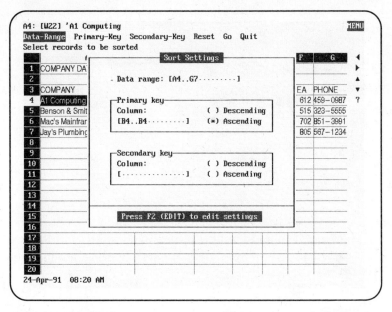

Fig. 12.4. *Entering the data range to sort in the Sort Settings dialog box.*

Note: To select the range from the 1-2-3 menu with the mouse or arrow keys, click the **Data-Range** menu option (or type **D**). Then point to the range in the worksheet.

You also can select *before* you select a command. To prespecify a range, make sure that you are in READY mode and press F4 to switch to POINT mode. Use the mouse or arrow keys to highlight a range and press Enter. 1-2-3 remembers this range for a subsequent command, unless you press Esc or move the cell pointer. When you select **/Data Sort** and choose **Data-range**, 1-2-3 displays your prespecified range in the Sort Settings dialog box.

Select **Primary-Key** and type **D3** (for STATE). For the sort order, select either **Ascending** or **Descending**. In the dialog box, click inside the parentheses to the left of **Ascending**. To select Ascending with the keyboard, type **A**. The asterisk means that **Ascending** is selected.

Finally, select **G**o from the menu to execute the sort. Figure 12.5 shows the database sorted in ascending order by state.

Cue:
Use /File Save before sorting your database.

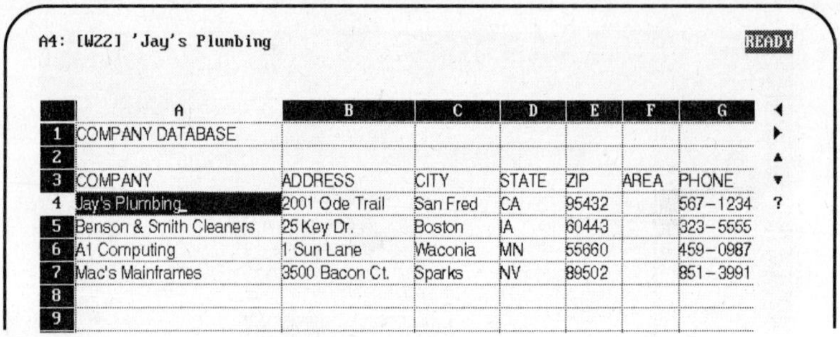
A4: [W22] 'Jay's Plumbing READY

	A	B	C	D	E	F	G
1	COMPANY DATABASE						
2							
3	COMPANY	ADDRESS	CITY	STATE	ZIP	AREA	PHONE
4	Jay's Plumbing_	2001 Ode Trail	San Fred	CA	95432		567–1234
5	Benson & Smith Cleaners	25 Key Dr.	Boston	IA	60443		323–5555
6	A1 Computing	1 Sun Lane	Waconia	MN	55660		459–0987
7	Mac's Mainframes	3500 Bacon Ct.	Sparks	NV	89502		851–3991
8							
9							

***Fig. 12.5.** The database sorted by the STATE field.*

/**D**ata **S**ort also is useful for adding new records in the proper position in an existing database. You add the new record to the bottom of the current database, expand the data range, and then sort the database again, using the desired sort key.

Using the Two-Key Sort

To see how a two-key sort works (sorting first by one key and then by another key within the first sort order), this example shows you how to add a new record to the end of the Company database and then reorder it, first by STATE and then by CITY within STATE.

Place the cursor in cell A8 and add the following entries to the indicated cells:

A8:	**Ralph's Bar**
B8:	**'10 Lilac**
C8:	**Carmel**
D8:	**CA**
E8:	**95309**
G8:	**'369-2468**

Your database now should look like figure 12.6.

After adding the Ralph's Bar record, select /**D**ata **S**ort. Notice that A4..G7 is still the **D**ata-Range. To include the new record, use the down-arrow key or the mouse to extend the highlighted area down, highlighting A4..G8. Because the STATE field is still selected as the **P**rimary-Key, you don't have to identify the field again. Select **S**econdary-Key, enter **C3**, and choose **A**scending for the sort order by CITY. Figure 12.7 shows the results of issuing the **G**o command after you have specified the two-key sort.

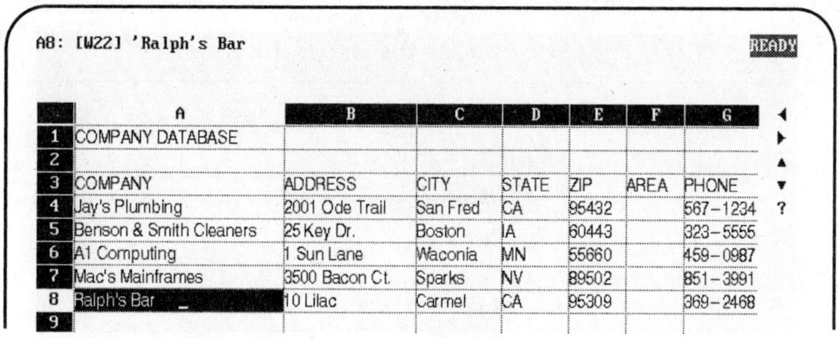

A8: [W22] 'Ralph's Bar READY

	A	B	C	D	E	F	G
1	COMPANY DATABASE						
2							
3	COMPANY	ADDRESS	CITY	STATE	ZIP	AREA	PHONE
4	Jay's Plumbing	2001 Ode Trail	San Fred	CA	95432		567-1234
5	Benson & Smith Cleaners	25 Key Dr.	Boston	IA	60443		323-5555
6	A1 Computing	1 Sun Lane	Waconia	MN	55660		459-0987
7	Mac's Mainframes	3500 Bacon Ct.	Sparks	NV	89502		851-3991
8	Ralph's Bar	10 Lilac	Carmel	CA	95309		369-2468
9							

Fig. 12.6. The database after adding a new record.

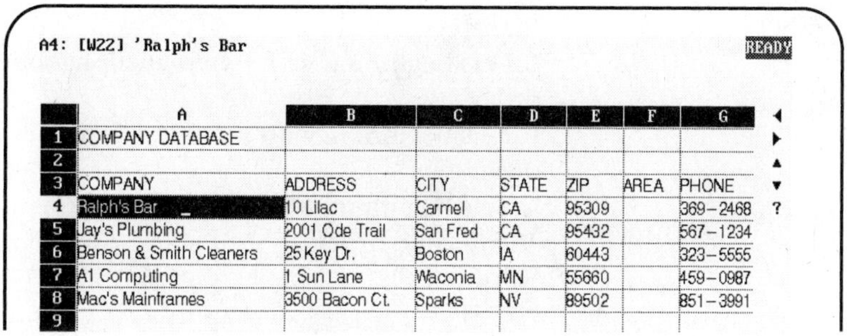

A4: [W22] 'Ralph's Bar READY

	A	B	C	D	E	F	G
1	COMPANY DATABASE						
2							
3	COMPANY	ADDRESS	CITY	STATE	ZIP	AREA	PHONE
4	Ralph's Bar	10 Lilac	Carmel	CA	95309		369-2468
5	Jay's Plumbing	2001 Ode Trail	San Fred	CA	95432		567-1234
6	Benson & Smith Cleaners	25 Key Dr.	Boston	IA	60443		323-5555
7	A1 Computing	1 Sun Lane	Waconia	MN	55660		459-0987
8	Mac's Mainframes	3500 Bacon Ct.	Sparks	NV	89502		851-3991
9							

Fig. 12.7. The database sorted by the STATE and CITY fields.

Records now are grouped in alphabetical order, first by state (California, Iowa, Minnesota, and Nevada), and then by city within state (Carmel, California, before San Fred, California). When you determine whether to use a primary or secondary sort key, be sure to request a reasonable sort. For example, you probably don't want to sort first by CITY and then by STATE within CITY.

Caution:
Do not include blank rows past the end of the database when you designate the sort range.

Determining the Sort Order

Certain aspects of the sort order are determined by the collating-sequence setting you chose when you installed 1-2-3. The three options for this setting are Numbers First, Numbers Last, and ASCII. For Numbers First and Numbers Last, 1-2-3 ignores capitalization. For ASCII, uppercase letters precede lowercase letters (Benson comes before benson, for example).

Table 12.1 shows the effects of each setting when you select **A**scending sort order (selecting **D**escending order reverses the orders shown).

Table 12.1
Collating Sequences for Ascending Order

Collating Sequence	Sort Order
Numbers First	Blank cells Labels beginning with numbers in numerical order Labels beginning with letters in alphabetical order Labels beginning with other characters in ASCII-value order Values
Numbers Last	Blank cells Labels beginning with letters in alphabetical order Labels beginning with numbers in numerical order Labels beginning with other characters in ASCII-value order Values
ASCII	Blank cells All labels in ASCII-value order Values

Cue:
You can use the Install program to change the order or precedence that 1-2-3 uses for sorting.

If you sort records based on a label field that contains numbers, you must make sure that all the values in the field are the same length (as in the ZIP field). For example, if you sort on the ADDRESS field (which you probably won't do), 1-2-3 sorts the address that starts with 2001 before the address that begins with 25. Because 1-2-3 looks at the numbers as labels, it compares the two fields character-by-character. Because the *20* in 2001 comes before *25*, the 2001 address comes first. To avoid inaccurate matching, add enough leading zeros to ensure that all values are the same length (that is, change 25 to 0025).

Restoring the Presort Order

Reminder:
Add a "counter" field to your database in case you want to restore records to their original order.

If you sort the original contents of the database on any field, such as the ADDRESS field (see fig. 12.8), you cannot easily restore the records to their original order. Therefore, you should save the worksheet file before you choose /Data Sort. To preserve the original order of the records in the database is to add a "record number" column to the database. The record number is just a column of consecutive numbers, one for each record. After you sort the database on a particular column, you can sort again on the record-number field to restore the records to their original order. Later in this chapter, you see how to use the /Data Fill command to enter these record numbers automatically.

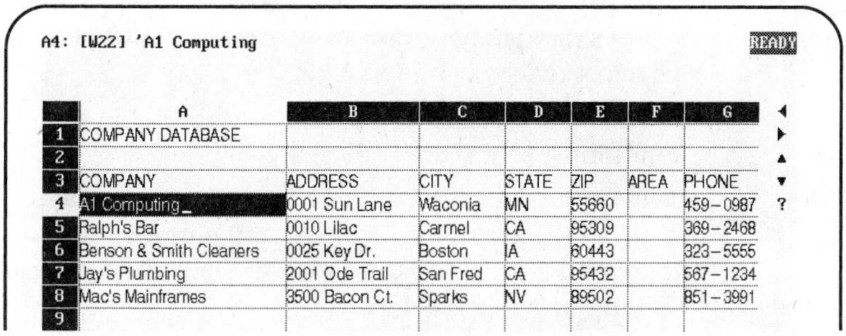

Fig. 12.8. The database sorted by the ADDRESS field after adding leading zeros to the addresses.

Searching for Records

You have learned how to use /Data Sort to reorganize records according to key fields. In this section of the chapter, you learn how to use /Data Query, the menu's other data-management command, to search for records and then edit, extract, or delete them.

The simplest way to search a 1-2-3 database is to look for records that meet certain conditions, or *criteria*. To determine which companies are in California, for example, you use a search operation to find all records with CA as the value in the STATE field. The STATE value CA is the criterion for this search.

After you locate the records you want, you have the option of editing the records, extracting them, or deleting them. If you *extract* a set of records from the database, 1-2-3 copies them to another section of the worksheet. For example, you can extract all records with a California address to another area of the worksheet and then print them.

Using Minimum Search Requirements

To initiate any search operation, you need to define the database and criteria to use and then select the appropriate operation from the /Data Query menu:

Input Criteria Output Find Extract Unique Delete Reset Quit

You use the first three options to define the ranges to use for search operations on the database. The next four options perform search functions. The last two options reset the ranges and end the Query command. The following table describes these options in more detail.

Option	Description
Input	Defines the database range to search; required for all searches
Criteria	Defines the worksheet range that contains the search conditions; required for all searches
Output	Defines the range to contain the records found as a result of the Extract or Unique search operations. 1-2-3 copies the matching records to the output range, leaving the original database intact.
Find	Moves down through a database and highlights records that match given criteria. You can enter or change data in the highlighted records.
Extract	Copies records based on a set of criteria from a database to another area of the worksheet
Unique	Similar to Extract but recognizes that some records in the database may be duplicates; eliminates duplicates when copying records to the output range
Delete	Deletes from the database all records that match the given criteria; shifts the remaining records to fill the gaps that remain
Reset	Removes all previous search-related ranges so that you can specify a different search location and conditions
Quit	Returns you to READY mode

To perform a Query operation, you must specify both an input range and a criteria range and select one of the four search options. Before issuing an Extract or Unique command, you also must specify an output range.

Determining the Input Range

The input range for the /Data Query command is the range of records to search. The specified area does not have to include the entire database. In the company database shown in figure 12.8, specifying an input range of A3..G8 defines the search area as the entire database. Entering A3..G4 as the input range limits the search area to the records for Minnesota.

Whether you search all or only a part of a database, you must include the field-name row in the input range. If field names occupy space on more than one row, specify only the bottom row to start the input range. In the company database, for example, you start the input range with row 3 because row 3 contains the field names.

To specify the input range, select /Data Query Input and type or point to a range or use an assigned range name. To enter the range using the Query Settings dialog box, select /Data Query, press the Edit (F2) key to edit the settings in the box, select Input range and then type a range or range name. Press Enter twice to return to the menu.

To enter the range using the mouse, point to the Input range field in the Query Settings dialog box and double-click. Type the range or range name and press Enter. Click OK to return to the menu. For this example, the Input range is A3..G8.

After you specify the Input range, you do not have to do so again unless the search area changes.

Entering the Criteria Range

To search for records that meet certain criteria, you must talk to 1-2-3 in terms the program understands. Suppose that you want to identify all records in the database that contain CA in the STATE field. With the database on-screen and 1-2-3 in READY mode, type **STATE** in cell A12 and **CA** in cell A13 (see fig. 12.9).

Caution:
When you specify the input range, include the row of field names with the database records.

Cells A12 and A13 are called the *criteria range*. They tell 1-2-3 to look for a field name called STATE and to find in that field records that contain CA. To help you remember where this range is, you can type **Criteria Range** in cell A11, as shown in figure 12.9. (1-2-3 does not use cell A11; only you do).

> *Note:* You normally place the criteria range to one side of the database range, not directly below it. In this example (fig. 12.9), the criteria range was placed below the database to show the entire operation on one screen.

To specify the criteria range, select /Data Query Criteria and type or point to a range or use an assigned range name. To enter the range using the Query Settings dialog box, select /Data Query, press the Edit (F2) key to edit the settings in the box, select Criteria and then type a range or range name. Press Enter twice to return to the menu.

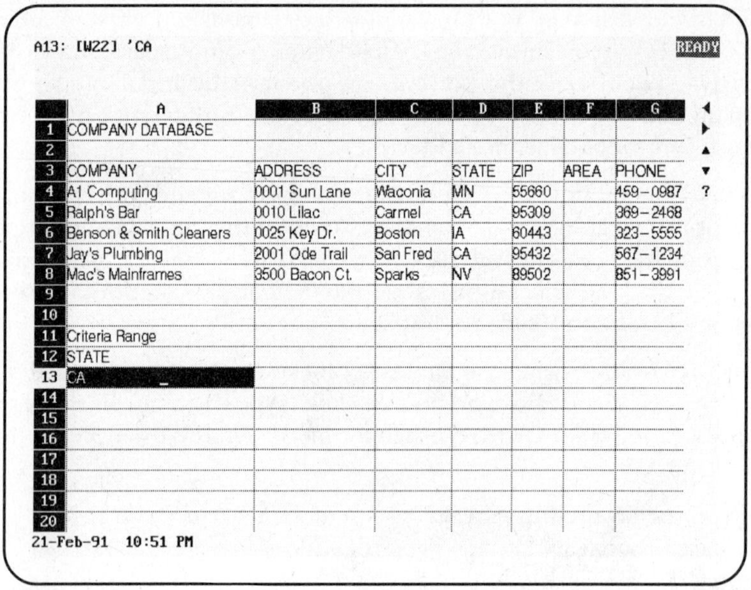

Fig. 12.9. Adding a criteria range to the worksheet.

To enter the range using the mouse, point to the **Criteria range** field in the Query Settings dialog box and double-click. Type the range or range name and press Enter. Click OK to return to the menu. For this example, the criteria range is A12..A13.

Cue:
Use the /Copy command to copy the desired field names to the Criteria range.

You can use numbers, labels, or formulas as criteria. A criteria range can be up to 32 columns wide and two or more rows deep. The first row must contain the field names of the search criteria, such as STATE in row 12 of figure 12.9. The rows below the field names contain the criteria, such as CA in row 13. The field names of the input range and the criteria range must match exactly.

By entering criteria in the worksheet and specifying the input and criteria ranges, you have completed the steps necessary to execute a **Find** or **Delete** command.

Using the Find Command

When you select **Find** from the /**Data Query** menu, 1-2-3 displays a high-lighted bar on the first record in the input range that meets the conditions specified in the criteria range, and the mode indicator changes from READY to FIND. In the current example, the highlighted bar rests on the first field of the first record that includes CA in the STATE field (see fig. 12.10).

```
A5: [W22] 'Ralph's Bar                                    FIND

          A                B        C       D      E      F      G    ◄
 1  COMPANY DATABASE                                                  ►
 2                                                                    ▲
 3  COMPANY            ADDRESS     CITY    STATE  ZIP    AREA  PHONE   ▼
 4  A1 Computing       0001 Sun Lane  Waconia  MN   55660       459-0987  ?
 5  Ralph's Bar        0010 Lilac   Carmel  CA     95309        369-2468
 6  Benson & Smith Cleaners  0025 Key Dr.  Boston  IA  60443    323-5555
 7  Jay's Plumbing     2001 Ode Trail  San Fred  CA  95432      567-1234
 8  Mac's Mainframes   3500 Bacon Ct.  Sparks  NV   89502       851-3991
 9
10
11  Criteria Range
12  STATE
13  CA
14
15
16
17
18
19
20
21-Feb-91  10:51 PM
```

Fig. 12.10. The first record highlighted during a FIND operation.

Use the down-arrow key again to move the highlighted bar to the next record that conforms to the criteria. Continue pressing the down-arrow key until you reach the last record that meets the search conditions (see fig. 12.11).

```
A7: [W22] 'Jay's Plumbing                                 FIND

          A                B        C       D      E      F      G    ◄
 1  COMPANY DATABASE                                                  ►
 2                                                                    ▲
 3  COMPANY            ADDRESS     CITY    STATE  ZIP    AREA  PHONE   ▼
 4  A1 Computing       0001 Sun Lane  Waconia  MN   55660       459-0987  ?
 5  Ralph's Bar        0010 Lilac   Carmel  CA     95309        369-2468
 6  Benson & Smith Cleaners  0025 Key Dr.  Boston  IA  60443    323-5555
 7  Jay's Plumbing     2001 Ode Trail  San Fred  CA  95432      567-1234
 8  Mac's Mainframes   3500 Bacon Ct.  Sparks  NV   89502       851-3991
 9
10
11  Criteria Range
12  STATE
13  CA
14
15
16
17
18
19
20
21-Feb-91  10:52 PM
```

Fig. 12.11. The last record matching the criteria highlighted during a find operation.

Reminder:
Use the up- and down-arrow keys to highlight records that meet the search criteria.

Use the down- and up-arrow keys to place the highlighted bar on the next or preceding record that meets the search criteria. Use the Home and End keys to reach the first and last matching records. The right-arrow and left-arrow keys move the cursor to different fields in the current highlighted record. You can enter new values for the fields or use the Edit key (F2) to update the current values in any field. If you change a record so that it no longer satisfies the Find criteria and then move away from that record, you cannot return to the record during the Find operation.

To end the Find operation and return to the /Data Query menu, press Enter or Esc. To return directly to READY mode, press Ctrl-Break.

Listing All Specified Records

Reminder:
Use /File Xtract to copy extracted records to a new file.

The Find command has limited use, especially in a large database, because you must scroll through the entire file to view each record that meets the specified criteria. As an alternative, you can use the Extract command to copy the matching records to an output range. You then can view, print, or even use the /File Xtract command on the extracted records contained in the output range.

Defining the Output Range

Reminder:
Field names in the criteria and output ranges must match exactly the corresponding field names in the input range.

Choose a blank area in the worksheet as the output range to receive records from an extract operation. Designate the range to the right of, or below, the database. In the first row of the output range, type or copy the field names of only those fields you want to extract. You do not have to include all the field names. The field names do not have to appear in the same order as they do in the database, although field names used in both the criteria and output ranges must match exactly the corresponding field names in the input range. To avoid mismatch errors, use the /Copy command to copy the database field names to the criteria and output ranges.

> **Note:** Because Release 2.3 incorporates Wysiwyg report-publishing features, Release 2.3 ignores the field-name label prefix when matching field names between input and output ranges. In earlier releases, if you centered a database field name and left-justified the corresponding field name in the output range, an extract operation based on that field name would not work. But as you can see in the ZIP field of figure 12.12, Release 2.3 matched the ZIP fields even though one was left-justified and the other was right-justiified.

```
E16: [W6] "ZIP                                                    READY

              A            B          C       D     E    F    G      ◄
   1  COMPANY DATABASE                                                ►
   2
   3  COMPANY       ADDRESS      CITY     STATE ZIP  AREA PHONE        ▲
   4  A1 Computing  0001 Sun Lane Waconia  MN    55660     459-0987   ?
   5  Ralph's Bar   0010 Lilac   Carmel   CA    95309     369-2468
   6  Benson & Smith Cleaners 0025 Key Dr. Boston IA  60443  323-5555
   7  Jay's Plumbing 2001 Ode Trail San Fred CA 95432    567-1234
   8  Mac's Mainframes 3500 Bacon Ct. Sparks NV 89502    851-3991
   9
  10
  11  Criteria Range
  12  STATE
  13  CA
  14
  15  Output Range
  16  COMPANY       ADDRESS      CITY     STATE ZIP  AREA PHONE
  17  Ralph's Bar   0010 Lilac   Carmel   CA    95309     369-2468
  18  Jay's Plumbing 2001 Ode Trail San Fred CA 95432    567-1234
  19
  20
  21-Feb-91  10:53 PM
```

Fig. 12.12. A full-record extract on an "exact match" label criterion.

Select /**D**ata **Q**uery **O**utput and type, point to, or name the range to contain the extracted records. To select the range using the Query Settings dialog box, select /**D**ata **Q**uery, press the Edit key (F2) to edit the settings in the box, press O and then type a range or range name. Press Enter twice to return to the menu.

To enter the range using the mouse, point to the **O**utput range field in the Query Settings dialog box and double-click. Type the range or range name and press Enter. Click OK to return to the menu.

You identify the output range as either the row of field names only or as the field-name row and the number of rows below the field names required to hold all the extracted records.

To limit the size of the extract area, enter the upper left to lower right cell coordinates of the entire output range. The first row in the specified range must contain the field names; the remaining rows must accommodate the maximum number of records you expect to receive from the extract operation. Use this method when you want to retain additional data that is located below the extract area. For example, as you can see in figure 12.12, naming A16..G18 as the output range assumes that there are two incoming records. If you do not allow sufficient room in the fixed-length output area, the extract operation aborts with the message Too many records for Output range.

Caution:
If you do not allow sufficient room in the output range for extracted records, the Extract operation aborts.

To create an open-ended extract area that does not define the number of incoming records, specify as the output range only the row that contains the output field names. For example, if you name A16..G16 as the output range for the database in figure 12.12, 1-2-3 starts placing extracted records in row 17 of the output range.

An extract operation first removes all existing data from the output range. If you use only the field-name row to specify the output area, all data below that row is destroyed to make room for the unknown number of incoming extracted records. Before you issue the Extract command, make sure that you do not need any of the data contained in cells below the output range.

Executing the Extract Command

To execute an Extract command, you must type the search conditions in the worksheet, enter the output field names in the worksheet, and set the input, criteria, and output ranges by using the menu or dialog box methods described previously. To accelerate the set-up process, you can establish standard input, criteria, and output areas.

For the company database example, you established the input, criteria, and output areas in the previous sections. If you select /Data Query Extract now, 1-2-3 extracts the two records from California companies.

Handling More Complicated Criteria Ranges

In addition to searching for an exact match to a single-label field, 1-2-3 enables a wide variety of record searches: on exact matches to numeric fields; on partial matches of field contents; on fields that meet formula conditions; on fields that meet all of several conditions; and on fields that meet either one condition or another. The following section focuses on some variations of queries on single fields.

Using Wild Cards in Criteria Ranges

You can use wild cards to match labels in database operations. In 1-2-3, two wild cards (? and *) act as place holders for one or more characters in an entry. The ? character instructs 1-2-3 to accept any single character as a replacement for the ?. For example, if you enter T? as a criterion for the field STATE, 1-2-3 looks for state abbreviations that begin with T and are two characters long. Thus, records with TX and TN meet the criterion.

The * character tells 1-2-3 to accept any and all characters that follow. You use the * character for field entries of unequal length.

With these wild cards (or any label criterion), you can use the tilde (~). The tilde tells 1-2-3 that you want all records *except* those that match the criterion.

Table 12.2 shows how you can use wild cards and the tilde in search operations.

Table 12.2
Using Wild Cards in Search Operations

Type	To Find
N?	Any two-character label that starts with *N* (NC, NJ, NY, and so on)
BO?L?	A five-character label such as BOWLE but not a shorter label like BOWL
BO?L*	A four-or-more-character label such as BOWL, BOWLE, BOLLESON, BOELING, and so on
SAN*	A three-or-more-character label that starts with SAN, followed by any number of characters (SANTA BARBARA and SAN FRANCISCO, for example)
SAN *	A four-or-more-character label that starts with SAN, followed by a space and any number of characters (SAN FRANCISCO, for example, but not SANTA BARBARA)
~N*	All strings that do *not* begin with the letter *N*

Use the ? and * wild cards when you are unsure of the spelling of a label or when you need to match several slightly different records. Always check which records match the wild cards by using /**D**ata **Q**uery **F**ind or /**D**ata **Q**uery **E**xtract before you use wild cards with the **D**elete command. If you are not careful, you may remove more records than you intend.

Using Formulas in Criteria Ranges

To set up formulas that query numeric or label fields in the database, you can use the following relational operators:

>	Greater than
>=	Greater than or equal to
<	Less than
<=	Less than or equal to

> =   Equal to
> <>   Not equal to

Create a formula that references the first field entry in the numeric column you want to search. 1-2-3 tests the formula on each cell down the column until the program reaches the end of the specified input range.

Because the criteria formula specifies which field to test, you can place the formula below any field name in the criteria range. (The locations for criteria formulas are, therefore, more flexible than text criteria, which must appear directly below the associated field name.) For example, you can use a formula to extract all records with an AREA code smaller than or equal to 700. First, type the formula **+F4<=700** in cell A13 (see fig. 12.13).

> *Note:* In Release 2.4, you also can use a short-hand syntax for criteria formulas. For example, the preceding formula, **+F4<=700** can be written as **'<=700**. You place this formula in the criteria range under the field name to which it applies, in this case, AREA. Also note that because the < (less than) symbol is an alternative way to display the 1-2-3 menu, you must type a label prefix, such as **'** (apostrophe), before you enter the formula.

```
A13: [W22] +F4<=700                                               READY

          A                    B            C        D     E    F      G      ◄
 1 |COMPANY DATABASE                                                           ►
 2 |                                                                           ▲
 3 |COMPANY              ADDRESS        CITY      STATE  ZIP  AREA  PHONE       ▼
 4 |A1 Computing         0001 Sun Lane  Waconia   MN     55660 612 459-0987    ?
 5 |Ralph's Bar          0010 Lilac     Carmel    CA     95309 916 369-2468
 6 |Benson & Smith Cleaners 0025 Key Dr. Boston   IA     60443 515 323-5555
 7 |Jay's Plumbing       2001 Ode Trail San Fred  CA     95432 805 567-1234
 8 |Mac's Mainframes     3500 Bacon Ct. Sparks    NV     89502 702 851-3991
 9 |
10 |
11 |Criteria Range
12 |STATE
13 |                   1
14 |
15 |Output Range
16 |COMPANY              AREA
17 |A1 Computing              612
18 |Benson & Smith Cleaners   515
19 |
20 |
21-Feb-91  10:57 PM
```

Fig. 12.13. A relational formula criterion to extract records.

Although the formula is displayed in the control panel, notice that 1-2-3 displays a one (1) in cell A13. After checking cell F4 to see whether the value in F4 was less than or equal to 700, 1-2-3 returned a one (1) for the criterion formula to indicate that the first record in the database does have a value that meets the criterion (612 is less than 700). 1-2-3 reevaluates the criterion formula for each record in the database. Those records whose AREA values cause the formula to be true (1) are extracted. If an AREA code for a record is greater than 700, 1-2-3 evaluates the formula as false (0) and that corresponding record is not extracted.

After you correctly specify the input, criteria, and output ranges, the extract operation produces two records in which AREA is less than or equal to 700.

To reference cells outside the database, use formulas that include absolute cell addressing. (For addressing information, refer to Chapter 4.) For example, suppose that immediately after you issue the preceding command, you decide to use 850 instead of 700 as the upper limit for extracted area codes. You can just edit the existing formula, or you can make fast changes easier by first returning to READY mode, entering the value **850** in cell F13, and typing the formula **+F4<=$F$13** as the criterion in cell A13.

With the program still in READY mode, press Query (F7) to repeat the most recent query operation (Extract, in this example) and eliminate the need to select /**Data Query Extract**. Use the shortcut method only when you do not want to change the locations of the input, criteria, and output ranges. As you can see from figure 12.14, four records matched and were extracted.

```
A13: [W22] +F4<=$F$13                                              READY

              A                 B          C       D     E    F     G
 1  COMPANY DATABASE
 2
 3  COMPANY              ADDRESS       CITY     STATE ZIP  AREA PHONE
 4  A1 Computing         0001 Sun Lane Waconia  MN    55660 612 459-0987
 5  Ralph's Bar          0010 Lilac    Carmel   CA    95309 916 369-2468
 6  Benson & Smith Cleaners 0025 Key Dr. Boston  IA    60443 515 323-5555
 7  Jay's Plumbing       2001 Ode Trail San Fred CA    95432 805 567-1234
 8  Mac's Mainframes     3500 Bacon Ct. Sparks   NV    89502 702 851-3991
 9
10
11  Criteria Range
12  STATE
13              1                      AREA   --------->  850
14
15  Output Range
16  COMPANY              AREA
17  A1 Computing              612
18  Benson & Smith Cleaners   515
19  Jay's Plumbing            805
20  Mac's Mainframes          702
21-Feb-91  10:58 PM
```

Fig. 12.14. A formula criterion that refers to a cell outside the database.

Setting Up AND Conditions

Now that you have seen how to base a Find or Extract operation on one criterion, you will learn how to use multiple criteria for your queries. You can set up multiple criteria as AND conditions (in which *all* the criteria must be met) or as OR conditions (in which any *one* criterion must be met). For example, searching a music department's library for sheet music requiring drums AND trumpets is likely to produce fewer selections than searching for music requiring drums OR trumpets.

You indicate two or more criteria, *all* of which must be met, by specifying all the conditions in a single row of the criteria range. For example, suppose that you want only records for companies not located in California and not in a city whose name starts with the letter *B*.

First, adjust your criteria range to add another field. Then, to clear out the AREA entry, use /Range Erase and select the range C13..F13. Next, add the field name to B12 by copying cell C3 to B12. Finally, adjust the size of the criteria range by using the /Data Query command and typing **A12..B13** in the dialog box for the Criteria field. Now you can add the desired criteria to the criteria range.

Place the formula '**< >CA** in cell A13 and place the criteria **~B*** in cell B13. Then issue the /Data Query Extract command. 1-2-3 extracts two records that meet both conditions (see fig. 12.15).

Setting Up OR Conditions

Criteria placed on the *same* row have the effect of a logical AND; they tell 1-2-3 to find or extract records based on this condition AND this one, and so on. Criteria placed on *different* rows have the effect of a logical OR; that is, find or extract records based on this condition OR that one, and so on.

Searching a single field for more than one condition is the simplest use of an OR condition. For example, you can extract records in which the STATE is MN or NV by placing MN in cell A13 and NV in cell A14 and expanding the criteria range to include the additional row.

You also can specify a logical OR condition on two or more different fields. For example, suppose that you want to search for records in which the state is not California OR the city does not start with the letter *S*.

First, use /Range Erase to erase cell B13. Next, place **~S*** in cell B14 to add the OR condition. Then adjust the criteria range to include the specified OR condition by expanding the criteria range down a row. When you issue the Extract command, 1-2-3 copies four records to the output range (see fig. 12.16).

```
A13: [W22] '<>CA                                                    READY

        A              B            C        D      E     F     G      ◄
 1  COMPANY DATABASE                                                    ►
 2                                                                      ▲
 3  COMPANY         ADDRESS       CITY     STATE  ZIP  AREA  PHONE      ▼
 4  A1 Computing    0001 Sun Lane Waconia  MN     55660  612 459-0987   ?
 5  Ralph's Bar     0010 Lilac    Carmel   CA     95309  916 369-2468
 6  Benson & Smith Cleaners 0025 Key Dr. Boston IA 60443 515 323-5555
 7  Jay's Plumbing  2001 Ode Trail San Fred CA    95432  805 567-1234
 8  Mac's Mainframes 3500 Bacon Ct. Sparks NV     89502  702 851-3991
 9
10
11  Criteria Range
12  STATE           CITY
13  <>CA       _    ~B*
14
15  Output Range
16  COMPANY         AREA
17  A1 Computing         612
18  Mac's Mainframes     702
19
20
24-Apr-91  08:23 AM
```

Fig. 12.15. *A two-field logical AND search.*

```
A13: [W22] '<>CA                                                    READY

        A              B            C        D      E     F     G      ◄
 1  COMPANY DATABASE                                                    ►
 2                                                                      ▲
 3  COMPANY         ADDRESS       CITY     STATE  ZIP  AREA  PHONE      ▼
 4  A1 Computing    0001 Sun Lane Waconia  MN     55660  612 459-0987   ?
 5  Ralph's Bar     0010 Lilac    Carmel   CA     95309  916 369-2468
 6  Benson & Smith Cleaners 0025 Key Dr. Boston IA 60443 515 323-5555
 7  Jay's Plumbing  2001 Ode Trail San Fred CA    95432  805 567-1234
 8  Mac's Mainframes 3500 Bacon Ct. Sparks NV     89502  702 851-3991
 9
10
11  Criteria Range
12  STATE           CITY
13  <>CA       _
14                  ~S*
15  Output Range
16  COMPANY         AREA
17  A1 Computing         612
18  Ralph's Bar          916
19  Benson & Smith Cleaners 515
20  Mac's Mainframes     702
24-Apr-91  08:24 AM
```

Fig. 12.16. *A logical OR search on two fields.*

Although Ralph's Bar does not meet the condition of not being in California, it does meet the condition of being in a city whose name does not start with *S*; this record therefore is extracted to the output range along with the records for companies that are not in California. To be selected, a record must meet only one condition OR the other.

To add additional OR criteria, drop to a new row, enter each new condition, and expand the criteria range.

Although no technical reason prevents you from mixing AND and OR logical searches, properly formulating such a mixed query may be difficult. Follow the format of placing each AND condition in the row immediately below the criteria field-name row and each OR condition in a separate row below the AND condition. Be careful, however, to ensure that each row in the criteria range specifies all AND conditions that apply. For example, if you want to search for records in which STATE equals CA AND CITY starts with *S* OR STATE equals NV AND CITY starts with *S*, enter the AND/OR conditions in the following cells:

> A13: **=CA**
> B13: **S***
> A14: **=NV**
> B14: **S***

Repeating the S* in cells B13 and B14 is critical because if 1-2-3 finds a blank cell in a criteria range, the program selects all records for the field name above that blank cell.

You should test the logic of your search conditions on a small sample database in which you can verify search results easily by scrolling through all records and noting which of them should be extracted. For example, if the database contains hundreds of records, you can test the preceding AND/OR search conditions on a small group of records in the database or use /Data Query Find to see which records will be selected.

Using String Searches

Reminder:
Use string functions to search for records based on the partial contents of a field.

To search for records, based on the partial contents of a field, you use functions in a formula. For example, suppose that you can remember only the street name *Bacon* for a record you want to extract from the database. You can use the formula @FIND("BACON",B4,0) as the search criterion in cell A13.

Note that although ERR is displayed in cell A13, the formula works properly when you issue the /Data Query Extract command (see fig. 12.17).

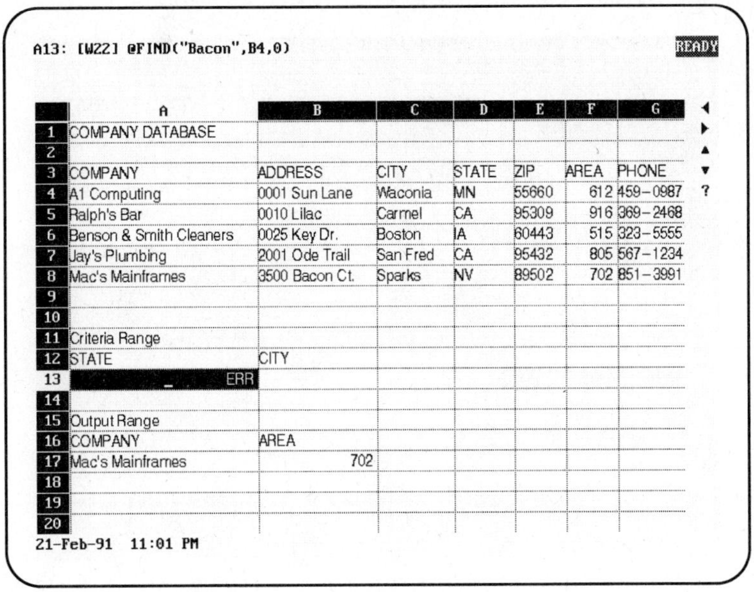

Fig. 12.17. *A function criteria used for a string search.*

Remember that the @FIND function returns the starting position of the search string (Bacon) in the string searched (the ADDRESS field). If @FIND does not find the search string, it returns ERR. Because "Bacon" does not occur in "0001 Sun Lane," the formula shows ERR. (Remember that the text string in the @FIND function must be enclosed in quotation marks.) As 1-2-3 checks each record, however, it matches and returns a true value for the fifth record. In criteria formulas, 1-2-3 treats both ERR and zero as false (nonmatching) values. (See Chapter 6 for a detailed discussion of 1-2-3 functions.)

Using Special Operators

To combine search conditions within a single field, use the special operators #AND# and #OR#. Use the special operator #NOT# to negate a search condition.

Use #AND# or #OR# to search on two or more conditions within the same field. For example, suppose that you want to extract all records with either "Bacon" or "Lilac" in their address. To match the records, use the following formula (see fig. 12.18):

@FIND("Bacon",B4,0)#OR#@FIND("Lilac",B4,0)

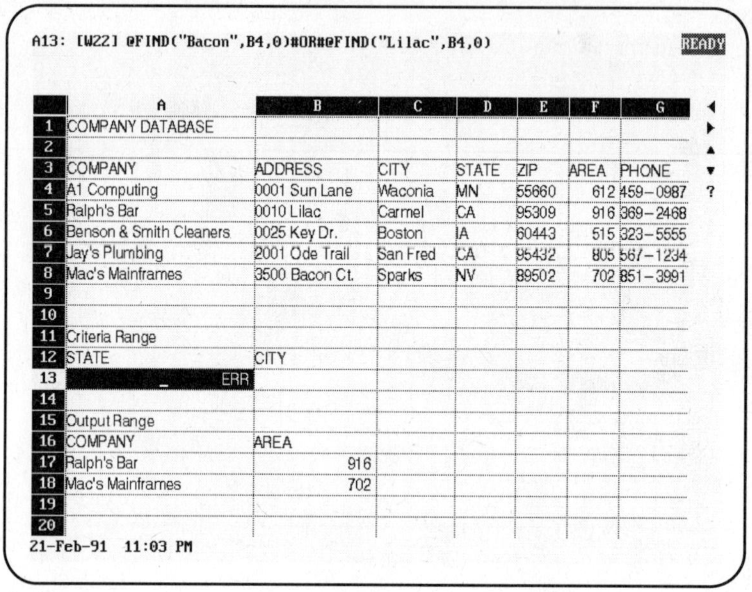

Fig. 12.18. The special operator #OR# used for extracting records.

You use the #AND#, #OR#, and #NOT# operators to enter (in one field) conditions that can be entered some other way (usually in at least two fields). For example, to find any California companies with the word *Bar* in their name, you can enter +D4="CA"#AND#@FIND("Bar",A4,0) in A13 or B13.

Use #NOT# at the beginning of a condition to negate that condition. For example, +D4="CA"#AND##NOT#@FIND("Bar",A4,0) would find all California companies without *Bar* in their name.

Unless you understand what @FIND does, using the @FIND function to search for matching records may produce unexpected results. Suppose, for example, that you wanted to find all records with a *2* or the word *Lilac* in their address. As you can see in figure 12.19, /Data Query Extract—using the criteria formula @FIND("2",B4,0)#OR#@FIND("Lilac",B4,0) as shown in the control panel—matched only two records instead of three. Why did it not also extract Jay's Plumbing?

The reason for this apparent error is simple: @FIND returns the *position* of the number *2* or the word *Lilac* in a string. But @FIND begins counting positions from zero (0). Because the address for Jay's Plumbing begins with 2, @FIND returns 0 as its position in the string. Because 1-2-3 treats a 0 result as false, 1-2-3 does not extract the Jay's Plumbing record.

To correct this problem, you must account for a possible zero return from @FIND. To do this, you add 1 to whatever value @FIND returns. Because

@FIND always returns ERR if the search string is not found, any value added to ERR still produces ERR. But if @FIND returns 0 and you add 1, you get 1. 1-2-3 then extracts that record. Figure 12.20 shows how to modify the criteria formula to extract the three records you want.

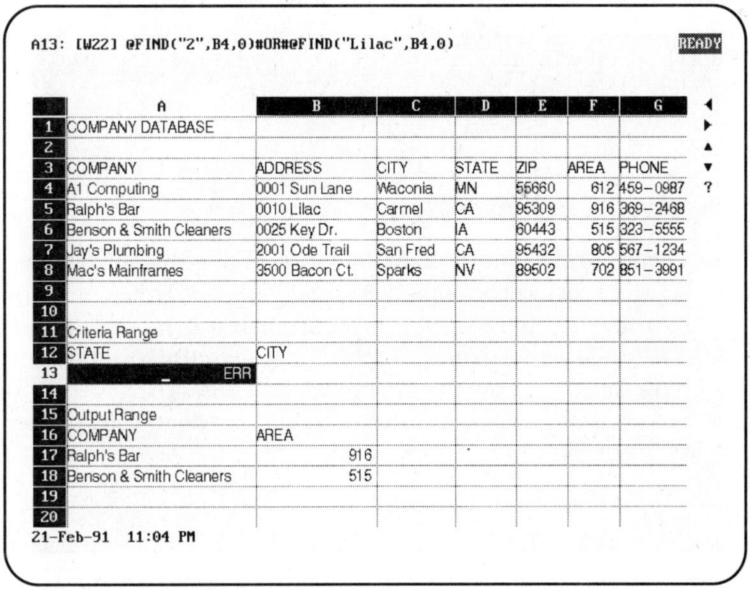

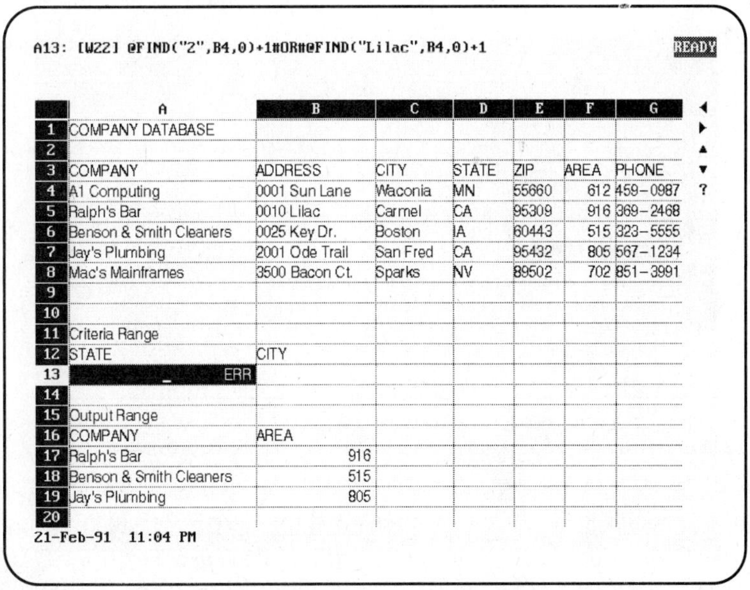

Fig. 12.19. A problem with the @FIND function.

Fig. 12.20. A solution for the problem with the @FIND function.

Performing Other Types of Searches

In addition to the Find and Extract options of the /Data Query command
already explained, you can use the /Data Query menu's Unique and Delete
commands for searches. By issuing the /Data Query Unique command, you
can produce (in the output range) a copy of the first occurrence of a record
that meets a specified criterion. The /Data Query Delete command enables
you to delete all records that meet a specified criterion.

Extracting Unique Records

Ordinarily, you use the Unique command to copy into the output area only
a small portion of each record that meets the criterion. For example, if you
want a list of the states in the database, set up an output range that includes
only the STATE field (cell A16 in fig. 12.21). To search all records, leave blank
the row below the field-name row in the criteria range. Then set the output
range at A16 and select /Data Query Unique to produce a list of the four
states in the database

```
A16: [W22] 'STATE                                                    READY

              A              B          C       D     E     F      G       ◄
  1 COMPANY DATABASE                                                        ►
  2
  3 COMPANY            ADDRESS        CITY     STATE ZIP   AREA  PHONE       ▲
  4 A1 Computing       0001 Sun Lane  Waconia  MN    55660  612 459-0987    ▼
  5 Ralph's Bar        0010 Lilac     Carmel   CA    95309  916 369-2468    ?
  6 Benson & Smith Cleaners 0025 Key Dr. Boston IA   60443  515 323-5555
  7 Jay's Plumbing     2001 Ode Trail San Fred CA    95432  805 567-1234
  8 Mac's Mainframes   3500 Bacon Ct. Sparks   NV    89502  702 851-3991
  9
 10
 11 Criteria Range
 12 STATE              CITY
 13
 14
 15 Output Range
 16 STATE          _
 17 MN
 18 CA
 19 IA
 20 NV
24-Apr-91  08:25 AM
```

Fig. 12.21. The result of issuing a /Data Query Unique command.

As another example, you can help prepare mailings from a large mailing-list
database by producing a list of the ZIP codes. To do so, you specify in the
output area only the field name ZIP, leave blank the row under field names
in the criteria range, and execute the Unique command.

Deleting Specified Records

As mentioned earlier, you can use the /Worksheet Delete Row command to remove rows from a worksheet. If you want a fast alternative to this "one-by-one" approach, use the /Data Query Delete command to remove unwanted records from your database files. Before you select Delete from the Query menu, you must specify the range of records to be searched (*input range*) and the conditions for the deletion (*criteria range*).

For example, suppose that you want to remove all records with a STATE field that begins with the letter *N*. To do so, use the criterion **N*** in cell A13. Then issue the /Data Query Delete command to delete the rows and remove all records for states that begin with *N*. The remaining records pack together, and the input range automatically adjusts.

Be extremely careful when you issue the /Data Query Delete command. To give you the opportunity to verify that you indeed want to select the Delete command, 1-2-3 displays the following menu, on which the leftmost, least dangerous command is highlighted:

    Cancel Delete

Choose Cancel to abort the Delete command. Select Delete to verify that you want to execute the delete operation.

Because the /Data Query Delete command does not show you which rows will be deleted, you can guard against deleting the wrong records by first saving the file or using the /Data Query Find (or /Data Query Extract) command to examine the records before you delete them.

Creating Data Tables

In many situations, the variables you use in your worksheet formulas are known quantities. For example, last year's sales summary deals with variables whose exact values are known. The results of calculations performed by using those values contain no uncertainties. Other situations, however, involve variables whose values are not known. Worksheet models for financial projections often fall into this category. For example, next year's cash-flow projection depends on prevailing interest rates. Although you can make an educated guess at what interest rates may be, you cannot predict them exactly.

Cue:
The /Data Table command automates the "what-if" process.

Data tables enable you to work with variables whose values are not known. With the /Data Table commands, you create tables that show how the results of formula calculations change as the variables used in the formulas change.

Suppose that you decide to buy a new car—a decision that necessitates a $12,000 loan. Area banks offer you several combinations of loan periods and interest rates. You can use a data table to calculate your monthly payment with each combination of period and interest rate.

The /Data Table commands also are used for database analysis. A data table designed for database analysis uses database statistical functions instead of formulas. These functions select data based on criteria and then use the data in calculations. For example, you can use a data table to find out how many clients you have in San Francisco or which city on your list has the highest sales volume.

This section shows you how to use the /Data Table commands to perform sensitivity, or what-if analysis, and database analysis. First, however, you need to understand some terms and concepts.

General Terms and Concepts

A *data table* is a range of answers for one or more formulas, presented in a row-and-column format. The answers are based on a set of input values you supply as part of the data table.

A *data table range* is a worksheet range that contains a data table.

A *variable* is a cell address used by the formula(s) in the data table. 1-2-3 changes the value of the variable each time 1-2-3 recalculates the formula(s) in the data table.

An *input cell* is a worksheet cell used by 1-2-3 for temporary storage during calculation of a data table. You must have one input cell for each cell variable in the formula. You replace the original cell addresses in the formula with the addresses of these input cells.

An *input value* is a specific value that 1-2-3 uses for the variable(s) in the formula(s) during the data-table calculations.

The *results area* is the portion of a data table that contains the calculation results. 1-2-3 calculates one result for each combination of input values. The data table's results area must be unprotected (refer to Chapter 4).

Caution:
Do not use logical formulas in a data table.

The formulas you select for a data table can contain values, strings, cell addresses, and functions. Do not use logical formulas, which always evaluate to either 0 or 1. Although a logical formula in a data table does not cause an error, the resulting 0 or 1 values generally are meaningless.

The Two Types of Data Tables

When you select /**D**ata **T**able, the following menu appears:

1   2   Reset

The menu selections correspond to the types of data tables 1-2-3 generates. The two table types contain different numbers of formulas and variables. In brief, the table types are as follows:

Data Table 1   One or more formulas with one variable

Data Table 2   One formula with two variables

Creating a Type 1 Data Table

A data table created with the /**D**ata **T**able **1** command shows the effect of changing one variable in one or more formulas. Before using this command, you must set up the data-table range and a single input cell.

The input cell can be a blank cell anywhere in the worksheet. The best practice is to identify the input cell by entering an appropriate label either above or to the left of the input cell.

The data-table range is a rectangular worksheet area. It can be placed in any empty worksheet location. The size of the data table-range can be calculated as follows:

- The range has one more column than the number of formulas.

- The range has one more row than the number of input values.

The general structure of a type 1 data-table range is as follows:

- The top-left cell in the data-table range is empty.

- The table's first row contains the formulas to calculate; each formula must refer to an input cell.

- The table's first column contains the input values to use when you recalculate the formulas.

After 1-2-3 completes the data table, each cell in the results area contains the result obtained by evaluating the formula at the top of that column with the input value to the left of that row.

Suppose, for example, that you plan to purchase a house in the $100,000 to $115,000 range, with a 30-year mortgage and a 10 percent or 11 percent interest rate. For each interest rate and price, you want to determine the monthly payment.

For this example, you can use cell B2 as the input cell, identifying it with a label in cell A2. You need one formula for each interest rate. You use the @PMT function, entered as follows in cell D2:

@PMT($B$2,0.10/12,360)

In cell E2, enter the following:

@PMT($B$2,0.11/12,360)

Because payments are monthly, each annual interest rate is divided by 12 to get the monthly interest rate. The *360* is the term of the loan in months.

Next, enter the four possible prices in cells C3 through C6. Select /Data Table 1, specify C2..E6 as the table range, and enter **B2** as the input cell. The resulting data table shows the mortgage payments on four different amounts at two different interest rates (see fig. 12.22). Cells D2 and E2 are formatted as **Text** so that you can see the formulas they contain.

D2: (T) [W20] @PMT($B$2,0.1/12,360)   READY

	A	B	C	D	E	F
1			/Data Table 1			
2	INPUT:			@PMT($B$2,0.1/12,360)	@PMT($B$2,0.11/12,360)	
3			100,000	$877.57	$952.32	
4			105,000	$921.45	$999.94	
5			110,000	$965.33	$1,047.56	
6			115,000	$1,009.21	$1,095.17	
7						
8						
9						

Fig. 12.22. /Data Table 1 used to calculate mortgage payments on four different house prices at two different interest rates.

Analyzing a 1-2-3 Database with /Data Table 1

You also can use /Data Table 1 to analyze the data in a 1-2-3 database. For example, if you have a database for tracking sales, you may want to use the /Data Table command to find the largest single sale made by an individual sales person in your office. Or you may want to find total sales by customer.

The structure of a data table for database analysis is similar to that for a what-if analysis. The upper left cell is empty, and the top row contains the formula(s) to be evaluated. The table also must have an input cell. The cell above the input cell contains the name of the database field to analyze. The formulas in the data table usually are database statistical functions.

The data table's leftmost column contains input values. These input values are the criteria for the analysis, rather than values for the formulas to use.

To calculate the results of the data table, 1-2-3 applies the formula at the top of the column to the database records, in each row of the data table, that meet the criteria values.

Imagine, for example, that you are the director of a week-long fishing tournament and that you are keeping a database of each contestant's catches. Each catch goes into one database record, which contains the contestant's name and the weight of the fish. At the end of the tournament, you want to calculate the total weight and the maximum weight of a single catch for each contestant. The database that handles this application is shown in figure 12.23.

```
A14: [W6]                                                           READY

        A     B      C             D                    E            F    ◀
  1             /Data Table 1 – – Database Analysis                       ▶
  2                                                                       ▲
  3   Angler Catch                                                        ▼
  4   Kidd    25                                                          ?
  5   Marks   19
  6   Alston  21
  7   Marks   24
  8   Alston  13
  9   Kidd    10
 10   Kidd    17
 11   Alston  11
 12                         Total Catch          Largest Catch
 13   Angler         @DSUM(A3..B11,1,A13..A14) @DMAX(A3..B11,1,A13..A14)
 14     _     Kidd            52                    25
 15           Marks           43                    24
 16           Alston          45                    21
 17
 18
 19
 20
 21–Feb–91  11:13 PM
```

***Fig. 12.23.** /Data Table 1 used to perform database analysis.*

In this data table, cell A14 is the input cell. Because you want to select records based on the Angler field, you enter the label **Angler** above the input cell, in cell A13.

The data table is in the range A3..B11. The three contestants' names are in the range C14..C16. The formulas are in cells D13 and E13.

To calculate the total weight caught by each contestant, enter in cell D13 the following formula:

> **@DSUM(A3..B11,1,A13..A14)**

For the maximum weight of a single catch for each contestant, enter in cell E13 the following formula:

> **@DMAX(A3..B11,1,A13..A14)**

Note that each of these functions uses the input cell (A14) and its identifying field name (A13) as the criteria range. Before evaluating the criteria range in these formulas, 1-2-3 inserts the input values from the data table one at a time into cell A14.

Select /**Data Table 1**, specify **C13..E16** as the table range, and enter **A14** as the input cell. 1-2-3 fills the data table with the results, as shown in figure 12.23. Cells D13 and E13 are formatted as **Text**.

Creating a Type 2 Data Table

The type 2 data table evaluates a single formula based on changes in two variables. To use /**Data Table 2**, you need two blank input cells, one for each variable. They can be located anywhere in the worksheet and need not be adjacent to each other. To identify the input cells, place an appropriate label in a cell next to or above each input cell.

The size of the data-table range is determined by the number of values for each variable. The range is one column wider than the number of values for the first variable and one row longer than the number of values for the second variable.

A major difference between /**Data Table 1** and /**Data Table 2** is the location of the formula to be evaluated. In /**Data Table 1**, the formulas are placed along the top row of the table, and the upper left corner is blank. With /**Data Table 2**, the upper left cell of the data-table range contains the formula to be evaluated (see fig. 12.24). As with /**Data Table 1**, this formula refers to the input cells.

The values for input cell 1 are listed below the formula. The values for input cell 2 are listed to the right of the formula. Be sure that the formula refers correctly to the two input cells so that the proper input values get plugged into the correct part of the formula.

```
D4: (C2) 548.21690735                                    READY
```

	A	B	C	D	E	F	G
1			/Data Table 2				
2							
3			@PMT(12000,B7/12,B8)	24	36	48	
4				9%	$548.22	$381.60	$298.62
5				10%	$553.74	$387.21	$304.35
6				11%	$559.29	$392.86	$310.15
7	INPUT 1:			12%	$564.88	$398.57	$316.01
8	INPUT 2:						
9							

Fig. 12.24. A table of loan payment amounts created with /Data Table 2.

1-2-3 calculates the results for the data table by evaluating the formula for each combination of values for input cells 1 and 2.

Suppose, for example, that you want to create a data table which shows the monthly payments on a $12,000 loan at 4 interest rates (9, 10, 11, and 12 percent) and 3 loan periods (24, 36, and 48 months).

First, locate input cell 1 in B7 and input cell 2 in B8. Put identifying labels in the adjacent cells (A7 and A8).

Enter the following @PMT formula in cell C3:

@PMT(12000,B7/12,B8)

As the formula is written, input cell 1 (B7) is for interest rates and input cell 2 (B8) is for periods. Enter the values for input cell 1 (interest rates) in the cells below the formula (C4..C7). Enter the periods in the cells next to the formula (D3..F3).

Now, select **/Data Table 2**. Specify **C3..F7** as the table range, enter **B7** as input cell 1, and enter **B8** as input cell 2. 1-2-3 calculates the data table, as shown in figure 12.24.

If the data table you create is larger than the screen, you can use **/Worksheet Titles** to freeze the input values on-screen as you scroll through the results area.

Analyzing a 1-2-3 Database with /Data Table 2

/Data Table 2 can be used to analyze database records that have two variables. Suppose, for example, that you have a sales database with the names of your salespeople, the items they sold, and the total of each sale. You want to see a data table that shows total sales by salesperson and item.

The structure of a data table for a database analysis is similar to that for a what-if analysis. That is, the upper left cell contains the formula to be evaluated (usually a database statistical function). The two input cells are in adjacent columns, and both are in the same row. The cells immediately above the input cells contain field names from the database used in the database analysis. You write the formula to include as the criteria range the two input cells and their associated field names.

The top row and left column of the data table contain the values or labels to use as criteria for the formula calculations. The criteria values for input cell 1 are in the left column of the table. The values for input cell 2 are in the top row of the table. Be sure that the data-table range input values correspond correctly with the input cells; otherwise, the results of the analysis will be erroneous.

Suppose that you want to create the data table shown in figure 12.25. To create a data table showing each sales representative's total sales of each item, you need a type 2 data table based on the SALESREP and ITEM fields in the database table.

```
A11: (T) [W21] @DSUM(A3..D9,3,F3..G4)                          READY

              A              B       C      D       E     F        G
 1                               /Data Table 2-- Database Analysis
 2
 3                  DATE SALESREP ITEM       AMOUNT      SALESREP ITEM
 4           19-Jul Kidd          Hair Tonic  49.99
 5           22-Jul Marks         Clipper     27.95
 6           25-Jul Alston        Waxer       76.97
 7           28-Jul Marks         Hair Tonic  49.99
 8           31-Jul Kidd          Clipper     27.95
 9           03-Aug Kidd          Waxer       76.97
10
11  @DSUM(A3..D9,3,F3..G4)  Hair Tonic Clipper  Waxer
12  Kidd                   49.99      27.95   76.97
13  Marks                  49.99      27.95   0
14  Alston                 0          0       76.97
15
16
17
18
19
20
21-Feb-91  11:21 PM
```

Fig. 12.25. /Data Table 2 used to perform database analysis.

Use cells F4 and G4 for the input cells and place the field names above them in cells F3 and G3.

Enter the following formula in cell A11:

@DSUM(A3..D9,3,F3..G4)

The criteria for input cell 1 (the input cell under SALESREP) are the sales representatives' names. You have three names; enter them in cells A12..A14. For input cell 2, the criteria are the items sold. Enter them in B11..D11. The entire data table is therefore in the range A11..D14. Note that the values or labels used as input values in a type 2 data table must match exactly the entries in the database.

When you are working with a large database, you can use /Data Query Unique to extract a nonduplicating list of all entries in a particular field and then use this list as the left column or (after transposing) the top row of the data-table range.

The next step is to select /Data Table 2 and specify **A11..D14** as the table range, **F4** as input cell 1, and **G4** as input cell 2. Figure 12.25 shows the results of the analysis.

Filling Ranges

/Data Fill fills a range of cells with a series of numbers, dates, or times that increase or decrease by a specified amount. /Data Fill is useful for restoring the order of records in a sorted database, building input values for data tables, or creating dates for a financial spreadsheet.

Reminder:
Use /Data Fill to enter a series of numbers or dates in a range of the worksheet.

When you issue the /Data Fill command, 1-2-3 first prompts you for the starting number of the series. The program then asks for the step value (or increment) to add to the preceding value. Finally, 1-2-3 prompts you for the ending value.

The /Data Fill command often is used to number the records in a database. You number records to preserve their original order before you issue the /Data Sort command. All you need to do is add a field to the database and use /Data Fill to fill the field with consecutive numbers. Then you can sort your database. If you find that the results of the sort are unacceptable, you re-sort the database on the numeric field created with /Data Fill to restore the order of the records in the database.

The /Data Fill command also can work with the /Data Table command to build a list of interest rates, as shown in figure 12.26. In the example illustrated by figure 12.26, you specify B6..B17 for the range of cells to be filled, .05 for the starting value, and .01 for the step value. For the ending value, let 1-2-3 default to 8,192, which is far beyond the ending value actually needed. The /Data Fill command, however, fills only the specified range and doesn't fill cells beyond the end of the range. You then can use the /**R**ange Format command to display the decimal values as percentages.

```
D2: (C2) @PMT(A2,B2/12,C2*12)                                    READY
```

	A	B	C	D	E	F	G	H
1	Principal	Interest	Term	Payment				
2	$30,000	10%	30	$263.27				
3								
4		Interest	Monthly					
5		Rate	Payments					
6		5%						
7		6%						
8		7%						
9		8%						
10		9%						
11		10%						
12		11%						
13		12%						
14		13%						
15		14%						
16		15%						
17		16%						
18								
19								
20								

```
21-Feb-91  11:32 PM
```

Fig. 12.26. *Filling a range of interest rates by using /Data Fill.*

Although regular numbers are used in the preceding example for the start, step, and stop values, you also can use formulas and functions. For example, you can use the cell formula +E4 for the step value. In this case, E4 contains either a number or a formula that evaluates to a number.

Reminder:
You can use formulas and functions for the start, step, and stop values in /Data Fill.

You also can use formulas and functions for the values, the most common functions being @DATE and @TIME. The step value can be a number of days, weeks, months, or years. (See Chapter 6 for more information about functions.)

Creating Frequency Distributions

The command for creating frequency distributions in 1-2-3 is /**Data** Distribution. You use a *frequency distribution* to determine how often a value occurs in a range of data. For example, you can use a frequency distribution to determine how many consumers from a random sample gave a rating of 10 (excellent) to a product (see fig. 12.27).

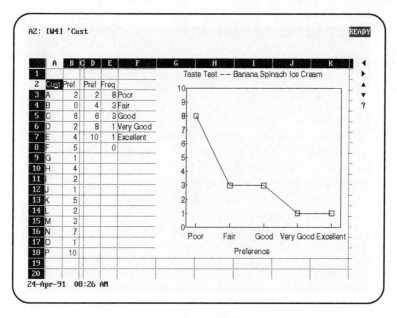

Fig. 12.27. */Data Distribution used to analyze taste preference data.*

To use the /**Data** **Distribution** command, you first specify a values range, which corresponds to the range of Taste Preference numbers in this example. After specifying B3..B18 for the values range, you set up the range of intervals at D3..D7, in what 1-2-3 calls the *bin range*. If the intervals are evenly spaced, you can use the /**Data** **Fill** command to enter the values for the bin range. If the intervals are not evenly spaced, you must enter the values manually.

When you specify these ranges and issue the /**Data** **Distribution** command, 1-2-3 creates the results column (E3..E8) to the right of the bin range (D3..D7). The results column, which shows the frequency distribution, is always in the column segment to the right of the bin range and extends down one extra row.

The values in the results column represent the frequency of the numbers in the values range for each interval. The first interval in the bin range is for values greater than zero and less than or equal to two; the second, for values greater than two and less than or equal to four, and so on. The last value in the results column, in cell E8, shows the frequency of leftover numbers (that is, the number of entries greater than the last interval).

The /**Data** **Distribution** command can help you create understandable results from a series of numbers. The results are graphed easily (see fig. 12.27). A manufacturer looking at this graph would probably start looking for another product or start trying to improve the taste of the current product. Banana Spinach Ice Cream probably will not be next summer's big seller!

Using the /Data Regression Command

The /Data Regression command performs multiple-regression analysis on data in a 1-2-3 worksheet. Most people have no need for this advanced feature. If you need to use it, 1-2-3 saves you the cost and inconvenience of buying a stand-alone statistical package for performing a regression analysis.

Cue:
Use /Data Regression to determine the relationship between sets of values.

Use /Data Regression to determine the relationship between one set of values (the dependent variable) and another (the independent variables). In a business setting, regression analysis has a number of uses, including relating sales to price, promotions, and other market factors; relating stock prices to earnings and interest rates; and relating production costs to production levels.

Think of linear regression as a way of determining the "best" line through a series of data points. Multiple regression does this for several variables simultaneously, determining the "best" line relating the dependent variable to the set of independent variables. Consider, for example, a data sample showing Annual Earnings versus Age. Figure 12.28 shows the data in the worksheet and plotted as an XY graph (use A7..A20 for the X-graph range and C7..C20 for the A-graph range).

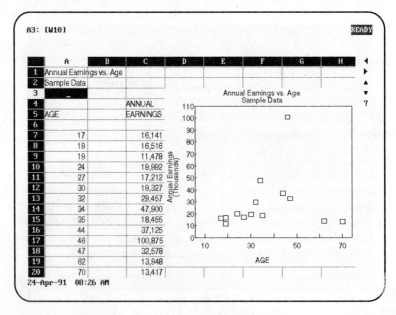

Fig. 12.28. Annual Earnings versus Age data and graph.

The /**Data Regression** command can determine simultaneously how to draw a line through these data points and how well the line fits the data. When you issue the command, 1-2-3 displays the following menu:

X-Range **Y**-Range Output-Range Intercept **R**eset **G**o Quit

Use the **X**-Range option to select one or more independent variables for the regression. The /**Data Regression** command can use as many as 16 independent variables. Because the variables in the regression are columns of values, any data in rows must be converted to columns with /**Range Trans** before you use the /**Data Regression** command. In this example, the **X**-Range is A7..A20.

The **Y**-Range option specifies the dependent variable. The **Y**-Range must be a single column; in this example, C7..C20 is the **Y**-Range.

The Output-Range option specifies the upper left corner of the results range. Select an unused section of the worksheet, because 1-2-3 writes the output over any existing cell contents. In this example, E5 was specified as the corner cell of the output range.

The Intercept option specifies whether to calculate the *y-axis intercept*, the value where the "best fit" line crosses the y-axis. The intercept value is the value of the dependent variable when the independent variables are zero. Calculating the intercept is the default. Use the default unless you know that the dependent variable must be zero when all the independent variables are zero.

Figure 12.29 shows the results of using the /**Data Regression G**o command in the Annual Earnings versus Age example. The results (in cells E5..H13) include the value of the intercept and the coefficient of the single independent variable that was specified with the **X**-Range option. The results also include several regression statistics that describe how well the regression line fits the data. In this case, the R-Squared value and the standard errors of the constant and the regression coefficient all indicate that the regression line does not explain much of the variation in the dependent variable.

The new data in column D is the computed regression line. These values consist of the constant plus the coefficient of the independent variable times its value in each row of the data. To calculate the regression line, type the formula **+$H$6+$G$12*A7** in cell D7. Then use the /**R**ange Format , (Comma) 0 command to format the result. Finally, use /**C**opy from D7..D7 to D8..D20 to copy the formula to the other cells in column D. When you copy the formula in D7 to the range D8..D20, the cell A7 changes to A8, A9, A10, and so on to A20. The other two cells in the formula (H6 and G12) remain the same because they are absolute addresses. The completed regression line can be plotted against the original data, as shown in figure 12.30.

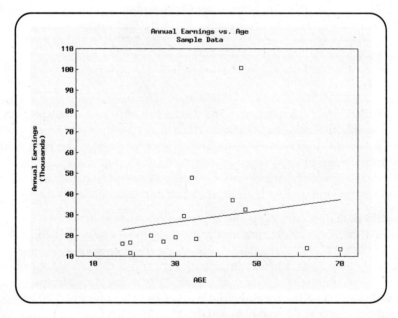

D7: (,0) +$H$6+$G$12*A7   READY

	A	B	C	D	E	F	G	H
1	Annual Earnings vs. Age							
2	Sample Data							
3								
4			ANNUAL	REGRESSION				
5	AGE		EARNINGS	LINE		Regression Output:		
6					Constant			18414.66
7	17		16,141	23,005	Std Err of Y Est			23930.20
8	19		16,516	23,545	R Squared			0.034195
9	19		11,478	23,545	No. of Observations			14
10	24		19,992	24,894	Degrees of Freedom			12
11	27		17,212	25,704				
12	30		19,327	26,514	X Coefficient(s)		269.9913	
13	32		29,457	27,054	Std Err of Coef.		414.2111	
14	34		47,900	27,594				
15	35		18,455	27,864				
16	44		37,125	30,294				
17	46		100,875	30,834				
18	47		32,578	31,104				
19	62		13,948	35,154				
20	70		13,417	37,314				

21-Feb-91 11:47 PM

Fig. 12.29. *The result of /Data Regression on Annual Earnings versus Age data.*

Fig. 12.30. *A graph of Annual Earnings versus Age data with a regression line.*

When you look at the Annual Earnings versus Age plot, you notice that income appears to rise with age until about age 50; then income begins to decline. You can use the /**D**ata **R**egression command to fit a line that describes such a relationship between Annual Earnings and Age.

In figure 12.31, a column of data is added in column B; this data is the square of the corresponding age in column A. To include this new column in the regression, specify the range **A7..B20** for the **X**-Range and then select **G**o to recalculate the regression output. Adjust the formulas in column D by changing D7 to +$H$6+$G$12*A7+$H$12*B7 (and then copying the formula to D8..D20).

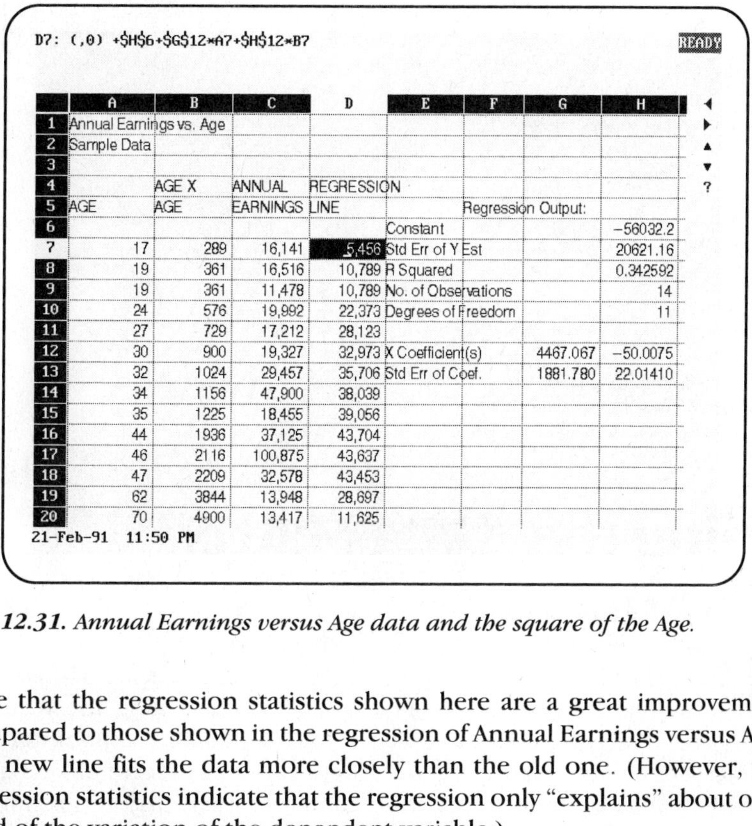

D7: (,0) +$H$6+$G$12*A7+$H$12*B7 READY

	A	B	C	D	E	F	G	H
1	Annual Earnings vs. Age							
2	Sample Data							
3								
4		AGE X	ANNUAL	REGRESSION				
5	AGE	AGE	EARNINGS	LINE		Regression Output:		
6					Constant			-56032.2
7	17	289	16,141	5,456	Std Err of Y Est			20621.16
8	19	361	16,516	10,789	R Squared			0.342592
9	19	361	11,478	10,789	No. of Observations			14
10	24	576	19,992	22,373	Degrees of Freedom			11
11	27	729	17,212	28,123				
12	30	900	19,327	32,973	X Coefficient(s)		4467.067	-50.0075
13	32	1024	29,457	35,706	Std Err of Coef.		1881.780	22.01410
14	34	1156	47,900	38,039				
15	35	1225	18,455	39,056				
16	44	1936	37,125	43,704				
17	46	2116	100,875	43,637				
18	47	2209	32,578	43,453				
19	62	3844	13,948	28,697				
20	70	4900	13,417	11,625				

21-Feb-91 11:50 PM

Fig. 12.31. *Annual Earnings versus Age data and the square of the Age.*

Note that the regression statistics shown here are a great improvement compared to those shown in the regression of Annual Earnings versus Age. The new line fits the data more closely than the old one. (However, the regression statistics indicate that the regression only "explains" about one-third of the variation of the dependent variable.)

To generate the new plot shown in figure 12.32, you must add the new regression coefficient (as mentioned earlier) to the equation that generates the regression line. Note that the regression line is now a parabola that rises until age 45 and then declines. The regression line generated by a multiple regression may or may not be a straight line, depending on the independent variables used.

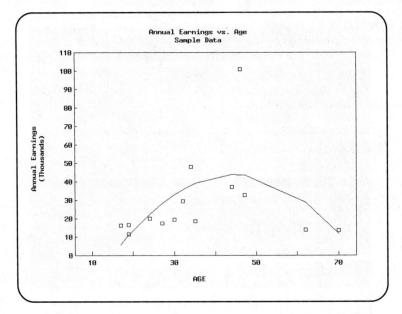

Fig. 12.32. *A graph of Annual Earnings versus Age data with a curved regression line.*

Using the /Data Matrix Command

The /Data Matrix command is a specialized mathematical command for solving simultaneous linear equations and manipulating the resulting solutions. This command is powerful but has limited application in a business setting. If you are using 1-2-3 for certain types of economic analysis or for scientific or engineering calculations, you may find this command valuable.

The /Data Matrix command's menu has two options: Invert and Multiply. The Invert option enables you to invert a nonsingular square matrix of up to 80 rows and columns. Just select the Invert option and highlight the range to invert. Then select an output range to hold the inverted solution matrix. You can place the output range anywhere in the worksheet—even on top of the matrix you are inverting.

The time required to invert a matrix is proportional to the cube of the number of rows and columns. A 25-by-25 matrix takes about 10 seconds, and an 80-by-80 matrix takes almost 5 minutes on a 16-MHz 80386 computer with no numeric coprocessor. If you are going to use 1-2-3 to invert matrices, you may want to invest in a numeric coprocessor for your computer.

The Multiply option multiplies two rectangular matrices together in accordance with the rules of matrix algebra. The number of columns in the first matrix must equal the number of rows in the second matrix. The resulting matrix has the same number of rows as the first matrix and the same number of columns as the second.

When you select /Data Matrix Multiply, 1-2-3 prompts you for three ranges: the first matrix, the second matrix, and the output range. Multiply is fast compared to Invert, but still may take some time if you multiply large matrices.

Loading Data from Other Programs

1-2-3 has several ways to import data from other applications. The Translate utility (refer to Chapter 7) has options for converting directly to 1-2-3 worksheets data from DIF, dBASE II, dBASE III, dBASE III Plus files, and from other file formats. You access the data by using the /File Retrieve or /File Combine commands.

Use the /File Import command to read the data from a text file into the worksheet. Depending on the format of the date in the text file, the files can be read directly to a range of cells or a column of cells. Specially formatted "numeric" data can be read directly to a range of worksheet cells. ASCII text can be stored as long labels in a single column, with one line of the file per cell. You then must disassemble these labels into the appropriate data values or fields by using functions or the /Data Parse command.

Finally, to read and write an ASCII sequential file directly from within the 1-2-3 advanced macro command programs, you can use certain advanced macro commands (see Chapter 14).

Using the /Data Parse Command

Cue:

Use /Data Parse to split long labels imported from text files into separate text, number, or date fields.

The /Data Parse command is a flexible, easy way to extract numeric, string, and date data from long labels and place that data in separate columns. For example, suppose that you have a disk file which contains a report of inventory data and that you want to load the ASCII file into 1-2-3. After using the /File Import command to load the file, you must reformat (*parse*) the data with the /Data Parse command.

The /File Import command loads the inventory data into the range A1..A8 (see fig. 12.33). Although the data appears to be formatted in a typical worksheet range, such as A1..G8, the display is misleading. The current cell-pointer location is A6; the entire contents of the row exist as a long label in that cell only.

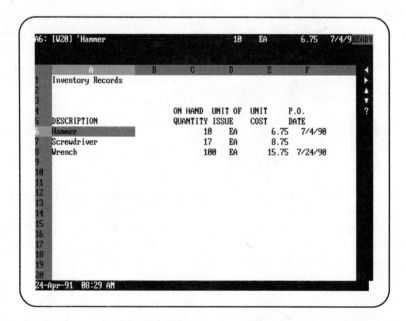

Fig. 12.33. The result of the /File Import command.

To break up the long label columns, move the cell pointer to the first cell you want to parse and select /Data Parse. You see the following menu:

    Format-Line Input-Column Output-Range Reset Go Quit

Use Format-Line to Create or Edit a line of formatting codes for the data to parse. The format line specifies how to split the long label into cells with numbers, labels, and dates.

Use Input-Column to specify the range of cells to parse. The input range (contained in just one column) consists of the cell containing the format line and all cells containing the long labels to parse.

Use Output-Range to specify the worksheet range in which 1-2-3 places the parsed data. You can specify a rectangular range or the single cell at the upper left of the range. The output data will have as many rows as there are long labels; the number of columns depends on the format line.

Reset clears the previously set Input-Column and Output-Range. Go performs the parse, based on the specified Input-Column, Format-Lines, and Output-Range.

To parse the data shown in figure 12.33, follow these steps:

1. Move the cell pointer to cell A4, the first cell in the range of data you want to break into columns. (You do not have to parse the title in cell A1.)

2. Parse the column headings in cells A4..A5 by using one format line; then parse the data by using another format line.

Different format lines are necessary because the data is a mixture of labels, numbers, and dates; and all the headings are labels. Select Format-Line Create. A suggested format line is inserted in the data at A4, in a step that moves the remaining worksheet contents down one line. Note that the data is now in the range A7..A9.

After you create a format line, you may need to edit it. To do so, select Format-Line again and choose Edit. Use the format line to mark the column positions and the type of data in those positions. /Data Parse uses the format line to break down the data and move it to the appropriate columns in the output range.

Format lines comprise combinations of certain letters and special characters. The letters denote the beginning position and the type of data; special symbols define the length of a field and the spacing. Note the following letters and symbols and what they do:

Letter/Symbol	Purpose
D	Marks beginning of a **Date** field
L	Marks beginning of a **Label** field
S	Marks beginning of a **Skip** position
T	Marks beginning of a **Time** field
V	Marks beginning of a **Value** field
>	Defines the continuation of a field; use one > for each position in the field (after the first position)
*	Defines blank spaces that may be part of the data in the next cell

Add as many format lines as you need in the data. In the inventory example, you need to enter another format line at cell A6 (which becomes A7 after you add the first format line in A4) and specify the format criteria for the data records that follow. Suggested format lines are shown in figure 12.34. To restore the **Parse** menu, press Enter after you finish editing.

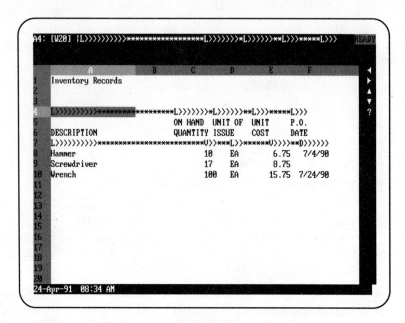

Fig. 12.34. Two format lines for the headings and data to parse.

After setting up two format lines in the Physical Inventory example, select **Input-Range** from the **Parse** menu. Point to or type the range **A4..A10**, which includes format lines, column headings, and data. Select **Output-Range** from the **Parse** menu and specify **A13** as the upper left corner of a blank range to accept the parsed data. Complete the operation by selecting the **G**o option; the results are shown in figure 12.35.

Cue:
Base the column width settings on the width of characters in text mode.

The data displayed in individual cells may not be exactly what you want. You can make a few changes in the format and column width, and you can add or delete information to make the newly parsed data more usable. These enhancements are not part of the /**D**ata **P**arse command but usually are necessary after you import and parse data.

To produce the final inventory database shown in figure 12.36, follow these steps:

1. Delete rows A3..A12 to remove the unparsed data and to move the parsed data up under the title.

2. Reformat the P.O. DATE range in column E to the Date 4 format.

3. Insert at column E a column for the inventory value (the P.O. DATE should now be column F).

4. Widen the new column E to 10 characters. Remember that the column width settings are based on the width of a character in text mode (no Wysiwyg).

5. Add the INVENTORY and VALUE headings in cells E3 and E4, respectively.

6. Enter in cell E5 the formula that computes the inventory value (+B5*D5).

7. Copy the formula in cell E5 to cells E6..E17.

8. Use the /Range Format command to change the format of cells D5..E7 to the comma-and-two-decimal-places display.

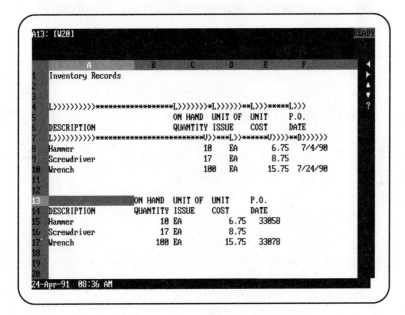

Fig. 12.35. *The result of the /Data Parse command.*

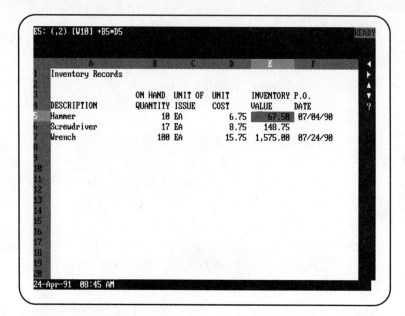

Fig. 12.36. Improving the appearance of parsed data.

If you are parsing a value that continues past the end of the field, 1-2-3 parses the data until it encounters a blank or until the value meets the next field in the format line. If you parse labels with several words separated by blanks, you need to make sure that the field widths in the format line are wide enough for the entire label. If you parse values, the field widths are less critical.

Experiment on small amounts of data until you are comfortable using the /Data Parse command. After you understand how this important command works, you may find many more ways to use it. Every time you develop a new application, consider whether existing data created with another software program can be imported and then changed to 1-2-3 format by using the /Data Parse command.

Summary

This chapter addressed all eight options on the /Data menu. The Sort and Query options, described extensively in the first half of the chapter, are true data-management commands that require database organization by field name. **F**ill, **T**able, **D**istribution, **M**atrix, **R**egression, and **P**arse manipulate data and can be used in database or worksheet applications.

Data management is one of 1-2-3's advanced capabilities. If you have mastered data management, you are a true "power user." You probably are already using 1-2-3 macros. If not, you can continue learning. Chapter 13 shows how to create and use keyboard macros, and Chapter 14 introduces you to the powerful advanced macro commands.

13

Using Macros

As you have seen so far, the worksheet, database, and graphics features of 1-2-3 give you many useful functions for everyday business needs. Yet 1-2-3 has another feature that enhances the value of these functions: the macro capability. In its most basic form, a macro is a collection of keystrokes saved as text in a worksheet range. 1-2-3 macros are a convenient way to automate the tasks you perform repeatedly, such as printing worksheets or changing global default settings. But macros and the advanced macro commands can do much more for you. With a more sophisticated macro, for example, you can construct business applications that function in the same way as applications written in programming languages such as BASIC, C, or FORTRAN.

This chapter shows you how to do the following:

- Develop macros

- Document macros

- Use LEARN mode to create macros

- Name and run macros

- Debug macros

- Build a simple macro library

- Use the 1-2-3 Macro Library Manager add-in

Chapter 14 introduces you to 1-2-3's *advanced macro commands* (a set of advanced programming commands) and helps you learn the functions and applications of those commands.

Introducing Macros

Reminder:
You can enter a macro exactly as you would any other label.

You can copy, edit, or move macros as you would any label. Consider the number of times you save and retrieve worksheet files, print reports, and perhaps set and reset worksheet formats. In each case, you perform the operation by pressing a series of keys—sometimes a rather lengthy series—on the computer's keyboard. By using a macro, you can reduce any number of keystrokes to a simple two-key abbreviation.

Consider, as an example, a simple macro that enters text. Suppose that your company's name is ABC Manufacturing, Incorporated. Typing this name as an entry in the worksheet takes 32 keystrokes (if you count pressing the Enter key). Now suppose that you want to place this text in numerous locations in your worksheets. You can type the entry's 32 keystrokes, copy the company name by using /Copy, or store the keystrokes in a macro. If you store the keystrokes in a macro, the next time you want to type your company's name, you can execute the 32 keystrokes by pressing just two keys.

Writing Some Sample Macros

The easiest way to understand macros is to write a few. The next two sections show you how to write two simple macros. The first macro enters text into a cell. The second macro executes a command specified in the macro.

Writing a Macro that Enters Text

In this section, you learn to create a macro that enters your company name in several locations in a worksheet.

Cue:
Before you create a macro, identify the keystrokes you want the macro to type for you.

Before you begin creating a macro, plan what you want the macro to do and then identify the keystrokes the macro is to type for you. In this case, you want a macro that enters a company name. You want the macro to type the letters, spaces, and punctuation that make up your company name. Then, as with any label, you want the macro to enter the typed characters into the cell by pressing the Enter key.

You start building your macro by storing the keystrokes as text in a worksheet cell. After you type the name, be sure to enter a tilde (~) to represent the Enter key. If you forget to add the tilde at the end of the macro, 1-2-3 acts as though you were entering the keystrokes at the keyboard and had not pressed Enter yet. Forgetting the tilde is one of the most common mistakes macro writers make.

Cell B3 in figure 13.1 shows the keystrokes, including the Enter (~) keystroke, you want 1-2-3 to type for you as part of the macro: `ABC Manufacturing, Incorporated~`

```
B3: [W27] 'ABC Manufacturing, Incorporated~                          READY

        A              B                  C      D      E      F    ◄
   1 │Name      │Macro              │         │      │      │      │  ►
   2 │          │                   │         │      │      │      │  ▲
   3 │\n        │ABC Manufacturing, Incorporated ~│  │      │      │  ▼
   4 │          │                   │         │      │      │      │  ?
   5 │          │                   │         │      │      │      │
   6 │          │                   │         │      │      │      │
   7 │          │                   │         │      │      │      │
   8 │          │                   │         │      │      │      │
   9 │          │                   │         │      │      │      │
```

Fig. 13.1. A simple macro for entering a company name.

Having entered the text you want the macro to type for you, you must name this sequence of keystrokes as a macro. To name this macro, follow these steps:

1. Move the cell pointer to cell B3 and select the /**R**ange Name Create command.

2. At the `Enter name:` prompt, type the name **\n**. In macros, the backslash (\) represents the Alt key.

3. At the `Enter range:` prompt, specify the range that contains the macro, cell B3. Because the cell pointer is already in this cell, just press Enter to indicate a single-cell range.

4. Document the macro as shown in figure 13.1. Place the macro name one cell to the left of the first line of the macro, in cell A3. Documenting the macro in this way helps you remember the macro's name.

Note: Most texts on 1-2-3 suggest placing the macro name in the cell to the left of the macro so that you can use the /**R**ange Name Labels **Right** command to apply the name to the macro. 1-2-3 doesn't require that you enter macro names; they serve as documentation only.

To *execute*, or run, this simple macro, just move the cell pointer to a cell where you want to enter the company name, press and hold down the Alt key, and then press **N**. 1-2-3 enters the sequence of characters identified as the macro \n. Figure 13.2 shows the results of moving the cell pointer to B10 and then running the \n macro. To save this macro for future use, save the file that contains the macro.

> *Note:* You also can save macros in a separate library file. See the section "Building a Simple Macro Library" later in this chapter for more information.

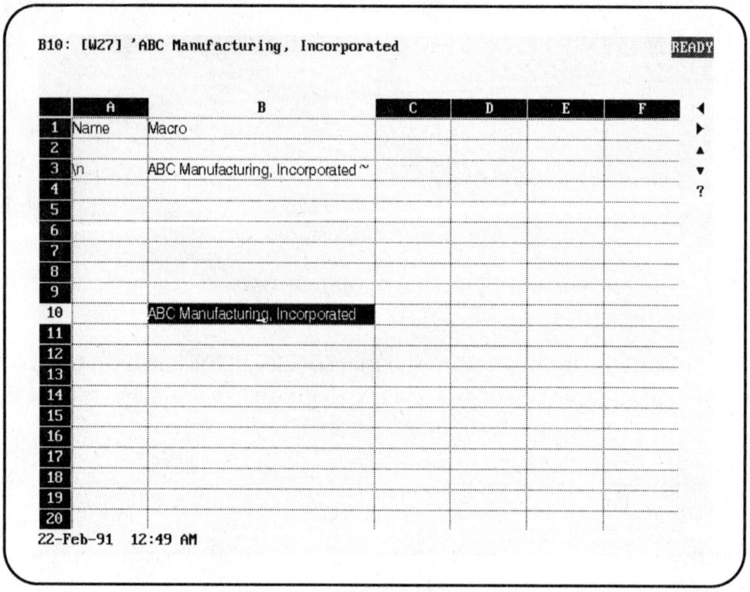

B10: [W27] 'ABC Manufacturing, Incorporated   READY

	A	B	C	D	E	F
1	Name	Macro				
2						
3	\n	ABC Manufacturing, Incorporated ~				
4						
5						
6						
7						
8						
9						
10		ABC Manufacturing, Incorporated				
11						
12						
13						
14						
15						
16						
17						
18						
19						
20						

22-Feb-91   12:49 AM

Fig. 13.2. The result of running the \n macro.

Writing a Simple Command Macro

In addition to macros that repeat text, you can write macros that repeat commands. If you follow the same procedure each time, macro writing can become second nature. This section describes a simple macro that enters commands. To create and name the macro, you use the same steps you used to create and name the macro that entered the company name.

First, plan what you want the command macro to do. For example, create a macro that changes the column width from the default 9-character width to a width of 14 characters. The keystrokes you normally use to enter this command are as follows:

1. Press the slash (/) to display the main menu.

2. Select **W**orksheet.

3. Select **C**olumn.

4. Select **S**et-Width.

5. Enter the number for the desired column width (**14**, in this example).

6. Press Enter.

You can create a macro to perform these operations. When you type this macro into a cell (remember to type an apostrophe before the slash to indicate a label entry), it should look like the following:

'/wcs14~

Notice that each character of the macro is what you normally press on the keyboard to enter this command. As with the first macro, the tilde (~) in this macro represents the Enter key.

Next, you need to name the macro. Because the macro changes the *column* width, you can call the macro \c. (The backslash represents the Alt key.) Remember that the name you assign to a macro should remind you of the macro's function.

In the following steps, you enter the macro name, which you use to run the macro, and document the name by placing it in the worksheet:

1. Place the macro name one cell to the left of the first line of the macro. If the text of the macro is in cell AA1, for example, type the name of the macro in cell Z1. This step documents the name of the macro.

2. With the cell pointer in cell Z1, choose the /**R**ange **N**ame **L**abels **R**ight command and press Enter. This command uses the label in cell Z1 (the macro name) to name the range one cell to the right (or cell AA1, which contains the macro).

3. To document the macro further, type an explanation next to each line of the macro. Place the explanation one cell to the right of each line of the macro. Figure 13.3 shows the \c macro with appropriate documentation.

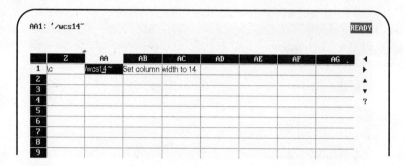

Fig. 13.3. *A simple command macro.*

After you name the macro, move the cell pointer to a column whose width you want to change. Press and hold down the Alt key and then press **C** to run the macro. The macro changes the current column width to 14 characters.

Guidelines for Developing Macros

Reminder:
Plan your macro
first before you try
to create it.

The steps for creating any macro are basic and conform to the following outline.

1. *Plan what you want the macro to do.* Write down the tasks you want the macro to perform and then arrange the steps in the order they should be completed.

2. *Identify the keystrokes the macro should repeat.* Keep in mind that basic macros are labels (text) that duplicate the keystrokes you want to replay.

3. *Find an area of the worksheet for the macro.* When you choose the area, be aware that executed macros read text from cells, starting with the top cell and working down through lower cells. Macros end when they come to a blank cell, a numeric cell, or a command that stops macro execution. To make certain that your macro stops executing at the last macro command, leave at least one blank cell below the last cell in the macro.

4. *Enter the keystrokes, keystroke equivalents, and commands into a cell or cells.* When you type a macro into the worksheet, you must enter each cell of the macro as text. Certain keystrokes (such as numbers) cause 1-2-3 to change from READY mode to VALUE

mode; other keystrokes (the / and the <, for example) change 1-2-3 to MENU mode. Therefore, if you are typing any of the following characters as the first character in a macro cell, you must place an apostrophe (') before that character:

- A number from 0 to 9

- /, +, –, @, #, $, ., <, (, \, or :

The apostrophe (') switches 1-2-3 from READY mode to LABEL mode. By using an apostrophe before any of the preceding characters and numbers, you ensure that 1-2-3 does not misinterpret your text entry. If any character not in this list is the first keystroke in the cell, 1-2-3 switches to LABEL mode and adds the apostrophe (') after you press Enter.

5. *Use range names rather than addresses in your macros.* 1-2-3 does not update addresses in a macro when you make changes to the worksheet. As a consequence, any copies, moves, insertions, or deletions can cause a macro to use incorrect addresses. To eliminate this problem, you use range names instead of addresses; range names in a macro (like range names in formulas) update their meaning when the worksheet changes.

Reminder:
Use range names to avoid cell reference problems in macros.

6. *Name the macro.* You use either the /**R**ange **N**ame **C**reate or the /**R**ange **N**ame **L**abels command to name the range of cells that contain the macro. You can use one of the following types of names:

- An Alt-*letter* name, such as \a

- A descriptive name, such as PRINT_BUDGET

- The name \0 (backslash zero), to run the macro each time you retrieve its worksheet file

Later sections in this chapter show you how to create and run a macro with each of these names.

7. *Document the macro.* You can document macros in several ways. Using a descriptive name is a first step. Another way is to enter documentation in the cells to the right of each line in the macro. The better you describe what the macro is doing, the easier it is to read and edit.

8. *Test and debug the macro.* Not all macros do exactly what you think they will when you write them. You may have to make changes to the text of the macro, or *debug* it, before it executes correctly.

Reminder:
Document your macro to help you remember what it does and why.

As your expertise increases and your macros become more complex, you still use the same basic steps to create a macro. Keep in mind that good planning and documentation are important for making macros run smoothly.

Using Macro Key Names

Reminder:
1-2-3 uses some special characters or words as equivalents for some keys and key combinations.

To identify certain keys and combinations of keys, 1-2-3 uses some special characters or words as key names. Table 13.1 summarizes these key names—the special characters and words you use in macros to represent keystrokes that are not alphanumeric characters. Many of the examples in this chapter use these key names. (See Chapters 2 and 3 for explanations of the direction and function keys.)

> *Note:* Some 1-2-3 keys, such as the tilde (~) and the braces ({ }), have special meanings in 1-2-3 macros. If you want to use these keys in a macro without invoking special meanings, enclose them in braces ({ }). For example, to have a macro enter a tilde as a character (instead of interpreting the tilde as the Enter key), type {~} in the macro.

Table 13.1
Summary of Macro Key Names

1-2-3 Key	Macro Key Name
Function Keys	
Help (F1)	{HELP}
Edit (F2)	{EDIT}
Name (F3)	{NAME}
Abs (F4)	{ABS}
Goto (F5)	{GOTO}
Window (F6)	{WINDOW}
Query (F7)	{QUERY}
Table (F8)	{TABLE}
Calc (F9)	{CALC}
Graph (F10)	{GRAPH}
App1 (Alt-F7)	{APP1}

1-2-3 Key	Macro Key Name
App2 (Alt-F8)	{APP2}
App3 (Alt-F9)	{APP3}
App4 (Alt-F10)	{APP4}
Cell Pointer-Movement Keys	
	{UP} or {U}
	{DOWN} or {D}
	{LEFT} or {L}
	{RIGHT} or {R}
Big Left (Ctrl- ←) or Back Tab (Shift-Tab)	{BIGLEFT}
Big Right (Ctrl- →) or Tab	{BIGRIGHT}
PgUp or PageUp	{PGUP}
PgDn or PageDown	{PGDN}
Home	{HOME}
End	{END}
Enter	~
Editing Keys	
Del	{DELETE} or {DEL}
Ins	{INSERT} or {INS}
Escape	{ESCAPE} or {ESC}
Backspace	{BACKSPACE} or {BS}
Special Keys	
Ctrl-Break in MENU mode	{BREAK}
~	{~}
{ (open brace)	{{}
} (close brace)	{}}
/ (slash), < (less than)	/ or {MENU}

You may have noticed that a few keys are not included in the table. These include Caps Lock, Num Lock, Scroll Lock, Compose (Alt-F1), Step (Alt-F2), Run (Alt-F3), Undo (Alt-F4), Learn (Alt-F5), Print Screen, and Shift. You cannot use these keystrokes in macros (although you will see in later sections that the Run command does have a macro substitute).

Note: Although you cannot include the Compose (Alt-F1) key in a macro, you can add LICS (Lotus International Character Set) characters to macro text and have the macro enter the characters when it runs. For more information about the Compose (Alt-F1) key and LICS characters, see Appendix C.

Caution:
Don't split macro key names across cells in a macro.

When you use the preceding key names in a macro, you must keep the entire key name in one cell. For example, you cannot split the key name {EDIT} into two cells: {ED in one cell and IT} in another. Also, be careful not to mix braces with parentheses. For example, avoid typing {DOWN).

Reminder:
Repeat certain key names by including a repetition factor.

You can repeat certain key names by including a repetition factor. A *repetition factor* tells 1-2-3 that you want a command repeated the specified number of times. For example, instead of typing {LEFT} three times, you can type {LEFT 3} or {L 3}. When you use repetition factors, be sure to place one space between the key name and the number of repetitions.

Planning the Layout of a Macro

Cue:
Use /Range Justify to edit a macro text cell to make the lines shorter.

Although a macro containing fewer than 240 characters can be entered in one cell, you should get into the practice of breaking apart a long macro down a column of cells. By limiting each cell to a single task or a few simple tasks, you can more easily debug, modify, and document a macro.

Figure 13.4, for example, shows two macros that execute the same sequence of keystrokes. The macros in figure 13.4 are enhancements to the macro in figure 13.1. Both macros enter the company name; move down two rows; enter the address; move down two rows again; and enter the city, state, and ZIP. In both cases, the named range is only one cell. \a is the range name given to the macro in B3, and \b is the range name given to the macro in the range B5..B9. Note that a macro must be in a single column. The \a macro is in the single cell B3. The \b macro is in the five cells B5 through B9.

```
B3: [W28] 'ABC Manufacturing, Incorporated~{D 2}'123 Industrial Drive~{D 2}READY
```

	A	B	C	D	E	F
1	Name	Macro				
2						
3	\a	ABC Manufacturing, Incorporated ~ {D 2}'123 Industrial Drive ~ {D 2}Reno,NV 89502 ~				
4						
5	\b	ABC Manufacturing, Incorporated ~	Company name			
6		{D 2}	Go down two cells			
7		'123 Industrial Drive~	Type address			
8		{D 2}	Go down two cells			
9		Reno,NV 89502~	Type city, state, and zip			
10						
11						
12						
13						
14						
15						
16						
17						
18						
19						
20						

```
25-Apr-91  07:26 PM
```

Fig. 13.4. Two different ways to write a macro to do the same task.

The \b macro works correctly whether you name just cell B5 or the range of cells B5..B9. Keep in mind that for simple keystroke macros as well as advanced macro command programs, 1-2-3 executes the keystrokes starting at the cell in the upper left corner of the range. After executing the keystrokes in B5, 1-2-3 moves down one cell and executes any keystrokes in that cell. Similarly, after completing those keystrokes, the program continues to move down and read until it encounters an empty cell, a cell that contains a numeric value, an error, or an advanced macro command that explicitly stops a macro. (These circumstances are discussed in Chapter 14.)

Although both macros perform the same functions, the \b macro is easier to read because it breaks the task into the following simple steps:

1. Type the company name.
2. Position the cell pointer.
3. Type the address.
4. Position the cell pointer again.
5. Type the city, state, and ZIP.

Macros are easier to read and understand later if you separate keystrokes and key names logically into separate cells.

Documenting Macros

As with other parts of a 1-2-3 worksheet, you should document your macros. The best way to do this is to place the comments next to the macro steps in the column to the right of the macro. Each line in the \b macro shown in figure 13.4 has a corresponding line of documentation in the cell to its right.

With these simple macros, identifying the tasks the macros perform is fairly easy. This sort of internal documentation is immensely helpful, however, with longer, more complex macros such as those discussed and demonstrated in the next chapter. Later, if you or someone else wants to make changes to the macro, these internal comments tell you the macro's purpose and its intended action.

Creating Macros with the Learn Feature

1-2-3 Release 2.3 offers a simplified way to create macros, called the Learn feature. To use Learn to create a macro, you select /Worksheet Learn Range and type or highlight a range to contain the macro. Then switch to LEARN mode; 1-2-3 records every keystroke you press. When you finish typing the macro, turn off LEARN mode. 1-2-3 places the saved keystrokes in a range you selected by using the /Worksheet Learn Range command.

You can try out this feature by creating a macro that sets the worksheet's global format to currency with two decimal places. First, select /Worksheet Learn Range. At the Enter learn range: prompt, enter the range for the macro by typing a range address or pointing to it. The range should be either a single cell or a single-column range. For this example, enter **A1..A3**.

After you enter the range location, create the macro by pressing Learn (Alt-F5). 1-2-3 displays the LEARN indicator at the bottom of the screen (see fig. 13.5). Everything you type from now on is recorded by 1-2-3. Carefully type the following keystrokes:

> **/wgfc**

When 1-2-3 asks for the number of decimal places, type **2** and press Enter.

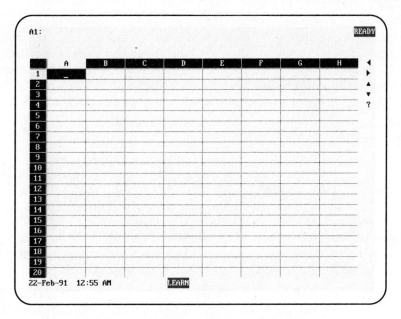

Fig. 13.5. The LEARN indicator displayed after pressing Alt-F5.

Press Learn (Alt-F5) again to turn off LEARN mode and press Enter. 1-2-3 displays the result of your keystrokes and commands in cell A1 (see fig. 13.6).

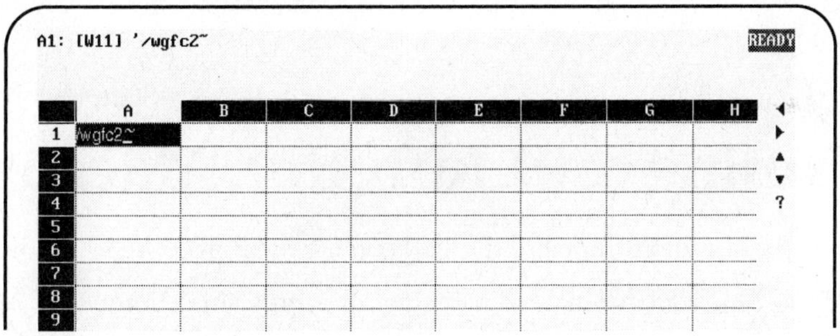

Fig. 13.6. A macro created with the Learn feature.

Now all you have to do is name and document the macro. The preceding section shows how to document the macro's contents. For details on naming macros, see the "Naming and Running Macros" section later in this chapter.

If the macro you enter is too large for the specified Learn range, you get the Learn range is full error message. If this happens, use the /Worksheet

Learn **R**ange command to make the range larger. When you get the error message, notice that 1-2-3 displays as much of the macro as the range permits. Press Esc to return to READY mode, select /**W**orksheet **L**earn **R**ange, and specify a new range directly under the preceding one. Next, activate Learn and continue creating your macro, starting where 1-2-3 left off. If you want to cancel the current range and start over again, use the /**W**orksheet **L**earn **C**ancel command. To erase a macro you created with Learn and start again, use /**W**orksheet **L**earn **E**rase.

Keep in mind that the Learn feature records all keystrokes you type, even your mistakes. In Learn mode, for example, if you type /**W** instead of /**R**, and you then press Esc to correct the error, the macro still contains the error, as well as the Esc keystroke. To correct an error in a short macro, just start again. If your macro is a long one, however, you may want to edit the macro rather than re-create it. You edit a macro created with Learn the same way you edit a normal macro or any other text entry—move to the cell containing the error and press Edit (F2). Make the corrections and press Enter.

To include an existing macro within the one you are recording, enter the range name of the macro you want to include, enclosed in braces. For example, to include a macro whose range name is MONTHS, enter {**MONTHS**}.

When you use Learn, 1-2-3 does not record any /**W**orksheet **L**earn commands, nor does 1-2-3 record the following keystrokes: Caps Lock, Num Lock, Scroll Lock, Compose (Alt-F1), Step (Alt-F2), Run (Alt-F3), Undo (Alt-F4), Learn (Alt-F5), Bookmark (Ctrl-F1), Shift, Print Screen, Ctrl-Break, and mouse actions.

Naming and Running Macros

The way you execute a macro depends on how you name it, as follows:

- Use Alt-*letter*, for macros named with \ and a single letter.

- Use Run (Alt-F3), for macros with descriptive names or to run macros by typing their addresses.

- Run the macro automatically, for macros named \0.

The following sections describe the three approaches to naming and running macros.

Using Alt-Letter Macros

One way to name a macro is to use the backslash key (\) and a letter. To run this macro, you hold down the Alt key and press the letter. For example, to run the first macro in this chapter (which you named \n), you hold down Alt and press **N**.

Because 1-2-3 does not differentiate between upper- and lowercase letters in a macro name, you can use either. Accordingly, \a, \B, and \C are all valid names for Alt-*letter* macros.

Single-letter macro names are limiting, however. You can create only 26 macros (\a to \z) in one file. Single-letter names are of little help when you are trying to identify what a macro does. Six months from now, for example, you may have trouble remembering what the \c macro does: does it copy a cell, change a column width, or type a company name?

Using Macros with Descriptive Names

You can give a macro a descriptive name of as many as 15 characters, as you would any range in the worksheet. To run a macro with a long name, you use Run (Alt-F3). Run displays a list of range names (including the Alt-*letter* macro names). You highlight the name of the macro you want to run and press Enter.

Reminder:
You can run any macro by pressing Run (Alt-F3) and selecting a name.

The longer names give you more flexibility; you can create any number of macros and give them names that indicate what they do. For example, instead of naming a macro to print your worksheet \p, you can name the macro PRINT_BUDGET.

> *Note:* If you create a macro name with more than one word, such as PRINT_BUDGET, be sure to use an underscore (_) and not a minus sign (–) to separate the words. 1-2-3 interprets a minus sign as subtraction, as in the range PRINT minus the range BUDGET.

Avoid using macro names that duplicate 1-2-3 keystroke equivalents, such as CALC or RIGHT, or any of the advanced macro commands listed in Chapter 14. Doing so leads to unpredictable and often incorrect results. Also avoid using cell addresses (such as IC1 or A4) as macro names.

Using Macros that Execute Automatically

Reminder:
A macro named \0 executes automatically when you retrieve the file that contains it.

The third way to name a macro is to give it the name \0 (backslash zero). This macro executes automatically when you load the worksheet. You use this type of macro to display data or execute commands before the user looks at the worksheet. Suppose, for example, that you have a worksheet with payroll information and you want to limit the number of people who can view this information. You create an automatic macro that asks for a password before it enables the user to see the file contents.

> ***Caution:*** \0 macros work automatically as long as the /**W**orksheet **G**lobal **D**efault **A**utoexec setting is **Y**es, which is the default. Any user can, however, change the setting to **N**o, in which case \0 macros are not automatically executed when the file is retrieved.

Figure 13.7 shows an automatic macro that moves the cell pointer to the bottom of column D. This macro executes the following keystrokes:

{GOTO}D7~{END}{DOWN 2}

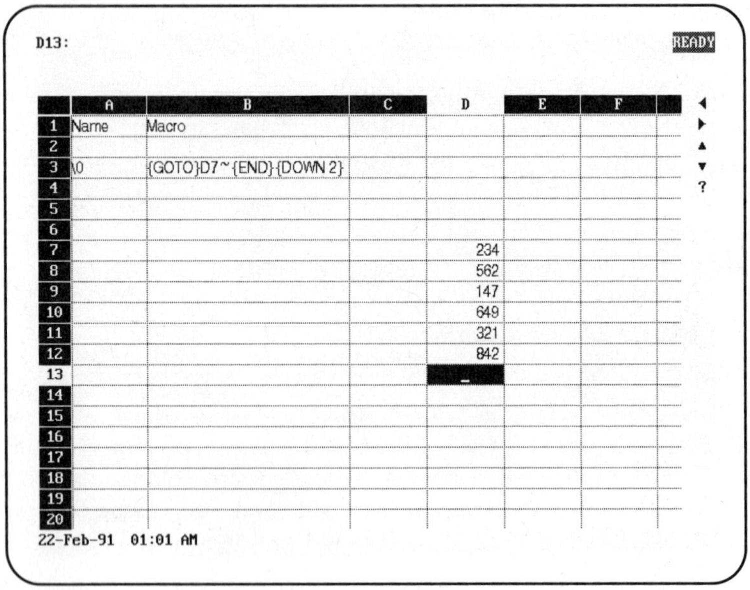

Fig. 13.7. A sample automatic macro.

The macro tells 1-2-3 to perform the following steps: press GoTo (F5), type **D7**, press Enter, press the End key, and then press the down-arrow key twice to move to the bottom of the column. These keystrokes are performed each time you retrieve the file that contains this macro. Note that the contents of cell B3 are as follows:

{GOTO}D7~{END}{DOWN 2}

Because a macro is a text label, it is preceded by an apostrophe. You can use any of the label prefixes (', ^, ", or \). The most common prefix, however, is the apostrophe.

To see how the preceding macro works on a column of numbers, type the numbers in cells D7 through D12, as shown in figure 13.7. Next, type the keystrokes the macro performs: press F5, type **D7**, and press Enter; then press the End key once (notice the END indicator at the bottom of the screen); and press the down-arrow key twice. You have just done what you want the macro to do.

Now move the cell pointer to cell B3, type the characters shown in cell B3 of figure 13.7. 1-2-3 collects the keystrokes as a label. By pressing Enter, you enter the label into cell B3.

Type '\0 in cell A3. Then select /**R**ange **N**ame **L**abels **R**ight and, with the cell pointer on cell A3, press Enter. Save and then retrieve the worksheet. The macro works automatically. If you want to repeat the macro after it runs when the file is retrieved, press Run (Alt-F3) and select \0 from the list of macro range names.

The four macros shown in figure 13.8 demonstrate many of the rules and conventions for naming and running macros. Here the macros are used only to demonstrate the three ways to name and run a macro. Each of these macros is discussed in detail in "Building a Simple Macro Library," later in this chapter.

> **Note:** Before you run a macro, be sure that you have positioned the cell pointer correctly or that the macro positions the cell pointer correctly. That is, make sure that the cell pointer is in the cell in which you want the macro to insert its text or start performing its commands.

To run any macro, press Run (Alt-F3). 1-2-3 lists all the range names in the current file. Figure 13.9 shows the full-screen listing of all range names after you press Run (Alt-F3) and then press Name (F3). To select the macro to run, highlight its name and press Enter.

Reminder:
1-2-3 executes the keystrokes in a macro starting with the first cell in the range.

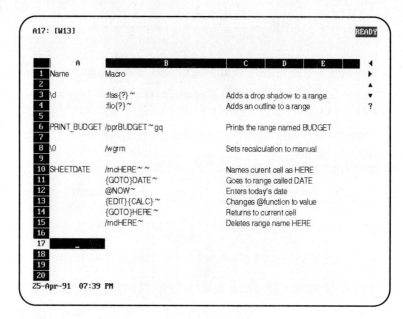

Fig. 13.8. Four macros that demonstrate naming rules (column A).

> **Note:** You also can use Run (Alt-F3) to start a macro at a cell other than its first cell. After you press Run (Alt-F3), type the cell address within the macro where you want 1-2-3 to begin and press Enter. You may want to start a macro at some other cell if you are testing or debugging it. See the following section, "Testing and Debugging Macros."

Testing and Debugging Macros

No matter how carefully you construct your macros, the first time you run them you may encounter errors. Programmers call these errors *bugs*; the process of eliminating the errors is called *debugging*.

1-2-3's Step feature is an extremely useful tool that helps make debugging fairly simple. When 1-2-3 is in STEP mode, a macro executes one step, or keystroke, at a time. STEP mode gives you a chance to see, in slow motion, exactly what your macro is doing.

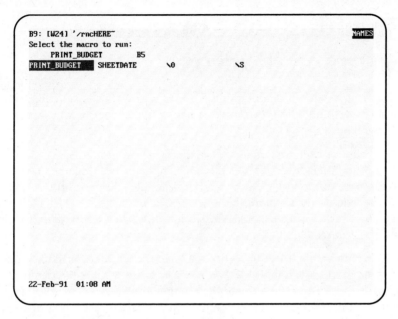

```
B9: [W24] '/rncHERE~                                          NAMES
Select the macro to run:
     PRINT_BUDGET          B5
PRINT_BUDGET   SHEETDATE        \0              \S
```

```
22-Feb-91  01:08 AM
```

Fig. 13.9. The result of pressing Run (Alt-F3).

To turn on STEP mode, press Step (Alt-F2). 1-2-3 displays the STEP indicator at the bottom of the screen. Now, run the macro. As soon as 1-2-3 executes the first keystroke of the macro, several things happen. 1-2-3 displays at the bottom of the screen the macro's cell address and the contents of that cell. The current macro instruction appears in reverse video. 1-2-3 then stops to enable you to see the effect of the first macro keystroke.

Reminder:
The Step (Alt-F2) key enables you to run a macro one keystroke at a time.

> *Note:* During STEP mode, if the macro pauses for user input, the STEP indicator changes to SST and flashes to alert you. Type any keystroke to continue debugging the macro.

If the keystroke works as you expect, press the space bar to tell 1-2-3 to execute the next keystroke in the macro.

Thanks to STEP mode, when an error occurs, you can pinpoint the error's location in the macro. After you identify the error, exit STEP mode by pressing Ctrl-Break. Use Edit (F2) to edit the cell in the macro that contains the error. Rerun the macro to make sure that the error you found is the only one. If another error occurs, find it by using Step (Alt-F2) again.

Watching for Common Errors in Macros

As you begin testing and debugging your macros, the material in this section should be helpful. When you test your macros, watch for the common errors described here.

If 1-2-3 cannot execute a macro as written, the program displays an error message and the address of the cell in which the error is located. Typically, this message points you to the error. Occasionally, however, the real error may precede the error identified in the error message. That is, 1-2-3 may have stopped executing keystrokes long before the error named in the message occurred.

Reminder:
When debugging a macro, check for common errors.

In the cell identified by the error message, check for the macro errors everyone seems to make. If 1-2-3 stops during one of the 1-2-3 commands, you probably forgot to complete the command by including a tilde (~) to represent the Enter key. Or you may have forgotten to press Q to quit a menu level. Sometimes, you have several menu levels to quit and must press Q more than once.

Even if 1-2-3 works all the way through a macro, the program may end with an error message or a beep. Remember that 1-2-3 continues to execute macro commands until it encounters an empty cell, a cell with a numeric value, or an advanced command that stops the macro. If 1-2-3 encounters data in the cell directly below the last line of the macro, the program may interpret that cell as part of the macro. Always use the /Range Erase command to empty the cell below the last line of your macro. If you discover that the cell is not empty, you may have identified one of the macro's problems.

If you get a message about an unrecognized macro key name or range name, followed by a cell address, check your key names and range names to make sure that they are spelled correctly. In addition, verify that you are using braces { } rather than parentheses ( ) or brackets [ ]; that you have the correct number and type of arguments for the key name; and that you do not have extra spaces in your macro, especially inside the braces { }.

Protecting Macros

If you create worksheet applications that others will use, you probably want to protect the macros used by an application from accidental erasure or alteration. Unlike most "programs," such as database management systems, 1-2-3 data and programs are in the same files. Even if you put all your macros at the end of the worksheet, the macros are still in the file; they can be changed by anyone who knows 1-2-3 well enough.

Many users create macros in the same worksheet that contains the models with which the macros are to be used. You can, however, maintain a separate library file containing nothing but macros (see the next section, "Building a Simple Macro Library," for details). Using a macro library is the best way to manage a large number of frequently used macros.

Most users store macros customized for a particular application in the same file that contains the application. To store macros in this way, place the macros together outside the area occupied by the main model. Storing the macros together makes finding and editing a macro easy and helps keep you from accidentally overwriting or erasing a macro as you create the model.

Caution:
Locate your macros in a worksheet area outside your main model.

Generally, you should place macros below and to the right of your worksheet model (see fig. 13.10). Be aware, however, that if you put the macros outside the range of your spreadsheet model, as shown, the End-Home key combination places the cell pointer at the lower right corner of the macros range, not the worksheet model range. If you place your macros in the worksheet as shown in figure 13.10, you may want to create a range name for the last cell in the model range (and also name the macro range). Then you can use the GoTo (F5) key to go to the bottom of the model and to the macro area.

Building a Simple Macro Library

A *macro library* is a file that contains macros you use frequently. By constructing a separate file that holds commonly used macros, you can run these macros anytime they are loaded. Such a library of macros can be used with any of your worksheets. The macros shown in figure 13.8 can be the basis of a macro library. Each of these macros is described in the following sections.

Cue:
Protect your macros from accidental erasure by saving them in a separate macro library file.

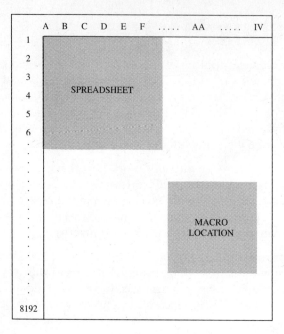

Fig. 13.10. *Positioning macros outside the work area.*

A Macro to Add a Drop Shadow to a Range

The first macro in figure 13.8 uses Wysiwyg commands to add a drop shadow and outline to a range of cells. The sequence of keystrokes is stored in cells B3 and B4 as follows:

> ':flss{?}~
> ':flo{?}~

If you have used the Wysiwyg add-in, you may be familiar with most of the keystrokes that make up this macro. Macro execution starts with an apostrophe (the label prefix) and then the **:** (colon), which activates the Wysiwyg command menu. The letters *flss* select the **:Formal Lines Shadow Set** menu commands. {?} is an advanced macro command that stops macro execution to accept any type of input from the user who is running the macro. In this macro, the user highlights, points to, or types a range that is to have a drop shadow. The tilde (~) completes the command.

The second line of the macro executes the **:Format Lines Outline** command and prompts for a range using the {?} macro command. Again, the tilde (~) completes the second Wysiwyg command.

If you have difficulty visualizing the sequence of keystrokes, try typing them, starting with the colon (:), which activates the main Wysiwyg command menu. Type **flss** and enter a range to have a drop shadow. Then type **flo** and specify the same range to add an outline to it.

The name of this macro is entered as \d in cell A3, the cell to the left of the cell that contains the macro (B3). Select /**R**ange **N**ame **C**reate to name the macro. At the prompts, type the name \d and the cell address **B3**.

You can run this macro in any of the following ways:

- Press Alt-D.

- Press Run (Alt-F3) and then choose the macro range name \d by highlighting it. Press Enter.

- Press Run (Alt-F3), press Esc, and move the cell pointer to the cell that contains the appropriate macro (B3, in this case). Press Enter.

A Macro To Print a Report

The second macro shown in figure 13.8 prints the worksheet range BUDGET, using the keystrokes stored in cell B6:

   '/pprBUDGET~gq

The macro starts with an apostrophe (the label prefix), followed by a / (slash), which activates the main 1-2-3 command menu. The letters *ppr* select the menu commands **P**rint **P**rinter **R**ange. *BUDGET* is the name of the range you want to print. The ~ (tilde) sets the print range (like pressing Enter). The letter *g* executes the **G**o print command. The letter *q* quits the menu.

Cue:
Save time by automating worksheet printing with a macro.

Using the /**R**ange **N**ame **C**reate command, name this macro PRINT_BUDGET. Cell C6 contains the documentation for the macro. To run the macro, use Run (Alt-F3).

A Macro To Set Worksheet Recalculation

The third macro shown in figure 13.8 sets worksheet recalculation to manual. The keystrokes, which mirror the manual ones, are shown in cell B8:

   '/wgrm

Because the macro's name in cell A8 is \0, this macro executes automatically when the file that contains this macro is retrieved (as long as the /Worksheet Global Default Autoexec setting is **Yes**). The macro starts with an apostrophe (the label prefix) and a / (slash) that activates the main 1-2-3 command menu. The letters *wgrm* select the menu commands **W**orksheet **G**lobal **R**ecalculation **M**anual.

In addition to running this macro when you retrieve or open the file, you can run the macro at other times. To run the macro, press Run (Alt-F3) and then choose the macro range name (\0) by highlighting it on the list of range names and pressing Enter.

A Macro To Date a Worksheet

The last macro in figure 13.8 records a date in the worksheet. This macro is handy, for example, if you want to record the date the worksheet was last edited. The obvious way to date a worksheet is to enter the @NOW function in the appropriate cell. But dating a worksheet in this way poses a problem. If you retrieve the worksheet a few days later, 1-2-3 recalculates the date, changing it to today's date, which defeats the purpose.

To solve this problem, use the following macro (it begins in cell B10):

```
'/rncHERE~~
{GOTO}DATE~
@NOW~
{EDIT}{CALC}~
{GOTO}HERE~
'/rndHERE~
```

This macro enters the date and ensures that it remains that date, no matter when you retrieve it. The macro assumes that a single cell with the range name DATE is somewhere in the worksheet.

> *Note:* For the SHEETDATE macro to work properly, the cell named DATE should be formatted as a date. To format the cell as a date, use **/R**ange **F**ormat **D**ate.

The first line uses **/R**ange **N**ame **C**reate to give the current cell location the name HERE. After the macro has finished dating the worksheet, the macro uses this range name to return the cell pointer to this location. The second and third lines go to the cell named DATE and insert the @NOW function.

The fourth line of the macro converts @NOW to the current date, by using Edit (F2) and Calc (F9). This conversion prevents further conversion of the date the next time you retrieve the worksheet. Finally, the macro returns the cell pointer to its original location and deletes the range name HERE.

Using the Macro Library Manager Add-In

After you have created a macro library, you can use the Macro Library Manager add-in to maintain the macros in the file. Like any add-in product, you must "attach" the Macro Library Manager to 1-2-3 Release 2.3 before you can use it. You also must "detach" the Macro Library Manager if you no longer want it to reside in memory. With the Macro Library Manager, you save a range of worksheet cells in a file with an MLB extension. You then can use this file through the /Add-In command while working in any 1-2-3 worksheet.

Attaching and Detaching the Macro Library Manager

To attach the Macro Library Manager, use the command /Add-In Attach. 1-2-3 displays files with the ADN extension (see fig. 13.11). Point to the file MACROMGR.ADN and press Enter. 1-2-3 displays the menu shown in figure 13.12.

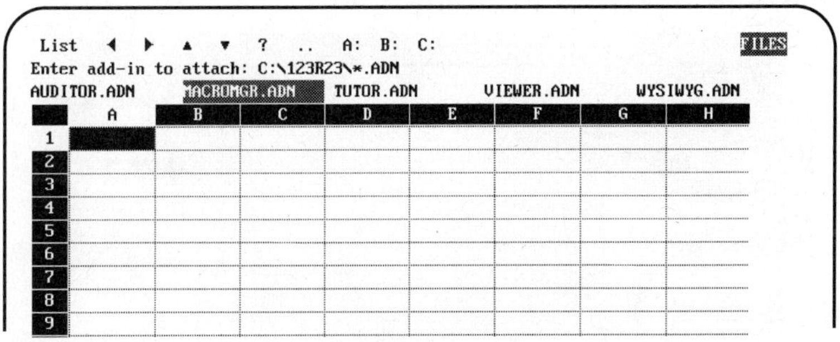

Fig. 13.11. ADN files displayed after selecting /Add-In Attach.

If you select **7**, **8**, **9**, or **10**, the Macro Library Manager is attached to the corresponding Alt-function key combination. For example, if you choose **7** from the menu, you can invoke the Macro Library Manager by pressing Alt-F7. If you choose **No-Key** from the menu, as shown in figure 13.12, you must invoke the program from the command menu by using /**Add-in I**nvoke.

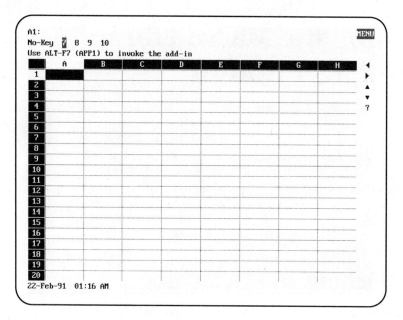

Fig. 13.12. *Assigning the Macro Library Manager add-in to an Alt-function key combination.*

To detach the Macro Library Manager, use /**Add-In D**etach. When 1-2-3 lists the add-in programs currently in memory (see fig. 13.13), highlight MACROMGR and press Enter.

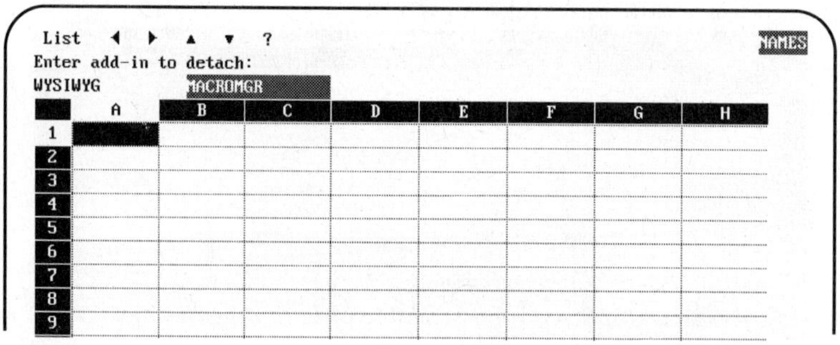

Fig. 13.13. *A list of resident add-in programs with /Add-in Detach.*

Invoking and Using
the Macro Library Manager

If you attach the Macro Library Manager to an Alt-function key combination, you invoke it by pressing those keys (for example, Alt-F7). If you choose **No-Key**, you must use the **/Add-In Invoke** command. When you issue this command, 1-2-3 displays the names of the add-in programs currently in memory. You invoke the add-in program by pointing to it and pressing Enter.

After you invoke the Macro Library Manger, 1-2-3 displays the menu shown in figure 13.14. To use this menu, you must have created a macro library. For example, you can use the worksheet and macros described in this chapter's "Building a Simple Macro Library" section.

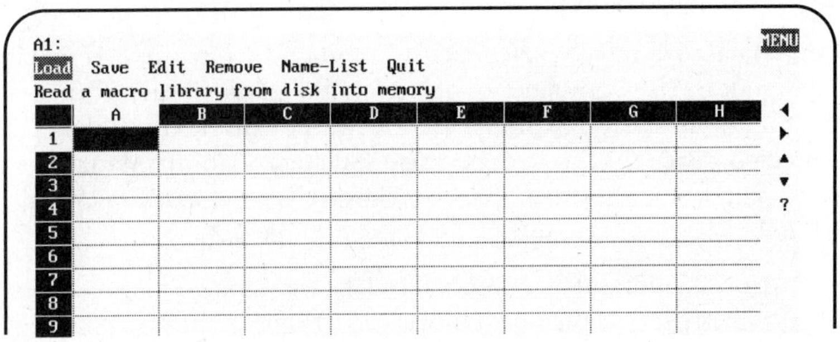

Fig. 13.14. The Macro Library Manager menu.

If you do not have a macro library in the current worksheet, press Esc to return to READY mode. Create a few macros in the current worksheet and then reinvoke the Macro Library Manager.

To save macros in a library file, you use the **Save** command from the Macro Library Manager menu. When you select **Save**, the add-in prompts first for the name of a macro library. Enter a new name for the MLB file that will hold the macros from the library. The add-in then prompts for the range of cells that contain the macros to put in this new MLB file. Highlight the range from your existing library. Finally, the add-in asks whether you want to set a password. A password prevents others from editing or viewing the macros in the MLB file in STEP mode but does not prevent someone from loading and using the library. To set a password, select **Yes**; select **No** if you don't want to use a password. If you set a password, be sure to remember the password you create. You will not be able to see it again.

Caution:
The Macro Library Manager does not ask you to confirm the password after you enter it.

After you save the macros in the MLB file, the add-in removes them from the current worksheet and returns to the Macro Library Manager menu. The macros are in the computer's memory and are still available. You can use them with any worksheet you retrieve. If you want to use the same MLB file in a subsequent session, you must attach and invoke the add-in and then use the Load command from the Macro Library Manager menu to load that library of macros.

When you choose the Load command to load a macro library into memory, the add-in may ask whether to Ignore or Overwrite the current range names in the worksheet. If your current worksheet contains range names that you want to keep, select Ignore to preserve the existing range names.

To remove a macro library from memory, use the Remove command from the Macro Library Manager menu. When you select Remove, the add-in displays the names of the currently loaded libraries. Highlight the library you want to remove and press Enter.

To edit a macro library, use the Edit command from the Macro Library Manager menu. This command copies a loaded macro library from memory into a range of the current worksheet. You must be careful to choose a blank, unprotected range for the data because the Macro Library Manager writes over existing data when it copies the library into a worksheet. Edit the individual cells in the usual way, by pressing Edit (F2).

The Name-List command from the Macro Library Manager menu copies a list of range names used by the macro library to a range in the worksheet. When you choose the Name-List command, the add-in displays the library names in the control panel. Select a library by pointing to it and pressing Enter. Then select an empty range in the worksheet, a range that you want to contain the macro range names, and press Enter. The add-in copies the range names to the worksheet range.

The Quit command from the Macro Library Manager menu, like other 1-2-3 Quit commands, affects only the menu and not the macro library.

Remember that the Macro Library Manager keeps the current library of macros in memory even after you erase a worksheet or load another worksheet into memory. You can use any of the macros in the current library with any worksheet you retrieve.

Moving Up to the Advanced Macro Commands

If the macros you write are increasingly large, consider using the advanced macro commands described in Chapter 14. You use some of these advanced macro commands in place of the menu commands.

The advanced macro commands are complete words; they are much less cryptic than simple macro commands, and thus are better suited for writing large programs. For example, in a macro program, you use the keystrokes /re to erase a range; in an advanced-macro command program, you use the command {BLANK}.

Reminder: Advanced macro commands are better suited for writing large programs.

The advanced macro commands also perform operations that go beyond what can be done from the main 1-2-3 command menu—operations such as reading and writing records to external files and recalculating only a portion of a worksheet. If this sounds like work you never want to do, relax. You don't ever have to use the advanced macro commands. If the limitations of your macro programs are increasingly restrictive and frustrating, however, consider moving up to the advanced macro commands.

Summary

This chapter gave you the information, and hopefully the confidence, you need to begin creating your own macros. You have seen how macros can save time, reduce repetition, and automate your worksheet models. The chapter defined a macro and walked you through the steps of creating some simple macros. The chapter also described the three ways to name and run macros, showed you how to debug and protect macros, and explained how to build a simple macro library. The chapter concluded with some ideas about moving up to 1-2-3's advanced macro commands, the focus of the next chapter.

14

Introducing the Advanced Macro Commands

In addition to the keystroke macro capabilities discussed in Chapter 13, 1-2-3 contains a set of advanced macro commands that offer many of the aspects of a full-featured programming language. You use the advanced macro commands to customize and automate 1-2-3 for your worksheet applications.

Chapter 13 shows you how to save time and streamline operations by using macros to automate keystrokes. After you learn the concepts and the advanced macro commands discussed in this chapter, you will be ready to develop programs that perform the following tasks:

- Create menu-driven models

- Accept and control input from a user

- Manipulate data in the worksheet

- Execute tasks a predetermined number of times

- Set up and print multiple reports

As you become more experienced with the advanced macro commands, you can take advantage of its full power to do the following:

- Disengage or redefine the function keys
- Develop a business accounting system
- Operate a 1-2-3 worksheet as a disk-based database

This chapter is designed to introduce you to the capabilities of programming with the advanced macro commands—not to teach programming theory and concepts. If you use 1-2-3 and want to learn some of the advanced techniques of macro programming, you should enjoy this chapter. The techniques presented can help you become a 1-2-3 macro expert.

Why Use the Advanced Macro Commands?

Programs created with the advanced macro commands give you added control and flexibility in the use of 1-2-3 worksheets. For example, you can develop a program that instructs and guides users as they enter data in a worksheet. With this program, you can ensure that different users enter data in the same way. Programs are especially nice for novice users who aren't familiar with 1-2-3's commands and operations; novices can use your program applications to update a worksheet, check figures, or even to create graphs with ease.

If you want to take 1-2-3 to its practical limits, the set of advanced macro commands is the proper vehicle and your creativity is the necessary fuel.

What Are the Advanced Macro Commands?

Reminder:
Invoke advanced macro commands from within macro command programs.

The 1-2-3 advanced macro commands are a set of 53 invisible commands. These commands are called *invisible* because, unlike the commands on the 1-2-3 menus and function keys, you cannot invoke the advanced macro commands from the keyboard.

The \h macro in figure 14.1 is an example of a program written with the advanced macro commands. The program displays a help menu, and the program shows a series of help screens.

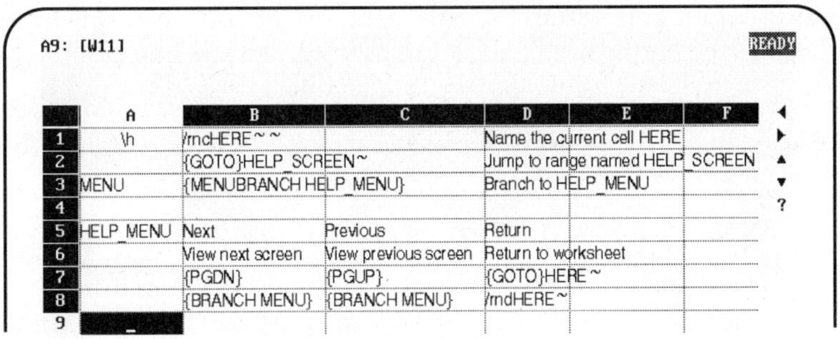

A9: [W11]   READY

	A	B	C	D	E	F
1	\h	/rncHERE~ ~		Name the current cell HERE		
2		{GOTO}HELP_SCREEN~		Jump to range named HELP_SCREEN		
3	MENU	{MENUBRANCH HELP_MENU}		Branch to HELP_MENU		
4						
5	HELP_MENU	Next	Previous	Return		
6		View next screen	View previous screen	Return to worksheet		
7		{PGDN}	{PGUP}	{GOTO}HERE ~		
8		{BRANCH MENU}	{BRANCH MENU}	/rndHERE ~		
9						

Fig. 14.1. *An advanced macro command program.*

The program in figure 14.1 begins by creating the range name HERE wherever the user has positioned the cell pointer before invoking the program. The second line displays a custom help screen. The third line uses the MENUBRANCH command to display a menu with three options: to select the next help screen, to select the preceding help screen, or to return to the original cell-pointer position in the worksheet. The BRANCH command in the last line of the Next and Previous menu options causes the program to redisplay the menu after the user has selected either of these options.

Notice that the program branches to range names rather than to cell addresses. As discussed in Chapter 13, you always should follow the convention of using range names instead of cell addresses. Not only does this practice make the program easier to read, but as you rearrange your worksheet, 1-2-3 updates the range-name addresses so that the program continues to operate on the correct cells and ranges.

Reminder:
All advanced macro commands are enclosed in braces ({ }).

Understanding Advanced Macro Command Syntax

The examples in this chapter show you how to incorporate the advanced macro commands into macros to produce complete, efficient programs. Like the key names used in keystroke macros (discussed in Chapter 13), all advanced macro commands are enclosed in braces. Just as you must represent the right-arrow key in a macro as {RIGHT}, you must enclose a command, such as QUIT, in braces: {QUIT}.

Like QUIT, some of the advanced macro commands are just a single command enclosed in braces. Many other commands, however, require additional arguments within the braces. An *argument* can consist of numbers, strings, cell addresses, range names, formulas, or functions.

Commands that take arguments have a grammar, or *syntax*, similar to the syntax used in 1-2-3 functions. The general syntax of these commands is as follows:

{COMMAND *argument1,argument2, . . . ,argumentN*}

Reminder:
The command name and the first argument are separated by a space.

The command name and the first argument are separated by a space. Arguments are separated by commas (with no spaces). As you study the syntax for the specific commands described in this chapter, keep in mind the importance of following the conventions for spacing and punctuation. In the following example:

{BRANCH *rangename*}

you are using the BRANCH command to transfer program control to a specific location in the program. The command BRANCH must be followed by the cell address or range name indicating where the program should branch. In this command, *rangename* is the argument.

> **Note:** If you are not sure of the syntax or purpose of an advanced macro command, type the opening brace ({) and then press the Help (F1) key. The Help system displays an alphabetical list of the valid commands and key names, such as {QUIT} and {CALC}. Press ↑ and ↓ to scroll through the list to find the command you want to use. Highlight the command and press Enter. Help shows you a description of the selected command, its syntax, and examples for its use.

Developing Programs with the Advanced Macro Commands

You begin a macro command program by defining the actions you want the program to perform and determining the sequence of those actions. Then you create the program, test it, debug it, and cross-check its results, as you would with any other macro.

Cue:
If you don't know how to create keystroke macros, read Chapter 13.

If you have created keystroke macros, you have a head start toward creating advanced macro command programs. These programs share many of the conventions used in the simple keystroke macros presented in Chapter 13. If you have not experimented with 1-2-3 macros, take some time to review

Chapter 13's simple keystroke macros before you try to develop advanced macro command programs. Also, review Chapter 13's discussions of creating, using, and debugging macros; many of the concepts are related to advanced macro command programs.

Carefully plan and position the advanced macro command programs in the worksheet, as you do with keystroke macros. You can locate your macros in a separate worksheet file and then use the /File Combine command to add the macro file to the current worksheet. Or create a macro library by using the Macro Library Manager add-in, as discussed in Chapter 13.

Creating the Program

You enter advanced macro command programs in a 1-2-3 worksheet as text cells. You must use a label prefix to start any line that begins with a character that is not a letter or a number (such as / or <) so that 1-2-3 does not interpret the characters that follow as numbers or commands. Remember to break up the program into separate cells; be sure that one macro command is within one cell. Additionally, you may want to include labels in the column to the left of the program to help you identify its parts. For example, if you have a program that asks the user for data and then checks that data, you may want to enter the label DATAENTRY at the start of the data-entry section of the program and the label CHECKDATA at the section with the commands that check the data for errors.

Also remember to document the program in the cells to the right of each program line. Because advanced macro command programs usually are more complex than keystroke macros, documenting each line is essential. A documented program, like the one shown in figure 14.1, is easier to debug and change than an undocumented one.

Reminder:
A documented program is easier to debug and change.

Naming and Running the Program

As described in Chapter 13, you have a choice of three types of names for a macro or an advanced macro command program. These types of names are as follows:

- Alt-*letter*, such as \h (see fig. 14.1)

- Descriptive range name, such as PRINT_BUDGET

- \0 (backslash zero), which runs when you retrieve the file that contains the macro

You use the /**R**ange **N**ame **C**reate or /**R**ange **N**ame **L**abels command to give the program one of these three types of names. You also should enter the name in the cell to the left of the program's first line. 1-2-3 does not use this name; it is for documentation purposes only.

You can give the same 1-2-3 range more than one name. For example, you can give a frequently used macro a descriptive name as well as an Alt-*letter* name. By doing so, you combine the benefit of the long, descriptive name (good for documentation) with the ease of use of the Alt-*letter* name.

To run the macro program, use one of the following methods:

- Press Alt and *letter*, for macros with *letter* names

- Press the Run (Alt-F3) key, for any macro

- Retrieve the file and run it automatically, for macros named \\0 (backslash zero)

Debugging a Program

After you develop and run a program, you may need to debug it. Like keystroke macros, macro programs are subject to such problems as missing tildes (~) and misspelled key names and range names.

To debug advanced macro command programs, use STEP mode in the same way you use it for simple keystroke macros. Before you execute the program, press Step (Alt-F2) to invoke STEP mode. Then execute your advanced macro command program. Press the space bar to single-step through each instruction in the program. When you discover an error, press Ctrl-Break to stop execution. Press Esc to clear the error message and then press F2 (Edit) to edit the program. Step through the program's execution again until all the errors are fixed, and the program runs correctly.

Listing the Advanced Macro Commands

This section lists alphabetically the 53 advanced macro commands. The list includes a description of each command; its syntax, showing the arguments required; and an example. The advanced macro commands can be grouped into six categories, according to their use or function in a program. These categories are as follows:

- Accepting input
- Controlling programs
- Making decisions
- Manipulating data
- Enhancing programs
- Manipulating files

Table 14.1 shows the commands grouped by category, along with a brief description of what they do. Use this table to determine which command to use for a particular task. Then you can turn to the alphabetical listing for a complete description and an example.

Table 14.1
Advanced Macro Commands by Category

Category: Accepting Input

Uses: Creates prompts, performs edit checks on data input, modifies 1-2-3 interface

Command	Description
{?}	Pauses macro execution for data entry from user
{FORM}	Interrupts macro execution for data entry into a form
{FORMBREAK}	Ends {FORM} command, cancels current form, and returns to macro
{GET}	Accepts single character from user
{GETLABEL}	Accepts label from user
{GETNUMBER}	Accepts number from user
{LOOK}	Places first character from type-ahead buffer into a cell

continues

Table 14.1 *(continued)*

Category: Controlling Programs

Uses: Controls program execution, runs subroutines, specifies operating system commands

Command	Description
{BRANCH}	Continues execution at new location in program
{BREAKOFF}	Disables {BREAK} key
{BREAKON}	Enables {BREAK} key
{DEFINE}	Specifies cells to store contents of subroutine arguments
{DISPATCH}	Branches indirectly to new location in program
{MENUBRANCH}	Displays a menu in the Control panel
{MENUCALL}	Similar to MENUBRANCH, except returns to statement after MENUCALL
{ONERROR}	Traps errors
{QUIT}	Ends program execution
{RESTART}	Cancels a subroutine
{RETURN}	Returns from a program subroutine
{*subroutine*}	Calls a subroutine
{SYSTEM}	Executes an operating system command
{WAIT}	Waits specified length of time

Category: Making Decisions

Uses: Tests for conditions, executes programs loops

Command	Description
{FOR}	Activates loop a specified number of times
{FORBREAK}	Ends {FOR} loop
{IF}	Conditionally executes statements after IF

Table 14.1 *(continued)*

Category: *Manipulating Data*

Uses: *Enters or erases data in a worksheet*

Command	Description
{APPENDBELOW}	Enters data *below* range and expands range to include the data
{APPENDRIGHT}	Enters data to *right* of range and expands range to include the data
{BLANK}	Erases cell or range
{CONTENTS}	Copies values to cells as labels
{LET}	Enters number or label into a cell
{PUT}	Enters number or label into specified row/column offset within a range

Category: *Enhancing Programs*

Uses: *Controls screen display and program operation, selectively recalculates worksheet*

Command	Description
{BEEP}	Sounds one of computer's four tones
{BORDERSOFF}	Suppresses display of worksheet frame
{BORDERSON}	Displays worksheet frame
{FRAMEOFF}	Suppresses display of worksheet frame
{FRAMEON}	Displays worksheet frame
{GRAPHOFF}	Removes graph displayed by GRAPHON
{GRAPHON}	Displays current graph and/or sets named graph
{INDICATE}	Changes control-panel mode indicator
{PANELOFF}	Suppresses display in control panel
{PANELON}	Reactivates display in control panel
{RECALC}	Recalculates portion of worksheet, row by row
{RECALCCOL}	Recalculates portion of worksheet, column by column
{WINDOWSOFF}	Suppresses redisplay of current window
{WINDOWSON}	Enables redisplay of current window

continues

Table 14.1 *(continued)*

Category: Manipulating Files

Uses: Opens, reads, writes, and closes text files

Command	Description
{CLOSE}	Closes file opened with {OPEN}
{FILESIZE}	Records size of open file
{GETPOS}	Records a file-pointer position
{OPEN}	Opens file for reading, writing, or both
{READ}	Copies characters from open file to worksheet
{READLN}	Copies next line from file to worksheet
{SETPOS}	Sets new position for file pointer
{WRITE}	Copies string to open file
{WRITELN}	Copies string plus carriage-return-line-feed sequence to open file

The ? Command

Reminder:
*During the pause,
the ? command
does not display a
prompt.*

The ? command pauses the program so that the user can enter any type of information. During the pause, no prompt is displayed in the control panel; the user can move the cell pointer to direct the location of the input. The program continues executing after the user presses Enter. The format for the ? command is as follows:

    {?}

For example, the following one-line program combines macro commands and an advanced macro command to create a file-retrieve program:

```
/fr{NAME}{?}~
```

This program displays all files in the current drive and directory and then pauses to accept input from the user. The user can either type the name of one of the displayed files or move the cell pointer to a file name and press Enter.

Even if you press Enter after typing an entry for the {?} command, you still must include a tilde (~) after the {?} command or move the cell pointer to another cell if you want 1-2-3 to accept your input.

The APPENDBELOW Command

The APPENDBELOW command copies the values in one range to the rows immediately below another range. As part of the copy operation, APPENDBELOW also expands the range to include the new data. The format of the APPENDBELOW command is as follows:

Reminder:
APPENDBELOW copies the contents of one range to another.

{APPENDBELOW *destination,source*}

APPENDBELOW copies the contents of *source* to *destination* and expands *destination* to include the new data below it. APPENDBELOW is a helpful companion to the FORM command. The two commands provide an easy way to copy data from an input form to a storage table or database range. Figure 14.2 shows a simple example that collects first- and last-name information, stores that information in a range called TABLE_1, and uses APPENDBELOW to record the data in the database range called TABLE_2. APPENDBELOW copies calculated values, not the actual formulas. In this respect, APPENDBELOW is similar to /**R**ange Value.

```
A22: [W11]                                                      READY

            A          B              C        D        E        F     ◄
    11   \a        {FORM TABLE_1}                                       ►
    12             {IF FIRST="Q"}{QUIT}                                 ▲
    13             {APPENDBELOW TABLE_2,TABLE_1}                        ▼
    14             {BRANCH \a}                                         ?
    15
    16             FIRST          LAST
    17  TABLE_1    Q              SMITH
    18
    19  TABLE_2
    20             BOB            JONES
    21             TOM            SMITH
    22        ▄
    23
    24
    25
    26
    27
    28
    29
    30
    26-Feb-91  11:40 AM
```

Fig. 14.2. The APPENDBELOW command used to copy data entered with the FORM command.

Three situations can cause the APPENDBELOW command to fail. The first is if the number of rows in the specified *source* exceeds the number of rows left in the worksheet below the specified *destination*. When this happens, APPENDBELOW aborts. For example, if only 100 rows are left in the worksheet, you cannot copy 200 rows of information.

A second situation that causes APPENDBELOW to fail is when executing the command would destroy data in the destination range by overwriting existing data. This safety feature prevents APPENDBELOW from destroying data in your worksheet.

The third situation is when the rows below the destination range are protected.

The APPENDRIGHT Command

APPENDRIGHT's operation mirrors that of APPENDBELOW, with one exception: APPENDRIGHT copies the values of *source* to the right of *destination*. (APPENDBELOW copies the contents of *source* to just below *destination*.) The APPENDRIGHT command uses the following format:

> {APPENDRIGHT *destination, source*}

APPENDRIGHT copies the contents of *source* to *destination* and expands *destination* to the right to include new data. APPENDRIGHT copies values, not the formulas, to *destination*.

If the destination range already contains data, is too small for the source data, or is protected, APPENDRIGHT ends with an error. Because 1-2-3 worksheets contain many more rows than columns, APPENDRIGHT runs out of space much sooner than APPENDBELOW. Figure 14.3 shows the result of changing the APPENDBELOW operation shown in figure 14.2 to APPENDRIGHT.

The BEEP Command

Cue:
Use BEEP to make the computer emit one of four sounds.

The BEEP command activates the computer's speaker system to produce one of four tones. Each argument (1 through 4) produces a different tone. The BEEP command commonly is used to alert the user to a specific condition in the program or to get the user's attention. The format of the BEEP command is as follows:

> {BEEP *number*} or {BEEP}

```
A35: [W11]                                                        READY

         A          B              C           D          E        F     ◀
 24     \a      {FORM TABLE_1}                                            ▶
 25             {IF FIRST="Q"}{QUIT}                                      ▲
 26             {APPENDRIGHT TABLE_2,TABLE_1}                             ▼
 27             {BRANCH \a}                                               ?
 28
 29             FIRST          LAST
 30 TABLE_1     Q              THOMAS
 31
 32 TABLE_2                                MAC        THOMAS
 33             BOB            JONES
 34             TOM            SMITH
 35     _
 36
 37
 38
 39
 40
 41
 42
 43
 26-Feb-91  11:41 AM
```

Fig. 14.3. The APPENDRIGHT command used to copy data entered with the FORM command.

BEEP sounds one of the computer's four beeps. Consider the following BEEP statement:

```
{IF A35>50}{BEEP 2}
```

This statement produces a sound if the condition presented in the IF statement is true. If the condition is not true, program control passes to the next cell below the IF statement.

The BLANK Command

The BLANK command erases a range of cells in the worksheet. Although this command works similarly to the /Range Erase command, using BLANK has an advantage over using /Range Erase in advanced macro command programs: Because BLANK does not use menus or force recalculation, it is faster than /Range Erase. The format of the BLANK command is as follows:

Reminder:
BLANK erases a range of cells.

{BLANK *location*}

BLANK erases the range defined by *location*. For example, the statement {BLANK RANGE_1} erases RANGE_1.

The BORDERSOFF Command

The BORDERSOFF command is identical to the FRAMEOFF command: Both commands remove the column border letters and row border numbers from the screen display. The format of the BORDERSOFF command is as follows:

{BORDERSOFF}

BORDERSOFF turns off the worksheet frame. See the FRAMEOFF command for more information.

The BORDERSON Command

The BORDERSON command redisplays the worksheet column border letters and row border numbers originally suppressed by a BORDERSOFF command. The format of the BORDERSON command is as follows:

{BORDERSON}

BORDERSON turns on the worksheet frame. Note that you must use the matching command to redisplay the borders. That is, if you used BORDERSOFF to turn off the frame display, use BORDERSON to turn it back on.

The BRANCH Command

The BRANCH command causes program control to pass unconditionally to the cell address indicated in the BRANCH statement. The program begins reading commands and statements at the cell location indicated in the *location* argument. Program control does not return to the line from which it was passed unless directed to do so by another BRANCH statement. Use the following syntax for BRANCH:

{BRANCH *location*}

BRANCH continues program execution in the cell specified by *location*. The following example shows you how to use BRANCH:

```
{GOTO}ENTRY~@COUNT(RANGE)~
{BRANCH START}
```

The first line places the cell pointer in the cell named ENTRY and then enters an @COUNT function. The second line passes program control to the cell named START, regardless of any commands that may follow the BRANCH command (in either the same cell location or in the cell below). 1-2-3 begins reading program commands in the cell with the range name START.

BRANCH is an unconditional command unless it is preceded by an IF conditional statement, as in the following example:

```
{IF C22="alpha"}{BRANCH G24}
{GOTO}S101~
```

For the IF statement to act as a conditional testing statement, the IF statement and the second command must be in the same cell. For more information, see the discussion of the IF command later in this chapter.

The BREAKOFF Command

The easiest way to stop a program is to issue a Ctrl-Break command. Although you want to use Ctrl-Break when you debug programs, you don't want a user to use Ctrl-Break to stop your macro program's execution. To prevent Ctrl-Break from stopping the execution of a program, use the BREAKOFF command.

Before you use a BREAKOFF statement, be certain that the program is fully debugged. You may need to issue a Ctrl-Break command to halt the program and make a "repair" while debugging the program.

Reminder:
Make sure that the program is fully debugged before using BREAKOFF.

The format of the BREAKOFF command is as follows:

{BREAKOFF}

Note: When the control panel contains a menu, you can halt program execution by pressing Esc, regardless of the presence of a BREAKOFF command.

The BREAKON Command

To restore the effect of Ctrl-Break, use the BREAKON command. The format of this command is as follows:

{BREAKON}

Reminder: *Ctrl-Break is turned back on when the macro program ends.*

Because any Ctrl-Break commands in the keyboard buffer are executed as soon as the BREAKON command is executed, be sure to place BREAKON where the program can stop safely. Figure 14.4 shows how you can use BREAKOFF and BREAKON.

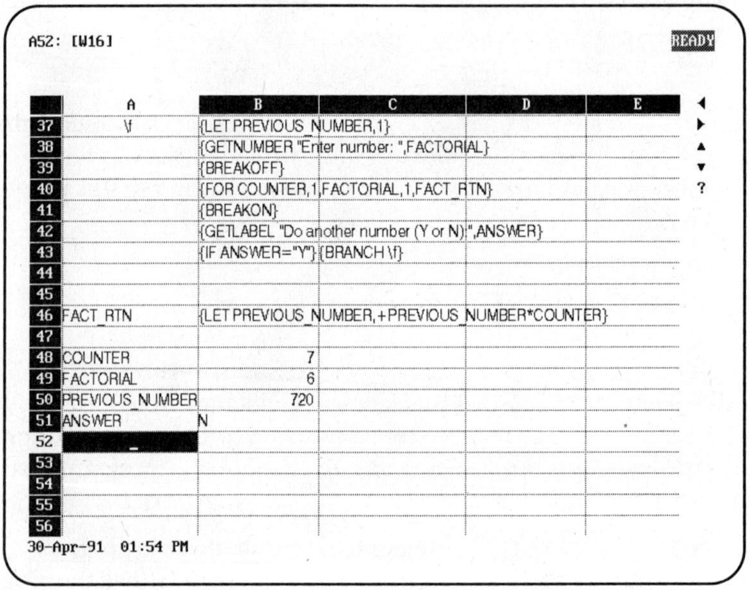

Fig. 14.4. *Use of the BREAKON and BREAKOFF commands.*

The CLOSE Command

Cue: *Use CLOSE to close a file and make sure that data is not damaged or lost.*

The CLOSE command closes an open file. If no file is open, the CLOSE command has no effect. CLOSE does not take an argument. The CLOSE command is particularly important for files that you write or modify; if you don't close a file, you can lose the last data written to the file. The format of the CLOSE command is as follows:

```
{CLOSE}
```

CLOSE closes a file opened with OPEN. Under most circumstances, 1-2-3 automatically closes a file you do not close. Nevertheless, you should develop the habit of using CLOSE when you finish using any file opened with OPEN. Use of the CLOSE command is shown in figure 14.5.

```
A65: [W11]                                                    READY

         A        B          C          D        E      F      G    ◄
    50 FILE_SIZE            \r          {OPEN "INPUT.TXT","R"}        ►
    51 NUM_REC                          {FILESIZE FILE_SIZE}         ▲
    52 REC_LEN   100                    {LET NUM_REC,FILE_SIZE/REC_LEN}  ▼
    53 POINTER                          {GETPOS POINTER}             ?
    54 COUNTER                          {FOR COUNTER,1,NUM_REC-1,1,READ_WRITE}
    55 INLINE                           {CLOSE}
    56
    57 READ_WRITE {READ REC_LEN,INLINE}
    58            {GETPOS POINTER}
    59            {OPEN "OUTPUT.TXT",R}{OPEN "OUTPUT.TXT",W}
    60            {OPEN "OUTPUT.TXT",A}
    61            {WRITELN INLINE}
    62            {CLOSE}
    63            {OPEN"INPUT.TXT",R}
    64            {SETPOS POINTER}
    65      ▄
    66
    67
    68
    69
    26-Feb-91  11:42 AM
```

Fig. 14.5. A program that uses the file manipulation commands.

The CONTENTS Command

The CONTENTS command copies the contents of one cell to another as a string. Optionally, CONTENTS also assigns a cell width or cell format to the cell that contains the string. If you do not specify either the width or format, 1-2-3 uses the column width or format of the source location to format the cell. The format of the CONTENTS command is as follows:

Cue:
Use CONTENTS to store a value in a cell and to change the width or format of the cell.

{CONTENTS *destination,source,width,format*}

CONTENTS stores the contents of *source* to *destination* as a string. Suppose that you want to copy the number 123.456 from cell SOURCE_1 to cell DEST_1 and change the number to a string while you copy. The statement for this operation is as follows:

```
{CONTENTS DEST_1,SOURCE_1}
```

The contents of cell DEST_1 are displayed as the string '123.456, with a left-aligned label-prefix character.

> *Note:* When CONTENTS makes a copy of the source cell number, the command also copies the way the number appears in the cell. For example, if the source cell is formatted as currency with 0 decimal places, the value 123.456 looks like $123, and CONTENTS copies the number to the destination cell as the string '$123. Similarly, if the source column width is 6, the number appears as 123.4, and the destination cell contains the string '123.4.

Suppose that you want to change the width of the string when you copy it. Instead of displaying the string as 123.456, you want to display it as 123.4. To get the result you want, change the statement as follows:

```
{CONTENTS DEST_2,SOURCE_1,6}
```

This second statement uses a width of 6 to display the string. 1-2-3 truncates the least significant digits of the number to create the string.

Suppose that you want to change the string's display format while you copy the source cell contents and change the destination cell width. The following string changes the display format to **Currency 0**:

```
{CONTENTS DEST_3,SOURCE_1,5,32}
```

The numbers to use for the format number in this statement are listed in table 14.2. The result of the statement is the number $123.

In the following examples of the CONTENTS command, the number in cell SOURCE_2 is 123.456; the width of the column that contains SOURCE_2 is 9; and the display format for cell SOURCE_2 is Fixed **2**.

The following command:

```
{CONTENTS DEST_4,SOURCE_2}
```

displays the label '123.46 in DEST_4, using the **Fixed 2** format.

The following command:

```
{CONTENTS DEST_5,SOURCE_2,4}
```

displays **** if a column is 4 characters wide.

The following command:

```
{CONTENTS DEST_6,SOURCE_2,5,0}
```

displays the label '123 in cell DEST_6, using the **Fixed 0** format.

The CONTENTS command is somewhat specialized but is useful in situations that require converting numeric values to formatted strings. Using the

Text format, CONTENTS can convert long numeric formulas to strings that are useful for debugging purposes.

Table 14.2
Numeric Format Codes for the CONTENTS Command

Code	Format of Destination String
0-15	Fixed, 0 to 15 decimal places
16-31	Scientific, 0 to 15 decimal places
32-47	Currency, 0 to 15 decimal places
48-63	Percent, 0 to 15 decimal places
64-79	Comma, 0 to 15 decimal places
112	+/– Bar Graph
113	General format
114	D1 (DD-MMM-YY)
115	D2 (DD-MM)
116	D3 (MMM-YY)
117	Text format
118	Hidden format
119	D6 (HH:MM:SS AMPM time format)
120	D7 (HH:MM AMPM time format)
121	D4 (Long International Date)
122	D5 (Short International Date)
123	D8 (Long International Time)
124	D9 (Short International Time)
127	Current default display format

The DEFINE Command

An important feature of 1-2-3's advanced macro commands is the capability of passing arguments to a subroutine call. To tell 1-2-3 where on the worksheet to place the arguments, a subroutine that takes arguments must contain the DEFINE command as its first statement. The format of the DEFINE command is as follows:

Reminder:
Use DEFINE if you use subroutines that pass arguments.

{DEFINE *loc1:Type1,...*}

DEFINE identifies the cells to contain the argument values. *Loc1*, *loc2*, and so on are cells or ranges in which 1-2-3 stores the argument values for the called subroutine.

Type1 is either S (or STRING) or V (or VALUE) and is optional; if not present, the default is STRING. If *loc* is defined as type STRING, 1-2-3 places the argument from the subroutine call into *loc1* as a label.

If *loc* is defined as type VALUE, the corresponding argument in the subroutine call is treated as a formula, range name, or number; 1-2-3 places the value of the argument in *loc*. If the corresponding argument in the subroutine call is not a valid number, string, or formula, 1-2-3 displays an error message. You do not, however, have to enclose a string in quotation marks or have a leading plus sign (+) in a formula that uses cell references.

Consider the program \d, shown in figure 14.6. \d has a subroutine that creates a list of four dates, each seven days apart, beginning with today. The subroutine takes one argument, @NOW. The DEFINE command stores the value of @NOW (today's date) in the cell called TODAY.

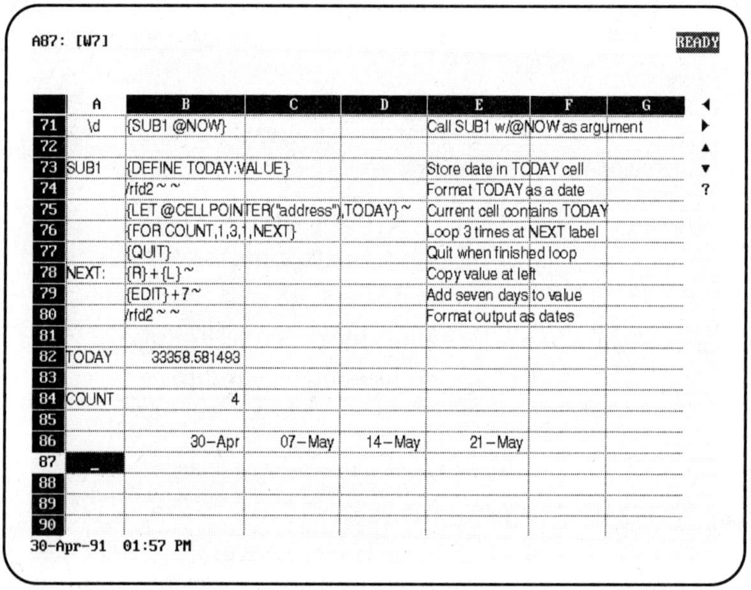

A87: [W7] READY

	A	B	C	D	E	F	G
71	\d	{SUB1 @NOW}			Call SUB1 w/@NOW as argument		
72							
73	SUB1	{DEFINE TODAY:VALUE}			Store date in TODAY cell		
74		/rfd2~~			Format TODAY as a date		
75		{LET @CELLPOINTER("address"),TODAY}~			Current cell contains TODAY		
76		{FOR COUNT,1,3,1,NEXT}			Loop 3 times at NEXT label		
77		{QUIT}			Quit when finished loop		
78	NEXT:	{R}+{L}~			Copy value at left		
79		{EDIT}+7~			Add seven days to value		
80		/rfd2~~			Format output as dates		
81							
82	TODAY	33358.581493					
83							
84	COUNT	4					
85							
86		30–Apr	07–May	14–May	21–May		
87							
88							
89							
90							

30-Apr-91 01:57 PM

***Fig. 14.6.** An example of a subroutine with parameters and a DEFINE statement.*

The rest of the program enters today's date in the current cell, formats the current cell and the three cells to the right as dates, and then enters the sequential dates.

The DISPATCH Command

The DISPATCH command is similar to the BRANCH command. The DISPATCH command, however, branches indirectly to a cell address or range name contained in the *location* cell. The format of the command is as follows:

{DISPATCH *location*}

The *location* argument is a cell address or range name that contains the destination of the DISPATCH. If the cell referred to by *location* does not contain a valid cell reference or range name, an error occurs and program execution either stops with an error message or transfers to an ONERROR command, if the macro contains an ONERROR command.

The location must contain a cell reference or range name that points to a single cell reference. If the location is either a multicell range or a range that contains a single cell, the DISPATCH command acts like a BRANCH statement and transfers execution directly to the location.

Reminder: DISPATCH must contain a cell reference.

In figure 14.7, the DISPATCH statement continues program execution in the cell called SUB_1 (which is in cell ANSWER, the location argument).

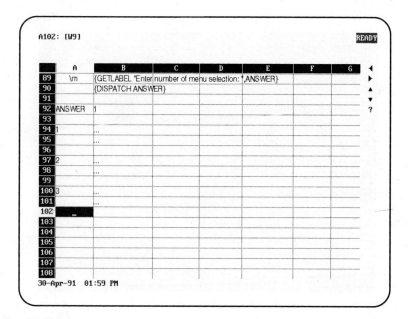

Fig. 14.7. *A macro that uses DISPATCH.*

The FILESIZE Command

The FILESIZE command returns the length of the file in bytes. The format of the command is as follows:

{FILESIZE *location*}

FILESIZE records the open file's size in *location*. The FILESIZE command determines the current length of the file and places this value in the cell referred to by *location*. *location* can be a cell reference or range name. For an example of the FILESIZE command, refer to figure 14.5.

The FOR and FORBREAK Commands

The FOR command executes a subroutine a specified number of times. A subroutine executed more than once is called a *loop*. The format of the FOR command is as follows:

{FOR *counter,start,stop,step,routine*}

counter is a blank cell that 1-2-3 uses to count the number of times the subroutine runs in the loop. 1-2-3 replaces any existing value in *counter*. *start* is the starting number for the counter, *stop* is the ending number, and *step* is the increment to add each time the subroutine runs; specify values, range names, or cell addresses. *routine* is the name of the subroutine to execute; specify a cell or range name.

If you have **nested** loops (one FOR loop inside another), you must be sure to complete the innermost loops before you complete the outer loop.

> **Caution:** Although you can have multiple loops in FOR structures, be careful of the logical flow from one loop to the next.

Notice how FOR is used in the simple example in figure 14.4. The FOR statement controls the number of times the program FACT_RTN executes. In this example, the FOR statement begins by using the range named COUNTER to keep track of the number of times the program should loop. The second argument, 1, is the start number for the counter; the next argument, FACTORIAL, is the stop number. The program keeps track of the looping process by comparing the counter against the stop number and stops executing if the counter value is larger than the stop number.

The FOR statement's next argument, 1, is the step number; this value is the increment to add. The last argument, FACT_RTN, is the name of the routine to execute.

The FORBREAK command terminates a FOR command loop before the loop has completed its number of iterations. FORBREAK then continues execution with the command following the FOR statement. For example, if FACT_RTN contains a test like the following:

```
{IF PREVIOUS_NUMBER>1000}{FORBREAK}
```

1-2-3 ends the loop as soon as the value in PREVIOUS_NUMBER exceeds 1,000.

The FORM Command

The FORM command temporarily interrupts macro execution so that the user can enter input into unprotected cells in a specified range. FORM, although similar to the /Range Input command, includes three additional options: branching to another line of advanced macro command instructions if the user enters certain keys, specifying a set of keystrokes as valid, and specifying a set of keystrokes as invalid. The format for the FORM command is as follows:

Reminder:
Use FORM to pause macro execution so that you can enter data into the unprotected cells in a range.

{FORM *input,call-table,include-keys,exclude-keys*}

FORM temporarily interrupts the macro so that a user can enter data into the *input* range—a worksheet range in which at least one cell has been unprotected with /Range Unprotect. The user enters data only in the unprotected cells.

Without the last three arguments, which are optional, FORM functions exactly like /Range Input: you can use any keys to enter data into and move between the unprotected cells.

You can use FORM's three optional arguments (*call-table, include-keys,* and *exclude-keys*) individually or in a combination of the *call-table* and the *include-keys* or *exclude-keys* arguments.

Call-table is a two-column range in which the first column lists the names of keys on the keyboard, such as {CALC} or {GRAPH}, and the second column lists the commands to be executed when the key is pressed.

Include-keys is a range of all keystrokes that are acceptable during execution of the FORM command. This list includes not only keystrokes entered into the unprotected field in the *input* range but also any other keys needed to operate the macro or to deal with an error condition.

Exclude-keys is a range listing all keystrokes that are unacceptable during the execution of the FORM command. By specifying the unacceptable keys, you implicitly identify the acceptable keys; you probably will use either the *include-keys* or the *exclude-keys* argument but not both.

To omit an optional argument, use one of the following command structures:

Structure	Result
{FORM *input*}	To omit all optional arguments
{FORM *input,call-table*}	To use only *call-table*
{FORM *input,,include-keys*}	To use only *include-keys*
{FORM *input,,,exclude-keys*}	To use only *exclude-keys*
{FORM *input,call-table,include-keys*}	To use *call-table* and *include-keys*
{FORM *input,call-table,,exclude-keys*}	To use *call-table* and *exclude-keys*

To complete execution of the FORM command, the user presses the key designated in the *call-table* or *include-keys* range to end the form. If the FORM command uses an *exclude-keys* range, the user presses Enter or Esc. 1-2-3 then continues execution of the macro program. When the user presses Enter or Esc, the cell pointer remains in its current position in the form.

Figure 14.8 shows an example of a form to accept data into the unprotected cells A93, B94, and A95 in the range INPUT. The *call-table* argument, KEYS, specifies the additional keystrokes to execute if the user presses F1 (HELP) or INS. If the user presses F1 (Help), the program beeps. If the user presses INS, the program uses the FORMBREAK command to break out of the form.

This example doesn't have an *include-keys* argument but does have an *exclude-keys* argument. The range EXCLUDE (D98..D101) shows the excluded keystrokes.

> *Note:* All three optional arguments for {FORM} (*call-table, include-keys,* and *exclude-keys*) are case-sensitive. For example, if your *include-keys* argument lists an uppercase B but not a lowercase b, only the uppercase B is accepted.

The FORMBREAK Command

The FORMBREAK command ends a FORM command and cancels the current form. The format of the command is as follows:

{FORMBREAK}

```
A102: [W10]                                                    READY

        A          B          C          D          E         F       G   ◄
   93          <- INPUT 1      \I        {FORM INPUT,KEYS,,EXCLUDE}          ►
   94  INPUT 2 ->                                                           ▲
   95          <- INPUT 3  KEYS      {HELP}        {BEEP 1}                  ▼
   96                                 {INS}         {FORMBREAK}
   97                                                                       ?
   98                      EXCLUDE   !
   99                                @
  100                                #
  101                                $
  102      _
  103
  104
  105
  106
  107
  108
  109
  110
  111
  112
   26-Feb-91  11:47 AM
```

Fig. 14.8. *The FORM command used to collect input and specify valid key-strokes.*

In addition to using FORMBREAK to end a FORM command and cancel the current form, you can use FORMBREAK with nested FORM commands. In this case, FORMBREAK ends the current form and returns you to the preceding form. For example, suppose that you use the FORM command to create an order-entry form that has a Vendor field. If the user presses Ins on the Vendor field, your program displays a second form, which lists vendor names. The user picks the name of the vendor or types a new name and presses Ins again. After the user presses Enter, your program issues a FORMBREAK command to return to the order-entry form.

Figure 14.8 shows an example of the FORMBREAK command.

The FRAMEOFF Command

The FRAMEOFF command removes the column border letters and row border numbers from the 1-2-3 display. The format of the command is as follows:

{FRAMEOFF}

FRAMEOFF suppresses display of the worksheet frame. After you execute a FRAMEOFF command in an advanced macro command program, 1-2-3

suppresses the worksheet-frame display until the program encounters a
FRAMEON command or completes execution.

The FRAMEON Command

The FRAMEON command redisplays the column border letters and row
border numbers originally suppressed by a FRAMEOFF command. The
format for the FRAMEON command is as follows:

    {FRAMEON}

FRAMEON redisplays the worksheet frame. The following sample program
uses FRAMEOFF and FRAMEON:

```
{FRAMEOFF}{?}~
{DOWN 2}
{FRAMEON}{?}~
{RIGHT 3}
{FRAMEOFF}{?}~
```

The program initially suppresses display of the worksheet frame until you
press a key, then redisplays the worksheet frame until you press a key, and
then again suppresses the worksheet frame until you press a key.

If you construct this macro yourself, note that even though the last
FRAMEOFF command doesn't have a matching FRAMEON command, the
worksheet frame redisplays when the macro program ends.

FRAMEON does not function in Wysiwyg graphics mode. To accomplish the
same effect as FRAMEON in Wysiwyg graphics mode, use the :Display
Options Frame 1-2-3 Quit Quit command sequence.

The GET Command

Reminder:
Use GET to place a
keystroke in a cell.

The GET command places a single keystroke into a target cell. You then can
analyze or test the keystroke and, based on the result of the test, change the
flow of the program. The format for the GET command is as follows:

    {GET *location*}

GET accepts a single keystroke into the range defined by *location*. The
following example shows how you can use GET:

```
{GET CAPTURE}
{IF CAPTURE="q"}/fs~r
{GOTO}SALES~
```

In this program, the GET statement traps individual keystrokes in a cell named CAPTURE. The second line evaluates CAPTURE. If the keystroke in CAPTURE is the letter Q, the file is saved automatically. If CAPTURE contains any other keystroke, /fs~r is ignored. In either case, control then passes to the third line of the program, which places the cell pointer in the cell with the range name SALES.

> ***Note:*** The GET command returns the trapped keystroke value as soon as the user presses a single key. If you are building a menu-driven worksheet program for a user, GET offers you a great advantage: the user does not have to press Enter after making a selection. With the three other major input commands—?, GETLABEL, and GETNUMBER—the user must press Enter to terminate input.

The GETLABEL Command

The GETLABEL command accepts any type of entry from the keyboard but stores the input as a label. The prompt, which must be enclosed in quotation marks, is displayed in the control panel. The format for the GETLABEL command is as follows:

Reminder:
Use GETLABEL to display a prompt and accept any type of input from the user into a cell.

{GETLABEL *"prompt",location*}

GETLABEL places the entry in *location* as a label when the user presses Enter. The following example shows the use of the GETLABEL command:

```
{GETLABEL "Enter order date (MM/DD/YY): ",ORDER_DATE}
{GOTO}ORDER_DATE~
{DOWN}~@DATEVALUE(ORDER_DATE)~/rfd1~
```

The GETLABEL statement displays a prompt and accepts a label into the cell named ORDER_DATE. The second line places the cell pointer in the ORDER_DATE cell. The third line places a formula in the cell below ORDER_DATE; this formula converts the label date to a numerical date and then formats the cell as a date.

Figure 14.9 shows how to improve the macro by using GETLABEL with the IF, BRANCH, and BEEP commands to add error handling. If the user enters a label that cannot be converted to a date, the second GETLABEL command (in the DATE_ERR macro) displays an error message; the program pauses until the user presses Enter and then branches back to prompt the user for a date in a correct format.

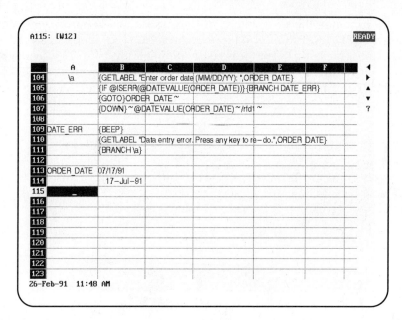

Fig. 14.9. The GETLABEL command used with other commands for string input.

The GETNUMBER Command

The GETNUMBER command accepts only numbers as entries. The format for the GETNUMBER command is as follows:

{GETNUMBER *"prompt", location*}

After the user types a number and presses Enter, 1-2-3 places the number in *location*. If the user presses Enter without having entered a number or tries to enter a label, 1-2-3 displays ERR in the cell. *prompt* is a string enclosed in quotation marks. 1-2-3 displays the prompt in the control panel.

In the following example, the GETNUMBER statement displays a prompt and accepts a number in cell CLASS_CODE:

```
{GETNUMBER "Classification code:",CLASS_CODE}
```

The GETPOS Command

The GETPOS command records the file pointer's current position. The format of this command is as follows:

{GETPOS *location*}

GETPOS records a file-pointer position in *location*. The current position of the file pointer is placed in the cell indicated by *location*, where *location* is either a cell or a range name.

The GETPOS command is useful for recording the file location of something you want to find again. You can use GETPOS to mark your current place in the file before you use SETPOS to move the file pointer to another position. You can use GETPOS to record the locations of important items in a quick-reference index. For an example of how to use GETPOS, refer to figure 14.5.

Reminder:
Use GETPOS to record the location of the file pointer.

> *Note:* As shown in figure 14.5, you can use GETPOS to mark your position in one file before opening another file. Then you can use SETPOS to return to the same position in the first file.

The GRAPHOFF Command

The GRAPHOFF command removes the named graph from the display and redisplays the worksheet. The format for using the GRAPHOFF command is as follows:

    {GRAPHOFF}

For more information about the GRAPHOFF command, read the following section about GRAPHON.

The GRAPHON Command

The GRAPHON command can set the currently named graph, display the currently named graph, or first set and then display the currently named graph. The format for the GRAPHON command is as follows:

    {GRAPHON *named-graph,*no-display}

GRAPHON displays the current graph or another named graph or sets the current graph without displaying it. To display a full-screen view of the currently named graph, use the command alone, as in the following example:

```
{GRAPHON}
```

To display a graph other than the current one, reset the currently named graph and then redisplay it. For example, if you have a graph setting named FIG_1, use the following structure:

```
{GRAPHON FIG_1}
```

In either of the preceding cases, 1-2-3 continues to display a full-sized version of the graph until the macro program completes execution or encounters one of the following commands:

- GRAPHOFF

- GRAPHON

- INDICATE

- ?

- Any command that displays a prompt or menu, such as GETLABEL or MENUCALL

To change the named graph but not display it, use the no-display argument. For example, if you want the graph setting named FIG_1 to be the current graph setting, but you don't want the graph displayed, use the following structure:

```
{GRAPHON FIG_1,no-display}
```

The IF Command

The IF statement uses IF-THEN-ELSE logic to evaluate the existence of certain numeric and string values. The advanced macro command IF, commonly used to control program flow and enable the program to perform based on criteria provided by the user, is the functional equivalent of the IF command in BASIC. The format of the IF command is as follows:

{IF *condition*}{*true*}
{*false*}

Reminder:
If condition is true, the statements following IF are executed.

IF executes a statement based on the result of *condition*. *condition* is a logical expression, such as +B3>100. If *condition* is *true*, 1-2-3 executes the remaining {*true*} commands on the same line as the IF command. If *condition* is *true*, the commands to execute ordinarily include a BRANCH command to skip the {*false*} statements. If *condition* is *false*, 1-2-3 executes the next line in the macro.

IF statements can check for a variety of conditions, including the position of the cell pointer, a specific numeric value, or a specific string value. In figure 14.10, for example, the IF statement checks to see whether the user entered a LAST_NAME of SMITH. If so, program control passes to the \b macro, which starts the program again. If LAST_NAME is not SMITH, the second line of SUB_3 executes, and the program continues by returning through the stack.

```
A133: [W14]                                                        READY

          A              B               C          D          E        ◄
 117      \b       {GETLABEL "What is your last name?",LAST_NAME}       ►
 118              {SUB_1}                                               ▲
 119                                                                    ▼
 120 SUB_1        {SUB_2}                                               ?
 121              {GETLABEL "What day is it?",DAY}
 122
 123 SUB_2        {SUB_3}
 124              {GETLABEL "How are you",HOW}
 125
 126 SUB_3        {IF LAST_NAME="SMITH"}{RESTART}{BRANCH \b}
 127              {GETLABEL "What is your first name?",FIRST_NAME}
 128
 129 LAST_NAME    Jones
 130 FIRST_NAME   Bob
 131 DAY          Tuesday
 132 HOW          Fine
 133      _
 134
 135
 136
26-Feb-91  12:32 PM
```

Fig. 14.10. The IF command used in a subroutine to check user input.

An IF statement is contained in a single cell. The part of the cell that follows the IF portion is called the *THEN clause*. The THEN clause executes only if the result of the logical test is true.

The second line of SUB_3 contains the *ELSE clause*, which executes if the result of the logical statement in the IF statement is false or if the program statements in the THEN clause do not transfer to another part of the macro. In the example in figure 14.10, the THEN clause contains a BRANCH statement so that the ELSE does not execute when the IF statement is true.

The IF statement adds significant strength to 1-2-3's advanced macro commands. The one disadvantage of an IF statement is that if the code in the THEN clause does not branch or execute a QUIT command, the program continues its execution right through the ELSE clause.

The INDICATE Command

The INDICATE command alters the mode indicator in the upper right corner of the 1-2-3 screen. This command commonly is used to provide custom indicators. The INDICATE command accepts a string argument that can be as long as the control panel (typically 80 characters). The format of the INDICATE command is as follows:

Cue:
Use INDICATE to display your indicators during macro execution.

{INDICATE *string*}

INDICATE resets the mode indicator to *string*. The following INDICATE command displays the message START in the upper right corner of the screen:

```
{INDICATE START}
```

> *Note:* In the preceding example, START is a string, but the INDI-CATE command also can use a range name or cell address for the *string* argument.

The START message displays until you exit 1-2-3, retrieve another file, or select /Worksheet Erase Yes. To restore the indicator to its preceding value, use the following command:

```
{INDICATE}
```

To blank out the indicator completely, use this command:

```
{INDICATE""}
```

The *string* argument is a string, a range name, or a cell address that contains a string. If the argument is a cell that contains a number, 1-2-3 displays an error message. You also can use a valid string formula for the string argument, such as {INDICATE @CELLPOINTER("address")}.

The LET Command

Cue:

Use LET to assign a value to a location without moving the cell pointer.

The LET command places a value or string in a target cell location without the cell pointer being at that location. LET is extremely useful for placing criteria in a database criterion range, for example. The format of the LET command is as follows:

{LET *location,expression*}

LET places the value of *expression* in *location*. The LET command can use numeric values, string values, or formulas. Suppose, for example, that the cell named FIRST contains the string "BOB", and LAST holds the string "JONES". The following statement stores "BOB JONES" in NAME:

```
{LET NAME,FIRST&" "&LAST}
```

Like the DEFINE command, the LET command enables you to specify :STRING and :VALUE (or :S and :V) suffixes after the argument. The :STRING suffix stores the text of the argument in *location*; the :VALUE suffix evaluates the argument as a string or numeric formula and places the result in *location*. When a suffix is not specified, LET stores the argument's numeric or string value if it is a valid formula; otherwise, the text of the argument is stored. For example, the following statement stores "BOB JONES" in NAME:

```
{LET NAME,FIRST&" "&LAST:VALUE}
```

The next statement, however, stores the string FIRST&" "&LAST in NAME:

```
{LET NAME,FIRST&" "&LAST:STRING}
```

Instead of using the LET command, you can move the cell pointer to the desired location with {GOTO} and enter the desired value into the cell. But the LET command has the major advantage of not disturbing the current location of the cell pointer. Furthermore, although you can enter numbers by using /Data Fill, you cannot use this command to enter string values. Overall, the LET command is a convenient, useful, and fast way to set the value of a cell from within a program.

The LOOK Command

The LOOK command checks the type-ahead buffer for keystrokes. The *type-ahead buffer* is a small storage area in memory where DOS holds a few keystrokes until they can be processed by a program such as 1-2-3. The format of the LOOK command is as follows:

{LOOK *location*}

LOOK places the first character from the type-ahead buffer into *location*. You can use the LOOK command to interrupt macro processing when the user presses a key. If LOOK detects something in the type-ahead buffer, it places a copy of the first keystroke in *location*.

Reminder:
LOOK copies the first keystroke in the type-ahead buffer to the specified locations.

When you include the LOOK command in a program, the user can type a character at any time; the macro finds that single character when it executes the LOOK command. An IF statement also can check the contents of *location*. Because the character is not removed from the type-ahead buffer, you must use the character or dispose of it before the program needs keyboard input or completes execution.

Although LOOK and GET are similar, they differ in an important way. GET pauses the macro until the user presses a key. GET places the keystroke into a cell, thus removing it from the type-ahead buffer. LOOK, however, places a *copy* of the keystroke into the cell specified by *location*, without pausing the macro or removing the keystroke from the buffer.

The \0 program shown in figure 14.11 uses the LOOK command. This program starts by placing the time the macro starts in the cell named COUNTER. Whenever the program encounters the LOOK command, 1-2-3 checks the keyboard type-ahead buffer and copies the first character found into the location called ANSWER.

```
A152: [W14]                                                    READY

           A              B            C          D         E      ◄
135          \0    {LET COUNTER,@NOW}                              ►
136 LOOK_ANSWER   {LOOK ANSWER}                                    ▲
137               {IF ANSWER<>""}{CHECK_ANSWER}                    ▼
138               {IF @NOW<=COUNTER+@TIME(0,0,30)}{BRANCH LOOK_ANSWER}  ?
139               {BEEP}
140               {GETLABEL "You're keeping me waiting.",ANSWER}{BRANCH \0}
141
142 CHECK_ANSWER  {GET ANSWER}
143               {IF ANSWER="q"}{QUIT}
144               {IF ANSWER="1"}/fs~ {LET COUNTER,@NOW}
145               {RESTART}{BRANCH LOOK_ANSWER}
146
147 ANSWER        q
148 COUNTER        02:49:30 PM
149               Please choose one of the following:
150               Q             Leave the macro
151               1             Save the file
152               _
153
154
26-Feb-91  12:32 PM
```

Fig. 14.11. The LOOK command used to examine the type-ahead buffer and to place the first keystroke in the specified location.

In this example, an IF statement checks the contents of ANSWER and branches to the CHECK_ANSWER macro if the user has typed a character. The IF command compares the contents of ANSWER to a null string. (A *null string* literally represents nothing.) You indicate a null string in a comparison test by placing two quotation marks side by side (" ").

The GET command at the beginning of the CHECK_ANSWER macro disposes of the keystroke that interrupted the loop. That is, GET removes the keystroke from the type-ahead buffer and places it in ANSWER.

The two IF statements in the CHECK_ANSWER macro form a simple test of the user's menu selections (one of the selections resets the time stored in COUNTER). If the user doesn't type a character, 1-2-3 executes the IF statement in cell B138. This IF statement tests whether the program has waited more than 30 seconds for user input and, if it has, prompts the user.

This example demonstrates a powerful use of the LOOK command. By storing the time the macro starts, you can give the user a limited amount of time to make a selection. You can either prompt the user if too much time elapses or make a default selection yourself. You can, for example, produce a macro that continues after a specified time even if the user doesn't make a selection.

The LOOK command is most helpful when you have a long program to process and you want to be able to stop processing at certain points in the program. At several places in the program, you can enter a LOOK command followed by an IF statement, as in figure 14.11. Then, if the user presses a key, the program stops the next time a LOOK command executes. If no key is pressed, the program continues processing. In such cases, the LOOK command is preferable to the GET command, which *always* stops the program to wait for an entry.

Cue:
Use the LOOK command to process long programs.

The MENUBRANCH Command

The MENUBRANCH command defines a menu with as many as eight options and displays it in the control panel. You select options from this menu in the same way you select options from a 1-2-3 menu. The format of the MENUBRANCH command follows:

{MENUBRANCH *location*}

MENUBRANCH executes a menu structure at *location*. You create, in from one to eight consecutive columns in the worksheet, the menu used by MENUBRANCH. Each column corresponds to one item in the menu. The upper left corner of the range named in a MENUBRANCH statement must refer to the first menu item; otherwise, you receive the error message Invalid use of Menu macro command.

Each menu item consists of three or more rows in the same column. The first row is the name of the menu option. All of the option names (taken together) must fit on the top line of the control panel (typically 80 characters); otherwise, 1-2-3 displays the error message mentioned in the preceding paragraph. Option names should begin with different letters. If two or more options begin with the same letter and the user tries to use the first-letter technique to choose an option, 1-2-3 selects the first option it finds with the letter you specified.

Cue:
Begin menu-option names with unique letters so that you can press the first letter of the option to select it.

The second row in the menu range contains the descriptions of the menu items. When the cell pointer highlights the name of a menu option, the corresponding description is displayed in the control panel under the menu option. Each description can contain as many as 80 characters of text. The description row must be present, even if it is blank.

The program command sequence begins in the third row. Because control branches to the individual programs, program control must be directed by statements at the end of each individual program.

The menu items must be in consecutive columns (with no blank columns between them). A blank column in *location* signals the end of the menu structure.

For an example of the MENUBRANCH command, refer to figure 14.1.

Note: If you have a multilevel menu structure, you can make the Esc key function as it does in the 1-2-3 command menus (backing up to the menu preceding the current menu). If the user presses Esc instead of selecting a menu item, 1-2-3 stops displaying the menu items and executes the next program command after the MENUBRANCH command. To make the program return to the preceding menu, add a BRANCH to the preceding MENUBRANCH.

The MENUCALL Command

Reminder:
MENUCALL returns program control to the statement after the MENUCALL command.

The MENUCALL command is identical to the MENUBRANCH command except that 1-2-3 executes the menu program as a subroutine. After executing an individual menu program, 1-2-3 continues executing the program at the cell immediately below the MENUCALL statement. The format of the MENUCALL command is as follows:

{MENUCALL *location*}

Figure 14.12 shows how to use a MENUCALL command to branch to a menu and then return to the macro's next line, which ends the macro.

When you use a MENUCALL, 1-2-3 returns to the statement immediately following the MENUCALL and reads a blank cell or a RETURN. In figure 14.12, 1-2-3 returns to the BRANCH statement, which then quits the macro.

The advantage of MENUCALL is that you can call the same menu from several places in a program and then return to the line after the calling point to continue execution. This advantage is true of subroutines in general.

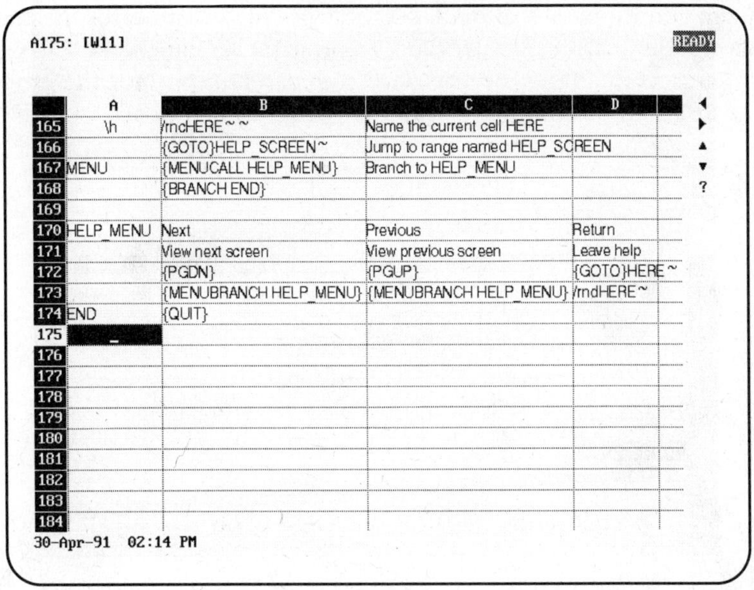

```
A175: [W11]                                                        READY

       A               B                    C                 D        ◄
165  \h        /rncHERE~ ~            Name the current cell HERE         ►
166            {GOTO}HELP_SCREEN~     Jump to range named HELP_SCREEN    ▲
167 MENU       {MENUCALL HELP_MENU}   Branch to HELP_MENU                ▼
168            {BRANCH END}                                              ?
169
170 HELP_MENU  Next                   Previous              Return
171            View next screen       View previous screen  Leave help
172            {PGDN}                 {PGUP}                {GOTO}HERE~
173            {MENUBRANCH HELP_MENU} {MENUBRANCH HELP_MENU} /rndHERE~
174 END        {QUIT}
175    _
176
177
178
179
180
181
182
183
184
30-Apr-91  02:14 PM
```

Fig. 14.12. The MENUCALL command used to branch to the macro's HELP_MENU.

The ONERROR Command

Normally, the processing of macro programs is interrupted if a system error, such as an open disk drive door, occurs during execution. The ONERROR command gives you a way to sidestep system errors that normally cause program termination. The general format of the command is as follows:

{ONERROR *branch,message*}

ONERROR traps an error and passes program control to the cell indicated by *branch*. You can record an error message in *message* (the optional second argument).

Because an ONERROR statement must be executed before it can trap an error, you may want to include an ONERROR statement near the start of your programs. Note, however, that only one ONERROR statement can be in effect at a time. When you write your programs, be sure to take precautions so that the correct ONERROR is active when its specific error is most probable.

The ONERROR statement shown in figure 14.13 acts as a safeguard against leaving drive A empty or not closing the drive door. If an error occurs,

Reminder:
Include the ONERROR statement near the start of the program.

program control passes to the DISK_ERR macro, and an error message is displayed. Because ONERROR causes a program to branch, the DISK_ERR macro must contain the {BRANCH \a} command to continue the program after a disk is inserted in drive A and the drive door is closed.

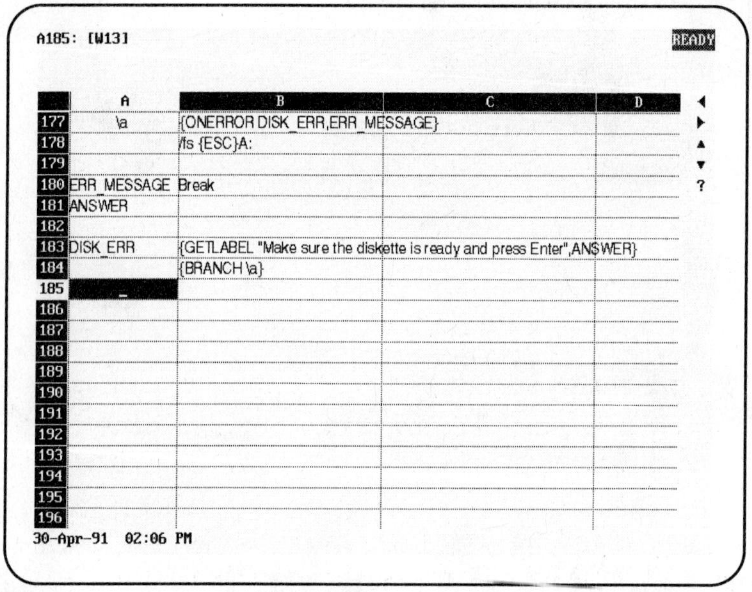

Fig. 14.13. *The ONERROR command used to prompt users to close the drive door.*

In this example, the ONERROR statement causes the program to branch to a cell called DISK_ERR if an error occurs. A copy of the error message that 1-2-3 issues is entered in a cell called ERR_MESSAGE. The first statement in the DISK_ERR routine uses GETLABEL to give the user a customized error message. The program pauses so that the user can press Enter, and then the program branches back to \a to try again.

In addition to the simple example shown in figure 14.13, you can use an ONERROR statement to examine the error message and branch to a subroutine to correct the error.

Ctrl-Break presents a special problem for the ONERROR statement. Because Ctrl-Break causes an error condition, the ONERROR statement is invoked automatically. In figure 14.13, Ctrl-Break is represented as Break. Because this sample macro does not check the error message, Ctrl-Break displays the `Make sure the diskette is ready and press Enter` **message.**

> *Caution:* The ONERROR command clears the subroutine stack, which may cause a macro to fail unexpectedly.

One possible technique for continuing the use of ONERROR is to disable Ctrl-Break after you debug your program. (Refer to the discussion of the BREAKOFF command, earlier in this chapter.) By disabling Ctrl-Break, you can prevent the confusion that may arise from the display of an untimely error message. Another technique is to issue immediately (as the first statement in your error-handling routine) another, similar ONERROR command to trap any additional errors, such as a second Ctrl-Break, immediately following the first error.

The OPEN Command

The OPEN command opens a disk file so that you can write to or read from that file. In the command's second argument, you can specify whether you want to read only, write only, or read from and write to the file.

1-2-3 enables only one file to be open at a time. If you want to work with more than one file in your application, you must open each file before using it; 1-2-3 closes an open file before opening and using the next file.

Reminder:
You can open only one file at a time; 1-2-3 closes an open file before opening another.

The format of the OPEN command is as follows:

> {OPEN *filename,access-mode*}

The *filename* argument can be a string, an expression with a string value, or a cell that contains a string or a string expression. The string must be a valid operating-system file name or path name. You can specify a file in the current directory by its name and extension. To specify a file in another directory, you may need to add a drive identification, a subdirectory path, or a complete operating-system path to the file name and extension.

The *access-mode* argument is one of four characters (R, W, A, and M) that specify whether you want to read only, write only, or both read and write to the file. These *access-mode* arguments are as follows:

Access-mode Argument	Description
"R"	Read access opens an existing file and enables the READ and READLN commands. You cannot write to a file opened with Read access.
"W"	Write access opens a new file and enables the WRITE and WRITELN commands. Any existing file with the specified name is erased and replaced by the new file.
"A"	Append access opens an existing file and enables both the READ (or READLN) and WRITE (or WRITELN) commands. Append access places the byte pointer at the end of the file.
"M"	Modify access opens an existing file and enables both READ (or READLN) and WRITE (or WRITELN) commands. You cannot use Modify access to create a file. Modify access places the byte pointer at the beginning of the file.

The OPEN command succeeds if it can open the file with the access you request. If the OPEN command succeeds, program execution continues with the cell below the OPEN statement. Any commands after OPEN in the current cell are ignored.

The OPEN command fails with an error if the disk drive is not ready. Use the ONERROR command to handle the possibility of such an error.

Cue:
To handle the possibility of errors during OPEN, use the ONERROR command.

If you specify an access mode of READ, APPEND, or MODIFY, but the file does not exist in the indicated directory, the OPEN command fails and program execution continues with the commands after the OPEN command in the current cell. To deal with the failure, you can place one or more commands in the same cell after the OPEN command; for example, you can use a BRANCH or a subroutine call to a macro that deals with the failure.

Following are some examples (with explanations) of the OPEN command:

```
{OPEN "PASTDUE",R}{BRANCH FIXIT}
```

Opens the existing file named PASTDUE in the current directory for reading; if the file cannot be opened, branches to the routine FIXIT

```
{OPEN "C:\DATA\CLIENTS.DAT",W}
```

Opens the new file named CLIENTS.DAT in drive C, subdirectory DATA, for writing

```
{OPEN FILE,A}{BRANCH RETRY}
```

Opens the file whose name is in the cell FILE for Append access; if the file cannot be opened, branches to the routine RETRY

```
{OPEN FILE,M}{BRANCH RETRY}
```

Opens the file whose name is in cell FILE for Modify access; if the file cannot be opened, branches to the routine RETRY

For an example that uses all the file commands except the READLN and WRITE commands (which are similar to the READ and WRITELN commands), refer to figure 14.5. In this example, the program named \r uses the OPEN command to open a file.

Figure 14.5 demonstrates the use of the file-manipulation commands to read data in 100-byte increments from one file (INPUT.TXT) and to write the same data to another file (OUTPUT.TXT) in lines that end with a carriage return and line feed.

As you look at the program in figure 14.5, take note of the items listed here:

- You must specify the value to use in REC_LEN before you execute the \r macro. This value determines the number of characters (bytes) to be read each time the READ_WRITE macro executes.

- The {OPEN "OUTPUT.TXT",R}{OPEN "OUTPUT.TXT",W} line creates OUTPUT.TXT if that file does not already exist. If the OPEN with Read access fails, OPEN with Write access creates the file. The subsequent OPEN, with an Append-access statement, places the file pointer at the end of the file so that the WRITELN command extends the file.

- GETPOS and SETPOS always refer to the currently open file (INPUT.TXT, in this example). OUPUT.TXT is closed when these commands are active.

The PANELOFF Command

The PANELOFF command freezes the control panel, suppressing the display of program commands in the control panel during program execution. Be aware, however, that the advanced macro commands MENUBRANCH, MENUCALL, GETLABEL, GETNUMBER, and INDICATE override the PANELOFF command. The format of the PANELOFF command is as follows:

{PANELOFF}

In the following example, PANELOFF suppresses display in the control
panel of the /Copy command in the second line of code:

```
{PANELOFF}
/cRANGE_1~RANGE_2~
```

> *Note:* When the macro ends, 1-2-3 restores the panel display as soon
> as the user moves the cell pointer or issues a command.

The PANELON Command

The PANELON command unfreezes the control panel. The format of the
PANELON command is as follows:

{PANELON}

Cue:
*Use PANELON at
the end of a macro
as a fast way to
restore the panel.*

PANELON reactivates the display in the control panel. In the following
example, PANELOFF freezes the control-panel display while RANGE_1 is
copied to RANGE_2; then PANELON reactivates the control panel:

```
{PANELOFF}
/cRANGE_1~RANGE_2~
{PANELON}
```

The PUT Command

The PUT command places a value within a range at the intersection of a
specified row and a column. The format of the PUT command is as follows:

{PUT *range,col,row,value*}

PUT places *value* into the specified cell within *range*. *range* is a range name
or cell address to contain the value. *col* is the column offset within the
range; *row* defines the row offset within the range. *value* is the value to
place in the cell. *col*, *row*, and *value* can be values, cells, or formulas.

Consider, for example, the following PUT statement:

```
{PUT TABLE,S1,S2,ARG4}
```

This statement places the contents of the cell named ARG4 in the range
named TABLE at the intersection defined by the values in cells S1 and S2.

Keep in mind that the row and column offset numbers used with the PUT command follow the same conventions followed by functions (the first column is number 0; the second is number 1; and so on). Also, the row and column values must not specify a location outside the range. If this happens, the macro fails, and 1-2-3 informs you that the PUT statement contains an invalid range.

The QUIT Command

The QUIT command forces the program to terminate unconditionally. Even without a QUIT command, the program terminates if it encounters a cell that is empty or contains an entry other than a string (unless the program is a subroutine called by another program). A good practice is always to include a QUIT statement in your program at the point at which you want execution to stop. (Conversely, do not put a QUIT command at the end of a program you intend to call as a subroutine.) The format of the QUIT command is as follows:

{QUIT}

QUIT halts program execution. In the following example, the QUIT command forces the program sequence to terminate unconditionally:

```
{HOME}/fs~r{QUIT}
```

When QUIT is preceded by an IF conditional testing statement, as in the following example, the program does not terminate unconditionally.

```
{GETNUMBER "Enter a number:", INPUT}
{IF INPUT<1}{QUIT}
```

The READ Command

The READ command reads a specified number of characters from the currently open file, beginning at the present file-pointer location. READ places the characters read from the file in the worksheet at the indicated cell location. The format of the READ command is as follows:

{READ *bytecount,location*}

READ copies the specified number of characters from a file to *location*. *bytecount* is the number of bytes to read, starting at the current position of the file pointer. *bytecount* can be any number between 0 and 240 (the maximum number of characters in a 1-2-3 label). *location* is the cell or range to contain the characters from the file.

READ places the specified number of characters from the file into *location* as a label. If *bytecount* is greater than the number of characters remaining in the file, 1-2-3 reads the remaining characters into the specified location. After the READ command executes, the file pointer is positioned at the character following the last character read.

The following statement transfers information from the open file into the cell named INLINE.

```
{READ REC_LEN,INLINE}
```

The amount of information transferred is determined by the contents of the cell named REC_LEN, which can contain either a value or a formula.

The READ command is useful when you want to read a specific number of characters into a specified location in the current worksheet. For example, a data file that contains fixed-length records can be read conveniently by a READ command with the *bytecount* argument specified as the record length.

In ASCII text files from a word processor or text editor, each line may end with a carriage-return-and-line-feed sequence, or the carriage-return-and-line-feed sequence may be only at the end of a paragraph. Often, ASCII text files with the carriage return and line feed at the end of each line can be read by using READLN (which reads a variable-length line) instead of READ (which reads a fixed number of characters).

The READLN Command

The READLN command reads one line of information (up to the next carriage return and line feed) from the currently open file, beginning at the file pointer's current position. The characters read are placed in the cell *location* in the current worksheet. The READLN command format is as follows:

{READLN *location*}

READLN copies the next line from the file to *location*. In the following example, READLN copies a line from an open file into the cell named HERE:

```
{READLN HERE}
```

Reminder:
Use READLN instead of READ to read lines delimited by a carriage return and line-feed.

Use READLN to read a line of text from a file whose lines are delimited by a carriage-return and line-feed combination. For example, use READLN to read the next line of an ASCII text file. ASCII text files (also referred to as *print files*) are created with 1-2-3's /**P**rint **F**ile command; 1-2-3 assigns the PRN file extension to these files.

If you attempt to read past the end of a file or if no file is open, the READ or READLN command is ignored and program execution continues in the same cell. Otherwise, after the READ or READLN command is completed, program execution continues on the next line. To handle the problem of an unexecuted READ or READLN statement, place a BRANCH or subroutine call after the READ or READLN.

The RECALC and RECALCCOL Commands

You can use the RECALC and RECALCCOL macro commands to recalculate a portion of the worksheet. Being able to recalculate only a portion of the worksheet is useful for large worksheets in which recalculation time is long and in which you need to recalculate certain values in the worksheet before you proceed to the next processing step. The formats for the commands for partial recalculation are as follows:

{RECALC *location,condition,iteration-number*}

and

{RECALCCOL *location,condition,iteration-number*}

In both formats, *location* is a range or range name that specifies the cell containing the formulas to recalculate. *condition* is either a logical expression or a reference to a cell. If you specify a cell for *condition*, the cell must be part of the recalculation range that contains a logical expression. If you include the *condition* argument, 1-2-3 recalculates the range repeatedly until the *condition* has a logical value of TRUE (<>0). *iteration-number* is the number of times to recalculate the formulas in *location*. If you include *iteration-number*, you must include *condition* also (use the value 1 to make *condition* always TRUE).

Reminder:
If you use a condition argument with RECALC or RECALCCOL, make sure that the reference is to a cell within the range.

The *condition* and *iteration-number* arguments are optional. If *condition* is a reference to a cell outside the recalculation range, the value of *condition*—either TRUE (1) or FALSE (0)—does not change, and *condition* does not control the partial recalculation.

The RECALC and RECALCCOL commands differ in the order in which cells in the specified range are recalculated. RECALC calculates all of the cells in the first row of the range, then all the cells in the second row, and so on. The RECALCCOL command calculates the cells in the first column of the range, then all the cells in the second column, and so on. With either command, 1-2-3 recalculates only cells within the specified range.

Use RECALC if the formula to be recalculated is below and to the left of the cells on which it depends. Use RECALCCOL if the formula is above and to the right of the cells on which it depends.

> **Caution:** You may have to use CALC if the formula to recalculate is above and to the left of cells on which it depends.

The formulas in the recalculation range can refer to values in cells outside the range; however, those values are not updated by RECALC or RECALCCOL. When either the RECALC or RECALCCOL command is executed, the partial recalculation occurs immediately, although the results do not appear on-screen until the screen is redrawn. Meanwhile, the recalculated numbers are used in calculations and conditional tests.

Cue:
Use PgUp and PgDn to redraw the screen.

If the macro program ends and you want to be sure that the recalculated numbers are on-screen, use the PgUp and PgDn keys to move the window away from and back to the recalculated range. The act of looking away and back again updates the screen and displays the current values in the recalculated range.

In a program, you may need to use CALC, RECALC, or RECALCCOL after commands such as LET, GETNUMBER, and ? or after such 1-2-3 commands as /Range Input. You do not need to recalculate after invoking such 1-2-3 commands as /Copy and /Move; 1-2-3 automatically recalculates the affected ranges after such commands, even during program execution.

The RESTART Command

Just as the main program can call subroutines, one subroutine can call another. As 1-2-3 moves from one subroutine to the next, it saves the addresses of where it has been. This technique is called *stacking*, or *saving addresses on a stack*. By saving the addresses on a stack, 1-2-3 can trace its way back through the subroutine calls to the main program.

Reminder:
Use RESTART to eliminate the contents of the 1 2-3 stack.

To prevent 1-2-3 from returning by the path it came, you can eliminate the stack by using the RESTART command. RESTART enables you to cancel a subroutine at any time during execution. Although seldom used, RESTART can be quite helpful. For example, 1-2-3's stack cannot exceed 32 nesting levels. If you attempt more calls than 32, the macro terminates with an error. You can clear the stack, however, by using RESTART.

The RESTART command normally is used with an IF statement under a conditional testing evaluation. The format for this command is as follows:

{RESTART}

RESTART cancels a subroutine. For an example of how you can use RESTART to prevent a user from entering incorrect data in a database, refer to figure 14.10. In this example, the \b macro first prompts the user for his or her last name. Then a call is made to SUB_1, which starts with a call to SUB_2. SUB_2, in turn, calls SUB_3.

The SUB_3 program first checks to see whether the user entered **SMITH** as a LAST_NAME. If the user entered **SMITH**, the program does not accept the entry; the program executes a RESTART and then a BRANCH back to the \b macro. If the user entered anything other than **SMITH**, SUB_3 prompts for the FIRST_NAME. When the user presses Enter, SUB_3 ends; control returns to the second line of SUB_2, which displays the prompt How are you. After the user enters something, SUB_2 ends, and the second line of SUB_1 executes.

The RETURN Command

The RETURN command indicates the end of subroutine execution and returns program control to the cell immediately below the cell that called the subroutine (or to other commands in the cell that contained the subroutine call). Do not confuse RETURN with QUIT, which ends the program completely. RETURN can be used with an IF statement to return conditionally from a subroutine. The form of this command is as follows:

Reminder:
Use RETURN to end a subroutine and return to the cell that called the subroutine.

{RETURN}

RETURN returns control from a subroutine. The macro shown in figure 14.14 demonstrates the RETURN command. The first line of the \a macro places the cell pointer in INPUT_1 and then calls the subroutine INPUT_SUB. After INPUT_SUB is executed, the RETURN command passes control to {HOME} (the entry that follows the subroutine call), placing the cell pointer in the HOME position.

1-2-3 also ends a subroutine and returns to the calling routine when the program encounters, while executing the subroutine, a cell that is blank or contains a numeric value. Therefore, the RETURN command in figure 14.14 really isn't necessary but serves as documentation.

```
A188: [W13]                                                    READY

          A          B            C          D          E       ◄
   176    \a      {GOTO}INPUT_1~                                 ►
   177            {INPUT_SUB}                                    ▲
   178            {HOME}                                         ▼
   179                                                           ?
   180 INPUT_SUB  {?}~
   181            {DOWN}
   182            {?}~
   183            {RIGHT}
   184            {?}~
   185            {RETURN}
   186
   187 INPUT_1
   188     _
   189
   190
   191
   192
   193
   194
   195
   26-Feb-91  12:35 PM
```

Fig. 14.14. *Use of the RETURN command.*

The SETPOS Command

The SETPOS command sets the position of the file pointer to a specified value. The format of the command is as follows:

{SETPOS *file-position*}

Reminder:
*SETPOS counts
positions from the
first character
(position 0) to the
last in the file.*

SETPOS sets a new position for a file pointer. The *file-position* argument is a number, or an expression resulting in a number, that specifies the character at which you want to position the pointer. The first character in the file is at position 0; the second is at position 1; and so on. Suppose, for example, that you have a database file with 100 records, each 20 bytes long. To access the first record, you can use the following commands:

```
{SETPOS 0}
{READ 20,buffer}
```

To read the 15th record, use the following commands:

```
{SETPOS (15-1)*20}
{READ 20,buffer}
```

Nothing prevents you from setting the file pointer past the end of the file. If the file pointer is set at or past the end of the file and a READ or READLN command is executed, the command does nothing; program execution continues with the next command on the same line as the READ or READLN. If the file pointer is set at or past the end of the file and a WRITE or WRITELN command is executed, 1-2-3 first extends the file to the length specified by the file pointer and then, starting at the file pointer, writes the characters.

> **Warning:** If you inadvertently set the file pointer to a large number with SETPOS and then write to the file, 1-2-3 attempts to expand the file and writes the text at the end of the file. If the file does not fit on the disk, the WRITE command does nothing; program execution continues with the next command on the same line as the WRITE command. If the file fits on the disk, 1-2-3 extends the file and writes the text at the end of the file.

If a file currently is not open, SETPOS does nothing; execution continues with the next command on the same line as the SETPOS command. Otherwise, when the SETPOS command is completed, execution continues on the next line of the program. You can place a BRANCH command or a subroutine call after the SETPOS command to handle the problem of an unexecuted statement. (SETPOS is shown in figure 14.5.)

The {*subroutine*} Command

A *subroutine* is an independent program that can be run from within the main program. Calling a subroutine is as easy as enclosing the name of a routine in braces—for example, {SUB}. To call a subroutine, you use the {*subroutine*} command. The format of this command is as follows:

{*subroutine argument1,argument2, . . . ,argumentN*}

subroutine is the name of the subroutine to call. You name a subroutine by using the /Range Name Create command, just as you used it to name the main program.

argument1, *argument2*, and so on are optional arguments for the subroutine. These arguments are cells, range names, strings, formulas, or functions.

When 1-2-3 encounters a subroutine name in braces, the program passes control to the named routine. Then, when the routine is finished (when 1-2-3 encounters a blank cell or a RETURN), program control passes to the next command in the same cell that contains the subroutine command or to the cell below it.

By using subroutines, you can decrease program-creation time. For example, instead of including the same program lines to display a help screen in each advanced macro command program you create, type the program lines once to create the help screen and then call those lines as a subroutine from each program.

By using subroutines, you can more easily isolate a problem. If you suspect that a subroutine is creating a problem, you can replace the call to the subroutine with BEEP. Then run the program. If the program runs correctly, beeping when the subroutine should be called, you know that the problem is in the subroutine.

Subroutines are easy to enhance. If you decide to add new commands, you can modify your subroutine once. All programs that call that subroutine reflect the new commands.

> **Caution:** 1-2-3 has a limit of 32 nesting levels on its stack.

The greatest benefit of a subroutine, however, is that any program in the same file can use it. Create the subroutine and then call it at any time from any program. When the subroutine is finished, program execution returns to the originating program.

The SYSTEM Command

Reminder:
SYSTEM executes any operating system or batch command.

The SYSTEM command executes any batch or operating-system command by using the following format:

> {SYSTEM *command*}

The following example shows how the SYSTEM command executes the batch command PARK:

> {SYSTEM PARK}

Reminder:
If you try to load a memory-resident program or use some batch commands, you may not be able to resume 1-2-3.

The operating-system command you execute with SYSTEM can be any operating-system or batch command. You can use as many as 127 characters to specify the command. Keep in mind a couple of warnings when you use SYSTEM. First, if you attempt to load a memory-resident program, you may not be able to resume 1-2-3. Second, some batch commands may not enable you to resume 1-2-3. For these two reasons, be particularly careful to save your files before you begin testing a macro that uses SYSTEM. Also remember that if all you want to do is access the operating system during a 1-2-3 session, the /System command provides a convenient alternative way to do this (although the same warnings apply).

The WAIT Command

The WAIT command causes the program to pause until an appointed time. The general format of the WAIT command is as follows:

{WAIT *argument*}

WAIT waits until the time or elapsed time specified by *argument*. The WAIT statement in the following example pauses the BEEP sequence for 0.5 seconds. (You can use this program to alert the user to the end of a long process.)

```
{BEEP 2}
{BEEP 4}
{BEEP 4}
{BEEP 2}
{BEEP 3}{WAIT @NOW+@TIME(0,0.5)}
{BEEP 2}
{BEEP 1}
```

The *argument* in the WAIT command must contain a date plus a time. If you want the program to wait until 6:00 p.m. today to continue, you can use the following expression:

{WAIT @INT(@NOW)+@TIME(18,00,00)}

In this example, @INT(@NOW) returns the serial number for 12:00 a.m. on today's date. Then +@TIME(18,00,00) adds 18 hours (or .75 days) to the serial number, causing the WAIT statement to pause macro execution until 6:00 p.m. today.

To make the program pause for 50 seconds, use the following expression:

{WAIT@NOW+@TIME(00,00,50)}

The WINDOWSOFF Command

The WINDOWSOFF command freezes the main part of the screen but enables the display of program commands in the control panel. The WINDOWSOFF command suppresses the current screen display, regardless of whether the program is executing.

Reminder:
WINDOWSOFF
freezes the main
part of the screen.

WINDOWSOFF is particularly useful when you are creating applications for beginning 1-2-3 users. WINDOWSOFF displays only the screen changes that the user *must* see; the command prevents the display of other changes that may confuse beginners. The format of the WINDOWSOFF command is as follows:

{WINDOWSOFF}

In the following example WINDOWSOFF suppresses the automatic screen-rebuilding associated with the /Copy command or the Calc (F9) key:

```
{WINDOWSOFF}
/cRANGE_1~RANGE_2~{CALC}
```

Cue:
Use
WINDOWSOFF to
reduce program
execution time.

The WINDOWSOFF and PANELOFF commands can have a significant effect on program execution time, in some cases reducing execution time by as much as 50 percent. Clearly, performance improvements depend on the particular application.

The program in figure 14.15 illustrates how to use WINDOWSOFF and PANELOFF to eliminate screen shifting and to reduce execution time for a graph "slide show" presentation. The program displays a sequence of graphs uninterrupted by intervening worksheet screens.

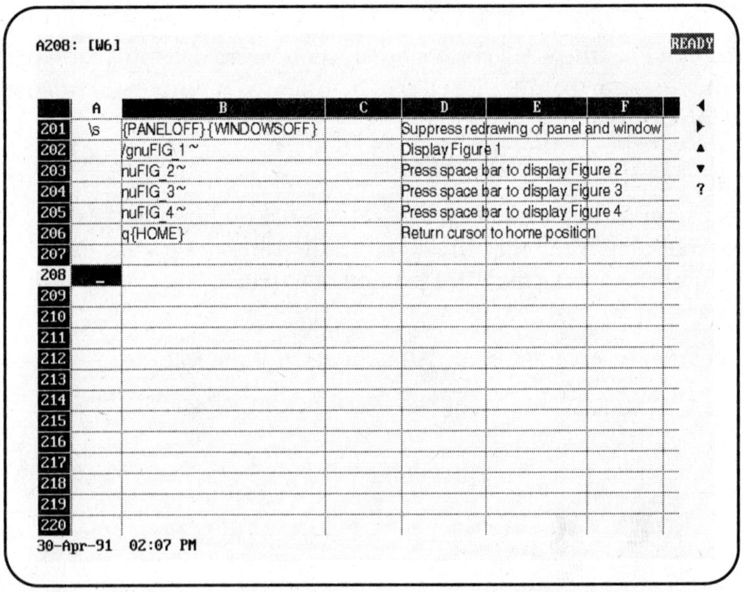

Fig. 14.15. The WINDOWSOFF command used for a graphics slide show.

Be aware that if an error occurs while WINDOWSOFF is in effect, normal updating of the worksheet window does not occur. Develop and test your programs without the WINDOWSOFF and WINDOWSON commands; then add these commands to the debugged and tested programs.

The WINDOWSON Command

The WINDOWSON command unfreezes the screen, enabling the display of executing program operations. This command commonly is used to enable the display of the 1-2-3 menu structures. The format of the WINDOWSON command is as follows:

> {WINDOWSON}

In figure 14.15, the WINDOWSON command activates display of the worksheet screen after all the graphs have been shown.

Cue:
Use WINDOWSON to enable the display of the 1-2-3 menu structures.

The WRITE Command

The WRITE command writes a string of text to the currently open file. The command's format is as follows:

> {WRITE *string*}

WRITE copies *string* to the open file. The *string* argument can be a literal string, a range name or cell reference to a single cell that contains a string, or a string expression. Because WRITE does not place a carriage-return-and-line-feed sequence at the end of the string, you can use several WRITE statements to concatenate text on a single line. WRITE is well suited to creating or updating a file that contains fixed-length database records. The WRITE command is used in much the same way as the WRITELN command. For example, to write the literal string, PAID, to an open file, you enter the following command:

Reminder:
WRITE does not append carriage returns or line feeds to the string.

```
{WRITE PAID}
```

If the file pointer is not at the end of the file, 1-2-3 overwrites existing characters in the file. If the file pointer is at the end of the file, 1-2-3 extends the file by the number of characters written. If the file pointer is past the end of the file (see the discussion of the SETPOS command), 1-2-3 extends the file by the length of the string.

The WRITELN Command

The WRITELN command is identical to the WRITE command except that WRITELN places a carriage-return-and-line-feed sequence after the last character written from the string. The WRITELN command format is as follows:

{WRITELN *string*}

WRITELN copies *string* (plus a carriage-return-line-feed sequence) to the open file. WRITELN is useful when the file being written or updated uses the carriage-return-and-line-feed sequence to mark the end of its lines or records. In many applications, several WRITE statements are used to write a line to the file; then a WRITELN is used to mark the end of the line. The WRITELN command is shown in figure 14.5.

The /x Commands

In addition to the 53 advanced macro commands, 1-2-3 includes a set of eight /x commands. These commands were included in 1-2-3 Release 1A to provide a "limited" programming capability that went beyond simple keystroke macros. All eight /x commands have advanced macro command counterparts. The eight /x commands and their advanced macro command counterparts include the following:

/x Command	Description	Advanced Macro Command Alternative
/xi	Sets up an if-then-else condition	{IF}
/xq	Quits execution	{QUIT}
/xg	Instructs a program to continue at a new location	{BRANCH}
/xc	Runs a subroutine	{*subroutine*}
/xr	Returns to the next line of the macro calling this subroutine	{RETURN}
/xm	Creates a menu	{MENUBRANCH}
/xn	Accepts input of numeric entries only	{GETNUMBER}
/xl	Accepts input of labels only	{GETLABEL}

Six of these commands (/xi, /xq, /xg, /xc, /xr, and /xm) work exactly like their advanced macro command counterparts. For example, /xq performs exactly like the advanced macro command QUIT. When inserted into a program, both commands produce the same result.

The other two /x commands (/xn and /xl) work a little differently from their advanced macro commands counterparts (GETNUMBER and GETLABEL). The /xn and /xl commands prompt the user for text and numeric data and then place the data in the current cell. For GETNUMBER and GETLABEL to do these same tasks, you must do some additional programming to identify the current cell as the location for the label or number entered.

/xn, unlike GETNUMBER, does not enable users to enter alphabetical characters (except for range names and cell addresses), nor does /xn enable the user to press Enter in response to the prompt. With GETNUMBER, a blank entry or a text entry has a numeric value of ERR. With /xn, however, a blank entry or a text entry results in an error message, and the user is again prompted for a number. This difference can be useful in some applications. For example, if you accidentally press Q (a letter) rather than 1, the /xn command returns an error message.

Except in the rare instances in which /xn and /xl perform differently from their advanced macro command counterparts, the /x commands should not be used in new programs developed in Release 2.3. The /x commands are useful, however, because they enable you to run and to easily modify in Release 2.3 any programs originally developed in Release 1A.

Summary

As you work with the 1-2-3 advanced macro commands, you discover that your powerful spreadsheet program has a rich programming language that can solve many application problems. But macro programs are slow, compared to lower level languages, such as assembly language, or even the higher level languages of C, Pascal, and BASIC. 1-2-3 does not always execute macro programming instructions with lightning speed. You almost always have a trade-off of capabilities; some applications may take a good deal of time to execute. But as you learn to integrate into worksheets the powerful worksheet functions, menu commands, macro key names, and advanced macro commands, you can develop seamless applications that offer a nice balance between programming and development time, as well as program-execution time.

Macro programming gives many 1-2-3 users a sense of satisfaction and accomplishment when they see their ideas transformed into working applications. This chapter provides the groundwork for developing such applications. Experiment with the sample macro programs; you have little chance of damaging or destroying anything, provided that you are prudent when you work with commands that manipulate disk files. Enjoy the adventure of exploring a new language and expressing new ideas!

As you become more experienced with the advanced macro commands, turn to other Que titles such as *1-2-3 Macro Library*, 3rd Edition, for help in becoming an expert advanced macro command programmer.

Part IV

1-2-3 Release 2.3 Command Reference

1-2-3 Command Reference

Worksheet Commands   /W

The /Worksheet commands control the display formats, screen organization, protection, and start-up settings for files. If you want to change these settings for only a portion of the worksheet, use the /Range commands. To change settings that affect the entire worksheet or file, however, use the /Worksheet commands shown on the 1-2-3 side of the pull-out command card in the back of this book.

Worksheet Global Format   */WGF*

Purpose

Defines the display format for numeric values and formulas in the worksheet. Formats previously entered with /Range Format are not affected.

Reminders

- Before you use /wgf, determine your most-used format for numeric data.

- If you want to format only a portion of the worksheet, use /Range Format instead of /wgf.

Procedures

1. Type **/wgf**.

2. Select one of the following formats:

Menu Item	*Description*
Fixed	Fixes the number of decimal places displayed. If the setting is three decimal places, for example, the number 1.2345 appears as 1.235.
Sci	Displays in scientific notation large or small numbers. In a two-decimal format, for example, the number 950000 appears as 9.50E+05.
Currency	Displays the default currency symbol (for example, $ or £) and commas. Currency format often is used for the first row and the bottom line of financial statements. In a two-decimal format, for example, 24500.254 appears as $24,500.25.
,	Marks thousands and multiples of thousands. In a 2-decimal format, for example, 24500.254 appears as 24,500.25.
General	Suppresses zeros after the decimal point, uses scientific notation for large or small numbers, and serves as the default decimal display
+/−	Creates horizontal bar graphs or time-duration graphs on computers that do not have graphics. A positive number appears as (+) symbols; a negative number, as (−) symbols. The number of symbols equals the integer value of the cell contents. For example, 6.23 appears as ++++++.
Percent	Displays a decimal number as a percentage followed by a percent sign (%). In a two-decimal format, for example, 0.346 appears as 34.60%.

Menu Item	Description
Date	Displays the date in one of five customary formats. One selection under **Date** formats the time display. The are the **Date** selections:

1 DD-MMM-YY	12-Jan-91
2 DD-MMM	12-Jan
3 MMM-YY	Jan-91
4 Long Int'l format (default MM/DD/YY)	01/12/91
5 Short Int'l format (default MM/DD)	01/12

Time:

1 HH:MM:SS AM/PM	1:04:34 PM
2 HH:MM AM/PM	1:04 PM
3 Long Int'l format (default HH:MM:SS)	13:04:34
4 Short Int'l format (default HH:MM)	13:04

Menu Item	Description
Text	Evaluates formulas as numbers but displays formulas as text. Numbers in cells appear in **General** format.
Hidden	Hides cell contents from display and printing but evaluates contents. Use this command to hide confidential notes or variables.

3. After you select **Fixed**, **Sci**, **Currency**, **,** (comma), or **Percent**, enter the number of decimal places. 1-2-3 normally truncates trailing zeros, but these appear for the number of decimal places you set.

4. Press Enter.

Important Cues

- Use /**Range** Format to format only a portion of the worksheet.

- Use **Text** format to display formulas as text while still using the numeric result from the formula.

- If you enter a number too large for the formatted cell, the cell fills with asterisks. To remove them, move the pointer to the cell, select /**Worksheet** Column Set-Width, and press the right-arrow key until the column is wide enough to display the entire number.

- To display non-USA formats with commands, use /**Worksheet Global Default Other International**. Using /**Worksheet Global Format** also can save memory. Individual cell formats set with /**Range Format** use more memory.

Cautions

- /wgf rounds displayed numbers to the specified decimal setting, but calculations are performed to 15-decimal precision. To keep apparently wrong values from being displayed, use @ROUND to round formula results so that calculated results match displayed values.

- Other users may enter percentage values incorrectly if you use the **Percent** format. You should include a screen prompt to remind operators to place a percent sign (%) after percentages so that 1-2-3 automatically divides the entry by 100.

For more information, see /**Range Format**, /**Worksheet Global Default**, *and Chapter 5.*

Worksheet Global Label-Prefix   /WGL

Purpose

Selects how you want text labels aligned throughout the worksheet.

Labels narrower than the cell width can be aligned to the left, right, or center. Labels longer than the cell width are left-aligned. Previously entered labels do not change.

Reminders

- Before you begin building the worksheet, decide how to align the labels. Use /wgl to select left-alignment (the default setting), right-alignment, or center-alignment.

- If you use /wgl after you begin to build the worksheet, existing labels are not affected. Any alignment previously set with /**Range Label** is not altered by /wgl.

- To change the alignment of labels in a single cell or a range of cells, use /**Range Label**.

Procedures

1. Type /**wgl**.

2. Select one of the following:

Menu Item	Description
Left	Aligns label with cell's left edge
Right	Aligns label with cell's right edge
Center	Centers label in a cell

3. Type the labels as you want them to appear on the worksheet.

Important Cues

- Align labels in a cell by entering one of the following prefixes before you type the label:

Label Prefix	Function
' (apostrophe)	Aligns label to the left (default)
" (quotation mark)	Aligns label to the right
^ (caret)	Centers label in the cell
\ (backslash)	Repeats character to fill the cell

Note: The backslash (\) label prefix cannot be selected with /wgl.

- The label prefix appears as the first character in the control panel when the cell pointer is positioned on a cell that contains a label. Use /**W**orksheet **G**lobal to show the global label prefix.

- You must enter a label prefix in front of labels that begin with a number or formula symbol. Supply a prefix such as in one of the following correct examples:

Correct	· Incorrect
'2207 Cheyenne Dr.	2207 Cheyenne Dr.
"34-567FB	34-567FB

- To turn a number into a label, place the cell pointer on the number you want to change and press Edit (F2). Then press Home to move the cursor to the beginning of the number; type the label prefix and press Enter. *Caution:* If you format numbers as text, formulas evaluate the characters as zeros.

- Because every line of macro code must be entered as a string, a label prefix *must* precede text used as macro code. For example, if your macro line begins with the command sequence /ppooc, you must precede the entry with a label prefix such as '/ppooc; otherwise, the keystrokes in the macro select the command instead of typing macro code.

- Preserve a formula that has an unidentified error by adding a label prefix before the formula. Consider the following formula:

  +B5*@PMT(B16B12/12,B14*12)

  If you enter this formula, 1-2-3 signals an error and enters EDIT mode. (The problem is a missing comma after B16.) If you cannot find the error, press Home to move to the beginning of the formula. Type an apostrophe and press Enter. The formula is accepted as a text label, and you can return to the formula later to look for the error and make the correction. Delete the apostrophe and press Enter after you make the correction.

- To turn a numeric label into a number, use EDIT mode and delete the label prefix.

Caution

Numbers or formulas preceded by a label prefix have the value of zero when evaluated by a numeric formula. In a database query, you must use text searches to search for numbers that have a label prefix.

For more information, see /**Range Label** *and Chapter 5.*

Worksheet Global Column-Width   /WGC

Purpose

Sets the column width for the entire worksheet. Column widths set with /Worksheet Column are not affected.

Reminder

Before you use /wgc, decide on the column widths you need for the worksheet and position the cell pointer so that an average column width shows.

Procedures

1. Type /**wgc**.

2. Enter a number for the column width used most frequently or press the right- or left-arrow key to increase or decrease the column width.

3. Press Enter.

Important Cues

- Use /Worksheet Column Set-Width to set individual columns so that numbers and labels display correctly. When the column width is too narrow for the value entered, asterisks display in the cell.

- Any global column width can be set to a new width with /Worksheet Global Column-Width. Column widths previously set with /Worksheet Column Set-Width keep their original setting.

- The default column width for all columns is 9 characters. Column width settings can range from 1 to 240 characters.

- You can see the current setting for the global column width by selecting /Worksheet Status.

Caution

If you use a split worksheet and change the column width in one or both windows, settings used in the bottom or right windows are lost when the windows are cleared. 1-2-3 keeps the column widths used in the top window of a horizontal split or the left window of a vertical split.

For more information, see /**Worksheet Column** *and Chapter 4.*

Worksheet Global Recalculation   /WGR

Purpose

Defines how worksheets recalculate and how many times they calculate.

Reminders

- You may need to use this command more than once. The first time, use it to set whether calculation is automatic or manual. The second time, use the menu to define how you want calculations done or how many times calculations should be done.

- Recalculation can be set to Automatic or Manual. Use Manual recalculation to increase data-entry speed on large worksheets or databases. By selecting either the Columnwise or Rowwise option, you can have 1-2-3 calculate formulas in a particular order. You also can use /wgr to calculate a formula many times to ensure that you achieve correct results.

- If you change recalculation to Columnwise or Rowwise, enter formulas in a specific order so that they are calculated correctly. 1-2-3's default settings are Natural and Automatic recalculation. In nearly all cases, you should leave recalculation in Natural mode.

Procedures

1. Type /**wgr**.

2. Select one of the following:

Menu Item	Description
Natural	Calculates formulas in the order the results are needed (the normal worksheet setting for the order of recalculation)
Columnwise	Starts at the top of column A and recalculates downward; then moves to column B
Rowwise	Starts at the beginning of row 1 and recalculates to the end; then continues through the following rows
Automatic	Recalculates whenever cell contents change (the normal worksheet setting for when recalculation occurs)
Manual	Recalculates only when you press Calc (F9) or when {CALC} is encountered in a macro. The CALC indicator appears at the bottom of the screen when recalculation is advised.
Iteration	Recalculates the worksheet a specified number of times.

3. If you select Iteration, enter a number from 1 to 50. The default setting is 1. Iteration works with Columnwise and Rowwise recalculations or with Natural recalculation when the worksheet contains a circular reference.

4. If you selected Columnwise or Rowwise recalculation, you may need to repeat Step 1 and select Iteration in Step 2. In Step 3, enter the number of recalculations necessary for correct results. Columnwise and Rowwise recalculations often require multiple calculations for all worksheet results to be correct.

Important Cues

- Display the current recalculation setting by selecting /**Worksheet Global**.

- **Columnwise** or **Rowwise** recalculation often requires multiple recalculations. Set the number of automatic recalculations by selecting /**wgr** and choosing **Iteration**.

Caution

When you use **Manual** recalculation, the screen display is not valid when the CALC indicator appears at the bottom of the screen. This indicator means that changes have been made to the worksheet and that you should press Calc (F9) so that 1-2-3 recalculates the worksheet to reflect the changes.

For more information, see /**Worksheet Status**, /**Worksheet Insert [Column, Row]** *and Chapter 4.*

Worksheet Global Protection   /WGP

Purpose

Protects the entire worksheet from being changed.

Cells previously marked with the /**Range Unprot** command are still unprotected when worksheet protection is on.

Reminder

Before you enable worksheet protection, save time by making sure that the worksheet is complete. After the worksheet is protected, you must disable protection or unprotect a range before you can modify the worksheet.

Procedures

1. Type /**wgp**.

2. Select one of the following options:

Menu Item	*Description*
Enable	Protects the worksheet. Only cells specified with /**Range Unprot** can be changed.
Disable	Unprotects the worksheet. Any cell can be changed.

Important Cues

- Before or after you protect the entire worksheet, you can use /**Range** Unprot to specify cells that can be changed.

- When global protection is enabled, protected cells display PR in the status line. Unprotected cells always display U in the status line.

- While /**Worksheet** Global **Protection** is enabled, the /**Range** Input commands restrict the cell pointer to cells unprotected by the /**Range** Unprot command. This arrangement makes movement between data-entry cells easier.

Cautions

- Macros that change cell content can change only unprotected cells. When you program macros, include code necessary to enable or disable protection.

- /Worksheet Erase is one of the few commands that can be used while /Worksheet Global **Protection** is enabled.

For more information, see /**Range** **Unprot**, /**Range** **Prot**, *and Chapter 4.*

Worksheet Global Default /WGD

Purpose

Specifies display formats and start-up settings for hardware.

With this command, you can control how 1-2-3 works with the printer; which disk and directory are accessed automatically; which international displays are used; and which type of clock is displayed. The settings can be saved so that each time you start 1-2-3, the specifications go into effect. For temporary changes, see the /**File** or /**Print** menu options.

Reminder

Before you set the interface for serial printers, find out the baud rate of your printer. The printer should be set to standard operating-system serial printer settings of 8 bits, no parity, and 1 stop bit (2 stop bits at 110 baud). These printer settings can be set with microswitches (DIP switches in your printer) and are normally preconfigured at the factory.

Procedures

1. Type **/wgd**.

2. Select from the following the setting you want to change:

Menu Item	*Description*
Printer	Specifies printer settings and connections. Choose from the following options:
Interface	Selects parallel or serial port from 8 settings, 1 through 8. The menu displays each of the 8 ports. The initial setting is 1 (Parallel 1).
AutoLF	Tells 1-2-3 whether your printer inserts its own line feed or whether 1-2-3 should insert a line feed. If the printer prints double spaces or overlapped printing, choose the opposite setting.
Left	Sets left margin. The default is 4, 0-240.
Right	Sets right margin. The default is 76, 0-240.
Top	Sets top margin. The default is 2, 0-32.
Bottom	Sets bottom margin. The default is 2, 0-32.
Pg-Length	Sets page length. The default is 66, 1-100.
Wait	Pauses for page insert
Setup	Creates initial printer-control code
Name	Selects from multiple printers
Delay	Specifies the amount of time 1-2-3 should wait for the printer to print (in minutes) before signalling an error. You can enter any number between 0 and 30. The default is 30.

Menu Item	Description
	Specify 0 if you want 1-2-3 to wait for the printer for an indeterminate length.
Quit	Returns to the /Worksheet Global Default menu.
Directory	Specifies directory for read or write operations. Press Esc to clear. Type the new directory and press Enter.
Status	Displays settings for /Worksheet Global Default
Update	Saves to disk the current global defaults for use during the next start-up
Other	Provides the following options:
International	Specifies display settings for **Punctuation, Currency, Date, Time,** and **Negative** formats
Help	Enables you to choose whether the Help file is immediately accessible from disk (**Instant**) or whether the Help file is on a removable disk (**Removable**)
Clock	Enables you to choose between **Standard** and **International** date and time formats or to have **None** displayed on the screen. Clock displays the date and time set by other commands, and Filename displays the file name instead of the date and time.
Undo	Offers two options: **Enable,** which enables the Undo feature; and **Disable,** which disables the Undo feature
Beep	Offers two options: **Yes,** which turns the computer's sound on; and **No,** which turns it off

Menu Item	Description
Add-In	Specifies the 1-2-3 add-ins you want to attach and invoke automatically each time you start 1-2-3
Expanded-Memory	Specifies how you want 1-2-3 to use expanded memory (assuming that you are using expanded memory)
Autoexec	Provides two options: **Yes**, which automatically executes autoexecute macros (\0); and **No**, which stops autoexecute macros from executing
Quit	Returns to the worksheet

Important Cue

Changes made with /Worksheet **G**lobal **D**efault are good only while 1-2-3 is running. To save the settings so that they load automatically at start-up, select /Worksheet **G**lobal **D**efault **U**pdate.

For more information, see Chapter 5.

Worksheet Global Zero   /WGZ

Purpose

Suppresses zeros in displays and printed reports so that only nonzero numbers appear; also enables you to display a label instead of a zero.

When /Worksheet **G**lobal **Z**ero is in effect, zeros from formulas and typed entries are hidden.

Reminder

Protect hidden zeros in the worksheet by using the /Worksheet **G**lobal **P**rotection and /**R**ange **U**nprot commands. Doing so prevents users new to 1-2-3 from typing over or erasing necessary hidden zero values or formulas.

Procedures

1. Type /**wgz**.
2. Choose one of the following options:

Menu Item	Description
No	Displays as zeros those cells containing a zero or a result of zero
Yes	Displays as blank those cells containing a zero or a result of zero
Label	Displays a custom label that replaces those cells containing a zero or zero result

3. If you choose Label, enter the label you want displayed. Precede the label with an apostrophe (') for left-alignment or with a caret ($^\wedge$) for right-alignment. The default label alignment is right-alignment.

Important Cues

- Zeros that continue to display are actually values greater than zero; however, their format displays them rounded to a zero value.

- Suppressed zeros in formulas and typed entries are still evaluated as zeros by other formulas.

Caution

If zeros are suppressed, you easily can erase or write over portions of the worksheet that appear blank but contain suppressed zeros. To prevent accidental erasures and typeovers, use /Worksheet Global Protection Enable and /Range Unprot.

For more information, see **/Worksheet Global Protection**, **/Range Prot**, **/Range Unprot**, *and Chapter 4.*

Worksheet Insert [Column, Row]　　　/WIC or /WIR

Purpose

Inserts one or more blank columns or rows in the worksheet. Use this command to add space for formulas, data, or text.

Reminder

Before you use /wi, do one of the following:

- Place the cell pointer in the column you want to move to the right when one or more columns are inserted.

- Place the cell pointer in the row you want to move down when one or more rows are inserted.

Procedures

1. Type /**wi**.

2. Select one of the following:

Menu Item	Description
Column	Inserts column(s) at the cell pointer; moves the current column right
Row	Inserts row(s) at the cell pointer; moves the current row down

3. If you choose **Column**, move the cell pointer right to highlight one cell for each column you want inserted.

   If you choose **Row**, move the cell pointer down to highlight one cell for each row you want inserted.

Important Cues

- Addresses and ranges adjust automatically to the new addresses created when columns or rows are inserted.

- Check all worksheet areas for composition, lines, and layout that may have changed. Use /**Move** to reposition labels, data, and formulas.

Cautions

- Cell addresses in macros do not adjust automatically. Adjust cell addresses in macros to reflect the inserted column(s) or row(s). Therefore, you always should use range names instead of cell addresses to ensure that your macros adjust correctly.

- Make certain that inserted columns and rows do not pass through databases, print ranges, or a column of macro code. Macros stop execution if they reach a blank cell. Database and data-entry macros may stop or work incorrectly if they encounter unexpected blank columns or rows in the database or data-entry areas.

*For more information, see /***Worksheet Delete** *and Chapter 4.*

Worksheet Delete   */WDC or /WDR*
[Column, Row]

Purpose

Deletes one or more columns or rows from the worksheet.

When you use /wd, the entire column or row and the information and formatting it contains are deleted from memory.

Reminders

- Before you delete a column or row, use the End and arrow keys to make sure that distant cells in that column or row do not contain needed data or formulas.

- Before you invoke /wd, place the cell pointer on the first column or row to be deleted.

Procedures

1. Type **/wd**.

2. Select one of the following:

Menu Item	Description
Column	Deletes column(s) at the cell pointer. Remaining columns to the right move left.
Row	Deletes row(s) at the cell pointer. Remaining rows below move up.

3. Specify a range containing the columns or rows you want deleted.

Important Cues

- /Worksheet Delete deletes all the data and formulas in the column or row. To erase the contents of cells but leave the blank cells in their location, use /**R**ange **E**rase.

- Formulas, named ranges, and ranges in command prompts are adjusted automatically to the new cell addresses after you delete a column or row.

- Use /**M**ove when you need to reposition a portion of the worksheet and cannot delete a column or row.

- Use Undo to reverse an accidental /Worksheet Delete action.

Cautions

- Formulas that refer to deleted cells have the value ERR.

- Deleting all cells belonging to a named range leaves the named range in formulas, but as an undefined name. You must redefine the name by using /**Range Name**.

- Deleting a row that passes through an area containing macros can create errors in the macros. Deleting code in the middle of the macro causes problems, and deleting a blank cell between two macros merges their code.

For more information, see /**Worksheet Insert**, /**Range Erase**, *and Chapter 4.*

Worksheet Column
[Set-Width, Reset-Width,
Hide, Display,   */WCR or /WCH or /WCS*
Column-Range]   *or /WCD or /WCC*

Purpose

Changes the column-display characteristics of one or more columns.

Columns wider than nine characters are needed to display large numbers, to display dates, and to prevent text from being covered by adjacent cell entries. Narrow column widths are useful for short entries, such as (Y/N), and for organizing the display layout.

Use **Hide** to hide columns you do not want to display or print. Redisplay these columns with the **Display** command.

Reminders

- Make certain that changing the width of a column does not destroy the appearance of displays in another portion of the worksheet.

- Move the cell pointer to the widest entry in the column before you use /wcs.

Procedures

1. Type /**wc**.

2. Select one of the following menu items:

Menu Item	Description
Set-Width	Sets a new column width
Reset-Width	Returns to the global width default
Hide	Hides the column(s) from view or from printing
Display	Displays the hidden column(s)
Column-Range	Sets the width of more than one column; provides the following options:
Set-Width	Sets new column widths
Reset-Width	Returns to the global width default

3. If you chose Set-Width, enter the new column width by typing the number of characters or by pressing the left- or right-arrow key to shrink or expand the column.

If you chose Hide or Display, indicate the columns you want changed. When you choose Display, hidden columns are displayed.

If you chose Column-Range, choose Set-Width or Reset-Width; indicate the columns you want to change and enter the column width as a number or press the left- or right-arrow key to shrink or expand the column.

Important Cues

- Asterisks appear in a cell whose column is too narrow to display numeric or date information.

- Text entries wider than the cell may be partially covered by text or numeric entries in the cell to the right.

- Use /Worksheet Global Column-Width to set the column width for columns that were not set individually with /Worksheet Column.

- Column width settings from /Worksheet Column override settings from /Worksheet Global Column-Width.

- You can use /wch to suppress columns in the current window without affecting the display in other windows. When the windows are cleared, the settings used in the top window of a horizontal split or the left window of a vertical split are kept; the settings used in the bottom or right windows are lost.

- When preparing reports, use /wch to hide the display of unnecessary data and reduce the number of printed columns.

Cautions

- Be sure that others who use your worksheet are aware of the hidden columns. Although the values and formulas of hidden columns work properly, the display may be confusing if data appears to be missing.

- When cells are hidden on an unprotected worksheet, ranges copied or moved to the hidden area overwrite existing data.

For more information, see Chapter 4.

Worksheet Erase   /WE

Purpose

Erases the current worksheet from memory, leaving a blank work-sheet on-screen.

Use this command to clear away old work after you have saved it and to start fresh with a blank worksheet.

Reminder

Be sure to save the worksheet before you use /Worksheet Erase.

Procedures

1. Type **/we**.

2. Select one of the following:

Menu Item	Description
No	Cancels the command, leaving the worksheet in memory
Yes	Erases the worksheet if it has not changed since last being saved. If the worksheet has been changed, and the changes have not been saved, a **No/Yes** prompt appears, asking whether you still want to erase the worksheet. Press **N** to keep; press **Y** to erase the worksheet and return to READY mode.

Caution

If you erase a worksheet from memory without first saving it, the worksheet is lost for good. Make sure that you save worksheets you want to use again.

*For more information, see /**File Save** and Chapter 4.*

Worksheet Titles /WT

Purpose

Displays row or column headings that may otherwise scroll off the screen.

Reminders

- You can freeze cell contents horizontally (in rows), vertically (in columns), or both ways.

- Rows are frozen across the top of the worksheet. Columns are frozen down the left edge.

Procedures

1. If you want column headings at the top of the screen, move the cell pointer so that the column headings you want frozen on-screen occupy the top row of the worksheet.

   If you want row headings along the leftmost edge of the screen, move the cell pointer so that the column containing the leftmost row headings is at the left edge of the screen.

   If you want both row and column headings, move the cell pointer so that the column headings are at the top of the screen and the row headings are in the leftmost column.

2. Move the cell pointer one row below the lowest row to be used as a title and one column to the right of the column(s) to be used as title(s).

3. Type **/wt**.

4. Select one of the following:

Menu Item	Description
Both	Creates titles from the rows above the cell pointer and from the columns to the left of the cell pointer

Menu Item	Description
Horizontal	Creates titles from the rows above the cell pointer
Vertical	Creates titles from the columns to the left of the cell pointer
Clear	Removes all frozen title areas so that all worksheet areas scroll

Important Cues

- To return the worksheet to normal, select the /Worksheet Titles Clear command.

- /Worksheet Titles does not work when you cannot display the titles and the cell pointer.

- If you split the worksheet into two windows with /Worksheet Window, each window can have its own titles.

- Press Home to move the cell pointer to the top left corner of the unfrozen area.

- Press GoTo (F5) to move the cell pointer inside the title area. This action creates duplicates of the frozen rows and columns. The double appearance can be confusing.

- The cell pointer can enter title areas when you are entering cell addresses in POINT mode.

- /Worksheet Titles can be useful for displaying protected screen areas when /Range Input is active. Position titles so that they display labels and instructions adjacent to the unprotected input range.

- /Worksheet Titles is especially useful for freezing column headings over a database or an accounting worksheet. You also can freeze rows of text that describe figures in adjacent cells.

For more information, see Chapter 4.

Worksheet Window   /WW

Purpose

Displays two parts of the worksheet at the same time. You can choose to split the worksheet horizontally or vertically. The two parts of the worksheet can scroll separately or together, following the same cell pointer movements.

Reminder

Before you use /ww, decide whether you want the worksheet split horizontally or vertically. If you want two horizontal windows, move the cell pointer to the top row of what is to be the lower window. To produce two vertical windows, move the cell pointer to the column that is to be the left edge of the right window. Position the cell pointer to create windows of the desired size. If you want equal-size windows, position the cell pointer midscreen.

Procedures

1. Type **/ww**.

2. Select one of the following:

Menu Item	Description
Horizontal	Splits the worksheet into two horizontal windows at the cell pointer
Vertical	Splits the worksheet into two vertical windows at the cell pointer
Sync	Synchronizes titles so that they move together. Windows are in sync when they are first opened.
Unsync	Unsynchronizes two windows so that they can move independently of each other. You can then simultaneously view different rows and columns in the worksheet. A window moves only when it contains the cell pointer.
Clear	Removes the right or bottom window

3. Repeat Steps 1 and 2 and select Unsync if you want the windows to move independently of each other. You can then simultaneously view different rows and columns in the worksheet.

Important Cues

- Each window can have different column widths. When /Worksheet Window Clear is selected, the settings used in the top or left window determine the column width for the remaining worksheet.

- Horizontal windows are useful when you work with databases. The criteria range and database column labels can appear in the upper window while the data or extracted data appears in the lower window.

- You can use /Worksheet Window to display messages, instructions, warnings, help text, and so on, without having to leave the worksheet.

Caution

Always clear windows and reposition the screen before you invoke windows in a macro. Macros that split windows may become confused if the window configuration differs from what the macros expect.

For more information, see Chapter 4.

Worksheet Status   /WS

Purpose

Displays the current global settings and hardware options. You also can use /ws to check available memory.

Reminder

You can check the worksheet's status whenever a worksheet is displayed. The screen displays the status of the following information:

Conventional memory

Expanded memory

EMS version

Cell pointers

Math coprocessor

Circular reference (one cell in the circular error)

Procedures

1. Type /**ws**.

2. Press any key to return to the worksheet.

Important Cues

- You can reduce the size of a worksheet, thereby increasing the memory available, by deleting unnecessary formulas, labels, and values. Use /Range Format Reset to reset the numeric format for unused areas; then save the revised worksheet to a file and retrieve a smaller version.

- The Circular Reference status displays a single cell within a ring of formulas that reference each other. The Circular Reference status shows only one cell address from this ring.

- You can use the 1-2-3 Release 2.3 Auditor add-in to quickly identify all of the circular references in your worksheet.

For more information, see Chapter 4 and Appendix B.

Worksheet Page   /WP

Purpose

Inserts page breaks in printed worksheets.

1-2-3 automatically inserts page breaks when the printing reaches the bottom margin. For some reports, however, you may want page breaks to occur at designated rows. The /Worksheet Page command indicates to the printer where selected page breaks should occur.

Reminders

- If you want to reuse the worksheet in a form without page breaks, save the worksheet before you insert the page breaks. The /Worksheet Page command inserts a row and inserts characters in that row, altering the worksheet so that it may be inconvenient for normal use.

- Before you use /wp, move the cell pointer to the leftmost column of the current print range and to the row where you want the page break to occur.

Procedures

1. Type /**wp**.

2. Press Enter. A row is inserted where the page is to break, and a double colon (: :) appears in the left column.

Important Cues

- Use /Worksheet Delete Row to delete the row containing a page break.

- /Worksheet **P**age overrides the /**P**rint File **O**ptions **O**ther Unformatted command, which normally suppresses page breaks. If you want to print to disk without using page breaks, make sure that you use /**R**ange **E**rase to remove the page-break markers.

- /Worksheet **P**age does not create page breaks that you can use with the Wysiwyg add-in's **:P**rint commands. You must use **:**Worksheet **P**age to create page breaks for **:P**rint.

Caution

Do not make entries in the row that contains the page-break marker (: :). Entries in this row do not print.

For more information, see **:Worksheet Page** *and Chapter 8.*

Worksheet Learn   /WL

Purpose

Specifies a worksheet range in which keystrokes are recorded when you turn on the Learn feature.

By recording your keystrokes, you can make macros quickly and efficiently. /**W**orksheet **L**earn saves you from having to write down or memorize the keystrokes for your macros and then from having to enter the macro code in the worksheet.

Reminders

- Decide where you want to store your macros. Ideally, macros should be stored to the right and below your active worksheet area so that when you make insertions or deletions in the worksheet, you don't affect your macros.

- Place the cell pointer at the top of the column in which you want keystrokes to be stored.

Procedures

To specify a range for recording keystrokes, do the following:

1. Type /**wlr**.

2. Highlight cells within a single column and press Enter.

3. When you are ready to begin recording keystrokes, press the Learn (Alt-F5) key combination. Enter all keystrokes to be recorded and press Learn (Alt-F5) to turn off the recording.

4. Press Calc (F9) or press Enter or move the cell pointer to transfer the captured keystrokes to the Learn range.

5. Go to the Learn range and edit the macro keystrokes, if necessary.

6. Name the macro with /**R**ange **N**ame **C**reate.

To clear or cancel a Learn range, do the following:

1. Type /**wl**.

2. Select one of the following:

Menu Item	Description
Cancel	Cancels an existing Learn range. This command does not erase any keystrokes in the Learn range.
Erase	Clears all the keystrokes presently recorded in the Learn range

3. If you choose **Erase**, a **No/Yes** menu appears. Choose **Yes** to erase the Learn range; choose **No** to cancel the command.

Important Cues

- Specify a long Learn range to allow plenty of room for the keystrokes to be stored. Each full command is recorded in a single cell. For example, /wir~ would be considered one complete command and would be the only keystrokes stored in a cell.

- If you don't specify a long enough Learn range, you get the message `Learn range is full`, and the Learn feature is turned off automatically. If you get this error message, press Esc to clear the error message, define a longer Learn range, and turn on the Learn feature again (by pressing Learn [Alt-F5]) to continue recording where you left off.

- When recording keystrokes, type the first letter of the commands in the menus so that your macros are easier to read. If you highlight menu options, the pointer movement keystrokes record. (If you choose the /Copy command by highlighting the option Copy instead of pressing **C**, for example, /{R2}~ records instead of /C.)

- Each time you turn on the Learn feature, keystrokes are recorded in the currently specified Learn range. If you already had keystrokes in the Learn range, the most recent keystrokes are appended to the keystrokes you already have recorded.

- If you make a mistake while recording keystrokes, you may want to start over again. Turn off recording by pressing Learn (Alt-F5) and use /Worksheet Learn Erase to clear what has been recorded. You then can turn on the Learn feature again.

For more information, see Chapter 4.

Range Commands   /R

/**R**ange commands control the display formats, protection, and manipulation of portions of the worksheet. (If you want to affect the entire worksheet, as by inserting an entire column, look at the /Worksheet command menu on the pull-out command card in the back of this book. Throughout this section, refer to the /**R**ange commands on the 1-2-3 side of the command card.)

Range Format   */RF*

Purpose

Prepares cells so that they display with a specific format for both values (numbers) and formula results.

/**R**ange Format formats a cell or range of cells so that numbers appear in a specific format: with fixed decimal places, as currency, with commas only, in scientific notation, or as dates. These formats affect both the screen display and printing.

Reminders

- Use /Worksheet Global Format to format the majority of the worksheet's cells that contain numeric data. Use /**R**ange Format to reset formats for areas that differ.

- Use /Worksheet Global Format to format new numbers entered throughout the worksheet. Numbers entered in ranges already formatted with /**R**ange Format are not affected.

- Move the cell pointer to the upper left corner of the range you want to format.

Procedures

1. Type /**rf**.

2. Select a format from the following menu items:

Menu Item	*Description*
Fixed	Fixes the number of decimal places displayed
Sci	Displays large or small numbers, using scientific notation
Currency	Displays currency symbols (such as $ or £) and commas
, (comma)	Inserts commas to mark thousands and multiples of thousands
General	Displays values with up to 10 decimals or in scientific notation
+/–	Creates horizontal bar graphs or time-duration graphs on computers that do not have graphics. Each symbol equals one whole number. Positive numbers display as plus (+) symbols; negative numbers, as minus (–) symbols.
Percent	Displays a decimal number as a whole number followed by a percent (%) sign
Date	Displays serial date numbers in the following five formats; provides the Time option, which offers four formats:

1 DD-MMM-YY	12-Jan-91
2 DD-MMM	12-Jan
3 MMM-YY	Jan-91
4 Long Intn'l (default MM/DD/YY)	01/12/91
5 Short Intn'l (default MM/DD)	01/12

Time:

1 HH:MM:SS AM/PM	1:04:34 PM
2 HH:MM AM/PM	1:04 PM
3 Long Intn'l (default HH:MM:SS)	13:04:34

Menu Item	Description
	4 Short Intn'l 13:04 (default HH:MM)
Text	Continues to evaluate formulas as numbers but displays formulas as text on-screen
Hidden	Hides contents from the display and printing but still evaluates contents
Reset	Returns the format to current /Worksheet Global format

3. If 1-2-3 prompts, enter the number of decimal places to be displayed. The full value of a cell—not the value displayed—is used for calculation. (See the first caution.)

4. If you select **Date** or **Time**, also select a format number to indicate how you want the date or time to appear.

5. Specify the range by entering the range address, highlighting the range, or using an assigned range name.

6. Verify that the specified range is correct.

7. Press Enter.

Important Cues

- /Range Format Hidden is the only format that affects labels. All other /Range Format commands work on values and numeric formulas.

- Dates and times are generated from serial date and time numbers created with @DATE, @DATEVALUE, @TIME, @NOW, and @TIMEVALUE.

- If you use a format other than General, asterisks fill the cell when a value is too large to fit the cell's current column width. (In the General format, values that are too large are displayed in scientific notation.)

- Use /Worksheet Global Default Other International to display non-USA formats or to determine the display of negative numbers in , (comma) or Currency format. Select one of these international format options: Punctuation, Currency, Date, or Time. Or select Negative and choose Parentheses or Sign to enclose negative numbers in parentheses or to precede negative numbers with a minus sign, respectively.

- /Range formats take precedence over /Worksheet Global formats.

Cautions

- /**R**ange Format rounds only the appearance of the displayed number. The command does not round the number used for calculation. This difference can cause displayed or printed numbers to appear to be incorrect. In some worksheets, such as mortgage tables, results may be significantly different than expected. Enclose numbers, formulas, or cell references in the @ROUND function to ensure that the values in calculations are truly rounded.

- Use the **F**ixed decimal format to enter percentage data. Use the **P**ercent format to display or print results. The **P**ercent format displays a decimal numeral in percentage form; a decimal numeral such as .23 is displayed as 23%. If the **P**ercent format is used for data entry, most users see numerals in percentage form (such as 23%) and attempt to enter similar percentages (.24 as 24, for example), producing grossly incorrect entries (such as 2,400%). If the **P**ercent format is used, numeric entries should be followed by a percent sign, as in 24%. The trailing percent sign causes 1-2-3 to divide the value by 100.

For more information, see /**Worksheet Global Format,** /**Worksheet Global Default,** *and Chapters 5 and 6.*

Range Label   /RL

Purpose

Selects how you want to align text labels in cells.

Labels narrower than the cell width can be aligned to the left, right, or center. To change how numbers appear on-screen, use either /**R**ange Format or /**W**orksheet Global Format.

Reminders

- Move the cell pointer to the upper left corner of the range containing the cells you want to align.

- Use /**W**orksheet Global Label-Prefix to align the majority of labels on the worksheet. After building the worksheet skeleton of text, align labels and set column widths by using /**R**ange Label and /**W**orksheet Column Set-Width.

Procedures

1. Type /**rl**.

2. Select one of the following menu items:

Menu Item	Description
Left	Aligns labels with cell's left edge
Right	Aligns labels with cell's right edge
Center	Centers labels in cell

3. Specify the range by entering the range address, highlighting the range, or using an assigned range name.

4. Press Enter.

Important Cues

- The label prefix appears on the first line of the control panel.

- Alignment works only for text smaller than the cell width. Text larger than the cell width is left-aligned. The text that exceeds the cell width squeezes out the cell's right edge.

- To align labels in a cell, enter one of the following label prefixes before typing the label:

Label Prefix	Function
' (apostrophe)	Aligns label to the left
" (quotation mark)	Aligns label to the right
^ (caret)	Centers label in the cell
\ (backslash)	Repeats character to fill a cell (This prefix cannot be selected from the menu.)

- The worksheet starts with labels left-aligned. Use /Worksheet Global Label-Prefix to set the label prefix used by text entries in areas not specified with /Range Label.

- /Range Label does not affect values (numeric cell entries). Values are always right-aligned.

- Labels beginning with numbers or formula symbols require label prefixes. Enter the label prefix before entering the numbers or symbols. This process is necessary for items such as addresses, part numbers, Social Security numbers, and phone numbers, as in the following examples:

Correct	Incorrect
'2207 Cheyenne Dr.	2207 Cheyenne Dr.
"34-567FB	34-567FB

- Use a label prefix to preserve formulas that have errors you haven't identified. For example, if you have a problem with the formula +B5*@PMT(B16B12/12,B14*12), and you don't have time to look for the error (a comma is missing after B16), use an apostrophe label prefix to turn the formula into text. Later, when you have more time, use EDIT mode to remove the apostrophe to change the text back to a formula. Then correct the formula error.

- Document formulas by inserting a label prefix before each formula and copying the formula as a label to the worksheet documentation area. Later, remove the label prefix from the original formula to restore it to its original, operable form.

Cautions

- **/Range Label Center** does not center labels on the screen or page. Use **:Text Align** to quickly center text within a range. If you prefer to work without Wysiwyg, center the text by moving the cell pointer with the text and following these steps:

  1. Enter the text if you have not done so already.

  2. Determine how many leading spaces are necessary to center the text on-screen.

  3. Press Edit (F2); then press Home. The cursor moves to the label prefix at the beginning of the text.

  4. Move the cell pointer right one character and insert spaces in front of the first character to center it.

  5. Press Enter.

- Macro code text must be in the form of labels. If you don't place a label prefix before the macro commands, such as **/wglr**, the keystrokes select menu items.

- Numbers or formulas preceded by label prefixes have a value of zero when evaluated by a numeric formula. In a database query, you must use text searches to search for these numbers that have label prefixes.

For more information, see **/Worksheet Global Label-Prefix,** **:Text Align,** **/Range Format,** *and Chapter 5.*

Range Erase   */RE*

Purpose

Erases the contents of a single cell or range of cells.

Reminders

- Use /Worksheet Erase if you want to erase the entire worksheet.

- If you have any doubts about erasing a range of cells, use /File Save to save the worksheet to a file before erasing the range. Erased cells cannot be recovered.

- Move the cell pointer to the upper left corner of the range to be erased.

Procedures

1. Type /**re**.

2. Specify the range to be erased: enter the range address, highlight the range, or use an assigned range name.

3. Press Enter.

Important Cues

- You can erase the contents of the current cell quickly by pressing Del.

- To erase protected cells, you first must remove worksheet protection by using /Worksheet **G**lobal **P**rotection **D**isable.

- Erasing data or formulas may produce an ERR display in formulas that depend on the erased data or formulas.

- Erasing a range does not change the format, label prefix (if set with /**R**ange **L**abel), or protection status assigned to the cell(s).

- If the Undo feature is enabled, you can press Undo (Alt-F4) if you accidentally erase the wrong range.

Cautions

- /Worksheet **D**elete can be dangerous if you use it to remove a record from a database. You can unintentionally delete a row that looks blank on-screen but contains cells with important data off-screen. Use instead /**Range Erase** and sort down empty records.

- Be careful not to erase formulas or values hidden with /**Worksheet Global Format Hidden** or /**Range Format Hidden**.

For more information, see /**Worksheet Delete,** /**Worksheet Erase,** *and Chapter 4.*

Range Name   /RN

Purpose

Assigns an alphabetical or alphanumeric name to a cell or a range of cells. (See the caution about alphanumeric range names.)

Reminders

- Instead of column-and-row cell addresses, use range names to make formulas and macros easy to read and understand and to make macros self-adjusting. If you frequently print specific areas of a worksheet or go to specific areas, you can name these locations and use the easily remembered range name when asked for the print range of the GoTo location.

- There are two types of range names: defined and undefined. A defined range name refers to a cell or range address and can be used in formulas or command prompts. An undefined range name has not been assigned an associated address or range and can be used only in formulas. Undefined range names are created when you use /**Worksheet Delete** to delete the data in a named range without first deleting the range name. Formulas that use undefined range names result in ERR.

Procedures

To create a range name that describes a single cell or range of cells, follow these steps:

1. Move the cell pointer to the cell or upper left corner of the range of cells to be named.

2. Type /**rn**.

3. Select **Create**.

4. When prompted to enter the range name, press Name (F3) to see a full-screen display of names already in use. If the name you want to use is listed, delete it before you create another range by that name. Press Esc to exit from the list.

5. Type a range name of as many as 15 characters and press Enter. Avoid using symbols other than the underline.

6. To specify the range to be named, enter the range address or highlight the range and press Enter.

To create range names from labels, follow these steps:

1. Move the cell pointer to the upper left corner of the column or row of labels.

2. Type **/rn**.

3. Select **Labels**.

4. Select one of the following menu items:

Menu Item	Description
Right	Uses the labels to name the cell to the right of each label
Down	Uses the labels to name the cell below each label
Left	Uses the labels to name the cell to the left of each label
Up	Uses the labels to name the cell above each label

5. By entering the range address or highlighting the range, specify the range of labels to be used as names and press Enter. Verify that the range encloses only labels.

To delete a range name, follow these steps:

1. Type **/rn**.

2. Select **Delete** to delete a single range name. Select **Reset** to delete all range names.

3. If you select **Delete**, highlight the range name and press Enter. The addresses in formulas of the deleted range names revert to normal cell addresses.

To display the names and addresses of existing range names, follow these steps:

1. Move the cell pointer to a clear area of the worksheet. (The area should be two columns wide and contain sufficient rows to hold all range names.)

2. Type **/rn**.

3. Select **Table**.

4. Press Enter to create a table of range names and their associated addresses.

Important Cues

- Use a range name when you enter a function. Instead of entering a function as **@SUM(P53..P65)**, for example, type it as **@SUM(EXPENSES)**.

- Similarly, use a range name when you respond to a prompt. For example, when the program requests a print range, provide a range name, as in the following:

    `Enter print range:` **JULREPORT**

- To move the cell pointer rapidly to the upper left corner of any range, press GoTo (F5) and then enter the range name or press Name (F3) to display a list of range names. After you have entered the range name or selected a name from the list, press Enter. Press Name (F3) twice if you have a large number of range names.

- You can press Name (F3) while you are building a formula. A list of range names displays, and you can select the name to use in the formula.

- To print a list of range names, use /**R**ange **N**ame **T**able. Then print the range of names and range addresses that 1-2-3 creates.

- /**M**ove moves range names with cells if the entire range is included in the block to be moved.

- Macro names are range names; therefore, macros must be named through the use of /rnc or /rnl.

Cautions

- A range name can be alphanumeric (as in SALES91), but avoid creating a range name that looks like a cell reference (for example, AD19). Such a range name does not function correctly in formulas.

- Use the underscore (_) instead of the hyphen in range names to avoid confusing 1-2-3. For example, the range name SALES_COST can be only a range name, but the name SALES-COST can be one name or a formula that subtracts the value in COST from the value in SALES.

- Always delete existing range names before re-creating them in a new location. If you don't delete an original range name, formulas that used the original name may be wrong.

- Do not delete columns or rows that form the corner of a named range. Doing so produces undefined range names.

- Moving the upper left or lower right corner of a named range shifts the cell addresses that the range name defines.

- When two named ranges have the same upper left corner, moving one of the corners moves the address location for both range names. To move a corner of overlapping named ranges, first delete one range name, move the range, and then re-create the deleted range name in its original location.

- /**R**ange **N**ame **T**able does not update itself automatically. If you move, copy, or change range names, you must re-create the range name table.

For more information, see Chapter 4.

Range Justify /*RJ*

Purpose

Fits text within a desired range by wrapping words to form complete paragraphs.

Use /**R**ange **J**ustify to join and word wrap automatically any lines of text in adjacent vertical cells to form a paragraph. /**R**ange **J**ustify redistributes words so that sentences are approximately the same length.

Reminders

- Delete any blank cells or values between vertically adjacent cells you want to join. Blank cells or values stop text from justifying.

- Move the cell pointer to the top of the column of text you want justified. Make sure that the cell pointer is in the first cell containing the text. In the first line of the control panel, you should see the first words of the text from the first row of the column.

- Remember that unless you specify a range for /rj, other cells are moved to reflect the justification. In figure R.1, a range has been specified in which the text is reformatted; this specification keeps the value in B10 from being displaced.

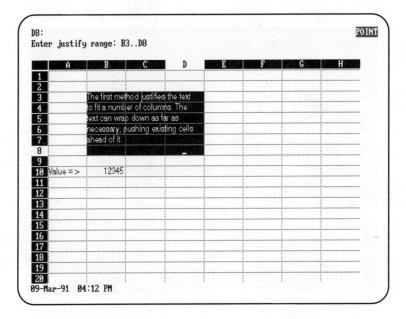

Fig. R.1. *The worksheet range marked for justification.*

Procedures

1. Type /**rj**.

2. Highlight the range in which you want the text to be justified. If you choose not to specify a range for the justification, highlight only the first row of the text column.

3. Press Enter, and the text is justified. If you specified a range, worksheet cells within the highlighted range are justified; cells outside the highlighted range are not moved.

Important Cues

- /**R**ange **J**ustify justifies all contiguous text in a column until justification is stopped by nonlabel cell contents (a blank cell, a formula, or a value).

- If you are uncertain about the results of /**R**ange **J**ustify, save the worksheet with /**F**ile **S**ave before using /**R**ange **J**ustify. You also can use Undo (Alt-F4) to restore the worksheet to its status before the command if you get unexpected results.

- Enter long lists of single-word labels as a single text line and justify the line down a column. Enter the words with a single space between them and make certain that the column width is only wide enough to contain the longest word.

- Use /**File Import** to import text from word processors (ASCII text files only). Text in 1-2-3 can be justified with /**Range Justify** to fit the worksheet.

- The Wysiwyg add-in's **:Text** commands are very easy to use to justify and edit text. If you are working with a large area of text that you need to justify or edit, try using **:Text Edit** instead of /**Range Justify**.

Cautions

- If the specified range is not large enough to hold the justified text, 1-2-3 displays an error message. To solve this problem, enlarge the range or move the text to a new location. If you enlarge the range, you may need to move other cell contents.

- Using /**Range Justify** on protected cells results in an error. Remove protection with /**Worksheet Global Protection Disable**.

For more information, see /**Move**, /**File Import**, /**Worksheet Page**, **:Text Edit**, *and Chapter 5.*

Range Prot and Range Unprot   /RP and /RU

Purpose

/**Range Prot** enables you to restore the identification of worksheet cells from unprotected to protected. /**Range Unprot** enables you to make changes to cells in a protected worksheet.

Use /**Range Unprot** and /**Worksheet Global Protection** to protect worksheets from accidental changes. /**Range Unprot** identifies which cells' contents can be changed when /**Worksheet Global Protection** is enabled. Cells not identified with /**Range Unprot** cannot be changed when /**Worksheet Global Protection** is enabled.

Reminder

Move the cell pointer to the upper left corner of the range you want to identify as unprotected. /**Worksheet Global Protection** may be enabled or disabled.

Procedures

To identify a cell or a range of cells as unprotected, follow these steps:

1. Type /**r**.

2. Select **Unprot.**

3. Specify the range to be identified as unprotected by typing the range address, highlighting the range, or using a range name.

4. Press Enter. On some displays, the contents of cells increase in intensity or change color. If you highlight an unprotected cell, U appears in the first line of the control panel.

To restore the potential for cell protection to an unprotected range, follow these steps:

1. Type **/r**.

2. Select **Prot.**

3. Specify the range by typing the range address, highlighting the range, or using an assigned range name.

4. Press Enter. The contents of cells not identified as unprotected are restored to normal intensity or color, and the U in the first line of the control panel line disappears.

Important Cues

- /Range **Prot** and /Range **Unprot** affect data entry only when /**Worksheet Global Protection** is enabled. The screen display of unprotected contents may be brighter or in a different color, depending on your graphics hardware. (See Chapter 4.)

- Use /**Range Input** to limit cell pointer movement to unprotected cells.

- Use /**Worksheet Global** to see whether worksheet protection is enabled or disabled.

Caution

Macros that make changes to cell contents do not work correctly if /**Worksheet Global Protection** is enabled and the macro attempts to change protected cells. Prevent this situation by limiting cell pointer movement to unprotected cells or by disabling worksheet protection when the macro starts. Macros should enable worksheet protection before they end.

For more information, see /**Worksheet Global Protection,** /**Range Input,** /**Worksheet Status,** *and Chapter 4.*

Range Input   /RI

Purpose

Restricts cell pointer movement to unprotected cells.

/Range Input is an excellent way to create fill-in-the-blank worksheets. Such worksheets prevent inexperienced users from making accidental changes to worksheet labels and formulas.

Reminders

- To use /Range Input effectively, organize your worksheet so that the data-entry cells are together. Include text and examples that show the operator the format and type of data to enter. Figure R.2 shows a worksheet arranged to maximize range input. In figure R.2, the input range is C6..E12.

```
D17: (C2) @PMT(LOAN AMOUNT,INTEREST/12,TERM*12)                    READY

        A       B       C         D        E       F       G       H
1
2                       LOAN CALCULATOR
3
4
5
6                       Price      $12,000.00
7                                      0.200
8
9
10                      Loan Amount  $9,600.00
11                      Interest         0.105 Annual %
12                      Term             4 Years
13
14
15
16
17                      Mo. Payment    $245.79
18
19
20
09-Mar-91  04:13 PM
```

Fig. R.2. *The Loan Calculator worksheet arranged to maximize /Range Input.*

- Before you use /Range Input, use /Range Unprot to identify unprotected data-entry cells. /Worksheet Global Protection does not have to be enabled.

- Move the cell pointer to one corner of a range that includes the unprotected data-entry cells.

Procedures

1. Type /**ri**.

2. Specify the input range to be displayed. Type the range address, highlight the range, or use an assigned range name.

3. Press Enter. The input range's upper left corner is moved to the screen's upper left corner. Cell pointer movements are restricted to unprotected cells in the designated input range.

4. Make data entries, using the arrow keys to move from cell to cell. Press Esc or Enter to exit from /**Range Input** and return to normal cell pointer movement.

Important Cues

- /**Range Input** restricts your key selections to Esc; Enter; Edit; Help; Home; End; and the left-, right-, up-, and down-arrow keys. Use standard alphanumeric keys for data entry and editing.

- /**Range Input** is most valuable when used within macros. Within macros, the command can be used to restrict data entry to one worksheet range for one part of the macro and to another worksheet range for another part of the macro.

For more information, see /**Range Name,** /**Range Unprot,** *and Chapter 4.*

Range Value   /RV

Purpose

Converts formulas in a range to their values so that you can copy only the values to a new location. This command rapidly converts formula results to unchanging values for database storage.

Reminders

- Check to see that the destination area is large enough to hold the copied values, which replace existing cell contents.

- Move the cell pointer to the upper left corner of the range containing the formulas.

- Ensure that the worksheet is calculated. If CALC shows at the bottom of the screen, press Calc (F9) to recalculate the worksheet. If the worksheet is linked to other files on disk, use /**File Admin Link-Refresh** to update linked values.

Procedures

1. Type **/rv**. 1-2-3 displays the prompt `Convert what?`.

2. Specify the source range by typing the range address, highlighting the range, or using a range name.

3. 1-2-3 displays the prompt `To where?`. Press Enter.

4. Specify the upper left corner cell of the destination range by typing a cell address or range name or by moving the cell pointer to this location.

5. Press Enter. The values appear in the destination range and preserve the numeric formats used in the original formulas.

Important Cues

*   **/R**ange **V**alue copies labels and string formulas and converts string (text) formulas to labels.

*   Use **/C**opy to copy formulas without changing them into values.

Cautions

*   **/R**ange **V**alue overwrites data in the destination range. Be sure that the destination range is large enough to receive the data without overwriting adjacent cell contents you don't want to alter.

*   If you make the destination range the same as the source range, formulas in the range are converted to their values. These values, however, overwrite the formulas they came from. The formulas are replaced permanently.

*For more information, see /***Copy**, /**File Admin Link-Refresh**, *and Chapter 4.*

Range Trans   /RT

Purpose

Reorders columns of data into rows of data or rows of data into columns of data.

/Range **T**rans is useful when you want to change data from spreadsheet format (headings on left, data in rows) to database format (headings on top, data in columns), or vice versa.

Reminders

*   Transpose the new data to a clear worksheet area. The transposed data overwrites any existing data.

- Move the cell pointer to the upper left corner of the range of cells you want to transpose.

Procedures

1. Type **/rt**. 1-2-3 displays the prompt `Transpose what?`.

2. Specify the range to be transposed: type the range address, highlight the range, or use an assigned range name and then press Enter.

3. When 1-2-3 displays the `To where?` prompt, move the cell pointer to the upper left corner of the destination cells where the transposed data is copied.

4. Press Enter.

*For more information, see /**Range Value** and Chapter 4.*

Range Search   /RS

Purpose

Finds or replaces text within a label or formula. The search and replace can be limited to a range.

Use this command to search databases quickly or to find locations on a worksheet. The command also is useful for finding and replacing cell references, functions, and range names in formulas.

Reminder

Place the cell pointer at one corner of the range to search.

Procedures

To find a text string in labels or formulas, do the following:

1. Type **/rs**. 1-2-3 displays the prompt `Enter range to search:`.

2. Type the cell addresses or highlight or type a range name to specify the range you want searched. Press Enter. 1-2-3 displays the prompt `Enter string to search for:`.

3. Enter the text string you want to find. You may use either upper- or lowercase text; the /**Range Search** command is not case-sensitive. Press Enter.

4. Choose one of the following:

Menu Item	Description
Formulas	Searches through formulas
Labels	Searches through labels
Both	Searches through both formulas and labels

5. Select **Find**. The cell containing the first occurrence of the string is highlighted.

6. Select one of the following:

Menu Item	Description
Next	Finds the next occurrence
Quit	Stops the search

7. When no more occurrences are found, press Esc or Enter to return to READY mode.

To replace one string with another, do the following:

1. Type /**rs**.

2. Type the cell addresses or highlight or type a range name to specify the range you want searched. Press Enter.

3. Enter the text string you want to find. You may use either upper- or lowercase text; the /**R**ange **S**earch command is not case-sensitive. Press Enter.

4. Choose one of the following:

Menu Item	Description
Formulas	Searches through formulas
Labels	Searches through labels
Both	Searches through both formulas and labels

5. Select **R**eplace.

6. Type the replacement string. Press Enter. The cell containing the first occurrence is highlighted.

7. Select one of the following:

Menu Item	Description
Replace	Replaces the found text with the replacement text and then finds the next occurrence
All	Replaces all occurrences of found text
Next	Finds the next occurrence without replacing the current text
Quit	Stops the search

8. When no more occurrences are found, press Esc or Enter to return to READY mode.

Important Cues

- Use the **R**eplace command to substitute one range name for another in formulas or one constant for another.

- Type the replacement text in the desired combination of upper- and lowercase letters.

- You cannot search for values that appear in cells by themselves. You can search for numbers only if they appear in a label or in a formula.

- You can search and replace any part of a formula: a number, a function, an operator, a range name, or a range.

Caution

Beware of replacing with **A**ll. 1-2-3 searches for the text string and finds it whether it is a whole word or part of another word. You can easily replace text or formulas you did not want to replace. Use the **R**eplace and **N**ext options to be on the safe side.

For more information, see Chapter 4.

Copy and Move Commands

The Copy and Move commands are used to copy or transfer the labels, values, and formulas among cells in the worksheet. You can use /Copy and /Move to copy or transfer the entry in one cell to another cell, from one cell to a new range, or from a range to another range. The commands described in this section of the command reference can be seen on the Copy and Move menus on the pull-out command card in the back of this book.

Copy /C

Purpose

Copies formulas, values, and labels to new locations. The copied data retains its format and its cell-protection status.

The cell addresses in copied formulas either change to reflect the new location or stay fixed, depending on whether you use relative or absolute cell references.

Reminders

- Make sure that the worksheets contain enough blank space to receive the cell or range of cells being copied. /Copy replaces the original contents of cells.

- If the receiving cell address is not close to the cell or range of cells being copied, make a note of the address before issuing /Copy so that you can type the To where? address. Pointing across a long distance to the To where? address can be tedious.

- Before you issue the /Copy command, move the cell pointer to the upper left corner of the range you want copied. If you are copying one cell, put the cell pointer on that cell.

Procedures

1. Type /c.

2. The Copy what? prompt requests the range of the cells to be copied. Enter the range to be copied by typing the range name or range address or by highlighting the range and press Enter.

3. At the To where? prompt, specify the upper left corner of the area where you want the duplicate to appear and press Enter. If you want multiple adjacent duplicates, you can specify the top left corner where each duplicate should appear.

4. Make sure that the copied formulas produce correct answers. If the answers are not correct, the copy procedure probably has adjusted cell addresses that should have remained fixed.

Important Cues

- /Copy creates duplicates of labels and values. Formulas that use relative cell references are adjusted to the new location; formulas that use absolute cell references remain fixed.

- You can make single or multiple copies, depending on the range you enter at the To where? prompt. Enter the ranges as follows:

Original Range Copy what?	*Desired* Copies	*Duplicate Range* To where?
One cell	Fill an area	Row, column, or range
Rectangular range	One duplicate	Upper left cell of duplicate, outside original range
Single column	Multiple columns	Adjacent cells across a row, formed from the top cell of each duplicate column
Single row	Multiple rows	Adjacent cells down a column, formed from the left cell in each duplicate row

Cautions

- Overlapping `Copy what?` and `To where?` ranges (original and duplicate) can cause formulas to yield incorrect results. To avoid producing incorrect results, move the cell pointer off the original cell before anchoring the `To where?` range with a period.

- If the range to be copied to does not have enough room to receive the copied range, the contents of the existing cells are covered by the copied data. To fix this problem, use /Move to move existing data; use /Worksheet Insert to insert blank columns or rows.

For more information, see **/Worksheet Insert Column**, **/Worksheet Insert Row**, **/Move**, **/Range Value**, **/Range Name**, *and Chapter 4.*

Move   /M

Purpose

Reorganizes the worksheet by moving blocks of labels, values, or formulas to different locations.

Cell references and range names used in formulas stay the same, which means that formula results do not change. You cannot move data across files.

Reminders

- Make sure that you have enough blank space in the receiving range to receive the cell or range of cells being moved. The moved data replaces the original contents of the cell.

- Before you issue the /Move command, position the cell pointer on the top left corner of the range to be moved. If you want to move one cell, place the cell pointer on that cell.

Procedures

1. Type /m.

2. The `Move what?` prompt requests the range of the cells to be moved. Highlight a range or enter one by typing the range name or range address and press Enter.

3. At the `To where?` prompt, enter the address of the single upper left corner of the range to which you want to move the cells. Do so by typing the cell address, typing a range name, or highlighting the cell with the cell pointer and pressing Enter.

Important Cues

- /Move does not change cell addresses. The range names and cell references in the formula remain the same.

- Use /Copy when you want to create at a new location a duplicate range of cells while keeping the original range intact.

- Range names move with the moved cells if the named area is completely enclosed or if you specify the range name at the `Move what?` prompt.

Cautions

- The contents of moved cells replace the contents of existing cells. To make room for moved cells, use /Move to move existing data; use /Worksheet Insert to insert rows or columns to provide additional room for copies.

- You cannot move an original so that the duplicate is beyond the worksheet boundary. Use /Worksheet Insert to insert additional rows or columns.

- Moving the anchor cell or the diagonally opposite cell of a named range or formula's range moves the corner(s) of the named range or formula's range to the new location as well.

If you have doubts about what is being moved, save the worksheet, delete the old range name, make the move, and then re-create the range name.

- Moving cell contents over the top of the corner in a formula's range creates an ERR in the referencing formula. The formula's range is replaced by ERR, and all dependent formulas show ERR.

- If a formula uses a named range, and cell contents are moved over a corner of the range, the name is replaced with ERR in the formula. The formula's results also display as ERR.

- Be careful when moving a named range that has the same upper left corner as another range. Moving one range changes the upper left corner of both named ranges but not to the same upper left cell unless the ranges are identical.

For more information, see /**Worksheet Insert,** /**Copy,** /**Range Name,** *and Chapter 4.*

File Commands /F

File commands are used to save and retrieve worksheets, extract a small worksheet from a larger worksheet, combine two worksheets, import ASCII data, and select the drive and directory for storage. Throughout this section, refer to the /File menu on the 1-2-3 side of the pull-out command card in the back of this book.

File Retrieve /FR

Purpose

Loads the requested file from disk.

Reminder

Before you retrieve a new file, use /File Save to save the current worksheet. When a new file is retrieved, it replaces the file currently displayed.

Procedures

1. Type /**fr.**

2. Select the name of the file you want to retrieve, either by typing the name or by using the right- or left-arrow key.

3. Press Enter.

Important Cues

- You can display a listing of file names by pressing Name (F3) in response to the `Enter name of file to retrieve:` prompt. Use the arrow keys to move to the file name you want and then press Enter. To return to the menu without making a selection, press Esc three times.

- Retrieve a single file from a different disk drive or directory by typing the drive designation, the path, and the file name, for example:

  `Name of file to retrieve:` **C:\123\FORECAST\JUNEV3**

  In this example, the file JUNEV3 is located on drive C in the FORECAST subdirectory of the 123 directory. To clear the previous path, you may have to press Esc twice after the prompt.

- Protected worksheets require a password. When you enter a password, be sure to use the same uppercase and lowercase letter combination you originally typed.

- If you attempt to retrieve from a network a file that is in use by someone else, 1-2-3 displays a Yes/No menu. Press **Y** if you want the file without having the reservation. Doing so enables you to use the file, although you cannot save it under the same name. Press **N** if you do not want to retrieve the file. See /File **A**dmin for more information on file reservations.

- When you start 1-2-3, the worksheet file loads automatically if you save the default directory under the name AUTO123.

- To change a drive or directory for the current work session, use the /File **D**irectory command.

- Use /**W**orksheet **G**lobal **D**efault **D**irectory to change the directory that 1-2-3 uses on start-up. Use /**W**orksheet **G**lobal **D**efault **U**pdate to save the settings to the disk.

Caution

The retrieved file replaces the file on-screen. Use /File **S**ave to store the current file or worksheet before retrieving a new one.

*For more information, see /*File **A**dmin, */*File **S**ave, */*File **C**ombine, */***W**orksheet **G**lobal **D**efault **D**irectory, */*File **D**ir, *and Chapter 7.*

File Save /FS

Purpose

Saves the current file and its settings.

/File Save stores files and worksheets so that they can be retrieved later.

Reminders

- Remember to save frequently to guard against data loss.

- Name files so that they are easy to remember and group together. If you give related files similar names (such as TRENDV1, TRENDV2, and TRENDV3), you can use the wild cards * and ? to copy and erase files.

Procedures

1. Move the cell pointer to the cell you want 1-2-3 to display the next time the file is retrieved.

2. Type **/fs**.

3. If the file has not been saved before, 1-2-3 prompts you for a name and displays a list of the worksheet files in the default directory. You can enter the file name for the worksheet by highlighting an existing name; by typing a new name; or by entering a new drive designation, path name, and file name.

4. Press Enter.

5. If a file already exists under the name you have selected, choose one of the following:

Menu Item	Description
Cancel	Cancels the save operation
Replace	Replaces an existing file with the current file
Backup	Saves the file and renames the existing file with the extension BAK

Important Cues

- Give file names of up to eight characters by using the letters A through Z, the numbers 0 through 9, and the underline character (_) or hyphen (-). Spaces cannot be used.

- Password protection prevents unauthorized access to 1-2-3 worksheets. If you save worksheets with a password, the password must be entered before the file can be retrieved. To save a file with a password, follow these steps:

  1. Type /**fs**.

  2. Type the file name, press the space bar, and press **P**.

  3. Press Enter.

  4. Type a password of up to 15 characters (no spaces) at the Enter password: prompt and press Enter. A graphics block appears in place of each letter. Be sure to remember the uppercase and lowercase letter combination. When you retrieve the file, you must enter the password in exactly the same way.

  5. After the verification prompt Verify password: appears, type the password again and press Enter.

     To change a protected file's password, use the Back space key to erase the [Password Protected] message displayed when you use /**F**ile **S**ave. Then repeat Steps 3 through 5.

- From the list of existing files on disk, you can select a file name to save to. When prompted for a name, press Esc to remove the default file name (if displayed). Press Name (F3), use the arrow keys to move to the file name you want to replace, and press Enter.

- Use /**F**ile **L**ist to display the size and the date of the existing files.

- If a file is too large to save in its entirety, use /**F**ile **X**tract to save portions of it to disk as separate files.

Cautions

- Saving a file under an existing file name replaces the old file. This means that you accidentally can write over files you want to keep. A safer practice is to use the **B**ackup option or to save each copy under a different name and to delete old versions later, using /**F**ile **E**rase or the operating system's ERASE command.

- After executing /File Save, do not remove your data disk until the light on the disk drive goes off. Pay no attention to the READY indicator. Wait several seconds after the READY indicator disappears before you remove the disk. If you remove the disk prematurely, information can be lost.

*For more information, see /**File Directory**, /**File Erase**, /**File Xtract**, and Chapter 7.*

File Combine   */FC*

Purpose

Combines values or formulas from a file on disk into the current file. Any part of a saved file can be combined with the current file.

Reminders

- Remember that /File Combine can be used three different ways: to copy the contents from the file on disk to the current file; to add values from the file on disk to the current file; and to subtract incoming values from the numeric values in the current file.

- Before starting the /File Combine operation, you must know the cell references or ranges you want from the disk and the name of the file on the disk.

- The /File Combine operation is easiest if the files on disk contain named ranges for the ranges to be combined with the current file in memory.

- Use /File Import and /Data Parse to bring ASCII files into the current worksheet and organize them. To send the file to an ASCII text file, use /Print File to print the file to disk.

- The format of the cells coming in from disk takes priority over the formats in the current file. Global formats, range names, and column widths do not change.

Procedures

1. Move the cell pointer to the upper left corner of the range in which the data is to be combined.

2. Type /**fc**.

3. Select one of the following choices:

Menu Item	*Description*
Copy	Copies incoming cell contents over the cells in the current worksheet. Cells in the current worksheet that correspond to blank incoming cells do not change. Labels and formulas in the current worksheet are replaced.
Add	Adds values from cells in the file worksheet to cells containing blanks or values in the current worksheet. Labels and formulas in the current worksheet are not changed.
Subtract	Subtracts values from cells in the file worksheet from the corresponding blanks or values in the current worksheet. Labels and formulas in the current worksheet are not changed.

4. Select how much of the saved worksheet file you want to use:

Menu Item	*Description*
Entire-File	Combines the entire file worksheet with the current worksheet. Use when the disk file has been created with /File **X**tract and contains only raw data.
Named/Specified-Range	Combines information from a named range or range address on the disk-based file into the current worksheet. Use when you want to retrieve only part of the information contained in a file on disk.

5. If you select Entire-File, choose a file name from the menu by pressing the right- or left-arrow key, by typing the file name, or by pressing Name (F3) to display a list of file names and then using the arrow keys to select one. Press Enter. If you select Named/Specified-Range, you are asked to enter the range name (or the range address) and the file name.

Important Cues

- If you frequently combine a small portion from a file, first give that portion a range name. Use /**R**ange Name to name the portion of the file and save the file back to disk. You then can use /**F**ile Combine and enter the range name as the part you want to combine.

- When creating worksheets, you can save time by using /**F**ile Xtract and /**F**ile Combine to merge parts of existing worksheets to form the new one.

- When you use /**F**ile Combine Add, cells in the incoming file that contain labels or string formulas are not added.

- Create a macro with /**F**ile Combine to consolidate worksheets.

- Use 1-2-3's file-linking capabilities to link cells in two worksheets.

Cautions

- /fcc combines values, labels, and formulas. All cell references, relative and absolute, are adjusted to reflect their new locations on the worksheet. Cell references are adjusted according to the upper left corner of the combined data range (the cell pointer location). Combined formulas adjust for the difference between the cell pointer and cell A1 on the current worksheet.

- Data copied into the current worksheet replaces existing data. Blank cells in the incoming worksheet take on the value of the cells in the current worksheet.

- Range names are not brought to the new worksheet when a file is combined. This arrangement prevents possible conflicts with range names in the current worksheet. After combining files, you must re-create range names with /**R**ange Name Create or /**R**ange Name Labels.

For more information, see /**Range Name Create**, /**Range Name Labels**, /**File Xtract**, *and Chapter 7.*

File Xtract   /FX

Purpose

Saves to disk a portion of the current worksheet as a separate file. You can save the portion as it appears on the worksheet (with formulas) or save only the results of the formulas.

Reminders

- Extracted ranges that include formulas should include the cells the formulas refer to; otherwise, the formulas are not correct.

- If the CALC indicator appears at the bottom of the screen, calculate the file before extracting values. Press Calc (F9) to calculate the file.

Procedures

1. Position the cell pointer at the upper left corner of the range you want to extract.

2. Type /**fx**.

3. Choose one of the following:

Menu Item	Description
Formulas	Saves as a new file the formulas and cell contents from the current file
Values	Saves as a new file the results from formulas and labels

4. Specify a file name other than that of the current worksheet.

5. Highlight the range of the worksheet to be extracted as a separate file. Enter the range by typing the range address (such as B23..D46), by typing the range name, or by moving the cell pointer to the opposite corner of the range and press Enter.

6. If the name already exists, choose one of the following:

Menu Item	Description
Cancel	Cancels the extract operation
Replace	Replaces the existing file with the extracted file
Backup	Saves the extracted file and renames the existing file with the extension BAK

Important Cues

- If you use /fxf to save a portion of a worksheet, the extracted file can function as a normal worksheet.

- To freeze a worksheet so that formulas and results don't change, extract a file with /fxv. The formulas are replaced with values.

- Use /fx to save memory when a worksheet becomes too large. Separate the worksheet into smaller worksheets that require less memory.

- Increase worksheet execution speed and save memory by breaking large worksheets into smaller ones with /fxf. Link the extracted worksheets so that they still pass data between them (see Chapter 3).

- You can protect an extracted file by using a password. For more information, read about /File Save, earlier in this section of the command reference.

Caution

Make sure that the extracted worksheet does not use values or formulas outside the extract range.

*For more information, see /***File Combine** *and Chapter 7.*

File Erase   /FE

Purpose

Erases 1-2-3 files from disk.

Use /fe to erase unnecessary files from disk so that you have more available disk space. You cannot erase files on disk that are in use with a reservation, as on a network drive. Use /Worksheet Erase to remove files from memory.

Reminders

- Use the operating system's ERASE or DEL command to remove a large number of files. From within 1-2-3, select the /System command, use ERASE or DEL at the system prompt, and return to 1-2-3 by typing **EXIT** and pressing Enter.

- You cannot restore an erased file. Before you erase a file, be sure that you do not need it.

Procedures

1. Type **/fe.**

2. Select the type of file you want to erase:

Menu Item	Description
Worksheet	Displays worksheet files with WK1 extensions
Print	Displays ASCII text files created with /**Print** or another program. The file extension must be PRN.
Graph	Displays files created with /**Graph**, which end with the extension PIC
Other	Displays all files in the current drive and directory

3. Type the path and the name of the file or use the arrow keys to highlight the file you want to erase and press Enter.

4. By selecting **Yes** or **No** from the menu, verify that you do or do not want to erase the file.

Important Cues

- You can erase files from different drives or directories either by specifying the drive designation, path, and file name, or by changing these settings with /**File Directory**.

- Press Name (F3) at step 3 to see a full-screen listing of files.

For more information, see /**File Directory**, /**File List**, *and Chapter 7.*

File List   /FL

Purpose

Displays all file names of a specific type that are stored on the current drive and directory.

/**File List** displays the size of the file (in bytes) and the date and time the file was created.

Reminder

Use /**File List** to select different directories and to display the current files.

Procedures

1. Type /**fl**.

2. Select the type of file you want to display:

Menu Item	Description
Worksheet	Displays worksheet files with WK extensions
Print	Displays ASCII text files created with /**Print** or another program. The file extension must be PRN.
Graph	Displays files created with /**Graph**, which end with the extension PIC
Other	Displays all files in the current drive and directory
Linked	Displays all files linked to the current file

3. Use the arrow keys to highlight individual file names and display their specific information. If the list of file names extends off the screen, use the arrow keys, PgDn, or PgUp to display the file names.

4. Display files from a different directory by moving the cursor to a directory name (such as BUDGET\) and pressing Enter. Move to a parent directory by pressing Backspace. You should press Esc to clear the path if you want to type a new path.

5. Press Enter to return to the worksheet.

Important Cues

- Use the /**File Admin Table** command to create a list of file information in the current worksheet. Be sure that you are in a blank part of the worksheet before you create a table; otherwise, data is erased.

- Use /fl to check your file listing before you use /**File Erase**. You don't want to erase files that are linked to files you still use.

- 1-2-3 displays the date and time each file was created so that you can find the most recent version of a file. (Date and time values are accurate only if you supply the correct entries when you start the computer. Date and time values can be reset at the system prompt through the DATE and TIME commands.)

For more information, see /**File Erase**, /**File Directory**, *and Chapter 7.*

File Import   */FI*

Purpose

Brings ASCII text files from other programs into 1-2-3 worksheets.

Many software programs use ASCII files to exchange data with other programs. Most databases, word processors, and spreadsheets have a method of printing ASCII files to disk.

Reminders

- Remember that you can use /File Import two different ways to transfer data into a 1-2-3 worksheet. The first method reads each row of ASCII characters as left-aligned labels in a column; the second method reads into separate cells text enclosed in quotation marks or numbers surrounded by spaces or separated by commas, colons, or semicolons.

- Be sure that you have enough room on the worksheet to receive the imported data; incoming characters replace the current cell contents. One row in an ASCII file is equal to one row on the worksheet. The number of columns depends on whether the incoming ASCII data is pure text (a single column) or delimited text (multiple columns).

Procedures

1. Move the cell pointer to the upper left corner of the range in which you want to import data.

2. Type /**fi**.

3. Choose how to import the ASCII file:

Menu Item	*Description*
Text	Makes each row of characters in the ASCII file a left-aligned label in the worksheet. Labels are in a single column from the cell pointer down.
Numbers	Enters each row of characters in the ASCII file into a row in the worksheet. Text enclosed in quotation marks is assigned to a cell as a label. Numbers surrounded by a space or separated by commas, colons, or semicolons are assigned to a cell as values. Other characters are ignored.

4. Select or type the name of the ASCII print file. Do not type the PRN extension.

5. Press Enter.

Important Cues

- 1-2-3 cannot import ASCII files that have more than 8,192 rows. Lines longer than 240 characters wrap to the next worksheet row. If necessary, you can use a word processor to read, modify, and divide the ASCII files into shorter lines before saving them to disk as ASCII files.

- You can separate ASCII text files that are not delimited by quotation marks, commas, colons, or semicolons. Use /File Import Text to bring the file into the worksheet. Use /Data Parse to separate the resulting long label into separate cells of data.

Cautions

- Incoming data replaces existing cell contents. If you are unsure of the size of the file you are importing, use the operating system's TYPE command to review the ASCII file.

- Word processing files contain special control codes that 1-2-3 cannot handle. Be sure to save your word processing document as an ASCII text or nondocument file before you try to import it into 1-2-3.

For more information, see /**Data Parse** *and Chapter 7.*

File Directory   /FD

Purpose

Changes the current disk drive or directory for the current work session.

Reminder

Sketching how the directories and subdirectories are arranged on your hard disk makes /File Directory easier to use. Include the types of files stored in different directories.

Procedures

1. Type /**fd**.

2. If the displayed drive and directory are correct, press Enter. If you want to change the settings, type a new drive letter and directory name; then press Enter.

Important Cues

- Access another drive and directory temporarily by selecting /**fr** or /**fs** and pressing Esc twice to clear the current drive and directory from the command line. Then type the drive designator and directory name, including a final backslash (\). You then can either type a file name or press Enter to see a list of file names on that drive or directory; move the cursor and press Enter to select a name from the list.

- Access another directory on the same drive by selecting /**fr** or /**fs** and pressing the Backspace key as many times as necessary to clear the current directory from the command line. Then type the directory name, including a final backslash (\). You then can either type a file name or press Enter to see a list of file names on that drive or directory; select a name from the list.

- Display current file names and directories by selecting /**File List**, choosing **Other**, and pressing **Name** (F3). Press Backspace to go to the parent directory.

- You can change 1-2-3's start-up drive and directory by using /**Worksheet Global Default Directory** to enter a new drive or directory. Save this new setting by using /wgdu.

Caution

When specifying drive letters and path names, be sure to enter the correct symbols. The most common mistakes include using a semi-colon (;) instead of a colon (:) after the drive designator, using a slash (/) instead of a backslash (\) between subdirectory names, and inserting spaces in names.

For more information, see /**Worksheet Global Default Update**, /**File List**, /**File Retrieve**, /**File Save**, *and Chapter 7.*

File Admin Reservation /FAR

Purpose

Controls the reservation status of a file on a network.

Reminder

/**File Admin Reservation** enables you to get or release a file's reservation so that you can make changes to a file and save it under the original file name.

Procedures

1. Type /**far**.

2. Choose one of the following commands:

Menu Item	Description
Get	Gets the file reservation for you after you have opened or retrieved the file and if no one has changed the file on disk after you opened it into memory. The read-only indicator (RO) disappears from screen.
Release	Releases the file reservation so that others can get the reservation. The read-only indicator (RO) appears on-screen.

Important Cues

- If you requested to get the reservation, but it was not available, a message appears to that effect.

- The /**File Save** command saves the worksheet only when you have the reservation for the file. Use the /farg command to get the reservation.

Caution

Do not release the reservation until you have saved the changes with /**File Save**. Releasing the reservation prevents you from making changes to the original file on disk.

For more information, see Chapter 7.

File Admin Table   /FAT

Purpose

Enters a table of files on the worksheet. You select which type of files is in the table.

Reminder

To set up the table, first find on the worksheet an area that is blank or unneeded. Information in the table overwrites information in the same worksheet location.

Procedures

1. Move the cell pointer to an area where the table does not destroy needed information.

2. Type /**fat**.

3. Choose one of the following commands:

Menu Item	Description
Worksheet	Enters a table of WK1 and WKS files
Print	Enters a table of PRN files
Graph	Enters a table of PIC graph files
Other	Enters a table of all files
Linked	Enters a table of files linked to the current file

4. If you choose **Worksheet**, **Print**, **Graph**, or **Other**, press Enter to enter a table for the current directory. If you want a table from another directory, type a different directory and press Enter.

5. Highlight the upper left corner of the range where you want the table and press Enter.

Important Cues

- Use /**File** List to see file information without creating a table on your worksheet.

- The table uses one row for each file plus one row for each directory. In addition, 1-2-3 erases one row at the bottom of the table (after the last entry). Disk files or linked files use four columns.

- The table columns for disk-based files are in the following order: file name, date, time, and file size. Use the /**R**ange **F**ormat command to format the date and time columns so that their entries appear as dates or times.

- The /fat command is an excellent way to read file information into a worksheet so that macros can operate on selected files.

- A table of linked files shows the path name for each linked file, if the path was included in the linking formula.

Caution

Information in the table overwrites information in the worksheet. If you are unsure how many files may be in a table, ensure that you are in a section of the worksheet that will not overwrite existing data.

For more information, see /**File Admin Reservation**, /**File List**, *and Chapter 7.*

File Admin Link-Refresh   /FAL

Purpose

Recalculates formulas in the current worksheet (on a network) that depend on data in other files on disk. Link-Refresh ensures that your worksheet uses current data.

Procedure

Type /**fal**.

Important Cue

Use the /File List Linked command to see whether other files are linked into the current file.

Caution

If the current file is linked to other files that may have changed, use Link-Refresh before printing or reviewing the final results. If you do not use Link-Refresh, your current file's results may be incorrect.

For more information, see /**File List Linked** *and Chapter 7.*

Print Commands   /P

The /**Print** commands print worksheet contents as values or formulas. Use /**Print Printer** to send output to the printer; use /**Print File** to send output (as an ASCII file) to disk; use /**Print Encoded** to send a print-encoded file to disk; use /**Print Background** to send output (as a print-encoded file) to disk and then to the printer in background mode. Refer to the /**Print** menu on the 1-2-3 side of the pull-out command card in the back of this book.

Print Printer   /PP

Purpose

Prints worksheet contents (values or formulas) to the printer.

Reminders

- Before you print, check the lower right corner of the screen to see whether the CALC indicator is displayed. If it is, press Calc (F9) and wait until the WAIT indicator stops flashing before you proceed with the /Print commands.

- /Print Printer prints the worksheet range directly to the printer.

- Remember that all /Print commands apply when output is printed directly to paper, but some do not apply when you use /Print File.

- Before you issue /Print Printer, move the cell pointer to the upper left corner of the range to be printed.

- Before printing, make sure that the printer is on, connected, and on-line.

Procedures

1. Type /pp.

2. Select Range to print a worksheet range.

3. Type the range address, highlight the range, or enter a range name to specify the range to be printed.

4. Select from the other print options explained in the /Print [Printer, File, Encoded, Background] commands section.

   For example, if the material to be printed is the beginning of a report or worksheet, adjust the top of the paper to the top of the print mechanism and select Align to align the printer and the top of the paper. If you are printing an additional part onto an existing page, do not align the paper.

5. Select Go to print.

Important Cues

- For information on printing a graph, see the :Print and PrintGraph sections of the command reference.

- You can use 1-2-3's /**Print** commands to set formats for your reports. Use commands from /**Print** [**P, F, E, B**] **O**ptions to control formats for printing.

- Print an ASCII text file to disk by using /**Print File**. Most popular software programs, including word processing and database programs, can import ASCII text files.

Caution

Do not manually adjust paper in the printer after the **Align** command has been given. Use the **Line** or **Page** command to move paper after it is aligned. Moving paper manually misaligns the paper and 1-2-3's line counter, resulting in large blank spaces in the printout.

*For more information, see /***Print File**, /***Print [Printer, File, Encoded, Background] Range***, and Chapter 8.*

Print File   /PF

Purpose

Prints worksheet contents as an ASCII text file to disk. ASCII text files are a common means of transferring data to and from different software packages.

Reminders

- Before you print the file, check the lower right corner of the screen to see whether the CALC indicator is displayed. If it is, press Calc (F9) and wait until the WAIT indicator stops flashing before you proceed with the /**Print** commands.

- Before you issue /**Print File**, move the cell pointer to the upper left corner of the range to be printed.

Procedures

To create an ASCII file for use in word processing, follow these steps:

1. Type /**pf**.

2. Type a file name in response to the `Enter name of text file:` prompt. Limit the file name to eight characters (don't use spaces). 1-2-3 automatically gives the file name a PRN extension.

3. Select **R**ange.

4. Type the range address, highlight the range, or use a range name to specify the range to be printed to disk.

5. Select **Options Margins None**.

6. Select **Other Unformatted** to remove headers, footers, and page breaks. (These print options can cause extra work in reformatting when the file is imported by another program.) Select **Quit** to return to the main **Print** menu.

7. Select **Go**.

To create an ASCII file to be used with a database program, follow these steps:

1. Reset all numbers and dates to a format understood by the database you are using.

2. Set column widths so that all data is displayed. Make a note of the column position in which each column begins and ends.

3. Type **/pf** and specify a file name.

4. Select **Range**.

5. Specify the range to be printed; you may not want to include field names at the top of databases. Specify the range by typing the range address, highlighting the range, or using an assigned range name.

6. Select **Options Margins None**.

7. Select **Other Unformatted** to remove headers, footers, and page breaks. Select **Quit**.

8. Select **Go**.

Important Cues

- To add multiple ranges of data to an ASCII text file, stay in the /**Print** menu; continue to choose new ranges and to select **Go**. The additional ranges append to the end of the ASCII text file you named with /**Print File**. When you quit the /**Print** menu, all final text ranges are printed to the ASCII file, and the file is closed so that you can no longer append data.

- To see an ASCII text file on-screen, return to the operating system. At the operating-system prompt, type the command **TYPE**, press the space bar, and type the path name and the name of the ASCII text file you want to review. For example, after the C> prompt you can enter **TYPE C:\123\BUDGET\VARIANCE.PRN** and press Ctrl-S to stop the data from scrolling off the screen. Press the space bar to continue scrolling.

- Before you print the file to disk, make sure that the columns are wide enough to display all the data. If a column is too narrow, values are changed to asterisks, and labels are truncated.

- Refer to your word processor's documentation for instructions on importing ASCII files. Refer to your database's documentation for instructions on importing column-delimited ASCII files.

Caution

Different database programs accept data in different formats; check to see in what form dates are imported and whether the receiving program accepts blank cells. Be sure to prepare your 1-2-3 file accordingly before printing to an ASCII file. As a general rule, remove numeric formats and align labels to the left before you print the data to disk. Because of an error in 1-2-3's method of calculating serial date numbers, dates in General format may be one day different from dates used in your database. If the right margin setting is too low, data may be moved to a following page when the file is printed to disk.

For more information, see **/Print Printer,** **/Print [Printer, File, Encoded, Background] Range,** *and Chapter 8.*

Print Encoded   /PE

Purpose

Prints worksheet contents (values or formulas) to an encoded file for later printing.

Reminders

- Before you print, check the lower right corner of the screen to see whether the CALC indicator is displayed. If it is, press Calc (F9) and wait until the WAIT indicator stops flashing before you proceed with the /Print commands.

- Remember that all /Print commands apply when output is printed directly to paper, but some do not apply when you use /Print Encoded.

- Before you issue /Print Encoded, move the cell pointer to the upper left corner of the range to be printed.

- /Print Encoded creates a file on disk that can later be sent to a printer through the operating system's COPY command.

Procedures

1. Type /**pe**.

2. Respond to the `Enter name of encoded file:` prompt. 1-2-3 automatically adds the file extension ENC.

3. Select **R**ange to print a worksheet range.

4. Type the range address, highlight the range, or enter a range name to specify the range to be printed.

5. Select from the other print options explained in this section of the command reference.

6. If the material to be printed is the beginning of a report or worksheet, adjust the top of the paper to the top of the print mechanism. Select **A**lign to align the printer and the top of the paper. If you are printing an additional part onto an existing page, do not align the paper.

7. Select **G**o to print.

Important Cues

- For information on printing a graph, see the **:P**rint and PrintGraph commands later in the command reference.

- You can use 1-2-3's print commands to set formats for your reports. Use commands from /**P**rint [**P**, **F**, **E**, **B**] **O**ptions to control formats for printing.

- Print an ASCII text file to disk by using /**P**rint **F**ile. Most popular software programs, including word processing and database programs, can import ASCII text files.

- You can print an encoded file by copying it to the printer at any time, whether or not 1-2-3 is in use. This capability is useful if you need to use a printer that isn't available where the PC is. When you create the ENC file, ensure that the designated printer is the same type that the file is to be copied to later. After a file has been created, use the COPY command to copy the encoded file to the printer. For example, to copy the FRCST.ENC file in the C:\123 directory to the printer on the first parallel port, type **COPY C:\123\FRCST.ENC/B LPT1** and press Enter. Do not forget the /B part of the command. If you use a PostScript or Apple LaserWriter printer connected to a serial port, use COM1 or COM2 instead of LPT1 or LPT2.

For more information, see Chapter 8.

Print Background   /PB

Purpose

Prints the current job to an encoded file and then to the printer in background mode.

Important Cues

- You must have the 1-2-3 BPRINT utility loaded before you can select /Print Background. To load the BPRINT utility, type **BPRINT** from the operating system before you access 1-2-3.

- The encoded file that /Print Background creates is only temporary. After 1-2-3 finishes printing the file in the background, it erases the temporary encoded file.

Procedure

Type /**pb**.

Cautions

- When you use /Print Background, 1-2-3 does not warn you whether anything is wrong with the printer (such as out of paper or a paper jam).

- Do not attempt to load BPRINT from the /System command while you are running 1-2-3. You must exit 1-2-3 with /Quit and load BPRINT first.

For more information, see **BPRINT** *in Chapter 8.*

Print [P, F, E, B]   /PPR or /PFR or
Range   /PER or /PBR

Purpose

Defines the area of the worksheet to be printed.

Reminders

- Check the lower right corner of the screen to see whether the CALC indicator is displayed. If it is, press Calc (F9) and wait until the WAIT indicator stops flashing before you proceed with the /Print commands.

- Before you print, move the cell pointer to the upper left corner of the range to be printed.

Procedures

To define the worksheet area to be printed, follow these steps:

1. Type /**pp** to print directly to the printer; type /**pf** to print to disk; type /**pe** to print an encoded file that can later be copied to a printer; or type /**pb** to print to the background. Specify a file name if one is requested. 1-2-3 adds the appropriate file extension for **File** or **Encoded** files.

2. Select **R**ange.

3. Type the range address, highlight the range, or enter an assigned range name to specify the range to be printed.

4. Verify that the range is correct and press Enter.

Important Cues

- /**Print [P, F, E, B] R**ange remembers the last print range used, which means that you can reprint the specified worksheet portion without reentering the range. You also can edit existing print ranges.

- Hidden columns within a print range do not print.

- To display the current print range, select **R**ange from the second-level /**Print** menu. The status line displays the current range address, and the specified range is highlighted on the screen.

- To display each corner of the range, press the period key (.). Each time you press the period key, the next corner is displayed.

- Use /**Print [P, F, E, B] O**ptions **B**orders to print headings at the top or side of every printed page. Use this technique, for example, when you want to print database field names at the top of every page.

- Use /**W**orksheet **P**age to insert mandatory page breaks in a range.

- After a range has been printed, 1-2-3 does not advance the paper to the top of the next page. Instead, 1-2-3 waits for you to print another range. To advance the paper, use the **P**age command on the main **Print** menu.

- If the print range is wider than the distance between the left and right margins, the remaining characters are printed on the following page (if printed to paper) or in the rows below the data (if printed to disk).

Caution

If you want long text labels to print, ensure that they are completely within the highlighted range. Highlighting only the cell containing text does not print text that extends beyond the cell.

*For more information, see /****Worksheet Page,** /****Print Printer,** /****Print File,** and Chapter 8.*

Print [P, F, E, B] Line   /PPL or /PFL or /PEL or /PBL

Purpose

Prints blank lines. Use this command to put spaces between ranges on the same paper.

Reminder

/**Print File Line** puts a blank line on paper or in the ENC or PRN file.

Procedures

1. Type /**pp**, /**pf**, /**pe**, or /**pb**.

2. Select **Line** to advance the paper one line or to insert a blank line in a file. Repeat the keystroke (or press Enter) as many times as necessary to advance the paper to the desired position.

Important Cue

Use this command to insert a blank line between printed ranges. You can get paper out of alignment with 1-2-3's internal line count if you change the position of paper in a printer manually (either by turning the platen knob or by pressing the printer's line feed button). Blank lines in the middle of printed output can signify that the printer and 1-2-3 are out of alignment. To realign the paper and reset 1-2-3, turn off the printer and roll the paper until the top of a page is aligned with the print head. Then turn on the printer again and use /**Print Printer Align** to reset 1-2-3.

For more information, see Chapter 8.

Print [P, F, E, B] Page /PPP or /PFP or /PEP or /PBP

Purpose

Ejects the page in the printer or marks the end of the current page in an ENC or PRN file. Paper alignment is maintained.

Reminders

- All /**P**rint commands apply when output is printed directly to paper, but some do not apply when output is directed to disk.

- Use /**W**orksheet **P**age to create a page break in a worksheet. When you print the worksheet, a new page begins at the page break.

Procedures

1. Type /**pp**, /**pf**, /**pe,** or /**pb**.

2. Select **P**age to advance to the next page and print the footer at the bottom of the page.

Important Cue

If the top of the paper is not in line with the print head when the paper is advanced, manually move the paper into position and reset 1-2-3 with /**P**rint **P**rinter **A**lign.

Cautions

- The length of the printed page may not match the length of the paper. Check the paper-length settings with /**P**rint [**P, F, E, B**] **O**ptions **P**g-Length. This problem also occurs when the page-length setting does not match the number-of-lines-per-inch setting.

- The paper in the printer can get out of alignment if you manually advance the paper to the top of the next page. This misalignment causes printing over the paper perforation and blanks in the middle of the page. To realign the paper and reset 1-2-3, turn off the printer and roll the paper until the top of a page is aligned with the print head. Then turn on the printer again and use /**P**rint **P**rinter **A**lign to reset 1-2-3.

For more information, see Chapter 8.

Print [P, F, E, B] *Options Header* /PPOH or/PFOH or /PEOH or /PBOH

Purpose

Prints a header below the top margin on each page. Use the **Header** option to print page numbers, dates, or a running title in the heading. Two blank lines are inserted after the header.

Reminders

- Use /Print [**P, F, E, B**] Options Borders to print column headings above data.

- A header uses the three lines below the top margin.

Procedures

1. Type **/pp**, **/pf**, **/pe**, or **/pb**.

2. Select **Header**.

3. Type a header as wide as the margin and paper width allow. The header can be up to 240 characters wide.

4. Press Enter.

Important Cues

- The date and page number can be printed automatically in a header. Enter an at sign (@) where you want the date to appear; enter a pound sign (#) where you want the page number. The # causes page numbering to begin with 1 and increase by 1 sequentially. Page numbering restarts at 1 when you issue an **Align** command.

- Break the header into as many as three centered segments by entering a vertical bar (|) between segments. For example, to print at page 21 a three-segment header that uses the computer's internal date of October 30, 1991, enter the following:

  @|Hill and Dale Landscaping|Page #

  The header appears as follows:

  ```
  30-Oct-91    Hill and Dale Landscaping    Page 21
  ```

- Create a header from cell contents by typing a backslash (\) in the header, followed by the cell reference that contains header information. Typing **\B12**, for example, creates a header out of the information in B12. This capability cannot be used in combination with other header data, and the cell contents are left-aligned in the header.

- Use **/Print [P, F, E, B]** Options Borders Rows to select worksheet rows that are printed above the data on each page. The **B**orders command is especially useful for printing database column headings above the data on each page.

For more information, see **/Print [Printer, File, Encoded, Background] Options Margins,** **/Print [Printer, File, Encoded, Background] Options Borders,** **/Print [Printer, Encoded, Background] Options Setup,** *and Chapter 8.*

Print [P, F, E, B] Options Footer /PPOF or /PFOF or /PEOF or /PBOF

Purpose

Prints a footer above the bottom margin of each page.

Reminders

- Use **/Print [P, F, E, B]** Options Footer to print, for example, a title, department heading, or identifier. Footers can be used to print page numbers and dates automatically.

- Footers reduce the size of the printed area by three rows.

Procedures

1. Type **/pp**, **/pf**, **/pe**, or **/pb**.

2. Select **F**ooter.

3. Type a footer as wide as the margin and paper width allow. The footer can be up to 240 characters wide.

4. Press Enter.

Important Cues

- Use the same cues listed in the preceding section on **O**ptions **H**eaders for creating footers that insert the date, page numbers, or data contained in cells.

- Footers occupy one line. Two blank lines are left between a footer and the body copy. The footer prints on the line above the bottom margin. To print the footer on the final page, select **Page** after **Go**.

For more information, see Chapter 8, **/Print [Printer, File, Encoded, Background] Options Header,** **/Print [Printer, File, Encoded, Background] Options Margins,** **/Print [Printer, File, Encoded, Background] Options Borders,** *and* **/Print [Printer, Encoded, Background] Options Setup**.

Print [P, F, E, B] Options Margins

/PPOM or /PFOM or /PEOM or /PBOM

Purpose

Changes the left, right, top, and bottom margins from the default margin settings.

Reminder

If you are not sure how margins align on the paper, turn the printer off and on to reposition the print head to the zero position. Adjust the paper so that the left paper edge and the top of the paper align with the print head. Choose the **Align** command from the second-level **/Print** menu. Now print a sample worksheet and check alignment.

Procedures

1. Type **/ppo**, **/pfo**, **/peo**, or **/pbo**.

2. Select **Margins**. Specify margins from the following options:

Menu Item	Description
Left	Sets 0 to 240 characters
Right	Sets greater than the left margin but not larger than 240
Top	Sets 0 to 32 lines
Bottom	Sets 0 to 32 lines
None	Sets the left, top, and bottom margins to 0 and the right margin to 240

Important Cues

- Most nonproportional fonts print at 10 characters per horizontal inch and 6 lines per vertical inch. Standard 8 1/2-by-11-inch paper is 85 characters wide and 66 lines long.

- When you want to print to disk, remember that you should set the left margin to 0 and the right margin to 240. These settings remove blank spaces on the left side of each row. Setting the right margin to 240 ensures that the maximum number of characters per row is printed to disk.

- Before printing to disk, select **None** for margins and **/Print File Options Other Unformatted** to remove page breaks, headers, and footers. Page breaks, headers, and footers confuse data transfer to a database. If you are importing the file to a word processor, use the word processor to insert margins, page breaks, headers, and footers.

Caution

If the line length is too short for the characters in a printed line, the additional characters are printed on the following page. To get a full-width print, use a condensed print setup string.

For more information, see **/Print File,** **/Print [Printer, Encoded, Background] Options Setup,** *and Chapter 8.*

Print [P, F, E, B] /PPOB or /PFOB
Options Borders or /PEOB or
/PBOB

Purpose

Prints row or column headings from the worksheet on every page of the printout.

Use row borders to print database field names as headings at the top of each page. Use column borders to print worksheet labels at the left of each page.

When specifying the print range, do not include the rows or columns containing the borders. Doing so causes the row or column borders to print twice, once from the print range and again from **Options Borders.**

Reminder

Before you issue /ppob, /pfob, or /pbob, move the cell pointer to the leftmost column of headings or to the top row of headings on the worksheet that you want repeated.

Procedures

1. Type **/ppob, /pfob, /peob,** or **/pbob**.

2. Select from the following menu items:

Menu Item	Description
Columns	Prints the selected columns at the left side of each page
Rows	Prints the selected rows at the top of each page

3. If necessary, press Esc to remove the current range. Move the cell pointer to the top row of the rows you want to use as a border or to the leftmost column you want to use. Press the period key (.) to anchor the first corner of the border. Then move the cell pointer, highlighting down for more rows or to the right for more columns. (You also can type a range name, if one exists.)

4. Press Enter.

Important Cue

Including borders is useful when you want to print multiple pages. If you want to print sections of a wide worksheet, you can further condense the columns by using /Worksheet Column Hide to hide blank or unnecessary columns.

Cautions

- If you include in the print range the rows or columns specified as borders, the rows or columns are printed twice.

- When you use /Print [P, F, E, B] Options Borders Columns or Rows, the cell pointer's current location becomes a border automatically. To clear the border selection, use /Print [P, F, E, B] Clear Borders.

For more information, see Chapter 8.

Print [P, E, B] Options Setup /PPOS or/PEOS or /PBOS

Purpose

Controls from within 1-2-3 the printing features offered by some printers.

The command gives you printing features controllable at the printer and not available through the other /Print [**P, E, B**] **O**ptions commands. Such features may include underlining or strike-through.

Reminders

- Your printer manual contains lists of printer setup codes (also known as *printer control codes* or *escape codes*). These codes may be shown two ways: as a decimal ASCII number representing a keyboard character or as the Escape key (Esc) followed by a character.

- 1-2-3 setup strings include decimal number codes (entered as three-digit numbers), preceded by a backslash (\). For example, the EPSON printer control code for condensed print is 15. The 1-2-3 setup string is \015.

- Some codes start with the Esc character, followed by other characters. Because the Esc character cannot be typed in the setup string, the ASCII decimal number for Esc (27) is used instead. For example, the EPSON printer code for emphasized print is Esc "E". In the 1-2-3 setup string, enter Esc "E" as \027E.

- Some printers retain previous control codes. Before sending a new code to the printer, clear the previous codes by turning the printer off and then on. You also can send the printer a reset code (\027@ for EPSON-compatible printers). Put the reset code in front of the new code you send. For example, the 1-2-3 printer setup string that resets previous codes and switches to emphasized printing mode is \027@\027E.

Procedures

1. Type **/ppos, /peos,** or **/pbos**.

2. Enter the setup string. If a setup string already has been entered, press Esc to clear the string. Each string must begin with a

backslash (\). Uppercase or lowercase letters must be typed as shown in the printer's manual.

3. Press Enter.

Important Cues

- Setup strings can be up to 39 characters long.

- You cannot combine some character sets or print modes. Your printer manual may list combinations that work for your printer.

- Use embedded setup strings in the print range to change printing features by row. Move the cell pointer to the leftmost cell in the print range row where you want the printing to change. Insert a row with /Worksheet Insert Row. Type two vertical bars (||) and then type the appropriate setup string. Notice that only one vertical bar appears. This setup string applies to all following rows. The row containing the double vertical bars does not print.

- When reading setup strings from the printer manual, don't confuse zero (0) with the letter O, or one (1) with the letter l.

- If you get the same several nonsense characters at the top of every printed page, you probably have those nonsense characters in your setup string, or you have selected the wrong type of printer.

Caution

Some printers retain the most recent printer control code. Clear the last code by turning off the printer for approximately five seconds or by preceding each setup string with the printer reset code. The reset code for EPSON-compatible printers is \027@.

For more information, see Chapter 8.

Print [P, F, E, B] Options Pg-Length /PPOP or /PFOP or /PEOP or /PBOP

Purpose

Specifies the number of lines per page by using a standard six lines per inch of page height.

Reminders

- Setting the lines per inch with a setup string creates an incorrect number of lines per page from this command. This command assumes six lines per inch.

- Determine the printing area available for body copy by taking the page height at six lines per inch and subtracting the top and bottom margins. Also subtract three lines for each header and footer.

Procedures

1. Type **/ppop**, **/pfop**, **/peop**, or **/pbop**.

2. Enter the number of lines per page if that number is different from the number shown. The page length can be 1 to 100 lines.

3. Press Enter.

Important Cue

Most printers print six lines per inch unless the ratio is changed with a setup string (printer control code). At six lines per inch, 11-inch-long paper has 66 lines, and 14-inch-long paper has 84 lines.

For more information, see **Print [Printer, File, Encoded, Background] Options Margins**, **/Print [Printer, Encoded, Background] Options Setup**, *and Chapter 8.*

Print [P, F, E, B,] Options Other
/PPOO or /PFOO or /PEOO or /PBOO

Purpose

Selects the form and formatting in which cells print. Worksheet contents can be printed as displayed on-screen or as formulas. You can print either option with or without formatting features.

Reminders

- **As**-Displayed (the default setting) is used with **F**ormatted for printing reports and data.

- Use **Cell**-Formulas with **F**ormatted to show formulas and cell contents. (Cell-Formulas often is used for documentation.)

- To print to disk the data to be used in a word processor or database, choose **As**-Displayed with **Unformatted**. If you are printing to disk (creating an ASCII file to export to a word processor or database), set the left, top, and bottom margins to 0 and the right margin to 240.

Procedures

1. Type **/ppoo**, **/pfoo**, **/peoo**, or **/pboo**.

2. Select the type of print from the following options:

Menu Item	Description
As-Displayed	Prints the range as displayed on-screen. This setting is the default setting.
Cell-Formulas	Prints the formula, label, or value contents of each cell on one line of the printout. Contents match information that appears in the control panel: address, protection status, cell format, formula or value, and annotation.
Formatted	Prints with page breaks, headers, and footers. This default setting is normally used for printing to paper.
Unformatted	Prints without page breaks, headers, or footers. This setting is normally used for printing to disk.

3. Select **Quit** to exit from the **Options** menu.

Important Cues

- Use **Cell-Formulas** to print documentation that shows the formulas and cell settings used to create the worksheet.

- In a **Cell-Formulas** listing, codes may appear that indicate cell contents and formatting. PR indicates a protected cell (if /wgpe has been selected); U indicates an unprotected cell. Other codes, such as F2 for "fixed to 2 decimal places," are compatible with control-panel codes for different formats.

- Document the worksheets by using the **Cell-Formulas** option to print a copy of all formulas. Use /**R**ange **N**ame **T**able to create a table of range names and addresses.

- Use Unformatted on files to be imported to databases. Databases expect ASCII-file data in a consistent order, and headers and footers can disrupt that order.

For more information, see /Print [Printer, File, Encoded, Background] Options Margins *and Chapter 8.*

Print [P, F, E, B]   */PPC or/PFC*
Clear   *or /PEC or /PBC*

Purpose

Clears some or all print settings and options.

Reminders

- Cleared formats return to default settings.

- This option is the only way to clear borders after they have been set.

Procedures

1. Type /**ppc**, /**pfc**, /**pec**, or /**pbc**.

2. Choose one of the following items:

Menu Item	Description
All	Clears all print options and resets all formats and setup strings to their defaults
Range	Clears the print range
Borders	Clears the borders and frame
Format	Resets the margins, page length, layout, fonts, colors, setup strings, and graph settings to the default setting

Important Cue

Use the /ppc, /pfc, /pec, /pbc commands in macros to cancel earlier print settings or to re-establish default settings you have specified. For example, use the /Worksheet Global Default Printer menu to create as default settings the settings you use most often for margins, the page length, and the setup string. Be sure to use /Worksheet Global Default

Update to update the configuration file to make these settings the default settings for future sessions. Then when you place a /ppca command at the beginning of a macro (or use the command interactively), the default settings you specify are entered automatically.

Caution

In 1-2-3, print parameters remain in effect until you give different instructions. If you want to provide a new set of parameters, use /ppca to ensure that you are starting from the default parameters.

For more information, see Chapter 8.

Print [P, F, E, B]   /PPA or /PFA
Align   or /PEA or /PBA

Purpose

Aligns 1-2-3's internal line counter with the physical page in the printer. Failure to use **Align** can cause blank gaps in the middle of printed documents.

Reminder

Use this command only after you have manually aligned the print head with the top of a sheet of printer paper. Use **Align** before printing for the first time or when printing to a printer that other operators have used.

Procedures

1. Position the printer paper so that the top of a page is aligned with the print head.

2. Type **/pp**, **/pf**, **/pe**, or **/pb**.

3. Select **Align** to synchronize 1-2-3 with the printer.

Cautions

- Printed pages may have gaps (blank lines) if you do not use this command.

- Align resets the page counter to 1 so that the page number automatically starts over at 1 after each **Align** command.

For more information, see Chapter 8.

Print [P, F, E, B] Go

**/PPG or /PFG
or /PEG or /PBG**

Purpose

Executes the /Print command, sending the print data in the range to the printer or file.

Reminders

- Before printing for the first time, align the top of the paper with the print head and choose the **Align** command from the second-level /**Print** menu.

- Use the /**Print** [**P, F, E, B**] **R**ange command to specify the range to print.

Procedure

Type /**ppg**, /**pfg**, /**peg**, or /**pbg**.

Important Cue

Printing to a file is not complete until you quit all print menus.

Caution

Use the /**Print** [**P, F, E, B**] **P**age command to eject pages and keep the printer aligned. If you manually eject pages, realign the paper and print head and choose /**Print** [**P, F, E, B**] **Align**.

For more information, see /**Print [Printer, File, Encoded, Background] Align** *and Chapter 8.*

Print [P, F, E, B] Quit

**/PPQ or /PFQ
or /PEQ or /PBQ**

Purpose

Closes the print job so that it completes correctly; returns to READY mode.

Reminder

To properly finish a print job, quit the /**Print** menu by using **Quit** or by pressing Esc or Ctrl-Break.

Procedure

Type **/ppq**, **/pfq**, **/peq**, or **/pbq**.

For more information, see Chapter 8.

Graph Commands /G

/**G**raph commands control the graph's appearance and specify worksheet ranges to be used as graph data. Store multiple graphs with /**G**raph **N**ame and display them at a later time. You can print either the current graph or a named graph. To send graphs to another program, use /**G**raph **S**ave to create a PIC. Throughout this section, refer to the /**G**raph menu on the 1-2-3 side of the pull-out command card at the back of this book.

Graph Type /GT

Purpose

Selects from among the 1-2-3 graph types: **L**ine; **B**ar; **X**Y; **S**tack-Bar; **P**ie; **H**LCO, or high-low-close-open (stock market); and **M**ixed (bar and line). Each type of graph is best suited for displaying and analyzing a specific type of data.

Reminders

- Before you can create a graph, you must create a worksheet that has the same number of cells in each x-axis and y-axis range, similar to the one in figure G.1. Each *y* data item must be in the same range position as the corresponding *x* value. Figure G.2 shows the bar graph produced from the worksheet displayed in figure G.1. (The legends and titles were added separately.)

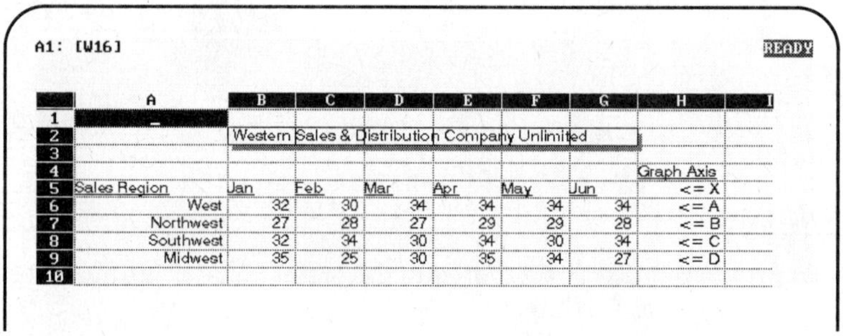
A1: [W16] READY

	A	B	C	D	E	F	G	H	I
1									
2		Western Sales & Distribution Company Unlimited							
3									
4								Graph Axis	
5	Sales Region	Jan	Feb	Mar	Apr	May	Jun	<= X	
6	West	32	30	34	34	34	34	<= A	
7	Northwest	27	28	27	29	29	28	<= B	
8	Southwest	32	34	30	34	30	34	<= C	
9	Midwest	35	25	30	35	34	27	<= D	
10									

Fig. G.1. *A worksheet with the same number of cells in each x-axis and y-axis range.*

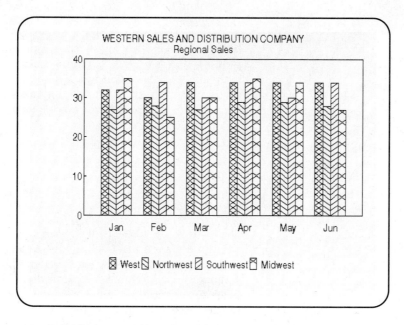

Fig. G.2. *The bar graph produced from the worksheet in figure G.1.*

- Except for pie graphs, graphs can have on the y-axis as many as six different series of data. The /Graph menu choices **A** through **F** are used to highlight the data series. The pie graph accepts data from only the A range.

Procedures

1. Type /**gt**.

2. Select the type of graph from the following options:

Menu Item	*Description*
Line	Usually depicts a continuous series of data. The change frequently occurs over time. Enter an x-axis label, such as months, in the X range from the /Graph menu. Line graphs can be altered to appear as area graphs.
Bar	Usually displays discrete data series. The x-axis often represents time. Comparative weights between different *y* values are easier to judge in bar graphs than in line charts. Enter x-axis labels in the X range from the /Graph menu.

Menu Item	Description
XY	Graphs data sets of x and y data; good for plotting clouds of data. (Unlike line graphs with labels on the x-axis and data on the y-axis, XY graphs have data on both axes.) Each x value can have between one and six y values. Enter x-axis data in the X range of the /Graph menu.
Stack-Bar	Shows how proportions change within the whole. Enter x-axis labels in the X range from the /Graph menu. A bar can have as many as six portions.
Pie	Shows how the whole is divided into component portions. Use only the A range to contain the values of each portion. The X range is used to label the pie wedges. 1-2-3 automatically calculates each portion's percentage from the A values.
HLCO	Tracks items that vary over time. High-low-close-open graphs are most commonly used in the stock market to show the price at which a stock opens and closes and its high and low during the day.
Mixed	Contains elements of both bar and line graphs and is therefore useful for relating trends in two distinct measurable quantities. Mixed graphs can have up to three bars and three lines.
Features	Varies the original graph type. Features provides the following options:
Vertical	Moves the x-axis to the bottom of the graph (default)
Horizontal	Moves the x-axis to the left side. The y-axis runs across the top, and the 2Y-axis runs across the bottom.
Stacked	Works with line, bar, XY, and mixed graphs containing two or more data sets. No plots values separately (default); **Yes** stacks values.

Menu Item	Description
Frame	Creates a frame around the graph. You can specify a frame around all or part of the graph.
3D-Effect	Creates a three-dimensional effect for a bar graph
Quit	Displays the /Graph menu

3. After you make your selection, the /Graph menu reappears.

4. If you already have highlighted the X range and ranges A through F to indicate the data to graph, select View. If you are beginning the graph, see /Graph **X A B C D E F** or /Graph **G**roup in this section.

Important Cues

- With 1-2-3, you can build graphs interactively. After selecting /Graph **T**ype and at least one x-axis and y-axis range, select View to see the graph as it is currently defined.

- When you save the worksheet to disk, you also save the most recently specified graph type and other graph settings.

- You can shade a pie graph's wedges with eight different shadings. You even can extract wedges from the pie. Use the B range to define the shade of a pie graph wedge and to extract the wedge from the pie. (To learn how to shade the pie graph, see /Graph **X A B C D E F** in this section.)

*For more information, see /***Graph X A B C D E F** *and Chapter 10.*

Graph X A B C D E F   /GX, /GA through /GF

Purpose

Specifies the worksheet ranges containing x-axis and y-axis data or labels.

Reminders

- The x-axis is the graph's horizontal (bottom) axis. The y-axis is the graph's vertical (left) axis. The labels or data assigned to the x-axis and the six possible sets of y-axis data (A through F) must have the same number of cells. To ensure that the x-axis and y-axis have an equal number of elements, place all the labels and data on adjacent rows.

- Pie graph ranges are different from those of other graph types. Pie graphs use only the A range for data. (The B range contains code numbers to control shading and the extraction of wedges from the pie.)

Procedures

1. Type /**g**.

2. From the following options, select the ranges for x-axis or y-axis data or labels to be entered:

Menu Item	Description
X	Enters x-axis label range. These are labels such as *Jan*, *Feb*, *Mar*, and so on. Creates labels for pie graph wedges and line, bar, and stacked-bar graphs (x-axis data range for XY graphs). The X range in figure G.3 is B5..G5.
A	Enters first y-axis data range, the only data range used by a pie graph
B	Enters second y-axis data range; enters pie graph shading values and extraction codes. (For more information, see this section's "Important Cues.")
C	Enters third y-axis data range
D to F	Enters fourth through sixth data ranges

3. Indicate the data range by entering the range address, entering a range name, or highlighting the range.

4. Press Enter.

Important Cues

- If the graph data is in adjacent rows or columns, you may be able to save time by using /**Graph Group**.

- To ease the task of keeping track of graph data and labels, put the data and labels in labeled rows.

- You do not need to change the /Graph menu settings when you change or update the data in the ranges. /Graph remembers all the settings.

- Use /Graph Reset Graph to clear all graph settings. Use /Graph Reset [X through F] to clear individual ranges and their associated settings.

- 1-2-3 automatically updates graphs when you input new data in the worksheet (for new data or labels in the x-axis and y-axis ranges). After you have set the graphs with the /Graph commands, you can view new graphs from the worksheet by pressing Graph (F10). If the computer beeps and no graph appears, you have not defined that graph, or the computer does not have graphics capability.

- Pie graphs do not use the x-axis and y-axis title options, grids, or scales.

- Pie graphs are limited because they often have too many elements in the A range, a situation that causes wedges to be small and labels to overlap. The A range is the only data range needed for pie graphs. Enter wedge labels in the X range, as you would for line graphs.

- Use the B range to enter the numbers from 1 to 18 that control the color or black-and-white patterns in each wedge. Add 100 to a shading code to extract one or more wedges from the pie.

Caution

If the graph has missing data or if the y values do not match the corresponding x positions, check to ensure that the x-axis and y-axis ranges have the same number of elements. The values in the y ranges (A through F) graph the corresponding x-range cells.

For more information, see /**Graph Type** *and Chapter 10.*

Graph Reset   /GR

Purpose

Cancels all or some of a graph's settings so that you can either create a new graph or exclude from a new graph one or more data ranges from the old graph.

Reminder

The **Graph** option of this command (see "Procedures") enables you to reset all graph parameters quickly.

Procedures

1. Type /**gr**.

2. Choose one of the following items:

Menu Item	Description
Graph	Resets all graph parameters but does not alter a graph named with /**Graph Name Create**. Use this option if you want to exclude all preceding graph parameters from the new graph.
X	Resets the X range and removes the labels (but not on XY graphs)
A through F	Resets a designated range and corresponding labels so that these are not displayed in the new graph
Ranges	Resets all data ranges and all data labels
Options	Resets all settings defined by /**Graph Options**
Quit	Returns to the /**Graph** menu

Important Cues

- Use /**Graph Type** to change the type of graph.

- The **Reset** command enables you to remove unwanted features from a graph quickly so that you can update it.

- Create templates of graphs that can be used with different sets of data by defining a graph, then removing its data ranges with **Reset**. Respecify the data ranges to create a graph with the same format.

Caution

If you delete too much from a graph, use /**F**ile **O**pen to retrieve the original file containing the original graph settings.

For more information, see Chapter 10.

Graph View   /GV

Purpose

Displays a graph on-screen.

Reminders

- What is displayed depends on the system hardware and the system configuration.

- On a nongraphics screen, no graph appears.

- If your system has a graphics card and either a monochrome display or a color monitor, you can see a graph instead of the worksheet on the screen after you select **V**iew. You must select /**G**raph **O**ptions **C**olor to see the graph in color.

Procedures

1. Select **V**iew from the /**G**raph menu when you are ready to see the graph you have created. The graph must be defined before you can view it.

2. Press any key to return to the /**G**raph menu.

3. Select **Q**uit to return to the worksheet and READY mode.

Important Cues

- You can use /**G**raph **V**iew to redraw the graph, but an easier way is to press Graph (F10). Graph (F10) is the equivalent of /**G**raph **V**iew, but the function key enables you to view a graph after making a change in the worksheet. You can use Graph (F10) without having to return to the /**G**raph menu. If your system doesn't have two monitors and graphics cards for each, you can use Graph (F10) to toggle back and forth between the worksheet and the graph. You therefore can use Graph (F10) to do rapid what-if analysis with graphics.

- If you want to see a portion of the worksheet at the same time that you see the graph, use the Wysiwyg add-in's :**Graph Add** command to add a graph to the worksheet.

- If you want to create a series of graphs and view the series, you must use /**Graph Name** to name each graph.

- If the screen is blank after you select **View**, make certain that you have defined the graph adequately, that your system has graphics capability, and that 1-2-3 was installed for your particular graphics device(s). Press any key to return to the /**Graph** menu. Then select **Quit** to return to the worksheet.

For more information, see Chapter 10.

Graph Save   /GS

Purpose

Saves the graph so that it can be printed with the 1-2-3 PrintGraph utility or from a different program.

/**Graph Save** saves a graph file that cannot be viewed or retrieved from within 1-2-3. This file can be used by graphics programs to improve the quality of 1-2-3 graphs.

Use /**Graph Name Create** and /**File Save** to save the graph's settings with the worksheet so that you can view multiple graphs.

Reminders

- Select **View** or press Graph (F10) to review the graph. Ensure that the graph has the correct scaling, labels, and titles.

- Check the screen's lower right corner for a CALC indicator. If CALC appears and the worksheet is still visible, press Calc (F9) to update all worksheet values before you save the graph.

- If you need to return to this graph later, use /**Graph Name Create** to save the graph settings; then use /**File Save** to save the worksheet to disk.

- The graph saved to a file is the current graph that displays on the screen.

Procedures

1. Type /**g**.
2. Select **Save**.

3. Enter a new file name, or use the right- or left-arrow key to highlight a name already displayed.

4. Press Enter.

Important Cues

- Saved graphs have the PIC file extensions. Other software programs may use a PIC file format.

- You must save a graph in PIC file format to print it from the PrintGraph utility.

Caution

If you need to save graph settings and the worksheet's graph display, name the graph with **/Graph Name Create** and then use **/File Save** to save the worksheet and graph together. **/Graph Save** saves information used only to transfer the graph to another program. Files saved with **/Graph Save** cannot be edited from the worksheet.

For more information, see **/Graph Name,** **/File Save,** *and Chapters 7 and 10.*

Graph Options Legend   */GOL*

Purpose

Legends indicate which line, bar, or point belongs to a specific y-axis data range.

Y-axis data is entered in ranges A, B, C, D, E, and F. Legend titles for each range also are assigned by A, B, C, D, E, and F. Figure G.2 shows a legend at the bottom of the bar graph, relating shading patterns to the division names West, Northwest, Southwest, and Midwest.

Reminder

As you create a graph, write on paper a list of the legend titles you want to associate with each data range (ranges A through F). If you already have created the graph, you can re-enter the A-through-F data ranges to see the associated legend ranges. To reenter these legends, follow the steps outlined in the following section.

Procedures

1. Type **/go.**

2. Select **Legend.**

3. Select one of the following items:

Menu Item	Description
A	Creates a legend for y-axis range A
B	Creates a legend for y-axis range B
C	Creates a legend for y-axis range C
D	Creates a legend for y-axis range D
E	Creates a legend for y-axis range E
F	Creates a legend for y-axis range F
Range	Assigns a legend to all ranges

4. If you choose **A** through **F**, enter the text for the legend. If you choose **Range**, specify the range containing the legends.

Important Cues

- 1-2-3 displays the legend along the bottom of the graph.

- 1-2-3 may cut a legend short if there is not enough room or if the legend exceeds the graph's frame. If this happens, re-enter a shorter legend.

- Create changeable legends by entering the text for a legend in cells. When /Graph Options Legend requests the legend title, you can enter a backslash (\) and the cell address or range name of a cell that holds the text.

Caution

If you relocate the data you used for a graph by using /Move, /Worksheet Insert, or /Worksheet Delete, 1-2-3 does not adjust cell addresses used to create legends. Create your graphs by using range names to describe data and legend ranges to prevent this problem.

For more information, see /**Range Name**, /**Graph X A B C D E F**, *and Chapters 4 and 10.*

Graph Options Format   /GOF

Purpose

Selects the symbols and lines that identify and connect data points.

Some line and XY graphs present information better if the data is linked with data points or if the data is represented by a series of data points linked with a solid line. Use /Graph Options Format to select the type of data points used for each data range (symbols, lines, or both).

Reminders

- Time-related data is usually best represented by a continuous series of related data. Trends and slopes are more obvious when they are represented with lines rather than a cluster of data points.

- Data-point clusters representing multiple readings around different x-axis values are likely candidates for symbols instead of lines. Symbols better reflect groupings. The symbol for each y-axis range is unique so that you can keep data separated.

Procedures

1. Type /**gof**.

2. Select the data ranges to be formatted:

Menu Item	Description
Graph	Selects a format for the entire graph
A to F	Selects a format for y-axis data points
Quit	Returns to the /Graph Options menu

3. Select the data point type:

Menu Item	Description
Lines	Connects data points with a line
Symbols	Encloses each data point in a symbol. Different ranges have different symbols. The **Symbols** option is most commonly used with XY graphs.
Both	Connects data points with a line and marks the data point
Neither	Selects neither lines nor symbols. Use /**Graph Options Data-Labels** to float labels or data within the graph.
Area	Fills the space between the line and the line or axis directly below

Important Cues

- Figure G.3 shows the line graph created from the data in figure G.1. The A and D data ranges, West and Midwest, are each plotted with a line. The B and C data ranges, Northwest and Southwest, are each plotted with a particular symbol.

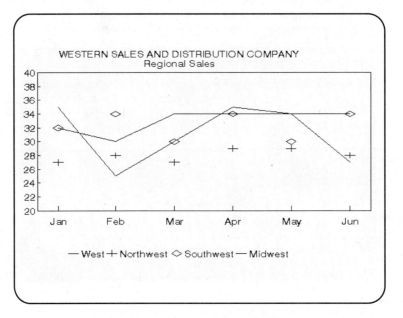

Fig. G.3. *A and C ranges plotted with lines, and B and D ranges plotted with symbols.*

- If you are plotting a regression analysis trend line (/**Data Regression**), set the data points as symbols only and the regression's calculated y values as a line. This arrangement highlights the trend as a straight line through a swarm of data points.

Caution

If your XY line graphs are a confusing jumble of crossed lines, you must sort the data in x-axis order by arranging each x,y data pair in ascending or descending x-axis order within the worksheet range. Be sure to sort the y-axis data with the corresponding x-axis data.

For more information, see Chapter 10.

Graph Options Titles   */GOT*

Purpose

Adds headings to the graph and to each axis. To increase the reader's understanding, use x-axis and y-axis titles.

Reminder

You must know the measurement units used in the x-axis and y-axis. 1-2-3 automatically scales graphs to fit accordingly and displays the scaling factor (for example, Thousands) along each axis.

Procedures

1. Type /**got**.

2. Select the title to be entered from the following options:

Menu	*Item*
First	Specifies the top heading of a graph
Second	Specifies a second heading of a graph
X-Axis	Specifies a title below the x-axis
Y-Axis	Specifies a title to the left of the y-axis

3. Type a title or enter the cell address of a cell containing a title. Use cell contents for a title by entering first a backslash (\) and then the cell address. If a title already exists, press Esc to cancel the title or press Enter to accept it.

4. Press Enter.

Caution

You can lose titles and headings contained in cell addresses if you move the cells with /**Move**, /**Worksheet Insert**, or /**Worksheet Delete**. Using range names instead of cell addresses solves this problem.

For more information, see /**Graph Options Data-Labels**, /**Graph Options Scale**, *and Chapter 10.*

Graph Options Grid /GOG

Purpose

Overlays a grid on a graph to enhance readability. The grid lines can be horizontal, vertical, or both.

Reminders

- Before you add a grid, create a graph to view.

- Grid lines cannot be used with pie graphs.

Procedures

1. Type /**gog**.

2. Select the type of grid from the following options:

Menu Item	*Description*
Horizontal	Draws horizontal grid lines over the current graph from each major y-axis division
Vertical	Draws vertical grid lines over the current graph from each major x-axis division
Both	Draws both horizontal and vertical grid lines
Clear	Removes all existing grid lines from a graph

Important Cues

- Select grid lines that run in a direction that enhances the presentation of data.

- Use grid lines sparingly. Inappropriate grid lines can make some line and XY graphs confusing.

- Use /**Graph Options Scale** to change the graph's scale, thereby changing the number of grid lines shown on the graph. Note that although this technique changes the number of grid lines, it also magnifies or reduces the graph's proportion.

- Some data-point graphs are more accurate if you use data labels. Use /**Graph Options Data-Labels** to create data labels that display precise numbers next to the point on the graph.

For more information, see /**Graph Options Scale**, /**Graph Options Data-Labels***, and Chapter 10.*

Graph Options Scale   /GOS

Purpose

Varies the scale along the y-axis. The x-axis scale can be varied on XY graphs.

Options within this command include the following:

- Making changes manually to the upper axis or lower axis end points

- Choosing formats for numeric display (Options are identical to those in /Worksheet Global Format or /Range Format.)

- Improving display of overlapping x-axis labels by skipping every specified occurrence, such as every second or third label

Use /Graph Options Scale to change the axes' end points manually, thereby expanding or contracting the graph scale. Changing the end points expands or contracts the visible portion of the graph.

Use /Graph Options Scale to format numbers and dates that appear on the axes. These formats are the same as /Range Format options.

Reminder

First create and view the graph. Notice which portions of the graph you want to view and which beginning and ending numbers you should use for the new X-scale or Y-scale. Also determine whether the x-axis labels overlap or seem crowded. You can thin the x-axis tick marks by using /Graph Options Scale Skip.

Procedures

1. Type /**gos**.

2. Select from the following options the axis or skip frequency to be changed:

Menu Item	Description
Y-Scale	Changes the y-axis scale or format
X-Scale	Changes the x-axis scale or format
Skip	Changes the frequency with which x-axis indicators display

3. If you select **Y**-Scale or **X**-Scale, choose from the following:

Menu Item	Description
Automatic	Automatically scales the graph to fill the screen; default (normal) selection
Manual	Overrides automatic scaling with scaling you select
Lower	Enters the lowest number for axis. Values are rounded.
Upper	Enters the highest number for axis. Values are rounded.
Format	Selects the formatting type and decimal display from the following options (see /Range Format for descriptions of these options):

Fixed	**+/−**
Sci	**Percent**
Currency	**Date**
,	**Text**
General	**Hidden**

Menu Item	Description
Indicator	Displays or suppresses the magnitude indicator (Thousands, Millions, and so on) that appears between the scale and axis titles. Select **Yes** to have 1-2-3 display its automatically calculated scaling factor; select **No** to suppress the display.
Display	(Y-Axis only) Specifies where you want to display the Y-axis in the graph, either on the **Right**, **Left**, **Both** sides, or **None** at all
Quit	Leaves this menu and returns to the /Graph Options menu

4. If you choose **Skip**, you must enter a number to indicate the intervals at which the x-axis scale tick marks are to appear. If you enter the number 25, for example, then the 1st, 26th, and 51st range entries appear. Y-axis tick-mark spacing cannot be controlled from the menu.

Important Cues

- Selecting a scale inside the minimum and maximum data points creates a graph that magnifies an area within the data.

- If data points have grossly different magnitudes, you may not be able to see all the data; some ranges may be too large for the graph, and others may be too small. Scale down values on the y-axis by entering a larger exponent. An exponent of 3, for example, means that numbers on the y-axis are divided by 10 to the third power (1,000).

*For more information, see /**Graph Options Grid** and Chapter 10.*

Graph Options Color or B&W   /GOC or /GOB

Purpose

Defines the color 1-2-3 tries to use to display graphs on the monitor. If you have a monochrome display, use /Graph Options B&W; if you have a color display, use /Graph Options Color.

Reminder

If you have a monochrome monitor, use /Graph Options B&W. If you need to print to a color printer, however, you must change to /Graph Options Color. Color monitors set to /Graph Options Color automatically print black and white on printers that are capable of only black-and-white print.

Procedures

To set the Color option, do the following:

Type /**goc**.

To set the B&W option, do the following:

Type /**gob**.

For more information, see Chapter 10.

Graph Options Data-Labels   /GOD

Purpose

Labels graph points from data contained in cells.

Graph labels can be numeric values that enhance the graph's accuracy or text labels that describe specific graph points. The labels for graph points come from worksheet ranges.

Reminders

- First create the graph. Then view the graph and note future label locations that correspond to data they represent. Figure G.4 shows three ranges: the X range, the A range, and A-range labels.

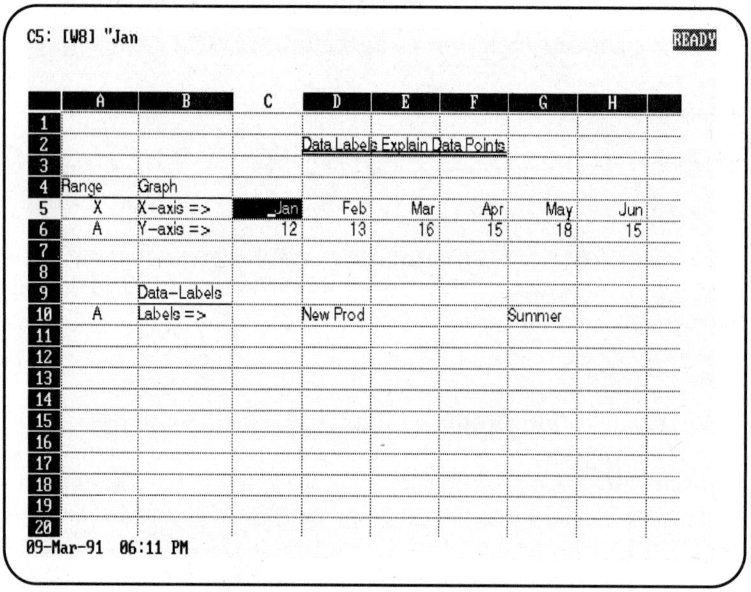

C5: [W8] "Jan								READY

	A	B	C	D	E	F	G	H
1								
2				Data Labels Explain Data Points				
3								
4	Range	Graph						
5	X	X–axis =>	Jan	Feb	Mar	Apr	May	Jun
6	A	Y–axis =>	12	13	16	15	18	15
7								
8								
9		Data–Labels						
10	A	Labels =>	New Prod			Summer		
11								
12								
13								
14								
15								
16								
17								
18								
19								
20								

09-Mar-91 06:11 PM

Fig. G.4. *X and A ranges used to plan the A-range labels.*

- Enter labels in an order corresponding to the order of the data-entry points they describe.

- Figure G.5 shows the resulting graph with labels to the right of the data points. Note that you do not have to enter a label for every data point.

Procedures

1. Type **/god**.

2. From the following options, select the data range you want to label:

Menu Item	Description
A through **F**	Enters the range to be labeled
Group	Enters at one time all the ranges to have labels. The **Columnwise** and **Rowwise** options appear. Select **Columnwise** if data sets are in a column; select **Rowwise** if data sets run across a row.
Quit	Returns to the **/Graph Options** menu

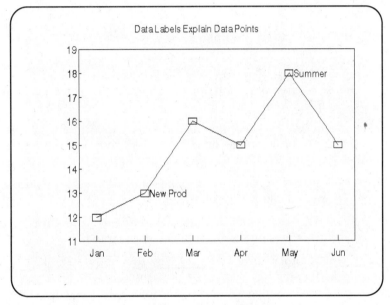

Fig. G.5. *The resulting graph with labels over the data points.*

3. Specify the range containing the labels. This range should be the same size as the range you selected for A through F. If you are grouping data ranges, the range selected here must be the same size as all the data ranges combined.

4. From the following options, select the data label location relative to the corresponding data points. (Note that in fig. G.5, the **Right** option was selected.)

Menu Item	Description
Center	Centers a label on a data point
Left	Aligns a label left of a data point
Above	Aligns a label above a data point
Right	Aligns a label right of a data point
Below	Aligns a label below a data point

5. Choose **Quit** or return to Step 2 to enter more data labels.

Important Cues

- Data labels can be formulas, values, or labels.

- Lines can have labels that are centered, left, right, above, or below. Bars can have labels that are above or below. If you choose a different option, the label appears above the bar. Pie graphs cannot have labels.

- Position floating labels that can be moved anywhere within the graph area by creating a set of labels assigned to invisible data points. To create floating labels, follow these steps:

  1. Set up two ranges that have the same number of cell locations and data points on the graph.

  2. In one range, enter floating labels in the left-to-right order in which you want them to appear in the graph.

  3. In the other range, enter the elevation of the y-axis labels. If the floating labels are to be positioned exactly where you want them, the cells in the elevation and label ranges must parallel actual data points in the x-axis and y-axis.

  4. Use /Graph **F** to enter the elevations for the F data range.

  5. Use /Graph Options Data-Labels **F** to specify the label range, and press Enter.

  6. Select **Center** to center the labels on the data points.

  7. To keep the F range data from plotting, use /Graph Options Format **F** Neither (invisible).

For more information, see /**Graph Options Titles**, /**Graph Options Scale**, *and Chapter 10.*

Graph Name *** /GN***

Purpose

Stores graph settings for later use with the same worksheet.

Because only one graph can be active at a time, use /Graph Name to name graphs and store their settings with the corresponding worksheets. To reproduce a stored graph, recall the graph and graph settings by name.

Reminders

- Before you can name a graph, you must create one that you can view.

- If you want to name a graph, make sure that it is the active graph.

- Before creating a table of graph names, make sure that you are in the file that contains the graphs you want to name.

Procedures

1. Type /**gn**.

2. From the following options, select the activity to name the file:

Menu Item	*Description*
Use	Retrieves previous graph settings with a saved graph name
Create	Creates for the active graph a name of up to 15 characters. Make sure that no graph currently has the same name.
Delete	Removes the settings and name for the graph name chosen from the menu. Be sure that you have the correct name; you are not given the option to cancel.
Reset	Erases all graph names and their settings
Table	Creates a table of graph names, types, and the first line of the graph title for names in the current file

3. If you are switching to a new graph, creating a name, or deleting or resetting names, specify the name. If you are creating a table of graph names, specify the location for the graph.

Important Cues

- Using /gn is the only way to store and recall graphs for later use with the same worksheet. /**Graph S**ave saves graphs as PIC files for use with PrintGraph and other graphic-enhancement programs.

- The graph table overwrites existing cell contents.

- The graph table has three columns and as many rows as there are names.

- Graphs recalled by /**Graph N**ame **U**se reflect changed data within the graph ranges.

- Create a slide-show effect by naming several graphs and recalling them in succession with a macro that controls /**Graph N**ame **U**se and uses the GRAPHON macro command with different graphs.

Cautions

- You can recall graphs in later work sessions only if you have first saved the graph settings with /**Graph N**ame **C**reate and then saved the worksheet with /**File S**ave. Even in the same work session, you cannot return to a previous graph unless you have saved the graph settings with /**Graph N**ame **C**reate.

- Respect the power of /**Graph N**ame **R**eset. It deletes all graph names in the current worksheet but does not reset the current graph parameters. The graph has no Yes/No confirmation step; when you press **R** for **R**eset, all graphs are gone.

For more information, see /**File Save**, /**File Retrieve**, *and Chapters 7 and 10.*

Graph Group   /GG

Purpose

Quickly selects the data ranges for a graph, X and A through F, when data is in adjacent rows and columns are in consecutive order. Designing worksheets with the /Graph Group command in mind can save you time later.

Reminder

In figure G.1, the /Graph Group range is B5..G9. /Graph Group automatically defines row 5 in this range as the X data range, row 6 as the A data range, row 7 as the B data range, and so on.

Procedures

1. Type /**gg**.

2. Specify the range containing **X** and **A** through **F** data values. The rows or columns must be adjacent and in the order X, A, B, C, and so on.

3. Select **C**olumnwise if the data ranges are in columns; select **R**owwise if the data ranges are in rows.

Important Cues

- /**G**raph **G**roup assigns data ranges in the order X, A, B, and so on. Rows or columns that exceed the seven data ranges are ignored.

- Selecting a range for /**G**raph **G**roup that contains blank rows or columns produces a graph containing blanks. For example, a rowwise group containing a blank row creates a bar graph with a missing set of bars.

*For more information, see /***Graph X, A, B, C, D, E, F,*** *and Chapter 10.*

Data Commands   /D

/**D**ata commands work on data tables and enable you to perform three functions: database selection and maintenance, data analysis, and data manipulation. One of the most used /**D**ata commands is **Q**uery. You use **Q**uery commands to rapidly find, update, extract, or delete information from within a large collection of data. You can use /**D**ata commands to perform many different types of data manipulation, such as sorting, filling ranges with numbers, and parsing imported data. Throughout this section, refer to the /**D**ata menu map on the 1-2-3 side of the pull-out command card at the back of this book.

Data Fill */DF*

Purpose

Fills a specified range with a series of equally incremented numbers, dates, times, or percentages.

Use /Data Fill to create date or numeric rows or columns, headings for depreciation tables, sensitivity analyses, data tables, or databases.

Reminder

Before you issue /Data Fill, move the cell pointer to the upper left corner of the range you want to fill. If you prespecify the range with F4 or the mouse, 1-2-3 does not try to reuse the preceding fill range.

Procedures

1. Type /**df**.

2. Specify the range to be filled: type the address (such as B23..D46), type a range name, or highlight the range.

3. When a Start value is requested, enter the starting number, date, or time in the filled range, and then press Enter. You also can reference a cell or range that results in a value. Use a number or time format that 1-2-3 recognizes. (The default value is 0.)

4. When a Step value is requested, type the positive or negative number by which you want the value to be incremented. Date or time Step values can use special units described in this entry's "Important Cues." (The default value is 1.)

5. Enter a Stop value. You can use a date or time in any date or time format except, if the step is negative, make sure that the Stop value is less than the Start value. /Data Fill fills the cells in the range column-by-column from top to bottom and from left to right until the Stop value is encountered or the range is full. (The default value is 8191.)

Important Cues

- If you do not supply a Stop value, 1-2-3 uses the default, which may give you results you don't want. Supply a Stop value if you want 1-2-3 to stop at a particular value before the entire range is filled.

- Use /Data Fill to fill a range of numbers in descending order. Enter a positive or negative Start value and enter a negative Step value. The Stop value must be less than the Start value.

- Use /Data Fill to create an index numbering system for database entries. You can then sort the database on any column and return to the original order by sorting on the index column. To index a database so that you can return to the original sort order, perform the following steps:

  1. Insert a column through the data.

  2. Use /Data Fill to fill the column with ascending numbers.

  3. Sort the data by any column. Include the column of index numbers in the sort range.

  4. To return to the original sort order, resort the data on the column containing the index numbers.

- Use data tables to change the input values in a formula so that you can see how the output changes. If the input values vary by constant amounts, use /df to create an input column or row for the data table.

Cautions

- Numbers generated by /Data Fill cover previous entries in the cell.

- If the Stop value is not large enough, a partial fill occurs. If the Stop value is smaller than the Start value, /df does not even start. Remember that if the increment is negative, the Stop value must be less than the Start value.

  For more information, see /**Data Table** *and Chapter 12.*

Data Table 1   /DT1

Purpose

Generates a table composed of one varying input value and the result from multiple formulas.

/Data Table 1 is useful for generating what-if models that show the results of changing a single variable.

Reminders

- /Data Table 1 is used to show how changes in one variable affect the output from one or more formulas.

- Formulas in /dt1 can include functions.

- To change two variables in a single formula, use /Data Table 2.

- Before executing /dt1, enter data and formulas as though you are solving for a single solution (see cells B4..C8 in fig. D.1).

```
C8: (C2) [W10] @PMT(C5,C4/12,C6*12)                                    READY
```

	A	B	C	D	E	F	G
1							
2		Data Table 1: One Input					
3							
4		Interest =	0.08	<= Input 1			
5		Balance =	$15,000.00				
6		Term =	4				
7							
8		Payment =	$366.19				
9							
10			Data Table 1				
11				+C8	<= Table Formula displayed		
12		Input 1 Values =>	0.065	$355.72	in Text Format		
13		=>	0.068	$357.80			
14		=>	0.070	$359.19			
15		=>	0.073	$361.29			
16		=>	0.075	$362.68			
17		=>	0.078	$364.79			
18		=>	0.080	$366.19			
19		=>	0.083	$368.31			
20		=>	0.085	$369.72			

```
09-Mar-91  06:25 PM
```

Fig. D.1. */Data Table 1: solving with single inputs.*

- In the leftmost column of the table, enter the numbers or text to be used as the replacement for the first variable (Input 1). In the second blank cell in the top row of the data table, type the address of the cell containing the formula or the formula itself. Enter additional formulas to the right on the same row. The upper left corner of the /Data Table 1 area (C11 in fig. D.1) remains blank.

- Display the cell addresses of the formulas at the top of the table by using /Range Format Text. You may need to widen the columns if you want to see entire formulas.

Procedures

1. Type /**dt1**.

2. Enter the table range so that it includes the Input 1 values or text in the leftmost column and the formulas in the top row. If a

range has been previously specified, press Esc and define the range: type the address, type a range name, or highlight the range.

3. Enter the address for Input 1 by moving the cell pointer to the cell in which the first input values are to be substituted. In figure D.1, the values from C12 to C20 are to be substituted into C4.

4. 1-2-3 then substitutes an Input 1 value into the designated cell and recalculates each formula at the top of the data table. After each substitution, the results are displayed in the data table. In figure D.1, the variable input for interest (.080) produces a monthly payment of $366.19. With /**Data Table 1**, you can see how sensitive the monthly payments are to variations in the interest rate.

Important Cues

- Make the formulas in the top row of the data table area easier to understand by using /**Range Name Create** to change address locations (such as C4) into descriptive text (such as *Interest*). /**Range Format Text** displays formulas as text, although the formulas still execute correctly.

- After you designate range and input values, you can enter new variables in the table and recalculate a new table by pressing Table (F8). You cannot recalculate a data table the same way you recalculate a worksheet—by setting **Global Recalculation** to Automatic, by pressing Calc (F9), or by placing {CALC} in a macro.

- If input values vary by a constant amount, create them by using /**Data Fill**.

- /**Data Table 1**, combined with @D functions, is useful for cross-tabulating information from a data table. For example, suppose that you have a database of checks with amount and account code. Using an @DSUM function as the data table formula and an input range of account codes generates a table of the total for each account code.

Cautions

- The data table covers existing information in cells.

- Press the Table key (F8) to repeat the most recent /**Data Table** command so that you update the table after worksheet changes.

For more information, see /**Data Fill** *and Chapter 12.*

Data Table 2 /DT2

Purpose

Generates a table composed of two varying input values and their effect on a single formula.

/Data Table 2 is useful for generating what-if models that show the results of changing two variables.

Reminders

- Formulas in /Data Table 2 can include functions.

- If you have to change a single input and see its result on many formulas, use /Data Table 1.

- Before executing /Data Table 2, enter data and formulas as though you were solving for a single solution (see cells B4..C8 in fig. D.2).

```
C8: (C2) [W12] @PMT(C5,C4/12,C6*12)                              READY
```

	A	B	C	D	E	F	G
1							
2		Data Table 2: Two Inputs					
3							
4		Interest =	0.08	<= Input 1			
5		Balance =	$15,000.00	<= Input 2			
6		Term =	4				
7							
8		Payment =	$366.19				
9							
10			Data Table 2	Input 2 Values =>			
11			+C8	12000	13000	14000	15000
12		Input 1 Values =>	0.065	$284.58	$308.29	$332.01	$355.72
13		=>	0.068	$286.24	$310.10	$333.95	$357.80
14		=>	0.070	$287.35	$311.30	$335.25	$359.19
15		=>	0.073	$289.03	$313.11	$337.20	$361.29
16		=>	0.075	$290.15	$314.33	$338.50	$362.68
17		=>	0.078	$291.83	$316.15	$340.47	$364.79
18		=>	0.080	$292.96	$317.37	$341.78	$366.19
19		=>	0.083	$294.65	$319.20	$343.76	$368.31
20		=>	0.085	$295.78	$320.43	$345.08	$369.72

```
09-Mar-91  06:29 PM
```

Fig. D.2. /Data Table 2: solving with two inputs and a single formula.

- In the leftmost column of the table, enter the numbers or text to be used by the first variable, Input 1 (C12..C20 in fig. D.2). In the top row of the table, enter the numbers or text to be used by the second variable, Input 2 (D11..G11). In the blank cell in the upper left corner of the table (C11), type the address of the cell containing the formula (+C8) or the formula itself.

• Make the cell address in the upper left corner of the table visible with /Range Format Text. You may need to widen the columns if you want to see all of the formula.

Procedures

1. Type /**dt2**.

2. Enter the table range so that it includes the Input 1 values in the leftmost column and the Input 2 values as the top row. If a range has been previously specified, press Esc and define the range: type the address, type an assigned range name, or highlight the range.

3. Enter the address for Input 1 (C4) by moving the cell pointer to the cell in which the first input values are to be substituted. In figure D.2, the values from C12 to C20 are to be substituted in C4 as the interest amount. Press Enter.

4. Enter the address for Input 2 (C5) by moving the cell pointer to the cell in which the second input values are to be substituted. In the example, the values from D11 to G11 are to be substituted in C5 as the principal amount. Press Enter.

5. 1-2-3 then substitutes Input 1 and Input 2 and recalculates the formula in C8. After each combination of substitutions, the formula in C8 calculates a new answer and displays it in the table. In the example, the variable inputs for interest (0.08) and balance ($15,000) produce a monthly payment of $366.19. The monthly payment formula (C8) is referenced in cell C11.

Important Cues

• Make the formula in the top left corner of the table range easier to understand by using /**Range Name Create** to change address locations (C4) to descriptive text (*Interest*). Make the formula visible with /**Range Format Text**.

• After you designate range and input values, you can change input values in the input column and row and recalculate a new table by pressing Table (F8).

• If input values are an evenly spaced series of numbers, create them with /**Data Fill**.

• /**Data Table 2**, combined with @D functions, is useful for cross-tabulating information from a database table.

For more information, see /**Data Fill** *and Chapter 12.*

Data Table Reset /DTR

Purpose

Resets the ranges you specified for all data tables.

Reminder

After you reset the data table ranges they are gone for good. If you are not sure whether you want to reset the data table ranges, save the file first with /File Save.

Procedures

Type **/dtr**.

For more information, see Chapter 12.

Data Sort /DS

Purpose

Sorts the database in ascending or descending order, according to the entries in one or two columns.

Reminders

- Sorting can be done on up to two fields (columns). The first sort field is the **Primary-Key**; the second is the **Secondary-Key**. Both keys can be sorted in ascending or descending order.

- Save a copy of the worksheet with /File Save before sorting. Save to a different name to preserve the original file.

- If you want to return after sorting to records (rows) that are in a specific order after sorting, insert a column and use /Data Fill to fill it with index numbers. Re-sort on the index numbers to return to the original order. Filling a range with sequential numbers is described in more detail in the /Data Fill entry.

Procedures

1. Type **/ds**.

2. Highlight the data range to be sorted. The range must include every field (column) in the database but does not have to include every record (row). Only records in the specified range are sorted, however. Do not include the field labels at the top of the database, or the labels are sorted with the data. Enter the range: type the address, type a range name, or highlight the range. Press Enter.

3. Move the cell pointer to the column of the database that is to be the **Primary-Key**; then press Enter.

4. Specify ascending or descending order by entering **A** or **D** and pressing Enter.

5. Select **Secondary-Key** if you want duplicate copies of the **Primary-Key** sorted. Move the cell pointer to the column of the database that is to be the **Secondary-Key** and then press Enter.

6. Specify ascending or descending order by selecting **A** or **D** and pressing Enter.

7. Select **Go**.

Important Cues

- Select **Quit** to return to READY mode at any time. Select **Reset** to clear previous settings.

- Sort settings are saved with the worksheet.

- During the Install process, you can change the order in which 1-2-3 sorts characters. The three sort precedences are ASCII, **Numbers First**, and **Numbers Last**. In ASCII and **Numbers First** formats, cell contents are sorted as follows:

  Blank spaces

  Special characters (!, #, $)

  Numeric characters

  Alpha characters

  Special compose characters

- In ASCII format, uppercase letters are sorted before lowercase; in **Numbers First** format, the case of characters is ignored. **Numbers Last** is similar to **Numbers First** except that numeric data is sorted after alpha characters.

Cautions

- If you sort a database without including the full width of records, the sorted portion is split from the nonsorted portion. Putting the records back together may be nearly impossible. If you saved the worksheet before sorting, you can retrieve the original file.

- Do not include blank rows or the data labels at the top of the database when you highlight the data range. Blank rows sort to the top or bottom of the database in ascending or descending order, and the data labels are sorted into the body of the database.

- Formulas in a sorted database may not be accurate because sorting switches rows to new locations. If the addresses do not use absolute and relative addressing correctly, the formulas in sorted records change. As a rule, use a relative address in a formula when the address refers to a cell in the same row. If the address refers to a cell outside the database, use an absolute address.

For more information, see /**Data Fill** *and Chapter 12.*

Data Query Input   /DQI

Purpose

Specifies a range of data records to be searched. The records can be within a worksheet's data table or within an external table. You can specify more than one data table.

Reminders

- You must indicate an input range before you use the Find, Extract, Unique, or Delete command from the /Data Query menu.

- The input range can be the entire database or a part of it.

- The input range must include the field names.

Procedures

1. Type /**dqi**.

2. At the `Enter input range:` prompt, specify the range of data records you want searched. Either type the range address or move the cell pointer to highlight the range. Be sure to include in the range the field names at the top of the range and portions of the records that may be off the screen.

Caution

Redefine the input range if you add one or more rows to the bottom of the range. A defined input range is adjusted automatically if you insert or delete rows or columns within the range.

For more information, see /**Data Query Output,** /**Data Query Criteria,** /**Data Query Find,** /**Data Query Extract,** *and Chapter 12.*

Data Query Criteria   /DQC

Purpose

Specifies the worksheet range containing the criteria that define which records are to be found.

Reminders

- You must indicate a criteria range before you use the Find, Extract, Unique, or Delete options of the /Data Query command.

- You do not need to include in the criteria and output ranges all the field names in the database. If you do include all the field names, however, you won't have to alter the criteria range to apply a criterion to a new field.

- The first row of the criteria range must contain field names that exactly match the field names of the database. Use the /Copy command to copy field names from input ranges to ensure that criteria and input range field names exactly match.

- The row below the first row of the criteria range contains the search criteria.

- You can use more than one criteria for a search.

- More than one row can contain criteria, but the row below the field names in the criteria range cannot be blank.

- Criteria can be numbers, labels, or formulas. Numbers and labels must be positioned directly below the field name to which they correspond.

- Criteria labels can contain wild-card characters. An asterisk (*) stands for any group of characters; a question mark (?) represents a single character.

- A tilde (~) before a label excludes that label from a search.

- Criteria can contain logical operators (<, <=, >, >=, <>).

- You can use #AND#, #NOT#, or #OR# to create compound logical formulas as criteria.

- Criteria on the same row of the criteria range are treated as if they were linked by #AND# for every condition to be met. Criteria on separate rows are treated as if they were linked by #OR# for any condition to be met.

Procedures

1. Type **/dqc**.

2. At the `Enter criteria range:` prompt, specify or highlight the range that contains field names and criteria. The range should contain at least two rows: the first row for field names from the top row of the database you want searched, and the second row for the criteria you specify. Allow two or more rows for criteria if you use them to specify #OR# conditions.

Important Cues

* Use wild cards in the criteria if you are unsure of spelling or want to find data that may have been misspelled. 1-2-3 searches only for exact matches for the characters in the criteria range.

* You can place the criteria range in the data-entry portion of the worksheet and use a split screen to view the criteria and output ranges simultaneously.

Cautions

* Including a blank row immediately below the field names in the criteria range causes all records to be found, retrieved, or deleted with **Query** commands.

* If you alter the number of rows in a defined criteria range, you must redefine the range to reflect the change.

For more information, see /**Data Query Input,** /**Data Query Find,** /**Data Query Extract,** *and Chapter 12.*

Data Query Output /DQO

Purpose

Assigns a location to which found records can be copied by the /Data Query Extract or /Data Query Unique commands.

Reminders

* You must indicate an output range before you use the Extract and Unique options of the /Data Query command. The Find and Delete options do not use an output range.

* Locate the output range so that there is nothing below its columns. Locate the output range so that it does not overlap the input or criteria ranges.

- You can limit the output range by specifying the size of the (multiple-row) range. Or you can ensure that the output range is unlimited in size if you specify the range as the single row of field names. That way, the results of the search can be listed in the unlimited area below the field names.

- The first row of the output range must contain field names that match the field names of the input and criteria ranges, but the field names in the output range can be in any order, and the label prefixes and the case of the letters can be different.

Procedures

1. Type /**dqo**.

2. At the Enter output range: prompt, specify or highlight the output field names. If you want a limited number of extracted records, include as many rows in the output range as you want extracted rows.

Caution

If you specify the row of field names as a single-row output range and use /**Data Query Extract** or /**Data Query Unique**, matching records are listed below the output range. Any information in the cells in the row-and-column path from directly below the output range through the bottom of the worksheet, however, are erased. If you want to preserve any information in those cells, specify the output range as a multiple-row range. That way, cells below the last row of the output range are not affected by any results of a search. If the output range is too small, you get the Too many records for output range error message and only a partial extract.

*For more information, see /**Data Query Input**, /**Data Query Criteria**, /**Data Query Extract**, /**Data Query Unique**, and Chapter 12.*

Data Query Find /DQF

Purpose

Finds records in the database that meet conditions you have set in the criteria range.

Reminders

- /**Data Query Find** moves the cell pointer to the first cell of the first record that meets the condition. By pressing the up- or down-arrow key, you can display previous or succeeding records that meet the criteria. Using /Data Query Find can be the best way to access a record in a database quickly.

- You must define the input range and criteria range before using /Data Query Find. Enter a criterion that specifies the type of records you want in the criteria range.

Procedures

1. Type /**dqf**.

2. The cell pointer highlights the first record that meets the criteria. You hear a beep if no record in the input range meets the criteria.

3. Press the up- or down-arrow key to move to the next record that meets the criteria. Pressing the Home key or the End key finds in the database the first or last record that meets the criteria.

4. You can edit contents within a record by moving the cell pointer right or left with the arrow keys. When the cell pointer highlights the cell you want to edit, press the Edit (F2) key and edit the cell contents. Press Enter when you finish editing.

5. Return to the /Data Query menu by pressing Enter or Esc when you are not in EDIT mode.

Important Cues

- After you enter the /Data Query commands and ranges, you can repeat the operation by changing the criteria and pressing the Query (F7) key.

- /dqf remembers the last input and criteria range used from the /Data Query menu. You do not have to enter the input and criteria range if they are the same as those used by the previous database command.

- Use wild cards (* or ?) in the criteria if you are unsure of the spelling or if you want to find data that may have been mis-spelled. 1-2-3 finds only exact matches for the characters in the criteria range.

- Before you delete records with /Data Query Delete, use /dqf to display the records to be deleted.

Cautions

- If /dqf does not find a record, use /Range Erase to erase old criteria from the criteria range. A space character may have been used to erase a field in the criteria range. If so, /dqf looks for a space in the database, a process that can result in no found records.

- If /dqf finds all records, use the /Data Query Criteria command to check the size of the criteria range. Do not include a blank row immediately below the field names in the criteria range; if you do, these commands find all records.

For more information, see /**Data Query Input**, /**Data Query Criteria**, *and Chapter 12.*

Data Query Extract   /DQE

Purpose

Copies to the output range of the worksheet those records that meet conditions set in the criteria range.

Reminders

- /Data Query Extract extracts copies of information from the input range that matches specific criteria found in the criteria range.

- You must define a 1-2-3 database complete with input, output, and criteria ranges. The output range must have field names entered exactly as they appear at the top of each database column.

- Choose an output range in a blank area of the worksheet. You can limit the output range to a specified number of rows, or you can give the output range an unlimited number of rows.

Procedure

Type /**dqe**.

Important Cues

- Records that match the criteria range are copied to the output range. If there is not enough room in the output range, 1-2-3 beeps, and an error message appears.

- After entering new criteria in the criteria range, press the Query (F7) key to repeat the most recent query.

- /dqe remembers the last input, criteria, and output ranges used from the /Data Query menu. You do not have to enter the ranges if they are the same as the previous ranges.

- Select the **Reset** command to clear all range settings.

- **/Data Query Unique** works the same way as /dqe, but **/Data Query Unique** extracts only unique records that meet the criteria.

Caution

If you select only the field names as the output range, you are given an unlimited amount of rows for the extracted report, but existing contents below the output field names are erased.

For more information, see **/Data Query Find, /Data Query Unique,** *and Chapter 12.*

Data Query Unique   /DQU

Purpose

Copies to the output range of the worksheet unique records that meet conditions set in the criteria.

Reminders

- **/Data Query Unique** extracts copies of information from the input range that match specific criteria found in the criteria range.

- You must define the input, output, and criteria ranges before using **/Data Query Unique**.

Procedure

Type **/dqu**.

Important Cues

- Nonduplicate records that match the criteria range are copied to the output range. If there is not enough room in the output range, 1-2-3 beeps, and an error message appears.

- Only field names in the output range are used to test whether a record has a duplicate. A single copy of all duplicates appears in the output range.

- To include duplicate records in the extract range, use **/Data Query Extract**.

- After entering new criteria in the criteria range or copying new headings into the output range, press the Query (F7) key to repeat the most recent query.

- /dqu remembers the last input, criteria, and output ranges used from the /**Data Query** menu. You do not have to enter the ranges if they are the same as the previous ranges.

- Select **Reset** to clear all range settings.

Cautions

- As with other /**Data Query** commands, the field names in the criteria range must match the field names in the database.

- If you select only the field names as the output range, you are given an unlimited number of rows for the extracted report, but existing contents below the output field names are erased.

For more information, see /**Data Query Input**, /**Data Query Output**, /**Data Query Criteria**, /**Data Query Find**, /**Data Query Extract**, *and Chapter 12.*

Data Query Delete   /DQD

Purpose

Removes from the input range any records that meet conditions in the criteria range.

Reminders

- Use /**Data Query Delete** to clean up the database and to remove records that are not current or that have been extracted to another area of the worksheet.

- You must define a 1-2-3 database complete with input and criteria ranges.

- Create a backup file before using /**Data Query Delete**. If data is incorrectly deleted, a copy of the worksheet is intact.

- To check which records are marked for deletion, select /**Data Query Find** after you enter the input and criteria ranges. Use the up- and down-arrow keys to display the records that meet the criteria.

- Another method of checking the records marked for deletion is to use /**Data Query Extract** to make a copy of the records. Check this copy against the records you want to delete.

Procedures

1. Type /**dqd**.

2. You are asked whether you want to delete the records. Select **Cancel** to stop the command and not delete records. Select **Delete** to remove the records from the input range.

3. Save the worksheet under a new file name by using **/File Save**. Do not save the worksheet under the same file name; doing so replaces the original database with the database from which records have been deleted.

Important Cues

- After entering new criteria, press the Query (F7) key to repeat the most recent query.

- Create a rolling database that stores only current records and removes old records to archive files. Use **/Data Query Extract** to extract old records from the file; save them to another worksheet by using **/File Xtract**. Then use **/dqd** to remove the old records from the database file.

Cautions

- As with other **/Data Query** commands, the field labels in the criteria range must match the field labels in the database. The labels can appear in a different order, but the spelling must match. The easiest and safest method of creating criteria labels is to use **/Copy**.

- You can inadvertently delete more than you want with **/dqd**, particularly if the row immediately below the field names in the criteria range is empty when you execute **/dqd**. Make sure that your criteria range is set up correctly before you use this command.

For more information, see **/Data Query Find**, **/Data Query Extract**, **/Worksheet Delete Row**, **/Range Erase**, *and Chapter 12.*

Data Query Reset   /DQR

Purpose

Clears the current input, criteria, and output ranges.

Procedure

Type **/dqr**.

For more information, see Chapter 12.

Data Distribution */DD*

Purpose

Creates a frequency distribution showing how often specific data occurs in a database.

For example, using data from a local consumer survey, you can have /**Data Distribution** determine how income is distributed. After you set up income brackets as a *bin*, /**Data Distribution** shows how many people's incomes fall within each bin. Figure D.3 shows an example of this type of distribution. The contents of column E (text values) were entered manually.

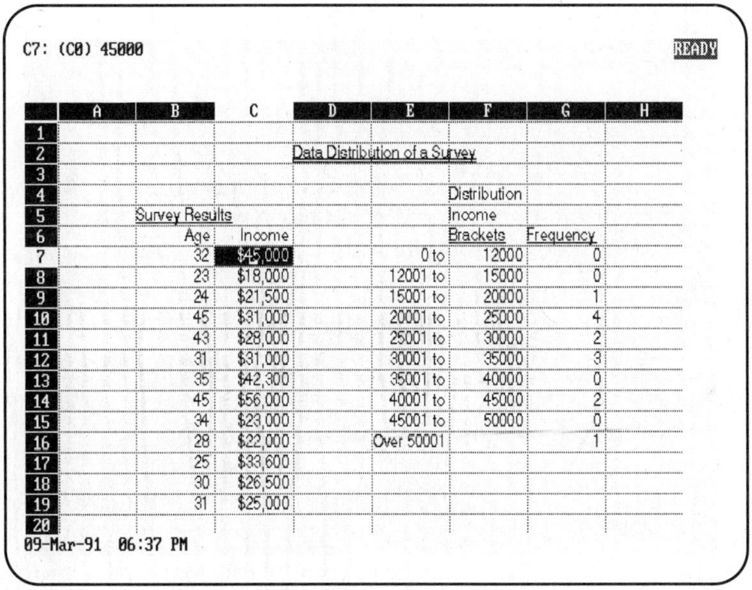

```
C7: (C0) 45000                                              READY

      A        B        C        D        E        F        G        H
 1
 2                              Data Distribution of a Survey
 3
 4                                         Distribution
 5            Survey Results               Income
 6                  Age   Income           Brackets  Frequency
 7                  32    $45,000     0 to   12000        0
 8                  23    $18,000  12001 to  15000        0
 9                  24    $21,500  15001 to  20000        1
10                  45    $31,000  20001 to  25000        4
11                  43    $28,000  25001 to  30000        2
12                  31    $31,000  30001 to  35000        3
13                  35    $42,300  35001 to  40000        0
14                  45    $56,000  40001 to  45000        2
15                  34    $23,000  45001 to  50000        0
16                  28    $22,000  Over 50001             1
17                  25    $33,600
18                  30    $26,500
19                  31    $25,000
20
09-Mar-91  06:37 PM
```

Fig. D.3. *An example of /Data Distribution.*

Reminders

- /**Data Distribution** works only on numeric values.

- Data must be arranged in a value range: a column, row, or rectangular range.

- You must move the cell pointer to a worksheet portion that has two adjacent blank columns. In the left column, enter the highest value for each entry in the bin range. Enter bin values in ascending order.

Procedures

1. Type /**dd**.

2. Enter the value range at the `Enter values range:` prompt, which contains the data being analyzed. The value range in figure D.3 is C7..C19.

3. Enter the bin range at the `Enter bin range:` prompt, type the range address, type a preset range name, or highlight the range. The bin range in figure D.3 is F7..F15.

4. The frequency distribution appears in the column to the right of the bin range. In figure D.3, the distribution appears in G7..G16. Notice that the frequency column extends one row beyond the bin range. The last frequency value is the number of values that are greater than the last bin value.

Important Cues

• Use /**Data Fill** to create a bin range with evenly distributed values.

• You can find distribution patterns of subgroups in the database by first using /**Data Query Extract** to create a select database. Use /dd to find the distribution in the subgroup.

• You can make data distribution tables easier to read by including a text column at the left of the bin range.

• Use @DCOUNT with /**Data Table 1** to determine the data distribution for text in a database. Enter the text being counted down the left column of the data table. The input cell is the cell in the criteria range into which you would insert text. The @DCOUNT function should be placed in the top row of the data table area.

• Use @DCOUNT if you want to count items that match more than one criterion. (/dd uses the bin as the only criterion.) Insert criteria in the criteria range by using /**Data Table 1** or /**Data Table 2**.

Cautions

• Text labels and blanks are evaluated as zero in the value's range.

• /dd overwrites any cell contents that previously existed in the frequency column.

*For more information, see /**Data Table 1, /Data Table 2, /Data Fill**, and Chapter 12.*

Data Matrix   /DM

Purpose

Multiplies column-and-row matrices of cells. Inverts columns and rows in square matrices.

Reminder

/Data Matrix, a specialized mathematical command, enables you to solve simultaneous linear equations. You also can do array math or array manipulations.

Procedures

To invert a matrix, follow these steps:

1. Type /**dm**.

2. Choose **Invert**. You can invert a nonsingular square matrix of up to 80 rows and columns.

3. Enter the range address or range name of the range you want to invert.

4. Type or highlight an output range to hold the inverted solution matrix. You can indicate or point to only the upper left corner of the output range. You can locate the output range anywhere on the worksheet, including on top of the matrix you are inverting.

5. Press Enter.

To multiply matrices, follow these steps:

1. Type /**dm**.

2. Choose **Multiply**. You can multiply two rectangular matrices together in accordance with the rules of matrix algebra.

3. Enter the range address or range name of the first range to multiply. The number of columns of the first range must equal the number of rows of the second range. The maximum size of the matrix is 80 rows by 80 columns.

4. Enter the range address or range name of the second range to multiply.

5. Enter an output range to hold the multiplied solution matrix. You can type or point to only the upper left corner of the output range, and then press Enter. The resulting matrix has the same number of rows as the first matrix, and the same number of columns as the second.

Caution

The output matrix overwrites existing cell contents.

For more information, see Chapter 12.

Data Regression   /DR

Purpose

Finds trends in data by using multiple linear regression techniques. Data regression calculates the best straight line relating dependent values to independent values.

Reminders

- /**Data Regression** measures the dependency of dependent values to independent values. The measure of this dependency is displayed as *R Squared*. The closer R Squared is to 1, the greater the dependency.

- A completed regression analysis produces the constant and X coefficients so that you can predict new values of Y from a given X. The following equation calculates Y values:

    Y = Constant + Coeff. of X1*X1 + Coeff. of X2*X2 + Coeff. of X3*X3 + ...

- If there is a single X for each Y, the formula is the familiar formula for a straight line:

    Y = Constant + Coeff. of X1*X1

- The *Constant* term is the location where the best-fit line intersects the y-axis.

- The output area always is nine rows in length and four columns wide.

Procedures

1. Type /**dr**.

2. Select **X-Range**; then specify the range containing up to 16 independent variables. The values must be in adjacent columns.

3. Select **Y-Range**; then specify the range containing a single column of dependent variables. This single column must have the same number of rows as the X-Range.

4. Select Intercept and choose one of the following items:

Menu Item	Description
Compute	Calculates the best-fit equation. The y-axis intercept finds its own value.
Zero	Calculates the best-fit equation but forces the equation to cross the y-axis at zero when all X values are zero

5. Select **Output-Range** and enter the cell address of the upper left corner of the output range.

6. Select **Go**.

Important Cues

*   You can enter a row of coefficient labels between the Degrees of Freedom row and the X Coefficient(s) rows that are not overwritten by the output range.

*   To create a best-fit straight line from the results of /**Data** **Regression**, execute /dr, sort the original X and Y data in ascending order by using X data as the primary sort field (so that the graph plots correctly), and then enter the following formula in the top cell of the calculated Y column:

    Ycalc = Xvalue * Coeff. of X1 + Constant

    Copy this formula down a column to produce all the calculated Y values for each real X value. Use the /**Graph** commands to generate an XY graph where the X range for the graph is the real X value. The A graph range is the original Y data, and the B graph range is the calculated Y data.

Caution

/**Data** **Regression** produces the warning `Cannot Invert Matrix` if one set of X values is proportional to another set of X values. Values are proportional when one set of X values can be multiplied by a constant to produce the second set of X values.

For more information, see the /**Graph** *commands and Chapter 12.*

Data Parse   /DP

Purpose

Separates the long labels resulting from /**File** **Import** into discrete text and numeric cell entries. The separated text and numbers are placed in individual cells in a row.

Reminders

- Import the data with /File Import Text. Each row of text from the file appears in a single cell. Rows of text appear down a single column.

- The long label resulting from /File Import Text may appear to be entries in more than one cell; however, the long label is located in the single cell at the far left of the worksheet.

- If the file you are importing includes numbers surrounded by spaces and text within quotation marks, use /File Import Numbers. This command automatically separates numbers and text in quotation marks into separate cells.

- Find in the worksheet a clear area to which the parsed data can be copied and then note the cell addresses of the corners. Move the cell pointer to the first cell in the column you want to parse.

- /Data Parse separates the long label by using the rules displayed in the format line. You can edit the format line if you want the data to be separated in a different way.

Procedures

1. Move the cell pointer to the first cell in the row where you want to begin parsing.

2. Type /**dp**.

3. Select Format-Line.

4. Select Create. A format line is inserted at the cell pointer, and the row of data moves down. This format line shows 1-2-3's best guess at how the data in the cell pointer should be separated.

5. You may want to edit the format line if a parsed area is not wide enough to include all the data in a field or if a field is not the correct type. If you want to change the format line, select Edit from the Format-Line menu. Edit the format line and press Enter.

6. If the imported data is in different formats, such as an uneven number of items or a mixture of field names and numbers, you must create additional format lines. Enter these lines at the row where the data format changed. Create additional format lines by selecting Quit and repeating the procedure.

7. Select Input-Column.

8. Specify the column containing the format line and the data it is to format. Do not highlight the columns to the right that appear to contain data, but do not.

9. Select **Output-Range**.

10. Move the cell pointer to the upper left corner of the range to receive the parsed data and press Enter.

11. Select **Go**.

Important Cues

- Figure D.4 shows two format lines generated automatically by 1-2-3. The first format line is for the field names; the second is for the data. The initial format lines separate inventory items that have a blank in the name. The asterisk (*) followed by an *L* shows where 1-2-3 thinks that a new field should begin.

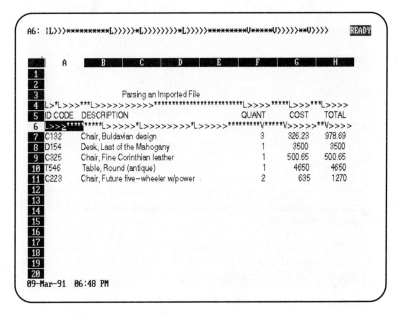

Fig. D.4. *Format lines for /Data Parse.*

- Use symbols to indicate the first character of a label (L), value (V), date (D), or time (T). You also can choose to skip a character (S), specify additional characters of the same type (>), or add a blank space (*) if the data is longer than the > symbols indicate.

- Editing keys can be used on the format line to change the parsing rules. In addition, you can use the up- and down-arrow keys, PgDn, and PgUp keys to scroll the information on-screen. Use this method to see whether the format line has assigned enough space for each piece of data being parsed.

Caution

The output range should be blank. Parsed data covers any information previously in the output range.

For more information, see /**File Import** *and Chapter 12.*

System, Add-In, and Quit Commands /S, /A, and /Q

Throughout this section, refer to the /Add-In menu on the 1-2-3 side of the pull-out command card at the back of this book.

System /S

Purpose

Leaves the current worksheet, exits from 1-2-3 temporarily so that you can run operating-system commands, and enables you to return to 1-2-3 and the worksheet.

Reminders

- Be certain that the programs you run from within 1-2-3 can fit in your computer's available memory. Do not load or run memory-resident programs from the system level.

- If you want to run an external operating-system command, be sure that the command is available on your disk drive or is on the path for a hard disk system.

Procedures

1. Type /**s**.

2. Type the internal operating-system commands or program names that you want to run.

3. When you finish running a program, return to the operating system.

4. Return to 1-2-3 from the operating-system prompt by typing **EXIT** and then pressing Enter.

Important Cue

For a complete discussion of the various operating-system commands, see *Using DOS* and *Que's MS-DOS 5 User's Guide*, Special Edition, both published by Que Corporation.

Caution

Do not attempt to run the BPRINT background printing utility from the /System command. You must leave 1-2-3 and run BPRINT before you start 1-2-3.

For more information, see Chapter 2.

Add-In Attach   /AA

Purpose

Loads an add-in application program into memory. Add-in applications are programs that work along with 1-2-3 to extend its capabilities. Release 2.3 comes with five add-in programs: Wysiwyg, the Macro Library Manager, Viewer, Auditor, and the 1-2-3 Release 2.3 Tutorial.

Assigns a function key (for example, Alt-F7) that you can use to invoke the add-in each time you want to use it.

Reminders

- Make sure that the add-in program is in the default 1-2-3 directory. Add-in programs have the extension ADN. The Wysiwyg add-in, for example, is WYSIWYG.ADN; the Macro Library Manager is MACROMGR.ADN. For more details, refer to the documentation for your add-in program.

- You may not have enough memory to attach an add-in unless you remove other memory-resident programs (such as SideKick) or detach other add-ins.

Procedures

1. Type /aa (or press Alt-F10 and select **Attach**).

2. Highlight the add-in name from the list of ADN files displayed. Press Enter.

3. Select one of the following items:

Menu Item	Description
No-Key	Does not assign the add-in to a function key. The add-in must be invoked with /Add-In **Invoke**.
7	Assigns the add-in to Alt-F7
8	Assigns the add-in to Alt-F8
9	Assigns the add-in to Alt-F9
10	Assigns the add-in to Alt-F10

Important Cues

- You can invoke an add-in by using the function key you assigned to the add-in when you attached it or by using the /Add-In Invoke command.

- If you want an add-in to attach automatically each time you start 1-2-3, use /Worksheet Global Default Other Add-In Set. Be sure to use /Worksheet Global Default Update to save the setting.

- When you don't have enough memory to attach an add-in, you get a `Memory Full` error message. If any other add-ins are attached, you can use /Add-In Detach to remove them from memory, allowing room for the other add-in. You also can exit from 1-2-3 and free up memory by removing any other memory-resident programs you may be using.

For more information, see Chapter 2.

Add-In [Detach, Clear]   */AD or /AC*

Purpose

Removes add-ins from memory so that you have more memory available for your spreadsheet or other add-ins.

Procedures

To remove an add-in from memory, do the following steps:

1. Type **/ad** (or press Alt-F10 and select **Detach**).

2. Highlight the add-in from the displayed list of attached add-ins. Press Enter.

3. Select **Quit** to leave the /Add-In menu.

To remove all add-ins from memory, do the following:

1. Type **/ac** (or press Alt-F10 and select **Clear**).

2. Select **Quit** to leave the /Add-In menu.

Important Cue

The /Add-In Detach and /Add-In Clear commands remove the application from memory during the current work session only. If you have an auto-attach add-in that you no longer want to attach automatically, use the /Worksheet Global Default Other Add-In Cancel command. Be sure to use /Worksheet Global Default Update to save the setting.

For more information, see Chapter 2.

Add-In Invoke   /AI

Purpose

Activates an add-in program that you have previously attached.

Use this command when you want to use the commands or functions in the add-in program.

Reminder

If you used /Worksheet Global Default Other Add-In Set to attach the add-in automatically, the add-in must be attached either with /Add-In Attach or automatically when 1-2-3 is loaded.

Procedures

If you did not assign a function key to the add-in or if you did not choose to attach the add-in automatically, do the following:

1. Type /**ai**.

2. Highlight the add-in from the list of attached add-ins. Press Enter.

    Refer to the add-in's documentation for specific instructions on using the add-in.

If you assigned a function key to the add-in, do the following:

Press Alt and the function key (F7-F10) you assigned to the add-in when you attached it. If you assigned the add-in to the F7 function key, for example, press Alt-F7 to invoke the add-in.

Refer to the add-in's documentation for specific operation instructions.

Important Cue

You can automatically attach and invoke the add-in by using /Worksheet **Default O**ther **Add-In S**et. Choose **Y**es in response to the prompt Automatically invoke this add-in whenever you start 1-2-3? Be sure to use /Worksheet **G**lobal **D**efault **U**pdate to save the setting.

For more information, see Chapter 2.

Quit /Q

Purpose

Leaves 1-2-3 for the current work session and returns to the operating system.

Reminder

Make sure that you have saved the current worksheet and graph before exiting from 1-2-3.

Procedures

1. Type /q.

2. Press **Y** to quit 1-2-3 and return to the operating system. Press **N** to return to 1-2-3 and the current worksheet.

3. If you made changes to the worksheet, press **Y** to quit without saving. Press **N** to return to the worksheet.

4. If you started 1-2-3 from the Lotus 1-2-3 Access menu, you return to it. From the Lotus 1-2-3 Access menu, choose **Exit** to leave 1-2-3. If you started 1-2-3 by typing **123**, you return to the operating system.

Important Cue

Use the DOS COPY or DISKCOPY command to create a backup of important files. To guard against data loss, be sure to make backup copies regularly and keep a weekly archival backup copy at a separate location. In most cases, the computer can be replaced, but the data and worksheets cannot.

Caution

Worksheets not saved with /**File Save** or /**File Xtract** are lost when you exit from 1-2-3. Changes to existing worksheets or graphs are not recorded unless the worksheet has been saved with /**File Save**.

For more information, see /**File Save**, /**File Xtract**, *and Chapter 2.*

:Worksheet Commands   :W

:Worksheet commands set column widths, row heights, and page breaks. Please refer to the :Worksheet menu on the Wysiwyg side of the pull-out command card in the back of this book.

Worksheet Column   :WC

Purpose

Sets column widths.

Reminders

- Make certain that changing the width of a column does not destroy the appearance of displays in another portion of the worksheet.

- Move the cell pointer to the widest entry in the column before you use :wc.

Procedures

1. Type :wc.

2. Select one of the following menu items:

Menu Item	Description
Set-Width	Sets the width for one or more columns in the worksheet
Reset-Width	Resets the width of one or more columns to the global default column width

3. If you selected Set-Width, specify the columns whose width you want to change. Then enter the new column width by typing the number of characters or by pressing the left- or right-arrow key to shrink or expand the column or by using the mouse icons.

4. If you selected Reset-Width, specify the columns whose widths you want to reset. 1-2-3 automatically sets the width of all specified columns to the global default column-width setting.

Important Cue

Unlike most Wysiwyg commands, the column widths you set with :wc remain in the worksheet even when Wysiwyg is not loaded. In other words, the column-width settings are saved with the worksheet file and not with the Wysiwyg format settings.

For more information, see Chapter 9.

Worksheet Row :WR

Purpose

Sets row heights in the worksheet.

Reminder

Make certain that changing the height of a row does not destroy the appearance of displays in another portion of the worksheet.

Procedures

1. Type **:wr**.

2. Select one of the following menu items:

Menu Item	Description
Set-Height	Sets the height for one or more rows in the worksheet
Auto	Sets the height of one or more rows to the height that best suits the largest font in the rows

3. If you selected Set-Height, specify the rows whose height you want to change. Then enter the new height by typing the number (in point sizes between 1 and 255), by pressing the up- or down-arrow key to shrink or expand the row, or by using the mouse icons.

   If you selected Auto, specify the rows whose height you want to reset. 1-2-3 automatically sets the height of all specified rows to the height that best fits the largest font used in those rows.

For more information, see Chapter 9.

Worksheet Page :WP

Purpose

Inserts or removes a page break in a worksheet.

Reminder

Before you use **:wp**, move the cell-pointer to the row or column in the worksheet with which you want to begin the new page. If you want to begin a new page with row 35, for example, move the cell-pointer to any cell in row 35.

Procedures

1. Type **:wp**.

2. Choose one of the following menu items:

Menu Item	Description
Row	Inserts a horizontal page break (begin a new page at a specific row)
Column	Inserts a vertical page break (begin a new page at a specific column)
Delete	Removes a page break from the current column or row
Quit	Returns to READY mode

Important Cues

- 1-2-3 only uses page breaks inserted with **:wp** when you print with the **:Print** command. To insert a page break to use with the **/Print** commands, type **/wp**.

- Use **:Display Options Page-Breaks No** to hide the page break lines that 1-2-3 displays.

- A row page break is inserted at the top of the current row. A column page break is inserted to the left of the current column.

For more information, see Chapter 9.

:Format Commands   :F

:Format commands set the display of ranges in the worksheet. You use :Format commands to format both the screen display and printed output. Throughout this section, refer to the :Format menu on the Wysiwyg side of the pull-out command card in the back of this book.

Format Font   :FF

Purpose

Specifies the fonts you want to use for ranges in a worksheet and for default fonts.

Reminder

Each Wysiwyg font set contains eight fonts. You can use any or all of these fonts in the worksheet; however, depending on the printer and printer memory, you may not be able to print all eight fonts.

Procedures

1. Type **:ff**.

2. Choose one of the following items:

Menu Item	Description
1-8	Sets characters in a range to a font in the current font set
Replace	Replaces one of the fonts in the current font set with a different font
Default	Replaces the current font settings with the fonts from the default font set or update the default font set with the current fonts
Library	Retrieves, erases, or saves a font library file on disk
Quit	Returns to READY mode

3. If you chose **1** through **8**, specify the range you want to display with the selected font.

4. If you chose **Default**, select **Restore** to cancel the current font settings and replace them with the fonts from the default font set; select **Update** to copy the current font settings into the default font set file on disk.

5. If you chose **Replace**, select one of the fonts in the current font set, **1-8**. Then select a new typeface from the following menu: **Swiss, Dutch, Courier, Xsymbol,** or **Other**. If you select **Other**, select one of the additional typefaces displayed. Finally, specify a font size by entering a number from 3 to 72, inclusive.

6. If you chose **Library**, select one of the following menu items:

Menu Item	Description
Retrieve	Retrieves the font settings from a font set file on disk and makes that the current font set

Menu Item	Description
Save	Saves the current font set in a font file on disk
Erase	Deletes a font file from disk

Then specify the name of the font file from which you want to retrieve settings, to which you want to save the current font set, or which you want to erase from disk. If you specified a font file to save that already exists, select Cancel to cancel the save or select Replace to save with the new font settings.

Important Cues

- When typing data, or when in :Text Edit mode, you also can specify a font format for a range with a formatting sequence. To use a formatting sequence, move the cursor to the first character you want to format, press Ctrl-a, and type one of the following formatting codes: **1F** (font 1 in the current font set), **2F** (font 2 in the current font set), **3F**, **4F**, **5F**, **6F**, **7F**, or **8F**. Then move the cursor to the last character you want to format and press Ctrl-n.

- If you select :Format Font Replace and specify a font size that

  you have not previously installed, 1-2-3 selects the font size nearest to the size you specified.

- When you replace a font, all data previously formatted with the font number changes to the new font.

For more information, see Chapter 9.

Format Bold   :FB

Purpose

Adds or removes a bold format to characters in a range.

Reminders

- 1-2-3 displays Wysiwyg format settings only when Wysiwyg is in memory.

- Before you use the :Format Bold command, move the cell-pointer to the first cell in the range you want to format or prespecify the range.

Procedures

1. Type :fb.

2. Select **Set** to add the bold format to a range; select **Clear** to remove a bold format from a range.

3. Specify the range you want to format, either by typing the cell address, highlighting the range, or typing or highlighting the range name.

Important Cue

When typing data, or when in **:Text Edit** mode, you also canspecify a bold format for a range with a formatting sequence. To use a formatting sequence, move the cursor to the first character you want to bold, press Ctrl-a, and type **b**. Then move the cursor to the last character you want to format and type Ctrl-n.

For more information, see Chapter 9.

Format Italics   :FI

Purpose

Adds or removes an italic format to (or from) characters in a range.

Reminders

• 1-2-3 displays Wysiwyg format settings only when Wysiwyg is in memory.

• Before you use the **:Format Italics** command, move the cell-pointer to the first cell in the range you want to format.

Procedures

1. Type **:fi**.

2. Select **Set** to add the italic format to characters in a range; select **Clear** to remove italic from characters in a range.

3. Specify the range you want to format, either by typing the cell address, highlighting the range, or typing or highlighting the range name.

Important Cue

When typing data, or when in **:Text Edit** mode, you also can specify an italic format for characters in a range with a formatting sequence. To use a formatting sequence, move the cursor to the first character you want to italicize, type Ctrl-a, and type **i**. Then move the cursor to the last character you want to format and type Ctrl-n.

For more information, see Chapter 9.

Format Underline *:FU*

Purpose

Adds or removes an underline to (or from) characters in a range.

Reminders

- 1-2-3 displays Wysiwyg format settings only when Wysiwyg is in memory.

- Before you use the **:Format Underline** command, move the cell-pointer to the first cell in the range you want to format.

Procedures

1. Type **:fu**.

2. Choose one of the following items:

Menu Item	*Description*
Single	Adds a single underline to characters in a range
Double	Adds a double underline to characters in a range
Wide	Adds a wide underline to characters in a range
Clear	Clears the underline from characters in a range

3. Specify the range you want to format, either by typing the cell address, highlighting the range, or typing or highlighting the range name.

Important Cues

- When typing data, or when in **:Text Edit** mode, you also can specify an underline format for characters in a range with a formatting sequence. To use a formatting sequence, move the cursor to the first character you want to underline, type Ctrl-a, and then type one of the following formatting codes: **1_** (single underline), **2_** (double underline), **3_** (wide underline). Then move the cursor to the last character you want to format and type Ctrl-n.

- **:Format Underline** does not underline blank cells. Use **:Format Line** to underline entire cells, regardless of the cell contents.

For more information, see Chapter 9.

Format Color :FC

Purpose

Specifies colors for data in a range, both for screen display and for printed output.

Reminders

- 1-2-3 displays Wysiwyg format settings only when Wysiwyg is in memory.

- Before you use the :Format Color command, move the cell-pointer to the first cell in the range you want to format.

Procedures

1. Type :fc.

2. Choose one of the following items:

Menu Item	Description
Text	Sets data in a range to a specified color
Background	Sets the background color for a range
Negative	Sets the color for negative values in a range
Reverse	Reverses the Background and Text colors in a range
Quit	Returns to READY mode

3. If you chose Text or Background, select one of the following colors: Normal, Red, Green, Dark-Blue, Cyan, Yellow, or Magenta.

   If you chose Negative, select Normal to use the same color as the Text color or select Red.

4. Specify the range you want to format, either by typing the cell address, highlighting the range, or typing or highlighting the range name.

Important Cues

- 1-2-3 uses the color you select for Text as the color for underlining in the range.

- You can display negative values in a color other than the Text color or red by selecting :Display Colors Neg and choosing an alternate color.

Caution

Some noncolor printers use very similar shading for different colors. If you are formatting the worksheet with many different colors, try previewing a page first with **:Print Preview**. Then select colors that work on both the display and your printer.

For more information, see Chapter 9.

Format Lines   :FL

Purpose

Specifies lines along the edges of cells and ranges on the worksheet.

Reminders

- 1-2-3 displays Wysiwyg format settings only when Wysiwyg is in memory.

- Before you use the **:Format Lines** command, move the cell-pointer to the first cell in the range you want to format.

Procedures

1. Type **:fl**.

2. Choose one of the following items:

Menu Item	Description
Outline	Creates a single-line outline around a range
Left	Creates a vertical line along the left edge of each cell in a range
Right	Creates a vertical line along the right edge of each cell in a range
Top	Creates a horizontal line along the top edge of each cell in a range
Bottom	Creates a horizontal line along the bottom edge of each cell in a range
All	Creates a single-line outline around every cell in a range
Double	Creates a double-line outline around all or part of a range
Wide	Creates a wide-line outline around all or part of a range

Menu Item	Description
Clear	Clears lines from cells in a range
Shadow	Creates a drop shadow outline below and to the right of a range or removes drop shadow

3. If you chose **Outline**, **Left**, **Right**, **Top**, **Bottom**, or **All**, specify the range you want to format.

   If you chose **Double**, **Wide**, or **Clear**, select one of the following menu items:

Menu Item	Description
Outline	Creates or removes an outline around a range
Left	Creates or removes a vertical line along the left edge of each cell in a range
Right	Creates or removes a vertical line along the right edge of each cell in a range
Top	Creates or removes a horizontal line along the top edge of each cell in a range
Bottom	Creates or removes a horizontal line along the bottom edge of each cell in a range
All	Creates or removes an outline of the specified width around every cell in a range

Then specify the range you want to format. If you chose **Shadow**, select **Set** to create a drop shadow outline or select **Clear** to remove a drop shadow outline. Then specify the range you want to format.

Figure F.1 shows several different line formats in a worksheet.

Important Cue

1-2-3 uses the color you select for **Text** as the color for the lines in the range.

For more information, see Chapter 9.

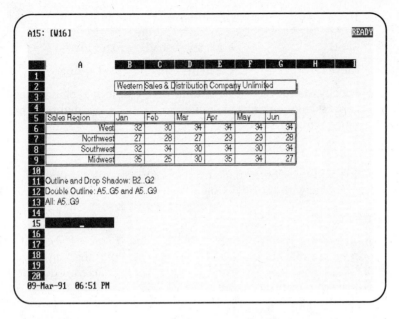

Fig. F.1. Outlines and drop shadows created with :Format Line.

Format Shade   :FS

Purpose

Adds or removes shading of a range.

Reminders

- 1-2-3 displays Wysiwyg format settings only when Wysiwyg is in memory.

- Before you use the :Format Shade command, move the cell-pointer to the first cell in the range you want to format.

Procedures

1. Type **:fs**.

2. Choose one of the following items:

Menu Item	Description
Light	Adds light shading to a range
Dark	Adds dark shading to a range

Menu Item	Description
Solid	Adds solid shading to a range
Clear	Clears the shading from a range

3. Specify the range you want to format, either by typing the cell address, highlighting the range, or typing or highlighting the range name.

Important Cue

Solid shading hides the data in a cell unless you select a different color for the data with **:Format Color Text**.

Caution

Solid shading always prints in black, even if you are using a color printer. For that reason, you should only use solid shading on areas of the worksheet that are blank or that contain data you do not want displayed in printed output.

For more information, see Chapter 9.

Format Reset   :FR

Purpose

Clears all format settings created with the **:Format** and **:Named-Style** commands from a range.

Reminders

- 1-2-3 displays Wysiwyg format settings only when Wysiwyg is in memory.

- Before you use the **:Format Reset** command, move the cell-pointer to the first cell in the range you want to reset.

Procedures

1. Type **:fr**.

2. Specify the range that contains the format settings you want to clear.

Important Cue

:Format Reset does not reset formats that are set with **/Range Format**, **/Worksheet Global Format**, or with special Wysiwyg formatting sequences.

For more information, see Chapter 9.

:Graph Commands :G

:Graph commands enable you to edit graphs and other graphics and to place them in the worksheet for display and for printing. Throughout this section, refer to the :Graph menu on the Wysiwyg side of the pull-out command card in the back of this book.

Graph Add :GA

Purpose

Inserts a graphic into the worksheet (both for display and for printing).

Reminder

Before you select :Graph Add, move the cell-pointer to the first cell in the range in which you want to add the graphic.

Procedures

1. Type :ga.

2. Choose one of the following items:

Menu Item	Description
Current	Inserts the current graph into the worksheet
Named	Inserts a named graph into the worksheet
PIC	Inserts a graphic in PIC format into the worksheet
Metafile	Inserts a graphic in metafile (CGM) format into the worksheet
Blank	Inserts a placeholder for a graphic into the worksheet

3. If you chose **Named**, **PIC**, or **Metafile**, specify from the list 1-2-3 shows the graph or graphic you want to display in the worksheet. Then specify the range into which you want to place the graphic.

   If you chose **Current** or **Blank**, specify the range into which you want to place the graphic.

Important Cues

- 1-2-3 automatically sizes the graphic you select so that it fits into the specified range.

- Use **:Graph Add B**lank when you haven't yet created the graph or graphic you want to insert into the worksheet.

For more information, see Chapter 11.

Graph Remove   **:GR**

Purpose

Removes a graphic from the worksheet.

Reminder

:Graph Remove does not delete a graph you created with /Graph; it only removes the display of the graph from the worksheet. You still can view the graph by pressing F10 or by selecting /Graph View.

Procedures

1. Type **:gr**.
2. Specify the graphic you want to remove from the worksheet by specifying a cell in the range that includes the graphic or by pressing F3 and selecting the name of the graph.

Important Cues

- Removing a graphic does not affect any data in the range in which you displayed the graphic.

- You can remove more than one graphic at the same time by specifying a range that contains all the graphics you want to remove.

Caution

Any edits you have made to a graphic with **:Graph Edit** are lost when you remove it.

For more information, see Chapter 11.

Graph Goto   **:GG**

Purpose

Moves the cell-pointer to the specified graphic.

Procedures

1. Type **:gg**.

2. Select the name of the graphic you want to move to by specifying a cell in the range that contains the graphic or by pressing F3 and selecting the name of the graphic.

Important Cue

If you have a small worksheet, use the mouse or arrow keys to move to the graphic.

For more information, see Chapter 11.

Graph Settings   *:GS*

Purpose

Sets the way a graphic is displayed in the worksheet.

Reminders

- Use **:Graph Settings** to replace one graphic with another, to hide the display of a graphic, to resize or move a graphic, to make a graphic opaque or transparent, and to synchronize updating a graph with changes in the worksheet's data.

- Before you select **:Graph Settings**, move the cell-pointer to a cell in the range that contains the graphic you want to work with.

Procedures

1. Type **:gs**.

2. Choose one of the following items:

Menu Item	Description
Graph	Replaces a graphic in the worksheet with a different graphic
Range	Moves or changes the size of a graphic
Sync	Synchronizes updating a graph with updates in the worksheet's data
Display	Displays the data in the graphic or displays the graphic as a shaded rectangle in the worksheet

Menu Item	Description
Opaque	Displays the data in the graphic (opaque) or displays the data in the range underneath the graphic (transparent)
Quit	Returns the worksheet to READY mode

3. If you chose **Graph**, select the graphic you want to replace by specifying a cell in the range that contains the graphic or by pressing F3 and selecting the graphic's name. Then choose one of the following items:

Menu Item	Description
Current	Replaces the graphic with the current graph
Named	Replaces the graphic with a named graph
PIC	Replaces the graphic with a graphic in PIC format
Metafile	Replaces the graphic with a graphic in metafile (CGM) format
Blank	Replaces the graphic with a placeholder for a graphic

If you chose **Named**, **PIC**, or **Metafile**, specify from the displayed list the graph or graphic you want to display in the worksheet.

4. If you chose **Range**, select the graphic you want to move or size by specifying a cell in the range that contains the graphic or by pressing F3 and selecting the graphic's name. Then use the arrow keys or the mouse to specify the new range for the graphic. Unlike **:Graph Move**, you must specify the entire range for the new graphic because 1-2-3 uses the new location information to resize the graphic as well as to move it.

If you chose **Sync**, select **Yes** if you want 1-2-3 to update the graph each time data in the worksheet is recalculated; select **No** if you want 1-2-3 to update the graph only when you select **:Graph Compute**. Then select the graphic you want to sync by specifying a cell in the range that contains the graphic or by pressing F3 and selecting the graphic's name.

If you chose **Display**, select **Yes** to display the graphic in the worksheet or select **No** to display a shaded rectangle instead of the data in the graphic. Then select the graphic you want to display by specifying a cell in the range that contains the graphic or by pressing F3 and selecting the graphic's name. If the graph is opaque, you see a shaded rectangle, but if it is transparent, you do not.

If you chose Opaque, select Yes to display the data in the graphic and select No to hide the graphic and display the data in the range underneath. Then select the graphic you want to display by specifying a cell in the range that contains the graphic or by pressing F3 and selecting the graphic's name.

Important Cues

- When you replace a graphic with **:Graph Settings Graph**, you do not replace any enhancements made to the graphic with **:Graph Edit**. If you want to remove the graphic and its enhancements, select **:Graph Remove**.

- It is quicker to use **:Graph Move** instead of **:Graph Settings Range** if you are moving a graphic but do not change the size.

- Use **:Graph Settings Display No** when you want to make many changes to the data in a worksheet because 1-2-3 does not need to redraw the graphics each time it recalculates the data. Don't forget to select **:Graph Settings Display Yes** to redisplay the graphics after you are done making changes.

- You can select multiple graphs to synchronize (or unsynchronize) display or to make opaque with **:Graph Settings Sync**, **:Graph Settings Display**, and **:Graph Settings Opaque** by specifying a range that contains all the graphs you want to work with.

Cautions

- If you unsynchronize graphs from their worksheet data, 1-2-3 does not update the graphs unless you select **:Graph Compute**. Be very sure you know about changes to the worksheet data if you choose to unsynchronize the graphs.

- Regardless of the setting you use for **:Graph Settings Display**, 1-2-3 always prints the data in a graphic and not a shaded rectangle.

For more information, see Chapter 11.

Graph Move   :GM

Purpose

Moves a graphic from one range to another in the worksheet.

Reminder

Before you select **:Graph Move**, move the cell-pointer to a cell in the range that contains the graphic.

Procedures

1. Type **:gm**.

2. Select the graphic you want to move by specifying a cell in the range that contains the graphic or by pressing F3 and selecting the name from the displayed list.

3. Specify the first cell in the range to which you want to move the graphic.

Important Cue

1-2-3 does not resize the graphic when you move it to a new range. To change the size of the range in which a graphic is displayed, use **:Graph Settings Range**.

Caution

Before you move a graphic, make sure that the range to which you are moving it does not contain data that you do not want to hide.

For more information, see Chapter 11.

Graph Zoom   :GZ

Purpose

Temporarily displays a graphic full screen.

Reminder

To view a graphic saved in a PIC file or metafile (CGM) format, select **:Graph View**.

Procedures

1. Type **:gz**.

2. Select the graphic you want to display by specifying a cell in the range that contains the graphic or by pressing F3 and selecting the name from the displayed list.

3. Press any key to remove the graphic from display and return to the worksheet.

For more information, see Chapter 11.

Graph Compute :GC

Purpose

Updates the data and display in graphics in the worksheet.

Reminder

When you select :Graph Compute, 1-2-3 recalculates all worksheets in memory and updates the current and named graphs. If you have resaved any graphics in PIC or metafile format, 1-2-3 also updates the files with the newly saved graphics.

Procedure

Type :gc.

Important Cues

- If you have deleted a PIC or metafile graphic file from disk before you select :Graph Compute, 1-2-3 blanks the display of the range that contained that graphic. The data underneath the display, however, is not affected.

- If you do not want 1-2-3 to update graphics in the worksheet each time 1-2-3 recalculates active worksheet files, select :Graph Settings Sync No.

For more information, see Chapter 11.

Graph View :GV

Purpose

Displays on the full screen a graphic saved in PIC or metafile format.

Reminder

To view a current graph, press F10 or select /Graph View.

Procedures

1. Type :gv.

2. Select PIC to display a list of graphs saved in PIC format; select Metafile to display a list of graphs saved in CGM format.

3. Select the graph you want to view from the list displayed.

4. Press any key to remove the graphic from display and return to the worksheet.

Important Cue

Use **:Graph View** to display graphs created and saved in PIC format.

For more information, see Chapter 11.

Graph Edit   :GE

Purpose

Edit a graph or graphic that you have positioned in the worksheet. Use **:Graph Edit** to create enhancements to the graph that are not available through the 1-2-3 /Graph commands. For example, you can add additional text, arrows, and freehand shapes.

Reminders

- To edit a graphic, you first must place it in the worksheet with **:Graph Add**.

- You can make two kinds of changes with the **:Graph Edit** commands—changes to the graphic appearance (such as background color) and changes to objects added to the graphic (such as arrows, additional text, and shapes).

- Remember that you use **:Graph Edit** to add or edit enhancements to a graphic only. If you want to change parts of the graph itself (things such as ranges, that you added to the graph with the /Graph commands) you must use the /Graph commands.

- Although you can use the direction keys to edit a graphic in the editing window, you will find it much easier to use the mouse. See Chapter 2 for information on mouse support in 1-2-3 Release 2.3.

- To use **:Graph Edit**, you first must place a graphic in the Wysiwyg graphics editing window. The graphics editing window is a temporary, separate display that 1-2-3 creates in which you edit a graphic. The procedure below explains how you add a graphic to the editing window.

Procedures

1. Type **:ge**.

2. Specify the graphic you want to copy into the graphics editing window by moving the cell-pointer to a cell in the range that contains the graphic or by pressing F3 and choosing the graph name.

Important Cue

You also can copy a graphic into the graphics editing window from READY mode by moving the mouse pointer to the graphic and double-clicking the left mouse button.

Caution

To use **:Graph Edit** and the graphics editing window, you must be in Wysiwyg graphics mode. If you aren't sure whether you are in graphics mode, make sure that Wysiwyg is in memory and then type **:dmg**.

For more information, see Chapter 11.

Graph Edit Add   :GEA

Purpose

Adds enhancements to a graphic.

Reminders

• Use **:Graph Edit Add** to include text, arrows, and shapes with a graphic displayed in the worksheet.

• Although you can use **:Graph Edit Add** with the direction keys, you will find it much easier to create and place objects if you use the mouse.

Procedures

1. Type **:gea**.

2. Choose one of the following items:

Menu Item	Description
Text	Adds text to a graphic
Line	Adds lines (both single line and multiple, connected lines) to a graphic
Polygon	Adds a polygon to a graphic
Arrow	Adds an arrow to a graphic
Rectangle	Adds a rectangle to a graphic
Ellipse	Adds a circle or ellipse to a graphic
Freehand	Adds a freehand form to a graphic

3. If you chose **Text**, type the characters you want to add to the graphic and press Enter. Then use the mouse or the direction keys to specify the location of the text in the graphics editing window. When you have moved the cell pointer to the location in which you want to place the graphic, press Enter or click the left mouse button.

If you chose **Line**, use the mouse or the direction keys to specify the location of the first point on the line in the graphics editing window. When you have moved the cell pointer to the location, press Enter or click the left mouse button. Then use the mouse or the arrow keys to draw the line. If you want to add a line connected to the first, press the space bar or click the left mouse button and draw the next line. Press Enter or double-click the left mouse button to finish drawing the line.

If you chose **Polygon**, use the mouse or the direction keys to specify the location of the first point in the polygon. When you have moved the cell pointer to the location, press Enter or click the left mouse button. Then use the mouse or the arrow keys to draw the first line of the polygon and press the space bar or click the left mouse button. Continue drawing sides of the polygon, finishing each side by pressing the space bar or clicking the left mouse button. When you have finished drawing the polygon, press Enter or double-click the left mouse button. (You don't need to draw the last side of a polygon—1-2-3 can finish the polygon if you press Enter or double-click the left mouse button.)

If you chose **Arrow**, use the mouse or the direction keys to specify the location of the first point on the arrow in the graphics editing window. When you have moved the cell pointer to the location, press Enter or click the left mouse button. Then use the mouse or the arrow keys to draw the arrow. If you want to add a line connected to the first, press the space bar or click the left mouse button and draw the next line. Press Enter or double-click the left mouse button to finish drawing the arrow. 1-2-3 places an arrowhead at the end of the line you drew.

If you chose **Rectangle** or **Ellipse**, use the mouse or the direction keys to specify the location of the first point of the rectangle or ellipse. When you have moved the cell pointer to the location, press Enter or click the left mouse button. Then use the direction keys or drag the mouse to stretch the rectangle or ellipse that 1-2-3 creates. When the rectangle or ellipse is the appropriate shape, press Enter or release the mouse button.

If you chose **Freehand**, use the mouse or the direction keys to specify the location of the first point of the shape. When you have moved the cell pointer to the location, press Enter or click the left mouse button. Then use the direction keys or drag the mouse to create the shape you want. Press Enter or release the mouse button to finish the shape.

Important Cues

- You can add a cell's contents to a graphic by selecting :Graph Edit Add Text, typing \ (backslash), and then specifying the cell address or range name.

- You can create a square from a rectangle or a circle from an ellipse by pressing Shift-Enter or pressing Shift and double-clicking the left mouse button to finish the object.

For more information, see Chapter 11.

Graph Edit Select   :GES

Purpose

Selects graphics and enhancements within the graphics editing window for editing.

Procedures

1. Type :ges.

2. Choose one of the following items:

Menu Item	Description
One	Selects one object (either the graphic or an enhancement)
All	Selects all objects (both the graphic and its enhancements) in the editing window
None	Cancels the selection of all objects (leaving no objects selected)
More/Less	Enables you to select more or fewer objects than are already selected
Cycle	Enables you to cycle through all objects and graphics so that you can select or not select each of them
Graph	Selects the graphic without its enhancements
Quit	Returns you to the :Graph Edit menu

3. If you chose **One**, move the cursor to the object and press Enter.

   If you chose **More/Less**, move the cursor to the object you want to select (or cancel as a selection) and press the space bar. Continue selecting objects (or canceling objects) by moving to the object and pressing the space bar. When you have finished, press Enter.

   If you chose **Cycle**, use the direction keys to cycle through the objects in the editing window. Press the space bar to select an object. When you have finished selecting objects, press Enter.

Important Cue

You can select a single object in the editing window by moving the cursor to the object and clicking the left mouse button. You can select several objects in the editing window by holding the left mouse button down and dragging the mouse over all the objects you want to select.

For more information, see Chapter 11.

Graph Edit Edit   :GEE

Purpose

Edit enhancements to a graphic that you created with other **:Graph Edit** commands.

Reminders

- Use **:Graph Edit Edit** to change or remove arrowheads, edit, align, or change the font of text enhancements and edit shapes you added to a graphic.

- You use **:Graph Edit Edit** to edit enhancements you make to graphics with other **:Graph Edit** commands. Use **/Graph** if you want to edit parts of a graph that you created with the **/Graph** commands.

Procedures

1. Type **:gee**.

2. Choose one of the following items:

Menu Item	Description
Text	Edits text in a text enhancement
Centering	Aligns text enhancements

Menu Item	Description
Font	Changes the font of text enhancements in a graphic
Line-Style	Changes the line-style of one or more shapes added to a graphic
Width	Changes the width of lines or of shape outlines
Arrowheads	Adds arrowheads to lines and edits existing arrowheads
Smoothing	Smooths (rounds) the edges of shapes added to a graphic

3. If you chose **Text**, move the cursor to the text you want to edit and press Enter or double-click the left mouse button. 1-2-3 displays the text in the control panel. Use the 1-2-3 editing keys to edit the text. When you are finished editing the line, press Enter or click the left mouse button.

If you chose **Centering**, select one of the following alignments: **Left**, **Center**, or **Right**. Then select the text enhancements that you want to align.

If you chose **Font**, select one of the eight fonts 1-2-3 displays. Then select the text enhancements that you want to change.

If you chose **Line-Style**, select one of the following line styles: **1**:Solid, **2**:Dashed, **3**:Dotted, **4**:Long-Dashed, **5**:Chain-Dotted, **6**:Chain-Dashed, or **7**:Hidden. Then select the objects that you want to change. You can change both lines and arrows and the outlines of shape enhancements, such as rectangles and circles.

If you chose **Width**, select one of the following width settings: **1**:Very-Narrow, **2**:Narrow, **3**:Medium, **4**:Wide, or **5**:Very-Wide. Then select the objects that you want to change. You can change both line and arrow widths and the widths of the outlines of shape enhancements, such as rectangles and circles.

If you chose **Arrowheads**, select one of the following options: **Switch** (moves the arrowhead to the other end of a line), **One** (adds an arrowhead at the end of a line), **Two** (adds arrowheads at both ends of a line), or **None** (removes the arrowheads from a line). Then select the lines or arrows that you want to change.

If you chose **Smoothing**, select one of the following smoothing styles:

Menu Item	Description
None	Removes smoothing (changes a circle into a square, for example) from objects that have been smoothed previously with **Tight** or **Medium**
Tight	Smoothes the edges of an outline, but doesn't change the shape (rounds the edges of a square, but doesn't change it into a circle, for example)
Medium	Completely rounds the edges of an outline, changing lines into curves (changes a square into a circle, for example)

Then select the shapes that you want to smooth.

Important Cues

- You can select a single object in the editing window by moving the cursor to the object and clicking the left mouse button. You can select several objects in the editing window by holding the left mouse button down and dragging the mouse over all the objects you want to select. However, you cannot select several objects with **:Graph Edit Edit Text**.

- If you have previously selected an object in the graphics editing window with **:Graph Edit Select**, you do not need to reselect the object in Step 3.

- Instead of using **:Graph Edit Edit Text** to edit a text enhancement in the graphics editing window, you also can move the cursor to the text and press F2.

For more information, see Chapter 11.

Graph Edit Color   :GEC

Purpose

Changes the color of graphics and enhancements within the graphics editing window.

Reminder

Even though 1-2-3 uses the colors you choose with **:Graph Edit Color** for both the display and printed output, not all printers can print in color. Check your printer specifications before you use **:Graph Edit Color** if your goal is to print graphics in color.

Procedures

1. Type **:gec**.

2. Choose one of the following items:

Menu Item	Description
Lines	Changes the color of a line, an arrow, or an outline
Inside	Changes the inside color of an object
Text	Changes the color of text enhancements
Map	Changes the color palette for the specified graphic
Background	Changes the background color of the range that contains the graphic
Quit	Returns you to the **:Graph Edit** menu

3. If you choose **Lines**, select the graphic or enhancements that you want to change and then choose one of the following colors: **Black, White, Red, Green, Dark-Blue, Cyan, Yellow, Magenta,** or **Hidden**.

   If you chose **Inside**, select the graphic or enhancements that you want to change. Then choose an inside color from the color palette that 1-2-3 displays.

   If you chose **Text**, select the text enhancements that you want to change and then choose one of the following colors: **Black, White, Red, Green, Dark-Blue, Cyan, Yellow, Magenta,** or **Hidden**.

   If you chose **Map**, select one of the eight colors you want to change on the color palette (**1-8**) or select **Quit** to return to the **:Graph Edit** menu. If you choose a color to change, 1-2-3 displays the color palette for the selected graphic and outlines the current color for the number or letter that you specified. Select a new color from the palette or press Esc to return to the **:Graph Edit Color Map** menu without changing the current selection.

   If you chose **Background**, choose a background color from the palette that 1-2-3 shows.

Important Cue

If you have previously selected an object in the graphics editing window with **:Graph Edit Select**, you do not need to reselect the object in Step 3.

For more information, see Chapter 11.

Graph Edit Transform :GET

Purpose

Changes the size and shape of graphics and enhancements within the graphics editing window.

Reminder

Some printers can rotate text only in 90-degree increments. Check your printer specifications before you use **:Graph Edit Transform** to rotate text in graphics to make sure that printed copies match the display.

Procedures

1. Type **:get**.

2. Choose one of the following items:

Menu Item	Description
Size	Resizes graphics or enhancements
Rotate	Rotates graphics or enhancements
Quarter-Turn	Rotates graphics or enhancements in 90-degree increments
X-Flip	Flips graphics or enhancements horizontally
Y-Flip	Flips graphics or enhancements vertically
Horizontal	Slants graphics or enhancements horizontally
Vertical	Slants graphics or enhancements vertically
Clear	Cancels all **:Graph Edit Transform** changes to the selected objects

3. Select the object (or objects) you want to transform.

If you chose **Size**, **Rotate**, **Horizontal**, or **Vertical**, use the direction keys or the mouse to adjust the graphics or enhancements. Press Enter to finish the transformation.

Important Cue

If you have previously selected an object in the graphics editing window with **:Graph Edit Select**, you do not need to reselect the object in Step 3.

For more information, see Chapter 11.

Graph Edit Rearrange *:GER*

Purpose

Rearranges graphics and enhancements within the graphics editing window.

Reminder

Use **:Graph Edit Rearrange** to copy and delete graphics and enhancements in the editing window, to move graphics and enhancements to the front or back of other objects, and to save graphics and enhancements from changes.

Procedures

1. Type **:ger**.

2. Choose one of the following items:

Menu Item	*Description*
Delete	Removes objects from the editing window
Restore	Retrieves the last object deleted from the editing window
Move	Moves objects within the editing window
Copy	Copies objects within the editing window
Lock	Protects an object from changes within the editing window
Unlock	Enables changes to an object within the editing window
Front	Moves an object in front of others in the editing window

Menu Item	Description
Back	Moves an object in back of others in the editing window

3. Select the object (or objects) you want to rearrange in the editing window.

   If you chose **Move** in step 2, use the mouse or the arrow keys to move the object. Press Enter to finish the move.

Important Cues

- If you have previously selected an object in the graphics editing window with **:Graph Edit Select**, you do not need to reselect the object in step 3.

- You can delete a previously selected object in the graphics editing window by pressing Delete.

- You can copy a previously selected object in the graphics editing window by pressing Insert.

Caution

:Graph Edit Rearrange Restore can restore only the most recently deleted object in the graphics editing window. If you have used **:Graph Edit Rearrange Delete** or the delete key more than once in an editing session, only the last object you deleted can be restored.

For more information, see Chapter 11.

Graph Edit View   :GEV

Purpose

Sets the size of areas in the graphics editing window.

Reminder

:Graph Edit View does not change the size or placement of graphics in the worksheet—only the size of areas in the graphics editing window.

Procedures

1. Type **:gev**.

2. Choose one of the following items:

Menu Item	Description
Full	Displays the graphics in the editing window at the normal size
In	Makes an area of the editing window full screen
Pan	Enables you to use + (plus), − (minus), and the other direction keys so that you can enlarge, reduce, or move graphics in the editing window
+	Enlarges the size of the contents of the editing window (up to a maximum of five times its previous size)
−	Reduces the size of the contents of the editing window (up to a maximum of five times its previous size)
Up	Moves the contents of the editing window up one-half screen in the editing window
Down	Moves the contents of the editing window down one-half screen in the editing window
Left	Moves the contents of the editing window left one-half screen in the editing window
Right	Moves the contents of the editing window right one-half screen in the editing window

3. If you chose **In**, use the arrow keys or the mouse to specify the first corner of the area you want to enlarge. Anchor the corner by pressing the space bar or by holding down the left mouse button. Then drag the mouse or use the arrow keys to specify the diagonally opposite corner of the area. Press Enter or release the mouse button to complete the command.

   If you chose **Pan**, use the +, −, and direction keys to move and size the graphics in the editing window.

Important Cues

- You can use the + (plus) and − (minus) keys to enlarge and reduce the contents of the graphics editing window instead of using **:Graph Edit View +** and **:Graph Edit View −**.

- You can use the up- and down-arrow keys to move the contents of the graphics editing window instead of using **:Graph Edit View Up** and **:Graph Edit View Down**.

For more information, see Chapter 11.

Graph Edit Options   *:GEO*

Purpose

Sets options for the graphics editing window, such as grid lines, the size of the cursor, and the text size in the graphic.

Reminder

Use **:Graph Edit Options Grid** when you want to see which parts of a graphic are located in the cells in the range that contains the graphic. The grid lines 1-2-3 displays in the graphics editing window are temporary and are not displayed when you return to the worksheet.

Procedures

1. Type **:geo**.

2. Choose one of the following items:

Menu Item	Description
Grid	Adds or clears grid lines in the graphics editing window
Cursor	Specifies the size of the cursor in the graphics editing window
Font-Magnification	Specifies the text size for graphics in the graphics editing window

3. If you chose **Grid**, select **No** to hide the grid lines or select **Yes** to display grid lines that correspond to the cells in the range that contains the graphic.

   If you chose **Cursor**, select **Small** to display the default editing cursor (a small cross); select **Big** to display the cursor as a large cross that fills the graphics editing window.

   If you chose **Font-Magnification**, specify the number (between 1 and 1000, inclusive) that corresponds to the percentage by which you want to enlarge (or reduce) the size of text you add to the graphic with other **:Graph Edit** commands. Specify 0 if you want to display the text as it is displayed in the graphic in the worksheet.

Important Cues

- When you are in the graphics editing window, you also can set and remove grid lines by pressing F4.

- When you return to the worksheet, 1-2-3 automatically scales the text in a graphic so that it corresponds to the size of the graphic as it fits in the specified range.

For more information, see Chapter 11.

Graph Edit Quit   :GEQ

Purpose

Leaves the graphic editing window and returns 1-2-3 to READY mode.

Reminder

You also can use Ctrl-Break to leave the graphic editing window and return to READY mode.

Procedure

Type **:geq**.

Important Cue

Any changes you made to a graphic with **:Graph E**dit are saved in the graph in memory when you leave the graphic editing window. However, you must use **/F**ile **S**ave to save the editing changes for the worksheet.

For more information, see Chapter 11.

:Print Commands   :P

:Print commands enable you to include Wysiwyg format settings in printed copies of the worksheets. You can print to either a printer, an encoded file, or to the background printing utility. Throughout this section, refer to the **:P**rint menu on the Wysiwyg side of the pull-out command card in the back of this book.

Print Go   :PG

Purpose

Prints the specified range to the current printer.

Reminders

- Before you print in 1-2-3, you first must specify the ranges and special print settings you want to use. See **:Print Range** for information on specifying the print range; see **:Print Layout** and **:Print Settings** for information on print settings.

- Before you select **:Print Go** make sure that the printer you want to use is selected and on-line. Otherwise, 1-2-3 cannot complete the print job. Select **:Print Config Printer** to select the current printer.

Procedure

Type **:pg**.

Important Cue

Use **:Print Go** when you want to print ranges that include Wysiwyg format settings. If you just want to print a quick, unformatted range, you also can use **/Print [Printer, File, Encoded, Background] Go**. (You must set a **Range** through the **/Print** menu, however.) Remember, however, that **/Print Go** does not print any Wysiwyg formats.

For more information, see Chapter 9.

Print File   :PF

Purpose

Prints the specified range to an encoded file on disk.

Reminders

- Before you print in 1-2-3, you first must specify the ranges and special print settings you want to use. See **:Print Range** for information on specifying the print range; see **:Print Layout** and **:Print Settings** for information on print settings.

- Before you select **:Print File** make sure that the printer you want to eventually use to print the file to is currently selected. Otherwise, the print settings 1-2-3 uses in the file may not be compatible with the printer. Select **:Print Config Printer** to select the current printer.

Procedures

1. Type **:pf**.
2. Specify the name of the file to be printed.

3. If you specify a file that already exists, select **C**ancel to return to READY mode without printing or select **R**eplace to overwrite the existing file with a file that contains the new output.

Important Cues

*   1-2-3 automatically adds the extension ENC to the file you print. If you want a different extension, include it when you specify the file name in Step 2.

*   Use **:P**rint **File** when you want to print ranges that include Wysiwyg format settings. If you just want to print a quick, unformatted range, you also can use **/P**rint **File**, **/P**rint **Encoded**, or **/P**rint **Background**. Remember, however, that **/P**rint **File**, **/P**rint **Encoded**, and **/P**rint **Background** do not print any Wysiwyg formats.

*   The file 1-2-3 creates with **:P**rint **File** is not an ASCII text file. Instead, it contains print codes specific to the printer so that 1-2-3 can include formatting information in the file. If you want to print an ASCII text file, select **/P**rint **File**.

Caution

Don't name print files with names that may be confused with other files you use because you are taking the chance of overwriting a file you may need. For example, don't name a print file with a name that begins with the characters 123 because it may coincide with a file that 1-2-3 uses.

For more information, see Chapter 9.

Print Background :PB

Purpose

Prints the specified range to an encoded file on disk and then to the printer in background mode.

Enables you to continue to work in 1-2-3 while printing.

Reminders

*   Before you print in 1-2-3, you first must specify the ranges and special print settings you want to use. See **:P**rint **R**ange for information on specifying the print range; see **:P**rint **Layout** and **:P**rint **Settings** for information on print settings.

*   Before you select **:P**rint **Background**, make sure that the printer you want to eventually use to print the file to is currently

selected. Otherwise, the print settings 1-2-3 uses in the file may not be compatible with the printer. Select **:Print Config Printer** to select the current printer.

- Before you can use background printing, you must load the 1-2-3 BPRINT utility from the operating system. See Chapter 9 for information on using BPRINT. Do not attempt to load BPRINT from the /System command. Use /Quit to exit 1-2-3 before loading BPRINT.

Procedure

Type **:pb**.

Important Cue

Use **:Print File** when you want to print ranges that include Wysiwyg format settings. If you just want to print a quick, unformatted range, you also can use /Print File, /Print Encoded, or /Print Background. Remember, however, that /Print File, /Print Encoded, and /Print Background do not print any Wysiwyg formats.

For more information, see Chapter 9.

Print Range :PR

Purpose

Specifies the ranges you want to print or clears all ranges from the print settings. 1-2-3 includes the format settings in the ranges you select when you print them.

Reminder

You must select **:Print Range** and specify ranges to print before you can select either **:Print Go** or **:Print File**. This step is true even if you have selected ranges with the /Print Range command.

Procedures

1. Type **:pr**.

2. Select **Set** to specify the range in the worksheet that you want to print; select **Clear** to cancel the ranges currently specified.

3. If you chose **Set**, specify the range you want to print. To specify the range, enter the range address or range name or use the arrow keys to highlight the range or range name.

Important Cues

- If you include a hidden column in the print range, 1-2-3 ignores that column when it prints.

- 1-2-3 displays the print range with dashed lines when you are in graphics mode.

For more information, see Chapter 9.

Print Config   :PC

Purpose

Sets options for the printer you want to use.

Reminders

- Before you use **:Print Config**, make sure that you have correctly installed the printers you have available through the 1-2-3 Install program.

- Use **:Print Config** to set the following printer options: the paper bin you want to use, the font cartridges you are using, the interface/port the printer is connected to, the printer you want to use, and the page orientation (landscape or portrait).

- Many configuration settings apply to selected printers only. If your printer does not use those settings, you can ignore those settings. For example, if you are using an Apple LaserWriter, you do not need to select **Bin**, **1st-Cart**, or **2nd-Cart** because the printer does not make use of these features.

Procedures

1. Type **:pc**.

2. Choose one of the following items:

Menu Item	Description
Printer	Specifies the printer you want to use (from the list of printers you selected during Install)
Interface	Specifies the interface/port with which the printer is connected
1st-Cart	Specifies the first font cartridge you are using in the printer

Menu Item	Description
2nd-Cart	Specifies the second font cartridge you are using in the printer
Orientation	Specifies whether you want to print in portrait or landscape mode
Bin	Specifies the paper bin you want to use
Quit	Returns to the **:P**rint menu

3. If you chose **Printer,** select from the displayed list of printers the number that corresponds to the printer you want to use. 1-2-3 displays only the names of the printers you selected during Install.

If you chose **Interface,** select the correct interface or port from the menu. If you specify a serial port, select the appropriate baud rate for the printer.

If you chose **1st-Cart** or **2nd-Cart,** select a cartridge from the list of available cartridges.

If you chose **Orientation,** select **Portrait** if you want to print across the width of the paper; select **Landscape** if you want to print across the length of the paper.

If you chose **Bin,** choose one of the following items:

Menu Item	Description
Reset	Clears the bin setting
Single-Sheet	Specifies single-sheet feed
Manual	Specifies manual paper-feed
Upper-Tray	Specifies the top bin on the printer
Lower-Tray	Specifies the bottom bin on the printer

Important Cues

- If you are using a printer that does not use font cartridges, specifying **1st-Cart** or **2nd-Cart** has no effect.

- If you are using a printer that does not have multiple bins, specifying **Bin** has no effect.

Cautions

- When you specify a **Printer** and **Interface,** 1-2-3 saves that information with the worksheet file. If you retrieve the file again to print, therefore, 1-2-3 defaults to the last **Printer** and **Interface** you specified with **:Print Config**.

- Do not select a font cartridge that you are not using in the printer because 1-2-3 may generate unexpected characters in the output.

- If you are using a printer that does not print in landscape mode, do not select **:Print Config Orientation Landscape**. If you do, 1-2-3 displays an error message when you attempt to print.

- Do not select **:Print Config Bin Single-Sheet** if your printer does not have a single-sheet feed option because 1-2-3 sends a form feed after each page, and this selection may confuse the printer and the paper alignment.

For more information, see Chapter 9.

Print Settings   :PS

Purpose

Specifies the settings for the printed output. You use **:Print Settings** to specify the following: the page number of the first and last pages you want to print, the number of copies you want to print, whether the printer should pause after each page, and whether you want to print the worksheet frame and grid.

Reminder

The print settings you specify with **:Print Settings** are not applicable to print jobs you create with **/Print**.

Procedures

1. Type **:ps**.

2. Choose one of the following items:

Menu Item	Description
Begin	Specifies the first page to print in the print job (from 1 to 9999, inclusive)
End	Specifies the last page to print in the print job (from 1 to 9999, inclusive)
Start-Number	Specifies the page number for the first page you print (from 1 to 9999, inclusive)

Menu Item	Description
Copies	Specifies the number of copies to print (from 1 to 99, inclusive)
Wait	Pauses the printer after printing each page
Grid	Specifies whether to print the worksheet grid
Frame	Specifies whether to print the worksheet frame
Reset	Resets all print settings to the default settings
Quit	Returns to the :Print menu

3. If you chose **Begin**, **End**, **Start-Number**, or **Copies**, specify the number.

If you chose **Grid** or **Frame**, select **No** if you do not want to print the worksheet grid or worksheet frame. Select **Yes** if you want to print the worksheet grid or worksheet frame.

If you chose **Wait**, select **No** if you do not want 1-2-3 to pause after it prints each page. Select **Yes** if you want 1-2-3 to pause after it prints each page.

Important Cues

- After you set the print settings, use **:Print Preview** to view the output on the screen before you print to a printer. It is far less time-consuming to make preliminary changes based on the previewed pages than to wait for printed output after each change to the settings.

- Use **:Print Layout Titles** to tell 1-2-3 to include a page number on pages of the printed output. **:Print Settings Begin, End** tell 1-2-3 which pages to print but do not print page numbers themselves.

Caution

With the exception of the frame and grid settings, none of the settings you specify with **:Print Settings** is saved with the file. You need to respecify the settings each time you begin a new 1-2-3 session, each time you reload Wysiwyg into memory, and each time you select /Worksheet Erase or /File New.

For more information, see Chapter 9.

Print Layout Page-Size :*PLP*

Purpose

Sets the size of the paper you are using to print.

Reminder

The default page size 1-2-3 assumes when you print is 8 1/2 inches by 11 inches.

Procedures

1. Type **:plp**.

2. Choose one of the following items:

Menu Item	Description
1:Letter	Standard 8 1/2-by-11-inch pages
2:A4	210 mm x 297 mm pages
3:80x66	8 1/2-by-11-inch fanfold pages
4:132x66	14-by-11-inch fanfold pages
5:80x72	8 1/2-by-12-inch fanfold pages
6:Legal	Standard 8 1/2-by-14-inch pages
7:B5	176 mm x 250 mm pages
Custom	Specifies a custom length and width

3. If you chose **Custom**, specify a page length and width. You can specify the size to be in inches, millimeters, or centimeters by typing **in**, **mm**, or **cm** after the length or width value.

Important Cue

Because 1-2-3 automatically formats print ranges so that they fit properly on each page, it is important that you specify the correct page size.

For more information, see Chapter 9.

Print Layout Margins   :PLM

Purpose

Sets new margin settings for printed output.

Reminder

The default page margins are 0.5 inches for the top, left, and right sides, and 0.55 inches for the bottom.

Procedures

1. Type **:plm**.

2. Select **L**eft, **R**ight, **T**op, **B**ottom, or **Q**uit.

3. If you chose **L**eft, **R**ight, **T**op, or **B**ottom, specify the number that corresponds to the new margin setting.

Important Cue

You can specify a margin size in a measurement different from the default by including a code with the new setting. If you want to specify a margin in inches, type **in** after the number; if you want to specify a margin in centimeters, type **cm** after the number; if you want to specify a margin in millimeters, type **mm** after the number. For example, to specify a right margin of 3 centimeters, select **:plmr** and type **3cm**.

Caution

You should not set left and right margins that together are larger than the width of the page. The same is true of the top and bottom margins. For example, if you are using a page that is 8 1/2 inches wide, you do not set a left margin of 4 inches and a right margin of 5 inches because the total margin size would be 9 inches, 1/2-inch larger than the paper is wide.

For more information, see Chapter 9.

Print Layout Titles   :PLT

Purpose

Sets the headers and footers you want to include on each page.

Reminder

Headers and footers are the lines you want to print at the top and bottom of each page. For example, if you wanted to include the date at the top of each page and the page number at the bottom of each page, you would specify a header that included the date and a footer that included the page number.

Procedures

1. Type **:plt**.

2. Choose one of the following items:

Menu Item	Description
Header	Specifies the text you want to print at the top of each page
Footer	Specifies the text you want to print at the bottom of each page
Clear	Removes the header and footer text
Quit	Returns you to the :**Print Layout** menu

3. If you chose **Header** or **Footer**, specify the text you want to print. You can enter any text you want (up to a maximum of 240 characters) or one of the following special characters:

@ — Prints the current date (formatted in the global international default date format)

— Prints the page number

| — Specifies the location in the header or footer for text. 1-2-3 left-aligns header and footer text unless you specify otherwise. To center text, type | and then the text you want to center; to right-align text, type another | and then the text you want to right-align. For example, the header @|Sales|# would print a header that has the date left-aligned, the centered title Sales, and the page number right-aligned.

\ — Specifies that you want to use the contents of a cell as the header or footer. To use a cell's contents in a header or footer, type \ followed by the cell address. For example, the footer **D2** would print the contents of cell D2 at the bottom of each page.

If you chose **Clear**, select **Header** to clear the header text, select **Footer** to clear the footer text, or select **B**oth to clear both the header and footer text.

Important Cues

- 1-2-3 prints the header on the line immediately below the top margin and prints two blank lines between the header and the first line of text; it prints the footer on the line immediately above the bottom margin and prints two blank lines between the last line of text on the page and the footer.

- You can format text in the header and footer by using the formatting sequences. See Chapter 2 for information on the Wysiwyg formatting sequences.

Caution

Although a header or footer can be up to 240 characters long, 1-2-3 only prints as much of the header or footer as it can fit on a single line across the page. If there is not enough room to print the entire line, 1-2-3 truncates the text.

For more information, see Chapter 9.

Print Layout Borders   :PLB

Purpose

Specifies the column and row borders you want to print at the left and top of each page and print range. This command is similar to the /**P**rint **P**rinter **O**ptions **B**orders command.

Reminder

Before you select **:P**rint **L**ayout **B**orders, move the cell-pointer to the first cell in the range that you want to use as a border.

Procedures

1. Type **:plb**.

2. Choose one of the following items:

Menu Item	Description
Top	Specifies the rows you want to print at the top of each page and at the top of every print range
Left	Specifies the columns you want to print at the left side of each page and to the left of every print range
Clear	Clears one or more borders
Quit	Returns to the :Print Layout menu

3. If you chose **Top** or **Left**, specify the range that contains the columns or rows you want to use as borders. You only need to include a single cell from each column you want to use as a left border and from each row you want to use as a top border.

   If you chose **Clear**, select **Top** to clear only the top border rows, select **Left** to clear only the left border columns, or select **All** to clear both the top and left borders.

Important Cue

Don't include the columns and rows you specified as borders when you specify a print range unless you want those columns and rows repeated in the output.

For more information, see Chapter 9.

Print Layout Compression   :PLC

Purpose

Shrinks or enlarges the font used for the print range.

Reminder

Use **:Print Layout Compression** when you want to try to print a large range on a single page.

Procedures

1. Type **:plc**.

2. Choose one of the following items:

Menu Item	Description
None	Turns off compression
Manual	Enables you to specify the percentage you want to shrink or enlarge the font used to print the range (between 15 and 1000).
Automatic	Tells 1-2-3 to attempt to shrink the print range so that it fits on a single page. 1-2-3 can shrink the print range up to a maximum of seven times smaller than normal

3. If you choose **Manual**, specify the amount you want to change the font. For example, if you want to double the size of the print range, select 200 (for 200 percent of the original size).

Important Cue

Do not include any page breaks in the print range if you are using **:Print Layout Compression** to shrink the range to a single page. 1-2-3 starts a new page at each page break, even if you have compressed the print range.

Caution

Depending on the printer you use and the font sizes you installed, some compression settings may not look the way you intended because the printer cannot print the fonts that would equal the percentage you specified.

For more information, see Chapter 9.

Print Layout Default   :PLD

Purpose

Updates the default layout settings 1-2-3 uses to print output through Wysiwyg.

Replaces the current layout settings with the default settings.

Reminder

Before you select **:Print Layout Default Update** to save the new default layout library, be sure that you have specified all the layout settings you want to include. Use the other **:Print Layout** commands to specify the settings.

Procedures

1. Type **:pld**.

2. Select **Restore** if you want to replace the current layout settings with the default settings; select Update if you want to save the current layout settings as the default settings (so that they are the initial layout settings you see each time you begin a new 1-2-3 session).

Important Cue

1-2-3 saves the default page layout settings in the file LAYOUT.CNF. When you select **:Print Layout Default Update**, 1-2-3 overwrites this file with a new file that contains the new settings.

Caution

After you update the default page layout file, the original settings are gone. If, for some reason, you want to recreate the original default layout settings file, clear all layout settings, set the page size to 8 1/2-by-11 inches, set the left, right, and top margins to 0.5 inches, set the bottom margin to 0.55 inches, and set compression to None.

For more information, see Chapter 9.

Print Layout Library :PLL

Purpose

Retrieves, creates, and edits page layout library files. A page layout library file contains the layout settings you specify for any given print job. For example, if you print a report each week for which you specify layout settings, you can create a page layout library file for that report. Then, each time you print the report, you can retrieve the library file instead of recreating the settings.

Reminder

Before you select :Print Layout Library to save a layout library file, be sure that you have specified all the layout settings you want to include in the library. Use the other :Print Layout commands to specify the settings.

Procedures

1. Type **:pll**.

2. Choose one of the following items:

Menu Item	Description
Retrieve	Replaces the current layout settings with the settings from a layout library file on disk
Save	Saves the current layout settings in a layout library file on disk
Erase	Erases a layout library file from disk

3. If you chose **Retrieve**, specify the name of the layout library file from which you want to retrieve layout settings.

   If you chose **Save**, specify the name you want to use for the layout library file. If a file with the specified name already exists, select Cancel to return to READY mode without saving the file or select Replace to save the file with the new layout settings.

   If you chose **Erase**, specify the name of the layout library file you want to delete from disk.

Important Cues

- When you save a layout library file, 1-2-3 automatically adds the extension ALS to the file. If you want to use a different extension, include that extension in the file name. Remember, however, that 1-2-3 does not automatically display library files with extensions other than ALS when you select **:Print Layout Library Retrieve** or **Erase**.

- Use names that you easily can identify with a set of layouts when you name a library file. For example, a name such as SALESRPT.ALS makes more sense than the name LIBRARY1.ALS for a set of layouts you want to use for a monthly sales report.

Caution

After you erase a library file, it is gone for good. Be sure that you no longer need a library file that you erase.

For more information, see Chapter 9.

Print Layout Quit   :PLQ

Purpose

Returns you to the **:Print** menu.

Reminder

Selecting **:Print Layout Quit** does not clear any of the layout settings you have specified.

Procedure

Type **:plq**.

For more information, see Chapter 9.

Print Preview   :PP

Purpose

Temporarily displays the specified print ranges as they appear when printed with **:Print Go** or **:Print File**.

Reminder

Before you print in 1-2-3, you first must specify the ranges and special print settings you want to use. See **:P**rint **R**ange for information on specifying the print range; see **:P**rint **L**ayout and **:P**rint **S**ettings for information on print settings.

Procedures

1. Type **:pp**.

2. 1-2-3 temporarily clears the screen and displays the first page of output on the screen. Type any key except Esc to display the next page or press Esc to redisplay the worksheet and return to READY mode.

Important Cue

Depending on the size of the ranges you are previewing and the number of format settings in those ranges, 1-2-3 may take some time to prepare the preview.

For more information, see Chapter 9.

Print Info   :PI

Purpose

Displays or clears the Wysiwyg print settings screen that contains the current print settings.

Reminder

You cannot specify print settings directly from **:P**rint **I**nfo; it is only for information.

Procedures

1. Type **:pi**.

2. 1-2-3 displays the print settings screen, or, if it already is displayed, removes the screen and redisplays the worksheet.

Important Cue

You also can view and remove the print settings screen by pressing F6 at any time while you are in the **:P**rint menu.

For more information, see Chapter 9.

:Display Commands :D

:Display commands specify the special Wysiwyg display characteristics you can set for a worksheet. Included in the :Display commands are format settings for the cell-pointer and worksheet background colors, for the number of rows displayed, for zooming the display of selected cells, and for displaying the worksheet frame as a ruler. Throughout this section, refer to the :Display menu on the Wysiwyg side of the pull-out command card in the back of this book.

Display Mode :DM

Purpose

Sets the display to either graphics or text mode and either color or monochrome.

Reminders

- Graphics mode is the default Wysiwyg display mode, in which the worksheet display echoes the way it would look when printed. All format settings you specify are displayed in graphics mode.

- Text mode is the default 1-2-3 display when Wysiwyg is not loaded in memory. Unlike the regular 1-2-3 display mode (when Wysiwyg is not in memory), you can continue to set formats; however, 1-2-3 does not display the formats in the worksheet until you reselect Graphics mode.

Procedure

1. Type :dm.

2. Choose one of the following items:

Menu Item	Description
Graphics	Displays the worksheet in graphics mode (the default Wysiwyg display)
Text	Displays the worksheet in text mode (so that it resembles the default 1-2-3 display when Wysiwyg is not in memory)
B&W	Displays the worksheet in monochrome (graphics mode only)
Color	Displays the worksheet in color (graphics mode only)

Important Cue

1-2-3 uses the display mode you select for the current session of 1-2-3 only. If you want to set the display mode permanently, specify the mode and then select **:Display** Default Update.

For more information, see Chapter 9.

Display Zoom   :DZ

Purpose

Enlarges or reduces the display of selected ranges in the worksheet. You can use **:Display Zoom** to get a better look at cell entries formatted with small fonts or to get an overview of a larger portion of the worksheet.

Reminder

Before you type **:dz**, move the cell pointer to the range you want to look at.

Procedures

1. Type **:dz**.

2. Choose one of the following items:

Menu Item	Description
Tiny	Displays cells at 63% of the standard display size
Small	Displays cells at 87% of the standard display size
Normal	Displays cells at their standard display size
Large	Displays cells at 125% of the standard display size
Huge	Displays cells at 150% of the standard display size
Manual	Displays cells at a specified size, between 25% and 400% of the standard display size

3. If you chose **Manual**, specify a new display size, between 25 and 400, inclusive.

Important Cue

1-2-3 uses the display size you select for the current session of 1-2-3 only. If you want to set the display size permanently, specify the size and then select **:Display Default Update**.

For more information, see Chapter 9.

Display Colors :DC

Purpose

Specifies the colors you want to use for the following worksheet characteristics: worksheet background, cell-pointer, worksheet frame, grid lines, format lines, negative values, drop shadows, labels and non-negative values, and unprotected cells.

Reminder

1-2-3 displays the colors you select only when Wysiwyg is in memory.

Procedures

1. Type **:dc**.

2. Choose one of the following items:

Menu Item	Description
Background	Sets the worksheet background color
Text	Sets the color for labels and non-negative values in the worksheet
Unprot	Sets the color for unprotected cells
Cell-Pointer	Sets the cell-pointer color
Grid	Sets the color of grid lines created with **:Display Options Grid**
Frame	Sets the color of the worksheet frame
Neg	Sets the color of negative values in the worksheet
Lines	Sets the color of format lines created with **:Format Lines**
Shadow	Sets the color of drop shadows created with **:Format Lines Shadow**

Menu Item	Description
Replace	Specifies alternate colors you want 1-2-3 to use with the worksheet display
Quit	Returns to the :Display menu

3. Choose one of the following colors: **Black**, **White**, **Red**, **Green**, **Dark-Blue**, **Cyan**, **Yellow**, or **Magenta**. Or select **Quit** to return to the **:**Display menu.

4. If you chose **Replace**, specify a new color by typing a number between **0** and **63**, inclusive, or by pressing the left- or right-arrow key (or the + and – keys) to increase or decrease the current value.

Important Cue

1-2-3 uses the display colors you select for the current session of 1-2-3 only. If you want to set the display colors permanently, specify the colors and then select **:**Display Default Update.

For more information, see Chapter 9.

Display Options   :DO

Purpose

:Display Options specifies the display of the following worksheet characteristics: the cell-pointer (solid or outline), the worksheet frame, grid lines, screen display intensity (brightness), and page-break lines.

Reminder

1-2-3 uses the display settings you select with **:**Display Options only when Wysiwyg is in memory.

Procedures

1. Type **:do**.

2. Choose one of the following items:

Menu Item	Description
Frame	Determines whether the worksheet frame is displayed or hidden
Grid	Determines whether grid lines are dis played or hidden

Menu Item	Description
Page-Breaks	Determines whether page-break lines (set with **:wp**) are displayed or hidden
Cell-Pointer	Determines whether 1-2-3 displays the cell-pointer as a solid rectangle or as an outline
Intensity	Sets the brightness of the screen display
Adapter	Selects the graphics video adapter
Quit	Returns to the **:Display** menu

3. If you chose **Frame**, choose one of the following items:

Menu Item	Description
1-2-3	Displays the default 1-2-3 worksheet frame used when Wysiwyg is not in memory
Enhanced	Displays the default Wysiwyg frame—column letters and row numbers are displayed in the center of separate rectangles
Relief	Displays the enhanced worksheet frame but changes the background color to gray and changes the display intensity to high
Special	Displays the worksheet frame as rulers in one of the following measurements: inches, centimeters (metric), points and picas, or 10-point characters
None	Hides the worksheet frame

4. If you chose **Frame Special** in Steps 2 and 3, choose one of the following items:

Menu Item	Description
Characters	Displays the worksheet frame as rulers measured in 10-point characters with six lines per inch
Inches	Displays the worksheet frame as rulers measured in inches

Menu Item	Description
Metric	Displays the worksheet frame as rulers measured in centimeters
Points/Picas	Displays the worksheet frame as rulers measured in points and picas

If you chose **Grid**, select **No** to hide the grid lines or select **Yes** to display grid lines.

If you chose **Page-Breaks**, select **No** to hide the page-break lines or select **Yes** to display the page-break lines.

If you chose **Cell-Pointer**, select **Solid** or **Outline** to specify the cell-pointer shape.

If you chose **Intensity**, select **Normal** to display the worksheet at the standard 1-2-3 screen display brightness or select **High** to display the worksheet at high intensity.

If you chose **Adapter**, select one of the following items:

Menu Item	Description
Auto	1-2-3 selects the graphics adapter you selected in Install.
1	VGA adapter
2	MCGA adapter
3	EGA adapter with enhanced color monitor
4	EGA adapter with monochrome monitor
5	EGA adapter with low-resolution color monitor
6	Hercules monochrome graphics adapter
7	CGA adapter
8	Compaq, Toshiba, or ATT-Olivetti 400 displays
9	No graphics adapter (text mode only)
Blink	EGA/VGA blinking attribute

Important Cue

1-2-3 uses the display options you select for the current session of 1-2-3 only. If you want to set the display options permanently, specify the options and then select **:Display Default Update**.

For more information, see Chapter 9.

Display Font-Directory :DF

Purpose

Specifies the directory in which 1-2-3 searches for the Wysiwyg fonts used to display and print worksheets and graphics (the font directory).

Procedures

1. Type **:df**.

2. Specify the directory that contains the font files you want to use when Wysiwyg is in memory.

Important Cues

- If you specify a directory that does not contain Wysiwyg font files, 1-2-3 uses the default 1-2-3 fonts that are displayed when Wysiwyg is not in memory.

- 1-2-3 uses the display font-directory you select for the current session of 1-2-3 only. If you want to set the font-directory permanently, specify the directory and then select **:Display Default Update**.

For more information, see Chapter 9.

Display Rows :DR

Purpose

Sets the number of rows that 1-2-3 displays in graphics mode (set with **:Display Mode Graphics**).

Reminder

1-2-3 uses the display rows setting you select with **:Display Rows** only when Wysiwyg is in memory.

Procedures

1. Type **:dr**.

2. Specify the number of rows you want 1-2-3 to display in graphics mode. Enter a number between 16 and 60, inclusive.

Important Cue

1-2-3 uses the display rows setting you select for the current session of 1-2-3 only. If you want to set the display rows setting permanently, specify the setting and then select **:**Display Default Update.

For more information, see Chapter 9.

Display Default :DD

Purpose

:Display Default restores the original Wysiwyg display settings or saves the new display settings you have specified with **:**Display commands in the Wysiwyg configuration file (WYSIWYG.CNF).

Reminder

1-2-3 uses the display setting you save with **:**Display Default each time you load Wysiwyg.

Procedures

1. Type **:dd**.

2. Select **R**estore to clear any new display settings you selected and use the display format settings from the configuration file.

   Select **U**pdate to save new display settings you selected with the **:**Display commands in the Wysiwyg configuration file.

Important Cue

After you save new settings with **:**Display Default, the previous settings in the Wysiwyg configuration file are lost.

For more information, see Chapter 9.

:Special Commands :S

:Special commands copy and move Wysiwyg formats. You can use the **:**Special commands to transfer Wysiwyg format information and graphics from one worksheet file to another or from one range in a worksheet to another. Throughout this section, refer to the **:**Special menu map on the Wysiwyg side of the pull-out command card in the back of this book.

Special Copy :*SC*

Purpose

Copies Wysiwyg format information from a range to one or more other ranges.

Reminders

- Before you begin, decide which range you want to copy Wysiwyg format information from and which range(s) you want to copy the formats to. Remember that all Wysiwyg format information in the FROM range is copied, including colors, shading, and lines.

- If the receiving address is not close to the FROM range, note the address before using :sc, so that you can type the TO address. Pointing across a long distance to the TO address can be error-prone.

Procedures

1. Type :sc.

2. The `Copy the attributes FROM:` prompt requests the range of the cells that contain the format information to be copied. Enter the range by typing the range name or range address or by highlighting the range.

3. Press Enter.

4. At the `Copy the attributes TO:` prompt, specify the upper left corner of the area where you want the duplicate Wysiwyg format information to appear.

5. Press Enter.

Important Cues

- If you copy Wysiwyg format information to a range that already contains Wysiwyg formats, 1-2-3 overwrites the old formats with the new settings.

- Use /Copy to copy data from one range to another.

- Use /Copy to copy formats set with /Range Format and /Worksheet Global Format.

Caution

Be sure that you check the ranges to which you are copying Wysiwyg format information before you do the copy. After you have copied new formats onto ranges, any previous Wysiwyg formats in those ranges are lost.

For more information, see Chapter 9.

Special Move   :*SM*

Purpose

Moves Wysiwyg format information from a range to one or more other ranges.

Reminders

- Before you begin, decide which range you want to move Wysiwyg format information from and which range(s) you want to move the formats to. Remember that all Wysiwyg format information in the FROM range is copied, including colors, shading, and lines.

- If the receiving address is not close to the FROM range, note the address before using :sm so that you can type the TO address. Pointing across a long distance to the TO address can be error-prone.

Procedures

1. Type **:sm**.

2. The `Move the attributes FROM:` prompt requests the range of the cells that contain the format information to be moved. Enter the range by typing the range name or range address or by highlighting the range.

3. Press Enter.

4. At the `Move the attributes TO:` prompt, specify the upper left corner of the area where you want the Wysiwyg format information to appear.

5. Press Enter.

Important Cues

- If you move Wysiwyg format information to a range that already contains Wysiwyg formats, 1-2-3 overwrites the old formats with the new settings.

- Use /Move to move data from one range to another.

- Use /Move to move formats set with /Range Format and /Worksheet Global Format.

Caution

Be sure that you check the ranges to which you are copying Wysiwyg format information before you do the copy. After you have copied new formats onto ranges, any previous Wysiwyg formats in those ranges are lost.

For more information, see Chapter 9.

Special Import   :SI

Purpose

Copies the formats, font set, graphics, and named styles from a Wysiwyg, Impress, or Allways format file into the current file.

Reminder

You can use :Special Import to copy formatting information from any FMT, FM3, or ALL formatting add-ins. Wysiwyg format files have the extension FMT; Impress files have the extenion FM3; Allways format files have the extension ALL.

Procedures

1. Type :si.

2. Choose one of the following items:

Menu Item	Description
All	Copies all formats, the font set, graphics, and named styles from a format file on disk into the current file
Named-Styles	Copies only the named styles from a format file on disk into the current file

Menu Item	Description
Fonts	Copies only the font set from a format file on disk into the current file
Graphs	Copies only the graphics from a format file on disk into the current file. Graphs copies all information about Wysiwyg graphics settings, including their positions in the worksheet, but does not delete any graphics already in place in the current file

3. Specify the name of the format file from which you want to copy formatting information.

Important Cues

• Remember that 1-2-3 copies the information in a format file into exactly the same cells as it appears in the file for which the format file originally was was created. For example, if you import information from a format file that contains information to bold cells A6 through B20, those cells are bold in the current file after the import.

• After you have imported the formatting information into the current file, 1-2-3 also updates the Wysiwyg format file for that worksheet file.

Caution

:Special Import overwrites any Wysiwyg format information that already exists for the current file. Be sure that you have saved the worksheet file before you do a :Special Import, just in case you need to return to the original format settings.

For more information, see Chapter 9.

Special Export   :SE

Purpose

Copies the formats, font set, graphics, and named styles from the current format file into another Wysiwyg or Allways format file on disk.

Reminder

You can use :Special Export to copy formatting information into any of the 1-2-3 formatting add-ins. However, because some Wysiwyg formats are not available in Allways, some formatting information (such as drop shadows, named styles, and wide lines) becomes lost if you copy into an ALL format file.

Procedures

1. Type **:se**.

2. Specify the name of the format file into which you want to copy information. If you are exporting formats into another Wysiwyg format file, you do not need to include the FMT extension; if you want to export information into an Allways file, include the FMT or ALL extension, respectively.

3. If you are copying information into a format file that already exists, choose one of the following items:

Menu Item	Description
Cancel	Cancels the command without exporting the formatting information
Replace	Replaces the formatting information in the format file on disk with the new information from the current format file

Important Cue

:Special Export does not copy graphs into the format file on disk; it copies only their positions in the worksheet and any special graphics formatting specified with the **:Graph Edit** commands.

Caution

:Special Export overwrites any Wysiwyg format information that already exists for the format file on disk. Be sure that you have saved a backup copy of the file before you do a **:Special Export**, just in case you need to return to the original format settings.

For more information, see Chapter 9.

:Text Commands   :T

:Text commands enable you to edit and enter text directly in the worksheet (as opposed to cell by cell in the control panel). The **:Text** commands are especially helpful when you are entering titles and longer passages of text in a worksheet. Throughout this section, refer to the **:Text** menu on the Wysiwyg side of the pull-out command card in the back of this book.

Text Edit   :TE

Purpose

:Text Edit enables you to edit labels within a specified text range.

Reminder

Before you select **:te**, move the cell pointer to the first cell in the range in which you want to edit text.

Procedures

To edit text in a specified text range, do the following:

1. Type **:te**.

2. Specify the text range (the range in which you want to edit text). **:Text Edit** edits only text within the range you specify.

3. Enter and edit text in the range. You can use the following editing keys while in text-editing mode:

Edit Key	Description
← or →	Moves the cursor one character to the left or right in the text range
↑ or ↓	Moves the cursor one line up or down in the text range
Backspace or Del	Deletes the character to the left or right of the cursor in the text range
Ctrl-← or Ctrl-→; Tab or Shift-Tab	Moves the cursor left to the beginning of the preceding word or right to the end of the next word
Ctrl-Enter	Creates an end-of-paragraph symbol and begins a new line in the text range
Enter	Begins a new line in the text range
Escape	Returns 1-2-3 to READY mode
Home and End	When typed once, moves the cursor to the first or last character in the line; when typed twice, moves the cursor to the first or last character in the text range

Edit Key	Description
Insert	Toggles between Insert and Overstrike editing modes
PgUp and PgDn	Moves the cursor up or down one screen
F3	Displays format options (such as bold, outline, font choices) that you can set on the text in the text range

4. Press Esc to quit editing text in the text range and to return to READY mode.

To set formats on text in the text range, do the following:

1. Type **:te**.

2. Specify the text range (the range in which you want to edit text). **:Text Edit** edits text only within the range you specify.

3. Move the cursor to the first character you want to format and press F3.

4. Choose one of the following items:

Menu Item	Description
Font	Specifies a font for the text
Bold	Bolds the text
Italics	Italicizes the text
Underline	Underlines the text
Color	Specifies a color for the text
+	Superscripts the text
–	Subscripts the text
Outline	Formats text so that only the outline of the characters is displayed
Normal	Removes formatting from the text

5. Move the cursor to the last character you want to format, press F3, and select **Normal**.

Important Cue

You can edit text in an existing text range (specified with **:Text Set**) at any time by double-clicking the left mouse button on any text in the range.

For more information, see Chapter 9.

Text Align   *:TA*

Purpose

Changes the label-alignment for labels in the specified text range.

Reminder

Before you select **:ta**, move the cell-pointer to the first cell in the range in which you want to change the label-alignment.

Procedures

1. Type **:ta**.

2. Choose one of the following items:

Menu Item	Description
Left	Left-aligns labels in the text range (aligns labels with the left edge of the text range)
Right	Right-aligns labels in the text range (aligns labels with the right edge of the text range)
Center	Centers labels in the text range (aligns labels so that they are centered in the text range)
Even	Aligns labels with both edges of the text range. Even does not align labels that end with a period (.), an exclamation point (!), a question mark (?), a colon (:), or an end-of-paragraph symbol (created with **:te**).

3. Specify the text range (the range in which you want to align labels). **:Text Align** aligns labels only within the range you specify.

Figure T.1 shows labels in two text ranges. The labels in range B2..B8 are centered; the labels in range D2..D8 are aligned evenly.

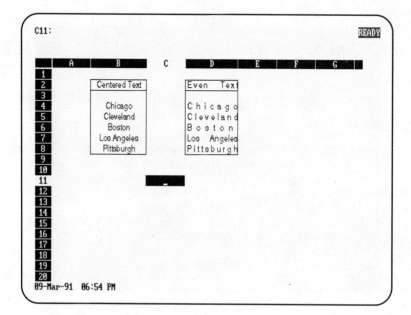

Fig. T.1. *Centered and even label alignment.*

Important Cue

1-2-3 displays labels that are longer than the width of the text range as left-aligned, regardless of which alignment you select.

For more information, see Chapter 9.

Text Reformat   :TR

Purpose

Justifies a column of labels so that the labels fit in the specified text range.

Reminder

Before you select **:tr**, move the cell pointer to the first cell in the column of labels that you want to justify.

Procedures

1. Type **:tr**.

2. Specify the text range (the range in which you want the labels to be displayed). You must include all rows in the column that you want to reformat, as well as any other columns that you want to use to justify the labels. 1-2-3 reformats the labels in the first column of the text range, by using the label-prefix of the first cell in the column so that the labels are justified within the entire text range. For example, if the first cell is right-aligned, 1-2-3 displays the labels in the first column of the text range at the right edge of the text range.

Important Cue

You cannot use **:tr** if global protection is set on. Type **/wgpd** to set global protection off before you select **:Text Reformat**.

For more information, see Chapter 9.

Text Set   *:TS*

Purpose

Specifies a text range that you can use with other **:Text** commands.

Reminder

Before you sclect **:ts**, move the cell-pointer to the first cell you want to include in the text range.

Procedures

1. Type **:ts**.

2. Specify the range of cells you want to include in the text range.

Important Cues

• 1-2-3 displays the format description {Text} in the control panel when the cell-pointer is located in a cell in a text range.

• You can edit text in an existing text range from READY mode by moving the cell-pointer to any cell in the text range and double-clicking the left mouse button. Then use the text range editing keys to edit the text.

For more information, see Chapter 9.

Text Clear :TC

Purpose

Clears the settings for a text range and removes any alignment in the range that was set with **:Text Align**.

Reminder

Before you select **:tc**, move the cell-pointer to the first cell you want to include in the range you want to clear.

Procedures

1. Type **:tc**.

2. Specify the text range you want to clear. The range you specify does not need to be exactly the same as a previously defined text range.

Important Cue

:Text Clear does not remove formats specified with the **:Text Edit** or **:Text Reformat** commands.

For more information, see Chapter 9.

:Named-Style Commands :N

:Named-Style commands define a set of Wysiwyg formats (such as cells you want displayed in bold face for titles or an entire report or schedule format) that you can save and reuse. Throughout this section, refer to the **:Named-Style** menu on the Wysiwyg side of the pull-out command card at the back of this book.

Named-Style 1 through Named-Style 8 :ND1 through :ND8

Purpose

Formats a range with a named-style set of Wysiwyg formats. Use these commands, in combination with **:Named-Style Define**, to set common Wysiwyg formats quickly.

Reminder

Before you format a range with a named-style set, you must define the named-style with the **:Named-Style Define** command.

Procedures

1. Type **:n**.

2. Select the named-style set you want to use for a range (or ranges) from the menu (1 through 8). 1-2-3 displays the name and description of each named-style set next to its corresponding number. You can select any of the eight named-style sets.

3. Specify the range or ranges that you want to format with the named style.

Important Cue

1-2-3 updates any cells you format with a named style when you change a named-style set with **:Named-Style Define**.

For more information, see Chapter 9.

Named-Style Define   :ND

Purpose

Defines and names a set of formats in a cell as a **Named-Style**. You can define up to eight different named-style sets.

Reminder

Before you select **:Named-Style Define**, be sure that you have formatted a cell with the Wysiwyg formats you want to use as the named-style set. Figure N.1 shows a cell formatted with Wysiwyg commands that can be used as a named-style set.

Procedures

1. Type **:nd**.

2. Select the number for the named style you want to define (1–8).

3. Specify the cell that contains the Wysiwyg formats you want to define as a named-style.

4. Enter a name (a maximum of six characters) for the named style.

5. Enter a description (a maximum of 37 characters) for the named-style set.

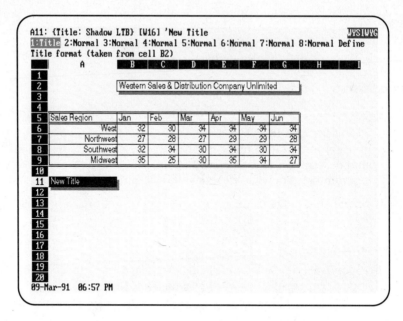

Fig. N.1. *Defining a cell's Wysiwyg formats as a named style.*

Important Cues

- When you define a :Named-Style, you should specify only the cell that contains the formats you want. You can specify a range of cells, but 1-2-3 uses the Wysiwyg formats from the first cell in the range only.

- After you have defined a named-style set, 1-2-3 displays its name and description after its number each time you select :n.

For more information, see Chapter 9.

Quit Command   :Q

Purpose

Leaves the Wysiwyg menu and returns 1-2-3 to READY mode.

Reminder

Unlike the /Quit command, :Quit does not exit from 1-2-3. You still must use the /Quit command when you want to exit 1-2-3.

Procedure

Type :q.

Important Cue

To use the Wysiwyg menu again, type **:** (colon) or reinvoke the Wysiwyg add-in if necessary.

PrintGraph Commands

PrintGraph commands print graphs that have been saved from the worksheet through /**G**raph **S**ave. PrintGraph is a supplemental 1-2-3 utility available through the Lotus 1-2-3 Access menu.

To access instructions to print a graph, select **P**rintGraph from the Lotus 1-2-3 Access menu or type PGRAPH at the operating-system prompt. Recall that you can access the operating-system prompt by selecting /**S**ystem. The PrintGraph utility must be in the default disk and directory. Throughout this section, refer to the PrintGraph menu on the pull-out command card at the back of this book.

PrintGraph Image-Select   *PI*

Purpose

Selects PIC (graph) files to be printed or viewed. Use **P**rintGraph **I**mage-Select to select multiple files that then print in sequence.

Reminders

- Use the worksheet to create and save a graph. When you save the graph and its settings to disk from the worksheet, the file name has a PIC extension. (For more information on creating and saving graphs, see the Graph section.)

- Remember that you can use **P**rintGraph **I**mage-Select to view graphs from within PrintGraph, but you cannot change graphs in PrintGraph. Use PrintGraph only to print previously saved graphs.

- Use **P**rintGraph **S**ettings **H**ardware **G**raphs-Directory to access the directory in which the PIC files are located.

Procedures

1. Select **I**mage-Select from PrintGraph's main menu. You see a list of the current directory's PIC files with their respective sizes and creation dates. Previously selected graph files (if any) are marked with a number sign (#) to the left of the file names, as shown in figure PG.1.

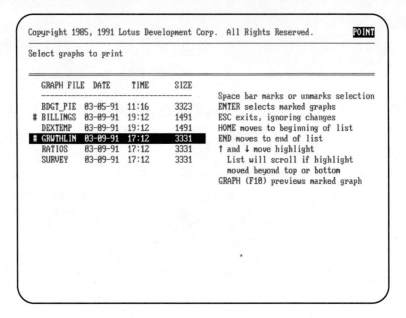

Fig. PG.1. *A list of PIC files displayed after choosing Image-Select.*

2. Use the down- and up-arrow keys to highlight the graph file names. To mark a graph to be printed, highlight the graph, and then press the space bar. Selected files are marked with a #. Remove # markings by highlighting the graph file name and again pressing the space bar.

3. To preview the graph on-screen, highlight the file name and press Graph (F10). Press any key to return to the **Image-Select** menu.

4. Press Enter to return to the **PrintGraph** menu. The graphs marked with # print when you select **G**o.

5. The selected graph file names appear on the left side of PrintGraph's main menu screen. Graphs print in the order selected.

Important Cues

- If you preview a graph on-screen, it does not look the same as the printed graph or the graph viewed from within the worksheet. PrintGraph's preview graphs use BLOCK1 characters and are not on the same scale as printed graphs. This preview function serves only as a reminder of which graph belongs to which file name.

- Previewing graphs from PrintGraph is possible only if you have hardware capable of graphics and if those capabilities are installed for 1-2-3.

*For more information, see /**Graph Save** and Chapter 10.*

PrintGraph Settings Image Size   *PSIS*

Purpose

Controls the location of the graph on the printed page, including the graph's size and its rotation.

The **Full** and **Half** settings automatically control graph location and rotation.

Reminders

- Settings selected from PrintGraph Settings Image Size control the printed appearance of graphs selected with **Image-Select**.

- If you want to print more than one graph per page, draw a thumbnail sketch of how the graphs should be arranged on the page and what their size and rotation should be.

Procedures

1. Select **Settings Image Size** from PrintGraph's menu.

2. From the following options, select the location/rotation of the graph(s) to be printed:

Menu Item	Description
Full	Prints large graphs on 8 1/2-by-11-inch paper; automatically sets rotation to 90 degrees to position the bottom of the graph on the paper's right edge
Half	Prints half-sized graphs to fit two graphs per page. Rotation is set to 0 degrees to position the graph upright.
Manual	Manually sets graph proportions, locations, and rotation
Quit	Returns to the preceding menu

3. If in Step 2 you selected **Full** or **Half**, skip to Step 5.

4. If in Step 2 you selected **Manual**, enter the proportions, location, and rotation for your graph from the following options:

Menu Item	Description
Top	Sets the margin in inches at the paper's top
Left	Sets the margin between the paper's left edge and the graph
Width	Sets the distance across the graph, measured across the direction of the paper feed
Height	Sets the graph's height, measured along the direction of the paper feed
Rotation	Sets counterclockwise the degrees of rotation. 90 degrees puts the bottom of the graph on the paper's right edge.
Quit	Returns to the preceding menu

5. Choose **Quit** or press Esc to return to the Settings Image menu.

Important Cues

- To print additional graphs on a single page, roll the paper backward to align the paper's serrations with the top of the printer's strike plate. Select **Align** to reset the top of form. Use **Settings Image Size Manual** to adjust graph locations, sizes, and rotations so that graphs do not overlap.

- Any changes to the graph's location, size, or rotation override any **Full** or **Half** selections you may have made.

- If you selected **Full** or **Half**, the graph prints with the same proportions as the on-screen graph (a ratio of about 1.385 along the x-axis to 1 along the y-axis). If you set the graph size manually, you can change these proportions. To maintain on-screen proportions, divide the desired x-axis length by 1.385 to get the appropriate y-axis setting.

- To rotate the graph and maintain on-screen proportions, use the **Height** or **Width** entry-area options to enter the x- and y-axis lengths as calculated in the preceding cue. The options are the following:

Menu Item	Rotation	Enter Length of
Height	0	Graph's y-axis
Width		Graph's x-axis
Height	90	Graph's x-axis
Width		Graph's y-axis
Height	180	Graph's y-axis
Width		Graph's x-axis
Height	270	Graph's x-axis
Width		Graph's y-axis

Caution

Graphs rotated at angles other than right angles are distorted.

For more information, see Chapter 10.

PrintGraph Settings Image Font   *PSIF*

Purpose

Determines which fonts (print styles) are used for alphanumeric characters in a printed graph. With this command, you can use one font for the title and another font for legends, other titles, and scale numbers.

Procedures

1. Access the main **PrintGraph** menu. The status of current PrintGraph settings appears below the double line.

2. Note the path to the Fonts-Directory under HARDWARE SETTINGS. If the path is not accurate, select **Settings Hardware Fonts-Directory** to specify the directory in which the FNT (font) files are located. Press Enter and then either choose **Quit** or press Esc to return to PrintGraph's **Settings** menu.

3. Note whether the default setting for font 1 and font 2 is BLOCK1. If you do not want to alter the default setting, proceed no further with this command. If you want to change one or both fonts, continue with the following steps.

4. Select **Image Font**.

5. Choose one of the following items:

Menu Item	Description
1	Specifies the print style for the top center title
2	Specifies the print style for other titles and legends

The screen displays the following list of font options:

```
BLOCK1
BLOCK2
BOLD
FORUM
ITALIC1
ITALIC2
LOTUS
ROMAN1
ROMAN2
SCRIPT1
SCRIPT2
```

The BLOCK1 default setting is preceded by the # marker and is highlighted. (The marker is not visible if you elect to specify font 2 before you choose font 1. See the "Important Cues" section.)

A number after a font name is an indication of print darkness. A font whose name ends with 2 has darker print than a font whose name ends with 1. Darker fonts are more evident on high-resolution printers and plotters.

6. To choose a different font, use the down-arrow, up-arrow, Home, or End key to point to the font you want.

7. Press the space bar to move the # marker to the desired font. Note that at this point the space bar is a toggle: repeatedly pressing the space bar turns the marker on and off.

8. Press Enter to select the font or press Esc if you want 1-2-3 to ignore the action and to exit from the font menu.

9. Repeat steps 5 through 8 if you want to select another font.

Important Cues

- If you first select menu item 1 in Step 5, the font selection you make affects both font 1 and font 2. You can, however, select menu item 2 before you choose 1. Selecting menu item 2 enables you to make font 2 different from font 1. To choose font 2, move the pointer to the desired font and press Enter. After you have altered font 2—and until you end the PrintGraph session or unless you use Reset to replace current, unsaved settings with the default settings stored in the PGRAPH.CNF file—you can make a change to font 1 without affecting font 2.

- For best results with a dot-matrix printer, use the BLOCK fonts and avoid the ITALIC and SCRIPT fonts. If you have a high-density dot-matrix printer, you should be able to use the BOLD, FORUM, and ROMAN fonts with good results.

- The lower portion of the status screen should show the selected fonts.

- Use **PrintGraph Settings Save** to make the PrintGraph Settings specifications the default in the PGRAPH.CNF file.

Cautions

- If you have a two-disk system, while you are using the PrintGraph program, do not remove from the system the disk containing the font files.

- You cannot specify a print style unless the directory that stores the font instructions has been specified correctly.

For more information, see Chapter 10.

PrintGraph Settings Image Range-Colors   PSIR

Purpose

Assigns available colors to specified graph ranges for printing.

Reminder

Before you can use **Range-Colors**, you must select a printer or plotter with **Settings Hardware Printer**.

Procedures

1. Select **Settings** from PrintGraph's menu.

2. If you have not yet designated a printer or plotter, select **Hardware Printer**. After you make the selection and press Esc, choose **Image Range-Colors**.

If you already have designated a printer or plotter, select **Image Range-Colors**. The **Range-Colors** menu displays the colors available on your system. Ranges X and A through F display only black if the system cannot print in color. If the system can print in color, use the right- and left-arrow keys and the Enter key to choose a range and its color.

The color of range X is the color of the graph, including the grid, scale numbers, and x- and y-axis labels. The color for each range from A through F is for each graphed data series and corresponding legend.

3. After you have assigned a color to one range, select another range and assign it a different color. Repeat this process until you have assigned a unique color to each range.

4. Select **Quit** or press Esc to leave the **Range-Colors** menu.

Caution

Before you can specify range colors, you must have a color-graphics printer or plotter that has been correctly installed. To install the printer or plotter, choose **Install** from the Lotus 1-2-3 Access menu and follow the instructions for establishing applicable printer or plotter driver sets. Use **Settings Hardware Interface** and **Settings Hardware Printer** to specify the current printer or plotter configuration.

For more information, see Chapter 10.

PrintGraph Settings Action   PSA

Purpose

Causes the printer to pause or stop between graphs.

Procedures

1. Select **Settings Action** from PrintGraph's menu.

2. Select **Pause Yes** to make the printer pause between graphs so that you can choose other print options or change the paper.

Or, select **Eject Yes** to print one graph per page by making the printer advance continuous-feed paper automatically to the next page after a graph is printed.

Important Cues

- If you choose **Pause Yes**, the computer pauses during printing and beeps as a signal for you to change printer or plotter settings, insert a new sheet of paper, or change plotter pens. To make the printing resume, press the space bar.

- If you select **P**ause **N**o (the default setting), PrintGraph prints graphs without pausing.

- If you choose Eject **N**o (the default setting), PrintGraph prints a second graph on a page if the page is long enough. If the page is not long enough, PrintGraph advances the paper to the top of the next page.

- Use **S**ettings **H**ardware **S**ize-**P**aper to alter the page length.

Cautions

- **S**ettings **A**ction **P**ause affects a printer differently on a network: the printing pauses, but PrintGraph gives no signal at the network device.

- Be sure to use **S**ettings **A**ction **P**ause **Y**es if your printer does not use continuous-feed paper or have an automatic sheet feeder.

For more information, see Chapter 10.

PrintGraph Settings Hardware   PSH

Purpose

Defines for PrintGraph which directories contain graphs and fonts, determines the type(s) of printer(s) to be used and how they connect to the PC, and specifies the paper size.

Figure PG.2 shows PrintGraph's **S**ettings **H**ardware menu. The selections you make from this menu are displayed under the title HARDWARE SETTINGS.

Reminders

- Use 1-2-3's main Install program (described in 1-2-3's reference manual) to install the printers and plotters to be used to print or plot graphs. You can install more than one printer and/or plotter at a time. PrintGraph cannot communicate to the printer or plotter until you install the printer or plotter with 1-2-3's main Install program.

- If you are using a printer or plotter connected to a serial port, check the printer's or plotter's manual to find the recommended baud rate (transmission rate).

Procedures

To change the directory containing the font or graph files, follow these steps:

1. Select **S**ettings **H**ardware from PrintGraph's menu.

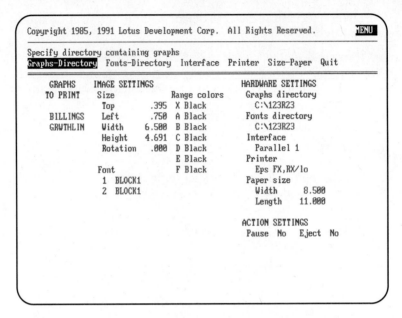

Fig. PG.2. *The PrintGraph Settings Hardware menu.*

2. From the following options, select the directory to be changed:

Menu Item	Description
Graphs-Directory	Changes directory where PIC files are located (for example, C:\123R23\RESULTS)
Fonts-Directory	Changes directory where font (FNT) files are located (for example, C:\123R23)

To change your PC's interface (hardware connection) used to communicate to the printer or plotter, follow these steps:

1. Select **Settings Hardware** from PrintGraph's menu.

2. Select **Interface**.

3. From the following options, select the interface that connects your printer or plotter to the PC:

Setting	Device
1	First parallel printer (most printers)
2	First serial printer (most plotters)

Setting	Device
3	Second parallel printer
4	Second serial printer
5 through **8**	The DOS devices LPT1: through LPT4: (usually used with printers connected to network)

4. If you selected a serial interface (options 2 or 4 in step 3), enter the baud rate (transmission rate). You can find the recommended baud rate in the printer's or plotter's manual.

To select which printer or plotter installation to use, follow these steps:

1. Select **Settings Hardware** from PrintGraph's menu.

2. Select **Printer**.

3. Use the down- and up-arrow keys to highlight the printer or plotter installation option to be selected. Some installation options may be listed more than once. If you use a printer or plotter with duplicate installation options, experiment with the duplicate listings; they offer different print intensities and resolution.

4. After you have highlighted the selection, press the space bar to mark your choice with a # sign. To remove the # sign, highlight the choice and press the space bar again.

5. Press Enter to return to the **Settings Hardware** menu.

To select a different page size, follow these steps:

1. Select **Settings Hardware** from PrintGraph's menu.

2. Select **Size-Paper**.

3. Enter separately (in inches) the new paper size for **Length** and **Width**.

4. Press Enter and then select **Quit** to return to the **Settings Hardware** menu.

Important Cue

If **Settings Hardware Printer** does not list an installation option for the printer, select a similar but earlier printer model from the same manufacturer. Also check with the printer's dealer and Lotus Development Corporation to obtain disks containing additional hardware installation options.

Caution

1-2-3 expects serial printers to communicate transmitted data according to a certain protocol. Most printers and plotters already are set to send data according to this protocol. The following are PrintGraph's transmission settings:

Data bits	8
Stop bits	1 (2 for 110 baud)
Parity	None

For more information, see Chapter 10.

PrintGraph Go, Align, and Page   *PG, PA, PP*

Purpose

Activates the printing process, specifies the printhead position as the top of the page, and advances the paper one page at a time, respectively.

Procedures

1. Check the status area of the PrintGraph screen to verify that the graphs selected have the correct image, hardware, and action settings necessary for the current printing.

2. Make sure that the printer has enough paper for the print job.

3. Position the printhead to the desired top-of-page position and make sure that the printer is on-line.

4. Select one or more of the following options:

Menu Item	*Description*
Go	Activates the printing operation
Align	Makes the current printhead position the top-of-form position
Page	Advances the paper one page when a key is pressed

Important Cue

If you want to change the page length, select Settings Hardware Size-Paper.

For more information, see Chapter 10.

Installing 1-2-3 Release 2.3

The Install program for installing 1-2-3 Release 2.3 makes installation almost automatic; after you start the program, you follow the on-screen instructions. You must install Release 2.3 on a hard disk; the Install program is designed for this type of installation.

The Install program begins by creating several subdirectories on your hard disk. Then the program copies the program files to the new appropriate subdirectory. The program also asks you to select the type of video display you have, as well as the type of printer. Before you install Release 2.3, verify the brand and model of your printer. The program can detect the type of video display you use. Finally, the Install program generates the font files needed to use the Wysiwyg add-in.

Installation takes about 15 to 20 minutes; you need another 15 to 20 minutes to generate the basic font set for the Wysiwyg feature. When you are ready to begin, turn on your computer and follow the instructions in this appendix.

Checking DOS Configuration

Before you install 1-2-3 Release 2.3 to run under DOS, you must complete a preliminary step: ensure that DOS is configured adequately to run 1-2-3 by checking your CONFIG.SYS file for the FILES statement. CONFIG.SYS is found on your hard disk in the root directory. Type **TYPE C:\CONFIG.SYS**

897

and press Enter to see the contents of CONFIG.SYS. The screen displays something like the following:

```
FILES=25
BUFFERS=20
DEVICE=C:\DOS\ANSI.SYS
```

The FILES statement tells DOS how many files can be open at one time. The minimum number of files that you must select is 20 (FILES=20). If you see no FILES statement, or if the number of files in the FILES statement is below 20, change the CONFIG.SYS file. You can edit CONFIG.SYS with any text editor, such as EDLIN, or with a word processor that can save files as ASCII unformatted text.

Also, make sure that your version of DOS is 2.1 or higher and verify that you have at least 512K of memory available for 1-2-3 and Wysiwyg (640K is recommended). On the hard disk, you need 7M of available disk space to load 1-2-3 and all of its companion programs (including Wysiwyg). Refer to the Lotus documentation for specific requirements about using 1-2-3 Release 2.3 with Microsoft Windows.

Using the Install Program

After installation is complete, be sure that you make backup copies of the original disks and store the originals in a safe place.

Upgrading to Release 2.3

Lotus recommends that users who upgrade to Release 2.3 from previous releases create a different directory for the new version. If you plan to follow the Lotus recommendation, go immediately to the next section, "Starting the Install Program."

Otherwise, refer to your Lotus documentation for information on how to use the same subdirectory you used for your previous release of 1-2-3.

Starting the Install Program

To install 1-2-3, place the Install disk in drive A. Switch to drive A by typing **A:** and pressing Enter. At the DOS A> prompt, type **INSTALL** and press

Enter. The first screen you see is 1-2-3's welcome screen (see fig. A.1). Read the information on-screen and then press Enter to continue the installation and to register your disks.

> *Note:* You also can install 1-2-3 from disk drive B, if necessary. Substitute B for A in the preceding paragraph and in the appropriate locations throughout this appendix.

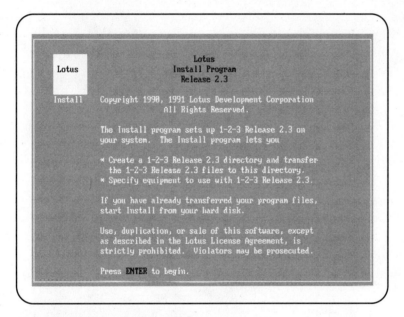

Fig. A.1. The 1-2-3 Install Welcome screen.

Registering Your Original Disks

To make your disks usable, you must register them by entering and saving your name and company name on the Install disk (enter your name again if you have no company name). Type your name and press Enter and then type your company name. Make sure that you type the information correctly. If everything is correct, press Enter to continue.

The Install program then asks if you want to record what you typed on the disk. Choose **Yes** and press Enter. The information you typed is recorded, and your copy of 1-2-3 now is registered. Your name and company name, along with a serial number, appear every time you start 1-2-3.

Choosing Files To Install

In the next step of the installation procedure, you choose the auxiliary programs that you want to install in addition to the 1-2-3 program (see fig. A.2). The default is to install all these additional programs except PrintGraph and Translate. To install everything, you need at least 7M of free disk space. To add or remove one or more of these choices from the installation, highlight the choice to add or remove and press the space bar. This action adds or removes the check mark from the item.

Note: When you highlight a program option, a dialog box on the right side of the screen lists the amount of disk space required by each program.

Fig. A.2. *The default screen for selecting the 1-2-3 and Add-in programs to install.*

The list of choices include the following:

Program	Description
1-2-3	Contains the 1-2-3 program files
Wysiwyg	Adds publishing features to 1-2-3 to improve the appearance of printouts and graphs
Add-ins	Adds auditing, file viewing features, and a macro library manager to 1-2-3
1-2-3-Go!	Teaches you how to use 1-2-3 with on-screen tutorials
Wysiwyg-Go!	Demonstrates how to use Wysiwyg to create presentation-quality reports and graphs
PrintGraph	Displays and prints graphs made with 1-2-3
Translate	Converts data from other programs to 1-2-3 and converts data from 1-2-3 to other programs

Wysiwyg is an add-in program that switches 1-2-3 to graphics mode so that you can see changes—such as underlines, boldface, and even graphs—on the screen in the worksheet.

The other 1-2-3 add-ins included with Release 2.3 include the Viewer add-in, the Auditor add-in, and the Macro Library Manager add-in. See Chapters 3 and 7 for information about the Viewer add-in. Appendix B covers the Auditor add-in. See Chapter 13 for a description of the Macro Library Manager add-in.

1-2-3-Go! is an on-line tutorial program that you can use to learn 1-2-3. Wysiwyg-Go! is a sophisticated demo program that shows you how to use the Wysiwyg add-in to enhance reports and graphs.

PrintGraph is a separate program, included with 1-2-3, which displays and prints graphs you define from 1-2-3 worksheet data. Note that Wysiwyg also enables you to print graphs.

Translate is a program that converts outside data files—such as those files created by Symphony and dBASE—as well as data file formats, such as DIF, to 1-2-3 format and vice versa.

Creating a Directory for the 1-2-3 Files

The next screen asks for the hard disk letter to use for the 1-2-3 files (see fig. A.3). Most often, you install programs on drive C. To install 1-2-3 on drive C, press Enter. To install 1-2-3 on a different drive, type the letter of the drive (for example, **D**) and press Enter.

After you choose the drive, you are asked to name the 1-2-3 directory that you want to store the 1-2-3 files. The default directory name is \123R23 (see fig. A.4). You can type another name. Press Enter to continue.

If the directory does not exist, the Install program creates the directory. First, the Install program asks you to confirm that you want the directory created, as shown in figure A.5. To change the directory name, press N and then press Enter. To confirm that the directory should be created, press Enter to accept the Y default.

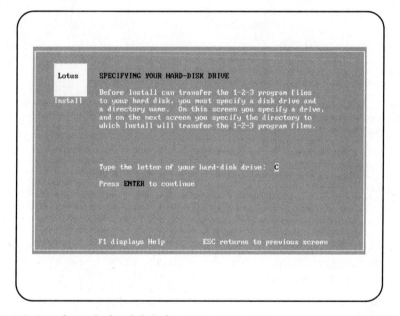

Fig. A.3. Specifying the hard disk drive to contain 1-2-3.

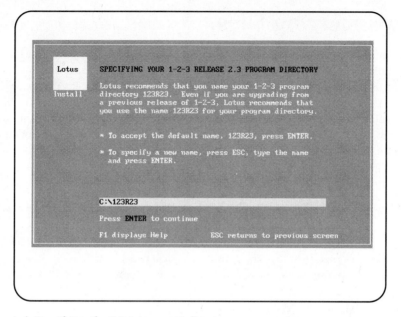

Fig. A.4. *Specifying the 1-2-3 program directory.*

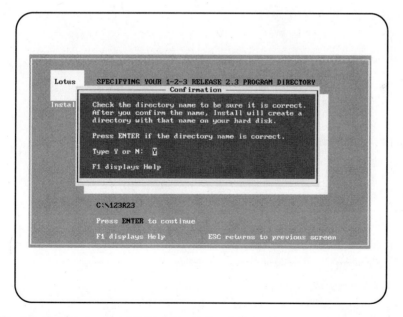

Fig. A.5. *Confirming the 1-2-3 program directory name.*

Transferring Files

Because the files on the installation disks are compressed, you cannot copy the files from the DOS prompt. After you name the drive and directory, the Install program begins transferring files to the hard disk. The program transfers files first from disk 1. After transferring the files from the disk, Install prompts you to insert the next disk. Follow the screen prompts to insert the correct disk. Install transfers only those programs you specified in the initial choices screen (see fig. A.2).

Configuring 1-2-3 for Your Computer

After the program transfers the system files, the second part of the installation begins (see fig. A.6). The first screen describes how to make selections in this part of the installation. Press Enter to continue to the Main menu (see fig. A.7).

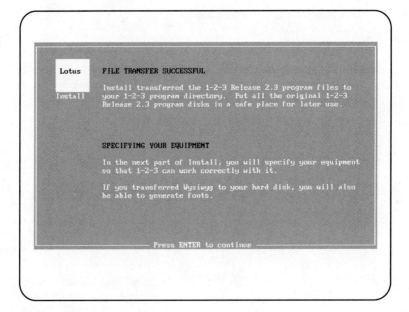

Fig. A.6. *Starting the second part of the installation process.*

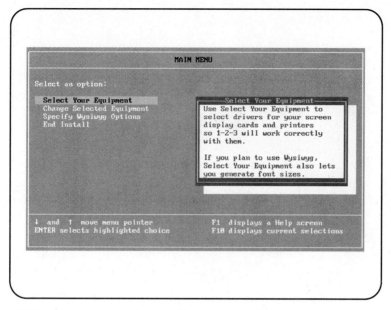

Fig. A.7. The main menu of the Install program.

In the Main menu, the first option, `Select Your Equipment`, is highlighted. To make a different selection, press the up- or down-arrow key to highlight the desired selection and then press Enter. Because you are installing 1-2-3 for the first time, press Enter to select the first option.

> *Note:* After you install 1-2-3 to your hard disk, you can change the configuration. For example, if you purchase a new printer, you must add the printer configuration. Choose `Change Selected Equipment` from the Main menu. See "Changing the 1-2-3 Configuration," later in this appendix.

Next, the Install program lists the type of video display that the program detects on your computer system. Figure A.8 shows the screen that appears when the program detects a Video Graphics Array (VGA). Make a note of the type of screen 1-2-3 detected for your computer and press Enter. When the Screen Display Selection menu appears, highlight the type of display detected and press Enter (see fig. A.9).

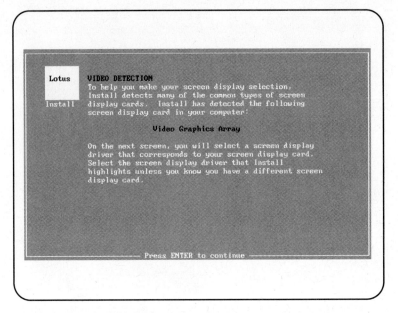

Fig. A.8. *Detecting the type of screen display.*

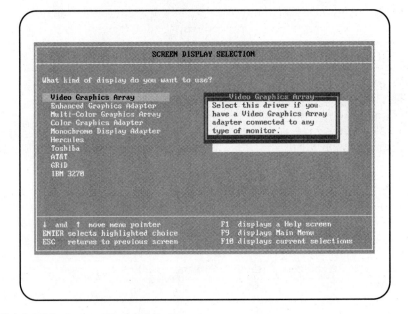

Fig. A.9. *The Screen Display Selection menu.*

Often a video display has more than one way of displaying information on-screen. After you select your type of display, the program lists the available modes for that display. Figure A.10 shows the modes available for a VGA type of display. If your video display offers more than one mode, choose the one that best suits your needs. The mode selected in figure A.10 displays 25 lines with 80 characters per line with a black background. After 1-2-3 is installed, you can change this selection.

If your video display does not offer different modes for displaying information on-screen, you do not see the screen in figure A.10. Instead, the Install program records the display you chose and moves on.

Next, you select a printer. First, you are asked whether you have a text printer (see fig. A.11). If you do not have a printer or do not want to install a printer now, select No and press Enter to continue. Otherwise, press Enter to select Yes.

Choosing Yes displays the Text Printer Selection menu (see fig. A.12). Highlight your model of printer and press Enter. In figure A.12, the highlight is on HP (Hewlett-Packard) as the brand of printer to install.

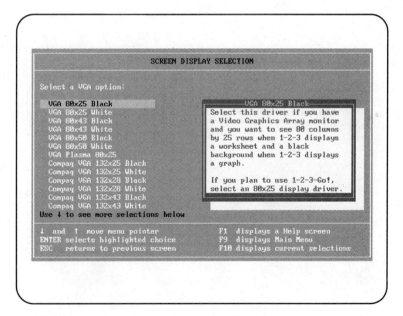

Fig. A.10. *Selecting the video display mode.*

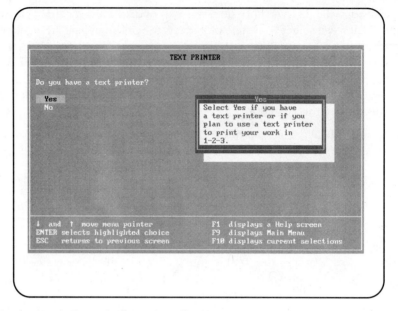

Fig. A.11. *Deciding whether to install a text printer.*

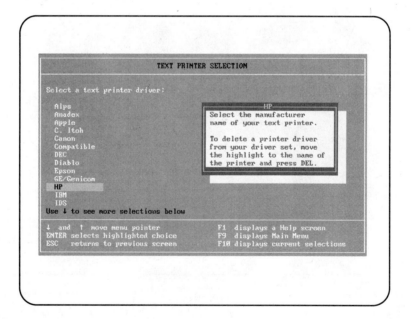

Fig. A.12. *The Text Printer Selection menu.*

After you select the brand of printer, you select the model. Figure A.13 shows the available HP models; in this figure, the LaserJet series is highlighted. After you highlight the correct model, press Enter.

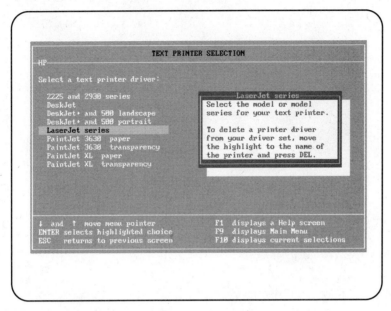

Fig. A.13. *Selecting a printer model.*

If your printer supports font cartridges (most laser printers and a few dot-matrix printers enable you to add fonts), you can choose the font cartridge you want to use with 1-2-3. If this option is one of your choices for your printer model, select the appropriate cartridge from the list displayed and press Enter.

After you install the printer, Install asks whether you want to install another text printer. Answering Yes returns you to the Text Printer Selection menu. To select another printer, follow the same procedure as you followed to select the first printer. If you have only one printer or if you do not want to install another printer at this time, press Enter to answer No (the default answer).

You then are asked if you have a graphics printer for printing Wysiwyg and PrintGraph graphs (see fig. A.14). If you do, leave the highlight on Yes and press Enter. Then select the graphics printer by using the same procedure previously described for selecting the text printer. If you don't have a graphics printer, select No and press Enter. Install then asks whether you have another graphics printer to install. Select Yes to return to the Graphics Printer Selection menu or press Enter to accept the default of No.

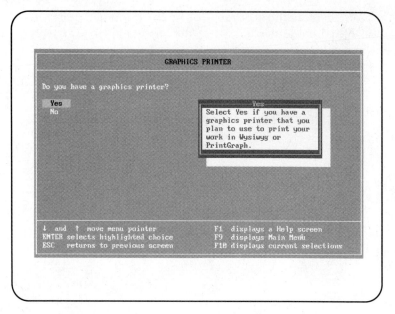

Fig. A.14. *Deciding whether to install a graphics printer.*

After you make your display and printer selections, the program prompts you to name your driver set or SET file (see fig. A.15). The SET file contains all the information from your responses to questions about your display and printer type. If you answer No to the prompt, the program names the file 123.SET. Alternatively, if you answer Yes, you then name the file something else.

If you name the SET file something other than 123.SET, you must supply the SET file's name when you start 1-2-3. For example, if you create a SET file called 60LINE.SET, when you start 1-2-3, type **123 60LINE** and press Enter. If you use the default name of 123.SET, you do not need to specify the SET name when you start 1-2-3.

For the first-time installation, choose No and press Enter to accept the default name. In "Changing the 1-2-3 Configuration," a later section of this appendix, you learn how to create and use more than one SET file.

The Install program transfers files to the hard disk to complete the installation. Which files transfer depends on your selection of video display and printer. Depending on your equipment setup, Install may ask you to insert one or more install disks.

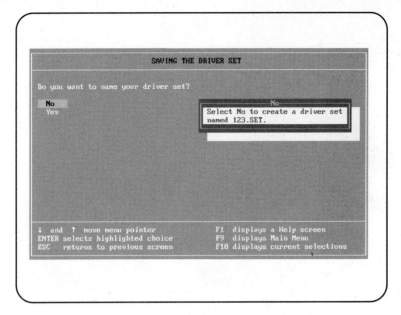

Fig. A.15. *Naming the driver set file (SET).*

Generating Fonts

After Install copies the needed files to the hard disk, you see a screen that tells you your next step is to generate fonts for the Wysiwyg program. (see fig. A.16).

Note: You do not see the screen in figure A.16 if you chose not to install the Wysiwyg add-in program.

Press Enter at the font generation screen to continue the installation process. Install displays the Generating Fonts menu (see fig. A.17). From this menu, you can choose between Basic, Medium, and Extended font sets. Each successive font set gives you a broader range of fonts and font sizes to choose from when you are in the Wysiwyg add-in, but each font set also takes a longer time to install and requires more disk space to store. For now, choose the Basic font set and press Enter. (You can install additional fonts later).

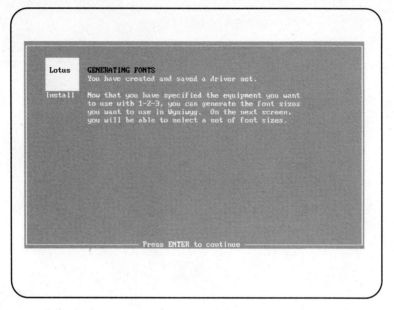

Fig. A.16. *The font generation screen.*

The Basic, Medium, and Extended options enable you to specify the font
sets you want Wysiwyg to generate. The following list details the meaning
of Basic, Medium, and Extended font sets:

Option	Definition
Basic	Generates Swiss, Dutch, Courier, and Xsymbol fonts in the following point size: 4, 6, 8, 10, 12, 14, 18, and 24. A Basic set takes the least amount of time to generate but has the fewest point sizes.
Medium	Generates the point sizes in the Basic set, plus 9, 11, 16, 20, and 36. Medium takes more time to generate than Basic and less time than Extended.
Extended	Generates the point sizes in the Medium set, plus 5, 7, 13, 30, 48, 60, and 72. An Extended set takes the most time to generate.

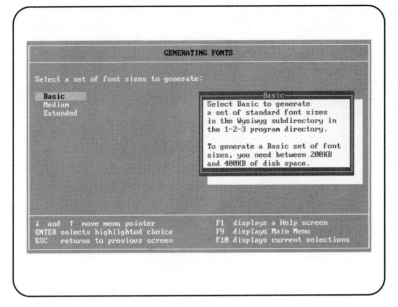

Fig. A.17. *The font generation menu.*

Install displays the font names and point sizes 1-2-3 creates during the generation process. The installation process generates the fonts needed to work with your printers and with your type of display. Installing the Basic font set on a 12 Mhz 286 computer takes about 20 minutes, but a 20 Mhz 386 computer requires only five minutes or so.

After generating the fonts, Install prompts you to press any key to return to the operating system prompt (see fig. A.18).

Changing the 1-2-3 Configuration

In some cases, you may want to change the configuration you created when you first installed 1-2-3. For example, if you purchase a new printer or a new video display, you must reconfigure 1-2-3 to take advantage of this new equipment. Also, to create additional SET files, you must use the Install program again.

After you install 1-2-3 on your hard disk, you can start and run the Install program easily. First, make the directory that contains 1-2-3 the current directory. For example, if the directory is C:\123R23, type **CD \123R23** at the operating system prompt and press Enter.

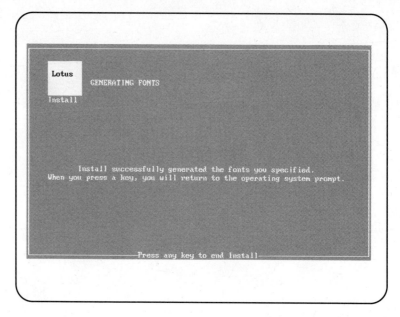

Fig. A.18. *The successful generation of fonts.*

Next, type **INSTALL** and press Enter. The program displays a welcome screen, which is similar to the screen you saw when you first installed 1-2-3. Press Enter to continue to the Main menu. From the Main menu, choose Change Selected Equipment. The Change Selected Equipment menu provides a list of menu selections (see fig. A.19).

These menu selections perform the following actions:

Options	*Description*
Return to Main Menu	Returns to the Main menu
Make Another Driver Set Current	Chooses a different SET file to use for 1-2-3
Modify the Current Driver Set	Changes the configuration of the current SET file (normally 123.SET)
Save the Current Driver Set	Saves all modifications to the current SET file to disk
Switch Mouse Buttons	Switches between left and right buttons
Add New Drivers to the Library	Adds drivers that come with new equipment
End Install	Exits the Install program

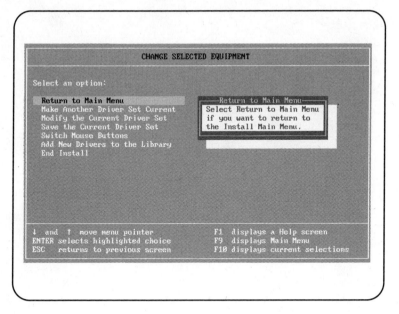

Fig. A.19. The Change Selected Equipment menu.

Modifying Printer or Video Display Drivers

If you purchase a new printer or video display, you may need to modify the current SET file. Select `Modify the Current Driver Set`. The Modify Current Driver Set menu appears (see fig. A.20). From this menu you can change options you selected during the initial installation, as well as some additional options. Press F10 to display a screen that shows the current selections.

The selections for display and printer on the Modify Current Driver Set menu are similar to the selections you saw when you first installed 1-2-3. For example, to change the video display, highlight `Text Display` and press Enter. The next screen shows a list of the available text display options. Scroll down the list until you see the type of display for your new monitor.

Note: The choice you made during the initial installation procedure is marked with an arrow next to the name.

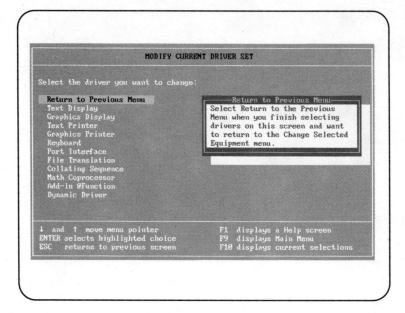

Fig. A.20. *The Modify Current Driver Set menu.*

Highlight the new choice and press Enter. Install changes the display choice to your new selection and then returns you to the Modify Current Driver Set menu. To make sure that Install made the change you want, press F10 and check the selection after `Text Display`.

Use this same process to change all the other selections in the current driver set. Another selection you may want to change is `Collating Sequence`.

Changing the Collating Sequence

You use the `Collating Sequence` option in the Modify Current Driver Set menu to change the sorting order that 1-2-3 uses. Highlight `Collating Sequence` and press Enter. You see a screen with a choice of three options (see fig. A.21). The following listing describes these options:

Options	Description
ASCII	Characters are sorted according to the ASCII table
Numbers first	Numbers are sorted before letters (the default)
Numbers last	Letters are sorted before numbers

Suppose, for example, that you have four entries:

123 Main Street
Adams Rib Plaza
4 Market Place
ADAMS RIB PLAZA

With the `Numbers first` option selected, sorting the four entries in ascending order results in the following:

123 Main Street
4 Market Place
Adams Rib Plaza
ADAMS RIB PLAZA

Sorting the four entries with the `Numbers last` option selected results in the following:

Adams Rib Plaza
ADAMS RIB PLAZA
123 Main Street
4 Market Place

In an ASCII table, each character is assigned a numeric value. Numbers have lower numeric values than letters. Uppercase letters have a lower numeric value than lowercase letters. Therefore, sorting the entries with the `ASCII` option selected results in the following order:

123 Main Street
4 Market Place
ADAMS RIB PLAZA
Adams Rib Plaza

These three options give you flexibility in sorting data. Make a selection by highlighting the option and pressing Enter. You return to the Modify Current Driver Set menu.

Switching Mouse Buttons

Another change you may want to make (particularly if you are left-handed) is the mouse button to use. Press Esc and choose the `Switch Mouse Buttons` selection from the Change Selected Equipment menu. You can change the mouse button you use to select items (see fig. A.22). The left mouse button is the default. Select `Right` or `Left` and press Enter. Install makes the change and returns you to the Change Selected Equipment menu.

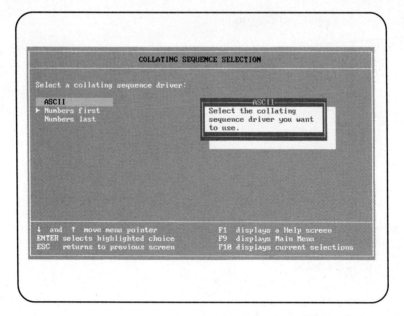

Fig. A.21. *The Collating Sequence Selection menu.*

Adding New Drivers

If you purchased new equipment, such as a new printer, sometimes the manufacturer includes a floppy disk with a 1-2-3 driver specifically designed for that printer. You use the Add New Drivers to the Library option under the Change Selected Equipment menu to add this driver file to your configuration.

When you choose Add New Drivers to the Library, Install asks you which disk drive contains the driver file you want to add. Insert the floppy disk that contains the printer driver. Type the drive letter that holds the driver disk and press Enter. Install copies the driver to your 1-2-3 directory and returns to the Change Selected Equipment menu. Now you can choose the Modify the Current Driver Set option, select Text Printer or Graphics Printer from the Modify Current Driver Set menu, and select this new printer from the list.

Saving Changes to a SET File

When you finish making selections from the Modify Current Driver Set menu, select the option `Return to Previous Menu`. This selection returns you to the Change Selected Equipment menu.

Select `Save the Current Driver Set`. You are prompted to name the SET file. The current set file, 123.SET, does not yet contain the changes you just made. You may want to save these changes either to 123.SET or to another name. By assigning a new name to the driver set, you can start 1-2-3, using either the original selections you made during initial installation or the new modifications. Two different SET files can be helpful if, for example, your monitor can display either 25 lines or 34 lines at one time on the screen. You can create a SET file for 1-2-3 that specifies the 34-line display and call the file 34LINE.SET.

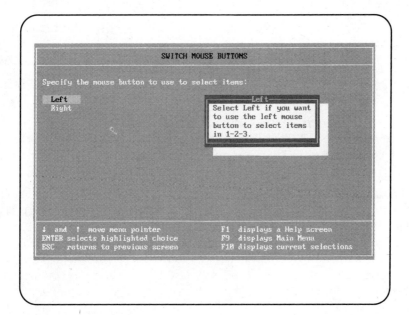

Fig. A.22. *Switching the mouse button you use to make selections in 1-2-3.*

If you want to use the new SET file, include the file name when you start 1-2-3. For example, at the operating system prompt you type:

123 34LINE

To save your changes to a name other than 123.SET, press Backspace to erase 123. Then type the new name. For example, type **34LINE**, as shown in figure A.23, and press Enter. Install creates the file 34LINE.SET in the \123R23 directory. To save your changes to the default name (123.SET), press Enter.

As you save the file, be prepared to insert any disks the Install program needs. Depending on the changes you made to the configuration, the Install program may need to copy files from these disks. You are prompted for the drive letter, and then you are prompted to place one of the disks in the drive.

Finally, the screen states that the installation was completed successfully. Press Enter to return to the Change Selected Equipment menu.

> *Note:* If you selected additional printers and/or displays, the Generating Fonts screen appears. To proceed, follow the instructions in the "Generating Fonts" section earlier in this appendix.

Making Another Driver Set Current

If you create multiple driver sets, you may want to make changes to the selections in the SET files other than the current driver set. Here, you need to make the driver SET file you want to change current. To perform this action, select Make Another Driver Set Current from the Change Selected Equipment menu.

Install prompts for the name of the driver set to modify (see fig. A.24). The default is 123. Use Backspace to erase 123, type the name of the SET file you want to use, and press Enter. Install then returns to the Change Selected Equipment menu. All displayed choices you see from here on are based on the selections in the different SET file. Save all modifications you make to this file by selecting the Save the Current Driver Set option.

Changing Wysiwyg Options

In addition to the Change Selected Equipment option, Install's Main menu contains a selection called Specify Wysiwyg Options. Using this option, you can generate more standard fonts or add fonts from an external source (see fig. A.25).

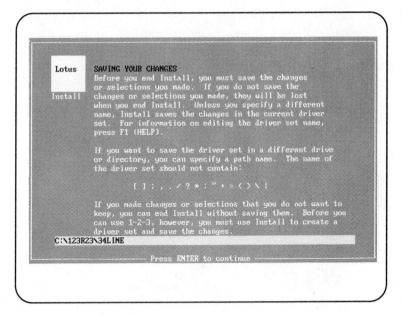

Fig. A.23. *Saving the SET file called 34LINE.*

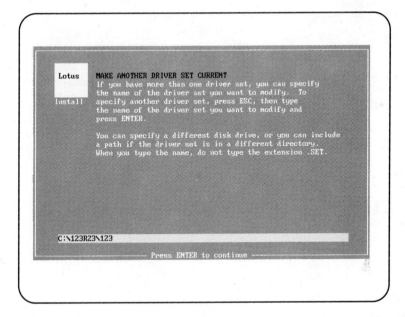

Fig. A.24. *Specifying another driver set file to use.*

If you choose the Generate Fonts, you see the screen shown in figure A.17. If you created the Basic font set and now want to create the Medium or Extended font set, you can make the change from this screen. For example, choose the Extended font set and press Enter. 1-2-3 generates the Extended Wysiwyg font set.

If you choose Add Fonts, 1-2-3 asks you which disk drive contains the fonts you want to add. These fonts are available from your dealer. Choose the drive, and 1-2-3 copies the fonts to your 1-2-3 directory.

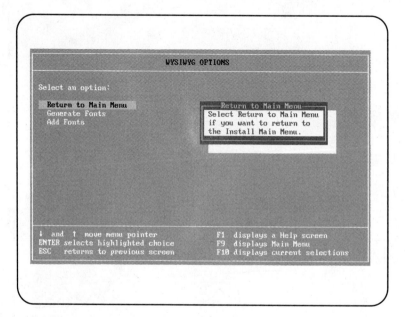

Fig. A.25. *The Wysiwyg Options menu.*

Exiting the Install Program

You can exit the Install program by returning to the main menu and selecting the End Install option. To display the main menu, press F9 from a menu screen or press Esc until you see the main menu.

After you select End Install, the program checks for any changes you have made but not saved to the driver set. If you have made changes but have not saved them, Install asks whether you want to save them before ending. Select Yes to save the changes to the current driver set or No to abandon the changes and press Enter.

Install then asks you to confirm that you want to end the program (see fig. A.26).

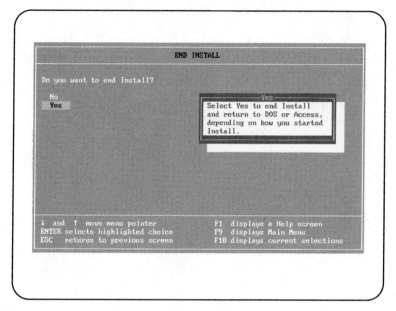

Fig. A.26. *Ending the Install program.*

Select Yes to confirm the exit and press Enter to return to DOS.

B

Using
the Auditor

1-2-3 Release 2.3 includes several add-in programs that enhance or expand upon the existing features of 1-2-3. Throughout this book, you saw and used some of these programs, such as Wysiwyg and the Macro Library Manager. This appendix describes Auditor, another add-in program.

You can use Auditor to diagnose the formulas in a worksheet and to help you verify the accuracy of your figures. You may find Auditor particularly useful when fine-tuning or debugging formulas. With Auditor, you can ensure that the formulas refer to the proper cells and that certain cells are used in the proper worksheet calculations. You also can use Auditor to find and correct circular references and to determine the recalculation order that 1-2-3 uses within a range.

This appendix shows you how to use Auditor to perform the following tasks:

- Highlight all formulas in the worksheet
- Find all cells that supply data to a formula
- Find all formulas that rely on a particular cell
- Trace the path of circular references
- Check the order of recalculation

Attaching and Detaching Auditor

Before you can use Auditor, you first must attach Auditor, just as you do with other add-in programs. To attach an add-in, select /Add-In Attach from 1-2-3's main menu. 1-2-3 displays a list of add-in program files with the extension ADN. Select AUDITOR.ADN and press Enter.

1-2-3 then asks for a function key you can assign to Auditor. You use the key to invoke (or run) the add-in. The key numbers 7 through 10 refer to the function keys labelled F7 through F10. After you choose one of these numbers, you can invoke the add-in by holding down the Alt key and pressing the function key you selected. For example, if you choose 10, you can invoke Auditor by holding down Alt and pressing F10.

> *Note:* If no add-in is attached to Alt-F10, you can use Alt-F10 to select the Add-in menu.

You also can assign No-Key to the add-in. If you don't assign a key to Auditor, you must invoke the add-in by using /Add-In Invoke. Select a key to assign to Auditor and press Enter. 1-2-3 assigns the key you select to Auditor and then returns to the /Add-In menu.

To remove Auditor from memory, use /Add-In Detach. 1-2-3 displays a list of currently attached add-in programs. You then can highlight AUDITOR and press Enter. For now, however, leave Auditor in memory so that you can try the features described in this appendix.

Invoking and Using Auditor

To invoke Auditor, hold down the Alt key and press the function key you assigned to Auditor. 1-2-3 displays the Auditor menu and Auditor Settings dialog box shown in figure B.1. Auditor is now in the computer's memory and is integrated with 1-2-3. You can use Auditor on the current worksheet or leave Auditor, load another worksheet, and then invoke Auditor again with the Alt-function key combination.

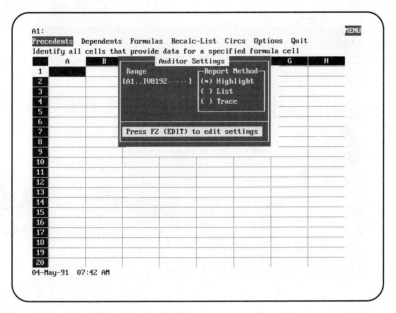

Fig. B.1. *The Auditor Settings dialog box.*

To leave Auditor and return to READY mode, select **Q**uit from the Auditor menu. From READY mode, you can select /**File R**etrieve to load a worksheet. You then redisplay Auditor by invoking the add-in, either with the Alt-function key combination or by using /**Add-In I**nvoke. For example, figure B.2 shows a sample cash flow worksheet and Auditor together in 1-2-3.

Understanding the Auditor Menu

The Auditor menu contains seven options. Table B.1 describes each of these options.

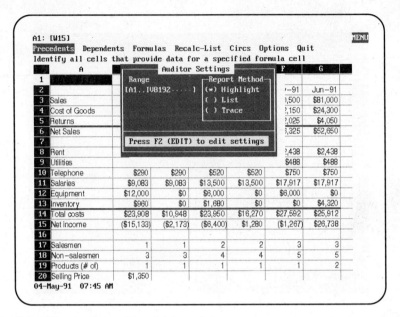

Fig. B.2. *Using Auditor with a 1-2-3 worksheet.*

Table B.1
Auditor Menu Selections

Option	Description
Precedents	Finds all cells that supply data to a formula
Dependents	Finds all formulas that depend on a specified cell
Formulas	Identifies all cells that contain formulas
Recalc-List	Shows the path that 1-2-3 follows when recalculating the worksheet
Circs	Lists all cells involved in a circular reference
Options	Modifies or resets the audit range and reporting method
Quit	Leaves Auditor and returns to 1-2-3

Setting the Audit Range

When you first run the add-in, Auditor assumes that you want to diagnose the entire worksheet—all cells from A1 to IV8192. Auditor calls this range the *audit range*. Auditor displays the current audit range under `Range` on the left side of the Auditor Settings dialog box, as shown in figure B.2. The Auditor Settings dialog box also enables you to select the `Report Method` used by Auditor. These reporting methods are detailed later in this chapter in the "Changing the Reporting Method" section.

Suppose, however, that you want to fine-tune only a small section of a large worksheet. You checked—and found correct—the rest of the worksheet. You want Auditor to diagnose only the last few changes you made. You normally change the audit range to include only those cells you modified. If these cells refer to other formulas or cells that are not in the range, this situation is okay. Auditor still identifies all outside cells if the cells are used by the audit range.

To change the audit range, select **O**ptions **A**udit-Range from the Auditor menu. Auditor highlights the current audit range in the worksheet and changes to POINT mode. Press Esc to unanchor the range and highlight a new range with the keyboard. For example, to specify the range in the sample cash flow worksheet shown in figure B.2, you highlight the range A2..G20. After you highlight the correct range of cells, press Enter. Auditor displays the new range in the Auditor Settings dialog box.

If the audit range is off by only one or two cells, you also can edit the current range in the Auditor Settings dialog box. Press F2 (Edit) to move inside the box. To select the range, type **R** or click on the current audit range. Auditor displays a small underline cursor at the end of the audit range. Use the arrow keys to move to the cell address and edit the address. When you finish, press Enter one time to accept the new range. Press Enter again or click OK to return to Auditor's main menu.

Finding Formulas

After you set the audit range, you are ready to try a reporting option, such as **F**ormulas. The Formulas option locates all cells in the worksheet that contain formulas. Select **F**ormulas; Auditor highlights the cells that contain formulas. If you have a color monitor, Auditor displays the cells in a different color. If you have a monochrome monitor, the cells show as high intensity. Figure B.3 shows the result of using Formulas on the cash flow worksheet.

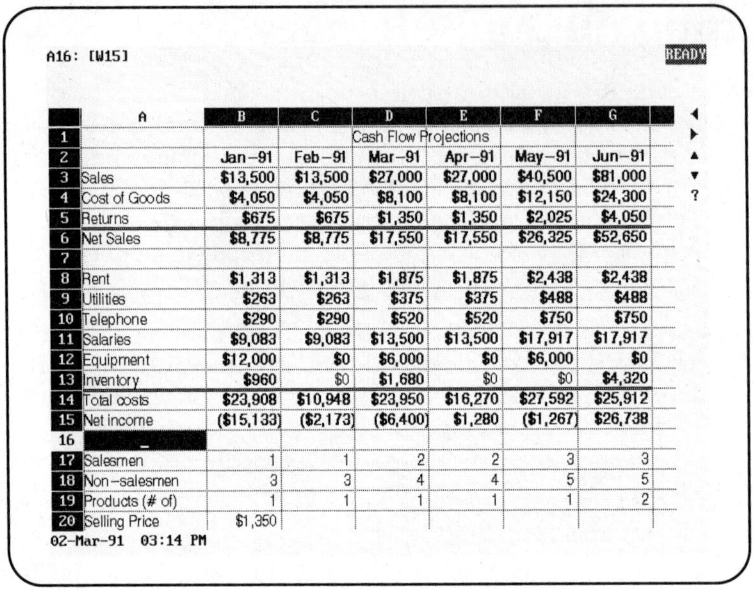

A16: [W15]   READY

A	B	C	D	E	F	G
1			Cash Flow Projections			
2	Jan–91	Feb–91	Mar–91	Apr–91	May–91	Jun–91
3 Sales	$13,500	$13,500	$27,000	$27,000	$40,500	$81,000
4 Cost of Goods	$4,050	$4,050	$8,100	$8,100	$12,150	$24,300
5 Returns	$675	$675	$1,350	$1,350	$2,025	$4,050
6 Net Sales	$8,775	$8,775	$17,550	$17,550	$26,325	$52,650
7						
8 Rent	$1,313	$1,313	$1,875	$1,875	$2,438	$2,438
9 Utilities	$263	$263	$375	$375	$488	$488
10 Telephone	$290	$290	$520	$520	$750	$750
11 Salaries	$9,083	$9,083	$13,500	$13,500	$17,917	$17,917
12 Equipment	$12,000	$0	$6,000	$0	$6,000	$0
13 Inventory	$960	$0	$1,680	$0	$0	$4,320
14 Total costs	$23,908	$10,948	$23,950	$16,270	$27,592	$25,912
15 Net income	($15,133)	($2,173)	($6,400)	$1,280	($1,267)	$26,738
16						
17 Salesmen	1	1	2	2	3	3
18 Non–salesmen	3	3	4	4	5	5
19 Products (# of)	1	1	1	1	1	2
20 Selling Price	$1,350					

02-Mar-91 03:14 PM

Fig. B.3. Auditor highlights (displays in bold text rather than reverse video) all cells that contain formulas.

You now can easily see all cells that hold formulas. As you examine these cells, you may spot an error in the formula. If you edit the cell to correct the mistake, Auditor keeps the cell highlighted. However, if the correction involves a change to the worksheet, such as moving cells, inserting or deleting rows and columns, or redefining range names, Auditor removes all highlights. You must select Formulas again to redisplay the formula cells.

Note: To remove the highlights from the worksheet without making changes, use the **Options Reset Highlight** command. "Resetting Auditor Options" later in this appendix describes how to select and use this option.

Changing the Reporting Method

In the preceding section, when you selected Formulas, Auditor highlighted all cells in the worksheet that matched that option. Highlighting matched cells works well for small worksheets, such as the cash flow example. But when you work with a large worksheet, you cannot see all the highlighted cells on one screen; you must scroll through the worksheet to see all the matching cells.

To correct this limitation, Auditor uses two other reporting methods to display the results of an option: you can create a list of matching cells in a separate range of the worksheet, or you can move a highlight through the worksheet and display one matching cell at a time. This second method is called *tracing* through the worksheet. You change the Auditor reporting method by selecting **Highlight**, **List**, or **Trace** from the Options menu.

By default, the Auditor reporting method is set to **Highlight**, to highlight matching cells, as described in the preceding example. To change to one of the other two reporting methods using the dialog box, press F2 (Edit) and then select Report **Method**. Select a reporting method by typing the highlighted letter. For example, to select **Trace**, press **T**. Notice that the asterisk moves from the word Highlight to Trace. Press Enter twice to return to the Auditor main menu.

> *Note:* To change the reporting method using the Auditor Settings dialog box and the mouse, press F2 (Edit) to activate the dialog box. Click on the word **Trace**. Click OK to return to the Auditor main menu.

Try the Formulas option again. This time, Auditor highlights the first cell that contains a formula and displays a menu with the options Forward, Backward, and Quit. Select **Forward** to trace through the worksheet and to find the next matching cell or **Backward** to move to the preceding matching formula cell. After you look at the formulas, select OK to return to the main menu.

Use the same procedure to change the reporting method to List. The only difference between selecting **List** and selecting **Trace** is that **List** also prompts for a range to contain the list of matching cell addresses and contents. Be sure to specify an empty range because Auditor does not write over existing data in the range.

Finding Formulas that Refer to One Cell (Dependents)

Before you make changes to a worksheet, make sure that you do not inadvertently change other parts of the worksheet that are correct. For example, if you change the value of one cell, the value of a formula in another area of the worksheet also can change if the formula depends on that cell's value. The formula also can depend directly or indirectly on a cell.

To find all formulas that may be affected by a change you make to a single cell, you use the **Dependents** option. Dependents finds all formulas in the audit range that depend on a specific cell. Select **Dependents**. Auditor prompts for the dependent source cell. Highlight or type the address of a cell whose value you may want to change. Then press Enter. Using the reporting method you chose (**Highlight**, **List**, or **Trace**), Auditor reports back to you all formulas (if any) that depend on the information in the cell.

For example, suppose you want to find all formulas that depend on cell B20 in the sample cash flow worksheet. You choose **Dependents** and specify cell B20. Auditor shows you all the formulas that directly or indirectly rely on the value in B20 for calculations. Figure B.4 shows the cells found for cell B20. For this figure, the reporting method is set to **Highlight**.

```
A16: [W15]                                                        READY

        A           B         C         D         E         F         G
 1                               Cash Flow Projections
 2                   Jan-91    Feb-91    Mar-91    Apr-91    May-91    Jun-91
 3  Sales           $13,500   $13,500   $27,000   $27,000   $40,500   $81,000
 4  Cost of Goods    $4,050    $4,050    $8,100    $8,100   $12,150   $24,300
 5  Returns            $675      $675    $1,350    $1,350    $2,025    $4,050
 6  Net Sales        $8,775    $8,775   $17,550   $17,550   $26,325   $52,650
 7
 8  Rent             $1,313    $1,313    $1,875    $1,875    $2,438    $2,438
 9  Utilities          $263      $263      $375      $375      $488      $488
10  Telephone          $290      $290      $520      $520      $750      $750
11  Salaries         $9,083    $9,083   $13,500   $13,500   $17,917   $17,917
12  Equipment       $12,000        $0    $6,000        $0    $6,000        $0
13  Inventory          $960        $0    $1,680        $0        $0    $4,320
14  Total costs     $23,908   $10,948   $23,950   $16,270   $27,592   $25,912
15  Net income     ($15,133)  ($2,173)  ($6,400)   $1,280   ($1,267)  $26,738
16
17  Salesmen              1         1         2         2         3         3
18  Non-salesmen          3         3         4         4         5         5
19  Products (# of)       1         1         1         1         1         2
20  Selling Price    $1,350
02-Mar-91  03:17 PM
```

Fig. B.4. *Highlighted formulas in cells B15..G15 refer to the specified cell (B20).*

Finding Cells Used by One Formula (Precedents)

Just as you want to know when formulas are affected by a change to a cell, you also may want to know every cell that a formula uses. For example, suppose that you want to revise a formula to make the formula more efficient. Before editing the formula, you may want to see every cell that supplies information to that formula.

Or perhaps, when you are debugging a formula, you cannot find the reason for an erroneous result. You need to verify that the cells you believe the formula is using are actually the cells involved in the result. After you track down all the cells the formula uses, you can better determine why the formula is giving you the wrong answer.

To find all the cells that supply information to a particular formula, use the **Precedents** option. Select **Precedents**. Auditor prompts for the formula to use. Point to or type the address of the cell that contains the formula and press Enter. Auditor finds all cells that the formula uses and displays the results in the chosen reporting method.

Figure B.5 shows the cells used by the formula in cell B15 (Net income). The reporting method selected is **Highlight**.

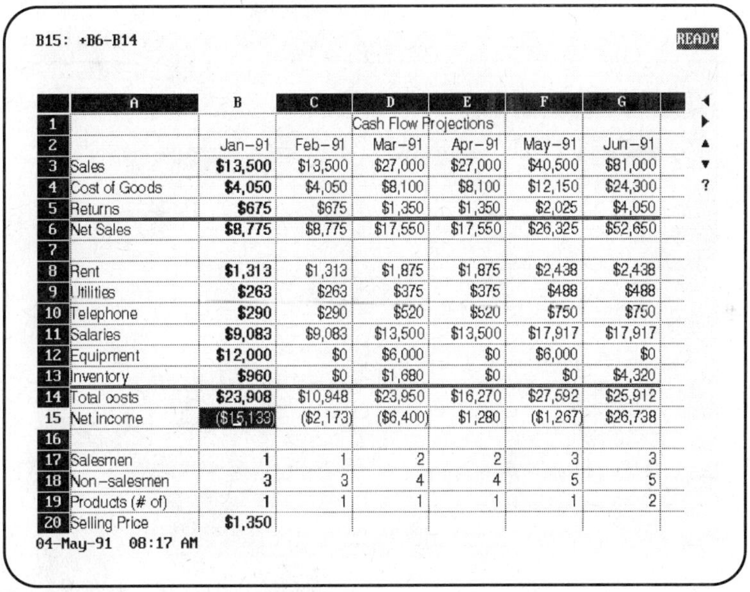

B15: +B6-B14   READY

	A	B	C	D	E	F	G
1				Cash Flow Projections			
2		Jan–91	Feb–91	Mar–91	Apr–91	May–91	Jun–91
3	Sales	$13,500	$13,500	$27,000	$27,000	$40,500	$81,000
4	Cost of Goods	$4,050	$4,050	$8,100	$8,100	$12,150	$24,300
5	Returns	$675	$675	$1,350	$1,350	$2,025	$4,050
6	Net Sales	$8,775	$8,775	$17,550	$17,550	$26,325	$52,650
7							
8	Rent	$1,313	$1,313	$1,875	$1,875	$2,438	$2,438
9	Utilities	$263	$263	$375	$375	$488	$488
10	Telephone	$290	$290	$520	$520	$750	$750
11	Salaries	$9,083	$9,083	$13,500	$13,500	$17,917	$17,917
12	Equipment	$12,000	$0	$6,000	$0	$6,000	$0
13	Inventory	$960	$0	$1,680	$0	$0	$4,320
14	Total costs	$23,908	$10,948	$23,950	$16,270	$27,592	$25,912
15	Net income	($15,133)	($2,173)	($6,400)	$1,280	($1,267)	$26,738
16							
17	Salesmen	1	1	2	2	3	3
18	Non–salesmen	3	3	4	4	5	5
19	Products (# of)	1	1	1	1	1	2
20	Selling Price	$1,350					

04-May-91   08:17 AM

Fig. B.5. *All cells that supply information to B15 (Net Income) include the highlighted ranges B3..B14 and B17..B20.*

Examining Circular References

In 1-2-3 worksheets, circular references are among the most complicated and difficult errors to correct. In rare cases, you intentionally create circular references to perform calculations. Usually, however, the CIRC indicator is an unwelcome surprise.

Circular references are hard to find because these errors often result from an indirect reference that seems a reasonable assumption to make in a formula. For example, in the cash flow worksheet, instead of having a single value for the number of salesmen to hire (shown in row 17), you want to make the number of salesmen contingent on net income. If net income is too far in the red (negative numbers), you reason, you may need to increase the number of salesmen to bring in more revenue.

Figure B.6 shows a formula in B17 that describes this reasoning—basically, if net income (B15) is in the red more than $10,000, you want to have two salesmen. Otherwise, one salesman is fine. If you enter this formula, however, 1-2-3 displays the CIRC indicator.

```
B17: (G) @IF(B15<-10000,2,1)                                    READY
```

	A	B	C	D	E	F	G
1				Cash Flow Projections			
2		Jan–91	Feb–91	Mar–91	Apr–91	May–91	Jun–91
3	Sales	$27,000	$13,500	$27,000	$27,000	$40,500	$81,000
4	Cost of Goods	$8,100	$4,050	$8,100	$8,100	$12,150	$24,300
5	Returns	$1,350	$675	$1,350	$1,350	$2,025	$4,050
6	Net Sales	$17,550	$8,775	$17,550	$17,550	$26,325	$52,650
7							
8	Rent	$1,500	$1,313	$1,875	$1,875	$2,438	$2,438
9	Utilities	$300	$263	$375	$375	$488	$488
10	Telephone	$490	$290	$520	$520	$750	$750
11	Salaries	$11,167	$9,083	$13,500	$13,500	$17,917	$17,917
12	Equipment	$15,000	($3,000)	$6,000	$0	$6,000	$0
13	Inventory	$720	$0	$1,680	$0	$0	$4,320
14	Total costs	$29,177	$7,948	$23,950	$16,270	$27,592	$25,912
15	Net income	($11,627)	$827	($6,400)	$1,280	($1,267)	$26,738
16							
17	Salesmen	2	1	2	2	3	3
18	Non–salesmen	3	3	4	4	5	5
19	Products (# of)	1	1	1	1	1	2
20	Selling Price	$1,350					

```
04-May-91  08:19 AM                            CIRC
```

Fig B.6. Cell B17 with a formula that creates a circular reference.

The Circs option of the Auditor menu helps you determine why a formula, such as the formula previously described, can cause a circular reference. Select Circs from the Auditor main menu. Auditor temporarily removes the worksheet from the screen and displays a list of the cells involved with circular references. (The worksheet may have more than one circular reference.) For example, figure B.7 shows two cells in the cash flow worksheet that are involved with a circular reference, B3 and B17.

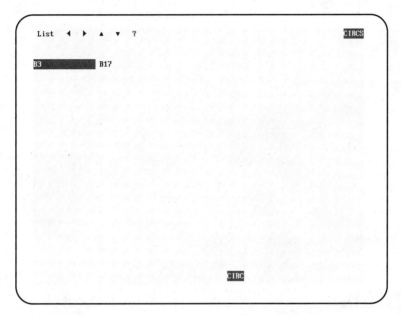

Fig. B.7. The two cells involved in a circular reference.

Highlight the cell to use (in this example, B17) and press Enter. Auditor then lists all the cells that refer to this cell. For cell B17 (the @IF formula in the cash flow example), the first cell that uses B17 is cell B3, or sales, as shown in figure B.8. Because the number of salesmen (B17) depends on net income (cell B15), and net income depends on sales (B3), and sales depends on number of salesmen, you found the circular reference.

To return from the Circs display, press Esc until you return to the Auditor menu. Select Quit to exit Auditor and to go to the worksheet to fix the problem.

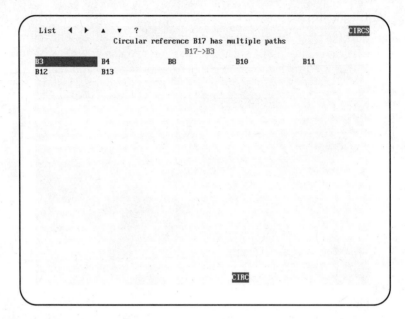

Fig. B.8. The cells responsible for the circular reference of cell B17.

Examining Recalculation Order

For some worksheets, the order 1-2-3 uses to recalculate the worksheet is important. For example, you may want to make sure that 1-2-3 recalculates net sales before recalculating net profit. You learned in this book that you can set the recalculation order to one of three methods: **N**atural, **C**olumnwise, and **R**owwise. You set recalculation order by using the /**W**orksheet **G**lobal **R**ecalculation option.

During recalculation, 1-2-3 may skip around the worksheet. For example, with **N**atural recalculation, 1-2-3 begins recalculating cells at the top of a column. But if a formula in a cell near the top of the column refers to a cell at the bottom of the column, 1-2-3 first goes to the bottom of the column and performs that calculation.

To determine the recalculation order that 1-2-3 uses in the audit range, use the **R**ecalc-List option. Before you use this option, change the reporting method to **T**race or **L**ist and then select **R**ecalc-List from the Auditor main menu. If you select **T**race for the reporting method, Auditor highlights the first cell that 1-2-3 calculates in the audit range. Select Forward to move to the next cell to be recalculated. Select **B**ackward to move back through the cells. Select **Q**uit to exit the **T**race display and return to Auditor.

If you selected **List** for the reporting method, Auditor copies the list of formula cells, in the order they recalculate to the range you specified. Figure B.9 shows the result of the **Recalc-List** option with the **List** reporting method. The recalculation order list actually extends from cell A22 to A97. Figure B.9 shows just a part of the result.

```
A22: [W15] 'Natural Recalculation List                              READY

            A           B      C      D      E      F      G      ◄
 22  Natural Recalculation List                                     ►
 23  B2: @DATE(91,1,1)                                              ▲
 24  C2: +B2+31                                                     ▼
 25  D2: +C2+31                                                     ?
 26  E2: +D2+31
 27  F2: +E2+31
 28  G2: +F2+31
 29  B13: ((+B17*B19*20)+(C17*C19*20)+(D17*D19*20))*12
 30  B12: (B17+B18)*3000
 31  B11: (B17*25000)/12+(B18*28000)/12
 32  B10: (B17*200)+(B18*20)*1.5
 33  B8: ((+B17*150+B18*300)*15)/12
 34  B9: +B8*0.2
 35  B14: @SUM(B13..B8)
 36  B3: (+B17*10)*B19*$B$20
 37  B5: +B3*0.05
 38  B4: (+$B$20*0.15)*(B19*20*B17)
 39  B6: +B3-B4-B5
 40  B15: +B6-B14
 41  C3: (+C17*10)*C19*$B$20
04-May-91  08:52 AM
```

Fig. B.9. The result of selecting the Recalc-List option for the cash flow worksheet.

Resetting Auditor Options

After you used Auditor to correct one worksheet, you also may want to check all other worksheets you manage. Before you retrieve another worksheet, you may want to reset the audit range and report method. Also, if you highlighted a range of cells by using **Highlight** and either **Precedents**, **Dependents**, or **Formulas**, you may want to turn off the highlighted cells.

To reset the audit range and reporting method, select **Options Reset Options**. Auditor resets the audit range to A1..IV8192 and the reporting method to **Highlight**. You can see these changes in the Auditor Settings dialog box. Select **Quit** to return to the Auditor main menu.

To remove the highlight set by the Auditor **Highlight** reporting method, select **Options Reset Highlight** from the Auditor menu. Auditor removes the highlights (or color) from cells in the worksheet. Select **Quit** twice to return to the worksheet and READY mode.

Compose Sequences for the Lotus International Character Set

The Lotus International Character Set (LICS) includes characters you may not find on your keyboard. These special characters include monetary symbols, mathematical symbols and operator signs, and diacritical marks.

To enter a character that is not on your keyboard, press Compose (Alt-F1) and then a series of keystrokes that Lotus calls a *compose sequence*. To create some characters, you can use one of several compose sequences. For example, to enter the British pound sign (£), press Compose (Alt-F1) and then type **L=** or **l=**. Depending on your hardware, some LICS characters may not display on your monitor or print from your printer. If a character does not display on your screen, print a sample range to see whether the character is available from your printer.

The following table lists the special characters, the characters' respective LICS codes, a description of each character, and the compose sequence— or sequences—that you use to create each character.

If you use some of these characters frequently, you easily can create macros to perform the compose sequences. You can store the macros in a macro library and access the characters at any time. (See Chapters 13 and 14 for information on how to create macros and macro libraries.)

You also can generate LICS characters by using the @CHAR function. For example, @CHAR(163) enters the British pound symbol (£) into the worksheet. See Chapter 6 for a complete discussion of the @CHAR function.

> *Note:* If you cannot print the correct character, and you double-checked the LICS code, the problem may be with the code page that is currently set for DOS. The *code page* refers to a set of codes that DOS uses for displaying characters. In the United States, 1-2-3 supports only one code page, #437 (English), which is the default. If your computer is set to run under a different code page, reset the code page to 437 to enable your computer to use 1-2-3 and 1-2-3's utility programs.

Standard ASCII Characters

The following table defines the LICS codes 32 through 127, which represent standard ASCII characters.

Table C.1
LICS Codes for Standard ASCII Characters

LICS code	Character	Description	Compose Sequence
32	Space	Space	
33	!	Exclamation point	
34	"	Double quotes	
35	#	Pound or number sign	+ +
36	$	Dollar sign	
37	%	Percent	
38	&	Ampersand	
39	'	Close single quote	
40	(	Open parenthesis	
41	)	Close parenthesis	

LICS code	Character	Description	Compose Sequence
42	*	Asterisk	
43	+	Plus	
44	,	Comma	
45	–	Minus	
46	.	Period	
47	/	Slash	
48	0	Zero	
49	1	One	
50	2	Two	
51	3	Three	
52	4	Four	
53	5	Five	
54	6	Six	
55	7	Seven	
56	8	Eight	
57	9	Nine	
58	:	Colon	
59	;	Semicolon	
60	<	Less-than symbol	
61	=	Equal sign	
62	>	Greater-than symbol	
63	?	Question mark	
64	@	At sign	aa or AA
65	A	A, Uppercase	
66	B	B, Uppercase	
67	C	C, Uppercase	
68	D	D, Uppercase	
69	E	E, Uppercase	
70	F	F, Uppercase	
71	G	G, Uppercase	
72	H	H, Uppercase	
73	I	I, Uppercase	
74	J	J, Uppercase	

continues

Table C.1 *(continued)*

LICS code	*Character*	*Description*	*Compose Sequence*
75	K	K, Uppercase	
76	L	L, Uppercase	
77	M	M, Uppercase	
78	N	N, Uppercase	
79	O	O, Uppercase	
80	P	P, Uppercase	
81	Q	Q, Uppercase	
82	R	R, Uppercase	
83	S	S, Uppercase	
84	T	T, Uppercase	
85	U	U, Uppercase	
86	V	V, Uppercase	
87	W	W, Uppercase	
88	X	X, Uppercase	
89	Y	Y, Uppercase	
90	Z	Z, Uppercase	
91	[	Open bracket	((
92	\	Backslash	//
93	]	Close bracket	))
94	^	Caret	vv
95	_	Underscore	
96	`	Open single quote	
97	a	a, lowercase	
98	b	b, lowercase	
99	c	c, lowercase	
100	d	d, lowercase	
101	e	e, lowercase	
102	f	f, lowercase	
103	g	g, lowercase	
104	h	h, lowercase	
105	i	i, lowercase	
106	j	j, lowercase	

LICS code	Character	Description	Compose Sequence
107	k	k, lowercase	
108	l	l, lowercase	
109	m	m, lowercase	
110	n	n, lowercase	
111	o	o, lowercase	
112	p	p, lowercase	
113	q	q, lowercase	
114	r	r, lowercase	
115	s	s, lowercase	
116	t	t, lowercase	
117	u	u, lowercase	
118	v	v, lowercase	
119	w	w, lowercase	
120	x	x, lowercase	
121	y	y, lowercase	
122	z	z, lowercase	
123	{	Open brace	(-
124	¦	Split vertical bar	^ /
125	}	Close brace	)-
126	~	Tilde	--
127		Delete	

International Characters and Special Symbols

This following table defines the LICS codes 128 through 255, which represent codes for letters and symbols from other languages and currencies.

To enter one of these characters, use the @CHAR function and the LICS code for the character or use Compose (Alt-F1) and the compose sequence listed in the table.

For some compose sequences, you must enter the sequence of keystrokes in the order shown in the table. Those compose sequences that must be typed exactly as shown are marked with an asterisk (*). Do not type the asterisk as part of the sequence.

Some characters also have more than one compose sequence. In these cases, the table lists all possible compose sequences.

Table C.2
LICS Codes for International Characters

LICS code	Character	Description	Compose Sequence
128	`	Grave, uppercase	* ` space bar
129	´	Acute, uppercase	* ´ space bar
130	^	Circumflex, uppercase	* ^ space bar
131	¨	Umlaut, uppercase	* " space bar
132	~	Tilde, uppercase	* ~ space bar
133	■	Unknown character (display only)	
134	■	Unknown character (display only)	
135	■	Unknown character (display only)	
136	■	Unknown character (display only)	
137	■	Unknown character (display only)	
138	■	Unknown character (display only)	
139	■	Unknown character (display only)	
140	■	Unknown character (display only)	
141	■	Unknown character (display only)	
142	■	Unknown character (display only)	
143	■	Unknown character (display only)	
144	`	Grave, lowercase	* space bar `

LICS code	Character	Description		Compose Sequence
145	´	Acute, lowercase	*	space bar ´
146	^	Circumflex, lowercase	*	space bar ^
147	¨	Umlaut, lowercase	*	space bar "
148	~	Tilde, lowercase	*	space bar ~
149	ı	i without dot, lowercase	i	space bar
150	–	Ordinal indicator	_	space bar
151	▲	Begin attribute (display only)		ba
152	▼	End attribute (display only)		ea
153	■	Unknown character (display only)		
154	•	Hard space (display only)		space bar space bar
155	←	Merge character (display only)		mg
156	■	Unknown character (display only)		
157	■	Unknown character (display only)		
158	■	Unknown character (display only)		
159	■	Unknown character (display only)		
160	ƒ	Guilder sign		ff
161	¡	Exclamation mark, inverted		!!
162	¢	Cent sign		C| c| C/ or c/
163	£	British pound sterling symbol		L= l= L- or l-
164	"	Open double quotes, low		"^
165	¥	Yen sign		Y= y= Y- or y-
166	Pt	Peseta sign	*	PT pt or Pt

continues

Table C.2 *(continued)*
LICS Codes for International Characters

LICS code	Character	Description	Compose Sequence
167	§	Section sign	SO so So or s0
168	¤	General currency sign	XO xo Xo or x0
169	©	Copyright sign	CO co or C0
170	ª	Feminine ordinal indicator	a_ or A_
171	<<	Much-less-than sign	<<
172	Δ	Delta	dd or DD
173	π	Pi	* PI pi or Pi
174	≥	Greater-than-or-equals sign	* >=
175	÷	Division sign	:-
176	°	Degree sign	^0
177	±	Plus-or-minus sign	+-
178	^{2}	2, superscript	^2
179	^{3}	3, superscript	^3
180	„	Close double quotes,low	" v
181	μ	Micron symbol or mu	* /u
182	¶	Paragraph sign	!P or !p
183	•	Middle dot	^.
184	™	Trademark sign	* TM tm or Tm
185	^{1}	1, superscript	^1
186	º	Masculine ordinal indicator	o_ or O_
187	>>	Much-greater-than sign	>>
188	¼	One-quarter fraction	* 14
189	½	One-half fraction	* 12
190	≤	Less-than-or-equals sign	* =<
191	¿	Question mark, inverted	??
192	À	A grave, uppercase	A`
193	Á	A acute, uppercase	A´
194	Â	A circumflex, uppercase	A^
195	Ã	A tilde, uppercase	A~

LICS code	Character	Description		Compose Sequence
196	Ä	A umlaut, uppercase		A"
197	Å	A ring, uppercase		A*
198	Æ	AE dipthong, uppercase	*	AE
199	Ç	C cedilla, uppercase		C,
200	È	E grave, uppercase		E`
201	É	E acute, uppercase		E´
202	Ê	E circumflex, uppercase		E ^
203	Ë	E umlaut, uppercase		E"
204	Ì	I grave, uppercase		I`
205	Í	I acute, uppercase		I´
206	Î	I circumflex, uppercase		I ^
207	Ï	I umlaut, uppercase		I"
208	Ð	Icelandic eth, uppercase		D-
209	Ñ	N tilde, uppercase		N~
210	Ò	O grave, uppercase		O`
211	Ó	O acute, uppercase		O´
212	Ô	O circumflex, uppercase		O ^
213	Õ	O tilde, uppercase		O~
214	Ö	O umlaut, uppercase		O"
215	Œ	OE dipthong, uppercase	*	OE
216	Ø	O slash, uppercase		O/
217	Ù	U grave, uppercase		U`
218	Ú	U acute, uppercase		U´
219	Û	U circumflex, uppercase		U ^
220	Ü	U umlaut, uppercase		U"
221	Ÿ	Y umlaut, uppercase		Y"
222	Þ	Icelandic thorn, uppercase		P-
223	β	Beta or German sharp, lowercase		ss
224	à	a grave, lowercase		a`
225	á	a acute, lowercase		a´
226	â	a circumflex, lowercase		a ^
227	ã	a tilde, lowercase		a~

continues

Table C.2 *(continued)*
LICS Codes for International Characters

LICS code	Character	Description	Compose Sequence
228	ä	a umlaut, lowercase	a"
229	å	a ring, lowercase	a*
230	æ	ae dipthong, lowercase	ae
231	ç	c cedilla, lowercase	c,
232	è	e grave, lowercase	e`
233	é	e acute, lowercase	e´
234	ê	e circumflex, lowercase	e^
235	ë	e umlaut, lowercase	e"
236	ì	i grave, lowercase	i`
237	í	i acute, lowercase	i´
238	î	i circumflex, lowercase	i^
239	ï	i umlaut, lowercase	i"
240	ð	Icelandic eth, lowercase	d-
241	ñ	n tilde, lowercase	n~
242	ò	o grave, lowercase	o`
243	ó	o acute, lowercase	o´
244	ô	o circumflex, lowercase	o^
245	õ	o tilde, lowercase	o~
246	ö	o umlaut, lowercase	o"
247	œ	oe dipthong, lowercase	oe
248	ø	o slash, lowercase	o/
249	ù	u grave, lowercase	u`
250	ú	u acute, lowercase	u´
251	û	u circumflex, lowercase	u^
252	ü	u umlaut, lowercase	u"
253	ÿ	y umlaut, lowercase	y"
254	þ	Icelandic thorn, lowercase	p-
255	■	Unknown character (display only)	

Allways Commands

R elease 2.2 of 1-2-3 is packaged with Allways, a desktop publishing add-in. Release 2.0 or 2.01 users can purchase Allways separately from Lotus Development Corporation. Allways does not claim to be a full-featured desktop publishing program, but this program may be all you need for many desktop publishing tasks involving 1-2-3 reports and graphs.

Like Wysiwyg, new with Release 2.3, you can use Allways to incorporate a variety of type fonts, lines, shadings, and other formatting features. In addition to enhanced text formatting, Allways enables you to embed 1-2-3 graphs in your printouts, add enhanced text to your printed graphs, and print 1-2-3 graphs and associated worksheet data from Allways.

This appendix contains a complete reference for the Allways commands. This easy-to-use Allways command reference should be used in addition to the 1-2-3 command reference that precedes Appendix A. (Note that the Wysiwyg commands at the end of the command reference are available only to those users who have the Wysiwyg add-in packaged with 1-2-3 Release 2.3.)

Allways Commands

Allways is an add-in program included with Release 2.2 (Release 2.01 users can buy the program separately). This "spreadsheet publishing" program, which works in conjunction with 1-2-3, enables you to produce professional-looking reports. In addition, Allways enables you to print graphs along with your worksheets—all without leaving 1-2-3.

Allways Menu Map

| Worksheet | Format | Graph | Layout | Print | Display | Special | Quit |

Allways Attach   */AA*

Purpose

Makes available a variety of fonts, lines, and shadings for use in printed reports. A report printed with Allways can look much more professional than one printed with 1-2-3. Figure AW.1 illustrates some of the formatting features you can use with Allways: lines, boxes, shading, fonts, underlining, and boldface.

Fig. AW.1.
A worksheet formatted with Allways.

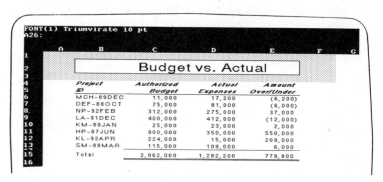

/**Allways** Attach also prints graphs without your having to exit from 1-2-3 and includes 1-2-3 graphs with reports.

Reminders

- Use the AWSETUP program to install Allways.

- Allways is an add-in program supplied with Release 2.2. (Users of Release 2.01 can buy Allways separately.) As with any add-in, Allways must be attached before it can be invoked. You can have Allways attach automatically whenever you load 1-2-3, or you can attach the add-in when you need to use it.

Procedures

1. Type **/aa** (or if you are using Release 2.01's Add-In Manager, press Alt-F10 and choose **Attach**).

2. Highlight ALLWAYS.ADN and press Enter.

3. Select one of the following:

Menu Item	Description
No-Key	Does not assign Allways to a function key. Allways must be invoked with **/A**dd-In **I**nvoke.
7	Assigns Allways to Alt-F7
8	Assigns Allways to Alt-F8
9	Assigns Allways to Alt-F9
10	Assigns Allways to Alt-F10

Note: With Release 2.01's Add-In Manager, you cannot use Alt-F10 to invoke an add-in.

Important Cues

- You can invoke Allways with the function key you assigned to it when you attached it, or you can invoke Allways with **/A**dd-In **I**nvoke. (If you are using Release 2.01's Add-In Manager, press Alt-F10 and then choose **I**nvoke.)

- If you don't have enough memory to attach the Allways add-in, you will get a `Memory Full` error message. If any other add-ins are attached, you can use **/A**dd-In **D**etach (in Release 2.01's Add-In Manager, press Alt-F10 and choose **D**etach) to remove them from memory, allowing room for the Allways add-in. You also can exit from 1-2-3 and free up memory by removing any other memory-resident programs you may be using.

- To quit Allways and go back to 1-2-3, choose **Q**uit from the Allways menu (Release 2.01 users should choose **123** from the Allways menu) or press Esc when the ALLWAYS indicator appears in the upper right corner of the screen.

- Use **/W**orksheet **G**lobal **D**efault **O**ther **A**dd-In **S**et to attach Allways automatically when 1-2-3 is loaded. (If you are using Release 2.01's Add-In Manager, press Alt-F10 and then choose **S**etup Set.)

Caution

Do not detach Allways before saving the worksheet; if you do, your formatting will be lost.

Worksheet Column Set-Width and
Worksheet Row Set-Height   /WCS and /WRS

Purpose

Precisely adjusts the width of the worksheet columns and the height of the worksheet rows. Allways enables column widths to be set in tenths of an inch and row heights to be set in point sizes. Because you can use different font sizes in a worksheet and see the sizes on-screen, you may discover that you need to change the width of a column or the height of a row.

Reminder

Place the cell pointer on the first row or column to be set. To change more than one adjacent column or row, press the period (.) key to anchor one corner of the range and then use the arrow keys to highlight the number of rows or columns.

Procedures

To change the width of a column, do the following:

1. Type **/wcs**

2. Type the new column width or press the right- and left-arrow keys to adjust the width one character at a time. To adjust the width one-tenth of a character at a time, press Ctrl and the right- or left-arrow key.

3. Press Enter.

To change the height of a row, do the following:

1. Type **/wrs**

2. Type the new row height in points or press the up- and down-arrow keys to adjust the point size one increment at a time.

3. Press Enter.

Important Cues

- To return to the original 1-2-3 column widths after adjusting column widths in Allways, use the **/W**orksheet **C**olumn **R**eset-Width command. (In Release 2.01, Allways uses **R**eset instead of **R**eset-Width.)

- The default row height setting is **Auto**. Allways automatically calculates the appropriate row height necessary for the font size you have chosen. The row height of a large font size, for example, is taller than that of a tiny font size.

- You can create a thick vertical line by shading a column with **/Format Shade** and then narrowing the column width. To create a thick horizontal line, shade a row and then narrow the row height.

Worksheet Page /WP

Purpose

Changes where Allways creates a page break. You can tell Allways at which row or column to start a new page.

Reminders

- To see where the current page breaks are, use **/Print Range Set** to define the area to be printed. A dashed line indicates where the page breaks are located.

- Place the cell pointer on the first row or column of the new page.

Procedures

To set a row page break, do the following:

1. Type **/wpr**

2. Position the pointer on the first row of the new page (if you haven't already) and press Enter.

To set a column page break, do the following:

1. Type **/wpc**

2. Position the pointer on the first column of the new page (if you haven't already) and press Enter. A dashed line appears to the left of the specified column to indicate the new page break.

Important Cue

To remove a page break, place the cell pointer on the first row or column of the page and select **/Worksheet Page Delete**.

Format Font   /FF

Purpose

Selects the font for a range of cells. The font consists of a typeface (for example, Times Roman), a point size, and sometimes an attribute (for example, heavy or italic).

Reminders

- Place the cell pointer on the first cell you want to format.

- If you want to choose a font from a laser cartridge, use the **/P**rint Configuration **C**artridge command to select the cartridge to use.

- The fonts available to choose from depend on your printer; Allways can print any font your printer is capable of printing.

- Allways includes three soft fonts: Courier, Times, and Triumvirate. If you have a dot-matrix printer, Allways uses your printer's graphics mode. If you have a laser printer, these fonts are automatically downloaded to your printer when you use them. Your printer may not have enough memory for larger fonts.

- Each worksheet can use eight different fonts. These eight fonts are stored in a "font set."

- Each worksheet can have its own font set. These font sets can be named and saved in font libraries, which you can use in other worksheets.

Procedures

To choose a font from the current font set, do the following:

1. Type **/ff**

2. Highlight the font or type the number (**1-8**) that appears next to the font.

3. Make sure that **U**se is highlighted in the menu. Press Enter.

4. Indicate the range by highlighting or by typing. Press Enter.

To use a font not in the current font set, do the following:

1. Type **/ff**

2. Specify the font to be replaced: highlight it or type the number (**1-8**) that appears next to the font. (Choose a font you don't need in the current worksheet.)

3. Select **R**eplace.

4. A list appears of all the fonts your printer can use. Highlight the font you want to add, or type the number next to the font. Press Enter.

5. Highlight the point size and press Enter.

6. If you want to use this new font, select **U**se and highlight the range for the font. Press Enter.

To save the current font set in a library, do the following:

1. Type **/ff**

2. Select **L**ibrary **S**ave.

3. Type a file name of as many as eight characters and press Enter. The file is saved under the extension .AFS.

To use a font library, do the following:

1. Type **/ff**

2. Select **L**ibrary **R**etrieve.

3. Allways displays a list of library files (.AFS extension). Highlight the name and press Enter. The eight fonts saved in this library display in the font box. Any of these fonts can now be used in the worksheet.

Important Cues

- Before choosing the **/F**ormat **F**ont command, you can select the range to format. To preselect the range, place the cell pointer on the first cell to format, press the period (.) key to anchor one corner of the range, and then place the cell pointer on the last cell to format. When you use **/F**ormat **F**ont, the range you have selected will be the default range to format.

- To choose a font in the current font set, you can use a "quick" key rather than the menu. First, select the range to format. Then press Alt and the desired font number.

- Create font libraries for combinations of fonts that you are likely to use in other worksheets.

- If you change the font size of a paragraph of text, you may find that the text requires more or fewer columns than it originally did. To respace the text, use the **/S**pecial **J**ustify command. This command is similar to 1-2-3's **/R**ange **J**ustify command, which "wordwraps" text within the range you define.

Caution

Your laser printer may not have enough memory to download soft fonts that have a large point size. If you get an Out of memory error message when you print, you need to specify a different-sized font or use an internal or cartridge font.

Format [Bold, Underline, Color] /FB, /FU, or /FC

Purpose

Boldfaces, single-underlines, or double-underlines a range of cells. The titles in figure AW.2 are boldfaced, the last number in each column is single-underlined, and the final totals are double-underlined.

Fig. AW.2.
A worksheet
formatted with
boldface,
single-, and
double-
underline.

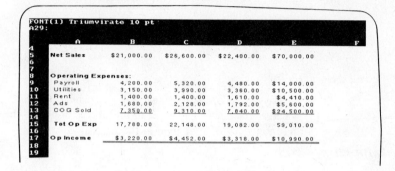

Changes the color of a range of cells (assuming that you have a color printer).

Reminder

Place the cell pointer on the first cell you want to format.

Procedures

To boldface a range, do the following:

1. Type **/fb**

2. Select Set.

3. Indicate the range by highlighting or typing. Press Enter.

To underline a range, do the following:

1. Type **/fu**

2. Select one of the following:

Menu Item	Description
Single	Places a single underline under the range
Double	Places a double underline under the range

3. Indicate the range by highlighting or typing. Press Enter.

To add color to a range, do the following:

1. Type **/fc**

2. Highlight the color or type the number (**1-8**) that appears next to the color. Press Enter.

3. Indicate the range by highlighting or by typing. Press Enter.

Important Cues

● Before choosing the **/**Format command, you can select the range to format. To preselect the range, place the cell pointer on the first cell to format, press the period (**.**) key to anchor one corner of the range, and then place the cell pointer on the last cell to format. When you use the **/**Format command, the range you have selected will be the default range.

● Another way to boldface a range is to use a "quick" key rather than the menu. First, select the range to format. Then press Alt-B. (Note: If the cell is already boldfaced, Alt-B cancels the boldface.)

● You also can underline by using a "quick" key: Alt-U. The first time you press Alt-U, the range will be single-underlined. The second time, it will be double-underlined; the third time, the underlining will be cleared.

● To cancel boldfacing from a cell or a range, use **/**Format **B**old Clear. To cancel underlining, use **/**Format **U**nderline **C**lear.

Format Lines   */FL*

Purpose

Draws horizontal or vertical lines; creates boxes around individual cells or an outline around a range of cells.

Reminder

Place the cell pointer in the upper left corner of the range you want to draw a line around.

Procedures

1. Type **/fl**

2. Select one of the following:

Menu Item	Description
Outline	Draws lines around the entire range, forming a single box
Left	Draws a line at the left side of each selected cell in the range
Right	Draws a line at the right side of each selected cell in the range

Top	Draws a line above each selected cell in the range
Bottom	Draws a line below each selected cell in the range
All	Draws lines around each selected cell in the range so that each cell is boxed (the same as choosing **L**eft, **R**ight, **T**op, and **B**ottom)

3. Indicate the range by highlighting or by typing. Press Enter.

Important Cues

- Before choosing the **/F**ormat command, you can select the range to format. To preselect the range, place the cell pointer on the first cell to format, press the period (.) to anchor one corner of the range, and then place the cell pointer on the last cell to format. When you use the **/F**ormat command, the range you have selected will be the default range.

- The "quick" key for drawing lines is Alt-L. The first time you press Alt-L, the range is outlined. The second time, the range will be boxed, and the third time all lines will be cleared.

- To remove lines, use **/F**ormat **L**ines **C**lear.

- To change the darkness of lines before you print, use **/L**ayout **O**ptions **L**ine-**W**eight (**L**ineWeight in Release 2.01). Choose among **N**ormal, **L**ight, and **H**eavy.

- If you need thicker vertical lines, shade a column with **/F**ormat **S**hade and then narrow the column width. To create thick horizontal lines, shade a row and then narrow the row height.

Format Shade /FS

Purpose

Highlights important areas on the printed spreadsheet. The column headings in figure AW.3 stand out because of their light background shading.

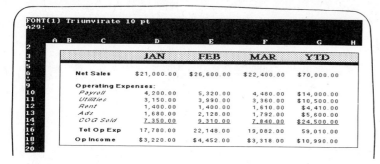

Fig. AW.3.
Headings
emphasized
with light and
solid shades.

Creates thick horizontal and vertical lines. The thick line underneath the column headings in figure AW.3 was created with a solid shade on a narrow row.

Reminder

Place the cell pointer in the upper left corner of the range you want to shade.

Procedures

1. Type **/fs**

2. Select one of the following:

Menu Item	Description
Light	Uses the lightest shading available
Dark	Uses a darker shading
Solid	Shades the range a solid black

3. Indicate the range by highlighting or by typing. Press Enter.

Important Cues

- Before choosing the **/F**ormat Shade command, you can select the range to format. To preselect the range, place the cell pointer on the first cell to format, press the period (**.**) to anchor the corner of the range, and then place the cell pointer on the last cell to format. When you use the **/F**ormat Shade command, the range you have selected will be the default range.

- The "quick" key for shading is Alt-S. The first time you press Alt-S, the range becomes lightly shaded. The second time, the shading becomes dark; the third time, the range is shaded solid. The fourth time you press Alt-S, all shading is cleared.

- To remove shading, use **/F**ormat Shade Clear.

Graph Add */GA*

Purpose

Prints a graph without requiring you to exit from 1-2-3 and load the PrintGraph program.

Places a 1-2-3 graph file (.PIC extension) in a spreadsheet report.

Defines the size of the range where the graph should print.

Reminders

- Create the graph in 1-2-3 and save it to a .PIC file by using 1-2-3's /Graph Save command.

- To print the graph in the middle of a report, insert rows or columns where you want the graph to appear.

- Place the cell pointer in the upper left corner of the area where you want the graph to appear in the report.

Procedures

1. Type /ga

2. Highlight the name of the graph from the displayed list of .PIC files. Press Enter.

3. Type or highlight the range where you want the graph to appear. This range defines the size of the graph, so be sure to indicate the width (number of columns) and height (number of rows) of the graph. Press Enter. A hatching pattern appears in the range.

Important Cues

- To see the actual graph, rather than the hatching pattern, on the screen, use the /Display Graphs Yes command.

- To eliminate a graph from the spreadsheet report, use /Graph Remove.

- To change the size of the graph range after you have added the graph, use /Graph Settings Range.

- Use the /Format Lines command to place an outline border around the graph after you have added it. Use /Format Shade to shade the background of the graph.

- With Allways, you can have up to 20 graphs per worksheet.

- To adjust the graph range precisely, you can change the row heights and column widths of the graph range by using the /Worksheet Row and /Worksheet Column commands.

- Use the **/Graph G**oto command to move the pointer to a particular graph you have added. This command is useful when you have many graphs in a large spreadsheet.

Caution

Be sure not to define the graph range so that it includes cells containing data; the graph range should include blank cells only.

Graph Settings   /GS

Purpose

Defines the print fonts for the text in the graph; defines the colors for the graph ranges. Places more white space around the graph and changes the graph's range.

Figure AW.4 shows the **Graph S**ettings menu along with the Graph Settings sheet where the current options are displayed.

```
GRAPH(1) A:\AWFIG9.PIC                                          MENU    0
PIC-File Fonts Scale Colors Range Margins Default Quit
Replace a graph in the worksheet with a different graph file

    .PIC file: A:\AWFIG9.PIC

    Fonts                              Range: A1..A1
      1: LOTUS      Scale: x 1.00
      2: ITALIC1    Scale: x 1.00

    Colors                             Margins (in inches)
      X: Black                             Left:   0.00
      A: Blue                             Right:   0.00
      B: Black                              Top:   0.00
      C: Black                           Bottom:   0.00
      D: Black
      E: Black
      F: Black



17
18
```

Fig. AW.4.
The Graph
Settings sheet.

Reminders

- Allways uses the fonts supplied with 1-2-3's PrintGraph program, so be sure that you have copied the PrintGraph disk to your 1-2-3 subdirectory. The font files have the extension .FNT.

- Use Allways' **/Graph A**dd command to insert the graph.

- Place the cell pointer anywhere within the graph range.

Procedures

To change the graph fonts, do the following:

1. Type **/gs**

2. If the cell pointer was not in the graph range, you will be asked to select a graph from a list of graphs you have added to the spreadsheet. Highlight the .PIC file name and press Enter.

3. Choose **Fonts**.

4. Select one of the following:

Menu Item	Description
1	Specifies the font for the top center title
2	Specifies the font for other titles and legends

5. Highlight the desired font from the displayed list. These are the fonts that come with 1-2-3's PrintGraph program. You also may type the number (**1-11**) that appears next to the font. Press Enter.

To set the font scaling factor (that is, relative size), do the following:

1. Type **/gs**

2. If the cell pointer was not in the graph range, you will be asked to select a graph from a list of graphs you have added to the spreadsheet. Highlight the .PIC file name and press Enter.

3. Choose **Scale**.

4. Select one of the following:

Menu Item	Description
1	Specifies the scaling factor for the first font (top center title)
2	Specifies the scaling factor for the second font (other titles and legends)

5. Type a number between .5 and 3, inclusive (1 is the default; .5 makes the font half the default size; 3 makes the font three times the default size). Press Enter.

To assign colors to graph data ranges, do the following:

1. Type **/gs**

2. If the cell pointer was not in the graph range, you will be asked to select a graph from a list of graphs you have added to the spreadsheet. Highlight the .PIC file name and press Enter.

3. Choose **Colors**.

4. Specify a range (**X, A, B, C, D, E,** or **F**).

5. Highlight the appropriate color from the displayed list, or type the number (**1-8**) that appears next to the color. Press Enter.

To change the graph range, do the following:

1. Type **/gs**

2. If the cell pointer was not in the graph range, you will be asked to select a graph from a list of graphs you have added to the spreadsheet. Highlight the .PIC file name and press Enter.

3. Choose **R**ange. The current graph range is highlighted on the screen.

4. Type the new range, or move the cell pointer and highlight the new range. Before specifying the new range, you can press Esc or Backspace to cancel the current range. Press Enter.

To change the margins around the graph, do the following:

1. Type **/gs**

2. If the cell pointer was not in the graph range, you will be asked to select a graph from a list of graphs you have added to the worksheet. Highlight the .PIC file name and press Enter.

3. Choose **M**argins.

4. Select one of the following:

Menu Item	Description
Left	Designates the left margin, the amount of space between the left edge of the graph range and the beginning of the graph
Right	Designates the right margin, the amount of space between the graph and the right side of the graph range
Top	Designates the top margin, the amount of space between the upper edge of the graph range and the top of the graph
Bottom	Designates the bottom margin, the amount of space between the graph and the bottom of the graph range

5. To specify the size (in inches) of the margin, type a number between 0 and 9.99, inclusive. The default is 0. Press Enter.

Important Cues

- To return the graph settings to their default values, choose **/G**raph **S**ettings **D**efault **R**estore. To permanently change the default settings, use **/G**raph **S**ettings **D**efault **U**pdate. The current settings will be stored as the default.

• You will see an error message if your font files (.FNT files) are not in the 1-2-3 program directory. If you haven't copied these files from the Print-Graph disk, do so. If the files are located in a different subdirectory, use the **/Graph** FontDirectory command to specify where the .FNT files are.

Layout PageSize and Layout Margins   */LP and /LM*

Purpose

Defines the size of paper (for example, letter, legal, or custom). Specifies the margins around the page.

Reminder

Attach and invoke the Allways add-in.

Procedures

To define the page size, do the following:

1. Type **/lp**

2. Highlight the page size from the displayed list, or type the number next to the page size. Press Enter.

3. If you chose **Custom**, you will be asked to enter the page width and page length in inches.

To set the margins, do the following:

1. Type **/lm**

2. Specify margins from these options:

Menu Item	*Description*
Left	Designates the left margin, the amount of space between the left edge of the paper and the printed worksheet
Right	Designates the right margin, the amount of space between the printed worksheet and the right edge of paper
Top	Designates the top margin, the amount of space between the top of the paper and the printed worksheet
Bottom	Designates the bottom margin, the amount of space between the printed worksheet and the bottom of the paper

3. Type a number between 0 and 99.99 inches, inclusive (default is 1.00). Press Enter.

Important Cues

- Allways' **/Layout Margins** command is similar to 1-2-3's **/Print Printer Options Margins** command. You should be aware, however, of several differences. In 1-2-3 the right and left margins are entered in characters, and the top and bottom margins refer to the number of lines; in Allways all the margins are entered in inches. Furthermore, the right margin in Allways is the space between the printed worksheet and the right edge of the page; in 1-2-3 the right margin is the number of characters that will print on the line.

- The margins you enter in 1-2-3's print options are not transferred into Allways.

- To specify landscape (sideways) mode on a laser printer, use the **/Print Configuration Orientation** command.

- To save the page layout settings, use the **/Layout Library Save** command and assign the settings a name (which will be given the extension .ALS). You can then retrieve the settings with other worksheets.

Layout Titles and Layout Borders /LT and /LB

Purpose

/Layout Titles prints a one-line title at the top or bottom of every page. This title is called a *header* or *footer*, respectively.

/Layout Borders prints a worksheet range (rows or columns) on every page. This range consists of cells that contain text to be used as a title called a *border*.

Reminder

Attach and invoke the Allways add-in.

Procedures

To specify headers and footers, do the following:

1. Type **/lt**

2. Choose from the following:

Menu Item	Description
Header	Designates a one-line title that prints at the top of each page
Footer	Designates a one-line title that prints at the bottom of each page

3. Type a title of as many as 240 characters. Press Enter.

To print column or row headings on each page, do the following:

1. Type **/lb**

2. Choose from the following:

Menu Item	Description
Top	Instructs Allways to print worksheet row(s) at the top of each page
Left	Instructs Allways to print worksheet column(s) at the left side of each page
Bottom	Instructs Allways to print worksheet row(s) at the bottom of each page

3. Move the cell pointer to the row or column to be used as a border. If the border has multiple rows or columns, press the period (.) key to anchor one corner of the range. Highlight the additional rows or columns. Press Enter.

Important Cues

- When specifying a border range, you need to include only one cell in the row for the top and bottom borders or one cell in the column for the left border. In other words, you do not need to highlight all the cells in the border.

- Just as in 1-2-3, the date and page number can be printed automatically in the header or footer. Enter an "at" sign (@) where you want the date to appear and a number sign (#) where you want the page number to appear.

- Break the header or footer into as many as three centered segments by entering a vertical bar (|).

- Allways' **/L**ayout **T**itles command is the equivalent of 1-2-3's **/P**rint **P**rinter **O**ptions [**H**eader, **F**ooter] commands. Similarly, Allways' **/L**ayout **B**orders command is the same as 1-2-3's **/P**rint **P**rinter **O**ptions **B**orders command.

- The headers, footers, and borders you enter in 1-2-3's print options are not transferred into Allways.

- To cancel headers or footers, use the **/L**ayout **T**itles **C**lear command. To cancel borders, use the **/L**ayout **B**orders **C**lear command.

- To save the page layout settings, use the **/L**ayout **L**ibrary **S**ave command and assign the settings a name (which will be given the extension .ALS). You can then retrieve the settings with other spreadsheets.

Caution

If you include in the print range the rows or columns specified as borders, the rows or columns will be printed twice.

Layout Options */LO*

Purpose

Places a grid on the worksheet and changes the weight of lines created with
/**Format** Line.

Reminder

Attach and invoke the Allways add-in.

Procedures

To change the weight of a line, do the following:

1. Type /**lol**

2. Choose one of the following weights:

Menu Item	Description
Normal	Selects the standard density of a line created with /**Format** Line
Light	Sets the density of a line created with /**Format** Line to about half that of the Normal setting
Heavy	Sets the density of a line created with /**Format** Line to about double that of the Normal setting

3. Select **Quit Quit** to return to Allways.

To set a grid on the worksheet, do the following:

1. Type /**log**

2. Select **Yes** to turn on the grid; select **No** to shut off the grid.

3. Select **Quit Quit** to return to Allways.

Important Cues

- If the densities of the lines are not heavy enough, you may set columns and rows to a suitable width and set the shading of those cells by using /**Format** **Shade** Solid.

- Use /**Layout** **Options** **Grid** **Yes** rather than /**Format** **Lines** All. With the former command, each cell is outlined with a dotted pattern. This grid stands out much less than lines.

- The grid covers every cell on the worksheet, whereas /**Format** **Lines** covers only specified ranges.

Layout Library /LL

Purpose

Enables you to make different settings and store each in a file of its own—a library—for easy recall.

Reminders

- Attach and invoke the Allways add-in.

- In the Layout menu, make all necessary changes pertaining to such things as page size, margins, borders, options, and titles.

Procedures

To save a library file, do the following:

1. Type **/lls**

2. Either select from the list one of the current library files to save to or type a new library file name; press Enter.

3. If you selected a file name from the menu, choose whether to Cancel the command or **R**eplace the existing library file with a new library file.

4. Select **Q**uit to return to Allways.

To retrieve a library file, do the following:

1. Type **/llr**

2. Either select from the list one of the current library files to retrieve or type a new library file name; press Enter.

3. Select **Q**uit to return to Allways.

To erase a library file, do the following:

1. Type **/lle**

2. Select a library file from the list or type a file name to erase; press Enter.

3. Select **Q**uit to return to Allways.

Important Cues

- When saving a file, you may select one of the names that are listed or type a new name and press Enter.

- When retrieving a library file, you may select one of the names listed or type a new name and press Enter.

Caution

When selecting **E**rase, make sure that the file you choose to erase is the one you want to erase. You are not prompted to verify your choice.

Layout Update *ILU*

Purpose

Replaces the current layout settings with the default settings or makes the current settings the default settings.

Reminder

Attach and invoke the Allways add-in.

Procedures

To return to the default layout settings, do the following:

1. Type **/ld**

2. Select **R**estore.

3. Select **Q**uit to return to Allways.

To make the current layout settings the default, do the following:

1. Type **/ld**

2. Select **U**pdate.

3. Select **Q**uit to return to Allways.

Important Cues

- Make sure that all layout settings are correct before selecting **/L**ayout **D**efault **U**pdate.

- Selecting **/L**ayout **D**efault **R**estore replaces all the current layout settings with the default settings. If you want to save the current settings, select **/L**ayout **L**ibrary **S**ave before restoring the defaults.

Print *IP*

Purpose

Prints the worksheet and/or graph that you have formatted with Allways. Specifies what you want to print.

Reminders

- Format the worksheet as you like; specify layout options.

- Make sure that Allways is configured with the correct printer information. You can use the **/P**rint **C**onfiguration command to check or change the current settings for **P**rinter, **I**nterface, **C**artridge, **O**rientation, **R**esolution, and **B**in. (The options available differ depending on which printer you have.)

- Place the cell pointer in the upper right corner of the range to be printed.

Procedures

1. Type **/p**

2. Select **R**ange Set.

3. Specify the range to be printed: type the range address or highlight the range. Press Enter.

4. Choose **S**ettings and select from the following (if necessary):

Menu Item	Description
Begin	Requests the number of the first page to print
End	Requests the number of the last page to print
First	Requests the first page number to be inserted into a header or footer
Copies	Requests the total number of copies to be printed
Wait	Pauses the printer for single-sheet feeding

5. Enter the requested response, according to the option selected in the preceding step.

6. Press Esc to go back to the preceding menu.

7. Select **G**o to begin printing.

Important Cues

- Allways' **/Print R**ange command is the equivalent of 1-2-3's **/Print P**rinter **R**ange command. 1-2-3's print range, however, is not transferred to Allways.

- The **/Print R**ange command puts dashed lines around each page in the print range. If you don't like where the page breaks are, use **/Worksheet P**age to set new page breaks before you print.

- You can specify 1-2-3 range names for your print ranges in Allways. When prompted for the print range, type the range name or press the Name (F3) key to choose from a list of names.

- You can select the range to print before choosing the **/Print R**ange command. To preselect the range, place the cell pointer on the first cell to print, press the period (.) to anchor one corner of the range, and then place the cell pointer on the last cell to print. When you use the **/Print R**ange command, Allways automatically fills in the selected range.

- Use **/Print S**ettings **C**lear to return the print settings to their defaults.

Caution

Your laser printer may not have enough memory to download soft fonts that have a large point size. If you get an Out of memory error message when you print, you need to specify a different-sized font or use an internal or cartridge font.

Print File   /PF

Purpose

Enables Allways to capture printing in a file.

Reminder

Use /fr in 1-2-3 to retrieve the worksheet to print.

Procedures

1. Type **/pf**

2. Select from the list or type the name of the file to contain the printed information.

3. Specify the range to print either by pointing or typing the range.

Important Cue

The /pf command prints a worksheet to a file in the same manner as if the worksheet were printed to the printer. From a DOS prompt, type **COPY /b** *filename*.**PRN PRN**, where *filename* is the name you typed or selected when Allways asked for a name. The file will be printed on a printer as if it were being printed from Allways.

Display   /D

Purpose

Sets the characteristics of the screen. You can set the colors of the screen's foreground and background, for example. You also can display the worksheet in **G**raphics mode ("what you see is what you get") or in **T**ext mode (like the display in 1-2-3).

Changes the size of the characters on-screen. You can reduce the characters so that you can see more of the worksheet at once on the screen, or you can magnify them to see small fonts more clearly. Figures AW.5 and AW.6 show the same worksheet at two different magnifications: "tiny" and "large."

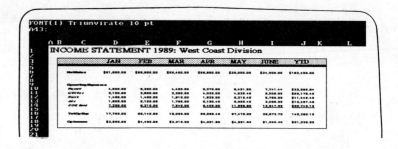

Fig. AW.5.
*A worksheet
zoomed at
the "tiny"
magnification
level.*

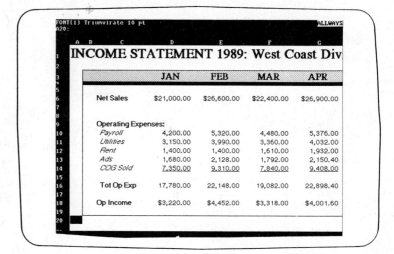

Fig. AW.6.
*A worksheet
zoomed at
the "large"
magnification
size.*

Turns on or off the display of graphs that have been added to the worksheet.

Reminder

The **/Display** commands do not affect the report printout; they simply change how the worksheet looks on the screen.

Procedures

1. Type **/d**

2. Select one of the following:

Menu Item	Description
Mode	Provides the options **G**raphics and **T**ext mode
Zoom	Provides the options **T**iny, **S**mall, **N**ormal, **L**arge, and **H**uge for character display. Figure AW.5 is an example of "tiny"; figure AW.6 is an example of "large."

Graphs	Enables you to choose whether to show graphs on the screen
Colors	Provides the options **B**ackground, **F**oreground, and **H**ighlight, for which you select colors (assuming that you have a color monitor)

3. Enter the requested response, according to the option selected in the preceding step.

Important Cues

- "Quick" keys are available for some of the display commands:

    Reduce (F4): reduces the display

    Enlarge (Shift-F4): enlarges the display

    Display (F6): switches between **G**raphics and **T**ext mode

    Graph (F10): turns the display of graphs on and off

- The /**D**isplay **G**raphs **Y**es command displays the actual graph, rather than the hatching pattern, on the screen. However, you will notice a delay whenever the screen redraws.

- In **G**raphics mode, the formatting displayed on-screen looks much as it does when printed. You must have a graphics monitor to see text in **G**raphics mode.

- You cannot see formatting on-screen in **T**ext mode. The control panel, however, displays the formatting instructions for the current cell. The **Z**oom feature also does not work in **T**ext mode.

Special Copy and Special Import   /SC and /SI

Purpose

/**S**pecial **C**opy applies the same formatting information contained in one cell or range of cells to another cell or range. The formatting that is copied includes the font, boldfacing, underlining, shading, color, and lines. Use Allways' **C**opy command to save time in formatting.

/**S**pecial **I**mport applies to all the formatting information contained in another worksheet on disk. The formatting that is imported includes the individual cell formats, the font set, layout, print range, and graphs. Use this command to format a worksheet that is laid out identically to an existing worksheet you have already formatted.

Reminders

- Save the file in 1-2-3 before copying or importing formats; if you make a mistake when defining the ranges, or if you get unexpected results, you can retrieve the file with its original formatting.

- Allways' /Special Copy and /Special Import commands do not copy data—only the formatting instructions. If you want to copy data, use 1-2-3's /Copy and /File Combine commands.

Procedures

To copy cell formats, do the following:

1. Type **/sc**

2. By highlighting or typing, indicate the range containing the format you are copying. Press Enter.

3. Indicate the range you are copying the format to. Press Enter. This range is now formatted identically to the original range.

To import a format, do the following:

1. Type **/si**

2. Enter the name of the file containing the format you want to copy. Press Enter. The current file now is formatted identically to the original file.

Important Cues

- Use the /Special Move command to move imported cell formats that do not match the current file exactly.

- Another command on the Special menu is Justify. This command is similar to 1-2-3's /Range Justify command, which "wordwraps" text within the range you define. If you change the font size of a paragraph of text, you may find that the text requires more or fewer columns than it originally did. The /Special Justify command respaces the text.

Caution

1-2-3's Undo command does not work in Allways. If you don't like the results of importing the formats from another file, you cannot reverse the operation. The only way to get rid of the new formats is to retrieve the original file (assuming that you saved it before importing).

Index

Free Catalog!

Mail us this registration form today, and we'll send you a free catalog featuring Que's complete line of best-selling books.

Name of Book _____

Name _____

Title _____

Phone (___) _____

Company _____

Address _____

City _____

State _____ ZIP _____

Please check the appropriate answers:

1. Where did you buy your Que book?
   - [ ] Bookstore (name: _____)
   - [ ] Computer store (name: _____)
   - [ ] Catalog (name: _____)
   - [ ] Direct from Que
   - [ ] Other: _____

2. How many computer books do you buy a year?
   - [ ] 1 or less
   - [ ] 2-5
   - [ ] 6-10
   - [ ] More than 10

3. How many Que books do you own?
   - [ ] 1
   - [ ] 2-5
   - [ ] 6-10
   - [ ] More than 10

4. How long have you been using this software?
   - [ ] Less than 6 months
   - [ ] 6 months to 1 year
   - [ ] 1-3 years
   - [ ] More than 3 years

5. What influenced your purchase of this Que book?
   - [ ] Personal recommendation
   - [ ] Advertisement
   - [ ] In-store display
   - [ ] Price
   - [ ] Que catalog
   - [ ] Que mailing
   - [ ] Que's reputation
   - [ ] Other: _____

6. How would you rate the overall content of the book?
   - [ ] Very good
   - [ ] Good
   - [ ] Satisfactory
   - [ ] Poor

7. What do you like *best* about this Que book?
   _____
   _____

8. What do you like *least* about this Que book?
   _____
   _____

9. Did you buy this book with your personal funds?
   - [ ] Yes
   - [ ] No

10. Please feel free to list any other comments you may have about this Que book.
   _____
   _____
   _____

QUе

Order Your Que Books Today!

Name _____

Title _____

Company _____

City _____

State _____ ZIP _____

Phone No. (___) _____

Method of Payment:

Check [ ]   (Please enclose in envelope.)

Charge My: VISA [ ]   MasterCard [ ]

American Express [ ]

Charge # _____

Expiration Date _____

Order No.	Title	Qty.	Price	Total

You can **FAX** your order to **1-317-573-2583**. Or call **1-800-428-5331, ext. ORDR** to order direct.
Please add $2.50 per title for shipping and handling.

Subtotal _____

Shipping & Handling _____

Total _____

QUе

BUSINESS REPLY MAIL
First Class Permit No. 9918   Indianapolis, IN

Postage will be paid by addressee

11711 N. College
Carmel, IN 46032

BUSINESS REPLY MAIL
First Class Permit No. 9918   Indianapolis, IN

Postage will be paid by addressee

11711 N. College
Carmel, IN 46032

Wysiwyg Menu Map

Worksheet Format Graph Print Display Special Text Named-Style Quit

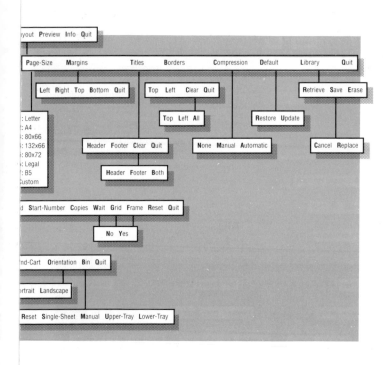

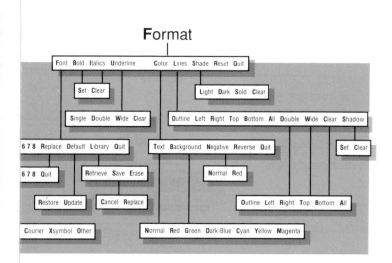

Format

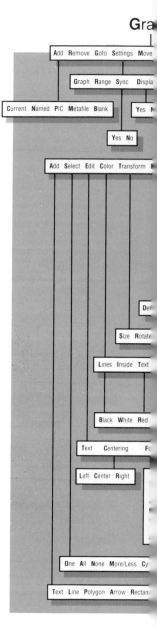

Text

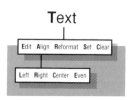

ɔh

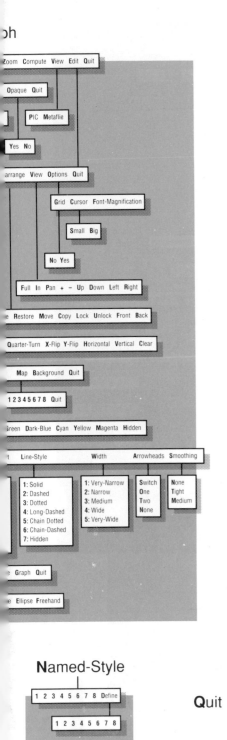

Zoom Compute View Edit Quit

Opaque Quit

PIC Metaflie

Yes No

arrange View Options Quit

Grid Cursor Font-Magnification

Small Big

No Yes

Full In Pan + – Up Down Left Right

Restore Move Copy Lock Unlock Front Back

Quarter-Turn X-Flip Y-Flip Horizontal Vertical Clear

Map Background Quit

1 2 3 4 5 6 7 8 Quit

Green Dark-Blue Cyan Yellow Magenta Hidden

Line-Style   Width   Arrowheads Smoothing

1: Solid   1: Very-Narrow   Switch   None
2: Dashed   2: Narrow   One   Tight
3: Dotted   3: Medium   Two   Medium
4: Long-Dashed   4: Wide   None
5: Chain Dotted   5: Very-Wide
6: Chain-Dashed
7: Hidden

Graph Quit

Ellipse Freehand

PrintGraph Menu Map

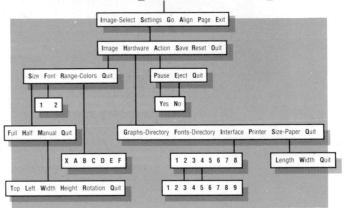

Image-Select Settings Go Align Page Exit

Image Hardware Action Save Reset Quit

Size Font Range-Colors Quit   Pause Eject Quit

1 2   Yes No

Full Half Manual Quit   Graphs-Directory Fonts-Directory Interface Printer Size-Paper Quit

X A B C D E F   1 2 3 4 5 6 7 8   Length Width Quit

Top Left Width Height Rotation Quit   1 2 3 4 5 6 7 8 9

Auditor Menu Map

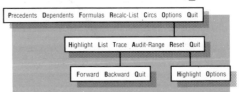

Precedents Dependents Formulas Recalc-List Circs Options Quit

Highlight List Trace Audit-Range Reset Quit

Forward Backward Quit   Highlight Options

Macro Library Manager Map

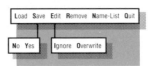

Load Save Edit Remove Name-List Quit

No Yes   Ignore Overwrite

Named-Style

1 2 3 4 5 6 7 8 Define   Quit

1 2 3 4 5 6 7 8

Special Edition

USING 1-2-3®
FOR DOS RELEASE 2.3
Command Chart